The Columbia Guide to the
Latin American Novel Since 1945

The Columbia Guides to Literature Since 1945

The Columbia Guides to Literature Since 1945

The Columbia Guide to the Literatures of Eastern Europe Since 1945, ed. Harold B. Segel

The Columbia Guide to American Indian Literatures Since 1945, ed. Eric Cheyfitz

The Columbia Guide to Contemporary African American Fiction, Darryl Dickson-Carr

The Columbia Guide to Asian American Literature Since 1945, Guiyou Huang

The Columbia Guide to East African Literature in English Since 1945, Simon Gikandi and Evan Mwangi

The Columbia Guide to Central African Literature in English Since 1945, Adrian Roscoe

The Columbia Guide to the
Latin American Novel Since 1945

Raymond Leslie Williams

Columbia University Press
New York

Columbia University Press
Publishers Since 1893
New York   Chichester, West Sussex

Copyright © 2007 Columbia University Press

Library of Congress Cataloging-in-Publication Data

Williams, Raymond L.
   The Columbia guide to the Latin American novel since 1945 / Raymond Leslie Williams.
      p. cm.—(The Columbia guide to literature since 1945)
   Includes bibliographical references and index.
   ISBN 978-0-231-12688-5 (cloth : alk. paper)
      1. Latin American fiction—20th century—History and criticism.   2. Latin American fiction—20th
century—Bio-bibliography.   I. Title.   II. Series.

   PQ7082.N7W546 2007
   813.640998—dc22

                              2007008726

Casebound editions of Columbia University Press books are printed on permanent and durable
acid-free paper.
Printed in the United States of America
c 10 9 8 7 6 5 4 3 2 1

Contents

Preface / *vii*

Part I

Introduction, Chronological Survey and Regional Survey / *1*

Introduction to the Latin American and Caribbean Novel / *3*

Chronological Survey / *15*

Regional Survey / *24*

Conclusion: The Post-1945 Novel, the Desire to Be Modern,

and Redemocratization / *73*

Part II

Nations, Topics, Biographies, Novels (A-Z) / *75*

Annotated Bibliography / *353*

Index / *367*

Preface

This critical study offers many features of a literary history of the modern Latin American and Caribbean novel as well as several features of an encyclopedia. Part 1 is organized along the lines of a four-part history of the Latin American novel from 1945 to 2005. Part 2 is more encyclopedic in approach, with entries appearing under the letters A through Z that succinctly explain the novelistic tradition of specific nations, topics, authors, and the content of selected individual novels. Part 3 consists of an annotated bibliography of studies on the Latin American and Caribbean novel. Most of the novels described, analyzed, or mentioned in this study were written in Spanish, and many of these novels have been translated into English. Some of the novels were originally written in Portuguese (in Brazil), French (in the Caribbean), Dutch (in the Caribbean), and English (in the Caribbean and the United States), and some of these novels have been translated into English and other languages.

I am grateful for the contributions to the research for this work provided by research assistants George Carlsen, Adrian Kane, Lila McDowell, Gabriela Miranda-Recinos, José Recinos. I want to thank Susan Pensak of Columbia University Press.

Part I

Introduction, Chronological Survey, and Regional Survey

Introduction to the Latin American and Caribbean Novel

The Colonial Legacy

The diverse peoples, languages, and cultures of the region today called Latin America and the Caribbean share a colonial legacy. Spain and Portugal ruled the region for approximately three centuries and other European nations have exercised a colonial presence. Taking into account its indigenous, African, and Iberian cultural heritages, the Mexican writer Carlos Fuentes has eschewed the very term *Latin America* and identified this vast region as "Indo-Afro-Ibero America." The numerous indigenous languages and cultures (literally hundreds, from Mapuche in Chile to Nahuatl in Mexico), the several African languages and cultures, and the several Western European languages and cultures (principally from Spain and Portugal, but including French, English, and Dutch) make the vast region that—for lack of a better term—we call Latin America and the Caribbean patently heterogeneous.

The colonial legacies that are important and still live topics of the Latin American and Caribbean novel today are also diverse in themselves. The colonial legacy from Spain has produced the writing of novels in the Spanish language in over twenty nations as well as Puerto Rico and the Unites States. Writing in Spanish, novelists from Mexico to Chile are still assessing the colonial legacy from Spain, some of whom have returned to the medieval roots of their "mother" language. The colonial legacy from Portugal is still being written about in the Portuguese language in Brazil, both in historic research and historical novels. France's colonial legacy is extant in the three "departments" they still govern in the Caribbean (Guadeloupe, Martinique, and French Guyana) and where novelists such as Maryse Condé write "Caribbbean" novels in French about their African and colonial identities, among other topics related to the colonial past. The colonial legacies of Great Britain and Holland are also the focus of fiction being written in English and Dutch in nations such as Jamaica and Suriname, among other parts of the Caribbean, often called the West Indies, where English and Dutch are spoken and written. Novelists such as Erna Brodber, who writes in English in Jamaica, and Astrid Roemer, who writes in Dutch in Suriname, are testimony to this part of the European legacy of colonialism.

Writers such as Carlos Fuentes in Mexico and Diamela Eltit in Chile, as well as many of their cohorts, have addressed a variety of issues related to these colonial legacies, some of which have been addressed in subtle and complex novels. In the broadest of terms, however, Latin American and Caribbean writers have addressed the colonial legacy in three general areas: in novels about the wars of independence (mostly dealing with nineteenth-century Enlightenment thought as well as the early nineteenth-century political conflicts themselves), in novels about about the Mexican Revolution (1910–1917), and in novels about the Cuban Revolution of 1959.

The literature about the independence period is vast, for numerous contemporary novelists have felt the need to reassess that key period of nation building in Latin America and the Caribbean. Thus, novelists such as Colombia's Gabriel García Márquez, who wrote the novel *El general en su laberinto* (1989, *The General in His Labyrinth*) on a prominent political figure of the independence, Simón Bolívar, were interested in rewriting the history of the foundation of the Latin American nations. Numerous historical novels about the nineteenth century have been written—reassessments of the empirical history, of Enlightenment thought, and of nineteenth-century foundational fictions that had proposed other versions of the period's history. These novels question, for example, whether or not the political independence of these nations represented an authentic cultural and economic independence. They also question the values of the old aristocracies that tended to remain in power after the political independence from Spain, Portugal, and the other European powers with interests in Latin America. The Argentine Ricardo Piglia's novel *Respiración artificial* (1979, *Artificial Respiration*) returns to the roots of Argentine nationhood in the nineteenth century, as he reviews in depth the nation's cultural and political history.

The literature about the Mexican Revolution is as vast as the literature of independence and the foundational fictions of the nineteenth century. The Mexican Revolution was a broad-based rebellion against not only the authoritarian regime of Porfirio Díaz but also a reaction against the old elite—the same families that had ruled Mexico since the colonial period. From Mariano Azuela's classic novel of the Mexican Revolution, *Los de abajo* (1915, *The Underdogs*) to the modern fictional critique of the postrevolutionary political establishment in Fuentes's modern classic, *La muerte de Artemio Cruz* (1962, *The Death of Artemio Cruz*), an entire series of novels were published in Mexico to create the genre called the novel of the Mexican Revolution. These novels cast a critical eye on not only the old regime surviving the regime of Porfirio Díaz, but also tended to portray the revolution itself as a chaotic conflict lacking the firm ideological clarity that the same political forces (and official historians) have attempted to portray it as having.

The other major disruption of the colonial legacy was the Cuban Revolution of 1959, and it also produced a vast literary response that took several directions. The Cuban Revolution produced a set of novels about Cuban society, politics, and culture before, during, and after the revolution. Guillermo Cabrera Infante, for example, offered a nostalgic reflection on life in Havana immediately before the revolution in his novel *Tres tristes tigres* (1967, *Three Sad Tigers*). On the other hand, Jesus Díez's *Las iniciales de la tierra* (1989, The initials of the land) is a historical work that explores the adventure of the Cuban Revolution and the efforts to construct a new nation in the 1960s.

The Cuban Revolution has also indirectly produced a substantive set of novels of exile and fiction of *cheísmo* (celebrating Ernesto "Che" Guevara) dealing with guerrilla insurgency. Writers such as the Peruvian Edmundo de los Ríos, whose novel *Los juegos verdaderos* (1968, The real games) deals with youthful political rebels who follow a Che Guevara–type guerrilla warfare path. Cuban writers from different generations, such as Reynaldo Arenas, Antonio Benítez Rojo, and Zoé Valdés, have written very different kinds of novels relating the experiences of Cuban exiles. Valdés is the youngest of the three, and her novels of the 1990s mostly set in Paris, a parody some of the clichés of exile fiction of the 1970s and 1980s, such as nostalgia for the homeland that is so common in fiction by writers in exile.

Beyond the Colonial Legacy: Contexts of the 1940s and 1950s

The colonial legacy of rule by elites, unequal distribution of wealth, and different forms of racial and gender discrimmination have survived well into the twentieth century in Latin America and the Caribbean. Most novels written since 1945 deal with this legacy in one way or another. In the first half of the twentieth century, the Latin American and Caribbean novel often present the social world in Manichean terms. Even the classic novels of the 1920s—*La vorágine* (1924, *The Vortex*) by the Colombian José Eustacio Rivera, *Don Segundo Sombra* (1926, *Don Segundo Sombra*) by the Argentine Ricardo Güiraldes, and *Doña Bárbara* (1929, *Doña Barbara*) by the Venezuelan Rómulo Gallegos—portrayed characters as stereotypes, little moral ambiguity, and a simplistic view of Latin American reality as "civilization" versus "barbarisim." These classic works, nevertheless, were canonized in Latin America in the 1930s and 1940s.

Among the early twentieth-century exceptions to this generalization, the avant-garde movements centered in cities such as Buenos Aires and Mexico City promoted modernist aesthetics and what they generally considered more "universal" approaches to storytelling. Writers such as the Guatemalan Miguel Angel Asturias and the Cuban Alejo Carpentier were involved with these same avant-garde movements in Europe, and in the 1940s Asturias and Carpentier began publishing fictions that reflected the interests of European avant-garde and modernist aesthetics.

In the 1940s and 1950s Latin American novelists began to successfully synthesize the long-standing sociopolitical commitment of the writer concerned with the colonial legacy and the new modernist aesthetics. Indeed, these writers of the 1940s and 1950s—Asturias, Carpentier, Agustín Yáñez, Clarice Lispector, Juan Rulfo, and others—were as politically committed as they were dedicated to the idea of writing a new national literature that would be both modern (which meant a variety of things) and universal (which also had numerous understandings).

The political scenario in the mid-1940s was as varied in Latin America and the Caribbean as its uneven socioeconomic development and its often unstable democracies. The end of World War II was of far less significance in Latin America than it was in Europe and the United States, although there were repercussions in some areas of the Hispanic world. In France's DOM (overseas departments) of Guadeloupe, Martinique, and French Guayana, the blacks who had participated in the European war now demanded more rights; the end of the war marked the growth of the *négritude* in much of the Caribbean. In Brazil the end of WWII marked the end of the neofascist government of Getúlio Vargas, who had headed the Estado Novo since the early 1930s.

The series of military dictatorships that had plagued several Central American states during the first half of the century finally waned in one of the parts of the region in 1945 in Guatemala, with the end of General Ubico's government, the establishment of democratic elections, and the reestablishment of the political rights and other freedoms of most democracies. The election of progressive Jacobo Arbenz in 1953, however, resulted in a reaction by local elites, who, in conjunction with the U.S. government (and U.S. airplanes dropping bombs on urban areas of Guatemala), demolished the short-lived democracy and reestablished favorable operations for the United Fruit Company. Years later a Guatemalan writer who had been a young child when his nation was attacked, Arturo Arias, wrote a novel of the experience, *Después de las bombas* (1979, *After the Bombs*).

In Argentina Juan Domingo Perón rose to power with massive popular support in the mid-1940s. In 1945 the military pressured him to resign from his positions as vice president and minister of labor, but he not only remained in power with ample popular support, he also took control of the nation in 1946, offering power to the working class and taking privilege from the upper-middle sectors by nationalizing the banks, urban transportation, the train system, and public services. This crucial and controversial period of Argentine history has been amply documented in novels published since the 1950s and in *La novela de Perón* (1985) by Tomás Eloy Martínez.

After World War II, Peru seemed to be on a democratic path, with the designation of Luis Bustamente y Rivero as president in 1945, but by 1948 a coup by General Manuel Odría resulted in a nearly decade-long authoritarian regime (1948–1956). Mario Vargas Llosa was a student during this period and later wrote the novel *Conversación en La Catedral* (1969, *Conversation in The Cathedral*) as his account of the brutal government in power during those years. In this elaborate portrayal of life in Peru in the 1950s, Vargas Llosa presents a sinister regime that perpetrates the most perverse aspects of the colonial legacy.

The 1940s were unstable years in Colombian and Venezuela. In Colombia the assassination of the Liberal Party's populist candidate Jorge Eliécer Gaitán on April 9, 1948, resulted in massive civil unrest, violence in the streets, and many deaths in Bogotá. This instability and decade-long conflict between the two traditional parties (the Liberal Party and the Conservative Party) led to the civil war of the 1950s (1948–1958) identified as La Violencia. The literary response to this conflict was the production of a large number of novels (over a hundred) published from the 1950s to the 1970s dealing with La Violencia. Most of them were detailed, bloody descriptions of questionable sociological or literary value, but some of the more accomplished novels from this war are Gabriel García Márquez's *La mala hora* (1962, *In Evil Hour*), Manuel Mejía Vallejo's *El día señalado* (1963, The signaled day), and Gustavo Alvarez Gardeazábal's *Cóndores no entierran todos los días* (1972, Condors do not bury every day). In *Cóndores no entierran todos los días* Alvarez Gardeazábal told horrific stories from his own youth, when he awoke in the morning to see cadavers on the streets of his hometown in the Valle del Cauca (the town of Tuluá)—a night's work by the professional assassins of the Conservative Party who were called *pájaros* ("birds"). In Venezuela President Rómulo Gallegos, a well-respected writer, was deposed from his presidential role after a few months, and this coup was a predecessor to the authoritarian government of Pérez Jiménez in the 1950s. Colombian Gabriel García Márquez worked in Venezuela as a journalist during this period and claims that one of the numerous models he used for writing his novel about the prototypical dictator, *El otoño del patriarca* (1975, *The Autumn of the Patriarch*), was based on his experience living under the government of Pérez Jiménez. Several Venezuelan novelists have fictionalized this period, including Miguel Otero Silva.

One of the most stable regimes in Latin America during the post-WWII period was in Mexico, where the PRM (Partido Revolucionario Mexicano, or Mexican Revolutionary Party) that had evolved since the early-century Mexican Revolution became the PRI (Partido Revolucionario Institucional). President Miguel Alemán led the PRI government in the early 1950s to what was described by some political and economic observers as the "Mexican Miracle," although critics of the regime point to the severe social and economic inequities that persisted in Mexico into the 1950s and beyond. In Mexico, as in most Latin American nations, there was a mass movement from the rural areas to the city, and Mexico

City followed a path of rapid growth in the entire post-WWII period. Carlos Fuentes attempted to capture the essence of this new urban life in one of the first urban novels to be published about this period in Mexico, *La región más transparente* (1958, *Where the Air Is Clear*). In this novel Fuentes was also highly critical of the new ruling class presiding over the Mexican Miracle.

In the 1940s and 1950s, then, writers such as Asturias, Carpentier, García Márquez, João Guimarães Rosa, Fuentes, and a host of others drew upon the venerable tradition of the Latin American writer as social critic, as voice of its indigenous traditions, its historic past and political present and its vast and heterogeneous cultures. In addition, these writers were interested in employing modernists aesthetics (including those of Jorge Luis Borges) to establish the groundwork for the new Latin American novel of the post-1945 period.

The Dictator Novel and Its Contexts: The Critique of the Colonial Legacy

As the writers of the 1960s Boom—Fuentes, García Márquez, Julio Cortázar, and Vargas Llosa—surveyed the political scene of Latin America in the early 1970s, the situation was dismal. A military dictatorship had been in power in Brazil since 1964, military governments were entrenched in Argentina, Uruguay, Haiti, the Dominican Republic, and Paraguay, and General Augusto Pinochet had just overthrown the democratically elected Unidad Popular government of Salvador Allende in 1973. As a response, these writers of the Boom and others decided to use the pen, writing novels dealing with real and fictionalized dictators to unmask the operations of not only the dictators that dominated Latin America at that moment but other strongmen who were part of the historic experience of these writers, such as two from the 1950s, General Pérez Jiménez of Venezuela and General Rojas Pinilla of Colombia. García Márquez had lived in both Colombia and Venezuela in the 1950s, so he had firsthand experience with such regimes.

The result was a series of novels about dictators, political authority, and the operations of power, from Alejo Carpentier's *El recurso del método* (1974, *Reasons of State*) and García Márquez's *El otoño del patriarca* to Mario Vargas Llosa's more recent *La fiesta del chivo* (2000, *The Feast of the Goat*).

The early masterpiece of the dictator novel was Asturias's *El Señor Presidente* (1946). Asturias had lived a good portion of his life under dictatorships in Guatemala. He was born in Guatemala in 1899, the year after Manuel Estrada Cabrera orchestrated the assassination of the extant president of Guatemala, ruling for two decades. Estrada Cabrera immediately militarized public education and passed a law to assure his control over workers. He signed a contract allowing the United Fruit Company into Guatemala under exceptionally favorable conditions, and his government made other deals that favored foreign investment, often to the detriment of local business interests and Guatemalan workers. Given the repression Asturias's family suffered under the Estrada Cabrera regime, his parents moved out of the capital to a rural area when Asturias was still a young boy. There Asturias was in close contact with the local Mayan population and learned to speak Quiché. His interest in indigenous cultures continued for the rest of his life and eventually became an important part of his fiction, including the novel *El Señor Presidente*.

In high school in Guatemala City, Asturias was a student activist against the dictatorship of Estrada Cabrera, which finally ended in 1920 when the National Assembly declared him mentally incompetent; he responded by ordering his soldiers to bomb the city. Nevertheless, the opposition did manage to imprison the dictator, ending his regime. Asturias began writing a short story in 1922 about the horrifying experience of living under the Estrada Cabrera regime; over a process of many years this story evolved into the novel *El Señor Presidente*. The novel itself does not name the dictator or refer to specific years; much of the focus, however, is on the machinations of Estrada Cabrera in the year 1916, with the torture and politically motivated jailings of the sort that Asturias himself had suffered as a student. In 1923 Asturias was forced into political exile in Europe, where he continued writing his novel. While in Great Britain and France, he studied topics such as Mayan culture, thus developing a more academic understanding of the people he had seen as a child.

After the military dictatorships of Generals José Orelana and Lázaro Chacón in the 1920s, Guatemala's legacy of authoritarian rule continued in the 1930s under General Jorge Ubico. Under his regime, opposition political activity was tightly controlled and the practice of forced labor was institutionalized. Asturias returned from Europe in 1933 to work with the political opposition to Ubico. Nevertheless, during this dictatorship Asturias was not able to publish his novel, though he continued writing and did finally publish it in 1946. Although directed mostly against the dictatorship of Estrada Cabrera, *El Señor Presidente* is really an amalgam of the consecutive repressive regimes in Guatemala during the first three decades of the twentieth century.

The background to the writing of *El Señor Presidente* and the lengthy process of writing it is one telling example of how the excesses of authoritarianism rule can inform the production of Latin American dictator novels. In Paraguay Augusto Roa Bastos went into political exile because of the regime of Alfredo Stroessner, but his novel *Yo, el Supremo* (1977, *I the Supreme*) is the result not only of the excesses of this dictatorship but also of the author's research on the legendary nineteenth-century Paraguayan dictator Dr. Francia. In this novel Roa Bastos's fictionalized rewriting of Paraguay's political history includes lengthy footnotes taken from historical documents on Dr. Francia's regime.

For Mario Vargas Llosa, the military dictatorship of Odría was a prototype of the most sinister aspects of the abuse of power, as he fictionalized this experience in *Conversación en La Catedral*. But Vargas Llosa continued writing about the uses and abuses of authority in novels such as *Pantaleón y las visitadoras* (1974, *Pantoja and His Special Service*) and *La guerra del fin del mundo* (1981, *The War of the End of the World*). Later in his career, however, he decided to research one of the classic dictatorships of Latin America—the regime of Batista in the Dominican Republic. Vargas Llosa's lifetime commitment to questioning authoritarian regimes culminated in one of the masterpieces of the dictator novel, the lengthy *La fiesta del chivo*.

Exile, Diaspora, and the Novel of Exile

The novel of exile or diaspora became prominent in Latin America during the military dictatorships of the 1970s and 1980s, particularly in Brazil, and the southern cone region of Argentina, Uruguay, and Chile. But the novel of exile has an important literary response to adverse political, social, and cultural conditions since WWII. From the 1940s to the 1990s, from George Lamming to the Cubans Guillermo Cabrera Infante and Severo Sarduy to Reynaldo Arenas and Zoé Valdés, Caribbean novelists have been writing in exile. Lamming went into exile from Barbardos to Great Britain in the early 1950s, then writing of his experience and that of the community of West Indies intellectuals in London. By the 1990s many of these writers, such as the Chilean Antonio Skármeta, the Argentine

Mempo Giardinelli, and the Brazilian Antonio Callado, had returned to their homelands and resumed their roles as committed intellectuals.

The conditions that motivate the diaspora vary: many writers in the Caribbean region have felt compelled to insert themselves in the cultural life of the metropole in order to improve their already limited possibilities of intentional dialogue and publication. Most novelists who write in French, English, and Dutch began their careers by publishing their first novels in Europe—France, Great Britain, and Holland. On the other hand, writers such as the Argentine Giardinelli and the Chileans Skármeta and Ariel Dorfman, as well as the Brazilian Callado, had already established publication credentials in their homelands and went into exile to avoid political repression, possible imprisonment, and even death under regimes with records for assassinating oppositional intellectuals. Some writers, such as the Mexican Federico Patán and the Chicano Rudolfo Anaya, have chosen what might be called an inner exile of remaining in their homelands and writing about different types of psychological dislocation. In both cases, however, the writer lives in a state of relative alienation from a dominant culture: Patán lives in Mexico as a Spaniard in exile; Anaya lives in New Mexico where he writes as a minority figure in the Unites States.

The novel of exile or diaspora has generally dealt with issues of displacement, cultural conflict, and nostalgia for the nation left behind, often presenting an idealized version of the nation remembered. In the 1970s and 1980s, in the writings of Skármeta and Giardinelli, these were common topics, as they had been for George Lamming when he wrote of the experience of exile in London in the 1950s. Many of these novelists have written of their experience and memories from their homeland; Reynaldo Arenas, for example, has published dramatic stories of repression and imprisonment in Cuba. Similarly, Lêdo Ivo of Brazil has written a novel about life in the city of Maceió (Brazil), *Ninho de cobras* (1973, *Snake's Nest*) that is basically a representation of conditions under the heavy-handed government of Getúlio Vargas in the 1930s and 1940s. Since the novel was published under the later military dictatorship of Brazil, readers have found parallels between the two, for Maceió is a town of violence and corruption. The Haitian case is somewhat different than much of the Caribbean and Latin America. The dictatorship of the Duvaliers (1956–1987) did result in the exile of a large number of writers and intellectuals.

In the 1990s—after several decades of exile fiction—Latin American writers have been reluctant to continue conventional approaches to displacement and cultural conflict. Cuban American Roberto Fernández, Cuban Zoé Valdés (writing in France), and Argentine Tununa Mercado (writing in Argentina after lengthy exile in Mexico) have all written texts that might be called postexile in the sense that they reject these topics and reflect critically on exile literature itself. Writing in the United States, Fernández has been just as satirical of idealized nostalgia for Cuba as has been Zoé Valdés writing about the Cuba she left behind in her youth.

Many Latin American novelists have written in exile without addressing exile issues directly. This is the case of the Cuban Cabrera Infante (who writes in Great Britain), the Cuban Severo Sarduy (who wrote in Paris until his death), the Argentines Flavia Company and Clara Obligado (both of whom write in Spain), and the Brazilian Silviano Santiago. Santiago's novel *Stella Manhattan* (1985) deals with exile from its setting in New York, although it covers a broad range of topics confronted by the generation in political exile from Brazil, including the vitality of leftist guerrillas and issues of gender. A group of academics have spent the better part of their adult lives as scholars in the United States and have had parallel careers as novelists, including Fernando Alegría, Lucía Guerra, and Alicia Borinsky. These novelists, although they have written, technically speaking, in exile, do not directly address their positions as exile writers. Rather, they use their experience in Latin America and the United States to tell their stories. Lucía Guerra, for example, has researched the life of a bicultural celebrity figure and written *Las noches de Carmen Miranda* (2002, The nights of Carmen Miranda).

Fictions of Resistance

Some writers did not have the option of exile from political repression or chose to remain in their homelands of social inequity in the post-WWII period. Many novelists chose exile as a response to some of the most repressive authoritarian regimes, such as the dictatorships of Pinochet in Chile (1973–1989), the Duvaliers in Haiti (1956–1987), and the "Process of National Reorganization" in Argentina (1976–1983). Some authors, however, did survive these regimes while remaining in the country, publishing books while many of their colleagues were censored, imprisoned, or murdered. Three such were were Diamela Eltit in Chile, Frankétienne in Haiti, and Ricardo Piglia in Argentina. In order to do this, they wrote subtle fictions of resistance—works so patently experimental or densely allegorical that the regimes did not interfere with the publication of these novels. Writers such as Ignacio Solares in Mexico and Adriano González León in Venezuela did not write under such severe conditions, but their works, too, could be considered fictions of resistance—subtle critiques written within the political establishements they were criticizing. Unlike writers who have assumed a position of "inner exile"—a state of distanced alienation from society—these writers of resistance are active participants in society, but in an oppositional way.

Eltit studied literature in Santiago during the 1970s during the dictatorship of Pinochet. Consequently, she belongs to the generation of writers who began writing in an inner exile situation within Chile; during the 1980s Eltit collaborated with young writers and artists to create a cultural scene of resistance to the military dictatorship. These writers and artists created innovative forms of popular theater, street happenings and visual arts that worked against the power structure without provoking direct confrontation. Her collaborators included young intellectuals with a broad range of literary and artistics interests such as Pedro Lemebel. Eltit's fiction is often read as political allegory, and she has spoken of "scenes of power," as well as ideology in essays and interviews, making her work a lengthy reflection on theory, politics, and literature. Eltit's most experimental novel is *Lumpérica* (1981, *E. Iluminata*), a work with no linear plot or anything comparable to a sequence of actions that might be constructed as a plot. Rather, it consists of a series of fragments and situations located in a plaza near Santiago. The experimental uses of space and language suggest an analysis of the historic roots of the Spanish language as a language of repression. Her novel *Por la patria* (1986, For the nation) is perhaps her fiction of resistance most directly comparable to the work of writers such as Frankétienne and Ricardo Piglia, for here she interrogates the roots of political power as it relates to language. Frankétienne was one of the few Haitian writers not to emigrate during the father-son Duvalier dictatorship of three decades in Haiti, nor to be imprisoned for his writing. In 1957 François Duvalier (also known as Papa Doc) began his twenty-nine-year rule of terror (supported by his brutal Tonton Macoutes), which continued after Papa Doc's death in

1971 when his son Jean-Claude Duvalier inherited the regime. Frankétienne is recognized for being the first writer to publish a novel in Haitian Creole in a nation where the standard had been to publish fiction in French; *Dézafi* (1975, Challenge), which is set during the Duvalier dictatorship, deals with the peasants in a small rural community. The impoverished and hopeless inhabitants of two villages suffer from hunger and fear, leading to a bizarre series of events. For writers of the Caribbean, language itself can be a political statement. For Frankétienne, political resistance to the Duvalier regime was writing *Dézafi* in Haitian Creole, followed by a novelistic experiment in the same language that might be called a lyrical essay, *Ultravocal* (1972, *Spiral*). Its fragmented, visionary, and tormented style not only defies the genre of the novel but seems to be an appropriate expression for the tortured existence of his island nation.

Writers of resistance from the southern cone region include Ricardo Piglia, Sylvia Molloy, Alejandra Pizarnik, and Luis Gusmán. They are as radical in their progressive politics as they are experimental in their approaches to writing. The fiction of Piglia is one of the most significant in Latin America since the early writings of Julio Cortázar. Piglia has published over five books of fiction, but these "fictions" can be read as meditations as well as political essays. Piglia's fiction is a major rewriting of Argentine history and literature just as the writing of Carlos Fuentes and Diamela Eltit is a reworking of much Latin American literature and history. Piglia has joined Fuentes and Eltit in search of the origins of the language and culture of the Americas: Eltit's investigation into the "mother language" in *Por la patria* has its equivalent in Piglia's questioning of the "father language" in *Respiración artificial*.

Respiración artificial opens with the question "Is there a story?" and then keeps the reader intrigued for the remainder of the novel, even though the action is minimal. This novel eventually becomes a lengthy meditation on Argentine cultural and political history. Near the end, the question arises in this novel—written during the military dictatorship—of how to speak the unspeakable. The multiple mediated narratives constantly evoke this question, always avoiding speaking the unspeakable, which would be the contestatory language against the military dictatorship in Argentina when *Respiración artificial* was written and published.

Molloy, Pizarnik, and Gusmán are the authors of subtle fictions that testify not only to resistance but also to the heterogeneity of postmodern writing in Argentina. Molloy's *En breve cárcel* (1981, *Certificate of Absence*) returns to the postmodern origins of Borges, the Borges who offers reflections on fictional texts, questioning the stability of the text itself. It is a self-conscious feminist work that defends its marginality and refuses to comply with the expectations of many readers. Pizarnik's *La condesa sangrienta* (1971, *The Bloody Countess*) has been read as a revisiting of the Dracula story in a postmodern world in which neither the truth of the moral or of the immoral are factors, for it recreates a fictional world in which morality is not an issue. More informed readings, however, point to a historical female Bluebeard—the Countess Báthory—and argue convincingly that Pizarnik does emphatically deal with moral issues. Gusmán's fourth novel, *En el corazón de junio* (1983, In the heart of June) sets forth a series of enigmas. Nevertheless, like *Artifical Respiration*, it attempts to speak the unspeakable.

Postmodern writers of the southern cone region write from the periphery of a periphery. The fiction of writers such as Eltit and Piglia questions the truth industry of much first world writing. Some writers of the post-Boom who wrote in exile faced the same issue of political repression but employed other strategies as a response; they tend to be less obscure and more accessible to their readers.

The fictions of the Mexican Ignacio Solares and the Venezuelan Adriano González León were written under regimes that projected institutionalized images of democracy and freedom of expression; neither Mexico nor Venezuela in the 1970s and 1980s was governed under a military dictatorship. Consequently, writers within these nations wrote fictions of resistance with the relative security of being safe from arrest. Mexican journalists and writers tend to understand the subtle limits of critique that the Mexican state will tolerate; the PRI is known to permit freedom of expression with limits well understood by the media industry. In the 1960s, when Adriano González León wrote *País portátil* (1968, Portable nation), guerrilla warfare was spreading throughout Latin America as a reponse to the social and economic equity of most Latin American societies, following the model of the Cuban Revolution.

Like Solares, Adriano González León has written all of his work within the borders of his nation. *País portátil* deals with urban revolutionaries in Caracas in the 1960s; it also expands to provide a larger sense of the city as well as the historical background to the protagonist's relatives, the Barazarte family. The basic present of the novel covers a span of a few hours, but the family story covers generations. Changes in time and narrative voice make this an intense story of tradition, political commitment, and urban guerrilla activity.

In summary, the fictions of resistance in Latin America, as written by novelists such as Eltit, Franketienne, Piglia, and others, are representative of the unique ways in which Latin American writers have responded to military and authoritarian regimes. In addition, writers such as Solares and González León have novelized critiques that reveal the operations of governments that have committed abuses with respect to human rights, the distribution of wealth, democratic ideals, and the like.

Women's Writing and Feminist Fiction

Since the 1980s, women's writing and feminist fiction have become an increasingly important part of the Latin American scene. The groundwork for this flowering of women's writing in Latin America, however, was laid in the previous decades by such prominent women writers as the Chilean María Luisa Bombal and the Argentines Marta Brunet and Beatriz Guido. These three novelists wrote most of their important work before 1945 and were followed by modern writers who set the stage for the 1980s, such as the Mexicans Rosario Castellanos and Elena Garro as well as the Brazilian Clarice Lispector. Each of these writers has also been increasingly recognized by scholars and readers of the literatures of Latin America and the Caribbean.

The most widely read Latin American woman writer of the 1970s and 1980s was Isabel Allende; she is universally recognized among scholars and critics for her first novel, *La casa de los espíritus* (1982, *The House of the Spirits*). Several other women writers, however, were equally or more productive, although they did not enjoy the commercial success of Allende. Among the women writers with established reputations in Latin America and the Caribbean were Elena Poniatowska, Elena Garro, Rosario Ferré, Luisa Valenzuela, Diamela Eltit, Albalucía Angel, Fanny Buitrago, Ana María Shua, Alicia Borinsky, Julieta Campos, Carmen Naranjo, Cristina Peri Rossi, Alejandra Pizarnik, and Armonía

Sommers. These women have been associated with several tendencies in Latin American fiction, from the post-Boom and exile writing to feminist and postmodern novels.

In addition, Brazilian writers Clarice Lispector, Helena Parente Cunha, Lya Luft, Hilda Hilst, and Nélida Piñón, as well as the Caribbean writer Maryse Condé and U.S. Latina novelists Sandra Cisneros, Ana Castillo, and Margarita Cota-Cardenas entered into a significant dialogue with the Latin American novel. Many of these writers set forth a specifically feminist project: writing in 1981, Brazilian writer Marina Colosanti has pointed to women as inheritors of earlier traditions and forgers of new ones. Helena Parente Cunha and Lispector from Brazil, as well as Chilean Diamela Eltit and Argentine Sylvia Molloy were well aware of this dual role. Women writers of the 1970s and 1980s were more sophisticated in their use of narrative technique and more affirmative about feminist issues than were writers of previous generations. They tend to use a variety of discourses (journalistic, instructional, legal) and in the process raise questions about the viability of the genre of the novel itself. Many of these women wrote for considerable portions of their careers while facing either political repression or exile.

Fanny Buitrago was generally less interested in innovation and feminist theory than Angel, Molloy, or other feminists. Buitrago has published a consistent body of fiction since the 1960s. She writes with an emphasis on oral tradition and modernist aesthetics. Her main interests are human relationships, and her characters tend to be isolated, abandoned, and constrained by social mores. Her most complex work is *Cola de zorro* (1970, Fox's tail), a family story, but not of the traditional sort. The three major characters in this work are connected by a man of mythical proportions. Buitrago's novels *Los pañamanes* (1979, The island men) and *Los amores de Afrodita* (1983, Aphrodite's loves) demonstrate her interest in stories that are accessible to a broad reading public, yet without the clichés of commercial literature. *Los amores de Afrodita* can be read as a volume of short stories, and similar volumes appeared throughout Latin America.

The fiction of Elena Poniatowska, Luisa Valenzuela, and Rosario Ferré has not been commercial enough to compete in sales with writers such as Allende and not experimental enough to be associated with postmodern writers. Nevertheless, these three novelists do have feminist interests, and their fiction is significant. Poniatowska's early writing was nonfiction, but she has published several novels more recently. From 1968 to 1990 she published the *testimonios* (testimonial novels) *Hasta no verte Jesús mío* (1969, *Here's to You, Jesusa*) and *La noche de Tlatelolco* (1971, *Massacre in Mexico*), the collection of short stories *De noche vienes* (1979, You come at night), the epistolary novel *Querido Diego, te abraza Quiela* (1978, *Dear Diego*), and the novel *La "Flor de Lis"* (1988, The flower of Lis). *Hasta no verte Jesús mío* is an oral history of a washerwoman. The plot of her later work, *La "Flor de Lis"* parallels Poniatowska's own life: the protagonist is from an aristocratic family background, emigrates from France to Mexico City, and eventually comes to understand the social and political realities of her adopted nation. In Poniatowska's work, the documentary spirit is constant, as is her search for social justice in Mexico.

Although she shares Poniatowska's interest in *testimonio*, Luisa Valenzuela has dedicated more of her career strictly to writing fiction. Valenzuela is just as political as Poniatowska, as is particularly evident in her work *Cola de lagartija* (1983, Lizard's tail). In this work, a character named Luisa Valenzuela confronts the chaotic process of writing and the increasingly absurd political and social world around her.

Rosario Ferré, Julieta Campos, Sandra Cisneros, Alejandra Pizarnik, Cristina Perri Rossi, Elizabeth Burgos, and Domitila Barrios published a heterogeneous array of works ranging from modernist fiction to *testimonio* narrative. Burgos is known for her collaboration with Rigoberta Menchú in their coauthored narrative of political struggles in Guatemala, *Me llamo Rigoberta Menchú y así me nació la conciencia* (1976, *I, Rigoberta Menchú*). Menchú relates the customs of her Native American people in a small farming community and the loss of her family members. This documentation of the excesses of the government became a polemical work in the 1990s. Barrios published two books of *literatura testimonial*, providing an account of her life in "*Si me permiten hablar . . .* " (1976, "If you'll let me speak"). Her religious experience with a group of Jehovah's Witnesses and her growing political awareness, political commitment, and political activity inform much of this *testimonio*. She also offers an eyewitness description of massacres in the mines. Her book *Aquí, también, Domitila* (1985, Here, too, Domitila), is a narrative about a hunger strike to protest the imprisonment of political prisoners.

Many women writers from Venezuela and Latina writers from the United States have been generally unknown beyond their respective national borders. Some scholars, nevertheless, have brought to the forefront the fiction of Venezuelan women writers, such as Milagros Matos-Gil, Ana Teresa Torres, and Laura Antillano. Sandra Cisneros, Ana Castillo, and Margarita Cota-Cárdenas have made innovative contributions to the novel as Latina writing in the United States, exploring themes of race and gender. These three writers in the United States question racism in Anglo-American society, while Castillo's *The Mixquihuala Letters* (1986) deals with internalized racism among Latinas. The connections between this novel and the Latin American novel written in Spanish are explicit. For example, Castillo states at the beginning of the novel that she writes "in memory of the master of the game, Julio Cortázar." Writing in the mode of Cortázar in *Hopscotch*, she indicates to the reader that "it is the author's duty to alert the reader that this is not a book to be read in the usual sequence. All letters are numbered to aid following any one of the author's proposed options." Cota-Cárdenas's *Puppet* (1985) is an innovative novel with respect to language, for this work both incorporates multiple languages and is a reflection on language. Cisneros's highly successful *The House on Mango Street* (1984) is a series of vignettes about a young girl growing up in a Latino section of Chicago. This is the most celebrated of Cisneros's works, all of which deal with gender and race.

In summary, the colonial legacy of Latin America and the Caribbean has been questioned and rejected most recently by women writers. The important predecessors to recent movements of redemocratization since the 1980s were the novels of dictators and the wide variety of fictions of resistance.

Chronological Survey

The colonial legacy, the 1960s Boom, and the international popularity of magical realist novelists have been the most widely recognized phenomena associated with the Latin American and Caribbean novel. In the mid-1940s the appearance of a series of now classic modernist novels signaled a change in the direction of Latin American fiction that preceded the popular novels of magical realism—the most widely recognized phenomenon associated with Latin American and Caribbean fiction. Following the lead of Borges and foreign modernists, these novelists of the 1940s rejected conventional and realist modes of writing, as well as the limits of much regionalist writing that had predominated in the 1920s and 1930s. Major novels that signaled this change in Latin America were Clarice Lispector's *Perto do coração selvagem* (1944, *Near the Wild Heart*), Miguel Angel Asturias's *El Señor Presidente*, Agustín Yáñez's *Al filo del agua* (1947, *The Edge of the Storm*), Graciliano Ramos's *Insônia* (1947, *Insomnia*), Leopoldo Marechal's *Adán Buenosayres* (1948), and Alejo Carpentier's *El reino de este mundo* (1949, *The Kingdom of This World*). Yáñez's *Al filo del agua* is still read in Mexico as a classic novel of modernist technique and of the repressive Mexican society that was typical before the Mexican Revolution of 1914–1917. Lispector, Asturias, Ramos, Marechal, and Carpentier have become national cultural icons and canonical writers of contemporary Latin America.

Borges's volume of short fiction, *Ficciones* (1944), was a key predecessor to this flourishing of the Latin American novel, for in this volume he reaffirmed the right of invention and the central role of imagination that had been often overlooked or ignored since the writings of the romantics. Indeed, the vast majority of Latin American novelists felt an obligation to imitate sociopolitical reality rather than engage in pure invention. In the stories of *Ficciones*, such as "The Secret Miracle" and "The Garden of Forking Paths," Borges took innovative and inventive approaches to time and space, openly challenging the very tenets of traditional realist-naturalist fiction.

With the appearance of the fiction of Asturias, Yáñez, Ramos, José Lins do Rêgo, and Carpentier, Latin American and Caribbean writers exercised the right of invention and employed stratagems commonly associated with modernist narrative: fragmented structure, multiple points of view, innovative use of language, interiorization, the use of neologisms, and the like. In the Latin American case these technical innovations came via European and North American modernists, particularly Proust, Joyce, Dos Passos, and Faulkner. The Latin American writers also participated in a shift of what was considered important in human experience and worthy of novelizing. In the 1950s many writers advocated these ideas, proposing the modernization and universalization of their respective national literatures in cultural magazines such as *Mito* in Colombia, *Sardio* in Venezuela, *Orígenes* in Cuba, and the *Revista Mexicana de Literatura* in Mexico.

Yáñez, Ramos, Marechal, Lins do Rêgo, and Carpentier were not as explicitly political in their novels as Asturias in *El Señor Presidente*, but they were equally interested in creating universal experience. In *Al filo del agua* Yáñez uses a multiplicity of strategies to recreate the experience of living in small-town, rural Mexico at the end of the repressive regime of dictator Porfirio Díaz; near the end of the book, the Mexican Revolution is breaking out. Ramos's collection of stories *Insônia* included modernist strategies as well, but Marechal's *Adán Buenosayres* is a lengthy and far more ambitious urban exploration of Greco-Roman classical mythology. In it Marechal explores psychological states, as does Do Rêgo in *Eurídice*. *El reino de este mundo* is Carpentier's rethinking and novelization of Latin American cultural issues—mostly related to national identity—that were in vogue in the 1940s and 1950s.

The 1950s produced some major modernist novels by authors such as Juan Rulfo, Lygia Fagundes Telles, David Viñas, Alejo Carpentier, and Miguel Otero Silva. A new generation of novelists, headed by Gabriel García Márquez, Julio Cortázar, and Carlos Fuentes, also began publishing their first fiction in the 1950s. Many of these writers were fascinated by Faulknerian modes of writing fiction, and Rulfo, Viñas, and García Márquez were among the most committed neo-Faulknerians: they used specific regional settings to tell universal human stories. Using the region of Jalisco, Mexico, as his setting, Rulfo creates the mythical town of Comala in his novel *Pedro Páramo* (1955, *Pedro Paramo*). García Márquez's *La hojarasca* (1955, *Leafstorm*) offers multiple points of view in the Faulknerian mode to relate universal human dramas of conflict and death. Juan Carlos Onetti was also a follower of Faulkner, although his novel *La vida breve* (1950, *The Brief Life*) is primarily a novel of existential anguish along the lines of the writings of Oreamuno and Cardoso.

Many novelists of the 1950s were engaged in a decade-long cultural debate about identity and modernization in the Americas. Carpentier had been theorizing about Latin American culture and its relationship to Europe for several years when he published *El reino de este mundo* and *Los pasos perdidos* (1953, *The Lost Steps*). The latter is a story of a return to origins, for the protagonist takes a trip down the Orinoco River that takes him back in time to the life of his youth and of primitive times. In both novels Carpentier explores issues of Latin American identity, and this exploration was part of a broader dialogue in the Caribbean as set forth by Francophone writer Aimé Césaire of Martinique.

The new generation of writers (born mostly in the 1920s and 1930s) was interested in modernizing Latin American culture by drawing on European and American modernist literary practices, their own cultural heritage, and a commitment to social change that was their response to the colonial legacy. Most of them were devoted followers of Jean Paul Sartre, whose theories of the *engagé* writer were cited from Mexico to Argentina. In Mexico this new generation was headed by Carlos Fuentes, who cofounded and codirected the *Revista Mexicana de Literatura* along with Emmanuel Carballo. With this journal Fuentes and his cohorts (known in Mexico as the Generation of Medio Siglo, the mid-century generation) intended to modernize and universalize Mexican culture. In Colombia the magazine *Mito* served a similar function, and the young writer Gabriel García Márquez was a collaborator with *Mito*, as was Alvaro Mutis. Throughout Latin America and the Caribbean groups of writers with similar interests founded magazines and journals to promote their ideas.

Fuentes, García Márquez, Cortázar, and Vargas Llosa also began writing fiction in the 1950s. Fuentes began his career with a volume of short stories with Mexican themes, but written in an inventive and fantastic mode, *Los días enmascarados* (1954, The masked days). His first novel, *La región más transparente*, revealed Fuentes's interest in modernizing Mexican literature and the Latin American novel. Using as a model such urban works as Dos Passos's *Manhattan Transfer* and Doblin's *Berlinalexanderplatz*, Fuentes created a vast panorama of Mexico City. Here and in *La muerte de Artemio Cruz* Fuentes employed the complete gamut of narrative strategies associated with literary modernism. In both novels he also delves into the history of Mexico as a key to understanding the present. García Márquez was equally interested in modernist strategies in his first novel, *Leafstorm*, clearly written in a Faulknerian mode. Cortázar and Vargas Llosa were mostly involved with short fiction in the 1950s, although Cortázar did publish his first novel, *Los premios* (*The Winners*) in 1958.

The 1950s witnessed similar movement toward modernization among writers throughout the Hispanic world. David Viñas of Argentina and Juan Carlos Onetti of Uruguay were among the most Faulknerian, as evidenced in the multiple narrators and use of space in Viñas's *Cayó sobre su rostro* (1955) and Onetti's *La vida breve*. In Brazil, Jorge Amado, João Guimarães Rosa, and Carlos Heitor Cony were writing with a growing awareness of modern literature in the West. Amado was yet to produce his major works, but Guimarães Rosa's *Grande Sertão: Veredas* (1956, *The Devil to Pay in the Backlands*) is a monumental work that incorporates Brazilian history, anthropology, indigenous cultures, and myth as well as impressive linguistic innovation. In the Hispanic U.S., one of the early novels to be recognized in the Chicano novelistic tradition was *Pocho* (1959) by José Antonio Villarreal.

International recognition of the new fiction of Latin America took the form of the Boom of the 1960s and early 1970s. The most celebrated figures of this Boom were Gabriel García Márquez, Carlos Fuentes, Mario Vargas Llosa, and Julio Cortázar. The Chilean José Donoso was often associated with the group, and several other writers of the same generation, such as the Mexican Elena Poniatowska and Rosario Castellanos, the Colombians Manuel Mejía Vallejo and Héctor Rojas Herazo, the Venezuelan Salvador Garmendia, the Cuban Guillermo Cabrera Infante, the Argentine Manuel Puig, and the Brazilians Jorge Amado, Clarice Lispector, Osmin Lins, Maria Alice Barroso, Carlos Heitor Cony, and Assis Brasil published novels comparable in quality to the major works of the Boom. In addition, by the late 1960s and early 1970s, a group of Chicano novelists, headed by Rolando Hinojosa, Tomás Rivera, and Rudolfo Anaya, began publishing novels that some scholars associated with the Boom.

The most recognized and now classic novels of the Boom were Fuentes's *La muerte de Artemio Cruz*, Vargas Llosa's *La ciudad y los perros* (1963, *The Time of the Hero*), Cortázar's *Rayuela* (1963, *Hopscotch*), and García Márquez's *Cien años de soledad* (1967, *One Hundred Years of Solitude*). Each of these works had considerable impact throughout the Hispanic world both in creating a broader readership for Latin American literature and in influencing later generations of writers. Vargas Llosa's *The Time of the Hero* was a polemical work in Peru and a best seller throughout Latin America. It tells a story considered scandalous in Peru: institutional corruption and devious sexual behavior pervade a military school well known in Lima. Fuentes's *The Death of Artemio Cruz* was an innovative technical experiment, because of its use of three narrative points of view, as well as work highly critical of the Mexican political establishment and their allies in the United States. The most experimental of all the novels of the Boom, however, was Cortázar's *Hopscotch*, a book that offers the reader several possible readings. The most heralded of the novels of the Boom was García Márquez's *One Hundred Years of Solitude*, the Colombian's magical realist tour de force that tells both a family story and the history of Latin America from its foundations to the twentieth century.

José Donoso had already published some fiction in the 1950s when he befriended Carlos Fuentes, the eventual spokesperson of the Boom, in the early 1960s. Donoso did not assume the political positions that characterized the four central figures of the Boom, but his ambitious and lengthy novel *El obsceno pájaro de la noche* (1969, *The Obscene Bird of the Night*) brought him considerable notoriety during the heyday of the Boom. It is a surreal experiment in which the reader must struggle to discern between dream and reality; characters change in character and identity.

Unlike Donoso, Salvador Garmendia and Manuel Mejía Vallejo did not associate with the writers of the Boom nor did they participate in their jetset lifestyle. For most of their writings careers, they remained in their respective homelands and were minimally recognized abroad. Nevertheless, they both published novels of quality similar to much of the writing of the Boom. Garmendia had been associated with the Sardio group in Venezuela in the 1950s, and published his early fiction during this period. His novels *Los pequeños seres* (1959, The little beings) and *Los habitantes* (1961, The inhabitants) were introspective and small-scale works dealing more with human relationships than the vast historical works of Fuentes and García Márquez. Mejía Vallejo's *El día señalado* consists of two story lines: one told by a third-person omniscient narrator dealing with a priest in a small town of Colombia and another told by a character who arrives at the town to commit an act of revenge. Both stories relate to the period of civil war in 1950s Colombia referred to as La Violencia.

At the margins of the Boom in Brazil, Jorge Amado, Clarice Lispector, Autran Dourado, Carlos Heitor Cony, and Assis Brasil were all publishing novels in the 1960s. Amado's *Dona Flor e seus dois maridos* (1969, *Dona Flor and Her Two Husbands*) is a now classic fantasy love story in the Latin American canon and Lispector's *A Paixão Segundo G. H.* (1964, *The Passion According to G.H.*) is an intimate work focusing on the existential anguish of an individual woman. Dourado's *A barca dos homens* (1961, A ship of men) is a work heavily laden with symbols and multiple voices of characters in intense relationships. A mirror image of these novels was a masculine version of individual angst in a limited space, centering on the forty-year-old male protagonist in Carlos Heitor Cony's *Antes, o Verão* (1964, Before, the summer). Two Mexican writers whose early fiction appeared in the 1960s on the margins of the Boom were Rosario Castellanos and Elena Garro. Castellano's *Oficio de tinieblas* (1962, Dark services) and Garro's *Los recuerdos del porvenir* (1963, *Memories of Days to Come*), like *El día señalado*, are novels of political violence with cultural implications in the development of the themes. These Mexican writers were concerned with women, feminist issues, and political persecution in many of their works. Indeed, they were pioneer feminists of Latin America who wrote ambitious modernist novels comparable in narrative technique to the most accomplished fiction of the Boom.

The 1970s and 1980s were characterized by the flourishing of a heterogeneous and compelling novelistic production. The cumulative effect of the work of novelists such as the Chilean Isabel Allende, the Puerto Rican Rosario Ferré, and the Brazilians Nélida Piñón and Clarice Lispector ushered in a new era for women writers in Latin America. In addition to the phenomenal rise of women's writing, scholars observed the appearance of a series of novels associated with a post-Boom of the Latin American novel. Other scholars, taking special note of the most radically innovative fiction, spoke of a now postmodern Latin American novel. The most significant cultural and political feature of this period was the rise of repressive military dictatorships in the 1970s and their fall in the late 1980s and 1990s. Since the 1980s, the human and cultural meaning of these dictatorships is still being accounted for by novelists. During the 1970s, in fact, enough Latin American writers published novels dealing with military regimes that the *dictator novel* became common usage.

Some Brazilian novelists publishing during this period, including Clarice Lispector, Jorge Amado, Autran Dourado, and Osman Lins, engaged in political, historical, and postmodern narratives comparable to those found among writers throughout the Spanish-speaking Americas. Lispector's novels in this period were *Uma apprendizagem ou o livro dos prazeres* (1969, Apprenticeships or the book of pleasures), *Agua viva* (1973, Live water), and *A Hora da Estrela* (1977, *The Hour of the Star*). The first of these three novels involves two individuals' search for identity, and Lispector's feminist concerns were increasingly evident. Jorge Amado continued his career as a novelist with *Tereza Batista cansada de guerra* (1972), a rewriting of popular *cordel* ballads, and Lins published the experimental *Avalovara* (1973, *Avalovara*). In Amado's playful text he creates an authorial narrator who supposedly knew a legendary heroine personally; Lins's experimental narrative offers the reader alternate structures and readings. Autran Dourado's novels of the 1970s and 1980s were written from the best tradition of modernist fiction, often with Faulknerian overtones.

The Chicano novel—now in dialogue with the Latin American Boom—flourished during this period, which produced some of the most compelling Chicano novels yet to appear. The main figures were Rolando Hinojosa, Tomás Rivera, Miguel Méndez, and Rudolfo Anaya. The coincidence of the Chicano political movement in the United States and the Boom of the Latin American novel were important factors for these Chicano writers, some of whom have spoken of their debts to the Latin American Boom novelists. Among the most notable of these dialogic novels were Rivera's *Y no se lo tragó la tierra* (1971, *And the Earth Did Not Devour Him*), Anaya's *Bless Me, Ultima* (1972), Méndez's *Peregrinos de Aztlán* (1974, *Pilgrims from Aztlán*), and Hinojosa's *Klail City y sus alrededores* (1975, *Klail City Death Trip*). These writers drew upon their own cultural history as Hispanics in the southwestern United States as well as Hispanic literary tradition, broadly conceived, to participate in a multicultural dialogue in the United States.

As was mentioned previously, in the ongoing discussions of the Latin American novel published since the 1960s Boom, some critics have referred to a post-Boom that represents, in effect, a continuation of the modernist project initiated in Latin America in the 1940s perpetuated by the writers of the Boom. Novelists such as Antonio Skármeta and Mempo Giardinelli do share generational attitudes that distance them from their immediate predecessors of the Boom. Nevertheless, their fiction represents a continuation of modernist aesthetics. These writers are by no means traditionalists; indeed, they employ the narrative strategies explored and refined by modernist writers since the 1940s. As such, Skármeta, Giardinelli, Allende, and a host of other Latin American storytellers belong to the tradition of the modernist novel—frequently adding a touch from their local tradition—be it orality, magical realism, or rewriting regional or national history.

The post-Boom represents a return to accessibility in the Latin American novel as well as more realism and pop elements that reflect a greater cultural autonomy and the revival of democracy in parts of the continent, according to Donald Shaw. Citing writers such as Skármeta, Shaw proposes that the assumptions made by the Boom writers—whether about literature or society—were directly contradicted in the next generation. Making reference to Giardinelli, Shaw emphasizes that the "extreme pessimism" characteristic of the Boom shifted to a new optimism in the post-Boom, although not all scholars uniformly agree that the Boom was necessarily so pessimistic. Giardinelli and others have also stated that their generation was defeated politically in Latin America, and that, consequently, they have lost much of the optimism conveyed by their earlier writing.

If the Boom was García Márquez's political statement and his magical realism set in Macondo, many of the writers associated with the post-Boom were politically committed storytellers whose writing can be seen as a post-Macondo phenomenon: they write either with or against the storytelling vitality and magic realist approaches of García Márquez. Writers such as Isabel Allende and Luis Sepúlveda produced a fiction with many overtones and stylistic characteristics from García Márquez's magical fictions. On the other hand, Colombian novelists such as Gustavo Alvarez Gardeazábal in *El bazar de los idiotas* (1974, *The Bazaar of the Idiots*) and Mario Tulio Aguilera Garramuno in *Breve historia de todas las cosas* (1975, A brief history of everything) have written parodies of *One Hundred Years of Solitude*.

Several writers and critics have pointed to the importance of the testimonial and a closer attachment to empirical reality among post-Boom writers. Isabel Allende, for example, believes that her writing breaks from two of the basic tenets of the Boom: she is neither "detached" nor "ironic." Several critics have argued that the Boom writers lacked a radical critique of society, embracing liberal solutions to mask their acceptance of the status quo. A more radical response to the political reality in Latin America was the post-Boom writing of Allende's *Of Love and Shadows* (1984 in the original Spanish as *De amor y de sombra*), Skármeta's *La insurrección* (1982, *The Insurrection*), and Elena Poniatowska's *La noche de Tlatelolco*. Similarly, several critics have suggested the importance of testimonials in post-Boom narrative.

In contrast, in studies of post-Boom fiction in Mexico other critics attempt to avoid the reduction of the Mexican novel to only the more accessible works. These scholars take into account the writing of novelists such as Juan García Ponce, Angelina Muñiz, and Humberto Guzmán, whose experiments with fiction are complex and elusive. The more accessible writers of Mexican fiction in the 1970s and 1980s who could be associated with a post-Boom are Sergio Galindo, Armando Ramírez, Arturo Azuela, Luis Zapata, Vicente Leñero, Luis Spota, and Jorge Ibarguengoitia. Galindo continued his modernist writing into the 1980s, publishing *Terciopelo violeta* (Violet velvet) in 1985 and *Otilia Rauda* in 1986. Arturo Azuela also published novels with a broad historical scope, beginning with a family story, *El tamaño del infierno* (1973, The size of hell). He followed with the story of a town, *Un tal José Salomé* (1975, Some guy named José Salomé), and a work about his own generation in the 1960s and 1970s, *Manifestación de silencios* (1979, Protest of silences). In *Chin-Chin el Teporocho* (1972, Chin-Chin from the Teporocho neighborhood), Ramírez focuses on everyday life in a working-class neighborhood in Mexico City and recreates a parody of the popular literature of soap operas and comic books. *La princesa del Palacio de Hierro* (1974, *The Princess of the Iron Palace*) by Gustavo Sainz was a reaction against the complexities of the fiction of the Boom and also against the hermetic qualities of the young and experimental Onda group in Mexico. In this novel an unnamed female protagonist relates a humorous story of failed relationships, sexual misadventures, and crime.

In Brazil critics do not write of their novelists as part of the Spanish American "post-Boom." Brazilian writers similar to the post-Boom in Spanish America, however, include novelists such as João Ubaldo Ribeiro, Márcio Souza, Autran Dourado, Oswaldo França Junior, and Carlos Heitor Cony. These writers tell linear stories, with interests ranging from rewriting the history of Brazil to mystery novels. They are among Brazil's most accomplished storytellers in the second half of the twentieth century and enjoy a wide readership in Brazil as well as abroad.

The term *post-Boom* has been useful to distinguish some tendencies of fiction published after the 1960s Boom. On the other hand, it was increasingly evident among critics that the radically heterogeneous Latin American novel of the 1970s and 1980s corresponded in many ways to what was being called postmodern fiction in the West. By the 1980s, it became appropriate to describe some of the new novels—although certainly not all of them—with a term that captured exactly what they were: *postmodern fiction*. Thus there has been a growing acceptance of the idea of a postmodern novel in Latin America. If the writers identified with the post-Boom tended to follow modernist aesthetics, postmodern writers have demonstrated diverging interests. These new interests have been particularly evident since 1968, with the novels of Manuel Puig, Severo Sarduy, José Emilio Pacheco, Ricardo Piglia, Diamela Eltit, and others.

Jorge Luis Borges has already been mentioned in the context of the rise of the modern novel in Latin America. A key moment for postmodern fiction in Latin America was the publication of his *Ficciones* in 1944. Moreover, several stories in this volume, such as "The Library of Babel" and "Pierre Menard, Author of the Quixote," can be seen as foundational texts for postmodern fiction of the 1970s and 1980s in Latin America. In them the boundary between the genres of fiction and the essay is blurred, opening the way for the fictionalized theoretical prose of writers such as Severo Sarduy, Ricardo Piglia, and José Balza. Borges's stories also tend to emphasize language as a theme in itself, questioning its capacity to effectively articulate reality and human subjectivity.

After Borges, important contributions to the later publication of Latin American postmodern fiction were two lengthy and elaborate modernist texts: João Guimarães Rosa's *Grande Sertão: Veredas* and Julio Cortázar's *Rayuela*. In *Grande Sertão: Veredas*, Guimarães Rosa began experimenting with the possibilities of the unresolved contradictions that are typical of much postmodern fiction. Cortázar's work in itself was not a fully elaborated postmodern work either, but its Morelli chapters at the end of the book were a radical proposal for postmodern fiction. In the late 1960s and 1970s the postmodern novel began to appear in Latin America, frequently under the signs of Borges, Guimarães Rosa, or Cortázar, and it was constituted by such experimental fictions as Cabrera Infante's *Tres tristes tigres*, Néstor Sánchez's *Siberia Blues* (1967), Puig's *La traición de Rita Hayworth* (1968, *Betrayed by Rita Hayworth*), and Lins's *Avalovara*.

Many of the roots of postmodern fiction can be related to numerous sources in Europe, North America, and Latin America. Nevertheless, the postmodern novel in Latin America is, to a large extent, a phenomenon that has frequently been in dialogue with Cortázar's self-conscious experimentation in *Hopscotch* as well as the fictional character Morelli's call for an "antinovel." Another important factor in the rise of postmodern fiction since 1968 was the first generalized presence of Joyce in Latin American literature in the 1960s. Joyce's entry into the general consciousness of the Latin American writer comes relatively late, and is not really noticeable until the appearance of works such as *Hopscotch* and *Three Trapped Tigers*.

A group of radically innovative novelists appeared on the Latin American literary scene in the 1970s and 1980s, including Diamela Eltit, Ricardo Piglia, Luis Rafael Sánchez, Héctor Libertella, Salvador Elizondo, Carmen Boullosa, Luis Arturo Ramos, José Balza, and R. H. Moreno-Durán. In their early writings, Libertella and Eltit were particularly interested in the type of linguistic innovations utilized by Sarduy. Seen in their totality, these postmodern writers and their cohorts offer radically diverse kinds of postmodernisms— perhaps a postmodern phenomenon in itself. Exponents of postmodern fiction in Brazil have been Ignácio de Loyola Brandão, Roberto Drummond, Rubem Fonseca, Ivan Angêlo, and Flávio Moreira da Costa. Loyola Brandão's *Zero* (1974) and *Não verás país nenhúm* (1981, *And Still the Earth*) are two of the most experimental and playful works of the period in Brazil.

The postmodern and transnational interests of the Latin American writer were evident in the 1990s, a period when the Latin American novel was a heterogeneous cultural manifestation of modernist, postmodern, post-postmodern, feminist, and gay fiction. These five modes overlap in many ways, frequently sharing a commitment not only to political and aesthetic critique but also the very subversion of the dominant discourses of power. Novelists still writing in a primarily modernist vein were associated in Latin America with the Boom and the post-Boom, Carlos Fuentes, Mario Vargas Llosa, Rosario Ferré, César Aira, Mempo Giardinelli, Isabel Allende, and Antonio Skármeta among them.

Laura Esquivel became one of the best-selling writers of the decade with her first novel, *Como agua para chocolate* (1990); in its English translation as *Like Water for Chocolate* this novel was received with considerable repercussions in the Americas throughout the 1990s. Postmodern writers such as Diamela Eltit, Alicia Borinsky, and Ricardo Piglia also continued publishing in the 1990s, as did a new generation of writers (born since 1955) that included novelists such as the Mexicans Jorge Volpi, Cristina Rivera-Garza, David Toscana, and Juan Villoro as well as the Brazilian Diogo Mainardi, the Chilean Alberto Fuguet, and the Bolivian Edmundo Paz Soldán. Feminist, gay, and lesbian writers, who became quite visible in the 1980s, went on writing in the 1990s. In Brazil and elsewhere they were often called the generation of the 1990s.

In the 1940s and 1950s writers such as Borges, Fuentes, and Cortázar called for a radical modernization of the Latin American novel. Their voices were heard not only in Spanish America but throughout the Hispanic world, including the U.S. southwest and the Caribbean regions where French and English are the dominant tongues. The 1990s fiction of Chicano writers Sandra Cisneros, Américo Paredes, John Rechy, and Tomás Villasenor, as well as the Haitian Edwidge Danticat and the Puerto Rican Giannina Braschi, are testimony to the radical modernization that has indeed taken place throughout Latin America in the 1990s. By the 1990s, postmodern and feminist fiction, as well as other heterogeneous discourses, challenged the more commercial and popular versions of traditional realism and modernist fiction of the Americas and beyond.

At the end of the century, the youngest generation of writers, most of whom were born in the 1960s and began publishing in the 1990s, began assuming their roles as writers with a presence in the Latin American literary scene. Polemics arose in several countries about their positioning as part of the cultural and literary traditions, their relationship with their predecessors in the 1960s Boom, and the effects of globalization, among other topics.

The young writers Alberto Fuguet and Sergio Gómez of Chile and Edmundo Paz Soldán of Bolivia have proposed an ambitious reconfiguration of the novelistic scene throughout Latin America to include their young group, which they designated as "McOndo" in opposition to what they saw as the international reading public's desire for Latin American writers to reduce their writing to the now tired schemes of magical realism. In Mexico Jorge Volpi, Ignacio Padilla, and colleagues of this generation claimed to create a crack in the established literary hierarchies and declared themselves the "generation of the crack." They use their numerous national and international literary prizes, as well as commercial success, as indicators of their cultural relevance. Similarly, in Brazil a new "generation of the 1990s" is claiming to supersede the grand figures of Brazilian letters. The success of these groups and the novels of the respective writers has been questioned by readers, writers, and critics. Nevertheless, writers of this generation, such as Bernardo Carvalho, Diogo Mainardi, Nelson de Oliveira, and Fernando Bonassi have given credence to the proposals that this new generation of the 1990s could well become a noteworthy group of writers in the near future. All have already published at least three books of fiction. Carvalho's recent novel *Nove Noites* (2002, Nine nights) is an intriguing fictionalization of the life of an American anthropologist who did research in Brazil in the late 1930s and early 1940s and then committed a mysterious suicide.

The recent rise of novelists such as the Mexicans Cristina Rivera Garza, David Toscana, Ignacio Solares, Carmen Boullosa, and Luis Arturo Ramos, the Brazilians Milton Hatoum, Bernardo Carvalho, and João Gilberto Noll, the Argentine Ricardo Piglia, and the Chilean Diamela Eltit are testimony to the ongoing high quality of Latin American fiction at the beginning of the twenty-first century. Many of these writers already have works published in translation beyond their national boundaries, and novels such as Cristina Rivera-Garza's *Nadie me verá llorar*, translated as *No One Will See Me Cry*, which appeared in English in 2003, and David Toscana's *Estación Tula*, translated as *Tula Station*, which appeared in English 2000, are two prominent examples of the strength of both the tradition and the innovation of the contemporary Latin American novel.

Regional Survey

The Mexican Novel: Context and Chronology

The major political contexts for the Mexican novel since 1945 are the Mexican Revolution of 1910–1917, the institutionalization of the political party in control during most of the post-WWII period, the PRI (Partido Revolucionario Institucional), and the massacre at the Plaza de Tlatelolco in Mexico City in 1968. During the Mexican Revolution, Mariano Azuela published *Los de abajo*, and his was only the first of a long series. In the 1940s, in fact, the old-school storyteller and social critic Azuela was still the most widely read novelist in Mexico. Even Mexican novels of the 1940s and 1950s that do not focus primarily on the revolution tend to have it in the background, making this event omnipresent in Mexican fiction.

The context for the Mexican Revolution was the *porfiriato*, the three-decade-long dictatorship of Porfirio Díaz that ended in 1910. During these three decades, Díaz favored a small and privileged elite, leaving the population at large marginal to the economy and the majority of the population impoverished. This elite was a remnant of the colonial legacy in Mexico. The revolution started in late 1910, under the leadership of an idealist, Francisco Madero, who eventually became a martyr. The other figures of the revolution who soon became prominent were Francisco "Pancho" Villa, Pascual Orozco, Emiliano Zapata, Venustantio Carranza, and Alvaro Obregón (their names are mentioned in Azuela's *Los de abajo*, as they are in much Mexican fiction of the revolution). "Pancho" Villa led revolutionary forces in the northern region of Mexico, and Emiliano Zapata led indigenous forces in the south; the latter expected the Mexican Revolution to mean social justice with respect to land distribution. The revolution itself became a chaotic struggle, with unlikely alliances and contradictory ideologies that were often difficult to decipher. Indeed, Azuela himself participated in the revolution, and his presentation in *Los de abajo* suggests that, in the end, self-interest predominated over ideology and the political ideals of many. In 1917 a revolutionary constitution was promulgated; it contained many provisions for progressive change that have been difficult to realize to this day.

For several decades after 1917, the revolution was in an administrative phase, with a series of governments that used the constitution of 1917 to justify and legitimate its power. The government of Lázaro Cárdenas in the 1930s is widely considered the most revolutionary and perhaps the closest to the ideals set forth in the Mexican constitution. Cárdenas carried out intense land reform and nationalized the petroleum industry. Since the post-WWII period many writers—certainly the majority—have been critical of the institutional party (PRI) as an authentic arm of the Mexican Revolution and its constitution.

Two major novels that focus on the Mexican Revolution in very different ways are Agustín Yáñez's *Al filo del agua* and Carlos Fuentes's *La muerte de Artemio Cruz*. Unlike Mariano Azuela before him and Fuentes after him, Yáñez is not really critical of the status quo in Mexico or the institutional attempts to carry out the revolutionary reforms set forth in the Mexican Revolution. The conflict in Yáñez's *Al filo del agua* is abstract and subtle. The setting for this novel is a small town in rural Mexico during a year-and-a-half period leading up to the Mexican Revolution in 1910. It begins with an "Acto preparatorio" that sets the tone for the novel in a series of sensory impressions and a static vision of the town ambience. From this point forward a tension is established between the static and mobile. Scholars have pointed to the importance of the universal human drama that unfolds. Rarely does one encounter a novel with such a seemingly perfect harmony between form and content as in this work, a masterpiece of narrative technique in Mexico. The two-part structure leads the reader through a process from fragmentation to harmony; the content of the novel also points to the fragmentation of the characters in the first half and the harmonious fulfillment of their desires when they join the revolution.

Yáñez's presentation of prerevolutionary Mexico makes the Mexican Revolution seem inevitable: the town is ready for change. Change and modernity seem to be "on the edge of the storm" and a positive alternative to the stultifying society of deeply embedded Hispanic tradition and the repressive *porfiriato*. By writing this novel in the 1940s, Yánez was implicitly supporting the status quo of Mexico's 1940s modernization; this process of the PRI's political agenda was being defined as the ongoing Mexican Revolution and a necessary reaction against the regime of Porfirio Díaz, against an old aristocracy that had ruled for centuries in Mexico, and against the most conservative values of the Catholic Church.

If *Al filo del agua* is read as a defense of the status quo of the 1940s, certainly Fuentes's *La muerte de Artemio* Cruz is far more critical. By using three alternating points of view, Fuentes tells the story of protagonist Artemio Cruz, who represents the new class of Mexicans that came into power with the Mexican Revolution and was moribund by the 1950s. In this novel Fuentes condemns Cruz and the corrupt Mexican society that he represents. Cruz is portrayed as the moral failure who betrays even his own ideals from an early period in his life—as a participant in the Mexican Revolution. The novel presents a series of moral tests for Cruz—all of which he fails. Nevertheless, he has led a life of wealth, power, and influence in modern Mexico. The period when this novel was written and published— the early 1960s—was one during which Fuentes was engaged in his most radical political activism as well as writing, and *La muerte de Artemio Cruz* is entirely representative of this stage of his work: Artemio basically sells out to American capitalism, but the supposed "Mexican miracle" of the 1940s and 1950s, in the view of Fuentes, is a failure.

The second important context, institutionalization of the PRI in Mexico, is a continuation of the story of the Mexican Revolution. For the three decades following the revolution, the ruling class carried out a variety of measures to consolidate its power and attempt to integrate a larger portion of the Mexican populace into the national economy than had been the case under the rule of Porfirio Díaz. Fuentes portrays this attempt, however, as a failure as well.

A very successful more recent novel questioning the institutional power of the PRI in Mexico was *El gran elector* (1993) by Ignacio Solares. In this work Solares creates a synthesis of several Mexican presidential figures in one character who is the prototype autocratic leader of the PRI. In this political satire Solares integrates actual speeches from several of these former presidents to ridicule the very discourse of power in Mexico.

The event simply referred to in Mexico as "Tlatelolco" was the massacre of students and workers who were protesting in the Plaza de Tlatelolco in Mexico City in 1968, drawing attention to the social injustice and political contradictions of the extant regime. For most Mexican intellectuals who were young adults in 1968, this event is considered a watershed in the Mexican political history of the century: it represented an enormous loss of faith in the possibilities of a democratic government in Mexico that might express the will of its citizens. Elena Poniatowska's *La noche de Tlatelolco* (1970) provides documentation on this event.

Beyond this focus on the Mexican Revolution, the PRI, and the national tragedy of Tlatelolco, the contemporary novel in Mexico follows many of the thematic and formal trends of the other regions of Latin America and the Caribbean. In addition, thematic interests specific to this region concern postrevolutionary society in Mexico since 1968. As is the case with the Andean region, the literature of Mexico has strong roots in indigenous culture and traditions that were amply fictionalized in the 1930s and 1940s. In Mexico this indigenous tradition in narrative found continuity in the fiction of the Rosario Castellanos; she became acquainted with local indigenous cultures by virtue of the fact that she was reared in Chiapas and lived close to the native population despite her own upper-middle-class background and European ancestry. In her novel *Oficio de tinieblas* Castellanos uses a historic uprising in Chiapas in 1867 as her setting, portraying the struggles of a priestess who led Chamula Indians in the rebellion. The author connects this rebellion to a traditional Chamula legend. She explores *indigenista* themes by portraying the encounter and conflict between two cultures, but in doing so she avoids many of the clichés associated with this type of literature when it was amply published in the 1930s and 1940s. She also characterizes the Indians as individuals—human beings—in a more convincing fashion than is typical of most indigenista literature.

The tradition of realist and social protest literature associated with the 1930s and 1940s also continued to mid-century in Mexico. Luis Spota followed closely in this tradition of direct social critique. Spota's *Casi el paraíso* (1956, Almost paradise) contains none of the flashy narrative techniques that characterize modernist fiction, but he did fascinate a large reading public in Mexico with his strong plots and his critique of middle-class mores and the abuse of power by the political establishment of the PRI. In *Casi el paraíso,* in particular, he criticizes café society in Mexico City.

With respect to the rise of fiction in Mexico, *Pedro Páramo* by Juan Rulfo, *La region más transparente* by Carlos Fuentes, and *El bordo* (1960, *The Precipice*) by Sergio Galindo established the continuity of modernistism as it had been pioneered by Asturias and Yáñez in the 1940s. These novels offer the geographic breadth and psychological depth of the most accomplished fiction of this period in Mexico. Galindo's novel is a story of human relationships within the small group of a family, focusing on an aunt. She suffers a tyranny that seems to be of her own making, and the tragedy of her life is inevitable from the beginning.

Besides Galindo, some of the most engaging writers of the generation of the writers of the Boom who were not part of this international scene in the 1960s were the Mexicans Rosario Castellanos and Elena Garro, along with the Nicaraguan Lizandro Chávez Alfaro and the Costa Rican Alfonso Chase. Comparable in depth to the best novels of the Boom, *Los recuerdos del porvenir* by Garro deals with life and death in the context of a world that is both real and unreal. The setting is a small town in Mexico before the *cristero* revolts of the 1920s, and this town has a special, even magical quality: it speaks with the voice of a character. Garro's insights on race, class, and gender make her a forerunner of much women's writing of the 1980s and 1990s.

Rulfo's *Pedro Páramo* and Fuentes's *La region más transparente* are more Faulknerian in tone and general conceptualization. *Pedro Páramo* is the story of a local boss or *cacique*, but it goes well beyond telling his story to explore in depth the personal and mythical resonances of his reign of power. Rulfo's setting is novel: all the characters are, in fact, dead and occupy a town that seems to be a hell. His minimalist and evocative style is exceptional in Latin American fiction of the mid-1950s. Following the tradition of many other characters of earlier Mexican novels, the cacique is yet another of the numerous protagonists in Mexican fiction whose position of wealth and power harks back to his role in the Mexican Revolution. The setting for *La región más transparente* is significant, for Fuentes presents a broad panorama of society in 1950s Mexico City. Fuentes is highly critical of the new ruling class in Mexico, satirizing the upper-middle class and politicians in power. At the same time, Fuentes's work is one of the most ambitious urban novels to have been published in the region and Latin America in general. In this sense, this was Fuentes's *Berlinalexanderplatz*—to cite Doblin's urban classic.

The most internationally visible continuity of the modern Latin American novel was the writing of the 1960s Boom of the Spanish American novel. In this region Carlos Fuentes was the representative of the Boom at the same time that he was, in fact, the de facto leader of the group in the sense that he articulated the political and aesthetic agenda of the writers of the Boom. His novels *La muerte de Artemio Cruz*, *Cambio de piel* (1967, *Change of Skin*), *Zona sagrada* (1967, *Holy Place*), and *Cumpleaños* (1969, *Birthday*) were major novels of the Boom. Other noteworthy novelists in this region to publish in the 1960s were the Mexicans Juan García Ponce, Fernando del Paso, and Vicente Leñero; each published a body of important fiction in later decades.

A first wave of postmodern fiction in Mexico was evident in the mid-1960s (approximately 1964–1968), with the publication of novels such as Vicente Leñero's *Los albañiles* (1964, The bricklayers), Salvador Elizondo's *Farabeuf* (1965), and José Emilio Pacheco's *Morirás lejos* (1968, *You Will Die in a Distant Land*). These writers seemed divorced from their immediate social and political context. Nevertheless, few of them would be accused of escapism after more than a superficial reading of their work, for they worked as oppositional writers more broadly and abstractly than the social critics of the previous generation. In *Los albañiles* Leñero questions the possibilities of establishing truth, a typical strategy of much postmodern fiction. The novel is about the identity of a murderer, but it also questions the ways in which truth is constructed and understood. Rather than attempting to propose a singular truth, this novel emphasizes the versions of truth that come to the fore. In addition to Leñero, this first wave of postmodern fiction in Mexico included the writings of José Emilio Pacheco, Salvador Elizondo, Gustavo Sainz, and José Agustín. Truth is primarily a matter of versions rather than a fixed quantity in Pacheco's *Morirás lejos* and Fuentes's *Cambio de piel*. Elizondo, Sainz, and Agustín published several experimental novels in the 1960s and the 1970s. Other important contributions to the Mexican postmodern were Sainz's *Gazapo* (1965) and Agustín's *De perfil* (1966, In portrait). These two novels can be seen as transitional works between the modernist stratagems of *Pedro Páramo* and *La muerte de Artemio Cruz* and the postmodernism of *Terra Nostra* (1975). The fiction of Gustavo Sainz and José Agustín questioned the conventional boundaries between elitist and popular culture, a common interest of many postmodern writers. Sainz's *Gazapo* affords the reader a sense of fiction and empirical reality as versions and possibilities; it was a noteworthy innovation for fiction in the region, bringing both the language of the youth and new technology into the Mexican novel. Sainz also writes beyond the colonial legacy; *Gazapo* is the first modern novel in Mexico in which the Mexican Revolution is totally absent.

This first wave of the postmodern in Mexico closes with the massacre at Tlatelolco and two experimental novels of 1968, Agustín's *Inventando que sueño* (1968, Inventing that I dream) and Elizondo's *El hipogeo secreto* (1968, The secret cave). Both are patently experimental with language and structure. *Inventando que sueño* consists of a set of stories that can be read separately or together as a novel and deal with alienated youth. In the cases of Agustín and Elizondo, history is the now, the present moment. Elizondo's metafiction is so experimental that writing a character does not imply creating a "real" character.

One reaction to the massacre at Tlatelolco was a type of escapism that emphasized technical experimentation in fiction. After this hyperexperimentation of the late 1960s and early 1970s in Mexico, most post-1968 postmodern fiction in Mexico became progressively less hermetic and more accessible. In addition to the work of Fuentes, the later postmodern writing in Mexico and Central America includes the work of the Mexicans Luis Arturo Ramos, Carmen Boullosa, María Luisa Puga, Brianda Domecq, and Ignacio Solares.

Fuentes has been at the avant-garde of the second wave of postmodern fiction in Mexico, publishing the postmodern *Cumpleaños*, *Terra Nostra*, *Una familia lejana* (1980, *Distant Relations*), *Gringo* viejo (1985, *Old Gringo*), and *Cristóbal nonato* (1987, *Christopher Unborn*). But Mexican postmodern fiction was abundant in the 1970s and 1980s, with the work of Salvador Elizondo, Gustavo Sainz, José Agustín, Héctor Manjarrez, María Luisa Puga, Sergio Fernández, Federico Patán, Luis Arturo Ramos, Sergio Pitol, Angelina Muñíz-Huberman, Ignacio Solares, and Carmen Boullosa.

"Displacement is the action of the novel," Fuentes has stated in an essay, and his five postmodern novels of this period are examples of this concept of action. *Cumpleaños* was written during Fuentes's initial creative stages of *Terra Nostra*, and the two novels share common conceptions: the descriptions of hermetically closed spaces occasionally evoke the equally hermetic space of El Escorial in *Terra Nostra*. The architectural constructs in *Cumpleaños*, like those of El Palacio in *Terra Nostra*, are quite severe and harsh. *Terra Nostra* is Fuentes's rewriting of the architecture of El Escorial, his major and culminating rereading of Latin American culture and history.

Terra Nostra also deals with the Latin American colonial legacy and cultural heritage from Spain; *Una familia lejana* considers similar issues with respect to France. Nevertheless, *Una familia lejana* suggests as much about Fuentes as a postmodern writer and his interests in literature, for this is the book that promotes the idea that living, in the end, is predicated on the act of telling stories. It also communicates that in a work of art the solution to an enigma is another enigma. *Una familia lejana*, *Gringo viejo*, and *Cristóbal nonato* continue the postmodern themes and strategies of *Cambio de piel*, *Birthday*, and *Terra Nostra*. Characters of multiple and transforming identities are evident in these three texts, and Fuentes flaunts the unresolved contradictions that are a sign of the postmodern.

Some of the postmodern innovators were more accessible than Pacheco, Agustín, and Elizondo. Luis Arturo Ramos, Sergio Pitol, Federico Patán, María Luisa Puga, and Brianda Domecq are postmodern writers of this type. Ramos, Pitol, and Puga tell stories with clearly defined plots, but, like the postmodern Fuentes in *Una familia lejana* and *Gringo viejo*, they engage the reader in subtle games and devices associated with the postmodern, such as cultivating unresolved contradictions and engaging in games of double coding in which characters, paradoxically, are not historical. Ramos's early writing, particularly his short fiction, had clear affinities with Cortázar. His most accomplished and patently postmodern novel, *Este era un gato* (1984, This was a cat), tells the story of Roger Copeland, a retired American marine captain who participated in the 1914 invasion of Veracruz. This novel communicates the sense of fragile identities that characterizes Fuentes's fiction in the 1980s. The text offers three possible conclusions, but ends in unresolved contradiction. Ramos's more recent fiction is also of considerable interest, including the short novel *La Señora de la Fuente y otras parábolas de fin de siglo* (1996, Mrs. de la Fuente and other end-of-the-century parables), *La casa del ahorcado* (1993, The house of the hung one), and *La mujer que quiso ser Dios* (2000, The woman that wanted to be God). In *La Señora de la Fuente y otras parábolas de fin de siglo* Ramos offers the reader a series of enigmatic short fictions that can be read as political allegories about an exhausted and corrupt nation. It is easy to read Ramos as a post-Tlatelolco product: his skepticism is typical of a generation that saw hope for social change and poltical reform vanish with the 1968 massacre.

Sergio Pitol's writings of the 1980s were metafictions in dialogue with film and literary texts. In *El tañido de una flauta* (1972, A flute's music), *Juegos florales* (1982, Flower arrangements), *El desfile de amor* (1984, The parade of love), *Domar a la divina garza* (1988, Taming the divine heron), and *La vida conyugal* (1991, Conjugal life) are metafictions of this sort. *El tañido de una flauta* is a dialogue with film and theory, but *Juegos florales* and *Domar a la divina garza* are Pitol's most innovative postmodern texts. The protagonist in *Juegos florales* travels to Europe to complete a text on Billie Upward also titled *Juegos florales*. He suffers in his attempts to deal with old relationships and his new text. *Juegos florales*, like the text within the text being written, is an ongoing Bakhtinian dialogue rather than a completed project. *Domar a la divina garza* is also a self-conscious Bakhtinian project, with a narrator who selects Bakhtin as the theorist who will be the basis for his novel. These and other factors make this a patently postmodern text that breaks down the conventional dichotomy between theory and fiction, disrupting the hierarchy of literary genres. Like *Terra Nostra*, it strives toward the encyclopedic.

María Luisa Puga and Brianda Domecq have published a substantive body of fiction. Puga has written *Las posibilidades del odio* (1978, The possibilities of hatred), *Cuando el aire es azul* (1980, When the air is blue), *Pánico o peligro* (1981, Panic or danger), *La forma del silencio* (1987, The form of silence), and *Antonia* (1989, Antonia), in addition to her fiction of the 1990s and the new century. Like the novels of Pitol, Puga's work often engages in the process of coming into being as she relates a story. *Pánico o peligro* is a metafiction that suggests narrating and living are basically the same activity where characters suffer unstable identities. *La forma del silencio* is a more self-conscious meditation on fiction, setting forth that reality constructs the novel and the novel constructs reality. Its focus on several decades since Tlatelelco reveals Puga to be a writer who, like Ramos, is skeptical of Mexican society's ability to make progress after 1968. Brianda Domecq has published the two innovative works *La insólita historia de la Santa de la Cabora* (1990, The strange story of Saint Cabora) and *Once días . . . y algo más* (1991, Eleven days . . . and more).

Federico Patán, Daniel Leyva, and Angelina Muñiz-Huberman are more technically innovative than Ramos, Pitol, Puga, and Domecq and are among the most hermetic Mexican writers of the period. The protagonist of Patán's *Ultimo exilio* (1986, The last exile) lives in the margins of a fictional and an everyday reality, but never with any sense of stability. He lives in physical exile, but his interior exile into fantasy and literature is more pronounced. Leyva's novels are among the most experimental to be published in Mexico in the 1980s. His *Una piñata llena de memoria* (1984, A piñata full of memories) recalls Cortázar's *Rayuela* in that it offers the reader the choice of several readings. Muñiz-Huberman's *Dulcinea encantada* (1992, Enchanted Dulcinea), like the works of Ramos and Patán, blurs the boundaries between fantasy and empirical reality. It is a metafiction that offers several intertextual readings, with references to writers such as Cervantes and Virginia Woolf.

Ignacio Solares and Carmen Boullosa wrote novels in the 1990s that can be read as fictions of resistance: *El gran elector* (1993, *The Great Mexican Electoral Game*, 1999) by Solares and *La milagrosa* (1993, The miracle maker) by Boullosa. Solares had already established a reputation as a writer interested in both history and fantasy in the novels *Puerta al cielo* (1976, Door to the sky), *Anónimo* (1979, Anonymous), *El árbol del deseo* (1980, The tree of desire), *La formula de la inmortalidad* (1982, The formula for immortality), *Serafín* (1985, Seraphim), *Casas de encantamiento* (1988, Charmed houses), and *Madero, el otro* (1989, Madero, the other). *El gran elector*, as explained earlier, is a novel about a Mexican president who represents a composite of all the Mexican presidents of the PRI since 1930. One postmodern aspect of several of these novels is that fact that everything, in the end, is discourse—different levels of speech—including the nation itself.

The fiction of Solares and Boullosa of the 1990s are critiques of Mexican politics, even though many of their referents do not deal directly with contemporary Mexican politics. Solares, Boullosa, and Ramos address the crisis of authority in Mexico in the latter part of the twentieth century, a crisis of a world presented with little transcendence and little truth. Their recent novels contain a multiplicity of differing discourses in unresolved contradiction.

With respect to recent popular fiction in Mexico, one of the most widely read works of the 1990s was Laura Esquivel's *Como agua para chocolate*. Esquivel later published the less successful *The Law of Love* (1995). Angeles Mastretta also participated in what some critics have called a "feminine Boom" in Mexico, publishing *Mexican Bolero* (1988), which had appeared in Spanish as *Arráncame la vida* and was widely read throughout the Hispanic world. Mastretta's ongoing work includes the novel *Lovesick* (1997), which had appeared in Mexico in the original Spanish as *Mal de amores*.

Many readers and critics in Mexico tended to take more seriously less commercially oriented writing, such as that of Elena Poniatowska, Sergio Galindo, Fernando del Paso, Elena Garro, Jesús Gardea, Silvia Molina, Vicente Leñero, Joaquín-Armando Chacón, Federico Campbell, Héctor Aguilar Camín, David Martín del Campo, Homero Aridjis, and Arturo Azuela. Poniatowska has enjoyed a distinguished career as a journalist and writer of testimonials in Mexico, although she also began to publish fiction in the 1980s, producing *Nada, nadie* (1988, *Nothing, Nobody: The Voices of the Mexico City Earthquake*, 1995), *La "Flor de Lis,"* and *Tinísima* (1992, *Tinísima*, 1995). All three novels are Poniatowska's fictionalized memoirs. Her novel *La piel del cielo* (2001, The skin of the sky) is a lengthy and ambitious Boom-type work that deals with the modernization of Mexican society since the 1920s, with a main character who is a pioneer Mexican scientist, and the novel's drama is the protagonist's attempts to insert science into Mexican national life. A post-Boom work of similar scope—most of twentieth-century Mexico—is Carlos

Fuentes's *The Years with Laura Díaz* (1999), which appeared originally in Spanish as *Los años con Laura Díaz*.

As mentioned previously, the newest generation of writers in this region—born since 1955—includes the Mexicans Cristina Rivera Garza, David Toscana, Juan Villoro, Jorge Volpi, Marta Cerda, Patricia Laurent Kullick, Luis Humberto Crosthwaite, Ignacio Padilla, and José Ramón Ruisánchez and the Central Americans Roberto Quesada, Rodrigo Rey Rosa, and Horacio Castellanos Mora. This generation has assumed several local, national and international identities, but, in many ways, they are a new generation of postmodern writers. A group headed by Volpi, Padilla, and others has successfully promoted itself in Mexico and Spain as the generation of the crack, but the word *crack* does not refer to drugs; rather, this term refers to the rejection of all previously established modes of writing. Many of their interests are similar to those of the generation of the 1990s in Brazil and throughout Latin America. They have particularly insisted on their right to ignore the more commercial trends of magical realism as well as the calls of literary nationalists that seem to require Mexican writers to write about Mexico. Volpi's *En busca de Klingsor* (1999, *In Search of Klingsor*), consequently, is set in Germany during WWII, with a novelistic structure that parallels the structure of Wagner's opera *Parsifal*. Like Poniatowska's *La piel del cielo*, the focus is on the development of science. Volpi attempts to build suspense around the voluminous of knowledge and texts transcribed in the novel. David Toscana, on the other hand, has crafted more deftly developed plots in his novels *Estación Tula* (1995, *Tula Station*), *Santa María del Circo* (1998, *Our Lady of the Circus*), and *Duelo por Miguel Pruneda* (2002, Mourning for Miguel Pruneda). In addition to his subtle and engaging plots, Toscana has a special sense for everyday life (and death), heritage, and history that escapes the commonplace and tired rhetoric often being rewritten in contemporary Mexican fiction.

Mexican writers of the same generation as Volpi, Cristina Rivera Garza, and Luis Humberto Crosthwaite, have written most of their fiction with some geographical or psychological relationship to borders, for Rivera Garza has been writing and teaching in San Diego and Tijuana and Crosthwaite has lived in Tijuana and other border areas. Rivera Garza is engaged in a wide range of fascinating border-crossing cultural experiments, including careful consideration of what it means to write in a "mother tongue" while living, reading, and translating in other languages. Her first novel, *Nadie me verá llorar* is a historical work that centers upon a nineteenth-century insane asylum; its total effect is to question not only nineteenth-century science but also the post-Enlightenment postulates of the rational that have constructed categories such as the sane and the insane. In her later fiction, including the novel *La cresta de Ilión* (2002, Ilion's hipbone), Rivera Garza explores subtle relations between human beings and the construction of gender. Crosthwaite is more interested in a kind of local neorealism than is Rivera Garza; his humorous novels include *La luna siempre será un amor difícil* (1994, *The Moon Will Forever Be a Distant Love*) and *Estrella de la Calle Sexta* (2000, Star of Sixth Street) and his fiction in general deals with issues related to border culture: the Spanish and English languages, biculturalism, and the like. He also questions conventional concepts of gender and genre, but tends to do so in playful, entertaining ways, with a keen eye for contradictions and the consequences of American cultural colonialism as he weaves through the popular culture of both Mexico and the United States. His most informed readers know Mexican rock groups from Tijuana, Mexico, as well as Mexican American pop culture in Los Angeles, California.

The novel is a heterogeneous genre in Mexico, a fact underscored by the region's multiple indigenous groups, its strong development of *mestizo* culture, as well as its historic proximity to the multiple literary influences of Europe and the United States from modernism to the postmodern. By the beginning of the twenty-first century, in addition to the tendencies already mentioned and factors of globalization, gay novelists, such as Luis Zapata, have been writing explicitly on issues of sexuality in the 1980s and 1990s in Mexico. Of the modernist writers, the novelists that stand out among the most accomplished in the region are Carlos Fuentes and Miguel Angel Asturias. The major post-Boom writers are Sergio Ramírez, Elena Poniatowska, Angeles Mastretta, and Laura Esquivel. Among the most innovative postmodern writers are José Emilio Pacheco, Gustavo Sainz, José Agustín, Federico Patán, Luis Arturo Ramos, Ignacio Solares, and Carmen Boullosa. Among the youngest innovators born since 1955, the writers with the most noteworthy novels already published include Cristina Rivera Garza, David Toscana, and Jorge Volpi.

The Central American Novel: Context and Chronology

Central American novelists of the twentieth century have generally written in the context of political instability, dictatorships, and the variety of consequences from the presence of the United Fruit Company in the region. The one exception is Costa Rica, which has been relatively stable, enjoyed democratic regimes, and has not had dealings with large foreign companies. Three major events mark the second half of the century: the overthrow of President Jacobo Arbenz of Guatemala by the United States in 1954, the rise of the Sandinistas in Nicaragua in the 1980s, and the civil war in El Salvador in the 1980s. An equally important factor, however, is the strong indigenous population in Central America, and this presence has been influential in both the political process and the literature of the region. Two Nobel laureates have been associated with the Maya presence in Guatemala: Miguel Angel Asturias's fiction has been closely associated with Mayan groups; Rigoberta Menchú's life and writing have created an awareness of the Mayan circumstance well beyond the borders of Guatemala.

These defining moments for the political and economic history of Central America had literary responses from a broad range of writers, including Asturias, the Nicaraguan poet and novelist Giaconda Belli, and the author of testimonials from El Salvador Manlio Argueta. Arturo Arias was a young child living in Guatemala when the CIA sponsored air attacks on the capital to overthrow the Arbenz government. Years later he wrote a novel about his childhood experience, one of the most heralded novels of the Central American region, *Después de las bombas*. Belli lived in Nicaragua under the authoritarian regime of Somoza and supported the Sandinista Revolution against Somoza. Her personal experience in Nicaragua during these key years is the central focus of her novel *La mujer habitada* (1988, The inhabited woman). Argueta wrote the testimonial of his experience in his book *Un día en la vida* (1980, *One Day in the Life*).

Novels such as Yolanda Oreamuno's *La ruta de su evasión* (Costa Rica, 1949, The route of her evasion), Rogelio Sinán's *Plenilunio* (Panama, 1947, Full moon), Luis Cardoza y Aragón's *Guatemala, las líneas de su mano* (1955, Guatemala, the lines of his hand) were pioneer works for the genre's modernization in the Central American region. Mario Monteforte Toledo wrote a set of three novels in this period that look back to the indigenista tradition in fiction as well as forward to more contemporary social and existential dramas. *Entre la piedra y la cruz* (Guatemala, 1948, Between the rock and the cross), *Donde acaban los caminos* (1953, Where the roads end), and *Una manera de morir* (1957, A manner of dying) can be associated in many ways with the interests of Asturias in the social and indigenista writing; at the same time, his interests in the individual in society linked him to Yáñez and Galindo in Mexico. In *Entre la piedra y la cruz* Monteforte Toledo shows some of the totalizing ambitions of the modernist novelist and the writers of the Boom, for it is a panoramic narrative that intends to exhibit the totality of the country. In this work the Indian protagonist Pedro Matzar is marginalized from the white world of Guatemalan society, but in the end the novel offers a note of optimism: he marries the white Margarita Castellanos, offering the cultural solution that the author imagined possible for the nation in the 1940s. The next two novels are less optimistic. In *Donde acaban los caminos* the solution of cultural hybridity seems to fail: the white doctor Zaúl Zamora concedes to societal pressure and cancels his plans to marry the indigenous María Xahil. Both novels offer hybrid configurations with epic and folkloric elements. *Una manera de morir* is more modernist in style, with erudite literary language and a harmonious structure based on contrast and counterpoint, but this is the least optimistic of Monteforte Toledo's works.

Some traditionalists, who still employed realist techniques, also prevailed well into the 1960s in Central America, and one of the best known of these writers is Joaquín Gutiérrez. His novel *Puerto Limón* (Costa Rica, 1950) deals with the 1934 banana workers' strike, but the social protest is articulated within a novel of characters' psychological development uncommon in such works.

Although best known for his now canonical *El Señor Presidente*, Asturias wrote several other novels of high quality and deep cultural exploration. His *Hombres de maíz* (1949, *Men of Maize*) represents an increased interest in Native American groups in Central America. In this digressive and elusive modernist work, Asturias relates the story of a conflict between the Indians, who strive to maintain their traditional ways of subsistence, and outsiders, who attempt to force them to change their ways. The conflict revolves around the cultivation of corn: the outsiders desire to interfere, even though corn is a sacred form of sustenance for the Indians.

The Central American nations have not produced a large number of novels closely allied with international postmodern culture, but novels such as Gioconda Belli's *La mujer habitada*, Roberto Quesada's *Los barcos* (Honduras, 1988, *The Ships*) and *The Big Banana* (1999), Rodrigo Rey Rosa's *Lo que soñó Sebastián* (Guatemala, 1994, What Sebastian dreamt), *El cojo bueno* (1996, The good one-legged man), *La orilla africana* (1999, The African shore), and *Piedras encantadas* (2001, Charmed stones), and Méndez Vides's *Las catacumbas* (Guatemala, 1987, The catacombs) and *El paraíso perdido* (1990, The lost paradise) can be related to some trends of postmodern fiction in Mexico and beyond.

Among the post-Boom writers in Central America, the Nicaraguan Sergio Ramírez has published short fiction and novels since the 1970s, including the novels *Tiempo de fulgor* (1970, Time of brilliance), *Castigo divino* (1998, Divine punishment), *Margarita, está linda la mar* (1998, Margarita, the sea is beautiful), and *Adiós, muchachos* (1999, Good-bye, boys). He has become one of the most widely read Central American writers throughout the Hispanic world. Much of his material is related to the social and political experience of having lived the Somoza dictatorship in Guatemala and of having been a leader of the Sandinista government. The Honduran Julio Escoto's *Rey del albor, Madrugada* (1993, King of dawn, Sunrise) is a novel of broad historic and geographic range, similar in this sense to the novels of the 1960s Boom. Its main theme—U.S. imperialism—also connects it to some of the writing of the Boom. Escoto had already published the novels *El árbol de los pañuelos* (1971, The napkin tree) and *Bajo el almendro, junto al volcán* (1988, Under the almond tree, next to the volcano). Carmen Naranjo's *Diario de una multitud* (1974, Diary of a multitude) is a pessimistic critique of Costa Rican society as well as a text with multiple voices that, in their totality, seek transcendence to overcome the dullness of everyday life in contemporary Costa Rica. *Sobrepunto* (1985, The point of overcoming) and other novels by Naranjo (over six) focus on stories of human relationships and, more specifically, feminist concerns within the context of the larger community. The Guatemalan Arturo Arias has been active as a writer and a scholar in the United States since the 1980s, serving in a variety of professional and intellectual settings, including the defense of Elizabeth Burgos's testimonial text *Yo me llamo Rigoberta Menchú y así me nació la conciencia* (1985, *I, Rigoberta Menchú: An Indian Woman in Guatemala*). His much acclaimed novel *Después de las bombas* is as aesthetically and politically allied with the writing of the Boom as the work of Ramírez: his later fiction includes *Jaguar en llamas* (1989, Jaguar in flames) and *Cascabel* (1998, Rattlesnake). The Costa Rican Samuel Rovinski and the Guatemalan Marco Antonio Flores belong to the generation of the Boom, although they published novels after the 1960s and are more readily associated with the post-Boom than the Boom.

Given the political strife and civil wars Central America during the 1970s and 1980s, it is logical that the post-Boom writing of this region includes documentary narrative that is often identified as testimonial. The most prominent of these writers is the previously mentioned Guatemalan indigenous activist Rigoberta Menchú whose *I, Rigoberta Menchú* has become virtually a canonical text of this genre over the past two decades of the century. In this region, as in some other regions of Latin America, the space previously considered "the margins" has become "the center," and this is the case with Rigoberta's personal testimonial to the abuse of the native population by the military dictatorship in Guatemala. The San Salvadoran Manlio Argueta's work is testimonial fiction dealing with the writer's experience in war-torn El Salvador and includes *El valle de las hamacas* (1968, The valley of hamocks), *Caperucita en la zona roja* (1977, *Little Red Riding Hood in the Red Light District*), *Un día en la vida* (1980, *One Day in the Life*), *Cuzcatlan* (1986, *Cuzcatlán: Where the Southern Sea Beats*), and *A Place Called Milagro de la Paz* (2000).

The Guatemalan Mario Roberto Morales also wrote the political novels *El esplendor de la pirámide* (1985, The splendor of the pyramid) and *Los demonios salvajes* (1978, The savage demons), the latter a protest work against dictatorships. The Guatemalan Edwin Cifuentes has published the novels *Libres por el tema* (1977, Free for the theme) and *El pueblo y los atentados* (1979, The town and the attempts). Guatemalan Miguel Angel Vásquez published a novel of social protest, *La semilla del fuego* (1976, The seed of the fire). Eduardo Bahr published *Fotografía del peñasco* (1969, The picture of the rocky terrain), Dante Liano published *El lugar de su quietud* (1989, The place of his peace), and Luis de León wrote *El mundo principia en Xibalbá* (1985, The world begins in Xibalbá).

The Caribbean Novel, the Caribbean Diaspora, and the U.S. Latino Novel: Contexts and Chronology

The Caribbean novel has been produced in multiethnic cultural settings, with the strong African heritage in the Caribbean, as well as its Amerindian original inhabitants, and significant immigration since the nineteenth century from India, Indonesia, and Asia. The Caribbean has extended to urban centers of the northeastern United States; its African heritage has been an important factor in the region's cultural unity. Cultural expression reached an ample awareness of these African roots in the 1920s and 1930s, and the literary manifestations of this awareness were the rise of Afro-Antillean poetry during this period and the *négritude* movement celebrating African identity. From the rise of the modernist novel with the fiction of the Cuban Alejo Carpentier to the more recent work of younger writers such as Zoé Valdés and Sandra Cisneros, the Caribbean and Latino novel have been a major presence in the Latin American cultural scene.

The Caribbean has many markers of recognition, for it is identified in the different languages of the region as *caribe, Antilles, West Indies, caraibe*, among other names. To speak of a Caribbean novel, of course, is to speak of a genre written in several languages that represent diverse European literary traditions; not only the Spaniards had colonial control in the region, but the British, French, and Dutch have had a historic presence there since the sixteenth and seventeenth centuries, and some nations, such as Haiti and the Dominican Republic, attained their independence in the early nineteenth century. On the other hand, independence came from the British and the Dutch in the Caribbean only after 1945; yet Guadeloupe, Martinique, and French Guyana have never gained independence and are currently Departments of France (DOM, overseas departments) rather than nations. Similarly, Puerto Rico has a special arrangement with the U.S. and is not an independent nation. Several prominent novelists write in French, Haitian Creole, English, Dutch, and various creole or hybrid-type languages. These novelists include Maryse Condé of Guadeloupe, who has published several novels in French, and Frank Martinus Arion, who has published several novels in Dutch as a writer from the former Dutch colony of Curaçao. Condé's work is increasingly available in English translation, and writers such as Arion also have some of their work translated into English; his *Double Play* appeared 1998 in English translation; it was originally published in Dutch in 1973. One of the prominent novelists of the Caribbean, George Lamming, writes in English.

The Caribbean region is marked by heterogeneity and hybridity, and this fact is particularly evident in the languages in which the literatures of the Caribbean are written. Fiction is written in Spanish in Cuba, Puerto Rico, and the Dominican Republic. In Guadeloupe, Martinique, and French Guayana, the novel has been written mostly in French, although some fiction has been published in a French creole. English has been the language of the novel in Jamaica, Trinidad/Tobago, and Barbados, as well as some Caribbean writers in the U.S., and Dutch the language of novels published by writers from Suriname and Curaçao. And if this situation were not complex enough already, there are variatations, with the use of some local creole languages: some Haitian writers, such as Frankétienne, have published novels not only in French but in Haitian Creole; writers in Suriname publish poetry in their creole, Srantongo; Frank Martinus Arion has written poetry in Papiamentu as well as fiction in Dutch; contemporary novelists from Martinique have published novels in both French and French Creole.

The end of WWII was more important in the Caribbean in several ways than was the case in the remainder of Latin America. Black soldiers from the Caribbean departments of France (Guadeloupe, Martinique, French Guyana) served in WWII, and once they returned to the Caribbean they were more affirmative in insisting on their rights as blacks, participating in the *négritude* movement. Since this period, the entire Caribbean region has been involved in an interlingual dialogue on Caribbean culture, a dialogue initiated by the Cuban Alejo Carpentier and the Martinicans Aimé Césaire and Frantz Fanon in the 1940s and 1950s. This attempt to address issues of a Caribbean cultural unity, identity, and political autonomy has been continued by intellectuals such as Eduoard Glissant from Martinique, Maryse Condé, Daniel Maxim, and Patrick Chamoiseau from Guadeloupe, and Antonio Benítez Rojo from Cuba, among others. Jacques Roumain's novel of social protest from Haiti, *Gouverneurs de la rosée* (1944) has been translated into Spanish and read throughout Latin America. Langston Hughes translated the English version as *Masters of the Dew*.

The novelists and intellectuals of the Caribbean region are still rewriting the history and the present circumstances of the colonial legacy, which in this region inherited a ruling elite not only from Spain but also from France, Great Britain, and Holland. In different parts of the Caribbean, however, the response to the colonial powers has varied considerably. In Haiti, for example, the *indigénisme* movement was a reaction to U.S. occupation of Haiti. This movement, led by Jean Price-Mars, was anti-American, ahistoric, and poetic in vision. It was a fully Caribbean-based movement of nationalist thought that rejected the values of the Enlightenment. On the other hand, the influential thinker Aimé Césaire from Martinique did not support decolonization; he was a product of the Enlightenment who wrote in favor of French societal reform in which Martinique would participate.

The singularly most important political event to take place in the entire Caribbean region during the post-WWII period, however, was the Cuban Revolution. Initially, the victory of Fidel Castro's relatively small group of guerrilla fighters over the corrupt dictatorship of Batista was seen as a ray of hope for progressive political forces throughout the Caribbean. Once the revolution was successful in creating a new regime, Havana was a cultural center for many Caribbean writers and intellectuals during the 1960s, most of whom visited the Cuban capital to participate in cultural festivals, literature conferences, literary prizes, and the like. The Cuban Casa de las Américas literary prizes were among the most prestigious of Latin America and the Caribbean region during the 1960s and 1970s. Guerrilla forces similar to those of Fidel Castro (and sometimes supported by the Cuban regime) appeared throughout the Caribbean, Central America, and Latin America in general from the early 1960s. Some of them, such as those in Colombia, have continued in their rural and urban guerrilla warfare to the beginning of the twenty-first century— for over four decades. There is a vast literature in the Caribbean region and beyond about the experience of first idealizing the possibility of revolutionary change, often followed by the disillusionment with revolution. There is also some literature related to rural and urban guerrilla warfare.

Fidel Castro began his guerrilla insurrection against the dictatorship of Batista in the early 1950s and led a rural guerrilla armed insurrection throughout the 1950s. When he triumphantly entered Havana in January of 1959, Mexican writer Carlos Fuentes was waiting with other Latin American intellectuals to celebrate this victory for the Latin American left. Guillermo Cabrera Infante's *Tres tristes tigres* is set in a decadent Havana of the 1950s, and many other Cuban novels have dealt with Cuban society before, during, and after the revolution. Lisandro Otero's early novel *La situación* (1963, The situation) relates the years of the Batista dictatorship in the 1950s. The use of several factual episodes provides the historical background; Otero recreates the atmosphere in Cuba before the second return of Batista to power in the early 1950s as well as early-century historical settings. He employs alternating chapters to provide both an external and interior vision of the events at hand, with differing class perspectives. The sense of being on the edge that Otero creates so masterfully corresponds to much postmodern fiction published later in Cuba. At the same time, he successfully portrays characters and a disappearing upper class in Cuba.

The novel in both traditional and modernist forms was being produced—almost surreptitiously—during the 1940s and 1950s in the Caribbean and by Latino writers in variousparts of the United States. Fiction writers such as the Puerto Ricans Emilio Díaz Valcárcel and Pedro Juan Soto have garnered the attention of scholars and critics in Latin America, Europe, and the United States. Writing in English in the Caribbean, V. S. Naipul, George Lamming, Wilson Harris, and Earl Lovelace participated in the establishment of foundational texts for their newly independent Caribbean nations.

The rise of the modernist novel in the Caribbean region was due primarily to the fiction of the Cubans Alejo Carpentier and José Lezama Lima as well as that of the Puerto Ricans Emilio Díaz Valcárcel and René Marqués. Carpentier has appropriately been described as the dean of Cuban novelists and is one of the major novelists of the Caribbean as well as Latin America in the twentieth century; he has been read widely since the 1940s and 1950s in the French, English, Dutch, and Hispanic Caribbean, and Boom writers such as Fuentes have expressed their admiration for Carpentier on numerous occasions. Carpentier wrote nine novels, and his fiction spans several decades that begin in the 1930s. Carpentier's main interests were history and time, but, like the other novelists of his generation, he was well aware of the presence of oral culture in Latin America, and traces of orality are discernible in his fiction. In the Dominican Republic an interest in modernizing the literary scene was evident with the appearance of the magazine *La Poesía Sorprendida* in 1943, and writers such as J. M. Sanz-Lajara, Aída Cartagena Portolatín, Marcio Veloz Maggiolo, Pedro Mir, and Pedro Verges have been active in revitalizing the novel in the region since the 1960s.

Before the appearance of *El reino de este mundo*, Carpentier had already published two books of fiction, as well as key essays. *El reino de este mundo* is a brief four-part novel set in Haiti during its early independence at the beginning of the nineteenth century. The novel relates the life of a character named Ti Noel as he develops in each of the book's four parts. This work provides a foundation for much of what later came to be known as magical realism in Latin American literature. As Carpentier understood the right of invention in the 1940s, the Latin American writer's special task was to express the "marvelous real." Carpentier himself referred to this book as an account rather than a novel, a fact probably related to his special interest in the marvelous quality of reality in the New World. This interest led him to seek historical accuracy in his fiction. The novel's four parts recount a rebellion, a massacre, the rule of Henri Christophe, and the coming of the mulattoes. The theme of this work is the struggle against tyranny, although some readers have found the novel's ending ambiguous.

Carpentier was a master of style; his compatriot José Lezama Lima wrote with such an awareness of style that in some of his fiction language itself becomes the central subject of the novel. Lezama Lima's novel *Paradiso* (1966) is a work that offers some of the linguistic complexities of Joyce; some critics consider it to be one of the most complex novels of the century in Latin America. In this work Lezama Lima tells the story of the Cemí family, covering several branches of the clan from the late nineteenth century to the 1930s, but centering on José Cemí. Lezama Lima's baroque language portrays the essence of the people and settings, and the author's explorations into various facets of adolescent sexuality, including homosexuality, are bold. Despite an ongoing impression of chaos and numerous lengthy digressions, the novel emphasizes unity and wholeness in the end.

The Cubans Lisandro Otero and Pablo Armando Fernández, like Carpentier, were more interested in history than Lezama Lima, and Otero's early novel *La situación* reflects this interest by relating the years of the Batista dictatorship in the 1950s; after *La situación* Otero has continued his creative work, publishing the historical novel *Temporada de ángeles* (1984, Period of angels) and a novel about sexuality and aging, *La travesía* (1995, The crossing). Fernández's *Los niños se despiden* (1968, The children say good-bye) covers a broad range of Cuban history from all periods. It is a fundamentally allegorical work that focuses on a utopian community, Sabanas, although the allegorical mode is not consistent throughout the novel.

The writing of Pedro Juan Soto in the 1950s foreshadows many of the issues confronted by writers of the Caribbean, of the Caribbean diaspora and of Latino writers in general, beginning with the fact that Soto's cultural and linguistic identity was frequently difficult for many readers and mainline critics to establish. He belonged to the generation of 1940 in Puerto Rico; many critics in the United States see him as a pioneer of Nuyorican literature. His volume of fiction *Spiks* (1956) communicates the difficult experiences of the Puerto Rican in New York. *Spiks* is generally considered a volume of short stories, but, like the Mexican José Agustín's *Inventando que sueño* and Sandra Cisneros's *House on Mango Street*, it contains enough unity and character development to be read as a novel. *Spiks* is an analysis of the immigration experience of Puerto Ricans in New York, and the title comes from the monolingual immigrant's phrase "I no spik English," which Soto included as a statement on behalf of the immigrant's identity and experience. *Spiks* consists of seven stories written from 1953 to 1956 that are intercalated with six brief texts identified as "miniatures." The book communicates the immigrant's urban experience in New York, with resonances of cultural experience dating back to the Spanish colonial legacy. In many ways, it reflects the experience of the Puerto Ricans living in their own urban space within the larger urban space called New York. Soto's vast body of fiction includes the novel *Usmaíl* (1959, U.S. Mail).

The rise of modernist fiction in Puerto Rico can also be directly attributed to the writing of Emilio Díaz Valcárcel and René Marqués. The tales of *El asedio* (1958, The siege) by Díaz Valcárcel represented some of his most accomplished fiction, including stories of his experience serving in the Korean War. He continued writing novels through the 1970s and 1980s, eventually moving toward stories of human relationships, such as *Dicen que de noche tú no duermes* (1985), a love story of two middle-age individuals who decide to meet on a Friday afternoon. A man of letters broadly recognized for his major work as a playwright, Marqués wrote primarily about Puerto Rico's political past and future. Among his fictional works, his novel *La víspera del hombre* (1958, The night before man) is a historical work set in the Puerto Rico of 1928 in which he draws parallels between the search for individual human dignity and the search for national dignity. *En una ciudad llamada San Juan* (1960, In a city called San Juan) is historical as well, with three aristocratic sisters whose lives reflect the political history of the nation. In addition to Díaz Valcárcel and Marqués, Abelardo Díaz Alfaro and José Luis González contributed to the rise of modernist fiction in Puerto Rico. González has written a series of novels critical of the cultural and political impact of the United States, including *La balada del otro* (1988, The ballad of the other) and *La llegada* (1980, The arrival).

The heterogeneity of Caribbean writing was evident in the 1960s with the production of a relatively new kind of writing that escapes easy classification: the *testimonio* or documentary-type novel, already described. The pioneer of this type of writing, which became much more widespread and fashionable later throughout Latin America, was Miguel Barnet. His *Biografía de un cimarrón* (1966, *An Autobiography of a Runaway Slave*) is a now classic book of this genre and relates the Afro-Cuban slave experience. Since writing this work, Barnet has continued producing works that can be related to both fiction and testimonial, having published other novels.

Much of the writing by Chicano writers in the United States has its roots in a desire similar to the testimonial—to share real-life experience in the form of fiction or fictionalized autobiography. Consequently, as Barnet, Carpentier, and Lezama Lima were increasingly recognized in the 1960s and 1970s, the U.S. Chicano writers Tomás Rivera, Rolando Hinojosa, Rudolfo Anaya, and Miguel Méndez were viewed as the founding fathers of the modern Chicano novel. In reality, the Chicano novel has its twentieth-century roots in the work of writers such as Josephina Niggli and José Antonio Villareal, who were writing in the 1940s and 1950s. Throughout the Caribbean and the Hispanic U.S., an important factor for the production of the new Latino fiction was the presence of the Boom: a large number of aspiring young Latino writers had read Gabriel García Márquez, Carlos Fuentes, Mario Vargas Llosa, and Julio Cortázar, as has become evident in their testimonies over the years as well as in their writing. Consequently, the connections between the Latin American tradition and the U.S. Latino tradition have been substantive, going beyond just a common language and culture. Ana Castillo, for example, dedicated one of her novels to Julio Cortázar.

At the opposite end of the spectrum from the linear-type fiction that shares intimate, personal experience (often the case of the testimonial) is the experimental and innovative fiction of the postmodern. The Caribbean region has been particularly productive of postmodern fiction, along with Brazil and Argentina, and the Cuban exile Severo Sarduy has had considerable impact throughout Latin America in the promotion of a postmodern-type writing. In addition to Sarduy, the leading figures of postmodern fiction written in the Spanish-speaking Caribbean are Cuba's Guillermo Cabrera Infante and Puerto Rico's Luis Rafael Sánchez and Edgardo Rodríguez Juliá. One of the pioneer works of the Caribbean postmodern was Cabrera Infante's *Tres tristes tigres*, and his interest in Joyce, which is most evident in this novel with respect to the use of language, is just one indicator of Cabrera Infante's postmodern directions. Innovative writers such as Frankétienne (formerly Franck Étienne) in Haiti, Maryse Condé in Guadeloupe, and Raphael Confiant in Martinique have also been associated with the postmodern. Several critics, in fact, have suggested that the hybrid–and-always-in-flux cultures of the Caribbean have always been "postmodern."

Sarduy's fiction differs considerably from Cabrera Infante's, but it is the most significant contribution to the Caribbean postmodern. Of his books the novel with the most impact on the Caribbean postmodern in particular and the Latin American postmodern in general is *Cobra* (1972), although none of Sarudy's work is as entertaining and accessible as Cabrera Infante's *Three Trapped Tigers*. Written more along the lines of the hermetic Lezama Lima than the playful Cabrera Infante, *Cobra* is Sarduy's novelistic reflection on language and writing. It was one of the early texts of Caribbean and Latin American post-modern fiction to blur the line between "fictional" and "theoretical" writing, and many young writers in other Latin American nations began to see the possibilities of the postmodern on the basis of having read *Cobra*. Sarduy parodies the theoretical writings of French theorist Jacques Derrida in the novel. The confluence of theory and practice in *Cobra* produces not an essence, but a lack of essence, thus pointing to the privileging of the artificial and superficial. Sarduy's novels *Matreya* (1978) and *Colibrí* (1983, Hummingbird) represent a continuation of the author's postmodern project. As in *Cobra*, the protagonists of these two novels are subjects in progress. A character named La Tremenda in *Matreya* is also identified as la Expansiva, la Divina, la Colonial, la Masiva, la Toda-Mena, and la Delirium. *Maitreya* opens in the mountains of Tibet with the death of the "maestro"—a Tibetan lama—the Chinese invasion of Tibet, and the monk's abandonment of the monasteries. The characters travel through India to Ceylon. From Ceylon the novel's various characters go to Sagua la Grande in Cuba. The twins who are born there spend time in New York and later travel to Iran and Algeria, but end up back in Ceylon. *Colibrí* begins with a group of youths wrestling in view of the wealthy and the military. It is a world of luxury and drugs where La Regenta (whose original sex is unknown) rules over her homosexual brothel. An athletic, blond boy, Colibrí, arrives in this setting and becomes an admired wrestler. After travels through the jungles, which include love affairs and other adventures, Colibrí returns to La Regenta's establishment and eventually takes it over. The uncertain and unstable identities of the narrator and the protagonist are the most clearly postmodern aspects of *Colibrí*.

With the publication of *La guaracha del Macho Camacho* (1976, *Macho Camacho's Beat*) in 1976, Luis Rafael Sánchez brought postmodern fiction to the forefront of Puerto Rican culture. He was already well-known in Puerto Rico for his short fiction and plays. The title of this novel in the original Spanish refers to the Puerto Rican music that permeates the text, and in between the layers of this music is a fragmented text with multiple narrators who offer the popular music, mass culture, and the heterogeneous cultural reality of everyday life in Puerto Rico. Sánchez appropriates a multiplicity of discourses in this novel, including the voices of a radio announcer (who appears in nineteen segments), television and radio commercials, popular singers, and many other voices of the mass media. Sánchez also parodies writers associated with high culture, such as José Donoso and Severo Sarduy. In addition, he makes allusions to a broad range of extraliterary cultural figures, from Mohammed Ali to Charlie Chaplin. Sánchez continues his postmodern project with his second novel, *La importancia de llamarse Daniel Santos* (1988, The importance of calling oneself Daniel Santos). In this work Sánchez neither creates nor debunks the myths surrounding the figure of a popular singer of the 1940s and 1950s, Daniel Santos, but questions how popular figures such as he are mythified and demythified. This novel is the story of an author's search for Daniel Santos. The author figure, who is identified in the text as a gay writer named Luis Rafael Sánchez, travels to numerous Latin American cities in search of Santos. Sánchez's search escapes generic definitions, as his book blurs the boundaries of fiction, biography, and testimonial.

The fiction of Edgardo Rodríguez Juliá, like that of Sánchez, escapes traditional genre definition. He also writes stories celebrating figures of popular culture. His first text, *Las tribulaciones de Jonás* (1981, The tribulations of Jonah), is a testimonial account of the renowned Puerto Rican political figure Luis Muñoz Marín. *El entierro de Cortijo* (1983,

Cortijo's Wake, 20054) deals with the wake of a legendary musician, Rafael Cortijo (1928–1932). His band was popular in Puerto Rico during the 1950s, and Rodríguez Juliá uses this figure to weave a narrative through working-class San Juan. This novel and *La noche oscura del Niño Avilés* (1984, The dark night of the Avilés boy) are texts for the active postmodern reader, offering a series of historical and fictional documents to decipher; neither work offers an overarching interpretive scheme. In a later work, the short novel *Una noche con Iris Chacón* (1986, A night with Iris Chacón), he relates three stories about popular culture in Puerto Rico. Rodríguez Juliá has also published *La renuncia del héroe Baltasar* (1974, *The Renunciation*).

The Dominican Republic and Haiti are not centers of postmodern fictional production in Latin America. Nevertheless, modernist writers Marci Veloz Maggiolo, Efraím Castillo, Andrés L. Mateo, and Manuel García Cartagena do exhibit some postmodern tendencies. Veloz Maggiolo demonstrated an interest in the postmodern with experiments such as *Florbella* (1986, Florbella) and *Materia prima* (1988, Raw material). Efraím Castillo, on the other hand, novelizes issues of American and Dominican cultures, questioning dominant U.S. values in his novels *Curriculum (el síndrome de la visa)* (1982, Curriculum, the syndrome of the visa) and *Intihuaman o Eva Again* (1983). Experimental and irreverent writers from Haiti—Frankétienne and Dany Laferrière–have contributed to a postmodern fiction of Haiti.

In summary, Caribbean postmodern fiction is one of the most heterogeneous of Latin America, to a large extent because of the multiple language and cultural groups that coexist in close geographic proximity. The remarkably hierarchical class structure of this region, as well as its proximity to the U.S., are also factors in the heterogeneity. The Caribbean region has been described as a culture of "performers." In very different ways, novels such as *Three Trapped Tigers*, *Cobra*, and *Macho Camacho's Beat* are, indeed, cultural performances. The postmodern writers of the Caribbean write with a full awareness of the provisional and precarious status of Caribbean culture, in close interaction with American culture and often dominated by it. Having been invaded by U.S. marines, nations such as Haiti and the Dominican Republic maintain a strong historic memory that is preserved in the novelistic tradition of the possible consequences of proximity to the United States.

Numerous Latino writers are in dialogue with Caribbean, Latin American, and international postmodern culture. They have also reacted against some of the assumptions of previous generations of Chicano writers with regard to Chicano nationalism and theories of identity and history. Feminist and gay writers have been prominent since the 1980s; Gloria Anzaldúa and Cherríe Moraga, known as poets and essayists, have been intellectual leaders in this response to the Chicano writing of the 1960s and 1970s. Some of the other major Latino writers of the 1980s and 1990s are the Chicanos Arturo Islas, Ana Castillo, Víctor Villaseñor, Mary Helen Ponce, Cecile Pineda, Luis Alberto Urrea, and the Puerto Rican Giannini Braschi (who has lived on the East Coast of the U.S.) As is the case of many writers located in the Caribbean, many of these novelists are involved in a variety of negotiations: between mainstream and marginal cultural groups as well as between more established and popular forms of writing. Islas's *Migrant Souls* (1990) can be seen as a postmodern narrative that negotiates forms of high art and mass culture. Like the Latin American postmodern, it is of substance, questioning compulsory heterosexuality. Victor Villaseñor's *Rain of Gold* (1991) has become something of a best seller with classic status, articulating themes of minority peoples. Ponce's 1989 novel *The Wedding* parodies many stereotypes of Hispanic culture.

Some Latin American fiction to appear after the 1960s Boom has been associated with a post-Boom. This is a line of writing that represents more continuity than disruption with the modernist novel and tends to be consistent with the aesthetic and political interests of writers such as Gabriel García Márquez, Carlos Fuentes, Tomás Rivera, and Rudolfo Anaya. Some of these writers question the value and viability of nationalism, as do their counterparts writing a more postmodern-type fiction. This post-Boom in the Caribbean and United Status has included novels by writers such as the Cubans Reinaldo Arenas, Antonio Benítez Rojo, Jesús Díaz, Matias Montes Huidobro, and Eliseo Alberto, the Latinos Rudolfo Anaya, Sandra Cisneros, Oscar Hijuelos, Lucha Corpi, and Americo Paredes, the Dominicans Pedro Mir and Pedro Verges, and the Puerto Ricans Rosario Ferré, Mayra Montero, and Olga Nolla. The later writings of Alejo Carpentier and Lisandro Otero can also be associated with the post-Boom in Latin America. Pedro Verges and Pedro Mir engage in rewriting the history of the Dominican Republic. They all tend to tell stories in a linear fashion, they still believe in reconstructing real historical events ("rewriting history"), and they are less interested in formal experimentation than most of the writers associated with the postmodern. In the 1980s women's writing became a strong presence in Latin American and Latino literature; novelists such as Cisneros and Ferré began to occupy central rather than marginal spaces in the Latin American and North American literary scene. Writers such as Edwidge Danticat from Haiti, Maryse Condé from Guadeloupe, and Astrid Roemer from Suriname share the interests of feminists throughout the Caribbean. The presence of Isabel Allende and Laura Esquivel in the American literary markets, of course, made an enormous contribution to this change. By the 1990s, in many ways, the former margins had become the center.

After the Boom of the Latin American novel, many writers who had participated in the Boom or published novels in the 1960s continued publishing novels that some critics have associated with the post-Boom. This is the case of Alejo Carpentier, who had published *El siglo de las luces* (*Explosion in a Cathedral*) in 1962 and then wrote books that really participate in the post-Boom, *El recurso del método* (1974, *Reasons of State*) and *Concierto barroco* (1974, Baroque concert). *Reasons of State* is Carpentier's contribution to the ever expanding genre of the dictator novel in Latin America. It is a satirical portrayal of an aging Latin American dictator living in France in the early part of the twentieth century. The title of the novel in the original Spanish parodies Descartes.

Cuban Eliseo Alberto has become a renowned writer only recently, having been awarded a prestigious literary prize (Premio Alfaguara de Novela) in 1998. Born in 1951, he has lived in exile in Mexico since the 1990s, after having established a literary reputation with a broad range of creative writing in Cuba. After publishing two novels written in Cuba, he has written two novels with strong plots and exceptional characters, *Caracol Beach* (1998) and *La fábula de José* (1999, José's story). In *Caracol Beach*, for example, the protagonist faces death, confrontation with his transvestite son, and the presence of African gods. *La fábula de José* consists of a conversation about the morality of assassination for the sake of love as well as a questioning of traditional ideas about nationalism.

Fiction writer and essayist Rosario Ferré is one of the foremost post-Boom writers of the Caribbean region and is well-known throughout Latin America in general and the Caribbean region in particular for her fiction and essays. Like many Caribbean writers, she is interested in politics, popular culture, and the relationship of the Hispanic culture of Puerto Rico with the Anglo culture of the United States. Unlike many of these writers, however, she has chosen a unique cultural/linguistic position: she has begun writing novels in English and publishing them afterward in Spanish translation, as is the case with the novel that appeared first in English as *The House on the Lagoon* (1995) and then in Spanish as *La casa de la laguna* (1996).

As Puerto Rican writers living on the island, Marya Montero and Olga Nolla share many interests with Ferré. Montero has published several novels, including *La trenza de la hermosa luna* (1987, Braid of the beautiful moon), *La última noche que pasé contigo* (1991, The last night I spent with you), and *Como un mensajero tuyo* (1998, As your messenger), all of which deal with both social history of the island and intimate relations among the characters. Nolla has published *La segunda hija* (1992, The second daughter) and *El castillo de la memoria* (1996, The castle of memory). The latter is a family saga and social history much along the lines of Ferré and a broad range of Latin American writers beyond Puerto Rico, such as Gabriel García Márquez and Isabel Allende.

Whereas Ferré has occupied a border position with respect to Puerto Rican and American culture; the Cuban writers Matías Montes Huidobro and Antonio Benítez Rojo have occupied slightly different cultural borders as Caribbean writers. Montes Huidobro has lived most of his adult life on a cultural border of the U.S. by leaving Cuba and assuming an academic position at the University of Hawaii. Most of his creative writing has been in theater, but he has also published a body of fiction that includes *Desterrados al fuego* (1975), his novel of the exile experience. The focus of the work is the detailed process of adaptation to a foreign culture and the assumption of a new identity. Benítez Rojo was an internationally recognized intellectual in Cuba in the 1960s, both as a creative writer and as a scholar. After going into exile in the U.S. and assuming duties as an academic at Amherst College, he has continued his career as a scholar and fiction writer. His novel *El mar de las lentejas* (1984, Sea of lentils) offers a broad, historical vision of the Spanish conquest of the Americas.

The Cubans Jesús Díaz and Senel Paz on the other hand, have dedicated their careers to writing while remaining on the island, producing fiction that is best associated with the post-Boom. Known in the Caribbean region since publishing his early short stories in the 1960s, Díaz has continued publishing novels throughout the latter half of the twentieth century. His novel *Las iniciales de la tierra* is an historical work that explores the adventure of the Cuban revolution and the efforts to construct a new nation. Paz is younger than Díaz (having been born in 1950 and beginning to publish fiction well after him), but has become a central fiction writer on the island since the 1980s. His first novel, *Un rey en el jardín* (1983, A king in the garden), is a fictionalized version of childhood memories during the Cuban Revolution.

Latino writing of this period has included both the mainstream and the marginalized. Among the Latino writers who have been most prominent during this period are Rudolfo Anaya, Sandra Cisneros, and Oscar Hijuelos. Anaya has been widely recognized since the publication of *Bless Me, Ultima* (1972), his now classic Chicano novel that is a celebration of a social collective unconscious and of the human spirit. Using the narrative strategies of modernism, Anaya tells the story of a young boy as an artist. Cisneros's most celebrated novel, *The House on Mango Street*, consists of narratives that affirm identity. Like her predecessors Tomás Rivera and Rolando Hinojosa, she exposes the reader to the realities of working-class life among Hispanic minorities. Oscar Hijuelos lives on the border between Caribbean and American cultures in New York as few writers do: he was born in New York City of Caribbean parents and has been educated in the United States. His novels, such as the Pulitzer Prize–winning *The Mambo Kings Play Songs of Love* (1989) and *A Simple Havana Melody* (2002), are a product of his unique bicultural background. All three of these novelists allude to a dominant Anglo society, although Cisneros offers a differing perspective on a society that not only dominates but is patriarchal. Less mainstream writers than Anaya, Cisneros, and Hijuelos, such as Nicholasa Mohr and Denise Chavez, have offered transgressive narratives about lesbian experience.

Some Latino writers have produced linear, post-Boom-type fictions (comparable to the Latin American post-Boom) in the form of detective novels. Two of the most productive Latino writers of this type of fiction have been Rudolfo Anaya and Lucha Corpi. Known for his celebrated novels of the 1970s that were unrelated to detective fiction, Anaya's later murder mysteries include *Zia Summer* (1996) and *Shaman Winter* (1999). Corpi, on the other hand, has been writing detective fiction from the beginning of her career, and her work includes *Eulogy for a Brown Angel* (1992) and *Black Widow's Wardrobe* (1999).

In the 1990s the heterogeneity of Caribbean and Latino fiction make generalizations and categorization increasingly difficult. Many of the writers are interested in issues of class, gender, and ethnicity in ways that associate them with the aesthetic interests of the postmodern as well as the political interests of the post-Boom. Writers born since 1955 possess life experiences radically different from previous generations, having been reared in a world without the 1968 experience, but with the growth of the media and globalization. In most cases they are acutely aware of their modernist tradition, from Borges to the writings of the Boom. Like their cohorts of the generation of the 1990s in Brazil and the generation of the crack in Mexico, they tend to reject the totalizing efforts and overt political writing that they associate with the 1960s writing of the Boom. Writers such as José Manuel Prieto, Ernesto Mestre, Manuel García Cartagena, Zoe Valdés, René Vásquez Díaz, Gianini Braschi, Julia Alvarez, Cristina Garcia, Judith Ortiz Coffer, Esmeralda Santiago, Mary Helen Ponce, Omar Torres, Virgil Suárez, Margarita Engle, Pablo Medina, Elías Miguel Muñoz, Roberto Fernández, and J. Joaquín Fraxedas are in many ways bicultural or multicultural and often write in a postnational context. Prieto, for example, was born in Havana, Cuba in 1962 and lived in Russia for twelve years, translating the works of Joseph Brodsky and Anna Akhmatova into Spanish. Author of the novel *Nocturnal Butterflies of the Russian Empire* (1999), he lives in Mexico City where he teaches Russian history. Mestre was born in Guantanamo, Cuba, in 1964 and emigrated with his family to Madrid, Spain, in 1972, and later that year to Miami. He received a BA in English literature from Tulane, lives in Brooklyn, and has published the novel *The Lazarus Rumba* (1999). The young writer from the Dominican Republic Manuel García Cartagena has published a first novel under the title *Aquiles Vargas, fantasma* (1989), a self-conscious metafiction that questions the political future of the Dominican Republic as well as the status of his book as a novel.

Five very different cases of the Caribbean diaspora among writers of this generation are the Cubans Zoé Valdés, René Vásquez Díaz, and Andrés Jorge, and the Puerto Rican Gianini Braschi. Zoé Valdés has been highly productive and widely acclaimed in the 1990s, having produced the novels *La nada cotidiana* (1995, *Yocandra in the Paradise of Nada*), *Te di la vida entera* (1996, *I Gave You All I Had*), *Café Nostalgia* (1998, Café nostalgia), *Sangre azul* (1998, Blue blood), *Traficantes de belleza* (1998, Beauty traffickers), *La hija del embajador* (1998, The ambassador's daughter), and *Querido primer novio* (2002, *Dear First Love*). As mentioned earlier, Valdés has spent recent years in exile in Paris, and her work has much to do with her status as a Cuban novelist who writes as a person uprooted from her homeland. Nevertheless, novels such as *Café nostalgia* represent an implicit critique of the genre of the Latin American "novel of exile" of the 1970s and 1980s. Thus, as a writer born in 1959, she distances herself from the previous generations of Caribbean exile writers who played out the now tired themes of feeling uprooted, nostalgic, and the like. *Café nostalgia* is her major work, and it is both an original reflection on nostalgia as well as an intimate and textured story of the protagonist's experience of the senses. It is also a subtle dialogue on this Cuban writer's relationship with other fictions of remembrance, such as those of Proust. The protagonist of *Yocandra in the Paradise of Nada* represents the first generation of Cubans born during or after the Cuban Revolution who sense the frustration and the related feelings of alienation from a socialist ideal. Both *Te di la vida entera* and *My Dear First Love* are love stories in which issues related to Cuban culture and politics are only background for intense descriptions of love and loss.

Having been born in 1952, René Vásquez Díaz is older than Valdés, but he also grew up with a generation less enchanted with the Cuban Revolution than earlier groups. He also shares a different sense of the role of nostalgia in exile fiction. He has an understanding for literary tradition, an art for playfulness, and a skill in story writing that make his novels *La era imaginaria* (1987, The imaginary era) and *Querido traidor* (1993, Dear traitor) important contributions to Caribbean writing. Jorge Andrés (born in 1960) has lived in Mexico in recent years, having published several novels. *Voyeurs* (2001) is Andrés's exploration of the invented time and space of a voyeur who is a painter and desires to paint the body of the nude woman whom he observes and imagines. In *Yo-yo boing!* (1998) Giannina Braschi flaunts experimentation, exile, and cultural borders in ways that distance her from Valdés and Vásquez Díaz, for her work is a celebration of a hybrid Spanish and English of the Puerto Rican diaspora as well as one that questions many cultural and literary traditions. Some portions of the novel are written in an invented form of a highly colloquial Spanglish.

Along the lines of their Caribbean and Latino counterparts on the East Coast of the United States, Chicano writers on the West Coast, such as Gloria Anzaldúa, Guillermo Gómez Peña, and Cherríe Moraga, do creative writing that is difficult to describe as novels. Their border writing questions the established norms of Anglo society and often reaffirms Hispanic identity in the United States. On the other hand, Latina writers Cristina García and Julia Alvarez have reached a broad U.S. readership to tell their transgressive stories of Latina women surviving in Anglo-American culture and society. In *How the García Girls Lost Their Accents*, Alvarez presents herself as both an insider and an outsider to standard Catholic religious practices. The sexual transgressions in the novels of Cristina García have brought her a wide readership, but they are still relatively moderate compared to the most transgressive feminist writers and the boldest postmodern Caribbean and Latino novelists.

With respect to the U.S. Hispanic novel, the strong Hispanic heritage in the southwestern U.S., as well as the significant Native American populations have been key factors in the development of Chicano novel fiction. The Chicanos Josephina Niggli and José Antonio Villareal were writing well before the "Boom" of Latin American literature or the flowering of the Chicano novel in the late 1960s and early 1970s. Niggli has become increasingly recognized as one of the pioneer Chicano writers of the twentieth century, although her writings are mostly in the areas of theater, history, and memoir. The other important precedent to the 1960s in Latino fiction was *Pocho* (1959) by José Antonio Villareal. At the same time, Latino writers such as Alejandro Morales, Roland Hinojosa-Smith, and Miguel Méndez are being published in Spanish in Latin America.

The Andean Region Novel (Colombia, Venezuela, Ecuador, Peru, Bolivia): Contexts and Chronology

The most prominent cultural and political contexts in the Andean region are the presence of indigenous groups and the increase of violence since the late 1940s, a violence that was mostly rural in the 1940s and 1950s in contrast to more recent urban violence. This is a culturally diverse region that includes not only a vast range of native American groups but also an Afro-Latin American population located primarily along the coasts of Venezuela, Colombia, Ecuador, and Peru. Well before 1945, the Andean region had established a strong tradition of social protest writing as well as works of Native American or indigenista themes. Indeed, the Ecuadorian Jorge Icaza's *Huasipungo* (1934) and the Peruvian Ciro Alegría's *El mundo es ancho y ajeno* (1941, *Broad and Alien Is the World*) are canonical works of indigenista fiction, which were attempts at portraying Native American cultural and political issues from a perspective that might be considered anthropologically sound. They attempted to avoid the clichés of romanticism and other simplified stereotypes of indigenous peoples.

Much of the Andean region was populated by Incas upon the arrival of Europeans in the sixteenth century; the northern part of the Andean region was the habitat for Chibchas and other groups. The native population has survived better in the Andean region than in many other parts of the Americas, and today Bolivia, Peru, Ecuador, and southern Colombia are predominantly indigenous or mestizo. The colonial legacy has left a much higher proportion of the indigenous population living at a lower socioeconomic level than those with European ancestry.

The most prominent author of indigenista themes in the Andean region in the post-WWII period was the Peruvian José María Arguedas; he wrote from the position of a bicultural individual who was reared in a Native American community and later educated in white and mestizo Peruvian society. He was born in the province of Andahuaylas in 1911 in southern Peru. His childhood experiences in Andahuaylas were key for his later fiction, for there he grew up in the world of indigenous groups. As one of Latin America's most accomplished exponents of *indigenismo*, he believed that the oral culture of the indigenous groups of Peru had not been recreated authentically in any novel. Convinced that social scientists had not done justice to the indigenous cause, he began writing fiction in the 1930s, publishing his first volume of short stories under the title *Agua* (Water) in 1935.

The cultural diversity of the Andean region was accentuated with the slave trade operated by the Spaniards during the colonial period. A center for the Spanish slave trade was Cartagena, Colombia; from there African slaves were distributed throughout the Andean region. Consequently, the northern coast of Colombia is predominantly African today, and much of the northern Colombian area is triethnic.

Manuel Zapata Olivella began his career with a political novel, *La calle 10* (1960, Tenth Street), providing an urban version of the same civil war fictionalized by Eduardo Caballero Calderón and many other Colombian novelists. Zapata Olivella produced other modernist novels: *En Chimá nace un santo* (1964, In Chimá a saint is born) and *Changó, el gran putas* (1984, Changó, the great son of a bitch). The latter is a lengthy and ambitious epic work that recalls some of the efforts of the 1960s Boom writers to produce "total" works.

The diversity of the novel in the Andean region has been underlined with the recent rise of women and gay writers of more international renown than had ever been the case before. The Colombian Laura Restrepo, the Bolivian Domitila Barrios de Chungara and Fernando Vallejo are three very different yet telling cases. Restrepo was trained as a journalist and was initially known in Colombia for her journalistic writing, later for her novels. She began publishing fiction in the 1980s, beginning with *Historia de un entusiasmo* (1986, History of an enthusiasm), and has grown to be a best-selling novelist in the Andean region in the 1990s. Two of her novels, *Leopardo al sol* (1993) and *Dulce compañía* (1995), have appeared in English: *Leopard in the Sun* and *Angel of Galilea*, respectively. The latter deals with a saint or an angel's role in an impoverished urban neighborhood in Colombia. Domitila Barrios de Chungara is an important Bolivian representative of testimonial writing, documenting the experiences and lives of miners in Bolivia. Fernando Vallejo has published a substantive number of novels since the mid-1980s and has been increasingly recognized as one of Colombia's most accomplished writers. He began with a trilogy that is a macabre satire of the elite social groups of Medellín. This trilogy, which began with *El fuego secreto* (1986, The secret fire), was also the first explicitly gay fiction to be published in Colombia. His more recent novels *El desbarrancadero* (2001) and *La Rambla paralela* (2002, The parallel avenue) are introspective and autobiographical reflections. Vallejo has been increasingly recognized as a major intellectual and writer throughout Latin America, making him one of the more prominent novelists of the Andean region to deal with gay themes.

The rise of modernist fiction in the Andean region during the 1940s and 1950s was signaled by the early writings of the Colombians Gabriel García Márquez, Eduardo Caballero Calderón, Manuel Mejía Vallejo, Héctor Rojas Herazo, and Alvaro Cepeda Samudio. Nevertheless, a group of lesser-known writers from the 1940s—Rafael Gómez Picón, Ernesto Camargo Martínez, Jaime Ardila Casamitjana, and Jaime Ibáñez—were the early pioneers of the modern novel in Colombia. In the remainder of the Andean region, novelists smitten by the modern included the Venezuelans Miguel Otero Silva, Salvador Garmendia, Ramón Díaz Sánchez, and Guillermo Meneses, the Ecuadorians Demetrio Aguilera Malta, Adalberto Ortiz, and Miguel Donoso Pareja, and the Peruvians Mario Vargas Llosa, Gustavo Valcárcel, Julio Ramón Ribeyro, Luis Loayza, and Sebastián Salazar Bondy.

These Andean writers were admirers of many European and North American writers, above all, the fiction of William Faulkner. They read translations by Borges and other editions of Faulkner's work published in Buenos Aires. García Márquez, Héctor Rojas Herazo, Alvaro Cepeda Samudio, and Miguel Otero Silva were among the most prominent Faulknerians in the 1950s and 1960s. As noted earlier, García Márquez's early work, particularly his first novel *La hojarasca*, was patently Faulknerian.

García Márquez, Cepeda Samudio, and Rojas Herazo were Faulknerian writers in the 1950s whose interest in modernizing Colombian and Latin American literature was witnessed by the publication of their novels *La hojarasca*, *La casa grande* (1962), and *Respirando el verano* (1962, Breathing the summer). The first novel by García Márquez and his initial use of the mythical town of Macondo, *La hojarasca* depicts life in Macondo in the early twentieth century, a period of a banana boom followed by an economic bust. The novel communicates a sense of decadence and dying through the three narrations of three different characters, all of whom are attending a wake. Numerous critics have pointed to the similarities with Faulkner's *As I Lay Dying*, and García Márquez is successful in creating an atmosphere of guilt, evil, and chaos, concluding with a note of hope that is typical of his early writing: the human spirit always prevails in his fiction of Macondo, despite ongoing suffering. (Chicano writers such as Tomás Rivera identified closely with this human plight and how the impoverished can prevail.) The third Faulknerian in this group of Colombian writers, Rojas Herazo, uses similar Faulknerian approaches to tell the story of a family and a town on the Caribbean coast that also become the focus of his later novels *En noviembre llega el arzobispo* (1967, The archbishop arrives in November) and *Celia se pudre* (1985, Celia is rotting). Rojas Herazo relates anecdotes of violent men and enduring women. Dying at an early age, Cepeda Samudio published no other novels. García Márquez continued his Macondo cycle with *El coronel no tiene quien le escriba* (1961, *No One Writes to the Colonel*) and *La mala hora*, two short novels that develop the characters of Macondo, telling stories of human dignity and of violence, with some touches of the humor that becomes so prominent later in his masterpiece *One Hundred Years of Solitude*.

Venezuelans Miguel Otero Silva and Ramón Díaz Sánchez played a role in Venezuela similar to the contribution of these three Colombians in their homeland. Otero Silva's interest in pursuing the modern novel was evidenced by the publication of his novel *Casas muertas* (1955, Dead houses), a work about a dying town that is malaria infested and ignored by the central government. In many ways this is the Venezuelan Macondo. Clearly, the author intends the town to be a metaphor for Venezuelan society, but the reader's awareness of this fact develops slowly. Given the miserable conditions, a general sense of hoplessness prevails. Using Faulknerian techniques, Otero Silva depends on extended flashbacks to reveal the underlying truths of the situation—one of death. Otero Silva's success in this subtle text is in engaging the reader in the individual characters before the social protest becomes too evident. Díaz Sánchez wrote in the tradition of social protest fiction, and his novel *Cumboto* (1950) reflects both that tradition and an interest in modernist innovations.

Manuel Mejía Vallejo's fictionalization of the period of La Violencia appears in his novel *El día señalado* by interweaving two plots by two different narrators, one dealing with the broad picture of the violent civil conflict, the other dealing with a youth seeking revenge against his father. A priest is the voice of love and human understanding, but the outcome of the novel underscores the overall hopelessness of the situation. Much of Mejía Vallejo's writing has an implicit tone of nostalgia, and this is the case of his later urban novel, *Aire de tango* (1973, Air of tango), his homage to the celebrated Argentine tango singer Carlos Gardel. The nostalgia suggests that somehow the past offered some intangible positive that is better than the hopeless present.

The Colombians Caballero Calderón and Mejía Vallejo create this sense of despair, and the Peruvian Gustavo Valcárcel creates an even stronger sense of hopelessness and loss in a prison novel, *La prisión* (1951, The prison). In this mostly first-person narrative, the protagonist shares dreams, memories, and observations. In the process of suffering in the prison, the protagonist is dehumanized and loses control of his narration and himself.

Julio Ramón Ribeyro, Oswaldo Reynoso, and Luis Loayza made contributions to the modernization of the Latin American novel in the 1960s that went fundamentally unnoticed beyond Peru at the time their works were published. Nevertheless, both were accomplished writers, as was evident early in Ribeyro's career with the publication of his novel *Los geniecillos dominicales* (Sunday temper) in 1965 and decades later when he received one of the most prestigious literary prizes of Latin America—the Premio de Novela Juan Rulfo. *Los geniecillos dominicales* deals with a young man who leaves his job to search for something more meaningful, then faces a series of related crises. Ribeyro offers an entertaining satire of certain literary clichés, a tone he mastered in his voluminous and superb short fiction. The protagonist of this novel has little respect for society's norms, as does the main character in Reynoso's *En octubre no hay milagros* (1965, In October there are no miracles). The protagonist of Luis Loayza's *Una piel de serpiente* (1964, Snake skin), on the other hand, is a revolutionary idealist who is easily manipulated by the established order.

The celebrated 1960s Boom of the Latin American novel had its point of departure in this area, for some of its key novels were published in the Andean region. The point of departure was the Peruvian Mario Vargas Llosa's *La ciudad y los perros* (1962, *The Time of the Hero*), and the other key novels of the Boom to appear in the Andean region were Vargas Llosa's *La casa verde* (1966, *The Green House*) and *Conversación en La Catedral* and García Márquez's *Cien años de soledad*. All these novels, as well as García Márquez's later *El otoño del patriarca*, have become modern classics of the Latin American literary tradition.

Many readers and critics consider these three novels of the 1960s the most brilliant period of Vargas Llosa's writing career. With *La ciudad y los perros* the author exploded onto the international literary scene throughout the Hispanic world, from Peru to Spain, with an intriguing plot, flashy narrative techniques, and a scandalous denunciation of the sacred institutions of Peru and Latin America. It was an immediate best seller throughout the Hispanic world, an unprecedented accomplishment at a time when few contemporary Latin American novels were read beyond national borders. The setting for this first novel is a military school in Lima that functions as a microcosm for Peruvian society. The multiple points of view and variety of points in time make the construction of the plot an adventure in itself. Vargas Llosa expands the technical possibilities and geographic scope in his next novel, the vast and ambitious *La casa verde*, set in a town in northern Peru (Piura) and in the jungles of the Amazon. In Piura a brothel becomes the scene for dramatic events of eventual mythic proportions, and in the jungle missionaries, Native American groups, government officials, and traders interact through a web of relations. The links between these two apparently different stories set in two different regions is a character called Sergeant Lituma, a native of Piura, and his Indian wife Bonifacia, whom he brings from the jungle. Other major characters include Don Anselmo, a harp player who builds a mythic brothel (the Green House) in Piura and later carries out a melodramatic affair with a blind orphan girl. The complex narrative engages the reader and creates an ambiguous sense of reality that seems to reflect the very experience of the characters themselves in their network of relationships. Consequently, the novel has a broad appeal for a wide range of readers.

For readers who find complex narratives a challenge, *Conversación en La Catedral* is Vargas Llosa's culminating masterpiece. Increasing the complexity of the narrative voices and temporal planes, Vargas Llosa focuses on the vicissitudes of the dictatorship of Manuel Odría in Peru from 1948 to 1956. This lengthy (two volumes in the original edition in Spanish) narrative has as its point of departure a conversation between two of the main characters in a bar in downtown Lima called The Cathedral. The novel begins with the question "At what point was Peru screwed over?" and then develops numerous possible answers to this question. In the process, the reader is privy to the decadent and violent world of all levels of Peruvian society. This work is also the culmination of Vargas Llosa's neo-Faulknerian mode of writing.

The zenith of the 1960s Boom both in the Andean region in particular and Latin America in general was García Márquez's *One Hundred Years of Solitude*. One of the most internationally acclaimed, widely read and rapidly translated novels in the history of Latin American literature, this novel popularized what in remaining decades of the century was the supposed emblem of Latin American culture: magical realism. The novel's fascinating plot and unforgettable characters have made it universally appealing. Read in a Latin American context, it is a deeply historical work as well, the culmination of Borges's implicit invitation in *Ficciones* to invent reality rather than merely imitate it. With respect to history, *One Hundred Years of Solitude* basically retells the unique history of both Colombia and Latin America, including some of the worst excesses of local oligarchs and foreign powers. The farcical presentation of the banana workers strike (and massacre) is, along with Cepeda Samudio's fictionalization of it in *La casa grande*, the first written public documentation of a national tragedy that had been obscured and forgotten by Colombia's institutionalized history and official historians. On a most basic level, *One Hundred Years of Solitude* is also a family story. In addition, much of what has been called "magical realism," in fact, comes directly from the oral tradition of Colombia's Caribbean coast.

After the 1960s Boom, some young writers searched for differing, nonmagical realist modes of writing and took the path suggested by Borges and Cortázar for an innovative and experimental fiction that a few critics have identified as postmodern. Others followed more linear and commercial routes, searching for a wider reading audience, and were identified by some critics as the post-Boom. The leading exponents of innovative and postmodern fiction in the Andean region of the 1970s and 1980s were the Colombians R. H. Moreno-Durán, Darío Jaramillo Agudelo, and Albalucía Angel, the Venezuelans José Balza and Oswaldo Trejo, the Bolivian Renato Prada Oropeza, and the Ecuadorian Jorge Enrique Adoum. A center for postmodern writing in the Andean region was Colombia, and it has its roots in the innovative novel *Mateo el flautista* (1968, Mateo the flutist) by Alberto Duque López.

Following the freedom for innovation suggested by the Argentines Borges and Cortázar and the Colombians García Márquez in *One Hundred Years of Solitude* and Alberto Duque López in *Mateo el flautista*, the postmodern innovators to appear on the scene in the 1970s were Andrés Caicedo, Umberto Valverde, Albalucía Angel, Marco Tulio Aguilera Garramuño, Rodrigo Parra Sandoval, and R. H. Moreno-Durán. Moreno-Durán published a substantial body of innovative fiction in the 1980s and 1990s; other postmodern fiction writers who published in this period were Darío Jaramillo Agudelo, Boris Salazar, Hugo Chaparro Valderrama, Héctor Abad Faciolince, and Orietta Lozano.

Moreno-Durán has had an ongoing postmodern fictional agenda in place since the late 1970s. He has explained in essays and interviews that he considers himself part of international postmodern culture as his primary identity and a Colombian second. This attitude is typical of a generation of writers who reject the dominant modes of nationalism that date back to the nineteenth century. The roots of his trilogy titled *Femina Suite* are to be found not only in the empirical reality of Colombia but also, as in the case of much postmodern fiction, in modernist literature. Many features of Moreno-Durán's first novel,

Juego de damas (1977, Women's game) can be associated with Cortázar's call for a new and innovative open novel proposed in *Hopscotch*. Women are important characters in most of his books; in *Juego de damas* they are intellectuals, beginning with their radicalized student life in the 1960s and passing through different stages of social climbing and the search for power. As in most of his fiction, the author develops elaborate relationships between language and power: he employs a series of strategies, including parody and euphemism, to subvert language. The two main characters of his second book, *Toque de Diana* (1981, Diana's call), are also intellectuals who engage in the linguistic and sexual exercises found in *Juego de damas*. In the third and most hermetic volume of the trilogy, *Finale capriccioso con Madonna* (1993, Capriccioso finale with Madonna), Moreno-Durán refers to both the eroticism of language and the language of eroticism. Several factors unify Moreno-Durán's trilogy as a single postmodern project, but, above all, the role of language itself as the main subject of all three books.

Moreno-Durán's *Los felinos del canciller* (1987, The chancellor's felines) lacks some of the hermetic qualities of his previous work and much postmodern fiction, and in this connection one might speak of an early postmodern attitude in the Andean region that produced relatively inaccesible works (the early Moreno-Durán, in this sense, corresponds to the early Severo Sarduy and the early Néstor Sánchez in Argentina) and a later, more accessible postmodern fiction. The difficulties and inaccessibility of many postmodern texts are replaced in *Los felinos del canceller* by wit: Rather than functioning as a barrier, Moreno-Durán's subtle manipulation of language is frequently the material of humor. This Colombian author continues his postmodern project with *El caballero de la invicta* (1993, The undefeated gentleman), which contains many of the same strategies already observed in his fiction.

Other postmodern novelists in Colombia are generally as demanding of their readers as Moreno-Durán. The fiction of Moreno-Durán and Angel is obviously removed from the type of modernity and magical realism pioneered by García Márquez. Creating a dialogue on fiction and philosophy, Aguilera Garramuño moves away from the context of Colombia and García Márquez, but he continues in the metafictional mode. The fiction of Darío Jaramillo Agudelo is an interesting case in the Andean region, for he writes in a postmodern mode while at the same time making an effort to reach a broader readership than is the case with Moreno-Durán, Angel, or many other innovative writers of his generation. All of his novels have an accessible and engaging story line. His first novel, *La muerte de Alec* (1983, The death of Alec), is a self-conscious meditation on the function of literature. It is an epistolary work directed to an unidentified "you." The characters are Colombian, but the novel is set in the United States. In this novel, as in some other postmodern fictions, the act of storytelling (giving order to a story) and interpretation (giving meaning to a story) become the predominant forces, taking precedence over other forms of understanding reality. Jaramillo Agudelo's fiction of the 1990s takes other directions beyond the postmodern.

Andrés Caicedo, Rodrigo Parra Sandoval, Alberto Duque López, and Umberto Valverde have conceived different kinds of postmodern projects. Caicedo's *¡Qué viva la música!* (1977, Let music live!), like the fiction of the first-generation postmoderns in Mexico of the Onda, involves a world of 1960s rock music and drugs. Beyond this obvious comparison, however, Caicedo has little in common with these young Mexican writers. *¡Qué viva la música!* is an experimental confrontation with a particular generation's cultural crisis in

1960s Colombia. Rodrigo Parra Sandoval's *El album secreto del Sagrado Corazón* (1978, The secret album of the Sacred Heart) is a collage of texts—books, newspapers, letters, documents, voices—representing an assault on the novel as a genre. The implied author suggests that the genre suffers limitations similar to those experienced by the protagonist, who lives in a very limiting and repressive religious seminary. Alberto Duque López proceeds similarly in *Mateo el flautista*, which in two parts offers two versions of the protagonist, Mateo. Umberto Valverde fictionalizes the popular culture of Caribbean music in *Bomba Camará* (1972) and *Celia Cruz* (1981).

A pioneer in experimental and postmodern fiction in Venezuela has been Oswaldo Trejo, whose books of fiction represent the most wildly experimental and self-conscious body of fiction ever published by a single writer in that nation. One of the most significant contemporary writers of Venezuelan postmodern fiction is José Balza, author of several volumes of fiction that escape genre classification. Like Moreno-Durán, he considers his books "exercises," blurring the line between fictional and essayistic discourses, writing fictions about literature and essays in a fictional mode. He sets forth a theory of the novel in his lengthy essay on *Don Quijote* titled "Este mar narrativo" (This narrative sea). In this essay, he privileges the unresolved contradictions of the novel that are typical of postmodern fiction, and he often returns to the correlations between the body and writing. Balza's early novels of the 1960s and 1970s were fundamentally modernist works, and his postmodern fiction consists of the novels *D* (1977), *Percusión* (1982, Percussion), and *Medianoche en video: 1/5* (1988, Midnight on video). He offers the subtitle *ejercicio narrativo* to the novel *D*, which relates, in a most general sense, a history of the modernization of Venezuela. Much of the story has been transcribed from cassette tapes, and at the end the author discusses the various problems with constructing this narrative. The postmodern worlds of his novels *Percusión* and *Medianoche en video 1/5* are fluid and provisional.

Postmodern fiction in Venezuela has also been produced by Alejandro Rossi, Francisco Massiani, Humberto Mata, Carlos Noguera, and Angel Gustavo Infante. A philosopher by training, Rossi has published several volumes of self-reflective metafictions, often written in the philosophical tone of Borges's fiction. His stories *El cielo de Sotero* (1987, The sky of Sotero) evoke this tone and self-reflective quality. Massiani has published entertaining and brief metafictions since the late 1960s, beginning with *Piedra de mar* (1968, Sea stone), which deals with an individual's personal crisis and his writing. The initial explorations into postmodern fiction by Mata, Noguera, and Infante, along with those by Balza, affirm the importance of innovative fiction in Venezuela.

The central figures for experimental fiction in Ecuador have been Jorge Enrique Adoum, Iván Eguez, and Abdón Ubidia. Despite the presence of Adoum, Ecuadorian fiction is more tradition bound than in Colombia or Venezuela. Iván Eguez has published several volumes of fiction since the 1970s and has written two novels with postmodern tendencies, *La Linares* (1976, Ms Linares) and *Pájara de memoria* (1984, Stream of memory). Abdón Ubidia has been relatively uninvolved with postmodern fictional exercises, although he does satirize multinational truth industries of mass communication in his entertainments titled *Divertimentos* (1989, Entertainments).

Martín Adán, the pioneer of experimental fiction in Peru, was a poet of the 1920s and 1930s whose one novel, *La casa de cartón* (1928, The house of cardboard), was an anomaly at the time. In the 1950s and 1960s a broader modernization of the Peruvian novel was effected by writers such as Mario Vargas Llosa, Julio Ramón Ribeyro, and Sebastián Salazar

Bondy. Peru is not a center of postmodern innovation. Nevertheless, modern writers, such as Vargas Llosa and Ribeyro have occasionally entered into dialogue with postmodern culture in some of their works. This is the case of the Vargas Llosa of the 1970s and novels such as *Pantaleón y las visitadoras* (1974, *Captain Pantoja and His Special Service*) and *La tía Julia y el escribidor* (1977, *Aunt Julia and the Script Writer*). With these two novels, the sober-toned, critical, and modernist Vargas Llosa turned away from his totalizing impulses and discovered some of the playful and humorous possibilities of fiction. As a postmodern text, *¿Quién mató a Palomino Molero?* (1986, *Who Killed Palomino Molero?*) is a search for fixed truths and a parodic play not only with the genre of the spy thriller but also with Vargas Llosa's own work. Ribeyro, like Vargas Llosa, is primarily a writer with the interests of a modernist, but some of his short fiction can be linked to the postmodern.

Renato Prada Oropeza and José W. Montes are the two figures most closely related to the postmodern in Bolivia, although the young writer Edmundo Paz Soldán has been more prominent in the 1990s. Prada Oropeza has been teaching in Mexico for the past two decades and is a literary critic and theorist of literature, practices that have been directly translated into his fiction. His novel *Mientras cae la noche* (1988, While the night falls) is a historiographic metafiction with several other characteristics of postmodern fiction, showing considerable affiliation with Borges and Cortázar's *Rayuela*. The humorous fictions of Montes exhibit some postmodern tendencies, but the vast majority of the novels published in Bolivia are far more conventional than the work of Prada Oropeza, Montes, or Paz Soldán. Montes is best known for his award-winning novel *Jonás y la ballena rosada* (1987, Jonah and the pink whale, winner of the Premio Casa de las Américas), but he has also recently published the lengthy novel *Sagrada arrogancia* (1998, Sacred arrogance).

The post-Boom in the Andean region was headed by some of the writers of the Boom, Gabriel García Márquez and Mario Vargas Llosa, as well as such prominent novelists as Manuel Mejía Vallejo, Salvador Garmendia, Fanny Buitrago, Gustavo Alvarez Gardeazábal, Germán Espinosa, Alvaro Mutis, Alfredo Bryce Echenique, Isaac Goldemberg, and, more recently, the Colombian Laura Restrepo. One of Espinosa's most accomplished novels, *Los cortejos del diablo* (1970, The courtship of the devil) is a historical work set in the colonial period. It tells the story of Juan de Mañozga, an inquisitor in Cartagena, Colombia, identified by some as the "Torquemada of the Indies." Espinosa's later novel, *Sinfonía del nuevo mundo* (1990, Symphony of the new world), is a historical novel involving Bolívar, with a well-developed plot directed to a broad reading public.

Alvarez Gardeazábal is the quintessential post-Boom novelist who publicly questioned some of the writers of the Boom and wrote best-selling novels that were widely read in Colombia during the 1970s and 1980s. His fiction is generally satirical of Colombian institutions and parodies the work of García Márquez. The most widely read of his works are *Cóndores no entierran todos los días* and *El bazar de los idiotas*, the latter already mentioned.

Fanny Buitrago, Alfredo Bryce Echenique, and Isaac Goldemberg have enjoyed both national and international commercial success with their post-Boom novels. Buitrago is best known in Colombia for novels and short stories that have appeared regularly since the 1960s. Her early writing, such as *Cola de zorro* (1970, Foxtail) is relatively complex, but her later novels *Los pañamanes* (1979, The island people) and *Los amores de Afrodita* (1983, Aphrodite's loves) demonstrate an interest in stories that are accessible to a broad reading public yet avoid the clichés of fiction for mass markets. *Los amores de Afrodita* can be read as a novel or as a set of short stories on topics related to love. Bryce Echenique's *Un mundo para Julius* (1970, *A World for Julius*) is a story of growing up in upper-middle-class Lima; but, more than a coming-of-age story, the novel satirizes this particular social class in a parody of its own language. His other post-Boom novels, which can be considered exercises in hyperbole and performance, are *Tantas veces Pedro* (1981, Pedro so many times), *La vida exagerada de Martín Román* (1981, The exaggerated life of Martín Román), *El hombre que hablaba de Octavia de Cádiz* (1985, The man that spoke of Octavia from Cádiz), and *La última mudanza de Felipe Carrillo* (1985, The last change of Felipe Carrillo). Goldemberg is a Jewish Peruvian writer who is best known for his poetry. His most acclaimed novel, *La vida a plazos de don Jacobo Lerner* (1975, *The Fragmented Life of Jacobo Lerner*), deals with the Jewish diaspora in Peru and the disenfranchisement of the protagonist.

A group of writers born since 1955 who have been prominent in the 1990s in the Andean region is headed by the Bolivian Edmundo Paz Soldán, the Colombians Héctor Abad Facciolince, Mario Mendoza, Santiago Gamboa, Jorge Franco Ramos, Hugo Chaparro Valderrama, Philip Potdevin, and Octavio Escobar Giraldo, and the Peruvians Jaime Bayly, Jorge Eduardo Benavides, Alonso Cueto, Melvin Ledgard, Peter Elmore, and Daniel Rodríguez Risco. Paz Soldán has been both an active novelist and spokesperson for his generation in the Andean region, publishing several novels and collaborating with the Chilean Alberto Fuguet in the publication of an anthology of his generation under the title *McOndo*, mentioned earlier. As postmodern writers of the generation after Moreno-Durán and Balza, they can also be identified as post-postmodern writers.

The most recent fiction of this generation in Colombia has been produced by Héctor Abad Facciolince, Hugo Chaparro Valderrama, Mario Mendoza, Santiago Gamboa, Jorge Franco Ramos, Philip Potdevin, and Octavio Escobar Giraldo. Each of these writers has published more than one novel in Colombia, and Abad Facciolince has a novel translated into English under the title *The Joy of Being Awake*, which appeared in Spanish as *Asuntos de un hidalgo disoluto* (1987). Chaparro Valderrama's *El capítulo de Fernelli* (1995, Fernelli's chapter) is a tribute to the Anglo-American detective genre, even though the narrator's main purpose in writing seems to be self-understanding. Philip Potdevin and Octavio Escobar Giraldo have published *Metatrón* (1995, Metatron) and *El último diario de Tony Flowers* (1995, The last diary of Tony Flowers), respectively, both novels with multiple literary allusions, even though these two authors claim that their cultural lives have been more significantly related to television than to literature. The lengthy *Metatrón* is encyclopedic in its cultural, historical, and literary scope and is easily comparable to other encyclopedic novels, such as Carlos Fuentes's *Terra Nostra* and Jorge Volpi's *En busca de Klingsor*.

With press clippings from the United States and Europe, the Colombians Santiago Gamboa, Mario Mendoza, and Jorge Franco have been involved in some of the international discussions related to the new generation of writers born in the 1960s that began publishing in the 1990s, which the Chilean Alberto Fuguet, the Bolivian Edmundo Paz Soldán, and their cohorts have identified as the McOndo generation and others have identified as the generation of the 1990s. As has been the case since the publication of the first innovative novels after García Márquez's *One Hundred Years of Solitude* in 1967, these novelists affirm their desire to take the Colombian novel in new directions beyond magic realism; they are particularly interested in exploring the meaning of the new urban spaces of Colombia as a generation that has lived urban life affected by drug trafficking and extreme violence. Gamboa appeared in the anthology of this generation compiled by Fuguet and Chilean Sergio Gómez. Mendoza was born in 1964 and, like Gamboa, left Colombia to study literature in Spain. He began publishing fiction in the early 1990s and has been awarded several literary prizes in the process of publishing the urban novels *La ciudad de los umbrales* (1992, Threshold city), *Scorpio City* (1998), *Relato de un asesino* (2001, An assassin's story), and *Satanás* (2002, Satan). Like Gamboa, he focuses on the tenuous and violent urban life of Bogotá, with anecdotes that emphasize both the deep individual suffering and the everyday commonplaces of death and violence. Jorge Franco gained considerable attention in Colombia with the publication of his first novel, *Rosario Tijeras* (1999, Rosario scissors), a work dealing with the paid assassins (*sicarios*) employed by the drug cartels in Medellín, Colombia. Although several novels dealing with drug culture (and its related violence) have appeared in Colombia and elsewhere, *Rosario Tijeras* has become one of the key texts on the subject. More recently, Franco Ramos has also published *Paraíso Travel* (2001, Paradise travel) and *Mala noche* (2003, Bad night), works that continue the urban accounts of violence, death, and human desperation.

In terms of literary production and the articulation of their role as writers of the generation of the 1990s, the Bolivian Edmundo Paz Soldán has been the most prominent voice of the Andean region. Author of the novels *Días de papel* (1992, Paper days), *Alrededor de la torre* (1997, Around the tower), *Río fugitivo* (1998, Fugitive river), *Sueños digitales* (2000, Digital dreams), and *La materia del deseo* (2001, The material of desire), he explores the concerns of his generation: globalization, the breakdown of the distinction between popular culture and high culture, and his relationship with previous forms of fiction, from the writing of the 1960s Boom to the spy thriller. Trained in literature at the University of California, Berkeley, Paz Soldán is in active dialogue with both the writers and the critics who are attempting to account for his generation's writing. Given his academic background and the substantive amount of critical and fictional writing he has published, Paz Soldán is far more aware of his past and his present as a Latin American writer than many of the other equally active but less scholarly informed spokespersons of this generation. For example, it is evident that Paz Soldán is aware of how his writing and that of his generation might be seen in the continuum of Andean literature; he is also fully aware of the major texts of the 1960s Boom, the theoretical writings on culture of the 1990s, and the issues of globalization that affect his own writing as well as the creative production of the generation of the 1990s throughout Latin America.

The Southern Cone Region Novel (Argentina, Chile, Uruguay, Paraguay): Contexts and Chronology

Heavily populated by European immigrants who came from not only Spain but also in considerable numbers from Italy, Eastern Europe, and Asia, the southern cone region was projecting economic and social plans comparable to those of the United States at the end of the nineteenth century. Nations such and Chile and Uruguay had established over a century of solid democratic political processes, with conventional political parties and a record of regular democratic elections. Two important political contexts of the post-WWII period, nevertheless, have been the rise of Juan Domingo Perón's populist and quasi-fascist state in Argentina and the presence of several brutal military dictatorships in the 1970s and 1980s in Chile, Argentina, Paraguay, and Uruguay. In the latter half of the twentieth century these nations have successfully worked toward redemocratization and regional economic integration. With the development of the Mercosur initiative, economic and cultural bonds were not only counted among these four nations but also in Brazil.

In the 1940s and 1950s a strong realist vein of literature of social protest and political critique was still being published in the southern cone region. In Argentina much of this writing had to do with the experience of living under the Perón regime in the 1940s and 1950s. Writers such as the Argentine Bernardo Verbitsky and the Uruguayan Gabriel Casaccia wrote critiques of working-class life in urban areas. Verbitsky's *Un noviazgo* (1956, An engagement) describes the effects of military dictatorships on the working class. Casaccia wrote several novels of political denunciation, including *La llaga* (1964, The wound) and *Los exiliados* (1966, The exiles). In Chile the generation of 1938 saw itself as social and political reformists, and writers such as Nicomedes Guzmán, Carlos Droguett, Juan Godoy, and Fernando Alegría wrote novels with social goals and a focus on the urban areas in contrast to the rural setting of earlier writing. Droguett and Alegría were among the most accomplished fiction writers of this generation. Droguett's *Eloy* (1960, Eloy) and *Patas de perro* (1965, Dog's feet) related the experience of characters on the margins of society. Alegría's *Los días contados* (1968, The numbered days) is set in Santiago's slums and tells the story of a boxer.

In the 1950s many writers of this region shared the political commitment of writers such as Droguett and Guzmán, but groups such as Uruguay's generation of 1945 and Chile's generation of the 1950s were also interested in modernizing Latin American literature and making it part of a "universal" (which basically meant "Western" and "modern") tradition. The rise of modernist fiction in the 1940s and 1950s in the southern cone region and the reaffirmation of the right of invention was signaled by the publication of novels such as Leopoldo Marechal's *Adán Buenosayres*, Juan Carlos Onetti's *La vida breve*, and David Viñas's *Cayó sobre su rostro*. Marechal's *Adán Buenosayres* is an ambitious and wide-ranging story of an Argentine intellectual during the 1920s, when writers in Argentina were in a heated debate over nationalist versus cosmopolitan or vanguardist literature. Since Marechal himself was a follower of Perón, he was either ignored or rejected by the intellectuals who opposed Perón (which, unfortunately for Marechal, was a substantial portion of the intellectuals). The first section of the novel is an "Indispensable Prologue" in which the author explains the book's basic organization. The narrator, who signs his name as Leopoldo Marechal, tells of the burial of Adán Buenosayres and that he has two of the deceased man's manuscripts, one titled *Cuaderno de Tapas Azules* ("The blue-covered notebook"), and the other called *Viaje a la Oscura Ciudad de Cacodelphia* ("Trip to the Dark City of Cacodelphia"). The first is a set of memoirs, the second an account of a descent into hell. The author-figure explains that he has decided to provide an account of Bueynosayres's life before these two texts and thus offers a seven-chapter text—the major portion of the novel. The characters of this novel are different types of intellectuals that Marechal satirizes. The author uses humorous, everday language to deflate the pretentious intellectual writing of many of his contemporaries.

Most novelists of the time wrote in a more sober tone, and this was the case of Onetti and Viñas, who offer the reader none of Marechal's humor. In Onetti's fiction of the early 1950s—*La vida breve* and *Los adioses* (1954, *The Goodbyes*)—he delves into severe forms of alienation. The protagonists of these works strive for any meaning in life, but eventually are reduced to enduring lives of nothingness. Disillusionment reigns in the always-gray world of Onetti. The protagonist is named Brausen, but he also has alter egos named Díaz Grey and Arce, leaving fixed identities impossible to establish. The characters are equally despondent in *Los adioses,* and the reader senses the same feeling of futility of Onetti's earlier work. In *Cayó sobre su rostro* Viñas presents the reader a more exterior vision of the fictionalized world than Onetti's and demonstrates that he is a master of narrative technique. He tends to open chapters in the middle of a key action—engaging the reader— later filling in the background. This procedure, along with subtle shifts in narrative point of view, make this novel far more complex than merely a debunking of some venerable military figures of Argentina's past. Viñas also uses alternating chapters to present the past and the present of the situation, as well as external dialogues intercalated with interior monologues. Years later the historical novel became fashionable in Latin America; *Cayó sobre su rostro* was a relatively early repudiation of Argentine official history.

The Chilean José Donoso and the Paraguayan Augusto Roa Bastos were not as fully committed to modernist writing practices in their early fictions as Marechal, Onetti, and Viñas, but they were by no means realists interested in the mimetic reproduction of reality. Donoso's *Coronación* (1957, *Coronation*) offers more in-depth psychological development than was common in the 1950s and characterizes an aging Chilean oligarch who lives a sterile life. The characterization of her and those around her is Donoso's subtle critique of the Chilean oligarchy. He is more strident in his critique of Chile's upper class in the later *Este domingo* (1966, *This Sunday*), a novel about the crisis of both a family and the oligarchy it represents. Roa Bastos is more historical in the sense that Viñas writes historical novels; his novel *Hijo de hombre* (1959, *Son of Man*) refers to the colonial period even though it focuses primarily on the period of the Chaco War of the 1930s. Its modernist ambitions make it an innovative novel in several ways: its use of the Guaraní language, its use of metaphor to transform the commonplace into something with more meaning, and the fact that the chapters can be read as virtually independent short stories.

As suggested in the discussion of Onetti and Viñas, dissatisfaction with life and the overtones of existential crisis are almost trademarks of fiction in this region during the 1950s. Novelists such as Eduardo Mallea, Mario Benedetti, and Manuel Rojas followed this pattern, writing books of generalized anguish and alienation. Mallea's *Los enemigos del alma* (1950, Enemies of the soul) and *Chaves* (1953) contain unfulfilled characters whose lives are minimal. The three main characters in *Los enemigos del alma* are disoriented and unable to find worthwhile paths in life, and the generally silent protagonist of *Chaves* seems unable to make any sense of life beyond the fulfillment of his most immediate and basic needs. In *Quién de nosotros* (1953, Who of us) Benedetti uses three characters and three narrative points of view to present his case for human alienation. Mazzanti's *El sustituto* (1954, The substitute) is a far more innovative piece of writing than any of these books on human alienation, with a style that represents the thought of the characters, although his ultimate theme is similar—alienation. Rojas's *Hijo de ladrón* (1951, *Born Guilty*) is shaped by the intensity, interiorization, and disorientation that characterizes the best of the fiction of this region in the 1950s.

Beatriz Guido and Manuel Mujica Lainez are modernist writers who approached topics that varied from the standard 1950s treatises on alienation. Guido recreates aspects of middle-class life in Buenos Aires in the 1920s in *La casa del ángel* (1954, The house of the angel), a narrative of an adolescent girl and her reaction to her father's male friend. It is a novel rich in revealing the thoughts, feelings, and fantasies of the young girl.

The transition figure between the high modernists and postmodern fiction in the southern cone region is Julio Cortázar, and the key novel in this transition was *Rayuela*. This novel, simply stated, was a revolutionary act in Latin America: it rejected numerous conventional modes of writing by proposing a kind of modernity the other writers of this period desired for Latin American culture; it rejected many of the already standard concepts of the modern novel in favor of total invention and a more postmodern aesthetic; it undermined established concepts of order in literature, culture, and society. *Rayuela* also suggested new roles for the reader and new ways of thinking of the act of reading itself. Cortázar offers the reader several types of reading, organizing the novel around three parts: the first two parts consist of fifty-six chapters telling Horacio Oliveira's story in Paris ("About That Side") and his story in Buenos Aires ("About This Side"); the third part, "About Other Sides," consists of "Expendable Chapters" that are narratives related to Horacio's story, quotations from other authors, proposals for radical new kinds of writing, newspaper clips, and the like. In this novel Horacio searches for understanding and encounters a series of other characters, including a double figure named Traveler and his lover, Maga. These encounters, as well as many other elements of the novel, have to do with breaking established patterns of thinking and living. The story of Horacio is the modernist text the reader can choose to read from the numerous potential stories *Rayuela* offers.

A key figure of the expendable chapters and Cortázar's proposal for a postmodern novel in Latin America is a writer named Morelli: this writer figure questions the tenets of both realist and modernist fiction, and in this sense Cortázar distinguishes himself from the other writers of the Boom who were fully committed to the modernist concept of the novel. Morelli invites writers to undermine Western concepts of representation and time as well as the very idea of linearity and plot. The postmodern reader of much of the innovative fiction by the likes of José Emilio Pacheco in Mexico, Severo Sarduy in Cuba, and Héctor Libertella in Argentina is fundamentally the active reader proposed by Morelli. In addition to hailing a new, postmodern reader, *Rayuela* undermines the concept of author.

With this novel Cortázar invited two generations of postmodern fiction writers in the southern cone region as well as Latin America in general to explore the possibilities and limits of radically undermining some of the most venerable assumptions of Western culture and thinking. For Cortázar, Western dualistic or Manichean thought is one tradition most in need of radical subversion. This radicalizing agenda became the new literary (and political) program for much postmodern and feminist writing that appeared in Latin America from the late 1960s to the early 1990s.

The southern cone region, along with Brazil, has become one of the most intensely productive regions in Latin America of postmodern fiction. Experimental and innovative postmodern writers such as Ricardo Piglia, Diamela Eltit, Sylvia Molloy, Alejandra Pizarnik, Héctor Libertella, and Armonía Sommers make this "periphery," paradoxically, a vital center. The early postmodern works in Argentina include Héctor Libertella's *El camino de los hiperbóreos* (1968, The road of southern nations), Néstor Sánchez's *Siberia Blues*, and Cortázar's *62: model para armar* (1968, *62: A Model Kit*). With these novels, as well as the fiction of Manuel Puig and Humberto Costantini's *Háblenme de Funes* (1970, Speak to me of Funes), it was obvious that Argentine fiction was undergoing a revolution of the sort Morelli had suggested in *Rayuela*. In Libertella's *El camino de los hiperbóreos*, for example, there is no traditional sense of plot other than the protagonist's vague search for something undefined. Libertella also subverts any sense of the individual by creating multiple identities in some characters. *Siberia Blues* and *62: A Model Kit* are radically experimental works with minimal adherence to such basics as sentence structure and characters as recognizable human beings. Costantini's *Háblenme de Funes* consists of a three-part structure of three vaguely related stories, the third of which is a metafiction dealing with a writer's creative process. In accordance with the linguistic experimentation of Sánchez and Cortázar, Costantini uses entirely different styles in the three parts of the book.

The postmodern writing of Manuel Puig consists of eight novels, beginning with *La traición de Rita Hayworth* (1968, *Betrayed by Rita Hayworth*). This novel fictionalized an active, postmodern reader with no controlling narrator to organize the anecdotal material. Rather, the novel is a multiplicity of voices that appear in the text as monologues or dialogues. It tells the story of a young boy with homosexual tendencies, and this in itself was a daring aspect of the work for a Latin American novel published in 1968. Puig's total work critiques gender-bound behavior and genre-bound limits for writing, particularly the novels *Heartbreak Tango* (1969), *The Buenos Aires Affair* (1973), and *El beso de la mujer araña* (1976, *Kiss of the Spider Woman*). They question authority and power, and truth remains elusive in all of Puig's writing.

After Cortázar, Libertella, and Puig, a second wave of postmodern fiction in Argentina came from writers who were well aware of such idols as Borges, Macedonio Fernández, and Cortázar, and this group includes Ricardo Piglia, Sylvia Molloy, Alejandra Pizarnik, and Luis Gusmán. Piglia's other books of fiction, including *Prisión perpetua* (1988, Perpetual prison) and *La ciudad ausente* (1992, The absent city), develop many of the same issues introduced in *Respiración artificial*. *Prisión perpetua* is less a novel than a series of ten related fictions. Questions about the authenticity of language and a "mother tongue" surface again. Piglia fictionalizes a postmodern active reader in both of these texts, and in *La ciudad ausente* (1992) he reaffirms his invitation to the postmodern reader to decipher the unspeakable, written in a language always at least once removed from the mother tongue. Sylvia Molloy, Alejandra Pizarnik, and Luis Gusmán are the authors of subtle fictions that are testimony to the heterogeneity of postmodern writing in Argentina. Molloy's *En breve cárcel* returns to the postmodern origins of Borges, the Borges who offers reflections on fictional texts, questioning the stability of the text itself.

The first indicator of a postmodern fiction in Chile appeared in 1968, the same year it appeared in much of Latin America. This narrative innovation in Chile was an experimental and relatively obscure novel written by an academic, Jorge Guzmán, under the title *Job-Boj* (1968). This novel was followed by such innovative works as José Donoso's *El obsceno pájaro de la noche* (1970, *The Obscene Bird of the Night*), and radical fictions by Mauricio Wacquez and Enrique Lihn. With the lengthy *El obsceno pájaro de la noche*, one of the most complex novels ever published by a Chilean writer, Donoso made a far more visible statement for a Chilean postmodern than had been the case with Guzmán's relatively ignored *Job-Boj*. Like Fuentes's *Terra Nostra* and Adoum's *Entre Marx y una mujer desnuda* (Between Marx and a nude woman), it is an anthology of postmodern devices and motifs.

Enrique Lihn is most widely known in Latin America as a poet, but he did write radically experimental novels. In his novels *La orquesta de cristal* (1976, The crystal orchestra) and *El arte de la palabra* (1980, The art of the word), Lihn's work is an attempt to critique the excessive rhetoric of the Spanish language. Writing under a dictatorship, Lihn creates in hermetic codes that parody the dominant discourses of power. The multiple footnotes of *La orquesta de crystal* and the metadiscourse of *El arte de la palabra* make language the main subject of these two novels. Mauricio Wacquez shows a similar interest with language itself, and demands the active participation of the postmodern reader in fictions such as *Excesos* (1971, Excesses) and *Paréntesis* (1975, Parenthesis).

A second wave of Chilean postmodern writers—Diamela Eltit, the later Donoso, and the young writers Alberto Fuguet and Antonio Ostornol—were a presence in Chile in the 1980s and 1990s. Eltit's project consists of several novels that have appeared since the 1980s, and she has become one of the most respected "writer's writers" and feminist intellectuals in Latin America today. Her first three works were written under the Pinochet dictatorship, a period during which Eltit and some of her cohorts attempted to produce a writing of resistance within the nation. Along with the writings of Piglia and Fuentes, her total work represents one of the most ambitious, challenging, and intense searches for authentic historic origins to be seen in Latin America. Her work is *problematic* in the positive sense of the word, and one of her most problematic novels is *Lumpérica* (1983, *E. Luminata*), which is highly fragmented, has no plot, and takes place—vaguely—in a public plaza in Santiago de Chile. The characters' relationship to the physical space of the plaza and to language might be seen as a substitute for "action." *Lumpérica* is a novel of unstable identities, provisional truths, and bodies in transformation. Her next novel, *Por la patria* (1986, For the country) is equally problematic. Alluding to political repression in Chile indirectly, Eltit once again writes historically. Returning to medieval epic wars, she inevitably associates these conflicts with the contemporary situation in Chile. She also explores the concept of linguistic incest in this novel.

In Eltit's *El cuarto mundo* (1988, *The Fourth World*), the family is the private space that becomes foreign in the symbolic world of the body. This novel deals with family relationships and is narrated by a young boy and by his twin sister. The first part of the novel ends with a family crisis centered on the mother's adultery. In the second part family tensions center on the incestuous relationship between the boy, María Chipia, and his twin sister. María Chipia begins the novel narrating as a fetus, and much of his narration consists of his attempt to understand the relationship between his own body, his mother's, and his sister's. The "fourth world" of the novel's title can be postulated as a space consisting of a periphery of a periphery, for example, marginal space on the periphery of an already peripheral Third World nation. Written under the Pinochet regime, Eltit's work offers an allegorical level of reading, as many novels written under dictatorships do.

Uruguay's postmodern writers include Híber Conteris, Armonía Sommers, Cristina Peri Rossi, Teresa Porzecanski, and Napoleón Baccino Ponce de León. As was the case in Buenos Aires and Santiago de Chile, innovative fiction in dialogue with international postmodern culture began appearing in Montevideo in the late 1960s. Conteris has not been a radical innovator, but he has written under the sign of Cortázar. He wrote his novel *El diez por ciento de la vida* (1986, *Ten Percent of Life*) in the Spanish language while in jail as a political prisoner from 1976 to 1983 during the military dictatorship. This novel can be read as detective fiction written under the influence of Raymond Chandler; it even has Marlowe and other Chandler characters in it, including Chandler himself. Like Piglia and some other postmodern writers from the southern cone, Conteris writes in a neutral nonliterary Spanish language that imitates translation—thus inviting the reader to question the possibility of writing in traditional and conventional literary Spanish.

Like several other postmodern texts from this region, *Ten Percent of Life* is an allegory of resistence. Conteris subverts the dominant discourses of the military by questioning the very idea of definite truths. As the novel develops, the active postmodern reader finds political clues hidden in this detective novel, making the work an allegorical fiction resisting the dictatorship. Conteris, like Piglia and Eltit, addresses the issue of speaking the unspeakable under these political conditions.

Other writers in Uruguay, such as Armonía Sommers, Cristina Peri Rossi, and Baccino Ponce de León, have demonstrated some postmodern tendencies. Sommers and Peri Rossi have been modernists from their early writings, and Sommers's modernist fiction dates back to her first novella, *La mujer desnuda* (1951, The nude woman), but her more postmodern fiction includes the three stories of *Tríptico darwiniano* (1982, Darwinian tryptic) and her technically experimental and complex novel *Sólo los elefantes encuentran mandrágora* (1983, Only elephants find mandrake). The feminist writing of Peri Rossi has included short fiction and novels, including the novels *El libro de mis primos* (1969, The book of my cousins) and *Nave de los locos* (1984, Ship of Fools). Peri Rossi's postmodern fiction blurs generic boundaries and is often discontinuous, an art of proliferation and digression. *Ship of Fools* is also a metafiction that questions the boundaries between painting and fiction. A historiograph metafiction, Baccino Ponce de León's *Maluco* (1990) also subverts multiple boundaries. Porzecanski has published several books of postmodern fiction, including the recent novel *Perfumes de Cartago* (1994, *Sun Inventions and Perfumes of Cartago*), *Una novella erotica* (2000, An erotic novella), and *Felicidades fugadas* (2002, Fleeting happiness).

Postmodern writers of the southern cone region write from the periphery of a periphery, for they are marginal as writers and marginalized geographically. One specificity of postmodern fiction of the southern cone region is the production of writing that constitutes complex allegories of resistance. Many of these writers necessarily turned to an allegorical mode that was their method of attempting to communicate the unspeakable. Some writers of the post-Boom who wrote in exile faced the same issue of political repression but employed other strategies as a response; they tend to be less allegorical, less obscure, and generally more accessible to their readers.

The southern cone region has also produced some of the major writers associated with the post-Boom: the Chileans Antonio Skármeta and Isabel Allende and the Argentines Mempo Giardinelli and Luisa Valenzuela are widely recognized as leading writers of their generation. All four have also had their lives and careers marked by the military dictatorships of their respective nations; all four have spent a considerable portion of their lives writing in exile. Their novels represent a continuation of the modernist project initiated in Latin America in the 1940s, with a return to the accessibility and realism many writers of the post-Boom felt were lost during the 1960s Boom.

Skármeta went into exile into Germany, where he wrote novels such as *Soñé que la nieve ardía* (1975, *I Dreamt the Snow Was Burning*) and *Ardiente paciencia* (1985, *Burning Patience*). In the former Skármeta deals with working-class individuals in an urban environment. The latter is a love story set in the crucial political period in Chile from 1969 to 1973 when Salvador Allende's Unidad Popular party was in power and gaining momentum. In *La insurrección* (1982, *The Insurrection*) and *Match Ball* (1989) Skármeta questions middle-class values in the context of the individualism found in athletic competition. In *No pasó nada* (1980, Nothing happened) Skármeta considers the complexities of living in exile as perceived by an adolescent. The author's regular use of colloquial language has been associated with the post-Boom. With the redemocratization of Chile, he returned to his homeland in the 1990s, and his more recent fiction written there includes *La boda del poeta* (1999, The poet's wedding), *La chica del trombone* (2001, The girl with the trombone), and *El baile de la victoria* (2003, The victory dance), winner of the Premio Planeta.

One of the most celebrated and widely read novelists of the post-Boom has been Isabel Allende. Her fast-moving plots and accessible works make her the post-Boom writer par excellence. She is best known for her first novel, *La casa de los espíritus*, her immensely successful assimilation of the procedures of magical realism and her family story from Chile. Her second novel, *De amor y de sombra*, was more directly political, dealing with the upheaval related to the military coup against Allende in 1973. *Eva Luna* (1987) is the story of a young woman whose picaresque adventures, from guerrilla warfare to passionate love, made this a best-selling novel. The same magical events in these novels that have made Allende an attractive writer for foreign readers have caused her to be rejected by the younger Latin American writers of the 1990s.

Neither Mempo Giardinelli nor Luisa Valenzuela has cultivated the U.S. readership of Allende and Skármeta in English translation, but both are widely read in Latin America, and Valenzuela's work has appeared in English translation. Giardinelli spent over a decade in political exile in Mexico, where he wrote some of his best-known novels, such as *Luna caliente* (1983, Hot moon) and *Que solos se quedan los muertos* (1985, How solitary the dead remain), both of which have well-developed and fast-moving plots. His major work and the centerpiece for his reception of the prestigious Rómulo Gallegos novel prize was *Santo Oficio de la memoria* (1991, Holy office of memory), his lengthy and ambitious family saga dealing with several generations of Italian immigrants to Argentina. It is a story of nation building. Having returned to Argentina in the 1980s, Giardinelli has been active on the literary and political scene and has published a novel of ecological concerns, *Imposible equilibrio* (1995, Impossible balance).

Valenzuela is as political as writers Piglia and Skármeta, as demonstrated in a body of fiction focused primarily on politics, language, and women. Her first novel of the 1970s, *El gato eficaz* (1972, The efficient cat) deals with a woman's playful—yet serious—dialogue with literature. The author tests the previous limits for women writers with respect to self-censorship and the erotic, frequently incorporating various types of language in her novels, including language not commonly used by middle-class women. *Cola de lagartija* is an overtly political work in which Valenzuela gives the narrator-protagonist her own name. The fictional Luisa Valenzuela of the novel confronts the chaotic process of writing and the increasingly absurd world around her.

The rise of the young generation of writers who began publishing in the 1990s was headed in the southern cone region by the Chileans Alberto Fuguet, Antonio Ostornol, Sergio Gómez, the Argentine Rodrigo Fresán, and the Uruguayan Henry Trujillo. Born in 1954, Ostornol is slightly older than many of this generation and has published several novels. Fuguet and Gómez are responsible for the publication of the polemical anthology *McOndo*, which placed together writers of this generation from throughout Latin America and Spain. They have proposed a new response to the magical realism of García Márquez and Allende. The writing of these young novelists is comparable to the concerns of the generation of the 1990s throughout Latin America, with its reaction to magical realism, its interest in the new urban experience, and its special relationship to popular culture and the mass media. The most internationally visible of these novelists is Fuguet, who has published novels in both Spanish and English.

Brazil and Its Context

The rise of the modernist novel in Lusophone Brazil in the 1940s corresponds to a broader movement throughout the Spanish-speaking Americas, from Mexico to Argentina. In Spanish America the 1940s were a period of reaffirming the right of invention, a movement led by Jorge Luis Borges and soon followed by the major novelists of the time. The fiction of Brazilians José Lins de Rêgo, Jorge Amado, Graciliano Ramos, and Rachel de Queiroz began a similar process in Brazil in the 1930s and 1940s with the publication of novels that employed the strategies of North American and European modernism comparable to those of Miguel Angel Asturias, Agustín Yáñez, Alejo Carpentier, and others in the Spanish-speaking Americas. Indeed, such strategies were not an entire novelty in Brazil, for modernist aesthetics had been introduced in Brazil in the 1920s with São Paulo's much heralded conference, a celebration of modern art (Semana de Arte Moderna), and the publication of works such as Mário de Andrade's *Macunaíma* in 1928. With the legacy of Brazil's modernismo and the end of the Estado Novo (the dictatorship of Gertúlio Vargas from 1937 to 1945), the Brazilian novel entered into a new phase, evincing a growing interest in being considered somehow modern and somehow universal. Works such as Clarice Lispector's *Perto do Coração Selvagem* as well as Rachel de Queiroz's *Tres Marias* (1939, The three Marias) and *O Galo de Ouro* (1950, The golden rooster) have loose connections with the new, modern novel that was arising in the 1940s throughout Latin America. José Lins do Rêgo's later novel, *Cangaceiros* (1953, Cangeceiros) was a work of social protest that also makes allusions to the modern novel.

In the novel, however, the Brazilian case does not follow the exact contours of the Spanish American novel in the second half of the twentieth century. The innovation and presence of Brazilian modernism since the 1920s, the powerful legacy of northeastern regionalism (and the northeastern tradition of the novel), and the military dictatorship of 1964 to 1985 are important factors in novelistic productions since 1945 that distinguish Brazil from its neighbors of the Latin American region. In Spanish America the 1920s vanguards were comparable to Brazilian modernism, but their impact on the novel was less notable in Spanish America than in Brazil; the regional tradition in Spanish America was in general weaker than in Brazil (with the possible exception of Colombia) and the military dictatorships in Spanish America were typical of only a few Spanish American nations—and not as lengthy as the twenty-one-year military regime in Brazil. Novelistic production in Argentina and Chile, which did suffer repressive military regimes, was affected in some ways comparable to Brazil. Writers in Brazil, Argentina, Uruguay, and Chile, for example, experienced censorship to similar degrees during the 1970s and had to employ subtle methods of writing to express their political resistance.

The 1940s and 1950s witnessed the continued publication of some conventional and often psychological novels that are best associated with realism and tradition. Octávio de Faria, for example, demonstrates an interest in reaffirming conservative, Catholic values in novels such as *Os Renegados* (1947, The renegades), *Os Loucos* (1952, The insane), and *O Senhor do Mundo* (1957, The man of the world). Lúcio Cardoso published a large amount of fiction in the realist mode from the 1930s to the 1960s, as did conventionalist realists such as Maria Alice Barroso before she became interested in the nouveau roman in the 1960s. Her novels *Os Posseiros* (1955, The squaters) and *História de um Casamento* (1960, History of a marriage) were bridge works that some readers associated with social realism, even though *História de um Casamento* is technically more associated with the innovations of the French novel. Her later *Quem Matou Pacífico?* (1969, Who killed Pacifico?) is a detective novel. Esdras do Nascimento began publishing novels in the 1960s, but his work is more comparable to the conventional, linear novels published in the 1940s and 1950s in much of Latin America.

The rise of modernist fiction (in the North American and European sense) in Brazil, the equivalent of the reaffirmation of the right of invention in Spanish America, was signaled by the publication of Clarice Lispector's *Perto do Coração Selvagem*, José Lins do Rêgo's *Eurídice* (1948), Graciliano Ramos's *Insônia*, João Guimarães Rosa's *Grande Sertão: Veredas*, and Jorge Amado's *Gabriela, Cravo e Canela* (1958, *Gabriela, Clove and Cinnamon*). Lispector's *Perto do Coração Selvagem* represented a distancing from the predominant mode of regionalism and a turn toward a more psychological fiction with the universal overtones often found in stories of human relations. Similarly, Lins do Rêgo explores the possibilities of the psychological novel with *Eurídice*, thus abandoning his own well-established interest in regional novels tied to the land of the northeast. Author of several previous works also bound to "the land" (the northeast region and its customs), Ramos was in the modernist mode when writing his volume of stories titled *Insônia*. They communicate a sense of unreality related to nightmares and insomnia. Guimarães Rosa's *Grande Sertão: Veredas* can also be associated with the regional tradition and is one of the most ambitious and totalizing modernist efforts of the century not only in Brazil but in all of Latin America, making it comparable to *Conversación en La Catedral* and *Terra Nostra*. It is a complex story of a reformed outlaw, as told by him, but with multiple layerings of plot and linguistic and mythical resonances. Its mythical and universal overtones distance it from more traditional regionalist texts. The 1950s fiction of Antonio Callado contributed to the new novel in Brazil, with psychological studies such as *A Madrona de Cedro* (1957). Callado continued writing psychological and social works, becoming more acutely politicized after the military coup. Amado had published works since the 1930s, but with *Gabriela, Clove and Cinnamon* ironic humor entered into his fiction in a significant way for the first time in this satire of Brazilian society.

Guimarães Rosa and Lispector are often associated with what was identified as the generation of 1956 in Brazil. Along with the creators of concrete poetry, they were committed to modernizing Brazilian letters and producing a culture more in step with the modernism of Europe and the United States, often manifesting itself in the desire to be "universal." The members of this intellectual cohort wanted to stimulate a lively cultural debate on literature and politics in the spirit of the 1920s in Brazil, and their work was similar to the work of the Sardío group in Venezuela and the efforts of Fuentes to promote modern literature in Mexico, with his *Revista Mexicana de Literatura*, as well as the group of writers in Colombia that published the magazine *Mito*. Writing in the spirit of this generation, Autran Dourado and Carlos Heitor Cony produced several novels in the 1960s. Autran Dourado's *A Barca dos Homens* was an important contribution to the modernization of the Brazilian novel, as were *Uma Vida em Segredo* (1964, *A Hidden Life*) and the widely read *Opera dos Mortos* (1967, Opera of the dead). Dourado continued publishing subtle fictions of human relations until the end of the century; his *O Risco do Bordado* (1973, *Pattern for a Tapestry*) is generally considered one of his masterpieces. Cony's early novels, *O Ventre* (1957, The Womb) and *Antes, o Verão* reflect his interest in human relations along the lines of Lispector and Dourado. The military dictatorship was a serious problem for progressive intellectuals such as Cony. With *Pessach: A Travessía* (1967, Passover: the crossing) the effects of the military coup and Cony's political transformation are evident. He quit writing fiction for two decades, only gaining prominence again as a novelist in the 1990s. Assis Brasil also published numerous novels from the 1960s to the 1980s that may be associated with the generation of 1956 and evolved from the conventional to the more innovative. His *Os Que Bebem Como as Cães* (1975, Those who drink like dogs) portrays prison experience as a response to the military dictatorship.

The lively cultural and political debate fostered by the generation of 1956, however, was squelched with the military coup of 1964, and novelistic production suffered the effects for the next two decades. Paradoxically, while Spanish American writers such as Gabriel García Márquez and Carlos Fuentes were enjoying the unprecedented international recognition that came with the Boom, writers in Brazil suffered a serious setback under the military regime. Some novelists, such as Carlos Heitor Cony, entered directly into the scenario by challenging the military with their writings. But they were soon jailed; Cony was briefly arrested, then freed. Others chose exile. During the years 1964 and 1965, several other writers who questioned or challenged the military were imprisoned, censored, or repressed. The years 1964 to 1968 (when many intellectuals in Spanish America were celebrating the Cuban Revolution) and the publication of landmark novels such as Vargas Llosa's *La casa verde* and García Márquez's *Cien años de soledad* were repressive ones in Brazil, and some critics labeled this dismal period *o sofoco* ("the suffocation"). This was when Jorge Amado published his relatively nonpolitical and entertaining *Dona Flor e seus dois maridos* (1966, *Dona Flor and Her Two Husbands*), although writers such as Cony and Callado found subtle ways to respond to repression in their fiction.

Indeed, one of the novelists who most successfully challenged the military government was Antonio Callado with novels such as *Quarup* (1967), *Bar Don Juan* (1971, *Don Juan's Bar*), *Reflexos do Baile* (1976, Reflections of the dance), *Sempreviva* (1981), and *Expedicão Montaigne* (1982, The Montaigne expedition). The protagonist of *Quarup* is a priest who becomes a revolutionary, but the novel presents an array of characters with varying utopian political ideals. In *Bar Don Juan* Callado takes a critical look at the leftist revolutionaries in Brazil in the early 1970s. He completes his overview of revolutionary activity in *Sempreviva*, in which revolutionaries are involved in a complex web of irrational forces. The protagonist returns to Brazil from political exile before the *abertura* ("opening" literally) and is caught in a nightmarish relationship with his allies on the left as well as on the right.

Some writers seemed to respond to the tense political atmosphere with formal experimentation, perhaps a political statement in itself. Two such novelists who wrote in dialogue with the French nouveau roman were Maria Alice Barroso and Oswaldo Carrea Louzada Filho. Barroso's early novels of the 1950s were of the social realism vein, but her work is linked to the strategies of Faulkner and the nouveau roman with *Um Simples Afeto Recíproco* (1962, A simple mutual affection) and *Um Nome para Matar* (1967, A name to kill). Louzada Filho takes a more disciplined approach to such techniques in his abstract novels *Dardará* (1965) and *Diario de Bordo* (1975, Travel journal).

In the 1950s and 1960s a small group of writers relatively disinterested in new literary techniques or innovation continued publishing realist fiction with strong, linear plots, often enjoying commercial success. A writer such as Moacir Costa Lopes, with no formal training in literature and no previous publications, wrote an adventure story based on his experience in the Brazilian military in WWII, *Maria de Cada Porto* (1959, Maria of each port), and it became an immediate best seller. He continued writing novels of action in the 1960s and 1970s. Similarly, Manoel Lobato wrote successful commercial novels in the 1960s and 1970s, beginning with *Mentira dos Limpos* (1967, Lie of the clean ones). Josué Guimarães also began publishing popular commercial fiction in the 1970s, with titles such as *Os Tambores Silenciosos* (1975, The silent drums) and *E Tarde para Saber* (1977, It's late to know).

As the reality of the military dictatorship became part of national cultural life in Brazil, some Brazilians called the years 1969 to 1974 the period of *vazio cultural* ("cultural gap"). But novelists did find ways to continue writing, turning to different expressions of inner exile or allegory, which were the methods of Clarice Lispector, Nélida Piñón, Erico Veríssimo, Antonio Callado, José J. Veiga, Lygia Fagundes Telles, Lêdo Ivo, and Autran Dourado. Attempting to publish in this period also produced a generation of censorship; the works associated with these conditions were Autran Dourado's *O Risco do Bordado*, Lispector's *Felicidade Clandestina* (1971, Clandestine happiness), Nélida Piñón's *Sala de Armas* (1973, Room of arms), Murilo Rubião's *O Pirotécnico Zacarias* (1974, Zacarias the pyrotechnician), and João Ubaldo Ribeiro's, *Sergeant Gertúlio* (1971).

Lygia Fagundes Telles has been a popular writer in Brazil since the 1960s, and her work fits into the general pattern of post-Boom writing in Spanish America. She began writing short fiction in the 1930s and published her first novel, *Ciranda de Pedra* (1954, The Marble Dance) in the 1950s. She is associated with the generation of 1945, who reacted against the radical experimentation of Brazil's modernism of the 1920s and 1930s. Nevertheless, she is a writer who knows how to use the narrative strategies of modernism well, often employing stream-of-consciousness techniques. She is a master of communicating a sense of wonder and fantasy. Much of her career has been dedicated to short fiction; her novels include *Verão no Aquário* (1963, Summer at the aquarium) and *As Meninas* (1973, The Girl in the Photograph).

Postmodern fiction had early precedents in Brazil, the most prominent being Mário de Andrade's experimental novel *Macunaíma* (1928), but the innovative writing of Guimarães Rosa and Lispector in the 1950s and 1960s were equally important forerunners. The turning point for experimental fiction in Brazil took place from the late 1960s through the early 1970s, as it did in the rest of Latin America, and the Brazilians most directly engaged in this early dialogue with international postmodern culture are Osman Lins, Ignácio de Loyola Brandão, and Flávio Moreira da Costa. Lins belonged to an earlier generation, but his novel *Avalovara* is one of the most boldly experimental Brazilian novels of the century and foundational for the production of postmodern fiction. It is a work of narrative fragments that the active postmodern reader must assemble, and it contains many other elements proposed by Morelli in Julio Cortázar's *Hopscotch*, a source for much postmodern writing in Brazil as much as in all of Latin America.

In addition to Lispector, Lins, Loyola Brandão, and Moreira da Costa, leading exponents of postmodern fiction in Brazil have been Roberto Drummond, Rubem Fonseca, João Gilberto Noll, Márcio Souza, Helena Parente Cunha, Sérgio Sant'Anna, Santiago Silviano, and Ivan Angêlo. Lispector, like Carlos Fuentes and Mario Vargas Llosa, was fundamentally an innovative modernist writer who was affected by the postmodern later in her career. Her feminist *A Hora da Estrela* is a metafiction that deals with the creative process and fictionalizes an active postmodern reader.

Moreira da Costa early on represented the new attitudes of the younger writers in Latin America. His novel *O Deastronauta: OK Jack Kerouac nós Estamos te Esperando em Copacabana* (1971, The Anti-astronaut: OK Jack Kerouac we are waiting for you in Copacabana) is a metafiction about a failed writer, with the irreverence and iconoclasm found in the fiction of Gustavo Sainz and José Agustín in Mexico in the 1960s and of Andrés Caicedo in Colombia in the 1970s. His later novels, *Cosa Nostra-Eu Vi a Mafia de Perto-Conforme Narrado por Tony Gomez* (1973, Our thing—I saw the mafia up-close, narrated by Tony Gomez) and *As Armas e os Barões* (1974, The arms and the barons) are wide-ranging and playful works integrating various kinds of texts.

Loyola Brandão is one of the most experimental of the Brazilian postmodern writers. His novel *Zero* (1974) was widely read, despite its innovative political statement, in the early 1970s and invites comparison with Cortázar's *A Manuel for Manuel* and Piglia's *Artificial Respiration*; the relationship between a police interrogator and his captive is portrayed as a complex game to be deciphered only by the most engaged postmodern reader. Loyola Brandão's *Não Verás País Nenhum* (1982, *And Still the Earth*) is a futuristic novel in which the "System" controls every movement of the nation's citizens, the real and unreal are difficult to distinguish, and the author openly recognizes his literary masters, including Isaac Asimov, Ray Bradbury, and Kurt Vonnegut. With a pervasive black humor, Loyola Brandão communicates a sense of exhaustion in Brazilian society that is a common trope in postmodern fiction. His text *Anônimo Célebre* (2002, The anonymous celebrity) is a continuation of several of the themes and strategies of the previous two novels, offering a critique of instant celebrities in societies of mass media and mass consumption such as Brazil. Certainly what many critics consider "postmodern" fiction is by no means an endorsement of the consumer society of late capitalism; to the contrary, writers such as Loyola Brandão are among the most critical of globalization.

The novels of Roberto Drummond are an iconoclastic and satirical rewriting of the history of Brazil since the 1950s, with considerable emphasis on pop culture. In *Sangue de Coca-Cola* (1983, Coca-Cola blood), Drummond appropriates the popular culture of the Mardi Gras carnival and delivers a performance comparable to Puig's appropriation of popular film and Luis Rafael Sánchez's incorporation of popular music in *Macho Camacho's Beat*. Underneath the beat of popular music in Brazil, however, is Drummond's rewriting of the recent history of Brazil's military dictatorships. *Hilda Furacão* (1991) is one of his most widely read novels in Brazil, a nostalgic and gently humorous look at student political life in the early 1960s, immediately before the 1964 coup. *Inês e Morta* (1993, Ines is dead) is a parable of how tyranny works and an inside look at the military dictatorship. Most of Drummond's novels are implicitly subversive, as is his last work, *Os Mortos não Dançam Valsa* (2002, The dead do not dance the waltz), a bizarre love story in which the lover's goal is to fulfill his deceased girlfriend's dream to dance a waltz overlooking the sea at Copacabana.

Sérgio Sant'Anna arose from 1960s counterculture and has been one of Brazil's foremost exponents of a postmodern fiction. In many ways his work can be seen as a Brazilian extension of the Mexican Onda group. His experimental *Confissões de Ralfo (uma autobiografia imaginária*) (1975, Confessions of Ralfo: an imaginary autobiography) had considerable impact in Brazil and has been called the "anti-*Don Quijote*" as a book with connections not only to Cervantes but also to Jack Kerouac. Seemingly a fantastic work, it offers a subtle political reading that deals with torture. Sant'Anna continued his iconoclastic ways with *Simulacros* (1977, Simulacra) and *Um Romance de Geração* (1980, A generational novel), the latter about a frustrated writer. He received the Jabuti prize for two novels in the 1980s, then publishing *Amazona* (1986, Amazonia), a parody of the political establishment. His recent short novel *Um Crime Delicado* (1997, A gentle crime) is a patently postmodern text with resonances of several novelistic genres.

Santiago Silviano is a leading exponent of postmodern fiction in Brazil; he is an academic and a writer who has earned a reputation as an experimentalist in both fiction and poetry. His early writing of the early 1970s has obvious connections with the French nouveau roman, but his later work is an inventive political metafiction that grows out of a more Brazilian cultural context. His novel *Stella Manhattan* is a work of unstable, fragile identities. The alter ego of another character, Stella Manhattan is forced from his native country by a father who is unhappy by his son's homosexuality and transvestism. It is a novel of complex relationships among unconventional characters, with the sexual complexities of characters in Sarduy's *Cobra* and the political intrigue of certain texts by Fuentes and Piglia.

Like Drummond, Rubem Fonseca and João Gilberto Noll have written postmodern novels with a broad appeal to their respective readerships in Brazil and abroad, where their novels have appeared in translation over the past two decades. Fonseca's novel *Bufo & Spallanzani* (1985) is a raucous parody of detective fiction, with a narrator-protagonist who is a compulsive writer in the process of creating a book with the title *Bufo & Spallanzani*. *Vastas Emocões e Pensamentos Imperfeitos* (1988, *The Lost Manuscript*) is a postmodern crime novel with a Brazilian film director as the narrator-protagonist. Noll began publishing fiction in the early 1980s, and his work tends to portray alienated characters attempting to survive in a disintegrating world. An opera star faces this situation in Noll's *Hotel Atlântico* (1997). His fragile characters also reflect on fiction, as does the narrator-protagonist in his recent *Berkeley em Bellagio* (2002, Berkeley in Bellagio).

Márcio Souza, Helena Parente Cunha, Per Johns, Márcia Denser, Ivan Angêlo, and Caio Fernando Abreu have also contributed to postmodern fiction in Brazil. Souza's *Galvez, Imperador do Acre* (1976, *The Emperor of the Amazon*) recalls some of his postmodern predecessors—including the innovative Brazilian modernist Oswald de Andrade—with its iconoclastic attitudes and random fragmentation. It is a parody of many kinds of texts, from nineteenth-century Brazilian literature to the modern Latin American novel in general. The work's antihero operates in the Amazon. Parente Cunha's *Mulher no Espelho* (1983, *Women Between Mirrors*) is an experiment in privileging the subjective to construct the meaning of a middle-aged woman's lived reality. The protagonist is a forty-five year-old Brazilian married to an extraordinarily domineering Brazilian man. She has three teenage sons. The narrative is her response to the otherness of female sexuality that has been repressed by her husband. She begins the novel by relating anecdotes of her youth and ends by reworking the terms of her existence. Parente Cunha's novel is an innovative fiction, and its most interesting technical device is the constant presence of a voice identified as "the woman who writes me."

Per John's postmodern trilogy consists of *As Aves de Cassandra* (1990, Cassandra's birds), *Cemitérios Marinhos as Vezes São Festivos* (1995, Marine cemeteries are sometimes festive), and *Navegante de Operetta* (1998, The operatic navigator). In his false search for meaning and characters, in which the narrator-protagonist expresses multiple personalities and presents multiple kinds of texts (fictions, essays, fables), the reader finds much that is intriguing and entertaining as well as little understanding of the main character or the society in which he lives. Ivan Angêlo's *A Festa* (1976, *The Celebration*) contains fragments that can be read in random order, as suggested by Morelli in Cortázar's *Hopscotch*. It is progressive both as a political text and an experimental fiction. Caio Fernando Abreu's *Onde Andará Dulce Veiga* (1990, *What Ever Happened to Dulce Veiga?*) is a playful and humorous postmodern text with numerous connections to international postmodern pop culture.

Some postmodern writers defy easy description and comparison with the other writers of their generation, and Chico Buarque is one of these exceptional writers. His four novels, *Fazenda Modelo: Novela Pecuária* (1975, Model farm: rural novel), *Estorvo* (1991, *Turbulence*), *Benjamin* (1995), and *Budapeste* (2003) fictionalize an active, postmodern reader. Buarque is also a subtle political writer. *Fazenda Modelo* is an allegory written in the context of an authoritarian society, and the fragmented and obsessed main character in *Estorvo* is also best understood when read in an allegorical fashion. His complex and ambiguous novel *Benjamin* moves between the past and present of the main character, who pursues a love affair with a woman of both his past and his present. Buarque has continued his challenging novelistic production with *Budapeste*.

Women writers in Latin America were prominent in the 1980s and 1990s, and Brazil did not diverge from this pattern. Writers such as Nélida Piñón, Lya Luft, Hilda Hilst, Márcia Denser, and Marilene Felinto were important figures in Brazil in this period, publishing new novels as well as new editions of earlier work. Patrícia Melo has entered the literary scene in Brazil more recently, meeting with considerable commercial success; Cíntia Moscovich writes with less commercial interests. Piñón has been active in the Brazilian literary scene since the 1960s, publishing several vast historical novels to acclaim. Miranda's fiction is similar to Piñón's in its historical breadth, although the recent *Clarice* (1999, Clarice) and *Dias and dias* (2002, Days and days) are intimate portrayals of the main characters. Hilst's *Qadós* (1973) is an experiment in blurring genre borders. Luft is more accessible, and two of her novels have appeared in English translation, *The Island of the Dead* (1986) and *The Red House* (1994). Both are works Luft describes as dealing with "close family relationships." Felinto has not been a highly productive fiction writer, but her first novel, *As Mulheres de Tijucopapo* (1982, *The Women of Tijucopapo*) is much recognized by critics as a search for origins. Melo's fast-moving works provide powerful and chilling insights into the minds of criminals and those on the margins of Brazilian society; her fiction has appeared in English under the titles *The Killer* (1997), *In Praise of Lies* (1999), and *Inferno* (2002); in Portuguese she has recently published *Valsa Negra* (2003, Black waltz). Cíntia Moscovich's first novel, *Duas Iguais: Manual de Amor e Equívocos Assemelhados* (1998, Two the same: love manual and similar errors) is a love story presented within a fragmented structure.

In Spanish America the novels of the 1970s that followed those of the 1960s Boom were often identified as a "post-Boom." These post-Boom novels are fundamentally modernist texts that were more accessible to a broader readership than the often more experimental and hermetic postmodern novels. Postmodern novels sometimes tell stories; post-Boom novels always do. In 1970s Brazil, as in 1970s Colombia, there was a repetition (in small scale) of the 1960s Boom in Spanish America, with the appearance of novels that had broad appeal and an international reception. With the election of Ernesto Geisel as the president of Brazil, there was a loosening of censorship and other repressive operations that were in force from 1974 to 1979; it was a period some Brazilians called the *descompressão* ("the decompression"). Brazilian novelists associated with this mid-seventies Boom and the changes of *descompressão* include Aguinaldo Silva, José Guimarães, Radam Nassar, Tania Fallace, Marcos Rey, Rubem Fonseca, Oswaldo França Junior, Plínio Marcos, and Alcione Araújo. Writers such as Loyola Brandão and Rubem Fonseca were in dialogue in many ways with international postmodern culture but also managed to attract a broad readership in Brazil. Josué Guimarães published several historical and conventional novels in the 1970s. Araújo's *Nem Mesmo Todo o Oceano* (1998,) is a lengthy (794-page) work that resonates with many types of novels, including the memoir, the bildungsroman, and the historical novel, and is a condemnation of the dictatorial state that arose out of the 1964 coup. The life of Oswaldo França Junior was clearly marked by the military government, and his novels of the 1960s and 1970s were indicative of this experience, with a strong emphasis on the absurd; his equally strong plots made him a widely read novelist in the late 1960s and 1970s.

Other writers of the Brazilian post-Boom (the Spanish American version) or *post-abertura* (as it was called in Brazil), many of whom had been publishing since the 1960s or 1970s, were Antonio Callado, João Ubaldo Ribeiro, Nélida Piñón, Carlos Heitor Cony, Autran Dourado, Patrícia Bins, and Fernando Gabeira. In the 1980s Callado published *A Expedicão Montaigne*, *Concerto Carioca* (1985, Carioca concert), and *Memórias de Aldenham House* (1989, Memories of Aldenham House), all three of which are constructed more for their value as entertainment than his revolutionary cycle of the 1960s and 1970s. Ribeiro published widely read novels throughout the 1980s and 1990s, including *Viva o Povo Brasileiro* (1989, *An Invincible Memory*), his family saga, national epic, and totalizing synthesis of Brazilian myth and culture. Bins published novels of human relations in the 1980s and 1990s that were the linear narratives in typical post-Boom style. *Pele Nua do Espelho* (1989, The mirror's naked skin) is a love story, and *Sarah e os Anjos* (1993, Sarah and the angels) deals with matters of sanity and insanity. Bins's novel *Caçada de Memórias* (1995, Hunt of memories) presents a male protagonist who has relationships with three women. Also writing in a linear mode was Marcelo Rubens Paiva, who enjoyed considerable commercial success in Brazil with *Feliz Ano Velho* (1982, *Happy Old Year*), one of many narratives that began to tell the truth about the atrocities of the military government. He later published a book inspired by the U.S. television show *The Twightlight Zone* titled *Blecaute* (1986, Blackout). Cony returned to the novel in the 1990s after having abandoned fiction writing, publishing *Quase Memória* (1995, Almost memory), winner of the Jabuti prize.

Two prominent ethnic writers of Brazil who are comparable to many post-Boom writers in Spanish America are Moacyr Scliar and Milton Hatoum. Scliar began writing in the late 1960s and has published over thirty books of fiction. His first novel, *A Guerra do Bom Fim* (1972, War with a happy ending) is about a Jewish boy growing up in Porto Alegre. Scliar writes in a more allegorical mode in *O Centauro no Jardim* (1980, *The Centaur in the*

Garden). One of the most accomplished and successful writers to appear on the literary scene has been Milton Hatoum. Born in the Amazon region, he began writing poetry and short fiction in the 1970s, later studying in São Paulo, Spain, and France. With interests in the ethnic history related to his Lebanese family background and human relations, he uses a sparse style to tell engaging stories. His first two novels, *Relato de um Certo Oriente* (1989, *The Tree of Seventh Heaven*) and *Dois Irmãos* (2000, *The Brothers*) have received the prestigious Jabuti prize in Brazil. These novels are family sagas that tell much of his personal experience, his Lebanese family's experience, and the experience of Brazil as a nation in the twentieth century.

Many of the novelists of *post-abertura*, who write after the end of the military dictatorship, were also publishing during the dictatorship. In the 1990s, however, a new generation of novelists began to publish their first works. Most of them had some previous experience writing journalism, publishing short stories, or both. As noted earlier, these writers, most of them born after 1955 (many since 1965), whom some critics have identified as a generation of the 1990s in Brazil, are comparable to a group of novelists in Spanish America of the same generation, such as the Chilean Alberto Fuguet and the Mexicans Jorge Volpi, Cristina Rivera Garza, and David Toscana. Many have particular interests in mass media and the Internet. Some claim that television and film are more important influences than literature per se. One of the main spokespersons for this generation of the 1990s in Brazil has been Nelson de Oliveira, and these young novelists include Diogo Mainardi, Bernardo Carvalho, Rubens Figueiredo, Mauro Pinheiro, Fernando Bonassi, João Batista Melo, Cíntia Moscovich, Carlos Ribeiro, and Nelson Motta. Nelson de Oliveira has published two anthologies of this new generation, *Geração 90: manuscritos de computador* (2001, The generation of the 1990s: computer manuscripts) and *Geração 90: os transgressores* (2002, The generation of the 1990s: the transgressors). These anthologies do not necessarily include all the fiction writers of this generation, and one of the most notable absences is that of Diogo Mainardi. Mainardi (born in 1962) and Pinheiro (born in 1957) have already seen a substantial number of works in print. Mainardi has been one of the most productive of the generation, having already published the novels *Malthus* (1989), *Arquipélago* (1992, Archipelago), *Contra o Brazil* (1998, Against Brazil), and *Polígano das Secas* (1995, Drought). The last is a satirical work that questions many Brazilian social and literary norms, including much of the writing that is considered monumental or virtually sacred to Brazilian letters, such as the regional novels of the northeast (the work of Graciliano Ramos, for example). Carvalho has already published several intriguing novels, and his recent *Nove Noites* (2002, Nine nights) is an engaging fictionalized inquiry into the life of an American anthropologist who mysteriously committed suicide in Brazil in 1939. Figueiredo (whom de Oliveira does include in his anthology *Geração 90*) has been equally productive, having published four novels that question many of the conventions of both society and literature. Bonassi has also been one of the most active participants of this generation, publishing *O Amor é uma Dor Feliz* (1997, Love and a happy pain), *Passaporte* (2001, Passport), and *Prova Contrária* (2003, Contrary proof).

Among the other novelists of this generation of the 1990s, Pinheiro has published the novels *Cemitério de Navios* (1993, Ship cemetery) and *Conçerto para Corda e Pescoço* (2000, Concert for string and neck). The protagonist of the latter work is a writer who lives at the margins of society with a fragile relationship to the written word. Motta's *So Canto da Sereia* (2002, Simply the mermaid chant) is subtitled *Um Noir Baiano*; it is a detective novel in the Bahia mode (the author promises the reader "sex, drugs, and Afro-jazz"). Batista Melo has gained attention in Brazil for his short fiction and has published his first novel under the title *Patagonia* (1998). Ribeiro's first novel, *O Chamado da Noite* (1997, The call of the night) sets characters in the postmodern culture of globalization, computers, and film.

Marcelo Mirisolo and Alfredo Guzik belong to this generation of the 1990s, but escape easy classification within any group or description. Both write about gender issues; Mirisolo is part of de Oliveira's anthology; Guzik is not. Nevertheless, Guzik is one of the few writers to deal with AIDS in a novel in Brazil; this is the focus of his *Risco de Vida* (1995, Life threat).

Observed in retrospect, the major Brazilian novelists in the second half of the twentieth century have been João Guimarães Rosa, Clarice Lispector, Jorge Amado, Autran Dourado, Rubem Fonseca, and Antonio Callado. They have all had an enormous impact on the literary scene in Brazil and Latin America in general, with recognition abroad in the form of translations and literary prizes. Each has written a body of work that was considered in some ways both innovative and substantive, at the same time that each of these six writers was remarkably productive—in most cases prolific. Guimarães Rosa and Callado were committed to the totalizing "national" project of writing about Brazil in the broadest of terms. Amado, Dourado, and Callado continued publishing throughout a good portion of the second half of the century, and writers such as Moacyr Scliar and Lygia Fagundes Telles have been productive novelists during the entire second half of the century as well. Among the younger inheritors of this novelistic tradition, Milton Hatoum is one of the writers who seems most aware of his role in Brazil both as an inheritor of tradition and innovation. Of the major writers of the century, João Guimarães Rosa, Jorge Amado, and Clarice Lispector have been the most widely read, studied, translated, and internationally recognized.

Conclusion: The Post-1945 Novel, the Desire to Be Modern, and Redemocratization

The Peruvian writer Mario Vargas Llosa and other intellectuals have proposed that great literature is a product of societies in crisis. Vargas Llosa suggests that this might partially explain phenomena such as the much renowned Russian novel of the nineteenth century and the voluminous outpouring of significant Latin American novels in the latter half of the twentieth century. The social and political contexts have been related to the Latin American writer in many ways: Nobel laureate Gabriel García Márquez claimed in 1975 that he would not write another novel until after the fall of Chilean dictator Augusto Pinochet; Carlos Fuentes was waiting for a victorious Fidel Castro in Havana in 1959 to celebrate the triumph of the Cuban Revolution; Julio Cortázar, Fuentes, and a host of others have cited the important social role and commitment of the Latin American writer. Indeed, the colonial legacy of Latin America left a markedly hierarchical society with deeply rooted inequities that have persisted well into the twenty-first century. The social and political role of the Latin American writer can easily be traced back to the nineteenth century. In the 1920s neo-Marxist critics such as the Peruvian José Carlos Mariátegui established a tradition of social critique inherited by post-WWII writers. In the post-WWII period many Latin American writers also cited Jean-Paul Sartre's positions on the socially committed writer, and being *engagé* was standard in the intellectual repertoire of most Latin American and Caribbean writers. Nevertheless, the precise details of political contexts, the political positions and roles of the writers is complex: the same Vargas Llosa who espoused revolutionary politics in the 1960s became openly critical of the Latin American left in the 1980s; Fuentes became persona non grata in Cuba in the late 1960s because he criticized Castro's record on human rights and freedom of expression; Aimé Césaire, who was a pioneer of postcolonial positions in the 1940s, is now considered masculinist by feminist critics in the Caribbean; Jorge Luis Borges, the father figure for Latin American novelists, often scoffed at the political role of the writer; even Gabriel García Márquez, one of the most consistent icons of the Latin American political left, claimed in the 1980s that the main role of the Latin American writer is simply "to tell good stories."

As Latin American and Caribbean societies have continued their processes of modernization and redemocratization in recent decades, Latin American novelists have expressed their ongoing, century-long desire to be modern in a variety of ways associated with modern and postmodern literature. Closer to their roots in the modern and their one-time idol Jean-Paul Sartre, Fuentes, Vargas Llosa and García Márquez have remained active political voices and authors who firmly believe in the potential of cultural practices to effect social change. More postmodern writers, such as Eltit and Piglia, have been more skeptical of totalizing literary and political projects.

The youngest generation of Latin American and Caribbean writers from each of the regions—from Mexico to the southern cone—has begun to assume new roles as novelists in an increasingly globalized economy with increased urban violence in cities such as Mexico City, Bogotá, and São Paulo. These writers of the generation of the 1990s have tended to reject much of the political agenda of their predecessors, focusing instead on the new urban violence and the prominence of extraliterary media. They have also begun to write novels with different attitudes toward issues common to the Latin American fiction of the 1970s and 1980s such as gender and exile.

In order to introduce this vast panorama of political contexts and fiction from Latin America and the Caribbean, part 1 has offered a general survey of some of the most prominent of the broad categories of political writing as well a general introduction to novels of social critique and the chronological development of the novel since 1945. Brief national overviews, topics, authors' biographies, and novels' synopses are provided in alphabetical order in part 2.

Part II

Nations, Topics, Biographies, and Novels

A

Abad Faciolince, Héctor [Biography] Colombian novelist, short story writer, essayist, editor, and translator, he is one of the leading writers of his generation, a generation that some writers in Colombia have described as the first to be born after the advent of national television and one that considers the media as important as the great classics of literature. This generation has also grown up in an urban setting of drug trafficking and widespread violence. Abad Faciolince, along with other Colombian writers of his generation, has been interested in fictionalizing this new urban experience, with particular emphasis on the precariousness of everyday life.

Born in Medellín (department of Antioquia), Colombia, in 1958, he has published a book of short stories, three novels, and a book of fiction, difficult to define within standard genres, under the title *Tratado de culinaria para mujeres tristes* (Culinary treatise for sad women). He studied journalism at the University of Antioquia (in Medellín, Colombia) and languages and literatures at the University of Turin in Italy. He has translated the fiction of several Italian writers into Spanish, including Umberto Eco. A writer who appeared on the literary scene in the 1990s, Abad Faciolince published his first volume of short stories, *Malos pensamientos* (Bad thoughts), in 1991. His first novel, *Asuntos de un hidalgo disoluto* (1994), was well received in Colom-

bia and soon appeared in English translation under the title *The Joy of Being Awake* (1996). It is a self-reflective metafiction that parodies traditional novel forms, a humorous entertainment of a seventy-two-year-old narcissist who uses the the Spanish picaresque to tell the story of his life since adolescence and follows irrational signs rather than rational systems of thought to understand his everyday life.

His experimental novel *Basura* (2000, Garbage) was awarded an international prize (Casa de las Americas, Cuba) for innovative fiction in the year it was published. In this work the protagonist is a writer who regularly throws his creations in the garbage, but the recovered pieces constitute a novel: a character collects and edits the pieces, constructing the book. This novel also includes parody of his compatriot Gabriel García Márquez. His recent novel *Angosta* (2004) is set in a decadent hotel populated by eccentric types, including a poet, a mathematician, two aging bohemians, and the owner of a bookstore. The title refers to a fictional city named Angosta located in the Andes. A representation of a Colombian-type urban space, Angosta has the geography and rigid class structure of several Colombian cities. Described by some critics as a combination of fiction and hyperrealism, this is one of Abad Faciolince's most elaborate and substantive novels. Abad Faciolince currently works as a journalist and editor in Bogotá, Colombia, where he writes on a broad range of literary, cultural, and political topics. He recently compiled a volume of these essays under the title *Palabras sueltas* (2002, Loose words).

Selected Work: *Asuntos de un hidalgo disoluto* (1994, *The Joy of Being Awake*, translation Nathan Budoff, 1996); *Tratado de culinaria para mujeres tristes* (1996); *Fragmentos de un amor furtivo* (1999); *Basura* (2000); *Oriente comienza en el Cairo* (2002); *Angosta* (2004).

Abbadón, el exterminador (1974, *Angel of Darkness*, by Ernesto Sábato. Translation by Andrew Hurley. New York: Ballantine, 1991) [**Novel**] An autobiographical novel in which Sábato himself is the protagonist, this work is a pastiche of several of his other writings, including references to fictional characters from previous works. Set in Buenos Aires in the early 1970s, it nevertheless has characters such as Hitler and Che Guevara, using space and time in ways similar to Jorge Luis Borges and Carlos Fuentes. Described by critics as dense, cerebral, and dark, its themes and characters are not developed chronologically, nor does the work show any gestures toward magical realism. Rather, it contains memoires, historical accounts, and interviews with persons who existed historically. The main theme is evilness, which appears to dominate the world by the end of the novel. Sábato also dies at the end, yet he seems to have achieved a vast understanding of the world and liberation from evil. The theme of revolution also appears with regularity. Not as internationally acclaimed as Sábato's earlier work or the novels of the 1960s Boom, it was read widely, nevertheless, in Argentina and much of Latin America.

Abeng (1984, by Michelle Cliff. Written in English. New York: Abbey) [**Novel**] One of the two novels by one of Jamaica's major women writers, *Abeng* reflects the complex dynamics women writers have been attempting to address as they confront the increasingly complex cultural environment of the Caribbean region. The protagonist, Clare Savage, also faces the colonial legacy of African slaves in Jamaica, for she is a light-skinned Afro-Jamaican. The main focus of the novel is her personal identity. Cliff, however, sees the issue in broad terms and, like writers such as the Cuban Alejo Carpentier and the Mexican Carlos Fuentes, she fictionalizes personal history as a metaphor for national history. Clare rejects the stereotype of Caribbean racial identity as binary. In the end Clare decides not to choose a racial identity and identifies with a peasant woman, Zoe, who symbolizes what it means to be a woman. Cliff's protagonist accepts the complexity of issues of race, class, and gender, and Cliff embraces this complexity and the idea of seeking wisdom.

Abreu, Caio Fernando [**Biography**] Brazilian novelist, short story writer, and journalist, he was one of the talented urban writers to appear on the Brazilian literary scene at a very young age in the late 1960s. Much of his writing describes urban decadence and poverty as well as the urban world of gay culture and generalized human anguish. His urban settings tend to be peripheries, the precise space often apartments, bars, and streets. Abreu also writes children's literature. Born in 1948 in Santiago (state of Rio Grande do Sul), he studied literature at the Universidade Federal de Rio Grande do Sul. He published his first short stories in 1966 and was awarded a prize in Brazil (Fernando Chinaglia) for his first book of fiction, *Inventário de Irremediável* (1970, Inventory of the irremedial), and published his first novel, *Límite Branco* (White border) that same year. The latter is a first-person narrative of adolescent experience in an urban setting. In 1988 he published a set of stories about adolescent alienation, *Os Dragões não Conhecem* *o Paraíso* (1990, *Dragons*). His second novel, the postmodern *Onde Andará Dulce Veiga* (1990, *What Ever Happened to Dulce Veiga?*) is a playful and humorous work that takes the reader through the urban pop culture scene of nocturnal São Paulo. He has also published the short stories *Morangos Mofados* (1982, Mouldy strawberries), *Mel & Girassóis* (1988, Honey and sunflowers), and *Triángulos das Aguas* (1983, Water triangle). The latter has been one of his most critically acclaimed works. It consists of three stories that describe human relationships and emotional states explained in abstract ways.

Selected Work: *Límite Branco* (1970); *Triángulos das Aguas* (1983); *Onde Andará Dulce Veiga* (1990; *What Ever Happened to Dulce Veiga?* translation Adiran Frizzi, 2001); *Bem Longe de Mariendbad* (1996).

Acosta, Oscar "Zeta" [Biography] Novelist and short story writer, he was an irreverent and iconoclastic pioneer in developing a Chicano novelistic aesthetic in the early 1970s in the United States. He was born in El Paso, Texas in 1935, studied law in California in the mid-1960s, began writing literature, and then disappeared on a trip in northern Mexico in 1974. His writings promoted ethnic identity, rejected the established order, and identified with the working class—commonplace topics and attitudes in U.S. Hispanic literature of the 1980s and 1990s. His representation of the U.S. minority experience and critique of it was marked by humor. This subversive humor and other factors have led critics to describe him as a Chicano Kerouac who traveled across the country in search of identity and the American Dream. His two novels were fictionalized autobiographies. The first, *The Autobiography of a Brown Buffalo* (1972) is his picaresque and satirical version of the author's self search in the process of participating in the struggle for Chicano rights in the United States. Associated with magical realism by some critics, Acosta underscores fictionality to question the viability of "factual" autobiography. Special use of the autobiographical form also raises questions about the genre for marginalized minority writers. With this experimental autobiography, Acosta rejects more conventional Chicano autobiographies, such as those written by Raymond Paredes, José Villareal, Ernesto Galarza, and others. The continuation of this story, *The Revolt of the Cockroach People* (1973), relates the political upheaval in Los Angeles in the early 1970s, with focus on a protagonist who is a Chicano lawyer named Buffalo Zeta Brown. In his narrative Acosta parodies a broad range of writers and cultural figures from both Anglo and Hispanic traditions, from Cervantes and Gabriel García Márquez to Federico García Lorca and James Cagney.

Selected Work: *The Autobiography of a Brown Buffalo* (1972); *The Revolt of the Cockroach People* (1973).

Adán Buenosayres (1948, by Leopoldo Marechal. Written in Spanish and untranslated. Buenos Aires: Sudamericana) **[Novel]** A modern Argentine classic, this lengthy (644-page) novel has been widely admired as a seminal work of the right of invention in Latin America. Drawing upon classical myths, Marechal sends his protagonist on an epic journey that eventually leads him to the "dark city of Cacodelphia." The novel is divided into three parts. The first, which contains five "books" (or chapters), deals with the protagonist, Adán Buenosayres, as well as his intellectual cohorts. The second part (the sixth book) is the protagonist's "notebook," and the third part (book 7) describes the trip to Cacodelphia. These books relate Adán's varying psychological, intellectual, and spiritual crises. Set in the 1920s in Buenos Aires, this novel satirizes and debunks many of the predominant ideas about literature and culture in vogue in Buenos Aires and throughout Latin America during the period.

Adioses, Los (1954, *The Goodbyes,* by Juan Carlos Onetti. *The Goodbyes and Others Stories.* Austin: University of Texas Press, 1990) [**Novel**] A continuation of Onetti's novel *A Brief Life, The Goodbyes* creates ambiguities in the narrated reality of the previous novel in the dismal setting of Onetti's fictional town of Santa María. The narrator is a detached figure who openly presents the events from his own point of view, which is often sordid and biased. This narrator-protagonist is a store owner who knows everything that his happening in the town. His broad knowledge of things, and the extreme detail of his descriptions, create an atmosphere of reliability. Nevertheless, he is hardly objective. This novel invites the reader to rethink what happens in the process of reading and writing. Ambiguity is the key to these processes and the centerpiece of Onetti's success. Consequently, this novel from 'the 1950s was a relatively early case in Latin America, along with those of Adolfo Bioy Casares and Jorge Luis Borges, of metafictional theorization. This interest in self-reflection on the creative process is one of several reasons that Onetti has become a legendary figure for the young writers of the 1990s in Latin America. Another edition of *Los adioses* appeared under the title *Farewells and a Grave with No Name* (translation Peter Bush, London: Quartet, 1992).

Adoum, Jorge Enrique [**Biography**] Ecuadorian novelist, poet, and essayist, he is one of the most experimental writers of the Andean region. One of the most innovative fictions ever published in twentieth-century Ecuador was Adoum's *Entre Marx y una mujer desnuda* (1976, Between Marx and a nude woman). A lengthy meditation on the novel and the nation of Ecuador, it is an encyclopedic work comparable in some ways to Fuentes's *Terra Nostra* and Cortázar's *Rayuela.* In fact, the novel's opening pages make direct references to Joyce and Cortázar. Perhaps the most telling feature of this work, however, is that the prologue begins on page 233 of a 311-page novel.

Selected Work: Entre Marx y una mujer desnuda (1976).

After the Bombs (See *Después de las bombas* by Arturo Arias) [**Novel**]

Afro–Latin American Novel [**Topic**] Fiction by Afro–Latin American writers has been a presence in Latin America throughout the century, and scholars have become increasingly attentive to this writing since the 1960s. In the 1920s the *creolité* movement, centered in the Caribbean region, which sought to highlight the African roots of Latin American culture, was an important force in the later production of the Afro–Latin American novel. Many Afro-Caribbean intellectuals looked to the United States and the Harlem Renaissance as a model, and Latin American writers in general have been well aware of the work of the entire Afro-American literary tradition, from Langston Hughes to James Baldwin. Essayists and theorists from the French Caribbean, such as Aimé Césaire and Eduourd Glissant, have been prominent in the conceptualization of an African identity in the Americas. More recently, Afro-Caribbean writers such as Maryse Condé and Daniel Maximim (both from Guadeloupe and writing in French), as well as Astrid Roemer (from Surinam and who writes in Dutch), have written of the experience of racism. Roemer's *Ergens Nergens* (1983, Nowhere, somewhere) tells of an African's experience in Holland. Scholarly introductions to the subject of Afro–Latin American fiction include the work of Richard Jackson and Marvin Lewis. In Brazil the first writer to use the term *Afro-brasileiro* was Darcy Ribeiro in *O Povo Brasileiro*, which was written before his death in 1997.

Major Afro–Latin American novelists to appear in the 1940s were Alejo Carpentier of Cuba, Jorge Amado and José Lins do Rêgo in Brazil, Quince Duncan in Central America, Adalberto Ortiz and Demetrio Aguilera Malta in Ecuador, and Arnoldo Palacios in Colombia, followed soon thereafter in the 1950s by Colombia's Manuel Zapata Olivella and Venezuela's Ramón Díaz Sánchez. Amado's numerous publications included many novels that celebrated African culture in Brazil. Zapata Olivella published the lengthy and comprehensive *Changó, el gran putas* (1983, Changó, the big SOB), his novel of the African diaspora in the Americas. In this work the author elaborates an African mythic vision of the origin of the universe and the subsequent movement to the Americas. The novel covers the African experience of imprisonment, being shipped to the Americas, and resistence. Historical cultural figures, such as Nat Turner in the U.S., François Mackandal in the Caribbean, and Benkos Bioho in Colombia, all appear in this novel. Zapata Olivella writes a broad fictionalized history, but his main focus is a Colombian story of resistance and liberation. Pioneer novels of the African tradition in Colombia were *Las estrellas son negras* (1949, The stars are black) by Arnold Palacios and *Las memorias del odio* (1953, Memories of hatred) by Rogerio Velásquez.

A seminal work of the African experience in the Americas was Carpentier's *El siglo de las luces* (1962, *Explosion in a Cathedral*), which includes a historic episode with the African slave rebel François Mackandal. Postmodern Afro–Latin American fiction writers include the Puerto Rican

Luis Rafael Sánchez and the Colombian Alberto Duque López.

Agosto (1990, August, by Rubem Fonseca. Written in Portuguese and untranslated. São Paulo: Companhia das Letras) [**Novel**] Set in August of 1954, this satirical book is a synthesis of historical fact and imaginative invention related to the characters and events of this turbulent period in Brazil's history. The centerpiece of the crisis is the 1954 suicide of President Getúlio Vargas and related events. During the time of the novel, which covers a period of several weeks, Vargas's regime was losing popular support as the government's corruption and abuse of power were also affecting its credibility with the middle class and the military. One of this government's most visible abuses of power was its attempt to assassinate opposition journalist Carlos Lacerda. Fonseca's version of this crisis focuses on a protagonist who is a detective who investigates the murder of Cláudio Aguiar, a well-known businessman. By combining the narrative strategies of detective fiction and the historical novel, Fonseca constructs a complex plot around numerous characters from the upper sectors of Brazilian society, as well as the police and organized crime figures. A narrator-figure speculates on the elaborate series of events in a way that is not common in nonfictional accounts. The narrator also makes the detective a sympathetic figure who is nearly overwhelmed by the corruption of Brazilian society. Critics have pointed out several parallels between the moral decadence of this society in 1954 and in 1990, when the novel was published.

Agua quemada (1981, *Burnt Water*, by Carlos Fuentes. Translation by Margaret Sayers Peden. New York: Farrar, Straus and Giroux, 1980) [**Novel**] Many critics consider this volume classic Fuentes, i.e., writings with themes and strategies that the Mexican writer used to establish his career in the 1950s and 1960s. Published in Spanish in a single volume of four stories titled *Agua quemada* ("burnt water") that could potentially be read as one novel, the book appeared in English under the same title, *Burnt Water*, but with a slightly different set of eleven stories. More specifically, *Agua quemada* in Spanish contains a quartet of stories; *Burnt Water* contains these stories, in addition to stories that Fuentes had published in Spanish much earlier. The term *burnt water* is a translation of the Aztec term referring to a volcano-ringed lake surrounding the ancient city of Tenochtitlán. Such paradoxical concepts—involving the blending of opposites—is one of Fuentes's main interests in this volume. These stories are set in modern Mexico City, yet they paradoxically exhibit an awareness of the historic past from the Aztec times, the colonial period, and the nineteenth century.

Aguilar, Rosario [Biography] A Nicaraguan novelist, she is one of Central America's leading women writers. She began writing in the late 1960s and continued through the Sandinista Revolution. Born in León, Nicaragua, in 1938, she moved with her family to the capital city of Managua in 1943. In the early 1950s she studied in the United States (in Louisiana and Texas) and she has also lived in Guatemala and Costa Rica. She has published a substantive body of fiction without every attempting to become a full-time writer by profession. She claims to have always written with an awareness of the venerable poetic tradition in Nicaragua, beginning to write fiction in the early 1960s, and publishing her first book of fiction, *Primavera sonámbula* (Somnambulate spring) in 1964. (This book and several other of her volumes of fiction are frequently referred to as "novels," for they contain long stories or novellas, depending on how the reader chooses to classify them.)

Her major novels are *El guerrillero* (1976, The guerrilla fighter) and *La niña blanca y los pájaros sin pies* (1992, The white girl and the birds without feet). *El guerrillero* is a historical novel divided into nineteen parts, set during the Somoza dictatorship. The protagonist is a school teacher who has relationships with three men: a subversive revolutionary, a sergeant in the military, and a judge. The triumph of the Sandinista Revolution at the end of the novel is a personal affirmation for her.

Selected Work: Primavera sonámbula (1964); *Quince barrotes de izquierda y derecha* (1965); *Rosa Sarmiento* (1968); *Aquel mar sin fondo ni playa* (1970); *Las doce y veintinueve* (1975); *El guerrillero* (1976); *La niña blanca y los pájaros sin pies* (1992, *The Last Chronicles of Terra Firma*, translation Edward Waters Hood, 1997); *La promesante* (2001).

Aguilar Camín, Héctor [Biography] Mexican novelist, short story writer, essayist, and journalist, he has been active in the Mexican cultural scene as an editor of several influential newspapers and magazines, holding key positions in progressive publications, such as the newspaper *La Jornada* and the magazine *Nexos*. A prominent public intellectual in Mexico City, he takes positions on a broad range of cultural and political topics; these subjects sometimes become matters of broad public discussion in Mexico. He was born in Chetumal (state of Quintana Roo) in 1946 and studied history at the undergraduate and graduate level, receiving a doctorate in history from the Colegio de México. He received a Guggenheim Fellowship in 1989. His novels tend to be historically based, well researched, with political implications, and often critical of key Mexican institutions. His widely read first novel, *Morir en el golfo* (1985, To die in the gulf) was critical of the state-owned petroleum industry in Mexico.

His second novel was *La guerra de Galio* (1990, Galio's war). *El resplandor de la madera* (1999, The shining of the wood) is his most lengthy (440 pages) and ambitious novel to date. It is a historical and ecological novel, with alternating chapters between past and present that tell the story of three generations of the Casares family in the Yucatán region of Mexico. His brief novel *Las mujeres de Adriano* (2001, Adriano's women) relates a character's affairs with several women, and this novel became a topic of ample discussion in Mexico. The protagonist attempts to defend the legitimacy of having five female lovers, fueling debates over sexual mores and the sociology of *machismo*.

Narrative: Morir en el golfo (1985); *La guerra de Galio* (1990); *Historias conversadas* (1992); *El error de la luna* (1995); *Un soplo en el río* (1998); *El resplandor de la madera* (1998); *Las mujeres de Adriano* (2001); *Mandatos del corazón* (2003).

Aguilera Garramuño, Marco Tulio [Biography] Colombian novelist, essayist, and short story writer, he was one of the first Colombian writers to parody his compatriot Gabriel García Márquez when he pubished his first novel, *Breve historia de todas las cosas* (1975, Brief history of everything). Aguilera Garramuño's work tends to be satiric and self-conscious. He particularly likes to ridicule standard sexual mores, playing with the erotic as part of sexuality and as part of a literary genre—the erotic novel. He was born in Bogotá, Colombia, in 1949, but spent his childhood in Costa Rica before moving with his family to Cali, Colombia, where he studied literature at the Universidad del Valle. Under the mentorship of the Colombian writer Gustavo Alvarez Gardeazábal, he began writing and participating in cultural life in Cali in the 1970s. He enjoyed considerable success in Colombia with the publication

of his humorous and satirical *Breve historia de todas las cosas*, a story of a small town in Costa Rica and a writer-figure who is the narrator. After publishing his first novel, he went to the University of Kansas in 1976 for an MA in Latin American literature and then moved from Kansas to Monterrey, Mexico, in 1978. The author returns to the real and the imagined in his fictional memoir, a novel titled *Buenabestia* (1992, Good beast). He continues with his fictionalized approaches to love and the erotic in *La pequeña maestra de violín* (2001, The little violin teacher). His novel *La hermosa vida* (2001, The beautiful life) is about an artist who writes on the basis of his dreams. In *El amor y la muerte* (2002, Love and death) the female protagonist lives her childhood in the Argentina of Perón, her marriage in Colombia, and her advanced adult years in Costa Rica and Nicaragua, where she is declared a Mother of the Revolution. Aguilera Garramuño continues writing fiction in a humorous vein, with particular focus on the conventions and duplicities of sexual relations. He currently lives in Xalapa, Mexico, where teaches, does editorial work, and writes fiction.

Selected Work: Breve historia de todas las cosas (1975); *Rostro con máscara: novela* (1979); *Paraísos hostiles* (1985); *Mujeres amadas* (1988); *El juego de las seducciones* (1989); *Los placeres perdidos* (1989); *Las noches de Ventura* (1992); *Buenabestia* (1992); *Esas fieras las mujeres* (1997); *La pequeña maestra de violín* (2001); *La hermosa vida* (2001); *El amor y la muerte* (2002).

Aguilera Malta, Demetrio [Biography] Ecuadorian novelist, poet, essayist, playwright and short story writer, he was associated with Ecuador's generation of 1930, which renewed the nation's conventional and conservative literary scene with their avant-garde writings in the 1930s. They desired a literature that was both aesthetically modern and politically progressive. He is one of Ecuador's major writers of the century, well known throughout the Hispanic world. He was a pioneer Afro–Latin American writer and an early magical realist who masterfully assimilated oral culture into his writing. Aguilera Malta was born in Guayaquil, Ecuador, in 1909 and died in Mexico City, where he was serving as Ecuador's ambassador to Mexico, in 1981. Before assuming the ambassadorship in Mexico, he had held numerous academic appointments in Ecuador and abroad and, in the late 1940s and early 1950s, had worked on the production of several films.

Aguilera Malta's writing career spanned the 1930s to the 1970s, and he is generally considered the major novelist of the century in Ecuador. His novel *Don Goyo* (1933) is an exceptionally well-crafted fiction, and many informed critics consider this work an early forerunner (by several decades) of the magical realism of writers such as Gabriel García Márquez. In this work Aguilera Malta tells the story of fishermen who live on an island near Guayaquil. The author contrasts two main characters—the legendary Don Goyo and a more earthly Cusombo. The dominant culture of the whites invades the island, interfering with life as it had been known there. The author creates a sense of a special and unusual world at the same time that he demonstrates the social and economic injustice of the situation imposed by the dominant culture. After nearly half a century *Don Goyo* appeared in English translation in 1980. His novels often denounce the exploitation of the indigenous peoples of Latin America. In the post-WWII period he is best known for his novels *Siete lunas, siete serpientes* (1970, *Seven Serpents and Seven Moons*) and *El secuestro del general* (1973, *Babelandia*), both of which deal with the abuse of political power. In *Siete lunas, siete serpi-*

entes the author creates a mythic town where the cultures of Africa, North America, and Europe meet. The magic elements that were subtle background material in *Don Goyo* are now fully exploited to create a novel of wild invention and rampant fantasy. Despite the fantasy element, as in his earlier work, Aguilera Malta demonstrates his concerns for social justice.

Selected Work: *Don Goyo* (1933, *Don Goyo*, translation John and Carolyn Brushwood, 1980); *La isla virgen* (1942); *Una cruz en la Sierra Maestra* (1960); *Los caballeros del sol* (1964, *La Caballaresca*, translation Willis Knapp Jones, 1967); *El Quijote de El Dorado: Orellana y el Río de las Amazonas, novela histórica* (1964); *El Quijote del diablo* (1964); *Un nuevo mar para el rey* (1965); *Siete lunas y siete serpientes* (1970, *Seven Serpents and Seven Moons*, translation Gregory Rabassa, 1981); *El secuestro del general* (1973, *Babelandia*, translation Peter Earle, 1973); *Jaguar* (1977); *Réquiem para el diablo* (1978).

Aguinis, Marcos [Biography] Argentine novelist, short story writer, essayist, and biographer, he is one of the most productive and widely read novelists in Argentina in recent years. He is also one of Latin America's most prominent Jewish Latin American writers. Born in Córdoba, Argentina, in 1935, he is the son of a Romanian Jewish immigrant to Argentina who moved to the small town of Cruz del Eje when he was a young child. His first language was Yiddish, and he claims to have learned Spanish with difficulty; the family moved back to Córdoba for his high school years, and in his youth he assisted his father in his household furnishing business. He received a classic Jewish education and as an adult writer claims to be agnostic. From an early age, he studied piano, and was an accomplished pianist until his early adulthood. Trained in Argentina and Europe, he did graduate work in medicine and psychiatry.

In 1958 he received his degree in medicine and surgery from the Universidad Nacional de Córdoba and moved with his wife to Río Cuarto, Argentina, where his first three children were born and he wrote his early books. He began publishing essays and fiction in the 1960s, and after personally identifying with the twelfth-century humanist Maimonides, eventually published a book-length essay on this intellectual under the title *Maimónides, un sabio de avanzada* (1963, Maimonides, a wise man ahead of his time). Several of his novels have been highly successful best sellers in Argentina in the 1980s and 1990s. After the military dictatorship, Aguinis was named subsecretary and then secretary of culture under the new democratic government of 1983. He has been awarded several national and international literary prizes, including the Planeta novel prize for his novel *La cruz invertida* (The inverted cross) in 1970.

His major novels are *La cruz invertida* (1970) and *La gesta del marrano* (1991, The gesture of the pig). The main characters in *La cruz invertida* are priests, and Aguinis is interested in the role of the traditional Catholic Church with respect to liberation theology. The progressive priests fail to reform the Church and are excommunicated. The protagonist is a young priest and progressive activist who supports subversive students opposing a repressive government. The author used mixed linguistic and cultural registers to avoid any direct connection to a specific Latin American country. In the end the institutions of the government and the Church prevail in their traditional mode. In *La gesta del marrano* he fictionalizes the history of the Spanish Inquisition with respect to the Jewish population in the Americas and relates this history to the identity crisis of one particular Jewish historical figure, Francisco Maldonado da Silva (1592–1639), a respected physician from Portugal who practiced medicine in the Chilean city of Concepción in the seventeenth century. Maldonado da Silva's father had been arrested and later converted to Catholicism and instructed his son to do the same. After thirteen years of imprisonment, he was burned to death under the laws of the Inquisition. Aguinis currently lives in Buenos Aires, where he is a practicing psychiatrist and writes fiction and essays.

Selected Work: *Refugiados. Crónica de un palestino* (1969); *La cruz invertida* (1970); *Cantata de los diablos* (1972); *La conspiración de los idiotas* (1978); *Profanación del amor* (1982); *La gesta del marrano* (1991); *La matriz del infierno* (1997); *Los iluminados* (2000); *Asalto al paraíso* (2003).

Aguirre, Eugenio [**Biography**] Mexican novelist and short story writer, he has been one of the most productive novelists in Mexico in recent decades. Among his voluminous writings, his historical ficton has had the most impact among critics and readers. He was born in Mexico City in 1946, where he studied law as an undergraduate and then received an MA in literature at the National University in Mexico City (UNAM). Most of his professional career has involved editorial and book distribution positions for the government. He has enjoyed success in promoting literary culture and the reading of books in Mexico and has served as president of the Mexican Association of Writers (1984–1986). He is best known for his historical novel *Gonzalo Guerrero* (1980, Gonzalo Guerrero), set in the sixteenth century—period of the conquest of Mexico by the Spaniards—which was widely read in Mexico and eventually appeared in a second edition in 1991. Aguirre's other novels cover a broad range of interests and themes, from childhood memories of early experiences at the beach and with the sea in *Un mundo de niño lleno de mar* (1985, A world of the child and the sea) to detective fiction in *El rumor que llegó del mar* (1986, The rumor that arrived from the sea). On the other hand, he explores Mexican *machismo* and the results of excessive paternal authority in *Cadáver exquisito* (1985, Exquisite cadaver).

Selected Work: *Jesucristo Pérez* (1973); *Pajar de imaginación* (1975); *El caballero de espadas* (1978); *Gonzalo Guerrero* (1980); *El testamento del diablo* (1982); *En el campo* (1983); *Pájaros de fuego* (1984); *Cadáver exquisito* (1985); *Segunda persona* (1985); *Lorencillo, el pirata del pañuelo rojo* (1986); *El rumor que llegó del mar* (1986); *La suerte de la fea* (1986); *Amor de mis amores* (1988); *Pasos de sangre* (1990); *El guerrero del sur* (1991); *El hombre baldío* (1992); *Los niños de colores* (1993); *Elena o el laberinto de la lujuria* (1994); *La fascinación de la bestia* (1994); *Desierto ardiente* (1995); *Cuarto cerrado* (1996); *Ángeles y demonios* (1996); *Lotería del deseo* (2003).

Agustín, José [Biography] Mexican novelist, short story writer, playwright, film director, and essayist, he is one of the iconoclastic figures of the century in his homeland. He and Gustavo Sainz were the leading figures in the publication of an irreverent, rebellious, and postmodern fiction of the mid-1960s that was identified locally within Mexico as the Onda. Taking inspiration from the U.S. 1960s counterculture, they debunked institutional elite culture. They wrote against not only the traditional writers of the 1930s and 1940s who told stories of the Mexican Revolution but also against the high modernism of Juan Rulfo and Carlos Fuentes. Unlike renowned public intellectuals in Mexico, such as Octavio Paz and Carlos Fuentes, they did not consider themselves spokespersons for political causes and, in fact, questioned the authority of spokespersons in any political or cultural realm. Agustín

was born in Acapulco in 1944 and was interested in North American popular culture from his youth. Rock music, the writings of J. D. Salinger, and the beat generation were important during his formative years and are clearly present in his first fictions. His first three novels, *La tumba* (1964, The tomb), *De perfil* (1966, In profile), and *Inventando que sueño* (1968, Inventing that I dream) were literary bombshells in Mexico and soon recognized throughout Latin America as an antiliterature that questioned many of the basic tenets of both traditional and modern fiction as they had been practiced until the 1960s in Mexico. Agustín's generation admired J. D. Salinger, and *De perfil* has often been compared to Salinger's *Catcher in the Rye* both for its humor and its portrayal of disaffected youth. In some respects it is difficult to classify these works of fiction as "novels"; *Inventando que sueño* has been read as a volume of short stories by some critics, as a novel by others. In any case, these works brought the hip Mexican language of 1960s youth culture, as well as its humor (along with many other elements of international postmodern culture), to Mexican literature. Agustín has a gift for using words that, in their context, are so appropriate that they are humorous. He continued fiction writing with *Abolición de la propiedad* (1969, Abolition of the property) and *Se está haciendo tarde (final en laguna)* (1973, It is getting late, end in the lake), and in the two works it is evident that he has no pretention of writing fiction of potential permanency, undermining the very idea of canonic or "classic" literature. His writing also suggests increasingly allegorical possibilities for reading, as is the case with his next works, *La mirada en el centro* (1977, The gaze in the center), *Ciudades desiertas* (1982, Desert cities), *Cerca del fuego* (1986, Close to the fire), *No hay censura* (1988,

There is no censorship), and *Dos horas de sol* (1994, Two hours of sun). His political and historical essays are humorous satires of the political establishment and its institutions in Mexico. Agustín has also written and directed two films: *Ya sé quién eres (te he estado observando)* (1970, I already know who you are, [I have been watching you]) and *La luz externa* (1973, The external light). He has published a film script in the form of a book, *Ahí viene la plaga* (1985, Here comes the plague).

Selected Work: La tumba (1964); *De perfil* (1966); *Inventando que sueño* (1968); *Abolición de la propiedad* (1969); *Se está haciendo tarde (final en la laguna)* (1973); *La mirada en el centro* (1977); *Ciudades desiertas* (1982); *Furor matutino* (1985); *Cerca del fuego* (1986); *No hay censura* (1988); *Luz interna* (1989); *Luz externa* (1990); *Dos horas de sol* (1994); *Amor del bueno* (1996); *Vida con mi viuda* (2004).

Aira, César [Biography] Argentine novelist, short story writer, translator, and essayist, he was born in Coronel Pringles, Argentina, in 1949 and has lived in Buenos Aires since 1967. He began publishing novels in the 1970s, and grew increasingly prominent in the 1980s and 1990s, earning a reputation as one of the leading novelists of his generation in Latin America; his heterogeneous fiction varies in tone, setting, and themes, but emphasizes Argentine history and social life. His early fictions were abstract and allegorical exercises in creating paradoxes. His first novel, *Moreira* (1975) is a brief experiment in allegory. *La luz argentina* (1983, The Argentine light) uses as its point of departure a married couple awaiting the birth of a child. Aira's later fiction tends to explore broader historical contexts. His multileveled *Canto castrato* (1984, Castrato song) is a historical novel set in the eighteenth century in Europe,

and its characters are engaged in an artistic journey that follows opera throughout European cities. It is also a love story dealing with political issues. With *Los fantasmas* (1990, The phantoms) he explores the fantastic and the absurd. *La liebre* (1991, The Hare) is set in nineteenth-century Argentina and is also a humorous exploration of the absurd in human existence: a scientist attempts to track down a rare type of rabbit that inhabits rural Argentina. *La mendiga* (1999, The beggar) relates the stories of everyday people in the neighborhood of Flores in Buenos Aires. Aira tells a very different kind of story in *El mago* (2002, The magician), depicting a magician with special powers.

Selected Work: Moreira (1975); *Ema, la cautiva* (1981); *La luz argentina* (1983); *La ovejas* (1984); *Canto castrato* (1984); *Una novela china* (1987); *Los fantasmas* (1990); *El bautismo* (1991); *La liebre* (1991, The Hare, translation Nick Caistor, 1991); *Embalse* (1992); *La guerra de los gimnasios* (1992); *La prueba* (1992); *El llanto* (1992); *Madre e hijo* (1993); *Como me hice monja* (1993); *El infinito* (1994); *La costurera y el viento* (1994); *Los misterios de Rosario* (1994); *Los dos payasos* (1995); *Abeja* (1996); *La trompeta de mimbre* (1998); *La serpiente* (1998); *El sueño* (1998); *Las curas milagrosas del Dr. Aria* (1998); *La mendiga* (1998); *El congreso de literatura* (1999); *El juego de los mundos* (2000); *Las tres fechas* (2001); *El mago* (2002); *El tilo* (2003); *La princesa primavera* (2003); *Diario de la hepatitis* (2003); *Mil gotas* (2003); *La noche de las flores* (2004); *Yo era una chica moderna* (2004).

Airó, Clemente [Biography] Colombian novelist and short story writer, he was active in the 1940s and 1950s and considered a pioneer Colombian writer of interior, psychological fiction. Born in Spain, he lived his entire adult life in Colombia. Relatively unknown outside of Colombia, he has been compared, nonetheless, to writers such as the Argentine Ernesto Sábato, the Spanish American master of existentialist fiction. Airo's fiction of existential anguish and alienation began with *Yugo de niebla* (1948, Yoke of clouds), a novel in which he portrays the desperation of several characters in a hopeless, negative environment. In this novel a transient couple rents a room in a pension hotel with the understanding that they will occupy the room only a short while. The third-person narrator functions as a character, revealing reality as the characters see it and eventually disclosing the couple's suicide. The first of these characters is the husband of the woman who owns the house, Patricio. He establishes the novel's tone on the basis of his lethargy and minimal economic existence. The frustrations and emptiness of the other characters then follow. The only characters seemingly not suffering from fundamental alienation is Alberta, a maid who finds some degree of fulfillment from her child. The major focus of the novel is the effect of the suicide on the dismal existences of the other characters.

In *Sombras al sol* (1951, Shadows toward the sun) and *La ciudad y el viento* (1961, The city and the wind) Airó broadens the setting of the pension hotel in *Yugo de niebla* to include the city of Bogotá. In *La ciudad y el viento* he novelizes a Bogotá in transition from elegant and aristocratic capital to violent crime-ridden modern city. In this work the civil war called La Violencia is the backdrop for a series of characters—everyday people such as a street person, a working woman, an alcoholic, and a politician—attempting to survive. He also published several volumes of short stories, including *Nueve estampas de alucinado* (1961, Nine portraits of hallucination).

Selected Work: *Yugo de niebla* (1948); *Sombras al sol* (1951); *Las letras y los días* (1956); *La ciudad y el viento* (1961); *El campo y el fuego* (1972); *Todo nunca es todo* (1982).

Alatriste, Sealtiel [Biography] Mexican novelist, essayist, and short story writer, he has been an important cultural force in Mexico in his role as editor as well as writer. His life and his writing have been characterized by diversity. He was born in Mexico City in 1949 and studied both business and literature as an undergraduate in Mexico City, later going to Cambridge University for an MA in Latin American studies (1975–1976). In Mexico he has held several editorial positions with publishers such as Alfaguara and Altea. His passion for film was evident in his first two novels, *Dreamfield* (1981) and *Por vivir en quinto patio* (1985, For living in the fifth patio). The latter also incorporated popular Mexican music of the 1940s; in this book Alatriste looks back to Spanish tradition and its *esperpento* of the Spanish writer Ramón del Valle-Inclán, a short and intriguing text that sets forth questions about human will, chance, and destiny. In 1994 he received a national novel prize for *Verdad de amor* (Truth of love). His more recent work is historic in nature. *El daño* (2000, The damage) is a fictional recreation of the life of writer Franz Kafka. *Conjura en la arcadia* (2003, Conspiracy in the arcadia) is set early in the twentieth century, a historical novel of political and personal intrigues among the new political leaders following the Mexican Revolution of 1910–1917.

Selected Work: *Dreamfield* (1981); *Por vivir en el quinto patio* (1985); *Tan pordiosero el cuerpo* (1987); *Quien sepa de amores* (1990); *En defensa de la envidia* (1992); *Verdad de amor* (1994); *La misma historia* (1995); *Los desiertos del alma* (1997); *El daño* (2000); *Conjura en la arcadia* (2003).

Alberto, Eliseo [Biography] A Cuban writer born in Arroyo Naranjo, Cuba, in

1951, he has published poetry and several novels as well as written film scripts. Early in his career he edited film magazines and later began writing literature in the early 1980s. His novel *La eternidad por fin comienza un lunes* (1992, Eternity finally begins on Monday) deals with a circus that travels throughout Latin America. He gained widespread recognition for his first novel, *Caracol Beach* (1998), which was awarded a prestigious international prize (Premio Alfaguara de Novela, 1998). Son of the celebrated Cuban poet Eliseo Diego, he was paid by the Cuban government to spy on his own father; the son chose to write the reports on his father as coauthor. The family nearly left Cuba in the early 1990s, but his father changed his mind at the last moment, deciding to live as an "inner exile" on the island. Nevertheless, in 1990 Eliseo Alberto left Cuba with Gabriel García Márquez in order to work on a project for television. The Cuban author recounts his personal story in a book titled *Informe contra mí mismo* (1997, Report against myself). He has taught fiction in Cuba and Mexico.

Eliseo Alberto's major novel to date is *Caracol Beach*, the protagonist of which is an aging Cuban who is night watchman in a Florida resort in the town of Caracol Beach. Pursued by the ghosts of his past as a war veteran, he would like to commit suicide in order to escape his circumstances. Incapable of actually committing suicide, however, he decides to place himself into situations in which he will be killed by someone else. This decision leads to a series of bizarre, irrational, and magical events that have made Eliseo Alberto a potential heir to García Márquez as a master of magical realism. His more recent novel, *La fábula de José*, is an allegorical work in which the main character, a criminal, accepts an offer to live in a zoo rather than a prison. Eliseo Alberto lives and writes in Mexico.

Selected Work: *La fogata roja* (1983); *La eternidad por fin comienza un lunes* (1992); *Caracol Beach* (1998, translation Edith Grossman, 1998); *La fábula de José* (2000); *Esther en alguna parte* (2005).

Alegría, Ciro [Biography] Peruvian novelist and short story writer, he is widely considered one of the masters of a fiction focusing on Native Americans, identified in Spanish as *indigenismo*. He was born in the northern part of Peru in an area called Sartimbaba in 1909 and died in 1967. In his childhood Alegría saw the exploitation of the Native American workers in the region where he grew up, and this experience marked his life and later writing. On the farm he heard the tales and experiences from the Indians and mestizos that later became material for his fiction. He studied in public schools with the renowned Peruvian poet César Vallejo, as well as at the Universidad Nacional in Lima, and later joined the Aprista party, which favored progressive social and economic policies. In 1931 he led a failed Aprista rebellion in Cajamarca, resulting in his being jailed and tortured. From 1934 to 1941 he was in political exile in Chile, where he wrote his three major novels of the 1930s and 1940s, including his now classic work *El mundo es ancho y ajeno* (1941, *Broad and Alien Is the World*). The other two are *La serpiente de oro* (1935, *The Golden Serpent*) and *Los perros hambrientos* (1939, The hungry dogs). In these and similar indigenista works, an outsider to the indigenous culture attempts to interpret the culture and in some way contribute to a fair and just treatment of the Native Americans by the dominant society. A major focus in all his writing is the relationship between man and nature. Rather than presenting the overwhelming nature that was most common in Latin American literature, he attempted to write of a nature that man could conquer. In *El mundo es ancho y* *ajeno* he narrates the end of the lives of the Rumi Indians, attempting to present a positive view of community life as well as of Quechua culture in general. *La serpiente de oro* is a plotless series of anecdotes that also deal with the relationship of man with nature. In the 1940s Alegría worked as a journalist in New York and taught at Columbia University. After his death in 1967 his wife published some of his writings posthumously, including the incomplete novel *Lázaro*. He wrote his major work before 1945, but his impact was strongest in the 1950s and 1960s.

Selected Work: *La serpiente de oro* (1935, *The Golden Serpent*, translation Harriet de Onis, 1943); *Los perros hambrientos* (1939); *El mundo es ancho y ajeno* (1941, *Broad and Alien Is the World*, translation Harriet de Onis, 1943); *Lázaro* (1972); *El dilema de Krause* (1979).

Alegría, Claribel [Biography] Novelist, testimonial writer, and poet from El Salvador, she is best known in the Hispanic world for her poetry. Nevertheless, she has also published fiction and testimonial works with explicitly feminist and political themes. Born in Estelí, Nicaragua, in 1924, she did her undergraduate studies at George Washington University, followed by periods of living in Argentina, Mexico, and other Latin American countries. She has collaborated with the Sandinistas in Nicaragua and has been an activist for human rights and especially women's rights in Central America; she has been particularly active since 1980 and the assassination of Archbishop Oscar Romero in Nicaragua. In recent years she has lived in both Nicaragua and the United States. Her poetry has been internationally recognized in a variety of ways, among them winning the prestigious Casa de las Américas Prize in Cuba in 1978 for her book *Sobrevivo* (I survive). She has collaborated on several writing projects with her husband, the North American journalist Darwin Flakoll. Their joint projects include testimonial writing such as *No me agarran viva: La mujer salvadoreña en lucha* (1983, *They Won't Take Me Alive*) and *Para romper el silencio: Resistencia y lucha en las cárceles salvadoreñas* (1987, Breaking the silence: resistance and struggle in the Salvadoran jails). In the latter they conduct interviews and tell the spectacular story of the escape from prison of members of the Peruvian Tupac Amaru Revolutionary Movement (MRTA). In their coauthored book *Death of Somoza* (1996) they recount the gripping story of the execution of Somoza in 1983 by Argentine guerrillas.

Alegría's novels tend to emphasize the magical and focus on the political, and this is the case in the three novellas of *Family Album* (1992). The first story, "The Talisman," recounts the experiences of the protagonist in school. The most political of the three, "Family Album," takes place during the Somoza dictatorship. The third story is more magical, and in all three the past affects the present of the characters. In *Louisa in Realityland* Alegría draws upon experiences from her youth to tell her personal story as well as the story of the brutal war in her homeland.

Selected Work: *Cenizas de Izalgo* (1964, *Ashes of Izalco: A Novel*, translation Darwin J. Flakoll, 1989); *Juego de espejos* (1970); *El detén* (1977); *Family album* (1982, *Family Album: Three Novellas*, translation Amanda Hopkinson, 1991); *Village of God and the Devil* (1985); *Luisa en el país de la realidad* (1987, *Luisa en Realityland*, translation Darwin J. Flakoll, 1987); *Y este poema-río* (1988); *Fuga de Canto Grande* (1996, *Tunnel to Canto Grande: The Story of the Most Daring Prison Escape in American History*, translation Darwin J. Flakoll, 1996); *Clave de mí* (1996).

Alegría, Fernando [Biography] Chilean essayist, novelist, and academic, he is associated with a group of writers in Chile referred to as the generation of 1938; these intellectuals saw themselves as committed to telling stories of ordinary people involved with real life. A prolific scholar and writer, he has written over forty scholarly and creative books. Alegría's creative writing is characterized by a smooth and entertaining development of plot with little concern for innovation per se, and his topics tend to be political. Born in 1918, he was educated in Chile, where he began writing fiction in the 1930s, publishing his first novel *Recabarren* in 1938 as a "novelized biography," which he later revised and published under the title *Como un árbol rojo* (1968, Like a red tree). His early political fiction included *Lautaro, joven libertador de Arauco* (1943, Lautario, young liberator of Arauco) and *Camaleón* (1950, Chameleon). *Caballo de copas* (1957, *My Horse González*) is an entertaining and lively story of a racehorse imported to the United States. He published his novel *Mañana los guerreros* (1965) in translation under the title *The Maypole Warriors* (1993, translation by Carlos Lozano). *Los días contados* (1968, The numbered days) deals with ordinary people in their ordinary lives. These characters become exceptional, however, as the narrator successfully portrays their range of humanity and emotion, their joy, sadness, and humor in various situations. The novel includes numerous interior monologues as Alegría moves with ease between the first and the third person. At the end of the novel one of the characters, Anita, speaks with the narrator-author figure identified as "Alegría," giving the novel a documentary tone. His more recent *Allende, mi vecino el presidente* (1989, *Allende: A Novel*) is his fictionalized biography of former president Salvador Allende. The Argentine writer Mario Benedetti wrote a prologue to his book *Coral de guerra* (1979, Choral of war), which communicates the brutal violence of the Pinochet regime in Chile. His short fiction includes *El cata-*

clismo (1960) and *Una especie de memoria* (1983).

His scholarly writing dates back to his student days; he published an academic treatise on poetry under the title *Ideas estéticas de la poesía moderna* in 1939 and a book-length essay on Thomas Mann in 1949 under the title *Ensayo sobre cinco temas de Thomas Mann*. He is broadly recognized in U.S. academia for his histories of the Spanish American novel, beginning with his now classic *Breve historia de la novela hispanoamericana* (1959). He is currently retired, after spending much of his adult life as a professor of Latin American literature at Stanford University.

Selected Work: *Recabarren* (1938); *Lautaro, joven libertador de Arauco* (1943, *Lautaro*, translation Delia Goetz, 1944); *Camaleón* (1950); *Caballo de copas* (1957, *My Horse González*, 1964); *Las noches del cazador* (1961); *Mañana los guerreros* (1965, *The Maypole Warrior*, translation Carlos Lozano 1993); *Los días contados* (1968); *Amerika, Amerikka, Amerikkka* (1970); *Coral de guerra* (1979); *Allende, mi vecino el presidente* (1989, *Allende: A Novel*, translation Frank Janney, 1993).

Alexis, Jacques Stephan [Biography] Haitian novelist and essayist, he was born in 1922. He wrote in French, but his work is known throughout the Caribbean, with translations available into English and Spanish of much of his work. Along with René Depestre, he was a leader in the *indigeniste* movement in Haiti in the 1930s and 1940s; both writers were interested in connecting Haiti to the rest of the Caribbean and Latin America, ending his nation's isolation and creating an inter-American dialogue. This indigenism produced several peasant novels in Haiti. Alexis's novel *Les arbres musiciens* (1957, The musical trees) is considered a final document of the *indigeniste* movement; drawing upon folk tradition and local tradition, Alexis describes a village in which the vodou priest is an admired leader and father figure.

Alexis is also associated with later post-negritude and post-*indigeniste* writing in Haiti. He participated in the historic First Congress of Black Writers and Artists in 1956, and in this meeting he read in an often-cited manifesto on the marvelous realism of Haitians; he proposed that the rich inheritance of Haitians be promoted as the true reflection of the people. Alexis also promoted fiction that became known as the novel of the land, along with Jacques Roumain. He was assassinated by the police of dictator "Papa Doc" Duvalier in 1961.

Selected Work: *Les arbres musiciens* (1957); *Compère Général Soleil* (1955, *El compadre general sol*, translation into Spanish, 1974); *General Sun my brother*, translation Carrol F. Coates, 1999); *L'espace d'un cillement* (1959, *En un abrir y cerrar de ojos*, translation into Spanish Jorge Zalamea, 1969; *In the Flicker of an Eyelid*, translation Carrol F. Coates, 2002).

Al filo del agua (1947, *The Edge of the Storm* by Agustín Yañez. Translation by Ethel Brinton. Austin: University of Texas Press, 1963) [**Novel**] A classic novel of the 1940s in Mexico, *Al filo del agua* is widely recognized as a landmark of the modern novel in Latin America. It has been called a novel of imminence, for the action takes place "at the edge of the storm"—the year and half period leading up to the Mexican Revolution that broke out in 1910. More than a historical novel, however, it is about patterns of human life. Set in a small village in the early twentieth century, it tells the stories of multiple inhabitants of a tradition-bound village at the outset of the revolution. Yáñez masterfully creates a sense for both the need to hold on to tradition and the desire for modernity and change. The author uses interior monologues, stream of consciousness, and a fragmented structure to communicate each individual's emotional and psychological state. The novel is a critique of the traditional Catholic Church and conventional mores of Mexican society at the outset of a major transformation. The past weighs heavily on the villagers, but Yáñez's probing of reality as ambiguous and complex, as well as his universal portrayal of the characters, make this one of the major novels of the century in Latin America.

Allende, Isabel [**Biography**] Chilean novelist, short story writer, and essayist, she has become one of the most widely read contemporary Latin American women writers. She is best known as the author of *La casa de los espíritus* (1982, *The House of the Spirits*), her first novel and an enormously successful incursion into the realm of magical realism. She was born in 1942 in Chile, and her father's first cousin was Salvador Allende, democratically elected leftist president of Chile from 1970 to 1973. In 1975 she went into exile in Venezuela, where she taught and worked as a journalist. When she was a young child her father disappeared, and the family moved into the house of her mother's parents. There she lived in a home that contained many stories that would be an important source for her future fiction, including books, photos, and old letters. This experience as well as the strong bond with her grandmother was made clear in *La casa de los espíritus*. In her youth she traveled with her mother and stepfather to Europe and the Middle East and later completed high school. She held government positions and worked as a journalist. She directly alluded to the political upheaval of the coup against President Allende in her second novel, *De amor y de sombra* (1984, *Of Love and Shadows*). *Eva Luna* is the story of a young woman who does not have the privileges and advantages of her sisters and learns to survive and encounters experiences such as guerrilla warfare, transsexuality, and passionate love. Her picaresque journey made *Eva Luna* a best-selling work. Allende has been living in the San Francisco Bay area in recent years, and her fourth novel, *El plan infinito* (1992, *The Infinite Plan*), is set in California. *El plan infinito* is a saga of a man's search for ideal love and his attempt to negotiate in personal terms his childhood of neglect and poverty. The two main characters are Gregory Reeves, the son of an itinerant preacher who grows up in a Hispanic barrio of Los Angeles and goes on to practice law in the Bay area, and Carmen Morales, a Mexican American friend who becomes a jewelry designer. She recounts the family history of both, using many situations and characters that American critics tended to view as simplistic stereotypes. Many other readers, however, appreciated her insights into the characters and her unpretentious style.

Her two major novels are *La casa de los espíritus* and *De amor y de sombra*. The former, which has been broadly commented upon by critics, is the story of four generations of the Trueba-del-Valle family, an amalgam of history and fiction, as well as numerous events that have associated her work with the magic realism of García Márquez. Women readers in particular have noted the strong and creative female characters in this novel and Allende's later work. The protagonist of *La casa de los espíritus*, in fact, has been seen as a representative of creativity and hope for Latin America. Allende continues the political history of Chile in *De amor y de sombra*, a novel that concerns other real events in Chile: the discovery in the village of Lonquén in 1978 of fifteen bodies in an abandoned mine.

Allende has also published a memoir of a trip she made through Chile, *My Invented Country* (2003). In her autobiographical personal memoir *Paula* (1994) Allende wrote an exorcism of death—the story of her family as told to her dying daughter. (In December of 1991 the author's daughter fell into a coma and died shortly thereafter.) In her idiosyncratic synthesis of legend, folklore, memoir, and fiction, Allende wrote about the joys of food and sex in *Afrodita: cuentos, recentas y otros afrodisiacos* (1998, *Aphrodite: A Memoir of the Senses*). She has also written a volume of short stories, *Los cuentos de Eva Luna* (1988, *The Stories of Eva Luna*).

Selected Work: *La casa de los espíritus* (1982, *The House of the Spirits*, translation Magda Bogdin, 1985); *De amor y de sombra* (1984, *Of Love and Shadows*, translation Margaret Sayers Peden, 1987); *Eva Luna* (1987, *Eva Luna*, translation Margaret Sayers Peden, 1988); *Los cuentos de Eva Luna* (1990, *The Stories of Eva Luna*, translation Margaret Sayers Peden, 1991); *El plan infinito* (1992, *The Infinite Plan*, translation Margaret Sayers Peden, 1993); *Paula* (1994, *Paula*, translation Margaret Sayers Peden, 1995); *Afrodita: cuentos, recentas y otros afrodisiacos* (1998, *Aphrodite: A Memoir of the Senses*, translation Margaret Sayers Peden, 1997) *Hija de la fortuna* (1999, *Daughter of Fortune*, translation Margaret Sayers Peden, 1999); *Retrato en sepia* (2001, *Portrait in Sepia*, translation Margaret Sayers Peden, 2001); *Zorro* (2005, translation Margaret Sayers Peden, 2005).

Alvarez, Julia [Biography] Novelist, short story writer, and poet from the Dominican Republic, she became a widely read Latina writer in the U.S. in the 1990s. She has taught at Middlebury College and has published a book of essays, *Something to Declare*. She was born in New York City in 1950 to parents from the Dominican Republic, who moved the family back to their homeland when she was three months old. In the 1950s her father was involved in the resistance against the dictatorship of Trujillo. The founders of this underground movement, the Mirabel sisters, were brutally murdered by the dictatorship just after the Alvarez family had moved back to New York City in 1960. Years later, based on this experience, Alvarez wrote her historical novel about the Mirabel sisters, *In the Time of the Butterflies* (1994). Without knowing the language or the culture well, Julia Alvarez attended the public schools of New York. This experience was a watershed for her, subjecting her to a necessarily intense linguistic and cultural circumstance. In many ways this experience led to the eventual writing of her major novel, *How the García Girls Lost Their Accents* (1991).

Julia Alvarez and her partner live in rural Vermont on an organic farm where she continues writing and promoting her farm literacy center in the Dominican Republic. Her most recent work is a book of poems, *The Woman I Kept to Myself* (2004). Among her diverse writings, she has published four novels.

Selected Work: *How the García Girls Lost their Accents* (1991); *In the Time of the Butterflies* (1994); *¡Yo!* (1997); *In the Name of Salomé* (2000).

Alvarez Gardeazábal, Gustavo [Biography] Colombian novelist, short story writer, journalist, and essayist, he has been a prominent public intellectual in Colombia since the early 1970s. An independent and vocal critic of the status quo, he has criticized both the progressive left and the conservative right in Colombia and Latin America as well as the two established traditional political parties in Colombia, the Liberal Party and the Conservative Party. His two main interests as a fiction writer are power and authority. A precocious figure in Colombia, he was publishing successful novels at an early age (his mid-twenties), focusing early on the historical

period of La Violencia in Colombia, a civil war between Liberals and Conservatives from 1948 to 1958. Born in Tuluá (department of Valle del Cauca) in 1945, he was an eyewitness to the brutality of La Violencia, for the streets of Tuluá were sometimes covered with cadavers in the morning when he awoke as a child. He studied literature at the Universidad del Valle, where he later taught. He has been an engaged and controversial journalist most of his career and, in recent years, has been involved in local, regional, and national politics, having served as both mayor of the small city of Tuluá and governor of the department of Valle del Cauca. His politics reflect his independence as thinker and actor; he regularly questions a broad range of Colombian institutions as the nation faces its multiple and ongoing crises. In his childhood in the Valle del Cauca region, deaths and violence were part of his daily life, and this became the focus of his widely read novel *Cóndores no entierran todos los días* (1972, Condors do not bury every day). In this novel he presents a fast-paced fictionalized version of the brutal violence the Conservatives exercised against the Liberals in the region of Tuluá. He demonstrates how a local political figure (nicknamed "The Condor") acquired and abused power. As Alvarez Gardeazábal's novelistic career developed, so did his career as professional journalist and politician. In *Dabeiba* (1972), he recreates a few hours in the life of inhabitants in a small town facing a natural disaster. His most widely read and studied work is *El bazar de los idiotas* (1974, *The Bazaar of the Idiots*), an entertaining story of two idiot brother with magical powers as well as a hilarious satire of Colombia's most revered institutions. In this novel he alternates chapters telling two story lines: the story of the idiot brothers in the Colombian town of Tuluá and the individual stories of a series of unique inhabitants of the town, each of whom suffers from some type of physical or mental defect and will eventually seek the help of the two brothers. Some critics have read this novel as a parody of García Márquez's *One Hundred Years of Solitude.*

In his later novels, *El titiritero* (1977, The puppeteer), *Los míos* (1991, My people), and *Pepe Botellas* (1984, Pepe Botellas), Alvarez Gardeazábal satirizes Colombia's basic institutions and creates situations featuring political power and characters seeking power.

His most innovative novel is *El titiritero*, a satire of how power is exercised in an academic setting. In *Pepe Botellas* he satirizes political opportunism by relating a semi-biographical story of a Cuban exile turned politician in Colombia; it is a study of the workings of demagogery. His most recent work is a novel dealing with drug traffickers and political conflict, *Comandante paraíso* (2002, Comandante paradise).

Selected Work: *Piedra pintada* (1965); *La tara del papa* (1972); *Cóndores no entierran todos los días* (1972); *Dabeiba* (1973); *El bazar de los idiotas* (1974, *The Bazaar of the Idiots*, translation Jonathan and Susan Tittler, 1991); *El titiritero* (1977); *Los míos* (1981); *Pepe Botellas* (1984); *El Divino* (1987); *El último gamonal* (1987); *Los sordos ya no hablan* (1991); *Las cicatrices de Don Antonio* (1997); *Comandante paraíso* (2002); *Las mujeres de la muerte* (2003).

Amado, Jorge [Biography] A prolific and internationally recognized Brazialian novelist, playwright, and essayist who began publishing in the 1930s, he published over twenty novels and numerous other books. Translated into forty-eight languages and published in fifty-two countries, he sold over one hundred million books and was described by the wife of the former president, Ruth Cardoso, as Brazil's "best ambassador." Born in 1912 on a cacao plantation in Bahia, he wrote many novels set in this region of the northeast, drawing upon the strong African traditions in that region and becoming known as a defender of the poor and the marginalized of Brazilian society. As a child, he was educated under the discipline of the Jesuits and later moved to Rio de Janeiro to study law. He worked as a journalist in the 1920s and was interested in literature at an early age. In 1931 he published his first novel, *O País do Carnival* (Carnival nation), which was well received in Brazil. A political activist in his youth, Amado became a member of the Brazilian Communist Party and was jailed in 1936. He was also imprisoned in the 1940s, going into political exile in the Soviet-bloc countries, including the Soviet Union and Czechoslovakia, where he continued writing. Returning to Brazil in 1952, he left the Communist Party in 1956. He became internationally acclaimed for his novel *Gabriela, Cravo e Canela* (1958, *Gabriela, Clove and Cinnamon*) and a member of the prestigious Academia Brasileira de Letras in 1959. Continuing in the satirical mode of *Gabriela*, he published the novelettes *A Morte e a Morte de Quincas Berro D'Agua* (1959, *The Two Deaths of Quincas Wateryell*) and *Os Velhos Marinheiros ou o Capitao de Longo Curso* (1961, *Home Is the Sailor*). He then published one of his most widely read works, *Dona Flor e Seus Dois Maridos* (1966, *Dona Flor and Her Two Husbands*), the story of a lower-middle-class cooking teacher who complements her second marriage (to a pharmacist) with the ghost of her more roguish first husband. From the 1970s to the 1990s Amado lived in a variety of settings in Brazil, the United States, and Europe and continued writing. In the late 1980s he wrote *The War of the Saints* in Paris. Set in the Brazilain city of Bahia, it is a historic tale about the descendents of the love between the Spaniard Francisco Romero Pérez y Pérez and Andreza da Anunciação, a dark mulatto girl.

Amado's supporters view him as a writer of the masses who is a master at depicting Brazil's colorful past, its oral tradition of popular culture and *literatura de cordel*, i.e., popular stories that many Brazilians consider the very essence of Brazilian life in the northeastern region in and around Bahia. His critics, however, have taken him to task for the simplicity of his style and his stereotypes of gender, race, and class in Brazil. His novelistic career is frequently divided into two periods. In the first, from the early 1930s to the 1950s, he was a militant social critic, publishing the novels *Jubiabá* (1935), *Terras do Sem Fim* (1943, *The Violent Land*), and *Os Subterraneos da Libertade* (1954, The underground workers for freedom), among other writings. In the second period, beginning with *Gabriela*, and continuing with *Dona Flor and Her Two Husbands*, he focuses more on entertainment and humor than the direct communication of social and political messages so transparent in his first phase.

Many contemporary writers have pointed to Amado's seminal importance as a professional and aesthetic model, and some of them consider his short novel *A Morte e a Morte de Quincas Berro D'Agua* a model of form. For example, the novelist João Ubaldo Ribeiro considered Amado both mentor and a model. One prominent Brazilian literary critic described Amado as "the solid proof that Brazil exists." He is a member of the Brazilian Academy of Letters and has received numerous national and international awards. Along with João Guimarães Rosa, Clarice Lispector, Antonio Callado, and Autran Dourado, Amado is one of the major Brazilian novelists of the twentieth century and one of the most widely read in Latin America. He died in 2001 at the age of eighty-nine in the city of Bahia that he had made internationally famous in his books.

Selected Work: *O País do Carnival* (1931); *Cacau* (1933); *Suor* (1934); *Jubiabá* (1935,

translation Margaret Neves, 1984); *Mar Morto* (1936; *Sea of Death*, translation Gregory Rabassa, 1984); *Capitaes da Areia* (1937; *Captains of the Sands*, translation Gregory Rabassa, 1988); *Terras do Sem Fim* (1943, *The Violent Land*, translation Samuel Putnam, 1945); *São Jorge dos Ilhéus* (1944); *Seara Vermelha* (1946); *Os Subterraneos da Libertade* (1954); *Gabriela, Cravo e Canela* (1958; *Gabriela, Clove and Cinnamon*, translation James L. Taylor and William L. Grossman, 1962); *A Morte e a Morte de Quincas Berro D'água* (1959; *The Two Deaths of Quincas Wateryell*, translation Emil Antonucci, 1965); *Os Vehlos Marinheiros ou o Capitao de Longo Curso* (1961; *Home Is the Sailor*, translation Barbara Shelby and Harriet de Onis, 1964); *Os Pastores da Noite* (1964); *Dona Flor e seus dois maridos* (1966; *Dona Flor and Her Two Husbands*, translation Harriet de Onis, 1969); *Tenda dos Milagres* (1969, *Tent of Miracles*, translation Barbara Shelby, 1971); *Tereza Batista Cansada de Guerra* (1972; *Tereza Batista: Home from the Wars*, translation Barbara Shelby, 1975); *Farda, Fardão, Camisole de Dormir* (1979, *Pen, Sword, Camisole*, translation Helen R. Lane, 1985); *Tocaia Grande* (1984, *Showdown*, translation Gregory Rabassa, 1988); *O Sumiço da Santa: Uma História de Feitiçaria* (1988, *The War of the Saints*, translation Gregory Rabassa, 1994); *A Descoberta da América Pelos Turcos ou de Como o Áraba Jamil Bichara, Desbravador de Florestas, de Visita a Cidade de Itabuna, para dar Abasto ao Corpo, ali lhe Ofereceram Fortuna e Casxamento ou Ainda os Esponsais de Adma* (1994); *O Compadre de Ogum* (1995).

Amaya Amador, Ramón [Biography] Honduran novelist, playwright, and essayist, he was born in Olanchito, Honduras, in 1916. He was a professional journalist who found ways to denounce social injustice in his novels when his journalistic voice was

censored. Much of his fiction was historical. Writing as a journalist in Honduras in
his youth, he opposed the dictatorshop of
Tiburcio Carías Andino. In 1946 Amaya
Amador emmigrated to Guatemala, where
he wrote for progressive newspapers. He
began writing fiction in the early 1950s and
had to take political exile in Argentina in
1954 with the military coup against the
government of Jacobo Arbenz in Guatemala. His first novel, *Prisión verde* (1950,
Green prison) was a *testimonio* of the exploitation of banana workers. His major
novel was *Con la misma herradura* (1993,
With the same tool), written in the early
1960s and published posthumously. It is a
historical novel of the seventeenth-century
expedition to the area of Mosquitos of two
Spanish friars. *El señor de la Siena* (1987,
The gentleman from Siena) deals with the
indigenous resistence to the Spanish con-
querors. *Los brujos de Itamateque* (1990,
The witches from Itamateque) is a historical novel that tells of a soldier executed in
1843 for practicing witchcraft.

Selected Work: *Prisión verde* (1950); *Rieles gringos* (1951); *Amanecer* (1953); *Con-
structores* (1958); *Cipotes* (1981); *El señor de
la sierra* (1987); *Operación Gorila* (1991); *Los
brujos de Ilamatepeque* (1987); *Con la
misma herradura* (1993); *Jacinta Peralta*
(1996); *Biografía de un machete* (1999); *Memorias de un canalla* (2004).

Ambert, Alba [Biography] Novelist, short
story writer, poet, scholar, and bilingual
educator, she began her career relatively
late as a creative writer after completing
her MA and PhD in psycholinguistics at
Harvard University and bilingual teaching
in the classroom. She was born in San Juan,
Puerto Rico, in 1946 to an impoverished
family; her mother died when she was two.
Nevertheless, she received her BA from the
University of Puerto Rico. Her writings include *Alphabets of Seeds* (2004), poetry, and

The Eighth Continent and Other Stories.
Her early fiction was a reconsideration of
her experience of childhood poverty in the
slums of San Juan and how to reconcile this
past with her later success as a middle-class
academic. She initially constructed this
story in an autobiographical novel written
in Spanish, *Porque hay silencio* (1987). Later
she rewrote this prize-winning novel in
English under the title *Perfect Silence* (1995)
and she was awarded the 1996 Carey Mc-
Williams Award by the *Multicultural Review*. The protagonist of this novel is a
Puerto Rican woman reared on the island
and later in the South Bronx. She successfully confronts the cycle of poverty that her
family has suffered for generations. Ambert
has also published several volumes of poetry, scholarly articles and books, and the
novels *The Eighth Continent* (1997) and *The
Passion for Magdalena Stein* (2004).

Selected Work: *Porque hay silencio* (1987);
Perfect Silence (1996); *The Eighth Continent*
(1997); *Por que soplan los vientos salvajes*
(1997); *The Passion for Magdalena Stein*
(2004).

Amor en los tiempos del cólera, El (1985,
Love in the Time of Cholera, by Gabriel
García Márquez. Translation by Edith
Grossman. New York: Knopf, 1988) **[Novel]**
One of García Márquez's most widely read
novels, this was his first book after having
received the Nobel Prize in Literature in
1982. This novel represents García Márquez's
return to his trademark magical realism, to
his Caribbean coastal region of Colombia,
i.e., the setting of his early fiction in the
mythical town of Macondo. This novel does
not take place in Macondo but in the Caribbean city of Cartagena de las Indias during the nineteenth century. This is a love
story on the surface, but García Márquez's
real interest is aging. His most lengthy
novel (over five hundred pages in the original Spanish), it does not represent as much

of the trademark García Márquez as some readers had expected, with relatively little of the magical realism, circular structures, and hyperbole that have characterized his work. Nevertheless, the ghost of a woman who waves at passing ships and the presence of a parrot who speaks Latin and French do remind the reader of the world of Macondo. The love story begins with Florentino Ariza who, at the age of seventeen, falls in love with Fermina Daza. Fermina's family, however, pressures her to marry the aristocratic Dr. Juvenal Urbino. Fifty years later Urbino dies, Florentino proposes to the widow, and their love is consummated on a riverboat ship.

Amphitryon (2000, *Shadow Without a Name*, by Ignacio Padilla. Translation by Peter Bush. New York: Farrar, Straus and Giroux, 2002) **[Novel]** Padilla is one of the members of the new wave or self-defined *Generación del Crack* in Mexico and he was awarded a prestigious prize for this novel, the Premio Primavera Novela (2000). His collaborator Jorge Volpi (the leader of this generation) has written a novel set in WWII Germany, and these young Mexican writers have made public statements to the effect that the Mexican novel should not be limited to the borders of their nation. This is a historical fiction set in wartime Europe during various periods—from the chaos of Austria at the end of World War I, the Nazi hierarchy of World War II, to the postwar years haunted by Nazi memories and the capture of Holocaust architect Adolf Eichmann in Buenos Aires in 1957. The enigmatic plotline of identity switches and strategy follows the usurpation of soldier Thadeus Dryer's identity by train guard Viktor Kretschmar over a game of chess. Years later General Dryer heads the Nazi's Project Amphitryon, where important members of the Reich are supplanted by trained doubles. Kretschmar's son is

brought under Dryer's wing and it is suggested that young Franz takes Eichmann's place in the gallows in Tel Aviv in 1960, allowing Eichmann to remain at large with a criminal underground at his command. The plot contains suspense and unresolved matters. The use of chess strategy, distant history, and murder is as reminiscent of Volpi as it is of the Mexican José Emilio Pacheco (who wrote a postmodern novel, *Morirás lejos* [1967, You will die in a distant land], set in Mexico, Germany, and the Middle East in the 1960s) and the Argentine master Jorge Luis Borges—who pioneered this type of fiction in the 1940s.

Anaya, Rodolfo [Biography] Lauded by some critics as the the godfather of the Chicano novel and by others as the father of Chicano storytelling, he has published novels, short stories, plays, poetry, and essays. One of the major Chicano novelists of the twentieth century, he has self-consciously attempted to recover the oral tradition of both Hispanic and Native American storytelling. In this way he attempts to relate not only to social and political history but also to mythological understandings of reality. He has been both praised and criticized for his tendency to present the past in an idealized manner, often with a nostalgic tone. Born in Pastura, New Mexico, in 1937, he completed graduate studies in English and in counseling in the late 1960s and early 1970s at the University of New Mexico. His writing represents his effort to reestablish the lost balance and harmony of the Native American regions of North America.

Anaya's most widely read work is his New Mexican trilogy *Bless me, Ultima* (1972), *The Heart of Aztlán* (1976), and *Tortuga* (1979). His work has been compared to the writings of Carlos Fuentes and Octavio Paz with respect to his interest in national psychology and individual identity. He received a prestigious national prize for

Chicano literature (Premio Quinto Sol) in 1972 for his first novel, *Bless Me, Ultima* (1972), widely considered a canonical work of Chicano literature; in it Antonio is the storyteller of the oral tradition. His stories are a rich expression of Mexican, Indian, and Anglo culture on both sides of the Mexican-U.S. border. In this work an indigenous folk healer attempts to heal the psychological wounds of the novel's protagonist, thus fictionalizing Anaya's belief that folk healers, or *curanderos*, are essential to all human communities. In this sense, *Bless Me, Ultima* has been read as a mythical and even mystical text rather than a strictly historic or political one, even though it does contain numerous historic elements and political overtones. In the fiction that follows, *Heart of Aztlán* (1976) and *Tortuga* (1979), he continues with his spiritual mission in fiction; his later work has also been associated with U.S. proletariate literature. In *Heart of Aztlán* Anaya follows the journey or mythic quest of the protagonist who searches for a personal integration as well as an integration within his community. The protagonist in *Tortuga* is in a boarding school and after this experience is a transformed man with a new consciousness. This is Anaya's third novel of apprenticeship and quest. In *Albuquerque* (1995), for which he was awarded the PEN Center USA West Award for Fiction, he follows the development of New Mexico by telling a family story over generations of yet another spiritual quest. Since the mid-1990s Anaya has also explored the genre of detective fiction in the novels *Zia Summer* (1995), *Shaman Winter* (1999), *Jalamanta* (1996), and *Rio Grande Fall* (1996). In his detective novels Anaya regularly uses a charismatic detective, Sonny Baca, to follow a trail of corruption, crime, black magic, and the like. Along this trail he faces enormous challenges within the context of New Mexican culture and his spiritual quest.

Anaya's work as a writer is an attempt to establish individual identity as part of a larger community. Conversely, Chicano community can be a vehicle for inner harmony. He has been a leader of the renaissance of Chicano literature in the U.S. as well as the Chicano novelist whose work is most easily comparable to the mythical overtones found in the fiction of Latin American masters Miguel Angel Asturias and Gabriel García Márquez. The characters in the fiction of Anaya (as in the work of García Márquez, Asturias, and his fellow Chicano writer Tomás Rivera) show the ability to endure despite difficult socioeconomic circumstances, offering a note of optimism. The recent publication of *The Anaya Reader* (2004) provides readers with a broad selection of his writings.

Selected Work: *Bless Me, Ultima* (1972, *Bendíceme Ultima*, 1992); *Heart of Aztlán* (1976); *Tortuga* (1979); *The Legend of La Llorona* (1984); *Lord of the Dawn: The Legend of Quetzalcoatl* (1987); *Albuquerque* (1995); *Zia Summer* (1995); *Rio Grande Fall* (1996); *Shaman Winter* (1999).

Angel, Albalucía [Biography] Colombian novelist and short story writer, she is one of Colombia's leading contemporary women writers and one of the few innovative, postmodern, and feminist writers in Colombia today. Author of six novels and a volume of short stories, she has lived outside of Colombia most of her adult life, residing in several European nations, including Great Britain, Italy, and the Scandanavian countries. Born in Pereira (department of Quindío), Colombia, in 1939, she came from a wealthy family in one of Colombia's premier coffee-producing regions. She did her undergraduate studies in literature and art at the Universidad de los Andes and continued with history of art in Paris and Rome. She worked as a folksinger in Europe and began writing in the late 1960s. She lived in Europe and

Colombia in the 1970s, returning to Colombia in 1975 from Europe to receive the Vivencias Novel Prize for her work *Estaba la pájara pinta sentada en el verde limón* (1975, The singing bird was on the green lemon tree).

Angel's early fiction reflects her experience in Europe. The novels *Los girasoles invierno* (1970, Sunflowers in the winter) and *Dos veces Alicia* (1972, Alice twice over) contain settings in Europe and the latter is her reinvention of Carroll's *Alice Through the Looking Glass*. *Estaba la pájara pinta sentada en el verde limón*, on the other hand, goes back to Angel's experience in Colombia during the period of La Violencia in the 1950s. Her interest in innovative fiction and feminism are apparent in her two major novels, *Misiá señora* (1982, The missus) and *Las andariegas* (1984, The travelers). *Misiá señora* is a three-part novel that tells the story of the protagonist Mariana's life in three stages. The gender issues of this novel include sexual harassment, the role of *machismo*, and the role of the Catholic Church. *Las andariegas* is an explicitly feminist work and her most radical novel to date. It is a search for both a feminist language and a female identity. These novels are part of a project that emanates directly from feminist theory and fiction. Of her total fiction, *Misiá señora* and *Las andariegas* are her most hermetic and feminist works. The former deals with different aspects of female sexuality and gender issues; the latter is a radical experiment that can be read as a double search: on the one hand, a search for female language, on the other, an evocation of feminine identity.

Her most recent novel, *Tierra de nadie* (2002, Land of no one), is a continuation of the spiritual search implicit in her two previous novels.

Selected Work: *Los girasoles invierno* (1970); *Dos veces Alicia* (1972); *Estaba la pájara pinta sentada en el verde limón* (1975);

Misiá señora (1982); *Las andariegas* (1984); *Tierra de nadie* (2002).

Angel of Darkness (See *Abbadón, el exterminador*) [**Novel**]

Angel of Galilea (See *Dulce Compañía*) [**Novel**]

Angêlo, Ivan [**Biography**] Brazilian novelist, journalist, and short story writer, he became a celebrated novelist with the publication of *A festa* (1976, The Celebration), which was awarded a national prize (Prêmio Jabuti). He was born in 1936 in Barbacan, Brazil, and began writing cultural journalism in his early twenties, publishing in newspapers and magazines in Belo Horizonte. Along with other enthusiastic young intellectuals in the state of Minas Gerais, he founded the literary magazine *Complemento*. Angêlo began writing his novel *A festa* in the early 1960s, but had to postpone its completion because of the military coup of 1964. After the coup he moved to São Paulo, where he was one of the chief editors of the *Jornal da Tarde*, a newspaper linked to the *Estado de São Paulo* until the mid-nineties. He worked as a newspaper editor in the remainder of the 1960s.

Two of his works, *A festa* and *A casa de vidro* (1979, The house of glass) are testimony to some of the worst memories of the military dictatorship in Brazil. *A festa* was successful not only among Brazilian readers, but was then translated into French, English, and eventually into German, garnering a prize in Germany. His first book of fiction was *Homen sofrendo no quarto* (1959, A man suffering in the room), which originally appeared under the title *Duas faces* and received a local prize in Belo Horizonte in 1959. His short fiction includes *A casa de vidro* and *A face horrível* (1986, The horrible face). *A festa* tells the dual story of a group of wealthy partygoers and a group of migrant workers that, over time, become involved with one another. It is divided into two parts: "Antes da festa" (dealing with victims of the 1960s military dictatorship) and "Depois da festa" (after the coup). The early editions published in Brazil emphasized the difference in the two parts by printing them in different colors; the two parts are preceded by seven short narratives set in different time frames. The presence of these narratives places into question the genre of *A festa* as short stories or novel. *Amor?* (1985, Love?) is written in diary form; the narrator-protagonist is a middle-aged Brazilian caught in a love triangle of self-doubt as he reflects on his relationship with his wife and his young lover, the latter having gone to Germany during the period he is writing his diary. In 1997 he published a novel for children, *Pode me beijar se . . .* (You can kiss me . . .).

Selected Work: *A festa* (1976, *The Celebration*, translation Thomas Colchie, 1982); *Amor?* (1985).

Anônimo Célebre, O (2002, by Ignacio de Loyola Brandão. Written in Portuguese and untranslated. São Paulo: Global, 2002) **[Novel]** Brandão is one of Brazil's more interesting postmodern writers, and this book offers the active postmodern reader a panoply of claims, texts, and devices. There are many types of experimentation: with fonts, poetic phrasing, and a relationship to popular culture through television and film. The text claims to be a "reality novel" along the lines of reality television. It is also an advice manual for how to be a celebrity, as well as a narrative of a body double for a well-known actor and his romantic past with a woman. Interspersed among the essays on celebrity and the erotic epistles are short histories of anonymous people who missed their chance for immortality, such as Kafka's nurse and Hemingway's friends.

The narrator appears on a talk show named Andrea about sex in all of its varieties. Later he discusses all of the name brand clothing, fad drugs, plastic surgery, and various roles in the entourage of any successful celebrity. The high life of the rich and famous is idolized in a clearly two-sided way, both demonstrating their fear of anonymity and an ironic praise of their exorbitant vices. In typical postmodern fashion, the text questions the ability of anyone to express anything of significance. More specifically, this narrative questions the ability of popular figures to express any meaning—despite their constant pandering to applause.

Años con Laura Díaz, Los (1999, *The Years with Laura Díaz*, by Carlos Fuentes. Translation by Alfred MacAdam. New York: Farrar, Straus and Giroux, 2000) **[Novel]** Fuentes is well-known for his broad-sweeping historical novels, such as *La muerte de Artemio Cruz* and *Terra Nostra*. *Los años con Laura Diaz* is a novel of this sort, following the basic historical pattern of his now classic *La muerte de Artemio Cruz*: this is the story of a Mexican woman, from the Mexican Revolution through the major historical events of twentieth-century Mexico or, more specifically, from 1905 to 1972. This historical family saga focuses on Laura, told in a setting with mysterious characters, lush settings, and the erotic. In addition to her husband, a charismatic labor leader, she has several men in her life (an aristocrat, a Spanish exile, an American), and they are all victims of history; she is more an agent of history and intellect than a real person with deep human emotions and reactions. Her perservance can be understood as the novel's most optimistic note. Fuentes offers the reader his insights into the political failures of Latin America in the twentieth century, this giving the novel the abstract and essayistic quality that has made Fuentes one of

Mexico's most widely read intellectuals as well as the nation's most criticized novelist. This is more a novel of ideas than of plot or character, as Fuentes adds one more building block to his rewriting of the entire cultural history of the Americas.

Antes (1989, Before, by Carmen Boullosa. Written in Spanish and untranslated. Mexico City: Vuelta) [**Novel**] Boullosa's second novel, this is a first-person narrative by a woman who reflects on her childhood and early adolescence, as told in sixteen chapters divided into seventy-three narrative segments. The unnamed narrator is born in 1954, the same year as Boullosa, leading some critics to consider the book a fictional autobiography. Indeed, there are numerous parallels between the lives of Boullosa and the protagonist. The innocence of the protagonist-as-child produces surprising and entertaining observations that have been described as exaggerations or magical thinking. Her upper-class family provides her with a comfortable life of privilege living in her two principal spaces: her home and her school. At home she lives with her two sisters, her father, and a woman named Esther who seems to be a mother figure, but from the protagonist's perspective not consistently so. In the process of piecing together her childhood experiences, which make the everyday seem larger than life, she attempts to understand herself. Although not considered one of Boullosa's major novels, *Antes* contributed significantly to establishing Boullosa as one of Mexico's most accomplished writers.

Antes, o verão (1964, Before, the summer, by Carlos Heitor Cony. Written in Portuguese and untranslated. São Paulo: Companhia das Letras.) [**Novel**] Originally published in 1964, this is an early work by one of Brazil's most productive novelists. After publishing a set of fictions in the 1960s, Cony became known in Brazil primarily as a journalist until returning to creative writing in the 1990s. *Antes, o verão*, a central book in his total fiction, deals with a middle-age protagonist who experiences an isolated life in a house facing the sea, despite living with his wife. A novel of delicate, subtle, and shadowy human relationships, it portrays an uncomfortable marriage of anguish and, eventually, of desperation. Cony fictionalizes everyday rituals of upper-middle-class and middle-age life showing considerable emptiness and touches of cynicism. The author blends an atmosphere of wind and sand with the monotony of everyday habits. With this novel, Cony consolidated his place as a major voice of the Brazilian fiction of the 1960s.

Antônio, João [**Biography**] Brazilian novelist and short fiction writer, he was born in São Paulo in 1937 and is one of the few authors of his generation from a working-class neighborhood of the capital. He was raised in this class setting and is associated with the plight of the urban poor in São Paulo and Rio de Janeiro. He studied theater and film at the USPE (University of São Paulo). In his fiction he uses the street jargon of everyday people, from pool players to bouncers. He is best known for his short fiction written during the military dictatorship: *Leão de chácara* (1975, The Bouncer), *Casa de loucos* (1976, House of lunatics), and *Dedeo-duro* (1982, The stoolie).

His focus on urban themes and use of colloquial urban language have made him an predecessor to the *Geração 90*.

Selected Work: *Leão de chácara* (1975); *Casa de loucos* (1976); *Dedeo-duro* (1982).

Arana, Federico [**Biography**] Mexican novelist, essayist, and fiction writer, he is associated with the group of young writers of the late 1960s and early 1970s identified in Mexico as the Onda. Gustavo Sainz and José Agustín had been the literary leaders of this rebellious group that brought North American rock-and-roll music, drugs, and the counterculture to Mexican narrative. Arana was born in Tizayuca (state of Hidalgo) in 1942, studied biology at the National University in Mexico City (UNAM), and has a made a career as a biology professor at the university level. His creative activities have been diverse, with enough involvement in music to compose for some films and enough expertise in painting to exhibit them in several countries.

Arana has published several books that are best described as "narratives," and the volume that most critics consider a "novel" is *Las jiras* (1973, The trips), which won an important novel prize in Mexico the same year it was published. It is the story of a group of Mexican youths dedicated to rock-and-roll music who search for direction in life. As is typical with the fiction of the Onda, this novel contains the plot and colloquial language of the youth of the period. His second volume of narrative, *Enciclopedia de latinoamericana omnisciencia* (1977, Encyclopedia of Latin American omniscience), consists of entertaining writings of various genres, including short stories and essays, and explores the future of Latin America. His short novel *Delgadina* (1978, Delgadina) relates a young woman's attempted romance under the reign of a possessive and authoritarian father. His essays cover a broad range of topics, from biology and ecology to the history of rock and roll.

Selected Work: *Las jiras* (1973); *Delgadina* (1978); *Yo mariachi* (1991).

Ardiles Gray, Julio [Biography] Argentine novelist, poet, playwright, and teacher, he was born in Tucumán in 1922. He has served as director of the literary supplement of the newspaper *La Gaceta* in Tucumán. Ardiles Gray has published short stories and several novels, and his fictions have been described as sagas. He has also

explored the fantastic in his shorter work. His early fiction relates experiences of growing up and the search for meaning by adults who reflect on childhood. His later novel, *El inocente* (1964, The innocent) also has a boy as protagonist who suffers from the social unrest of 1930s Argentina.

Selected Work: *Elegía* (1952); *La grieta* (1952); *Los amigos lejanos* (1956); *Los médanos ciegos* (1956); *El inocente* (1964); *Las puertas del paraíso* (1968); *Como una sombra cada tarde* (1980).

Arenas, Reinaldo [Biography] Cuban novelist born in Holguín (Oriente), Cuba, in 1943, he wrote fiction both in Cuba and later in exile. He was praised as a child prodigy by the eminent Cuban writer José Lezama Lima and other intellectuals in Cuba. As a youth, he worked in the National Library in Havana. He suffered numerous difficulties as a gay writer under the regime of Fidel Castro; he was imprisoned for eighteen months between 1974 and 1976. Once in exile (coming with the Mariel group to the U.S. in 1980), he was a virulent critic of Fidel Castro's regime in Cuba. He gained international acclaim in the Hispanic world with his first novels, *Celestino antes del alba* (1968, Celestino before dawn) and *El mundo alucinante* (1969, Hallucinations). In *Celestino antes del alba* he tells the story of a mentally challenged child's life on a farm, with ample digressions for the imagination. In general, his novels are autobiographical, historical, and highly imaginative works. His novel *El palacio de las blanquísimas mofetas* (1983, The Palace of the White Skunks) appeared first in French in 1975, then in German in 1977, and finally in the original Spanish in 1980. Two versions of *Otra vez el mar* (1982, Farewell to the Sea) were lost in Cuba before the novel was published in 1982. After his exile from Cuba to the U.S., he lived in New York, remaining consistently critical of the

Cuban government. In his polemical biography he described his suffering in a Cuban prison, where he was condemned for being a homosexual. His posthumously published novel *El asalto* (1991, The assault), like much of Borges's fiction, is similar to detective fiction written in the context of a labyrinth. More specifically, the detective chases a character who turns out to be a consummate sleuth. The protagonist sees his own identity threatened by his increasing resemblance with his mother. Arenas was extremely concerned about the abuse of power in general, however, and power and authority are the central topics of this novel. In *El portero* (1990, The Doorman), Arenas constructs a narrator whose voice is that of the Cuban community in the U.S.; the central focus of this novel is escape from imprisonment. *La loma del angel* (1995, The hillock of the angel) is based on the nineteenth-century Cuban novel *Cecilia Valdés* by Cirilo Villaverde, but Arenas's approach to this now classic slave novel is at times simplistic and slapstick, at other times so elaborate that critics of Latin American literature call it neobaroque.

His major work, *El mundo alucinante*, is a historical novel based on the life of an eighteenth-century Mexican friar, Servando Teresa de Mier (1765–1827). Freely exercising the right of invention, Arenas juxtaposes contemporary and eighteenth-century historical figures, portraying Fray Servando as a reformer in constant conflict in his attempts to change the world. As a dissident who was prosecuted by the Spanish Inquisition, the protagonist shared the experience of Arenas in Cuba. For the protagonist, the world is a prison that operates irrationally, and the only escape is fantasy. At the end of his life (similar to the end of a character's life in *The Doorman*), Arenas suffered from AIDS, leading him to commit suicide in 1990.

Arenas's *Celestino antes del alba*, *El mundo alucinante*, *La vieja rosa* (1980, The

old rose), *Termina el desfile* (1981, The parade ends), *El central* (1981), *Cantando en el pozo* (1982, Singing in the Well, 1987), *Otra vez el mar* (1982, Farewell to the Sea, 1985), *El palacio de las blanquísimas mofetas, Arturo, la estrella más brillante* (1984, Arturo, the most brilliant star), and his novel *The Doorman* (1989) are also a part of his post-Boom production. The narrator of *Celestino antes del alba* is a mentally challenged child who describes his impoverished, difficult life in a poor rural area of Cuba. He and his cousin Celestino imagine a life of fantasy. In *Otra vez el mar* he relates the horrifying tale of a disenchanted revolutionary poet as part of Arenas's ongoing critique of the Cuban government. *El palacio de las blanquísimas mofetas* is a surreal work that relates the real life and the fantasy life of a child in pre-Castro Cuba.

Selected Work: *Celestino antes del alba* (1968); *El mundo alucinante* (1969, *Hallucinations*, translation Andrew Hurley, 1994); *La vieja rosa* (1980, *Old Rose*, translation Ann Tashi Slater and Andrew Hurley, 1989); *Termina el desfile* (1981); *El central* (1981, *El central: A Cuban Sugar Mill*, translation Anthony Kerrigan, 1984); *Otra vez el mar* (1982, *Farewell to the Sea*, translation Andrew Hurley, 1985); *El palacio de las blanquísimas mofetas* (1983, *The Palace of the White Skunks*, translation Andrew Hurley, 1990); *Cantando en el pozo* (1982, *Singing from the Well*, translation Andrew Hurley, 1987); *Arturo, la estrella más brillante* (1984); *El portero* (1987, *The Doorman*, translation Doris M. Koch, 1991); *Viaje a la Habana* (1990); *El color del verano* (1991, *The color of summer*, translation Andrew Hurley 2000); *El asalto* (1991, *The Assault* translation Andrew Hurley, 1994); *La Loma del Angel* (1995, *Graveyard of the Angels*, 1997); *Adiós a mamá: De la Habana a Nueva York* (1996).

Argentina [Nation] The Argentine novel of the second half of the twentieth century inherited a robust literary tradition dating back to classic nineteenth-century texts that are still the subject of discussion in both essays and books of fiction. An avant-garde movement in Buenos Aires in the 1920s, as well as the presence of Jorge Luis Borges and Victoria Ocampo introduced Argentina to an ongoing international dialogue on modernity. Pioneer women writers in Argentina, such as Silvina Bullrich, Estela Canto, and Beatriz Guido, laid the foundation for the strong presence of women writers in the second half of the century.

Argentine culture and literature of the post-1945 period have been affected by the government of Juan Domingo Perón and, later, the military dictatorship. The major novelists of this period have been Adolfo Bioy Casares, Julio Cortázar, Leopoldo Marechal, Ricardo Piglia, Manuel Puig, and David Viñas. Prominent novelists of the post-Boom and the postmodern during the 1970s and 1980s have been Marcos Aguinis, César Aira, Alicia Borinsky, Mempo Giardinelli, Luis Gusmán, Héctor Libertella, Tomás Eloy Martínez, Sylvia Molloy, and Luisa Valenzuela. Of the new writers of the 1990s, Rodrigo Fresán has been the most noteworthy.

(Others noted: Julio Ardiles Grey, Haroldo Conti, Humberto Costantini, Marco Denevi, Antonio Di Benedetto, Martín Caparrós, Carlos Catania, Aline Diancanu, Gerardo Mario Goloboff, Angélica Gorodischer, Eduardo Gudiño Kieffer, Liliana Heker, Enrique Medina, H. Murena, Ernesto Sábato, Ana María Shua, Alicia Steimberg.)

Arguedas, José María [Biography] Peruvian novelist, essayist, he was born in the province of Andahuaylas in 1911 in southern Peru. His childhood experiences in Andahuaylas were key for his later fiction, for there he grew up in the world of the Indians, even though he was white. Along with Rosario Castellanos and Ciro Alegría, he was one of Latin America's most ac-

complished exponents of *indigenismo*: he was convinced that the oral culture of the indigenous groups of Peru had not been captured authentically in any novel and he was fully committed to accomplishing this. He was also convinced that historians and social scientists had not done justice to the Indian cause and attempted to do so in his writing as both an anthropologist and a novelist. He spent most of his life among educated intellectuals in Lima after moving there as an adolescent with his impoverished family. He lived a marginal existence throughout his early adult years, taking any job possible to survive and pursue his studies in Lima's Universidad Nacional Mayor de San Marcos. His association with leftist intellectuals and political groups resulted in his being jailed in 1937 for several months. He began writing in the 1930s, publishing his first volume of three short stories under the title *Agua* (Water) in 1935. In 1940 he published his first novel, *Yawar fiesta* (1941, *Yawar fiesta*), his preliminary attempt at entering the Indian world. The special relationship of the Indians with nature is emphasized by the fact that the Marañón River is a member of the community as a character in the novel. In this work the narrator-protagonist comes to the Indian village as a stranger and then is gradually made a part of the culture. The work that brought him to prominence in Peru is *Los ríos profundos* (1958, *Deep Rivers*), a story of Ernesto, a child torn between two worlds—the culture of the Native Americans and the urban culture of the whites. It is also the story of the oppressed versus the dominant groups. In *Todas las sangres* (1964, All bloods) two brothers are in conflict over the future order of power in Peru and, once again, Arguedas gives the reader a special entrance in the world of Indian culture, as seen from the inside. Arguedas's fiction is rich in oral culture, folklore, and the natural environment of the Native Americans of Peru. A posthumously published book, *El zorro de arriba y el zorro de abajo* (1971) appeared later in a critical edition edited by Julio Ortega under the title *The Fox from Up Above and the Fox from Down Below: Critical Edition*, translated by Frances Horning Barraclough. Arguedas began writing this unfinished book as a reaction to the disappearance of indigenous culture in Peru; he describes the degeneration of a port town where all human identity seems in the process of being destroyed. He committed suicide in 1969 as an alienated intellectual suffering great psychological pain when he ended his life. Scholars of Latin American literature, as well as writers such as Mario Vargas Llosa, consider Arguedas one of the most accomplished Latin American writers of *indigenista* themes.

Selected Work: *Yawar fiesta* (1941, translation Frances Horning Barraclough, 1941); *Diamantes y pedernales* (1954); *Los ríos profundos* (1958, *Deep Rivers*, translation Frances Horning Barraclough, 1978); *Todas las sangres* (1964); *El zorro de arriba y el zorro de abajo* (1971, *The Fox from Up Above and the Fox from Down Below: Critical Edition*, editor Julio Ortega, translation Frances Horning Barraclough).

Argueta, Manlio [Biography] Novelist, poet, and short story writer from El Salvador, he was born in San Miguel, El Salvador, in 1935. He began writing in the 1950s before studying social sciences at the University of El Salvador in the 1960s. Along with Roque Dalton, Argueta was the cofounder of a literary group, Círculo Literario Universitario. In 1969 he received a regional prize for his poetry, the Premio Centroamericano de Poesía, and in 1977 Cuba's prestigious Casa de las Américas prize for *Caperucita en la zona roja* (1978). In 1980 he was awarded a national novel prize in El Salvador. He spent much of his adult life in exile in Costa Rica, writing there for twenty-one years, but he currently

lives in El Salvador. He has also become one of Central America's leading exponents of the documentary writing referred to as *testimonio*, even though he has remained active in film, theater, and children's literature as well as continuing to write poetry. His early novels, *El valle de las hamacas* (1968, The valley of the hammocks) and *Caperucita en la zona roja* (1978, *Little Red Ridinghood in the Red Light District*, 1998), fictionalize the political repression and social injustices of El Salvador. The latter revolves around the relationship of two young lovers in a setting of political conflict. Combining techniques of the *testimonio* and the new novel, he tells a love story and a political story using colloquial speech. The focus is urban violence in the city of San Salvador in the late 1970s.

He is most recognized for *Un día en la vida* (1980, *One Day in the Life*), which has been translated into English, French, German, and several other languages.

Selected Work: *El valle de las hamacas* (1968); *Caperucita en la zona roja* (1977, *Little Red Ridinghood in the Red Light District*, translation Edward Waters Hood, 1998); *Un día en la vida* (1980, *One Day in the Life*, translation B. Brow, 1983); *Cuzatlán, donde bate la Mar del Sur* (1988, *Cuzcatlán: Where the Southern Sea Beats*, translation C. Hansen, 1987); *Milagro de la paz* (1995, *A Place Called Milagro de la Paz*, translation Michael B. Miller, 2000); *Siglo de o(g)ro: bio-no-vela-circular* (1997).

Arias, Abelardo [Biography] Argentine novelist, short story writer, playwright, and translator, he was born in Córdoba, Argentina, in 1918. He studied the novel in France with a scholarship from the French government and has served as director of the law library at the University of Buenos Aires. Arias has published chronicles of his European experience in France and Italy. In his fiction he was interested in the psychological exploration of his characters and occasionally employed the techniques of film to carry out his characterizations.

Selected Work: *Alamos talados* (1942); *El gran cobarde* (1956); *La vara de fuego* (1957); *Límite de clase* (1964); *Minotauroamor* (1966); *Polvo y espanto* (1971); *De tales cuales* (1973).

Arias, Arturo [Biography] Guatemalan novelist, short story writer, and essayist, he has been actively involved in U.S. academia for the latter part of the century. Born in 1950 in Guatemala, he studied in the U.S. and in France, completing a doctorate in sociology at the University of Paris. He has taught at San Francisco State University and the University of Redlands and has held administrative positions, such as president of the Guatemalan section of the Comunidad Latinoamericana de Escritores (1989) and president of the Latin American Studies Association (2003).

Arias has published novels and essays since the late 1970s. His *Gestos ceremonials: Narrativa centroamericana, 1960–1990* (1998) is a study of Central American fiction from 1960 to 1990. He edited a volume of essays on the testimonial writer Rigoberta Menchú under the title *The Rigoberto Menchú Controversy* (2001). His major work is *Después de las bombas* (1979, *After the Bombs*, 1990), in which he tells the story of a child's growing up in Guatemala after the bombing of Guatemala City in 1954. One of the leading post-Boom writers of the Central American region, Arias lives in Redlands, California.

Selected Work: *Después de las bombas* (1979, *After the Bombs*, translation Asa Satz, 1990); *Itzam Ná* (1981); *Jaguar en llamas* (1989); *Cascabel* (1998, *Rattlesnake*, translation Jill Robbins, 2003); *Sopa de Caracol* (2002).

Aridjis, Homero [Biography] Novelist, poet, and essayist, he is one of the major intellectual figures in Mexico today. Known primarily as a poet and essayist, since the late 1970s he has published a number of historical novels, including some that look back to prehistoric Mexico. He was born in Contepec (state of Michoacán) in 1940 and studied journalism and creative writing in his youth. He has been awarded a broad range of prizes and awards, including a Guggenheim Fellowship. Aridjis has studied and taught in the United States. Among his numerous activities, he has directed a movement of one hundred prominent Mexican intellectuals (the Grupo de los Cien or "group of one hundred") to serve as a moral conscience in Mexico for a variety of causes, but primarily as an ecological movement.

Aridjis's best-known novels are *Memorias del nuevo mundo* (1988, Memories of the new world) and *Gran teatro del fin del mundo* (1989, Great theater of the end of the world), both historical works. In *Memorias del nuevo mundo* his main character is Juan Cabezón, who came to the New World with Columbus. Numerous other well-known figures from the period appear, from Hernán Cortés to La Malinche. *Gran teatro del fin del mundo* is set in the period of Philip II of Spain, with language that harks back to the sixteenth century and techniques taken from theater. His later novel, *El señor de los últimos días* (1994, The lord of the last days) takes the reader back to the year ad 1000 and tells the story of daily life in a monastery in Spain as well as the perenniel conflict between Christians and Arabs. *La leyenda de los soles* (1994, The legend of the suns) is a recreation of Aztec myths of life and death cycles and set in the year 2027. Mexico City is inhabited by fifty million people and buried in its own garbage. It is a work of political corruption and ecological disaster.

Selected Work: *El poeta niño* (1971); *Noche de independencia* (1978); *1492, vida y tiempos de Juan Cabezón de Castilla* (1985, *1492—The Life and Times of Juan Cabezón of Castile: A Novel*, translation Betty Ferber,

1991); *Memorias del nuevo mundo* (1988); *Gran teatro del fin del mundo* (1989); *El señor de los últimos días* (1994, *The Lord of the Last Days: Visions of the Year 1000*, translation Betty Ferber, 1995); *La leyenda de los soles* (1994); *¿En quién piensas cuando haces el amor?* (1996); *La montaña de las mariposas* (2000); *La zona del silencio* (2002).

Arpa y la sombra, El (1979, *The Harp and the Shadow*, by Alejo Carpentier. Translation by Thomas Christensen and Carol Christensen. San Francisco: Mercury House, 1990) [**Novel**] Written while the author was dying of cancer, this short (159-page) novel projects the author as Christopher Columbus. It consists of three parts: "The Harp," "The Hand," and "The Shadow." The basic setting is the nineteenth century as Columbus is being considered for canonization, and in one section the protagonist reminisces on his deathbed. In this version of the story, Columbus seduces Queen Isabella in order to convince her to support his adventure. Thus history is moved by passion rather than political or economic motives. Columbus was never canonized, leaving some critics to speculate that this lack of official recognition was an allusion to Carpentier never having received the Nobel Prize in Literature. Columbus sees a monstrous mine of gold, which exists only in his imagination, rather than an unspoiled tropical paradise. A technical masterpiece, *El arpa y la sombra* is a carefully documented and detailed work that is another of Carpentier's tour-de-force exercises in ornate, neobaroque writing.

Arráncame la vida (1985, *Mexican Bolero*, by Angeles Mastretta. Translation by Ann Wright. London: Viking, 1989) [**Novel**] The first novel by this immensely popular Mexican novelist, it was one of the most widely read in Latin America in the 1990s. Set in the 1930s in Puebla, it relates the story of a woman who marries into one of the most wealthy and influential families in Mexico. The book is fiction rather than nonfiction or *testimonio*; nevertheless, the story is based on the life of Margarita Richardi, who married into the Avila Camacho family, of which one member served as president in the 1950s. The narrator-protagonist, Catalina Guzmán, is the woman, and her husband, Andrés Ascencio, is a fictional version of Maximino Avila Camacho, a powerful political figure who served as governor of the state of Puebla in the late 1930s. Catalina narrates her story in a linear fashion, with none of the self-referential play that characterizes much postmodern fiction. She attempts to protest against some of the inhuman treatment of their employees and becomes involved in other liberating adventures, such as an extramarital love affair. At the end of the novel the reader is left to judge whether Catalina poisoned her husband as a final act of liberation or whether she remained submissive and he died of natural causes. The novel is a critique not only of Mexico's *machismo* but also of the woman who acquiesces to *machismo*.

Arreola, Juan José [**Biography**] Mexican short story writer, playwright, essayist, and novelist, he was born in Zapotlán (Ciudad Guzmán) in the state of Jalisco in 1928. He has worked from the age of eleven in a variety of occupations related to the cultural and literary world of Mexico. In his youth he was particularly involved with theater, and he has translated European plays into Spanish. Arreola is best known as a writer of short fiction, and his volume of short stories *Confabulario* (1952) was a seminal book for the entry of the fantastic into Mexico.

Arreola has written one novel, *La feria* (1963, *The Fair*, 1977), set in his region of Jalisco, with a fragmented structure. It contains a series of voices that relate anecdotes, mostly in the first person, and these characters are an Indian who refers to his claims to land, a shoemaker who attempts to become a farmer, a young boy who describes his sexual desires, and several others characters, including some prostitutes. The novel's 228 fragments offer only minimal coherence.

Selected Work: La feria (1963, The Fair, translation John Upton, 1977).

Artificial Respiration (See *Respiración artificial* by Ricardo Piglia) [**Novel**]

Astillero, El (1961, *The Shipyard,* by Juan Carlos Onetti. Translation by Rachel Caffyn. New York: Scribners, 1968) [**Novel**] Most of Onetti's fiction is centered in the mythical town of Santa María; like his role model William Faulkner, Onetti used a fictional place to attempt to create universal experience. In this novel Onetti wanted to expose life as a game with no meaning other than playing the game itself. He suggests that this may be the best for which the human race can hope. The protagonist, Larsen, views life this way, and the other characters seem to share this vision. Larsen returns to his home in Santa María in disgrace, committed to achieving some kind of success by accepting a position as the manager of an old shipyard. The shipyard has broken windows and rusty machinery, but Larsen and his employees go through the motions of operating the shipyard as if everything were in normal working order. Some critics have read the novel as a metaphor for the degeneration and inertia of Uruguayan society of the time (late 1950s and early 1960s). A short novel at 190 pages, it is considered one of Onetti's masterpieces.

Asturias, Miguel Ángel [**Biography**] Guatemalan novelist, short story writer, translator, editor, poet, and playwright, he is one of the major novelists of the century in Latin America. His novels deal with the political and economic history of Central America and reveal a deep awareness of indigenous cultural traditions. He was awarded the Nobel Prize in Literature in 1967, one year after having received the Lenin Peace Prize; there is a general consensus that he received this award primarily for his novel *El Señor Presidente* (1946, *The President*). He was born in Guatemala City in 1899, was educated there, lived in both Europe and Latin America, and died in 1974. He studied law and wrote a thesis for his degree that already demonstrated his concern for social causes, focusing on the social problems of Native American groups. After his political activities led to his incarceration, he went into exile in London and Paris in 1924. In Paris he studied Mayan archeology and moved in the intellectual circles of surrealism, Dada, and the other avant-garde movements in fashion as well as meeting writers such as James Joyce, André Breton, Pablo Neruda, and Louis Aragon. These experiences helped orient Asturias toward the modernist novels he began to write in Paris and eventually published in the 1940s and 1950s. His first fiction, *Leyendas de Guatemala* (Legends of Guatemala), appeared in 1930, and was an attempt to incorporate Indian culture and oral tradition in modern fiction. He returned to this type of project with *Hombres de maíz* (1949, *Men of Maiz*), a novel more about cultural than political conflict. In this work he fuses Native American tradition, magic, and myth.

Asturias's major novel is *El Señor Presidente*, his surreal and experimental denunciation of dictatorships. The book refers to a historical dictator in Guatemala (Cabrera), yet the author maintains a distance from the dictator as person, making him the generic Latin American dictator and the novel of broad political and cultural interest. The atmosphere of oppression is portrayed through an pervasive sense of fear and paranoia. His use of experimental language and surrealist images make *El Señor Presidente* a pioneering work and a rare success at combining the strategies of the avant-garde with an attractive plot and political message. In the end Asturias also offers the reader some glimpse of hope, despite the ugly and perverse world that the characters inhabit.

Selected Work: *El Señor Presidente* (1946, *The President*, translation Frances Partridge, 1963); *Hombres de maíz* (1949, *Men of Maiz*, translation Gerald Martin, 1975); *Viento fuerte* (1950, *Strong Wind*, translation Gregory Rabassa, 1968); *El Papa Verde* (1954, *The Green Pope*, translation Gregory Rabassa, 1971); *Week-end en Guatemala* (1956); *Los ojos de los enterrados* (1960, *The Eyes of the Enterred*, translation Gregory Rabassa, 1974); *Mulata de tal* (1963, *Mulata*, translation Gregory Rabassa, 1967); *Maladrón* (1969); *Viernes de dolores* (1972).

Aura (1962, by Carlos Fuentes. Translation by Lysander Kemp. New York: Farrar, Straus and Giroux, 1968) [**Novel**] One of Fuentes's early novels, this brief work is an homage to the European tradition of the Gothic novel. In this novelette a young historian responds to a newspaper advertisement and goes to the home of Consuelo de Llorente to edit the papers of her deceased husband. The protagonist, however, finds immediate distraction from his editorial work: he is fascinated by an attraction to Consuelo's niece Aura. As the plot develops, the rational order of things seems to break down and the two women, Consuelo and Aura, become increasingly similar. In a dramatic finale to this the novel, the young historian has an affair with the Consuelo/Aura figure. Working with the figure of the double and an innovative use of the second person "you" that

is *tú* in Spanish, Fuentes created one of his early masterpieces.

Avalovara (1973, by Osman Lins. Translation by Gregory Rabassa. Austin: University of Texas Press, 1979) [**Novel**] At the time of its publication *Avalovara* was one of the most radical novelistic experiments to have ever appeared in Brazil as well as being noteworthy in Latin America in general. An outgrowth of the theories proposed by Jorge Luis Borges, Julio Cortázar, and Umberto Eco, *Avalovara* is a series of fragments that the reader has multiple possibilities of ordering. The reader encounters a male character from Brazil who seeks paradise by pursuing three women: the remote and hermetic Roos, an intellectual whom he pursues across Europe, the more down-to-earth and sensitive Cecília, and the enigmatic and abstract woman, whose identity is an ideogram rather than a name, who represents the exotic. Written in an immediate present, the narrative unfolds in a series of scenarios that are frequently enigmatic.

Avilés Fabila, René [**Biography**] Mexican novelist, short story writer, journalist, and essayist, he is recognized as one of the nation's most humorous, critical, and satirical writers. He was born in Mexico City in 1940 and reared by his mother, who was a schoolteacher. Of a working-class and leftist family, Avilés Fabila has been active in progressive politics for a lifetime, inspired by the writings of Marx, Max Weber, Che Guevara, and numerous other Marxist thinkers. In addition to these Marxists, other important authors for his literary and cultural education were Jorge Luis Borges, Juan José Arreola, Gustave Flaubert, D. H. Lawrence, and Oscar Wilde. In the early 1960s he received a creative writing scholarship from the Centro de Escritores Mexicanos, and his writing mentors there were

Juan Rulfo and Juan José Arreola. Avilés Fabila studied foreign relations in both Mexico City and the Sorbonne in Paris. In 1969 he published his first volume of short stories, *Hacia el fin del mundo* (Toward the end of the world), and he has continued writing fiction throughout his career, having published over fifteen volumes of short fiction. His first novel, *Los juegos* (1967, The games) caused a scandal in Mexico because of its strident critique of Mexican middle-class conventions, including those of some of its writers. His well-developed satirical voice was evident in his critique of the abuses of political power in *El gran solitario del palacio* (1970, The great solitary man in the palace). In this novel Avilés also touches upon one of the most popular topics of Mexican fiction of the latter half of the century: the 1968 massacre of students and workers at the Plaza of Tlatelolco. The novels that followed, *Tantadel* (1975) and *La canción de Odette* (1982, The song of Odette), deal with personal and sexual relations—all related by means of the author's trademark black humor. In the latter the identity of the protagonist is increasingly ambiguous as the novel progresses. His protagonist in *Requiem por un suicida* (1993, Requiem for a suicide) is a skeptical philosopher who considers suicide from the novel's first line, and this act is the central subject of the remainder of the novel. Since publishing this novel, Avilés Fabila has remained active as a journalist and writer of short fiction. With the publication of his complete work (*Obras completas*), he has published five novels, three volumes of autobiographical writings, one volume of essays and articles, and thirteen volumes of short stories. His novels have not been translated into English, but his short fiction can be read in translation: "Return Home," translation by Carolyn Brushwood (*New Letters*, 1985); "Miriam," translation by Carolyn Brushwood (*Tamaqua*, 1993).

Selected Work: *Los juegos* (1967); *El gran solitario del palacio* (1970); *Tantadel* (1975); *La canción de Odette* (1982); *Réquiem por un suicida* (1993).

Azuela, Arturo [Biography] Mexican novelist and academic, he came to fiction writing relatively late in life after studying mathematics and after teaching both mathematics and physics. Grandson of the renowned novelist Mariano Azuela (1873–1952), he was born in Mexico City in 1938. He holds a BA history from the National University in Mexico City (UNAM) and has also done graduate work in history at the same institution. Rather than following the common Latin American path to the novel—journalism and/or the short story—he began publishing novels in the 1970s, and his work was quite well received by Mexican critics and readers in the 1970s and 1980s. He is more known for his compelling plots—usually written in the context of Mexican history—than any particular interest in technical innovation. His first novel, *El tamaño del infierno* (1974, The size of hell), is a historical novel that tells Mexican history by means of a family story. *Un tal José Salomé* (1975, A guy named José Salomé) is set on the periphery of Mexico City, relating a story of the marginalized as seen by the protagonist, José Salomé. Azuela moves back and forth between the events of 1968 and the recent past in *Manifestación de silencios* (1979, March of silence), a fragmented and self-conscious text that is a contemplation of the watershed year of 1968 in Mexican political history. In contrast, *La casa de las mil vírgenes* (1983, The house of a thousand virgins) and *El don de la palabra* (1984, The gift of the word) are not as fragmented, although their stories are not entirely linear, either. The former is the story of a house and a neighborhood in Mexico City, Santa María la Ribera, told in a chronological fashion in the most general sense. *El don de la palabra* is a narrative about a forty-five-year-old Mexican actress's present life in Mexico as it relates to her past in Spain. Azuela distances himself from his typically broad perspectives on Mexican history and society in *El matemático* (1989, The mathematician)—the focus is on one individual's anguish and doubts as he faces his immediate past and his immediate future.

Selected Work: *El tamaño del infierno* (1974); *Un tal José Salomé* (1975); *Manifestación de silencios* (1979, *Shadows of Silence: A Novel*, translation E. C. Murray, 1985); *La casa de las mil vírgenes* (1983); *El don de la palabra* (1984); *El matemático* (1989); *La mar de utopías* (1991); *Estuche para dos violines* (1994). *Extravíos y maravillas* (2001); *Alameda de Santa Maria* (2003); *Los ríos de la memoria* (2003).

Azuela, Mariano [Biography] A prolific Mexican novelist associated primarily with the pre-1945 period, he has been widely read in Latin America throughout most of the twentieth century. Author of the classic novel *Los de abajo* (1915, *The Underdogs*), he was a realist and a social critic who questioned the political commitment of all leaders.

Azuela was born in the town of Lagos de Moreno in the state of Jalisco in 1873. He studied medicine and became a doctor and began writing fiction journalism and fiction at the turn of the century. His first novel, *María Luisa* (1907), treated his experiences as a student. He was a supporter of President Madera, a local political leader in his hometown of Lagos de Moreno. With the fall of Madera and the outbreak of the Mexican Revolution, he joined the forces of revolutionary leader Julián Medina (serving as a medical doctor for the troops) and eventually fled to El Paso, Texas, where he wrote his classic novel *Los de abajo*. In this novel he questioned the ideological bases of the Mexican Revolution. In 1949, after writing over twenty novels, he received the National Prize for Literature. Azuela died in 1952, becoming the model against whom many of the modern and postmodern novelists in Mexico would write for the better part of the second half of the century.

Selected Work: *María Luisa* (1907); *Los fracasados* (1908); *Mala yerba* (1909); *Andrés Pérez, maderista* (1911); *Sin amor* (1912); *Los de abajo* (1915, *The Underdogs*, translation Frederick H. Fornoff, 1992); *Los caciques* (1917); *Las moscas* (1918); *Domitilo quiere ser diputado* (1918); *Las tribulaciones de uma familia decente* (1918); *La malhora* (1923); *El desquite* (1925); *La luciérnaga* (1932); *El camarada Pantoja* (1937); *San Gabriel de Valdivias, comunidad indígena* (1938); *Avanzada* (1939); *Regina Landa* (1939); *Nueva burguesía* (1941); *La marchanta* (1944); *La mujer domada* (1946); *Sendas perdidas* (1949); *La maldición* (1955); *Esa sangre* (1956).

B

Bag of Stories, A (By Edna Van Steen. Translation by David George. Pittsburgh: Latin American Literary Review Press, 1991) **[Novel]** This volume of short stories contains nine stories from *Antes do Amanhecer* (1977, Before sunrise) and five from *Até Sempre* (1985, Until forever), offering the English-speaking world a fine introduction to a well-known writer in Brazil. Like the fiction of the Mexican Sergio Galindo and the Brazilian Autran Dourado, these stories are sophisticated yet accessible small screen accounts of human relationships rather than broad panoramic narratives of Brazil. In these fictions Van Steen weaves together textual patterns and social contexts, satirizing some of Brazil's most venerable cultural institutions, including the concept of *saudade*. In addition to issues of individual identity and human relationships, the stories deal with ethnic origin, sexuality, and gender; she questions the very concept of gender itself. In the story "Forever After" the protagonist undertakes a quest for her ethnic roots. These stories offer the foreign reader an insight into why some critics consider Van Steen one of Brazil's most respected women writers.

Balza, José [Biography] Venezuelan novelist, short story writer, and essayist born in Delta del Orinoco in 1939, he is one of the leading exponents of self-conscious, experimental, and postmodern fiction in Venezuela. His writing also tends to cross over genre boundaries; some of his texts are difficult to define as either fiction or essay. Volumes titled *Transfigurable* (1983, Transformable) and *Este mar narrativo* (1987, This narrative sea) are basically essays on fiction that have become his theory. On the other hand, his volume *Tres ejercicios narrativos* (1992, Three narrative exercises) and his volume titled *El vencedor: ejercicios narrativos* (1989, The winner: narrative exercises) are on the borderline of fiction and essay.

The *Tres ejercicios narrativos* were originally published as three separate short novels with no linear plot, no dialogue, and no memorable character development. Rather, a narrative voice communicates an always changing stream of changing meditations on the events as they occur. The earliest of these *ejercicios* is his first novel, *Marzo anterior*. He began publishing in the 1960s and was widely known throughout intellectual circles in Latin America by the 1990s. In *Marzo anterior* (1965, The previous March) the first-person narrator assumes an actual present to relate a complex story of human relationships. An experi-

mental piece of narrative in its time, this novel creates a strong identification between the narrator and the reader. His later novel *Percusión* (1982, Percussion) is a Proustian exercise in using images, words, and flashbacks to evoke the past. In this case the past is the author figure's childhood four decades earlier, a series of circular episodes relating to his rediscovered youth. An underlying desire for transformation and life renewed is evident throughout the novel as well as numerous references to Giardano Bruno and his work on the art of memory. His later novel, *Medianoche en video 1/5* (Midnight in video 1/5) appeared in French under the title *La Fleur de Minuit* (1992). His short fiction includes *La mujer de espaldas y otros relatos* (1990, The woman on her back and other stories).

In 1991 Balza received Venezuela's national prize for literature. He lives in Caracas, where he teaches and writes.

Selected Work: *Marzo anterior* (1965) *Largo* (1968); *Siete palmeras plantadas en el mismo lugar* (1974); *D* (1977); *Percusión* (1982); *Medianoche en video 1/5* (1988); *Tres ejercicios narrativos* (1992); *Después Caracas* (1995); *La mujer de la roca: ejercicios narrativos* (1997).

Bar Don Juan (1971, *Bar Don Juan*, by Antonio Callado. Translation by Barbara Shelby. New York: Knopf, 1972) **[Novel]** One of this Brazilian novelist's most acclaimed novels, its setting is the military dictatorship in Brazil during the 1960s. The main characters are leftists whom the reader sees in action immediately before and after the military coup of 1964 in Brazil. They meet at a bar in Rio de Janeiro in the hope of collaborating with revolutionaries from Bolivia and Cuba. The Brazilian left, however, is too festive in its attitude and too inefficient in orchestrating its plans to ever enjoy any success. All in all, the revolutionaries are too idealistic and innocent to effect political change. The novel is a follow-up to his previous work, *Quarup* (1967), and addresses specific circumstances in Brazil: the defeat of the Peasant League movement, the military takeover, and the resultant devastation of the trade union movement. Callado critiques the individualistic, self-centered motives of many of the urban revolutionaries, yet also underscores the hopelessness of living under the military dictatorship.

Barbados [Nation] This Caribbean island gained independence from Great Britain in 1966, so its national literary production is relatively recent. Writers George Lamming, Paule Marshall, and Kamau Brathwaite have published both anticolonial and postcolonial texts as the foundational figures of this new nation. The culture is both British and African; 98 percent of the population is of African descent, and the spoken language is Bajan, an English creole. One of the island's major writers, Brathwaite, is best known as a poet who has experimented with a broad range of cultural possibilities in his writing, from oral culture to computer-generated visual texts. He also published several books of "proems" (comparable to writers such as Hilda Hilst and Clarice Lispector in Brazil) that use a combination of poetry and prose.

Major novelists of Barbardos are George Lamming, Austin Clark, and Paule Marshall.

Barletta, Leónidas [Biography] Argentine novelist, poet, playwright, and essayist, he was associated with the Boedo group of writers in Buenos Aires in the 1920s who wrote proletariate literature. He was born in 1902 and died in 1975. His colleagues in the Boedo group included novelists Roberto Arlt, Elías Castelnuovo, and Max Dickman; their fiction tended to deal with the social problems of working people. Boedo was generally more concerned with issues of national identity and social class than what they considered the more effete direction of their counterparts in the Florida group of Buenos Aires. Nevertheless, Boedo and Florida were not as much in total opposition as one might think: there was considerable interaction between the two groups. Barletta's novel *Royal Circo* (1927, Royal circus) suggests that the author was as interested in individual psychology as class conflict, and he fictionalizes how working people share compassion, among other topics. He continued writing into the 1950s and 1960s.

Selected Work: *Maria Fernanda* (1924); *Vidas perdidas* (1926); *Royal Circo* (1927); *Vigilia por una pasión* (1932); *La ciudad de un hombre* (1943); *Historia de perros* (1950); *Primer cielo de Buenos Aires* (1960); *De espaldas a la luna* (1964); *Aunque llueva* (1970); *Un señor de levita* (1972).

Barnet, Miguel [Biography] Cuban writer of documentary fiction known in Latin America as *testimonio,* he has become recognized as a pioneer figure of this type of writing. Considered by some traditionalists an inferior type of fiction, testimonial has gained considerable status since the 1980s with the critical and theoretical work of scholars who have successfully argued in defense of the testimonial as a valid literary genre. The writings of Barnet and the Burgos/Menchú text *Me llamo Rigoberto Menchú y así me nació la conciencia* have been important for this process of validating the *testimonio.* In addition to writing documentary novels, Barnet has written critical and theoretical texts about this hybridized genre.

Born in Havana in 1940, Barnet is from an upper-middle-class family and attended American schools until the outbreak of the

Cuban Revolution in 1959. He has written his entire adult life in Cuba, collaborating with several Cuban journals and magazines, including *Unión* and *La Gaceta de Cuba*. He began writing poetry in the early 1960s, publishing several books, the first of which was *La piedra fina y el pavoreal* (1963, The fine stone and the peacock). His two books of documentary fiction, or *testimonio*, are *Biografía de un cimarrón* (1966, *An Autobiography of a Runaway Slave*) and *Canción de Rachel* (1969, *Rachel's Song*). An edition of the latter novel appeared in Argentina under the incorrect title of *La canción de Rachel*.

Barnet's major novel, which has been amply studied by scholars and commented upon by critics throughout Latin America, is *Biografía de un cimarrón*. It has become a symbol of the new literature of the Cuban Revolution. The reader of this testimonial is inevitably confronted with the question of whether the book is really the voice of an old runaway slave or of a young Cuban anthropologist. The book is based on the life of Esteban Montejo, an Afro-Cuban born approximately in 1860 whom Barnet interviewed at length in a nursing home. Montejo proved to be an articulate and witty individual whose exceptional background included having been a slave, a maroon, a laborer, and a soldier in Cuba's wars of independence. When Montejo shared anecdotes about Afro-Cuban religious practices, routine in the soldiers' barracks, his daily life on the run (along with living in caves to avoid being sent back to sugar factories), and the like, the book *An Autobiography of a Runaway Slave* took form. A first-person narrative, this book contains four parts: an introduction, the slavery period, the abolition of slavery, and the war of independence. The combination of this book and the critical studies on it by scholars such as Elizabeth Sklodowska and Roberto

González Echevarría (as well as Barnet's own essays on this genre) have radically changed the understanding of what constitutes "Latin American literature" in the latter half of the twentieth century.

Novel: *Biografía de un cimarrón* (1966, *An Autobiography of a Runaway Slave*, translation Jocasta Innes, 1966); *La sagrada familia* (1967); *Gallego* (1981); *La bella de Alhambra*; *Canción de Rachel* (1969, *Rachel's Song*, translation W. Nick Hill, 1991); *La vida real* (1986); *Oficio de ángel* (1989); *Actas del final* (2000).

Barreto, Benito [Biography] Brazilian novelist and journalist, he is known as a writer with well-defined social and regional interests. Born in Dores de Guanhães (state of Minas Gerais) in 1929, he began publishing novels in the early 1960s and has won several Brazilian literary prizes. His work has been translated into Russian, Czechoslovakian, and German. In his work he portrays class conflict, regionalism typical of the state of Minas Gerais, and a world of clear dichotomies, most frequently between exploiter and the exploited. Barreto's early works, *Plataforma Vazia* (1962, Empty platform), *Capela dos Homens* (1968, Chapel of men), *Mutirão para Matar* (1974, Armed to kill), and *Cafaia* (1976, Cafaia) are those of a writer of political commitment, but one who is also a master of modern fiction; he employs the conventional techniques of plot construction as well as more sophisticated strategies, such as the use of multiple points of view. In *Plataforma Vazia* the main characters go on an existential odyssey, beginning with a train trip, but suffer anguish and defeat. Alfredo and Matilde are the two main characters of this volume, as they are in his next two novels. The conflicts that Barreto constructs between his characters and society are viewed through the lens of a writer committed to social change, as was the case of many writers of his generation who were influenced by both Marxism and Jean-Paul Sartre: Barreto is indisputably committed or engagé.

Selected Work: *Plataforma Vazia* (1962); *Capela dos Homens* (1968); *Mutirão para Matar* (1974); *Cafaia* (1976); *Um Caso de Fidelidade* (2000).

Barroso, Maria Alice [Biography] Novelist of considerable visibility in Brazil in the 1960s and 1970s, she was recognized as an innovative presence in the early 1960s. She has held several administrative posts related to culture and academia. She was born in Miracema (state of Rio de Janeiro) in 1926 and has worked as both an editor and a library director. After teaching English and French in the late 1940s, she received a degree in library science in 1955. Among her other administrative positions, she was the director of the Hemeroteca Pública do Estado da Guandabara (1968–1970) and general director of the Biblioteca Nacional in 1984. Among her prizes and recognitions she was awarded the Walmap Prize in 1967, the Silvio Romero Medal in 1970, and the Cavaleiro de Ordem do Mérito Educativo in 1972.

Her early novels, *Os Posseiros* (1955, The poachers) and *História de um Casamento* (1960, Story of a marriage), were associated with social realism and early attempts at developing literary techniques associated with the modern novel. *Os Posseiros* centers around land conflict; this novel was published in Russian translation with the support of Jorge Amado. She employs three narrators in *História de um Casamento*, the story of a marriage imposed by parents. Barroso's conversion to modernist literary techniques, which critics have compared to both Faulkner and the French *nouveau roman*, are evident in *Um Simples Afeto Recíproco* (1962, A simple mutual affection) and the lengthy (521-page) *Um Nome para*

Matar (1967, A name to kill). The latter is a historical novel that communicates an individual's attitude about history, but it involves a playful sense of reality and fantasy that some readers have compared to the magical realist fiction of García Márquez. Her later *Quem Matou Pacífico?* (1969, Who killed Pacífico?) is a detective novel with touches of ironic humor. Much of her fiction is centered around her invented town of Parada de Deus, a setting of ongoing violence, but always tempered with her ironic tone and sense for life as a comedy. In *Um Dia Vamos Rir Disso Tudo* (1976, One day we will laugh about this) she continues her humorous comedy in a postmodern vein. *O Globo da Morte* (1981, The ball of death) is a continuation of the murder mystery genre, but also contains numerous linguistic experiments. Some of her fiction is self-conscious metafiction; in *Um Simples Afeto Recíproco* and *A Saga do Cavalo Indomado* (1988, The saga of the wild horse) an author figure intervenes to question the characters; it represents a return to the original narrated physical spaces of her earlier writing; the patriarch of Parada de Deus also returns.

Selected Work: *Os Posseiros* (1955); *História de um Casamento* (1960); *Um Simples Afeto Recípcroco* (1962); *Um Nome para Matar* (1967); *Quem matou Pacífico?* (1969); *O Globo da Morte: Divino das Flores* (1981); *Um Dia Vamos Rir Disso Tudo* (1976); *A Saga do Cavalo Indomado* (1988); *A Morte do Presidente ou a Amiga de Mamãe* (1994).

Bazar de los idiotas, El (1974, *The Bazaar of the Idiots*, by Gustavo Alvarez Gardeazábal. Translation by Jonathan and Susan Tittler. Pittsburgh: Latin American Literary Review Press, 1991) **[Novel]** One of the most widely read novels in Colombia by one of the nation's most popular novelists, this work is also one of the early parodies of García Márquez's *One Hundred Years of*

Solitude. Alvarez Gardeazábal's novel ridicules not only the magical world of Macondo but also many of Colombia's most venerable institutions, from its conservative Catholic Church to its plethora of annual beauty contests. The two main characters are a pair of mentally challenged brothers who discover they are capable of miraculous feats, curing the ill when they masturbate. The town of Tuluá becomes nationally and then internationally famous as the infirm make their pilgrimage to the town to be cured. The chapters alternate between telling the story of the idiots and portraying each of the sick characters who will eventually seek the assistance of the miraculous brothers. This was one of the early spoofs of García Márquez's magical world of Macondo and a noteworthy predecessor to the *McOndo* anthology edited by Fuguet and Gómez as well as the *Generación del Crack* in Mexico and the generation of the 1990s in Brazil.

Beleño, Joaquín [Biography] Panamanian novelist and journalist, he was born in Panama City in 1921 and studied both public administration and business. He worked as a day laborer in the Canal Zone and later as a journalist for the Panamanian newspaper *La Hora*. He wrote social protest fiction, and his best-known novel is a critique of working conditions in the Canal Zone, *Luna verde* (1951, Green moon). He was awarded the Ricardo Miró national literature prize for best novel in 1950, 1959, and 1965.

Selected Work: *Luna verde* (1951); *Gamboa road gang* (1960); *Curundú* (1963); *Flor de banana* (1965).

Belize [Nation] A Caribbean and Central American nation that gained independence in 1981, it has a brief and recent literary history. In the early 1990s the majority of the population spoke English, as a large number of people spoke Spanish, and minority indigenous groups spoke indigenous languages. The major novelist of Beliz is Zee Edgell.

Bellatín, Mario [Biography] Mexican novelist and short story writer, he is currently gaining a reputation as one of Latin America's more accomplished younger writers. He belongs to the generation of Mexican writers that became visible in the 1990s, rejecting the writing associated with magical realism and the 1960s Boom. His urban fiction is easily comparable to that of other writers throughout Latin America who have been identified in Brazil and elsewhere as the generation of the 1990s, even though Bellatín has not been directly associated with Mexico's *Generación del Crack*. He was born in Mexico City in 1960, and his creative efforts have been supported by a fellowship from the Mexican government (Sistema Nacional de Creadores de Arte) since 1999; he received a fellowship from the Guggenheim Foundation in 2002.

Bellatín likes to construct exceptional fictional scenarios as the initial settings for his equally exotic characters. Bellatin's characters inhabit a world of solitude and fragility that questions reason. *Canon perpetuo* (1999, Perpetual canon) consists of three novellas, one of which carries the title of the volume. His recent *Perros heroes* (2003, Dog heroes) claims to be a treatise on the future of the Americas, using animals as his point of departure in the fictive construct. If the novel is indeed read as a projection of the future of the Americas, it points to a degraded and dismal future reminiscent of such apocalyptic texts as Fuentes's *Cristóbal nonato*, for Bellatín represents a world in which human beings are reduced to the life of animals. The situation is similar in *Salón de belleza* (1999, Beauty parlor), only in this case the special scenario is a beauty parlor. Bellatín's work, along with the novels of Cristina Rivera Garza, David Toscana, and Jorge Volpi, is generally considered among the most promising of the Mexican writers of the generation of the 1990s.

Selected Work: *Canon perpetuo* (1999); *Salón de belleza* (1999); *Flores* (2002); *Perros héroes* (2003).

Belli, Giaconda [Biography] Nicaraguan novelist, essayist, and poet, she was a supporter of the Sandinista Revolution who currently lives in Los Angeles, California. She has published several volumes of poetry and short fiction. Born in Managua in 1948, she began writing poetry at an early age, which she has published throughout her career. She received a national poetry prize in Nicaragua in 1972 and the Casa de las Américas Prize in Cuba in 1978, establishing a reputation as a poet who could speak to the erotic as well as the political.

Belli is best known for her novel *La mujer habitada* (1989, *The Inhabited Woman*), a work that contains many of the elements of her poetry (the erotic and politics) as well as a love story. At the end of this novel Belli offers reaffirmations for a positive future that goes beyond immediate political conflict. Belli writes with an awareness of magical realist procedures, and *La mujer habitada* makes allusions to García Márquez's language, tone, and the magical realism of *One Hundred Years of Solitude*.

Selected Work: *La mujer habitada* (1989, *The Inhabited Woman*, translation Kathleen March, 1994); *Sofia de los presagios* (1990); *Wasala* (1995).

Benedetti, Mario [Biography] A prolific Uruguayan novelist, short story writer, poet, essayist, playwright, and journalist, he is associated with the generation of forty-five in Uruguay, or the "critical generation." This group of intellectuals rejected the pure aesthetics of some writers in vogue at the time in Uruguay and Argentina and was interested in social reality and its multiple contradictions. Indeed, Benedetti has become the prototype of the "committed" or engagé writer in Latin America; he has been a strident political voice throughout his lengthy and distinguished writing career and has often used dark humor to communicate his message. Benedetti was born in Paso de los Toros, Uruguay, in 1920 and has dedicated a lifetime to writing, publishing over fifty books. His family moved from rural Uruguay to Montevideo when he was four years old, and he considers himself an urban writer of the capital.

Along with his compatriot Juan Carlos Onetti, Benedetti was committed to taking Uruguayan literature from the countryside to the city, a move that meant rejecting the nostalgic and folkloric elements of much rural literature and placing emphasis on the individual in the context of modern society. To a large extent, in Benedetti's case, this also meant a critique of the modernization of Uruguay. He began writing poetry in the 1940s. He gained early renown for his first novel, *Quién de nosotros?* (1953, Who of us?), and his first volume of short stories, *Montevideanos* (1959, Those from Montevideo). His novels *La tregua* (1960, *The Truce*) and *Gracias por el fuego* (1965, Thanks for the fire) were early examples of his skills as a craftsman of fiction and of his commitment to political and social change. His volume *El cumpleaños de Juan Angel* (1971, Juan Angel's birthday) can be read as poetry or a novel—the author has called it "a novel written in verse."

After the military coup of 1973 in Uruguay, Benedetti went into political exile, living in Argentina, Peru, Cuba, and Spain. Among his many writings in exile, he published the novel *Primavera con una esquina rota* (1982, Spring with a broken corner). In recent years he has resided in Spain and Uruguay.

Most critics agree that Benedetti's major novel is *La tregua*, a work with political resonances dealing with a fifty-year old protagonist and his young wife. This novel engages the reader in questions about authenticity in a nation preoccupied with projecting positive external imagery but lacking in substantive values. As these questions are developed, *La tregua* also questions human relations in general and male-female relations in particular. With the Cuban Revolution and an ongoing political and economic crisis in Uruguay, Benedetti became increasingly more political in his writing after *La tregua*.

In *La borra del café* (1993) an individual struggles to become an artist. Opening in Montevideo, the novel describes the protagonist's unstable childhood moving from one place to another with his family. Benedetti likes to redefine and rename the world around him, and the young artist in this book does the same. His recent volume *El porvenir de un pasado* (2003, The future of a past) is a collection of short fictions written in an allegorical mode, along with some poems. Replete with Benedetti's trademark dark humor, the work fictionalizes scenarios that frequently relate to aging and death.

Selected Work: *Quién de nosotros?* (1953); *La tregua* (1960, *The Truce*, translation Benjamin Graham, 1969); *Gracias por el fuego* (1965); *El cumpleaños de Juan Angel* (1971, *Juan Angel's Birthday*, 1974); *Primavera con una esquina rota* (1982); *La borra del café* (1993).

Benítez Rojo, Antonio [Biography] Cuban novelist and essayist, he was in exile in the U.S. Since leaving Cuba in 1980 until his recent death in 2004, he served on the faculty at Amherst College. Along with Guillermo Cabrera Infante and Severo Sarduy, he belongs to the first generation of Cuban writers in exile from the Cuban Revolution. Since the 1960s he had been an internationally recognized intellectual in Cuba, both as a scholar and as a writer; consequently, his exile to the U.S. was a major event for Latin American intellectuals.

Born in 1931, Benítez Rojo gained critical acclaim in Cuba with the publication of the prize-winning volumes of short stories *Tute de reyes* (1967) and *El escudo de hojas secas* (1969). At the time he was writing under the sign of Julio Cortázar, combining the Argentine writer's fantastic (and blurring the boundary between the fantastic and the real) with his own interest in Caribbean cultural history. Some critics consider him the best short story writer produced by the Cuban Revolution.

As well as a premier fiction writer, Benítez Rojo is known as a cultural critic of the Caribbean region. His widely cited essay *La isla que se repite* (1989, *The Repeating Island*, 1992) has gained him considerable renown as one of the most lucid and informed critics of Caribbean culture. In this work Benítez Rojo attempts to define Caribbean culture within not only a historical and cultural context but also the context of discussions of international postmodern culture; he views Caribbean culture as a postmodern culture of performance that resists modernity. Among his books of fiction his historical treatment of the Spanish conquest in his novel *El mar de las lentejas* (1979, *Sea of Lentils*) is his best known. Other fiction to appear in English is a volume of short stories titled *The Magic Dog and Other Stories* (1990). Benítez Rojo can also be read in English in the more recent *A View from the Mangrove* (translation James Maraniss, 1998).

Selected Work: *Los inquilinos* (1976); *El mar de las lentejas* (1979, *Sea of Lentils*, translation James Maraniss, 1990); *Mujer en traje de batalla* (2001).

Benjamin (1995, *Benjamin*, by Chico Buarque. Translation by Clifford E. Landers. São Paulo: Companhia das Letras, 1997) [**Novel**] Chico Buarque was first known as a popular singer and most widely recognized in Latin America in that sphere. He composed and sang music against the dictatorship in Brazil (1964–1989). His second novel, *Benjamin*, uses the dictatorship as a backdrop to the complex and engaging story of an aging former leftist activist, now a fifty-year-old model named Benjamin. In the 1960s Benjamin lost his lover, Castana Beatriz, who was also a leftist activist assassinated by government special forces. Benjamin becomes obsessed with the memory of Castana Beatriz and, some three decades later, equally obsessed with a young woman, Ariela Masé, who resembles Castana Beatriz physically and might be her daughter. Benjamin attempts to establish a relationship with Ariela, but in the end she leades him to an assassination identical to the one suffered by Castana Beatriz. The novel's circular structure and other details communicate a cynical attitude to the possibilities of social and political change. The postdictatorship nation is empty of values and openly consumerist in orientation.

Berkeley em Bellagio (2002, Berkeley in Bellagio, by João Gilberto Noll. Written in Portuguese and untranslated. Rio de Janeiro: Objetiva) [**Novel**] Noll is one of Brazil's most accomplished postmodern novelists, and in this work the narrator is a Brazilian writer with a fellowship in Bellagio, Italy, to write a novel. In Bellagio he has a relationship with other artists and scholars and imagines life back in his hometown of Porto Alegre and in Berkeley, California, both of which are part of his past experi-

ence. With no continuous plotline, the narrative consists of a series of digressions about a variety of topics, above all, his concern for the loss of his past and his native tongue (*língua materna*) both as a vehicle of communication and as the vehicle of his creative writing as a novelist. The story is told alternating between first and third person. In this novel a narcissistic and openly gay writer figure occasionally admits that he sometimes forgets his narrative line and that nothing really "happens" to build a consistent plot. Nevertheless, Noll's concerns with language and culture make him one of the most interesting and provocative novelists writing in Brazil in the early twenty-first century.

Besieged City (See *Cidade Sitiada, A,* by Clarice Lispector) [**Novel**]

Beso de la mujer araña, El (1976, *Kiss of the Spider Woman,* by Manuel Puig. Translation by Thomas Colchie. New York: Knopf, 1979) [**Novel**] Along with *Betrayed by Rita Hayworth,* this fourth novel is one of the two most widely acclaimed of Puig's novels. Gay themes had appeared in a variety of subtle ways in Latin American literature well before the publication of *Kiss of the Spider Woman,* but this novel was one of the seminal Latin American novels to open the topic to a broad and mainstream readership. Puig explores the power of politics and gender, as well as how the process of sexual liberation and political liberation can be parallel. The plot involves the relationship between two men imprisoned in an unnamed Latin American nation (similar to Argentina) during a period of political repression: a homosexual window dresser and a dedicated leftist urban guerrilla. Their identities seem fixed at the beginning of the novel, yet blur by the end, questioning the viability of fixed sexual and political identities. The author includes an elaborate set of nine unnumbered footnotes in chapters 3 through 11 of this sixteen-chapter novel; these footnotes on sexuality and gender invite the reader to contemplate these issues in the broadest context, beyond the immediate circumstance of the two characters.

Bins, Patricia [Biography] A Brazilian novelist, short story writer, translator, artist, and journalist, she was born in Rio de Janeiro in 1930, where she now lives. When she was a child her family moved to Belo Horizonte, where she studied English language and culture. As an adolescent, she was then reared in Porto Alegre and received a traditional education that was European in its orientation. Bins has spoken of the contrasts in her life and work; for example, the contrast between her interior, European life and the exterior, Brazilian social life of her youth. She later studied English at the University of Michigan. Bins began journalistic writing in the 1970s and published her first book of short stories, *O Assassinato dos Pombos* (The assassination of the pigeons) in 1982. It is a volume of short fictions and chronicles everyday life. She has written occasional pieces for the newspaper *Correio do Povo* as well as literary and cultural journalism for other newspapers and magazines in Brazil.

Bins's first novel, *Jogo de Fiar* (1983, Game of confidence), begins a series of works that are interconnected. *Antes que o Amor Acabe* (1984, Before love ends) and *Janela do Sonho* (1986, Window of dreams) continue her saga of intimate human relationships, the contradictions between psychological/emotional life and exterior/social life, and the very act of writing novels. In general, her fiction deals with human relations, and her novel *Pele Nua do Espelho* (1989, Nude skin of the mirror) is

an intimate love story that also involves memory. *Sarah e os Anjos* (1993, Sarah and the angels) questions the categories of sanity and insanity; in it Bins uses experiments with the exploration of dreams as well as techniques such as mise en abyme. In *Caçada de Memórias* (1995, Hunt for memories) the male narrator-protagonist searches through the past, present, and future in dealing with his passionate relationship with three women. Several of the topics and interests of her previous novels, including insanity and the passionate feelings a character unilaterally feels toward others, appear in this work.

Bins's work is comparable to the small screen novelists from Mexico, such as Sergio Galindo and Juan García Ponce, as well as the work of Clarice Lispector from Brazil and Elena Garro from Mexico.

Selected Work: *Jogo de Fiar* (1983); *Antes que o Amor Acabe* (1984); *Janela do Sonho* (1986); *Pele Nua do Espelho* (1989, translated into Spanish as *La piel desnuda del espejo*, 1995); *Theodora* (1991); *Sarah e os anjos* (1993); *Caçada de memórias* (1995); *Instantes do Mundo* (1999).

Biografía de un cimarrón (1966, *Autobiography of a Runaway Slave*, by Miguel Barnet. Translation by Jocasta Innes. New York: Pantheon, 1968) **[Novel]** Based on the life of a runaway slave in Cuba, this book has become a classic *testimonio* in Latin America. It is the product of the real person Esteban Montejo telling his exceptional life story to author Miguel Barnet, who recreated the story as a first-person narrative. The book's four formal divisions offer an introduction to Montejo's life and circumstances, a description of the slavery period, the abolition of slavery, and the war of independence. Before the publication of this book the testimonial suffered from an uncertain staus in academic circles. *Biografía* *de un cimarrón* has become a watershed work in changing the perception that the testimonial is an inferior genre.

Bioy Casares, Adolfo [Biography] Argentine novelist, short story writer, and essayist, he was a well-known collaborator of Jorge Luis Borges. Along with Borges he had an enormous impact on Argentine literature and the modernization of Latin American fiction in general. He is frequently described as either a fantastic or metaphysical writer. For Bioy Casares and Borges Latin American literature of the 1920s and 1930s was often suffering from an excessive nationalism and a narrow provincialism. These two Argentine intellectuals looked not only to Anglo-American modernism for a change of direction for Argentine literature: they looked to surrealism and the other movements of the European avant-garde for both models and inspiration to freely exercise the right of invention in Latin American literature. Borges is generally more widely recognized in this role; nevertheless, Borges published his *Ficciones* in 1944, several years after Bioy Casares's *La invención de Morel* (*The Invention of Morel*), which first appeared in Spanish in 1937.

Bioy Casares was born in Buenos Aires in 1914, the only child of wealthy parents. In the early 1940s he began playful and inventive collaborative writing projects with Borges. Undeniably, Borges was the mentor and master in the relationship, but the benefits of their collaboration were mutual. From his youth Bioy Casares traveled regularly to France, the home of his father, so his life and his writings were the very definition of being cosmopolitan. His post-WWII fiction includes *Plan de evasión* (1945, *A Plan for Escape*) and *Sueño de los héroes* (1954, *The Dream of Heroes*). Both novels postulate invented realities as part of an attempt to solve problems in the real world. Later he published *Diario de la guerra del cerdo* (1969, *Diary of the War of the Pig*) and *Dormir al sol* (1973, *Asleep in the Sun*). According to Bioy Casares himself, he "suffered" from the influences of surrealism and the techniques of James Joyce. In the mid-1970s Bioy Casares began writing a type of diary that consisted of brief notes about such diverse and unrelated topics as his dreams, conversations, historical memory, films he had recently seen, the uses and abuses of language, abstract philosophical and literary reflections, the death of his dogs, and his numerous relationships with different women. These notes were published posthumously in a lengthy (888-page) volume edited by Daniel Martino titled *Descanso de caminantes* (2001, The walkers' rest). In these notes Bioy Casares makes numerous references to the writers who were his literary company, including Borges, Silvina Bullrich, Ernesto Sábato, Estela Canto, and Eduardo Mallea. In this lengthy volume Bioy Casares freely exhibits the digressive tendencies and gentle irony that characterize much of his fiction.

Scholars and the author himself agreed that his major novel was *La invención de Morel*, his fantastic tale about a fugitive from Venezuela who writes a diary and finds strange inhabitants who are three-dimensional movie images. He falls in love with a woman named Faustine and activates a machine to situate himself near her, thus making himself as lifeless as she. This novella (120 pages in length) has been read as Bioy's homage to the genre of film as well as a parable of the relationship between reader and text. In a provocative prologue to this book, Borges described it as a "perfect" novel, an ironic comment, given the fact that Bioy Casares's fiction was considered far from perfect, taking into account the predominant norms for fiction in the 1940s. With this novel and most of his writings, Bioy Casares was fundamentally misunderstood by his contemporaries in Latin America. Even though his major novel was published before 1945, its major impact was after 1945—in the 1960s and 1970s. Several young writers of the 1990s—such as Rodrigo Fresán and Edmundo Paz Soldán—refer to Bioy Casares as the pioneer writer concerned with technology and art.

Selected Work: *La invención de Morel* (1937, *The Invention of Morel and Other Stories*, translation Ruth L. C. Simms, 1964); *Plan de evasión* (1945, *A Plan for Escape*, translation Suzanne Jill Levine, 1975); *Sueño de los héroes* (1954, *The Dream of Heroes*, translation Diana Thorold, 1988); *Diario de la guerra del cerdo* (1969, *Diary of the War of the Pig*, translation G. Yates and D. A. Woodruff, 1972); *Dormir al sol* (1973, *Asleep in the Sun*, translation Suzanne Jill Levine, 1978); *La aventura de un fotógrafo en La Plata* (1985, *The Adventures of a Photographer in La Plata*, translation Suzanne Jill Levine, 1991).

Bless Me, Ultima (1972, Rudolfo Anaya. Written in English. Berkeley: TQS, 1972) [**Novel**] A key novel of the period of the flowering of the Chicano novel during the 1970s, it is widely considered a canonical text of the modern Chicano novel. The author believes that folk healers—*curanderos*—are important members of all communities, and in this novel a *curandera* named Ultima attempts to heal the psychological wounds of the protagonist, Antonio. He is seven years old when his apprenticeship begins, and during the year of narrative time that Ultima spends with Antonio's family the child experiences the loss of childhood innocence, the physical brutality of the adult world, the meaning of evil, doubts about his own Catholic faith, and a type of reconciliation with Ultima herself. Ultima has been described as an earth mother figure as well as a universal spirit, and she feels a spiritual tie with Antonio at the end. Anaya has a gift for describing rural New Mexican landscape in his fiction, and in this novel there are multiple allusions to traditional indigenous gods, ancient gardens, and the like, in a setting in which the separation between man and nature has not yet taken place. The novel contains numerous historical notes and political overtones, but some readers and critics have observed the mythical and mystical aspects of the work. *Bless me, Ultima* is one of the best-selling Chicano works; Anaya shares with Gabriel García Márquez and Sandra Cisneros the ability to create fictions that are accessible to both the cultural community he represents and a broader literary establishment. His symbolic patterns and mythic structures have been appreciated by a broad range of readers, including a readership in Latin America for this novel in its Spanish translation.

Boda del poeta, La (1999, Poet's wedding, by Antonio Skármeta. Written in Spanish and untranslated. Barcelona: Plaza y Janés) [**Novel**] One of the recent novels by one of Latin America's major novelists of the generation often associated with the post-Boom, it contains a prologue in which the author claims to be related to one of the novel's main characters, Esteban Coppeta. Based on childhood memories from the city of Antofogasta in northern Chile, Skármeta also tells the sad story of the island of Gema, a small community in the Adriatic Sea. Most of the action takes place in the second decade of the twentieth century, just before World War I. It follows the lives of the most distinguished inhabitants of the poverty-stricken island: the Coppeta brothers (Reino and Esteban), Alia Emar (the beautiful woman of the island), and Jerónimo Franck (Austrian in self exile and owner of a story, El Europeo). The marriage of Emar and Franck is the central event of the novel and the axis around which the rest of the plot evolves. The narrative covers a variety of historical moments in the island, but all are in reference to this "party of the century." Esteban Coppeta is the poet who has an affair with Emar and then finds refuge in Chile. Skármeta is a master storyteller, and this novel, which questions the veracity of history, is full of spicy anecdotes and sexual encounters to keep the interest of a broad range of readers.

Bolaño, Roberto [Biography] Chilean novelist, short story writer, and poet, he was born in Santiago, Chile, in 1953. His family moved to Mexico City in 1968, where he attended school until he was fifteen. The writers he most admired in his youth were the Mexican poet Efraím Huerta and the Chilean poet Enrique Lihn. The Bolaño family moved back to Chile in 1972, but, with the military coup of 1973, Roberto left his homeland permanently, moving first to Mexico and then to Spain. He began writing poetry in the mid-1970s. He was rapidly gaining a reputation as one of the most talented writers of his generation in Chile—and increasingly recognized in Latin America and Spain—when he died tragically in 2003. Slightly older than the writers of the generation of the 1990s or McOndo group, yet slightly younger than the postmodern group of Diamela Eltit, Ricardo Piglia, and their contemporaries, Bolaño wrote as a relatively solitary and unheralded figure most of his life.

In addition to his impressive group of novels, he published fine short fiction, including a volume of short stories titled *Llamadas telefónicas* (1997, Telephone calls). In 1998 he was awarded the important Premio Herralde de Novela in Spain, providing him with more visibility in the Hispanic world than he had ever enjoyed. Much of his postmodern fiction is a rewriting of the existentialist overtones of the Uruguayan Juan Carlos Onetti and and the Argentine Daniel Moyano as well as a dialogue with

international postmodern culture. His characters—many of whom are literary and/or historical figures—inhabit a contradictory and absurd fictional universe, suffer from different forms of delirium, and tend to have extreme personalities; they contemplate life in Chile, national culture, and more personal themes, such as the meanings of friendship, memory, and death. *La literatura nazi en América* (1996, Nazi literature in America) is a narrative that can be read as a novel or short fiction; it consists of a series of fictional entries in a literary dictionary of Nazi writers and, consequently, is a parody of much literary history as well as a political statement. *Estrella distante* (1996, Distant Star) also has a political referent, using the Chile of President Salvador Allende in 1971–72 as its basic setting and focusing on two unorthodox characters: a poet from Concepción (Chile) and a writer who copies verses from the Bible. Eventually, the two characters blend together with mixed identities, in Borgesian bifurcations. Unlikely crimes and surprising relationships are the centerpieces of two related novels, *Los detectives salvajes* (1998, The savage detectives) and *Amuleto* (1999, Amulet), both of which were much heralded by critics in Spain and Latin America. In *Los detectives salvajes* two detectives search for a writer who disappeared after the Mexican Revolution, although this search takes place decades after this civil war. Given its length, its multiple characters who appear on different continents, and Bolaño's interest in experimentation, *Los detectives salvajes* has been compared to novels such as Cortázar's *Rayuela*, Marechal's *Adán Buenosayres,* and Lezama Lima's *Paradiso.*

In his *Nocturno de Chile* (2000, By Night in Chile) Bolaño pushes the limits of the absurd and, in his internal reverie, often falls into a surreal mode with encounters as unlikely as a Marxist teacher giving the

Chilean dictator Pinochet lessons in politics. The protagonist, who is the teacher and an aging priest, literary critic, and poet, travels to Europe and back to Chile. This is a "writer's novel" par excellence: the narrator is in dialogue with some of the nation's major writers, including the Nobel laureate poet Pablo Neruda and the now deceased novelist José Donoso. In this work Bolaño weaves between the real world of post-Allende's Chile and the surreal world of the protagonist's dreams. An aging writer, priest, and teacher, Sebastián Urrutia Lacroix, travels from Chile to Europe and back while contemplating nature, urban society, and the culture of contemporary Chile. Eventually, he confronts paradoxes of life and death. This is one of the more intriguing meditations to appear in Latin America on the role of literature and national culture since Ricardo Piglia's *Artificial Respiration* (originally published in 1979 in Spanish). With *Una novelita lumpen* (2002, A lumpen novella) Bolaño changes the setting to Rome, so his typically extreme characters are now engaged in new types of experiences, including the discovery of some of the best and worst aspects of sexuality.

Selected Work: Consejos de un discípulo de Morrison a un fanático de Joyce (1984); *La pista de hielo* (1993); *La senda de los elefantes* (1994); *Estrella distante* (1996 *Distant Star,* translation Chris Andrews, 2004); *Literatura nazi en América* (1996); *Los detectives salvajes* (1998); *Amuleto* (1999); *Nocturno de Chile* (2000, *By Night in Chile,* translation Chris Andrews, 2003); *Una novelita lumpen* (2002); *El gaucho insufrible* (2003).

Bolivia [Nation] The Bolivian novel of the second half of the twentieth century inherited a literary tradition dating back to the nineteenth century. The Bolivian mining industry and social conflict have been a constant presence as well as the indigenous population. Augusto Céspedes (b. 1904) wrote realist and critical novels about working conditions in the mines.

Noteworthy novelists in recent years have been Renato Prada Oropeza, Edmundo Paz Soladán, and José Montes.

Bombal, María Luisa [Biography] Chilean novelist and short story writer, she was one of the pioneer women novelists in Latin America during the 1930s and 1940s. Her reputation has grown throughout the latter half of the twentieth century. She was born in 1910 and died in 1980. Some critics have pointed to her fiction of the 1930s as having anticipated the magical realism of Spanish American literature popularized decades later. She spent her adolescence in France, returning to Chile in 1931 after pursuing studies in French literature at the Sorbonne. During her stay in France she attended lectures given by Paul Valéry and participated in a variety of other cultural activities, including a literary workshop in which she wrote a story in French and was awarded a prize. In her youth she also practiced creative writing in Spanish and read many of the Western classics. In 1933 she moved to Buenos Aires, where she joined the group associated with the prestigious Argentine literary magazine *Sur,* befriending its director, Victoria Ocampo.

Bombal sets her works in *casas de campo* (large rural homes of the landed elite) in Chile, but without any of the folkloric overtones of Latin American rural fiction of the period. Thus she avoids nostalgia and uses images of water, mist, and dampness as consistent metaphors for her protagonists' unhappiness and alienation. The mist also creates an atmosphere of uncertainty.

Bombal is best known for her novel *La última niebla* (1934, *House of Mist*), which appeared in English as one of two volumes under the title *House of Mist and the*

Shouded Woman. As a response to the predominantly realist modes of writing in vogue in Latin America at the time, *La última niebla* was a relatively avant-garde work exploring female subjectivity. It deals with a female protagonist and her fantasized lover; she compensates for a disappointing marriage by remembering an intense love affair. The reader sees reality only as the protagonist sees it, without the settings of the realist novel. The leitmotif of mist predominates, serving as the element between the real world and the fantasy world of the protagonist. Although she wrote before 1945, her major impact was after World War II. A pioneer woman writer in Latin America, her work is comparable to the early fiction of the Brazilian Clarice Lispector and the Mexican Elena Garro.

Selected Work: *La última niebla* (1934, *House of Mist and the Shouded Woman*, translation the author, 1947, 1948); *La amortajada* (1938).

Bonasi, Fernando [Biography] Brazilian novelist, playwright, film director, screenwriter, and poet, he was born in 1962 in São Paulo. Bonasi is part of the youngest generation of Latin American writers, born since 1955, that Brazilian critics such as Nelson de Oliveira have identified as the generation of the 1990s. In addition to working as a journalist, he has written several pieces of theater and directed several film and television productions. His short film *Faça Você Mesmo* (Make yourself) won several international prizes in Latin America. In 1996 he published a volume of short stories that he claimed to have collected on the street: *100 Histórias Colhidas na Rua* (100 stories collected on the street). On the surface, *O Amor é uma Dor Feliz* (1997, Love is a merry pain) deals with a common theme in Brazilian fiction: the conflicted and violent city of São Paulo and characters who are young university students (one of whom is the narrator), but the novel also offers the reader some surprises and a broad range of topics. *O Céu e o Fundo do Mar* (1999, The sky is the bottom of the sea) is a novella set in two time periods: contemporary Brazil and the Brazil of the dictatorship, and deals with a wife of one of the individuals who "disappeared" for political reasons as well as a small-time drug trafficker. This novel has been successfully adapted to both the screen and theater. His innovative volume of fiction *Passaporte* (2001, Passport) can be read as a set of humorous travel stories or as a loosely organized novel. *Prova Contrária* (2003, Opposite evidence) is a highly experimental fiction in which the author announces the identity of the three main narrators in an introduction and then uses subtitles to describe a variety of settings and situations. Along with Rodrigo Fresán in Argentina and Mexicans such as Jorge Volpi, David Toscana and Mario Bellatín, Bonasi is one of the more talented and innovative of this generation in Latin America and the Caribbean.

Selected Work: *Crimes Conjugais* (1994); *Subúrbio* (1994); *O Amor é uma Dor Feliz* (1997); *O Céu e o Fundo do Mar* (1999); *Passaporte* (2001); *Prova Contrária* (2003).

Boom [Topic] A term widely applied to the Spanish American novel of the 1960s and most closely associated with the fiction of the Argentine Julio Cortázar, the Mexican Carlos Fuentes, the Colombian Gabriel García Márquez, and the Peruvian Mario Vargas Llosa. The Chilean José Donoso was a friend of and close collaborator with these four novelists and is often included as a member of the group. The Boom was a result of numerous institutions, individuals, and circumstances, among them the Cuban Revolution (which bonded many Latin American intellectuals in the 1960s), the Harper and Row publishing house in the United States, the Spanish literary agent

Carmen Balcells, the Spanish publishing company Seix Barral, the publication of the literary magazine *Mundo Nuevo* by Emir Rodríguez Monegal beginning in the mid-1960s, and the appearance on the scene of such capable translators as Gregory Rabassa and Suzanne Jill Levine. Later, Margaret Sayers Peden, Edith Grossman, and Alfred MacAdam completed highly successful translations for the writers of the Boom. Carlos Fuentes was an important figure in making all these factors work together.

The major novels of the Boom published in the 1960s were García Márquez's *One Hundred Years of Solitude* (1967), Julio Cortázar's *Hopscotch* (1963), Vargas Llosa's *The Time of the Hero* (1963), *The Green House* (1966), and *Conversation in The Cathedral* (1969), and Fuentes's *The Death of Artemio Cruz* (1963) and *A Change of Skin* (1967). The novels of the Boom tended to be lengthy, complex, and totalizing works directly associated with high modernist fiction of the Anglo-American world, for Anglo-American models such as James Joyce, John Dos Passos, and William Faulkner were their models.

Cortázar died in 1984, but the other writers of the Boom have continued publishing novels through the 1970s, 1980s, and 1990s. As their popularity grew in Latin America and beyond, the writers of the Boom suffered growing criticism in their respective homelands, usually based on politics, although some noteworthy critiques of the literary quality of their works appeared. García Márquez was widely critized in Colombia in the 1970s, but generally praised after he was awarded the Nobel Prize in Literature in 1982. Some scholars in Latin America, Europe, and the United States have also expressed critical judgments about the ever mutating political and aesthetic agendas of the writers of the Boom. Such renowned scholars as Jean Franco and Hernán Vidal have written at length about the Boom in a critical fashion, questioning their political consistency as leftist intellectuals. Nevertheless, novels of the Boom are widely read and generally considered the canonical works of the century in Latin America. Writers of the post-Boom of the 1970s and 1980s attempted to write against the prevailing modes of the Boom, and novelists associated with the postmodern and the later generation of the 1990s have tended to reject the overt political stances of the Boom. The young writers of the 1990s have often rejected García Márquez (and his magical realism) and Fuentes (and his totalizing efforts), while often embracing the storytelling capacity of Vargas Llosa as well as the numerous innovations pioneered by both Borges and Cortázar.

Boquitas pintadas (1969, *Heartbreak* Tango, by Manuel Puig. Translation by Suzanne Jill Levine. New York: Dutton, 1981) [**Novel**] Drawing upon the popular form of the serialized novel (or *folletín* in Spanish), Manuel Puig utilizes art forms associated with both popular culture and more elite literatures. This second novel by the Argentine master is set in the Argentine village of Vallejos in 1947 and tells the story of the women in the life of Juan Carlos Etchepare, an attractive man who loves drinking and seducing women. After a newspaper announces his death of consumption, an array of his former women provide texts that portray their relationships and fantasies. These texts include his own diaries and love letters as well as the women's sources of fantasies: radio serials, tango lyrics, movie magazines, and the like. The story culminates in female revenge. In this novel Puig writes in the Hispanic tradition of Don Juan literature and in parody of the serial novel that was most popular in Argentina. The parody implies a critique of male macho figures as well as of a variety of popular fictions forms. This novel conforms to the basic structural pattern of Puig's other novels: eight chapters in the first half of the novel, eight in the second. This work followed *La traición de Rita Hayworth* and confirmed Puig's place as a major figure on the Latin American literary scene after the Boom.

Bordo, El (1960, *The Precipice*, by Sergio Galindo. Translation by John and Carolyn Brushwood. Austin: University of Texas Press, 1969) [**Novel**] In contrast with the broad and panoramic national vision offered by many of the novels of the 1960s Boom, Galindo wrote more discrete novels of human relationships that some critics have called "small screen" novels. *El bordo* is a classic Galindo fiction that many critics consider his best work. It portrays the relationships within a single family, focusing on an aunt, Joaquina, who is the dominant figure, mourning lost opportunities for self-realization and living a tragic life. She endures the tyranny of spending her entire life attempting to compensate for the life she has seen but missed. By using a well-calculated series of events and details, Galindo gradually builds the anticipation of an impending tragedy that was inevitable from the novel's opening pages. At the time of its original publication in Spanish it was exceptional in its portrayal of human problems in the absence of economic factors—and without the character of the landless peasant that was often present in Mexican fiction from the 1930s to the 1960s. The writing of Galindo is comparable to the fiction of the same period of writers such as Clarice Lispector of Brazil, Sergio Pitol of Mexico, and José Donoso of Chile.

Borges, Jorge Luis [**Biography**] Argentine short story writer, essayist, and poet, he never published a novel. Nevertheless, few writers of any genre had as much impact as Borges on the Latin American novel of the remainder of the century after 1945. Indeed, three generations of Latin American novelists writing since the 1950s have been, to different degrees, devotees of Borges. His intellectual contributions hark back to the 1920s, when he was a leader of the *vanguardia* in Latin America. More specifically, he was active in internationalizing the European avant-garde by promoting its modernist tenets in Buenos Aires, which, in turn, had an impact throughout Latin America.

Borges's contributions were numerous, but his major importance was in reaffirming the right of invention in the 1940s: he showed both his contemporaries and several future generations of Latin American writers that novelists need not only to replicate or imitate reality (as several generations of realists had done in Latin America) but also to invent it. This reaffirmation represented a paradigm shift for the Latin American writer who had been committed to social critique and the imitation of social and political reality in fiction. For novelists of modernist interests Borges was a central figure; later generations of writers more associated with the postmodern also found inspiration in Borges and his collaborator Bioy Casares.

The centerpiece of Borges's fiction for Latin American novelists has been a volume of short fictions, *Ficciones* (1944), a work that contains such canonized stories as "The Garden of Forking Paths," "The Secret Miracle," and "Pierre Menard, Author of the Quijote." The first two stories were groundbreaking models for the modernist fiction in Latin America that flowered in the 1940s and 1950s; "Pierre Menard, Author of the Quijote" and several other stories that focused on language and writing per se were a significant precedent and model for much postmodern writing that appeared in the 1970s and 1980s in Latin America.

One indicator of Borges's presence well into the twenty-first century is the vast amount of writing on Borges not only by scholars but by the writers themselves. The Brazilian novelist Luis Fernando Veríssimo, for example, has written a novel with Borges as a main character, *Borges e os Orangotangos Eternos* (2001, *Borges and the Eternal Orangutans*, 2005), and the Argentine writer has been a character or referent in numerous Latin American short stories. In Argentina and much of Latin America Borges is more than a major writer; he is now a cultural icon.

Borges e os Orangotangos Eternos (2001, *Borges and the Eternal Orangutans*, by Luis Fernando Veríssimo. Translated by Margaret Jull Costa. New York: New Directions, 2005) [**Novel**] One of popular writer Veríssimo's most "literary" works, this novel is a tongue-in-cheek murder mystery that is also a parody of the writings of Argentine writer Jorge Luis Borges. The story is controlled by an unreliable narrator named Vogelstein, who is a Brazilian national and a scholar interested in the work of the American writer Edgar Allan Poe. Vogelstein travels from Brazil to Buenos Aires for a conference of the Sociedade Israfel, a group dedicated to the study of Poe. A participant in the conference, Rokopf, is murdered in his hotel room. Playing off many themes and motifs of Borges, this entertaining book is a postmodern rewriting of the Argentine master.

Borinsky, Alicia [**Biography**] Argentine novelist, poet, and scholar born in 1945, she went into exile into the U.S. in the 1970s, completing a PhD in Latin American literature at the University of Pittsburgh, later teaching at Johns Hopkins University before assuming a professorship in Latin American literature at Boston University, where she currently teaches. A disciple of Jorge Luis Borges and Felisberto Hernández, she is a master of irreverent humor and the ludic. Her *Theoretical Fables* (1993) includes essays on major modern fiction writers, and in this book she demonstrates how fiction can operate as theory, in addition to other subjects. She has published amply as a scholar of Latin American literature and began creative writing in the 1980s.

Her first novel, the satirical *Mina cruel* (1989) appeared in English as *Mean Woman* (1993). *Sueños del seductor abandonado* (1995), which appeared in English as *Dreams of the Abandoned Seducer* (1998), shows a vaudeville quality and air of parody that permeates Borinsky's fiction. In *Cine continuado* (1997, All-night movie) Borinsky continues her work in the *novela de espectáculo* (novel as spectacle) as she has characters changing not only their clothes but transforming in a series of anecdotes that underline the cruelty of a postdictatorial Argentine society. *Cine continuado* is a type of performance, using the visual effects of film and classic tango songs as chapter titles. It is a feminist work that parodies masculinist habits and culture. Women search for their identity in memory and struggle to survive in a brutally masculine world. A postmodern and open work, it leads the reader through a series of images and wordplay rather than toward any fixed conclusion. Borinsky suggests that society should not be judged as moral or immoral. Rather, she develops what might be called an "aesthetics of the amoral" that makes her comparable to Argentine predecessor Enrique Medina, who pushed the limits of decency and human cruelty with his writings of the 1970s. Borinsky received the 1996 Latino

Literature Award, given by the Institute of Latin American Writers, for *Dreams of the Abandoned Seducer*.

Selected Work: *Mina cruel* (1989, *Mean Woman*, translation Cola Franzen, 2003); *Sueños del seductor abandonado* (1995, *Dreams of the Abandoned Seducer*, translation Cola Franzen, 1998); *Cine continuado* (1997, *All Night Movie*, translation Cola Franzen, 2002).

Boullosa, Carmen [Biography] Mexican novelist, poet, playwright, short story writer, and essayist, she began her literary career by publishing poetry in the 1970s, but by the late 1980s was well on her way to a successful career as a novelist. She was born in Mexico City in 1954 and studied literature at the National University in the capital (UNAM). She remained in Mexico City until the late 1990s, when she moved to New York. In her novels she addresses topics such as memory, history, and gender, and her fiction is a dialogue with international postmodern fiction.

Boullosa gained immediate attention in Mexico with her first two novels, *Mejor desaparece* (1987, Better to disappear) and *Antes* (1991, Before), the latter of which received a prestigious national literary prize in Mexico, the Premio Villarrutia. Both are first-person texts that question patriarchal authority and contain a subtle element of paranoia. *Mejor desaparece* is a reflection on memory, built around a fragmented structure. Boullosa followed with two historical novels, *Son vacas, somos puercos* (1991, *They're Cows, We're Pigs*) and *El médico de los piratas* (1992, The doctor of the pirates), both of which are set in the Caribbean. In the former Boullosa appropriates the form of the colonial travel chronicle and even parodies the language of chroniclers such as Cabeza de la Vaca and Bernal Díaz del Castillo. She also draws upon the picaresque tradition, using first-person narrators who are *pícaro* types. But Boullosa is not a traditional writer, and she also uses postmodern strategies to mock any pretense of really telling history. She returns to Mexico in the novels that immediately followed, *La milagrosa* (1993, *The Miracle Maker*), *Duerme* (1994, Sleep), and *Cielos de la tierra* (1997, Heavens on earth), three works with many connections to postmodern fiction. *La milagrosa* is the story of a religious faith healer; it questions the limits of reason and rational explanation. In *Duerme* she uses a linear narrative to tell a complex story involving intertextual games. On the surface it is a novel of adventure about a European marauder in the New World, but it can be read as both a light novel and a more highbrow work. This is a historical novel in which she successfully combines archaic Spanish with modern language. *Treinta años* (1998, *Leaving Tabasco*) is perhaps her most self-consciously feminist text, focused on the body and memory. Boullosa moves to allegory with *De un salto descabalga la reina* (2002, *Cleopatra Dismounts*), a historical novel set in the times of Cleopatra and Mark Antony in which Cleopatra narrates stories to postpone her death.

Boullosa is among the most prominent postmodern women novelists writing in Latin America, along with figures such as the Chilean Diamela Eltit and the Argentine Sylvia Molloy. She currently lives in New York, where she writes.

Selected Work: *Mejor desaparece* (1987); *Antes* (1989); *Son vacas, somos puercos* (1991, *They're Cows, We're Pigs*, translation Leland Chambers, 1997); *Llanto: novelas imposibles* (1992); *La milagrosa* (1993, *The Miracle Maker*, translation Amanda Hopkinson, 1994); *Duerme* (1994); *Cielos de la tierra* (1997); *Treinta años* (1998, *Leaving Tabasco*, translation Geoff Hargreaves,

2001); *De un salto descabalga la reina* (2002, *Cleopatra Dismounts*, translation Geoff Hargraves, 2003); *La otra mano de Lepanto* (2005).

Brandão, Ignácio de Loyola [Biography] Brazilian novelist, short story writer, and essayist, he became known in Brazil in the late 1960s as a short story writer. He published the volume of stories *Depois do Sol* (After the sun) in 1965, and then followed with more stories in *Bebel que a Cidade Comeu* (1968, Bebel that the city consumed). Both these volumes present the dehumanization and inhumanity of urban life in the large cities of Brazil. Born in Araquera (state of São Paulo) in 1936, he has made a reputation not only as one of Brazil's first-rate short story writers and novelists but also as an oppositional and controversial intellectual figure during the military dictatorship.

Brandão's major novel and most controversial work, *Zéro* (1974, *Zero*), was originally published in Rome in 1974 and then appeared the following year in its first Brazilian edition. It was given an award as the best Brazilian novel of the year by the Fundacão Cultural de Brasília. Nevertheless, it was soon banished by military government's minister of justice, even though there is no explicit political commentary. *Zéro* is a hybrid text of newspaper clippings, movies, drama, and the like, and its radical aesthetics are matched by its strident social critique. Brandão's *Não Verás País Nenhum* (1982, *And Still the Earth*) has also been widely read in Brazil, the subject of ample critical commentary.

Selected Work: *Bebel que a Cidade Comeu* (1968); *Zéro* (1974, *Zero,* translation Ellen Watson, 2003); *Dentes ao Sol* (1976); *Não Verás País Nenhum* (1982, *And Still the Earth*, translation Ellen Watson, 1985); *O Beijo não Vem da Boca* (1985); *O Ganhador*

(1987); *O Anjo do Adeus* (1995); *Veia Bailarina* (1997); *O Anônimo Célebre* (2002).

Brasil, Assis (Francisco de Assis Almedia Brasil) [Biography] Brazilian novelist, journalist, and literary critic, he has written critical studies on novelists such as João Guimarães Rosa, Clarice Lispector, and Graciliano Ramos. Born in Paraíba, Brazil, in 1932, his readings of Faulkner were important for his later work. He has lived for lengthy periods of his life in the Brazilian cities of Fortaleza and Rio de Janeiro and began writing in the 1960s. In his novelistic tetralogy about Piauí, which many critics consider his best fiction, he depicts barren lives. *O Salto do Cavalo Cobridor* (1968, The leap of the horse) deals with aging in a patriarchal society; it portrays the suffering of four characters. Brasil is also well known for *Beira Rio, Beira Vida* (1965, Rivershore, lifeshore), the work that many critics consider his most accomplished novel. In it he denounces the suffering of Brazil's poor and marginalized.

In the 1970s Assis Brasil published four novels he identified as a *Ciclo do Terror* (Cycle of Terror). The first of these novels, *Os que Bebem como os Cães* (1975, Those who drink like dogs) was awarded a prestigious national prize (Prêmio Walmap) and portrays individual suffering and ongoing dehumanization in prison. *O Aprendizado da Morte* (1975, The death's learning) is a continuation of this novel. *Deus, o Sol, Shakespeare* (1978, God, sun, Shakespeare) is an experimental novel deploying a variety of texts: poems, letters, photographs, and the like. The last novel in the cycle, *Os Crocodrilos* (1980, The crocodiles), can be read as theater of the absurd. *Sodoma está Velha* (1985, Sodom is old) is the story of a brtual life in the marginal urban setting of the *favela*. Assis Brasil is a highly productive fiction writer who likes to create fictions that function as part of larger cycles. Consequently, his novelistic cycles include a *Cuarteto de Copacabana,* a *Tetralogia Piauiense,* a *Ciclo do Terror,* and a *Ciclo Minha Patria.*

Selected Work: Aventura no Mar (1955); *Verdes Mares Bravios* (1953; a young readers book); *Beira Rio, Beira Vida* (1965); *A Filha do Meio Quilo* (1966); *O Salto do Cavalo Cobrador* (1968); *Pacamão* (1969); *A Volta do Herói* (1974); *A Rebelião dos Orfãos* (1975); *Os que Bebem como os Cães* (1975); *Tiúbe, a Mestiça* (1975); *O Aprendizado da Morte* (1975); *Deus, o Sol, Shakespeare* (1978); *O Destino da Carne* (1982); *Os Crocodrilos* (1980); *Sodama está Velha* (1985); *Nassau, Sangue e Amor no Trópico* (1990); *Villegagnon, Paixão e Guerra na Guanabara* (1991); *Jovita, missão trágica no Paraguai* (1992); *Tiradentes Poder Oculto o Livra de Forva* (1993); *Paraguaçu e Caramuru* (1995); *Bandeirantes os Comandos da Morte* (1999).

Brazil [Nation] The Brazilian novel of the second half of the twentieth century inherited a tradition of innovation dating back to the nineteenth century master Machado de Assis and the modernista movement initiated in 1922 during the Semana de Arte Moderna. Continuity among innovators and experimentalists in Brazil during the post-WWII period is to be found in the novels of Clarice Lispector, João Guimarães Rosa, Hilda Hilst, Osman Lins, João Gilberto Noll, Silviano Santiago and Chico Buarque.

Many of the writers during this post-WWII period lived through the military dictatorship of 1964–1989, and this political repression created different responses— some more direct than others—among the novelists. For example, novelists Antonio Callado, Chico Buarque, and Iván Angêlo responded in very different ways. Callado with direct critique, Buarque with subtle allegory, and Angêlo with indirect criticism.

The major novelists of this period have been Jorge Amado, Antonio Callado, Autran Dourado, Rubem Fonseca, Milton Hatoum, Clarice Lispector, and João Guimarães Rosa.

(Others noted: Caio Fernando Abreu, Benito Barreto, Maria Alice Barroso, Patricia Bins, Fernando Bonasi, Assis Brasil, Bernardo Carvalho, Carlos Heitor Cony, Sonia Coutinho, Márcia Denser, Roberto Drummond, Alfredo Guzik, Iván Ivo, Diogo Mainardi, Ana Miranda, Cíntia Móscovich, Raduan Nassar, Nelson de Oliveira, Marcelo Rubens Paiva, Renta Pallotini, Mário Palmério, Nélida Piñón, Adélia Prado, Mário Prata, Rachel de Queiroz, Graciliano Ramos, José Lins de Rêgo, Carlos Ribeiro, Darcy Ribeiro, Murilo Rubião, Fernando Tavares Sabino, Herberto Sales, Sergio Sant'Anna, Moaçir Scliar, Abel Silva, Márcio Souza, Edna Van Steen, Zulmira Ribeiro Tavares, Lygia Fagundes Telles, Cristovão Tezza, Antônio Torres, Dalton Jérson Trevisan, João Silverio Trevisan, José J. Veiga, Erico Veríssimo, Luis Fernando Veríssimo, Luiz Vilela, Rui Zink.)

Brodber, Erna [Biography] Caribbean novelist, essayist, and academic, she was born in Jamaica in 1940 and has published several novels. She writes fiction to fill in the gaps left by the social sciences in the study of race and gender in the Caribbean regin. She thinks of herself more as a sociologist than a creative writer. Her main interest is the sociology of slavery from when Africans were captured and taken to the Americas. Brodber writes with a keen awareness of herself as a black woman.

She pursued undergraduate and graduate studies in the social sciences in London, Canada, and the United States in order to learn the history of African peoples in the Caribbean. She has published several several scholarly articles in the discipline of sociology. In the early 1970s, as a response to class and race prejudice, she began writing fiction as a form of therapy. She was teaching in areas such as human growth and development at the University of the West Indies when she wrote the novel *Jane and Louisa Will Soon Come Home* as a kind of case history for her students. Rejecting the methods of social scientists who study human behavior as a detached observor, Brodber feels a commitment to sharing her "research" and her stories with the people about whom she writes. Thus, for the author, *Jane and Louisa Will Soon Come* is a contribution to black sociology.

Brodber continued her blending of fiction and social science research in her novel *Myal* (1988). In this book she explored the links between different groups of the African diaspora—the Afro-Americans and the Afro-Jamaicans. This novel was the fictional version of an academic book in essay form that she also wrote: *American Connection*. Both her novel and her academic study were projects parallel to the wide-ranging novel of the African diaspora of the Americas published by Manuel Zapata Olivella in Colombia under the title *Changó, el gran putas*.

She sees her task as a writer as that of an "intellectual worker." This work connects to numerous Afro-Latin American writers, but particularly to Caribbean writers such as George Lamming and the Afro-Colombian writer Manuel Zapata Olivella.

Selected Work: *Jane and Louisa Will Soon Come Home* (1980); *Myal* (1988); *Lousiana* (1994).

Brothers, The (See *Dois irmãos* by Milton Hatoum) [**Novel**]

Brunet, Marta [**Biography**] A pioneer Chilean novelist born in Chillán, in southern Chile, in 1897, she published much of her fiction before the WWII period, but her introspective novels have earned her a considerable readership in Latin America since 1945. They tend to deal with issues of individual identity and self-realization, and she is also interested in how women are affected by their social roles. Reared in a rural area, this background was important for much of her later writing. She was homeschooled as a child; in addition, she traveled to Europe for three years with her parents, returning to Chile in 1914. On the return trip she visited Argentina, Uruguay, and Brazil. By the time her travels were over she had met many of the major intellectuals of the time, including Proust, Unamuno, Joyce, Ortega y Gasset, and Azorín. In 1925 she moved to Santiago, where she worked as a journalist and became involved with the intellectual life of the capital. She published her first fiction in the 1920s and continued writing in the 1930s. She served in the Chilean diplomatic corps; while working in the Chilean embassy in Argentina in the 1950s, Brunet launched a project for the dissemination of Chilean literature there. Her last novel, *Amasijo* (1962, Dough), was controversial in its portrayal of a woman's anguish at her solitary life. Her eight novels and sixty short stories gave her wide recognition in Latin America. She died in 1967.

Her major novel, *Humo hacia el sur* (1946, Smoke toward the south), is an ambitious and complex work that portrays life in a lumbermill town in the early part of the century. The novel offers description and analysis of all the social classes of the town, but with particular emphasis on the women. These powerful women prove to be even more politically effective than the men who appear to be in charge. Brunet's work is recognized as the production of one of the pioneer feminist writers of the century.

Selected Work: *Montaña adentro* (1923); *Bestia dañina* (1926); *María Rosa, Flor del Guillén* (1927); *Bienvenido* (1929); *Humo hacia el sur* (1946); *La mampara* (1946); *María nadie* (1957); *Amasijo* (1962).

Bryce Echenique, Alfredo [Biography] Peruvian novelist, short story writer, and essayist born in Lima in 1939, he has become one of the most prominent contemporary novelists in Peru and a major figure of the post-Boom in Latin America. He is widely recognized for his ability to combine wit and gossip to produce often charming narratives, a reputation gained from his first novel, *Un mundo para Julius*. He has described himself as a writer who creates in order to survive a limited, even boring, everyday existence and as an activity to fill in the voids of a solitary life in which he claims to always position himself "in the corner" rather than in the mainstream. Much of his fiction is autobiographical, and his later work, such as *La última mudanza de Felipe Carrillo* (1988, The last changes of Felipe Carrillo), is less humorous in tone than his early narratives, and more skeptical. Since moving to Europe in the mid-1960s, he has taught in both Paris and Montepellier.

Bryce Echenique was educated as a child in private Catholic schools in Lima, with teachers from the United States and Great Britain, and then studied law in the Universidad Nacional de San Marcos in Lima. His family traces its roots back to Spanish royalty. Since the mid-1960s he has lived in various cities in France, Italy, and Great Britain, with regular trips back to Peru to reacquaint himself with the Peruvian language that he recreates with exceptional mastery in his novels. His preferred writers are Cervantes, Rabelais, Sterne, and Stendhal, in that order, although, among Latin American writers, he often speaks of the Mexican fiction writer Juan Rulfo and the Peruvian poet César Vallejo. Hemingway and Proust have also been important models.

Bryce Echenique began writing in Perrugia, Italy, in 1965, launching his literary career with the publication of the volume of short stories *Huerto cerrado* (1968, Closed garden). After receiving an honorable mention for this volume in the Casa de las Americas Prize in Cuba, he began writing a short story that expanded in length in the process of writing—eventually becoming a lengthy first novel, *Un mundo para Julius* (1971, *A World for Julius*). In addition to over nine novels, he has published several volumes of short fiction, essays, and memoirs, the last under the title *Permiso para vivir: antimemorias* (1993, Permission to live: anti-memories).

His major novel is *Un mundo para Julius*, the story of a young boy's growing up in upper-middle-class Lima. It is a satire of the language and social mores of this group in Peru and was hailed as an antioligarchical and even revolutionary work that seemed in step with the revolutionary military government in power at the time. (The author himself, however, has pointed out that he wrote the work two years before the beginning of this revolutionary government.) From this first novel Bryce Echenique established himself as a master of language, particularly with respect to his exceptional ability to recreate the nuances of dialogue. Latin American critics speak of the success of the trademark "tonito de Bryce," referring to his ability to capture the appropriate tone in his dialogues.

In his more recent work, *La amigdalitis de Tarzán* (1999, *Tarzan's Tonsillitis*), he turns to the epistolary genre to tell the story of the relationship between a Peruvian singer and a Chilean-Salvadorian woman; the former loses a set of letters he had written over a ten-year period. With this loss he attempts to reconstruct ten years of life with her—meeting her in Rome, their love affair in Paris, and later complications. As in some of Bryce Echenique's other writing, the reader concludes that literature is a form of survival and love is a form of salvation. Along with writers such as the Argentine Mempo Giardinelli and the Chilean Antonio Skármeta, Bryce Echenique is a major figure in the post-Boom of the Latin American novel.

Selected Work: *Un mundo para Julius* (1971, *A World for Julius*, translation Dick Gerdes, 1992); *Tantas veces Pedro* (1974); *La vida exagerada de Martín Romaña* (1981); *El hombre que hablaba de Octavia de Cádiz* (1985); *La última mudanza de Felipe Carrillo* (1988); *Dos señoras conversan* (1990); *No me esperen en abril* (1995); *Reo de nocturnidad* (1997); *Guía triste de París* (1999); *La amigdalitis de Tarzán* (1999, *Tarzan's Tonsillitis*, translation Alfred MacAdam, 2001); *Puerto de mi amada* (2002).

Buarque, Chico (Francisco Buarque de Hollanda) [Biography] Brazilian music composer, artist, playwright, and novelist, he was born in Rio de Janeiro in 1944. He is internationally recognized as a celebrity recording artist and poet-songwriter but has also been involved with theater and, more recently, the writing of innovative fiction. Both his music and his fiction have been critical of the military dictatorship in Brazil (1964–1989) and of Brazil's consumer, free-market economy of the 1990s. Many of his songs were written for films. His family moved to São Paulo when he was an infant, and he did not return to Rio de Janeiro until 1966, the same year he married actress Marieta Severo, with whom he was married for three decades. Chico Buarque went to Europe as a child: his father, the distinguished historian Sérgio Buarque de Hollanda, received a professorship at the University of Rome in 1953, and the family resided in Rome from 1952 to 1954. He began his professional career in music in the mid-1960s and he gained rapid popularity through television appearances. His first long-playing albums appeared in 1966 and 1968, popularizing music that some critics have

described as "post-Bossa Nova" and others have compared to that of Bob Dylan.

Buarque became politicized to some extent as a reaction against the military government in the 1960s and went into political exile to Italy in the late 1960s and the early 1970s. His politics have placed him in sympathy with a variety of progressive movements, including the workers' movement of Lula since the 1980s, and he campaigned for President Lula as presidential candidate during his first presidential campaign in 1989. In the 1970s he publicly supported the government of Fidel Castro in Cuba.

Buarque began writing fiction in 1975 with the publication of *Fazenda modelo: novela pecuária* (1975, Model farm: rural novel), an allegorical depiction of an authoritarian society, which was a best seller in Brazil. After writing several plays and the children's story *Chapeuzinho amarelo* (1979, Little yellow hat), he returned to fiction with *Estorvo* (1991, *Turbulence*) and *Benjamin* (1995). *Benjamin* is an engaging and challenging text that moves between the past and the present of the main character, who pursues a love affair with women of both his past and his present. The subtle background to this novel is the military dictatorship, and Benjamin presents a skeptical view of Brazil's postdictatorship consumer society.

Now functioning as a writer as much as a musician, Buarque was interviewed in 1999 by the Chilean writer Antonio Skármeta as part of Skármeta's series of conversations with writers. He has also written the plays *Roda viva* (1968, Live wheel), *Calabar, elógio da traição* (1973, Calabar, in praise of betrayal), *Gota d'água* (1975, Drop of water, coauthored with Paulo Pontes), and *Opera do malandro* (1978). Given the sociopolitical content of many of his writings, he had to deal with censorship under the military dictatorship. His novels *Estorvo* and *Benjamin* have been made into films, the latter of which has been the most successful. His third novel *Budapeste* (2003, *Budapest*), winner of the 2004 National Award for literature Premio Jabuti, experiments with the sounds of Portuguese and Hungarian. The story follows José Costa, a middle-aged ghostwriter of autobiographies in Rio de Janeiro.

Selected Work: *Fazenda modelo: novela pecuária* (1975); *Estorvo* (1991, *Turbulence*, translation Peter Bush, 1992); *Benjamin* (1995, *Benjamin*, translation Clifford E. Landers, 1997); *Budapeste* (2003, *Budapest*, translation Alison Entrekin, 2005).

Buenos Aires Affair, The (1973, *The Buenos Aires Affair*, by Manuel Puig. Translation by Suzanne Jill Levine. New York: Dutton, 1976) [**Novel**] Based on the model of detective fiction, Puig's third novel both imitates and parodies its model. He structured this work exactly as he did all his other novels, in two parts, each of which contains eight chapters. *The Buenos Aires Affair* is Puig's homage to a genre popular in Argentina since the 1940s, detective fiction. As in *El beso de la mujer araña*, Puig questions gender-based behavior, genre-based thinking, and traditional concepts of authority and truth. This tongue-in-cheek thriller involves the abduction of a woman, a threat of sexual violation and murder, and a portrait of two destroyed lives. The two psychologically dependent main characters are a solitary and tormented sculptor and a successful art critic, the latter of which is troubled by guilt and suffers from sexual failures because of the guilt feelings. The crime around which the novel is constructed transpires on May 21, 1969, but the novel moves freely between 1930 in Buenos Aires (where both characters are born) and 1969 in the same city. This novel continues Puig's trajectory as a novelist who writes fiction that is both popular and innovative, that both challenges and confirms the legitimacy of conventional forms.

Bufo & Spallanzani (1985, *Bufo & Spallanzani*, by Rubem Fonseca. Translation by Cliff E. Landers. New York: Dutton, 1990) [**Novel**] Fonseca had already established his place as one of Brazil's most accomplished modern fiction writers and master of the detective fiction genre by the time he published *Bufo & Spallanzani*, a novel that has been critically acclaimed in its translations into English, Spanish, and other languages. In this humorous parody of the crime novel, Fonseca creates a protagonist who is a writer that becomes involved with a woman who is also writing a novel titled *Bufo & Spallanzani*. With her death a detective begins his search for the author of the crime, and his short list of suspects includes the writer-protagonist and her husband. The writer-protagonist fears that the detective will uncover his "dark past" (or *pasado negro*, which is the title of this novel in its Spanish translation). This detective is exceptionally intellectual in his approach, using scientific knowledge as the basis for much of the rationale of his investigation. The novel begins in the classic mode for the genre: a crime and an initial investigation. In this case, however, the protagonist, a writer, is also the narrator, so he relates the story of being investigated as well as other aspects of his own story, such as his literary background and preferences. He seeks refuge from the police investigation in the writing of his novel, also titled *Bufo & Spallanzani*. Eventually, however, he is arrested by the police and tortured. In the end the writer reveals that his wife's death was the result of a mercy killing she had requested because of an incurable illness.

Buitrago, Fanny [**Biography**] Colombian novelist and short story writer, she is one of the leading contemporary women writers in Colombia. Recipient of numerous short story prizes, she is a master storyteller who is interested in topics such as human relationships, love, death, personal fulfillment, and acceptance. She was born in Barranquilla, Colombia, in 1945, and grew up in Cali, which she considers her home. She took refuge in literature at an early age and still speaks of her admiration for books such as Lewis Carroll's *Alice in Wonderland*. Buitrago has spent most of her adult life in Bogotá, with the exception of one-year visits to Iowa and Sweden, respectively. Her first literary work was a play, *El hombre de paja* (1964, Scarecrow), which won a literary prize in 1964 and is her only published play.

Buitrago began publishing short fiction in newspapers in Venezuela and Mexico in the early 1960s and stunned the conservative literati in Colombia by winning a national literary prize at age eighteen for *El hostigante verano de los dioses* (1963, The harassing summer of the gods), a novel about disaffected youth. In this text a narrator-protagonist alternates chapters with the three other main characters, each of whom also narrate. It is not only a story of disaffection but also of a generation's boredom. Since publishing this first novel at a young age, Buitrago has spent a lifetime publishing a regular series of novels and volumes of short stories. In 1968 she was a finalist in the Seix Barral Novel Prize competition with her novel *Cola de zorro* (1970, Fox tail), a complex work in which she novelizes concepts and tells a family story of three generations. This challenging work has received critical acclaim among academics but has been ignored by the larger reading public in Colombia and beyond. Her volume of short stories *La otra gente* (1973, The other people) deals with the tortured relationships between husbands and wives, abandoned children, and the like. Her subsequent volume

of short stories, *Bahia Sonora,* is set on a multicultural (unnamed) island in the Caribbean, which Colombian readers will recognize as San Andrés, and draws upon oral tradition there. Her later novel *Los pañamanes* (1979, The island men) draws upon the same setting and folk tradition. Her only novel to appear in English translation is *Señora Honeycomb*, which was published in the original Spanish as *Señora de miel*. In this work Buitrago turns to popular culture to broaden her reading public, a strategy that has been successful in recent years in Colombia.

Selected Work: *El hostigante verano de los dioses* (1963); *Cola de zorro* (1970); *Los pañamanes* (1979); *Señora de miel* (1989, *Señora Honeycomb*, translation Margaret Sayers Peden, 1996); *Bello animal* (2002).

Bullrich, Silvina (Silvina Bullrich Palenque) [**Biography**] Argentine novelist, short story writer, essayist, and translator, she was one of the most productive women writers of the century in Latin America. She was a realist who portrayed the situation of women and challenged the conventional values of middle-class Argentine society. She questioned how women could survive in a patriarchal society and was also interested in seeing how women and men, bonded in marriage, might contribute to the betterment of a troubled Argentine nation. She was born in Buenos Aires in 1915, spent most of her youth in France (where her father was a diplomat), and received a superb education both in France and in her home. She read amply from her father's collection of French and Russian literature, remaining a Francophile her entire life. She began writing poetry in the 1930s and publishing short novels in the 1940s.

In her early novels, *Bodas de cristal* (1952, Crystal wedding) and *Teléfono ocupado* (1955, Busy signal), Bullrich portrays rebellious, emancipated women. In the former the protagonist reflects on her fifteen-year marriage. *Teléfono ocupado* is a Kafkaesque tale of an extortion attempt. Her most widely read novel, *Los burgueses* (1964, The boursoisie), is the first work of a trilogy that offers an ironic and satirical view of the landed gentry. The basic setting is a family reunion at the *estancia* (or plantation) of the patriarch. It is a first-person narration in which the narrative voice changes throughout the novel. By means of these different narratives, the reader perceives a changing society and a meanness of spirit among the elite. *La creciente* (1965, The flood) continues the critique, but now the target is the urban political class. The later *Mañana digo basta* (1968, Tomorrow I will say enough) consists of a fictionalized diary of a forty-nine-year-old woman who is a widow and mother of three. Bullrich died in 1990 as a pioneering woman writer of the century in Argentina.

Selected Work: *La redoma del primer angel* (1943); *La tercera versión* (1944); *El compradito* (1945); *Bodas de cristal* (1952); *Teléfono ocupado* (1955); *Mientras los demás viven* (1958); *Un momento muy largo* (1961); *Los burgueses* (1964); *Los salvadores de la patria* (1965); *El hechicero* (1966); *La creciente* (1967); *Mañana digo basta* (1968, *Tomorrow I'll Say Enough*, translation Julia Shriek Smith, 1996); *El calor humano* (1970); *Los monstruos sagrados* (1971); *Los pasajeros del jardín* (1971); *Mal don* (1973); *Los despiadados* (1978); *Saloma* (1979); *La mujer postergada* (1982); *Los pasajeros del jardín* (1995).

Burel, Hugo [Biography] Uruguayan novelist, journalist, and short story writer, he was born in Montevideo in 1951 and has led a dual career as journalist and fiction writer. His fiction is so inventive that much of it is in the realm of the fantastic, close to science fiction. He became known in Uruguay in the mid-1970s by winning short story contests and he has continued winning prizes, including the prestigious Juan Rulfo international short story contest. His fiction tends to involve complex human and textual relationships, with a particular eye for the absurd. He has published several volumes of short stories and novels. His first novel, *Matías no baja* (1986, Matías does not descend), offers a humorous and sometimes grotesque view of the 1970s military dictatorship in Uruguay. *Tampoco la pena dura* (1989, The pain does not last either) involves a set of characters easily associated with 1960s culture in pursuit of their passions. In *Crónica del gato que huye* (1995, Chronicle of the cat that flees) the author looks forward to the end of the century as a phantasmagoric and nightmarish experience. Burel looks back to the Perón regime in Argentina in the 1950s in *Los dados de Dios* (1997, God's dice), telling the story of a married Argentine woman who has a relationship with an Uruguayan artist. His recent *El autor de mis días* (2000, The author of my days) is a playful, self-conscious text dealing with intertextuality and the relationship between writers and technology such as personal computers and CDs.

Selected Work: *Matías no baja* (1986); *Tampoco la pena dura* (1989); *Crónica del gato que huye* (1995); *Los dados de Dios* (1997); *El autor de mis días* (2000); *El guerrero del crepúsculo* (2001).

Burgos, Elizabeth (See Menchú, Rigoberta and *Me llamo Rigoberta Menchú y así me nació la conciencia* by Elizabeth Burgos and Rigoberta Menchú) [**Biography**]

Burgos Cantor, Roberto [Biography] Colombian novelist and short story writer, he was born in Cartagena, Colombia, in 1948, and later moved to Bogotá, where he studied law and political science at the Universidad Nacional in Bogotá. Burgos Cantor gained a reputation at an early age as being one of Colombia's most talented young short fiction writers, winning the Premio Nacional de Cuentos (national short story prize) in 1970. His volume of short stories *Lo Amador* (On Amador) was amply praised among journalists and critics in Colombia. His major novel, *El patio de los vientos perdidos* (1984, The patio of the lost winds), also evokes his past on the Caribbean coast. *De gozos y desvelos* (1987, Pleasures and insomnias) is his novelistic book of fiction consisting of four anecdotes of human relationships centered around a young girl's statement that her grandmother never explained to her how to tell whether or not one is truly loved by others. Unable to fully understand matters such as these, Burgos's characters seem lost in a world of dreams and nightmares. Burgos lives in Bogotá with his family, where he practices law, works as an editor, and writes.

Selected Work: *El patio de los vientos perdidos* (1984); *De gozos y desvelos* (1987); *El vuelo de la paloma* (1992); *Pavana del ángel* (1995).

Buscando o seu Mindinho: Um Almanaque Auricular (2002, Looking for Mr. Pinky: an auricular almanac, by Mário Prata. Written in Portuguese and untranslated. Rio de Janeiro: Objectiva) **[Novel]** Prata has a reputation in Brazil for writing the eccentric; this narrative is an almanac of stories, anecdotes, and random texts all related to the little finger. The author explains in the introduction that a deceased acquaintance, "seu Mindinho" (Mr. Pinky), had inexplicably left him an edited collection of items related to the little finger, which, in his lack of the right small finger,

had helped define his name and identity. Mindinho explains in prefaces to each piece why he chose to incorporate the writing in his pinky finger almanac. These preambles include clues to the life story of Mindinho and the loss of his wife Glorinha, who also lacks a little finger. The pieces themselves range from an account explaining the hereditary trait of missing a little finger in Mindinho's ancestors to a screenplay for a Western miniseries. This narrative is indebted to parodies of popular writing genres, all of which involve the little finger.

Butazzoni, Fernando [Biography] Uruguayan novelist, short story writer, literary critic, screenwriter, and journalist, he was born in Montevideo in 1952 and went into political exile in 1972 during the military dictatorship. He has lived in Chile, Nicaragua, Sweden, Italy, and Cuba as well as in Central America and the Middle East when working as a journalist. In 1985 he returned to Montevideo and has been living and writing there since. Politics and history are the central topics for most of Butazzoni's writings. His fiction has been translated into several languages and praised for its suggestive qualities. His first book, the stories *Los días de nuestra sangre* (1979, The days of our blood), was awarded the prestigious Casa de las Américas prize in 1979. His first novel, *La noche abierta* (1982, The open night), which was awarded an important literary prize in Costa Rica, depicts the political crisis in Uruguay in the 1960s and 1970s. His novel *Príncipe de la muerte* (1993, Prince of death) is a vast historical work set in the nineteenth century.

Selected Work: *La noche abierta* (1982); *El tigre y la nieve* (1986); *La danza de los payasos perdidos* (1988); *Príncipe de la muerte* (1993); *La noche en que Gardel lloró en mi alcoba* (1996); *Mendoza miente* (1998); *Libro de brujas* (2001).

Caballeros del sol, Los (1964, *La Caballer-esca*, by Demetrio Aguilera Malta. Translation by Willis Knapp Jones. Carbondale: Southern Illinois University Press, 1967) [**Novel**] Gabriel García Márquez is the best-known of the several novelists who have written a novel about one of the folk heroes of Latin American politics, Simón Bolívar. His novel *The General in His Labyrinth*, however, was anticipated by several other fictional versions of Bolívar's life, including this fine novel by one of Ecuador's most accomplished novelists of the twentieth century, Demetrio Aguilera Malta. Here history is seen through the passions and tensions of Bolívar's love affair with Manuela Saenz (a matter that caught García Márquez's attention too). Bolívar and Saenz are caught up in two passions: one for each other and the other for the cause of Spanish American independence. Manuela's passion is most directly focused on Bolívar; he, however, is so intent on defining the political destiny of the region that this effort takes priority over his romantic relationship. Aguilera-Malta offers a novel in which historical details permeate the work and the future of Latin America alternates between hope and despair.

Caballero Calderón, Eduardo [**Biography**] Colombian novelist, essayist, and journalist, he has been a prominent intellectual figure in Colombia since the 1950s and has been prolific, publishing ten novels, four volumes of short stories, two books of memoirs, and hundreds of journalistic pieces. He was born in 1910 and belongs to one of the known families of Colombia's landed aristocracy, the Caballeros. He has written a book of articles, in fact, on the subject of the estate or *hacienda* that has belonged to his family since 1560, and this book is titled *Tipocoque: estampas de provincia* (1950, Tipocoque: scenes from the provinces). Much of Caballero Calderón's writing is an attempt to defend traditional values of this rural region located in the department of Boyacá in Colombia as well as the Hispanic cultural tradition inherited from Spain. He began creative writing as an adolescent and studied law without ever receiving a degree. In 1925 he published his first novel, the relatively unknown *Caminos subterráneos* (1925, Underground roads). In the 1930s he became active in national politics and began writing journalism. In 1933 he worked as chief of information for the government, and in the late 1930s he was based in various Latin American countries as foreign correspondent, first for the newspaper *El Espectador* and later for *El Tiempo*. He served as a government attaché in Spain in 1946 and used his stay in Spain to visit other European countries. In the 1940s he became involved in the literary world and in 1945 published his first novel to be nationally recognized, *El arte de vivir sin soñar* (1943, The art of living without dreaming).

In addition to defending traditional Hispanic values, Caballero Calderón's writing deals with the relationship between rural and urban values, problems of land and land distribution in Colombia, concepts of good and evil, and the general issue of cultural identity in the Americas. His two major novels are *El cristo de espaldas* (1952, Christ on his back) and *El buen salvaje* (1966, The noble savage). In *El cristo de espaldas* the protagonist is a young priest who attempts to mediate the conflicting interests in a town, gaining a certain spiritual triumph even though the ecclesiastic order forces him out of the town in defeat. *El buen sal-*

vaje is a metafiction on a topic common in modern Latin American literature: the Latin American intellectual's experience living in Paris. While in France the protagonist writes his novel, which consists of drafts for various types of potential novels. This satirical work is Caballero Calderón's most complex and sophisticated novel.

Selected Work: Caminos subterráneos (1925); *El arte de vivir sin soñar* (1943); *El cristo de espaldas* (1952); *Siervo sin tierra* (1954); *La penúltima hora* (1955); *Manuel Pacho* (1962); *El buen salvaje* (1966); *Caín* (1969); *El azote del sapo* (1975); *Historia de dos hermanos* (1976).

Cabeza de la hidra, La (1978, *The Hydra Head*, by Carlos Fuentes. Translation by Margaret Sayers Peden. New York: Farrar, Straus and Giroux, 1979) [**Novel**] Fuentes's contribution to the genre of detective fiction, this novel contains many of the classic devices of this genre at the same time that it is more a parody and pastiche of the spy thriller than a strict replica. In the context of his total work Fuentes places this novel in the cycle of writings that he calls *El Tiempo Político* (political time) along with *El sillón del águila* (2002, *The Eagle's Throne*) and the untitled novelistic project known as "El camino a Texas." In *La cabeza de la hidra* political time is linear time, and the plot moves with the speed of detective fiction and the spy thriller. The protagonist is Felix Maldonado, a stereotypic bureaucrat in the Mexican government who finds himself involuntarily implicated in a plot to assassinate the president. A complex series of events also reveals a plot to steal Mexico's oil reserves. Maldonado's double dies, and he assumes the identity of Diego Velásquez after deciding to play up a physical resemblance to the Spanish painter of that name. But this pseudo-detective novel becomes even more complex when Maldonado assumes other identities, such as Humphry Bogart and Woody Allen. Not one of Fuentes's major novels, *La cabeza de la hidra* is, nevertheless, one of the author's most entertaining and widely read books.

Cabrera Infante, Guillermo [**Biography**] Cuban novelist, short story writer, screenplay writer, and essayist, he has been one of the leading Latin American novelists since the 1960s. He is a witty and humorous writer who is often compared to James Joyce and Laurence Sterne and has been a pioneer in narrative experimentation in Latin America. After enthusiastically supporting Castro's revolution, Cabrera Infante held several government posts and was sent to Belgium in 1961 as Cuba's cultural attaché. In 1965, however, he became disillusioned with the government and took refuge in London, where he continues to reside. Since that move he has been a polemical and controversial political figure in Latin America. He was born in Gibara, a small town in Oriente province of Cuba, in 1929. His parents founded the Communist Party of Cuba when he was a young child, and he saw them arrested for political reasons and jailed for several months. Later the family moved to Havana, where they lived in poverty. Cabrera Infante became interested in literature while studying at the university and began a variety of creative activities after quitting his college studies. He attended a journalism school and became involved with the literary magazine *Bohemia* and later founded another magazine, *Nueva Generación*. He began creative writing in the early 1950s, and in 1952 he was jailed for publishing a story that included profanities in English. In the 1950s Cabrera Infante became involved in clandestine activities against the Batista dictatorship. In the late 1950s he began publishing some of the stories that eventually became the volume *Así en la paz como en la guerra* (1960, In peace as in war), fictions with political overtones that revealed the violence in Havana under the dictatorship in the 1950s. Cabrera Infante's recent writings that have appeared in English translation are included in the volume *Writes of Passage* (1994, translated by J. Boyas and P. Brookesmith).

His major novel, *Tres tristes tigres* (1967, *Three Trapped Tigers*), is a work with a tone of nostalgia set in Havana in the period immediately preceding the Cuban Revolution. It is a novel of constant movement and a sense of being on the brink of change. The main characters are highly creative and entertaining types, including a photographer, a television actor, and a writer. These characters, as well as other voices, are masters of language play, making this novel a hilarious tribute to the writing of James Joyce. Along with the writing of Borges and Julio Cortázar's *Hopscotch*, this work was a key predecessor to postmodern fiction of the 1970s and 1980s in Latin America.

Cabrera has had a lifetime passion for film, and he published a volume of essays in 1962, *Arcadia todas las noches* (Arcade every night), on five Hollywood film directors: Orson Welles, Alfred Hitchcock, Howard Hawks, John Houston, and Vincente Minnelli. He has used numerous cinematographic techniques in his fictions and has written the screenplay for three motion pictures that have been produced, including the film *Under the Volcano* (1972, Hollywood Universal).

Selected Work: *Tres tristes tigres* (1967, *Three Trapped Tigers*, translation Suzanne Jill Levine, 1971); *Vista del amanecer en el trópico* (1974, *View of Dawn in the Tropics*, translation Suzanne Jill Levine, 1978); *La Habana para un Infante difunto* (1979, *Infantes Inferno*, translation Suzanne Jill Levine, 1984).

Caicedo, Andrés [Biography] Colombian novelist and film critic born in 1950, he rose to prominence in his youth before dying tragically in 1977. Fascinated with film, rock music, and drug culture, he was comparable to the writers of the Mexican Onda when he appeared on the Colombian literary scene in the 1970s with short fiction and his one novel, *¡Que viva la música!* (1977, Let music live). He was the editor of a magazine *Ojo al Cine* during the early 1970s and was well known in Colombia for his work on film. His novel *¡Que viva la música!* was an anomaly in Colombia at the time of its publication, with its focus on youthful counterculture. In this novel the protagonist is obsessed with music; she lives for the night life of Cali and its intense 1960s musical scene. At the beginning of the novel she is innocent to this cultural life, but then becomes a follower of American rock music. She adopts an American lifestyle that she eventually rejects when she changes to salsa and gets to know Bárbaro. Her life becomes violent in the company of Bárbaro, who attacks Americans living in Cali. By the end of the novel she is working as a prostitute. *¡Que viva la música!* captures many of the complex cultural ambiguities of some sectors of Colombian society in the 1970s.

Caicedo's other writings were brief articles on film and three volumes of short stories. The volume *El atravesado* (1975, The crossed one) consists of one story, and *Angelitos empantanados o historias para jovencitos* (1977, Swamped little angels and other stories for children) and *Berenice* (1978) consist of several stories each. Caicedo's legacy in Colombia, however, rests with his one groundbreaking and iconoclastic novel. Although Caicedo wrote only one novel, his impact on Colombian literature has been enormous. He rebelled against the dominant modes of fiction writing in Colombia, which had been either novels about La Violencia (led by Manuel Mejía Vallejo) or the magical realism of Gabriel García Márquez. Caicedo can also be read as a forerunner to the urban interests of writers of the generation of the 1990s, such as the Colombians Santiago Gamboa and Mario Mendoza.

Selected Work: ¡Que viva la música! (1977).

Callado, Antonio [Biography] Brazilian novelist, essayist, playwright, and journalist, he is widely recognized as one of the major writers of the century in his homeland and as one of the most political writers of the period of the military dictatorship. Born in Niterói, Brazil, in 1917, he studied law in his native state, has lived for periods in Great Britain and France, and has had a prominent career as one of Brazil's leading journalists, working for the newspaper *Correio da Manhã* in Rio de Janeiro, the BBC in London, and in the newspaper *O Globo.* He lived in political exile in Great Britain for six years. In 1992 he began writing a column for the São Paulo newspaper *A Folha de São Paulo.*

Callado began writing novels in the 1950s, publishing his first one, *Assunção de Salviano* in 1954, a book about a character who feigns religious commitment to have contact with working people and win them over to the revolutionary cause. Written with a linear plot and simple language, this first work was uncharacteristic of his total fiction and his most celebrated political novel is *Bar Don Juan* (1971, *Bar Don Juan*). His fiction tends to portray social conflict as it is affected by the political context of the dictatorship. He is also quite well known for his lengthy and fragmented novel *Quarup* (1967), in which the protagonist comes into contact with a variety of groups suffering Brazil's social and political problems. Set in the Amazon, it offers a broad, moralistic view of the nation, as well as a parody of its ideologies. In *Bar Don Juan* the clientele in a bar suffers the emptiness and futility of living under a military dictatorship. It follows the fate of leftist activists immediately before and after the 1964 military coup. The plot involves the leftist group meeting in a bar in Rio de Janeiro to make plans to join forces with insurgents from Cuba and Bolivia. Callado is critical of the group's festive attitude and political failures. Both of these novels were best sellers in Brazil.

Of his later works *Reflexos de Baile* (1976, Reflections of a dance) is his most complex and fragmented technical experiment; *Sempreviva* (1981) is the story of a political exile who returns to Brazil before the *apertura,* or "opening," whose new life in Brazil is a nightmare. The homeland is now as much a risk as it is a refuge. The Brazilians that the protagonist encounters are in two groups: the leftists with whom he is an ally and the communists whom he opposes. Along with Guimarães Rosa, Clarice Lispector, and Autran Dourado, Callado is one of the major Brazilian novelists of the century. Like Guimarães Rosa, his main interest in writing was the broad, national project. Nevertheless, his fiction of the 1980s was more directed toward entertainment than critical national projects.

Selected Work: Assunção de Salviano (1954); *A Madona de Cedro* (1957); *Quarup* (1967, *Quarup,* translation Barbara Shelby, 1970); *Bar Don Juan* (1971, *Don Juan's Bar,* translation Barbara Shelby, 1972); *Reflejos do baile* (1976); *Sempreviva* (1981); *A Expedicão Montaigne* (1982); *Concerto carioca* (1985); *Memórias de Aldenhan House* (1980).

Cambio de piel (1967, *A Change of Skin,* by Carlos Fuentes. Translation Sam Hileman. New York: Farrar, Straus and Giroux, 1968) **[Novel]** One of Fuentes's most lengthy and complex novels, it is also one of his early experiments with characters of multiple identities, rather than the double identities that he had already been exploring. This is the postmodern Fuentes, with a novel set in Mexico in the 1960s, recounting the experiences of two couples who spend a weekend together in the Mexican town of Cholula. In this "present" Javier and his wife Elizabeth drive from Mexico City to the beach in Veracruz with Franz and his young lover Isabel. After the car breaks down in Cholula, the couples switch partners for the evening. At midnight they explore the Aztec pyramid Cholula. The identities of the characters are not always fixed and separate as the novel progresses; Fuentes also takes the reader through multiple digressions in time and space, going back in time to the pre-Columbia era and in space to other continents. This novel set the stage for Fuentes's transhistorical carnival that appeared in the mid-1970s, *Terra nostra* (1975).

Campbell, Federico [Biography] Mexican novelist, journalist, short story writer, translator, and essayist from the border city of Tijuana, he is associated with border writing. Much of his work has to do with politics and power, and his essays *La invención del poder* (1994, The invention of power) deal with these subjects. Born in Tijuana in 1941, he studied there for elementary school before going to Hermosillo, Sonora, for his high school studies in 1957 and 1958 and then to Mexico City for university-level studies, eventually completing a degree in law. He traveled to the United States and Europe in the early 1960s. He also studied journalism in the United States and was practicing journalism in the early 1960s when he began writing his first stories. He has always viewed journalism as a "necessary evil" for his writing—a method for survival. In 1963 he attended the writing workshops offered by Juan Arreola, and his first stories appeared in print that year. In 1967 and 1968 he was involved with the antigovernment movements in both the north of Mexico and in Mexico City. He began writing novels in a period of Mexican literary history (the 1970s) of intense experimentalism, and his early fiction was experimental and self-conscious. He had finished writing the novella *Todo lo de las focas* (Everything about seals) in the early 1970s, but had difficulty publishing it for several years. Much of his writing shares qualities of international postmodern fiction. In his first novel, *Pretexta* (1979, Pretext), he explores the methods of characterization of his main character and critiques the Mexican government and power structure from 1968 to 1978, a period of crisis after the Tlatelolco massacre and the government of Luis Echeverría from 1972 to 1978. In this book Campbell also questions the use of disinformation under the Echeverría regime. His novella *Todo lo de las focas* (1982) is a postmodern experimental exploration of the adolescent self and ambivalent border spaces. *Tijuanenses* (1989, Tijuana: Stories on the Border) is generally considered a set of stories that might be read as a novel, and most of the anecdotes treat border issues. His recent novels, *Transpeninsular* (2000, Transpeninsular) and *La clave Morse* (2001, Morse code) are ambiguous and challenging experiments with memory, history, and space. *Transpeninsular* refers to the two peninsulas that he knows well: the Italian peninsula and the peninsula of Baja California. The plot is based on a potential assassination or suicide of an academic in Baja California. *La clave Morse* refers to his father, who was a telegrapher. He has also written a book of essays on detective novels, *Máscara negra* (1995), as well as a volume of short essays on diverse topics under the title *Post scriptum triste* (1994).

Selected Work: Pretexta (1979); *Todo lo de las focas* (1982); *Tijuanenses* (1989, *Tijuana:*

Stories on the Border, translation Debra Castillo, 1995); *Transpeninsular* (2000); *La clave Morse* (2001).

Campos, Julieta [Biography] Cuban/Mexican novelist, essayist, short story writer, and translator, she has been a leading novelist and literary critic in Mexico since the 1960s. She was born in Havana, Cuba, in 1932, and studied literature there before receiving a scholarship to study in France. In Paris she married a Mexican academic, became a Mexican citizen in 1954, and has resided there since 1955. Campos has published several well-respected volumes of literary criticism and theory. In her complex fiction she has been interested in the deep, inner characterization of her characters as well as the nature of fiction as verbal construct. Her work invites comparison with such postmodern writers as the Mexicans Salvador Elizondo and José Emilio Pacheco. Her first novel, *Muerte por agua* (1965, Death by water), is an exploration of the psyche and the relations among the three main characters who suffer from an inability to communicate. *Tiene los cabellos rojizos y se llama Sabina* (1974, *She Has Reddish Hair and Her Name Is Sabina*) and *El miedo a perder a Eurídice* (1979, *Fear of Losing Eurydice*) are self-conscious metafictions. In the former the character is a writer who writes about a situation identical to that of himself and the action is minimal. *El miedo de perder a Eurídice* also contains a character who is a writer, and the book is a theory of fiction as much as a "novel." Her work has been widely recognized in Mexico and studied by scholars in the United States and Europe.

Selected Work: *Muerte por agua* (1965); *Celina o los gatos* (1968, *Celina or the Cats*, translation Leland H. Chambers, 1995); *Tiene los cabellos rojizos y se llama Sabina* (1974, *She Has Reddish Hair and Her Name Is Sabina*, translation Leland Chambers, 1993); *El miedo de perder a Eurídice* (1979, *Fear of Losing Eurydice*, translation Leland Chambers, 1993).

Canto, Estela [Biography] Argentine novelist, translator, and journalist, she was born in Buenos Aires in 1920, studying at Saint Lucy English School in the Argentine capital, and from an early age was a reader of Bernard Shaw, Tolstoy, Proust, and Thomas Mann. She was the editor of *Nuestras Mujeres*, a cultural magazine directed to women readers. She has translated numerous novels from English and French. Canto was known for her close relationship with Jorge Luis Borges before her death in 1994, and she was part of the literary group of Borges and Bioy Casares in Buenos Aires. She belonged to the generation of Argentine writers who were affected by the regime of Perón and wrote of the decadence of the Argentine upper middle class in the years leading up to the Perón government. Her first book of fiction was a group of short stories titled *Los espejos de la sombra* (1945, The mirrors of the shadow) and her first novel, *El muro de mármol* (The marble wall), appeared in 1945 and won an important literary prize in Buenos Aires (Premio Municipal). According to the author, one of her best novels was *El retrato y la imagen* (1950, Portrait and image). In this and her next novel, *El hombre del crepúsculo* (1953, The man of the twilight), she explored the emotional states and psychology of her characters, and was awarded the Medal of Honor from the Argentine Writer's Society in 1953. *La noche y el barro* (1962, The night and the mud) and *Isabel entre las plantas* (1966, Isabel among the plants) represented a change in her focus; the former deals with the Latin American international jet set of literature, culture, and business. Her novel *La hora detenida* (1974, The stopped hour) deals with the night that Evita Perón died. She also published several novels under pseudonyms.

Selected Work: El muro de mármol (1945); *El retrato y la imagen* (1950); *El hombre del crepúsculo* (1953); *La noche y el barro* (1962); *Isabel entre las plantas* (1966); *La hora detenida* (1974).

Caparrós, Martín [Biography] Argentine novelist, essayist, editor, and journalist, he started working for the newspaper *Noticias* in 1953. Between 1976 and 1983 he lived in Paris and Madrid, completing a degree in history in Paris. His journalistic interests have been wide-ranging, for he has written on topics as diverse as culture, sports, bullfighting, radio, and television, and his related work has been as director of several cultural and popular magazines in Argentina. He has published critical editions of Voltaire as well as historical studies on Argentina political history. Caparrós has published six novels. His most ambitious fictional project is a 941-page novel titled *La historia* (1999, History), which can be read in the context of other vast and totalizing historical projects in Latin America, such as Carlos Fuentes's *Terra Nostra* and João Guimarães Rosa's *Grande Sertão: Veredas*. His historical interests begin with the creation and continue through Western and Argentine historical time. *La historia* is also a postmodern metafiction that questions how history is written while it explains how the novel itself is written. His recent book, a fictionalized biography titled *Amor y anarquía: la vida urgente de Soledad Rosas, 1974–1998* (2003, Love and anarchy: the urgent life of Soledad Rosas, 1974–1998), is an account of the life of Soledad Rosas, an Argentine citizen who left her comfortable upper-middle-class life in Buenos Aires in 1997 and was arrested in Turin, Italy, a year later, accused of being the most dangerous terrorist of Italy. Soon

thereafter she was found dead, hung in prison. A story of love and anarchy, it deals with a theme present in Caparrós's fiction: how the state can produce its own worst enemies.

Selected Work: *Ansay o los infortunios de la Gloria* (1984); *No velas a los muertos* (1986); *El tercer cuerpo* (1990); *La noche anterior* (1990); *La historia* (1999); *Un día en la vida de Dios* (2001); *Amor y anarquía: la vida urgente de Soledad Rosas, 1974–1998* (2003).

Caramelo (2002, by Sandra Cisneros. Written in English. New York: Knopf) **[Novel]** The third novel by one of the most prominent Chicana writers in the United States today, *Caramelo* is a story of growing up as a young Chicana in the United States. It is also the story of her grandmother. Cisneros fictionalizes the experience of being both visible and invisible as a minority person in the United States. Taking this topic a step beyond what had already been explored by minority writers such as Ralph Ellison, Cisneros sets up a comparative scenario, contrasting the experience of a Chicana in the United States with that of a Chicana in Mexico. The story is narrated primarily by Lala, who relates a series of family trips between Chicago and Mexico City. Lala's experiences are juxtaposed with those of her grandmother and other family members. The grandmother's voice provides a counterpoint to Lala, and the parallels between the grandmother and Lala help the latter understand herself more fully. Cisneros focuses on how race and gender affect individual lives in nations such as the United State and Mexico, and her conclusions offer hope to minority women who find their identity affirmed by self-understanding.

Cardoso, Lúcio [Biography] Brazilian novelist and poet whose writings spanned the 1930s to the 1950s, he is one of Brazil's most respected chroniclers of the traditional values of that period. He was born in Minas Gerais, Brazil, in 1914, published eleven books, and died in 1968. He began writing pioneer novels of intimate human relationships at a time when the predominant novelistic mode in Brazil was the social novel of the the northeastern region. His most recognized works are *Maleita* (1934, Malaria) and *Crônica da Casa Assassinada* (1959, Chronicle of the assassinated house). In the latter novel, a lengthy work of over four hundred pages, a young woman's arrival at a traditional household results in complex psychological tensions. Cardozo is widely recognized as an important early contributor to psychologically oriented fiction in Brazil.

Selected Work: Maleita (1934); *Mãos Vazias* (1938); *O desconhecido* (1940); *A Profesora Hilda* (1946); *Inácio* (1946); *O Enfeitiçedo* (1954); *Crônica da casa assassinada* (1959).

Carnival (1985, by Wilson Harris. Written in English. London: Faber and Faber) [**Novel**] A Caribbean text that recalls some aspects of *Biografía de un cimarrón* by Miguel Barnet, this novel has an author who functions as a collaborator with the main character. The novel recreates conversations between Everyman Masters and his biographer Jonathan Weyl. They are both racially mixed and of the same class. Hours before his death, Masters encourages Weyl to write a fictionalized version, a "biography of spirt," of his life. The first chapter relates Master's last sexual encounter. The text moves from third to first person, undermining the idea of narrative authority. Eschewing the idea of the documentary truth of a Latin American *testimonio*, this text seeks imaginative truth. The novel ends with the marriage of the protagonist to his wife. Sexual identity, however, is challenged at the end, and Harris questions fixed categories of gender, race, and class.

Carpentier, Alejo [**Biography**] Cuban novelist, essayist, and short story writer, he was one of the most influential Latin American writers of the century. Some writers of the Boom, such as Carlos Fuentes, consider him the founding father of the modern novel in Latin America. Critics often describe him as the master of the dense, allusive, neobaroque style. Carpentier was born in Havana in 1904 and spent much of his youth, and later life, in France, the homeland of his father. After a distinguished career as the author of over twenty books, he died in 1980. He was reared in a large home with an ample book collection owned by his father, which led him to reading many of the Spanish and French classics at a young age. He had the privilege of attending two of the most elite private high schools in Havana. His family traveled throughout Europe, once going as far as Russia. He did considerable studies in both music and architecture, resulting in the strong presence of both in his writing. When he was a college student, however, the family fortune changed, for he was abandoned by his father and had to support the family himself through a combination of his writing and work in the advertising business. In the 1920s and 1930s Carpentier became increasingly politicized and involved with the avant-garde of cultural movements in Cuba, including the recognition of African movements as a source of inspiration. After being jailed as a political dissident, he escaped Cuba in 1928 for France, where he was a collaborator with Robert Desnos and other surrealists. His early interests in the European avant-garde, progressive politics, and the Afro-American movement all became integral parts of his novelistic vision in the coming decades.

Carpentier's major works are of uniformly high quality, but most critics agree that his major works are *El reino de este mundo* (1949, *The Kingdom of This World*), and *El siglo de las luces* (1963, *Explosion in a Cathedral*). *The Kingdom of This World* is set in Haiti and tells the story of a black king on this island, Henri Christophe, and a slave, Ti Noel. The novel's four parts concern a rebellion lead by a mythic leader named MacKandal, a massacre and a yellow fever epidemic, the rule of Henri Christophe, and the arrival of the mulattoes. The life of Ti Noel follows a pattern parallel to these four parts, as Carpentier develops his novel, which portrays the ongoing struggle against tyranny, a conflict between Africans and whites, and the opposition between the powerful and the oppressed. The novel is stylized enough to escape any association with traditional realism. *El siglo de las luces* is set in the Napoleanic era and the French Revolution. Victor Hughes, an obscure figure in French history, comes into contact with an aristocratic family in colonial Havana. In this work Carpentier introduces the reader to the cultural heritage of the Caribbean and Cuba in particular, with particular focus on cultural roots in France and Spain.

Some critics have read his later work, *El arpa y la sombra* (1979, *The Harp and the Shadow*) as a covert autobiography as well as a reflection on the fate of his works. More literally, it is a fictional narrative about the life of Christopher Columbus and his fate as a historical figure. In line with much of Carpentier's writing, this novel is laden with allusions to Western literary tradition, from classical antiquity to the modern Caribbean.

Selected Work: ¡Ecué-Yamba-O! (1933); *Viaje a la semilla* (1944, *Journey Back to the Source*, 1970); *El reino de este mundo* (1949, *The Kingdom of This World*, translation Harriet de Onis, 1957); *Los pasos perdidos* (1953, *The Lost Steps*, translation Harriet de Onis, 1956); *El acoso* (1956, *Manhunt*, 1959; translation Alfred MacAdam as *The Chase*, 1989); *El siglo de las luces* (1962, *Explosion in a Cathedral*, translation John Sturrock, 1963); *Concierto barroco* (1974, *Baroque Concert*, translation A. Zataz, 1974); *El recurso del método* (1974, *Reasons of State*, translation Frances Partridge, 1976); *El arpa y la sombra* (*The Harp and the Shadow*, translation T. Christensen and C. Christensen, 1979).

Carvalho, Bernardo [Biography] Brazilian experimental fiction writer, he was born in Rio de Janeiro in 1960 and has already published several novels, short stories, and plays. He worked as a correspondent for the *Fohla de São Paulo* in Paris and New York. He has been identified in Brazil as a prominent writer of his generation and consequently part of what critics such as Nelson de Oliveira have identified as the generation of the 1990s. Both his high level of productivity and the positive critical response to his work have made him one of the most noteworthy writers of this young generation. Paradox, ambiguity, and unresolved contradiction are common elements in his work. His first book of fiction is a volume of eleven short stories titled *Aberracão* (1993, Aberration). The action of his first novel, *Onze* (1995, Eleven), takes place in such diverse settings as the outskirts of Rio de Janeiro, Paris, and New York. A variety of equally diverse characters (from beggars to diplomats) appear in the ever changing spaces of this experimental novel. *Os Bêbados e os Sonâmbulos* (1996, The drinkers and the sleepwalkers) deals with gender and identity issues: a Brazilian military officer suffering from a brain tumor and losing his memory as he embarks on a search for origins. In *As*

Iniciais (1999, The beginners) the narrator is a writer who spends years in the process of deciphering or interpreting. His recent work, *Medo de Sade* (2000, Fear of Sade), is related to detective fiction and has been criticized for lacking the ambiguities of his earlier work.

Two of his most noteworthy novels to date are *Nove Noites* (2002, Nine nights) and *Mongólia* (2003, Mongolia). In *Nove Noites* he fictionalizes the real story of Buel Quain, a twenty-seven-year-old American graduate student of anthropology who committed suicide in the hinterlands of Brazil in 1938. He was completing his work at Columbia University when he went to Brazil and met Lévi-Strauss. He developed the story on the basis of indirect evidence and speculation: a contemporary novelist-figure, doing retrospective research, narrates much of the text; a contemporary of Buel Quain who is a *sertanejo* (rural inhabitant) in Brazil narrates other narrative fragments. *Mongólia* is a combination travel account and fiction.

Selected Work: Onze (1995); *Os Bêbados e os Sonâmbulos* (1996); *As Iniciais* (1999); *Medo de Sade* (2000); *Nove Noites* (2002); *Mongólia* (2003).

Carvalho-Neto, Paulo de [Biography] Known as a novelist and foklorist, Carvalho-Neto was born in 1923. His fiction draws upon a broad range of cultural sources, from the Iberian Peninsula in the Middle Ages to modern poetry. He has written the novels *Meu Tio Atahualpa* (1972, My uncle Atahualpa), *Los Ilustres Maestros* (1975, The illustrious masters), *Suomi* (1986), all of which are harsh critiques of social injustice in Brazil.

His later novel *Praça Mauá* (1991, Maua Square) is a new kind of critique in Carvalho-Neto's work, for now he uses the town square as a microcosm of Brazil and focuses on the relationships between men and women. The novel is replete with distraught lovers, and the text is supported with drawings and texts from Spain's ancient *pliegos sueltos* and Portugal's *cantigas d'amigo*. Other poetic prose draws upon the more modern tradition in Latin American poetry. The lovers all suffer from excesses such as ludic madness and some are devoured by each other. They live the chaos and urban morass of Brazil and, in the end, they seem to represent its excesses. Often as obscene as he is erudite, Carvalho-Neto seems to be a representation of the schizophrenia of his characters and his nation. In any case, he is always entertaining.

Selected Work: Meu Tio Atahualpa (1972); *Los Ilustres Maestros* (1975); *Suomi* (1986); *Praça Mauá* (1991).

Casa de los espíritus, La (1982, *The House of the Spirits*, by Isabel Allende. Translation by Magda Bogin. New York: Knopf, 1985) [Novel] Allende's first and most successful novel among critics and scholars, *La casa de los espíritus* recounts the story of the Trueba-del-Valle family through four generations. The historical context for this family story is Chilean society and politics from the beginning of the twentieth century to the military coup of Augusto Pinochet in 1973. The plot is developed in a sequential and chronological fashion, suggesting a certain belief in the concept of historical progress. It is Allende's first testimony of political repression in Chile, presenting women who are imaginative and even heroic individuals who resist patriarchal authority. The novel also contains magical events; this novel, published fifteen years after García Márquez's *One Hundred Years of Solitude*, did much to popularize magical realism once again in Latin America, Europe, and the United States, after it appeared to have been exhausted by the

1970s in much of the Hispanic world and in academic circles worldwide.

Casa do Poeta Trágico, A (1997, The house of the tragic poet, by Carlos Heitor Cony. Written in Portuguese and untranslated. São Paulo: Companhia das Letras) [**Novel**] Brazilian fiction and film offer abundant stories of men facing their middle-age crisis by falling in love with younger women. At the outset Cony seems to be pursuing this standard story line, for here a middle-age advertising executive, Augusto Richet, becomes obsessed with a young woman named Mona. After an excursion to Pompeii, they do marry. But in this case the couple slowly drifts apart and eventually get divorced. Richet becomes a shell of his former self and Mona gets remarried as she returns to her homeland of Italy to pursue her career as a rising business-woman. Cony follow his usual pattern of a well-constructed work, in this case a three-part novel to develop the story, which covers a two-decade marriage. The novel's settings offer the author ample opportunity to share his erudition with the reader via Richet, who is as obsessed with classical Pompeii as he is with Mona. Unfortunately, that tends to be the case of all of Cony's characters, who are incapable of establishing and maintaining meaningful human relationships. This is a novel of cynicism and emptiness.

Casa grande, La (1962, *La casa grande*, by Alvaro Cepeda Samudio. Translation by Seymour Menton. Austin: University of Texas Press, 1991) [**Novel**] Relatively un-known outside of Colombia until the mete-oric rise of Gabriel García Márquez placed Colombian literature on the international literary map, Cepeda Samudio was an ad-mired writer in Colombia in the 1950s and 1960s. *La casa grande* is known to be the first novel to fictionalize the horror and violence of the 1928 massacre of striking banana workers in Colombia. Along with Gabriel García Márquez's *La hojarasca* (1955, *Leafstorm*), *La casa grande* was a pioneer modern novel in Colombia and, like the García Márquez novel, patently Faulknerian in structure and tone. In addition to the 1928 banana workers' strike, *La casa grande* presents the story of a family that dominates the town and occupies *la casa grande* (the big house). A tour de force in narrative technique, the novel consists of ten unnumbered chapters, each containing a different method of developing a story set in a time frame immediately preceding and following the massacre. The principal characters are the family that has dominated the entire town from the *casa grande*, an imposing edifice visible to all. Cepeda Samudio's technique was novel in comparison to the typically violent and sanguinary novels of La Violencia in Colombia: the history and the story of the massacre are told without ever actually depicting the major event itself.

Casa verde, La (1966, *The Green House*, by Mario Vargas Llosa. Translation by Gregory Rabassa. New York: Harper and Row, 1973) [**Novel**] Widely acclaimed by critics as one of Vargas Llosa's most accomplished novels, *The Green House* is the author's second novel and one of the lengthy, complex, Faulknerian works of his early fiction. Set in such diverse spaces as the coastal, desert region of northern Peru, and the Amazon jungle, this novel consists of four parts with several chapters each and develops the story of numerous characters who interact, transform, and change in relationships with one another as the novel progresses and the situations change. This work has been likened to the fluvial webs of the Amazon with its maze of main rivers, tributaries, and small streams; reality as it is experienced in *The Green House* is in continual flux. Nevertheless, there are several hidden story lines that interweave to relate anecdotes of exploitation, betrayal, and modernization. Vargas Llosa began his novelistic career with this critique of two of Peru's most venerable institutions: the military and the Church. Based on some factual cultural and economic history of Peru, this novel also contains ample narrative segments in which Vargas Llosa began to develop his interest in romancelike fiction.

Casaccia, Gabriel (Benigo Casaccia Bibolini) [Biography] Paraguayan novelist who was born in 1907 and died in 1980, he is one of Paraguay's major literary figures of the century. Writing in the realist mode, he began publishing in the early 1950s. He lived through one of Latin America's most repressive long-term dictatorships, that of Alfredo Stroessner, who took power in Paraguay in 1954. This dictator eliminated civil rights and militarized Paraguay throughout the 1950s and 1960s. Casaccai's two major novels on political repression are *La llaga* (1964, The wound) and *Los exiliados* (1966, The exiled). *La llaga* involves a plot to overthrow the government as well as the three main characters; a mother, her son, and her lover. The intimate characterization of the three, through the use of interior monologues, makes their presence in the novel as important as the political plot. In *Los exiliados* Casaccia takes the story of these revolutionaries across the border, where they live in exile. It is the story of their gradual process of disintegration, with focus on a character who spends two decades dreaming of a return that will never happen.

Selected Work: La babosa (1952); *La llaga* (1963); *Los exiliados* (1966).

Castellanos, Rosario [Biography] Mexican novelist, short story writer, poet, and essayist, she wrote in defense of the Indian population in Mexico and of women. She is widely recognized as one of Mexico's major women writers of the twentieth century and as a leading exponent of *indigenismo* in Latin America. Castellanos was born in Mexico City in 1925 but brought up in Comitán in the state of Chiapas until her family moved back to Mexico City when she was seventeen years old. An important childhood experience was being reared by an Indian nursemaid who told her stories of Indian myths and life. Once in Mexico City, the adolescent Castellanos began writing poetry, and she published her first book of poems in 1948. After completing an MA in philosophy in Mexico City (UNAM) and graduate studies in literature in Spain, she accepted a position in the Instituto Nacional Indigenista in 1956 and soon thereafter began writing novels. In the 1960s she dedicated herself to writing fiction and essays as well as teaching literature at the university level. She is broadly recognized as a poet and as the author of the short stories *Ciudad real* (1960, *City of Kings*) and *Los convidados de agosto* (1964, The guests of August). Much of her poetry, short fiction, and essayistic work has appeared in a volume in English titled *A Rosario Castellanos Reader* (edited and with a critical introduction by Maureen Ahern; translated by Maureen Ahern and others, 1988) She was named Mexico's ambassador to Israel in 1971 and died there in an accident in 1974.

Castellanos's two major novels are *Balún Canán* (1957, *Nine Guardians*) and *Oficio de tinieblas* (1962, *The Book of Lamentations*). The former is an autobiographical novel that deals with the two worlds of the author's life, i.e., her early life of indigenous Mexico and her later life of mestizo modern Mexico. *Oficio de tinieblas*, generally considered her most accomplished work, is based on a historical event: the 1867 uprising of Chamula Indians in Chiapas, although the most consistent time frame is the 1930s, a period of social and economic reforms in Mexico. The story deals with the interaction between the *ladinos* (non-Indians) and the Tzotzil Indians. Castellanos fictionalizes the conflict by successfully portraying the Indians as individuals. The novel develops in three stages: an introduction to the world of the Tzotzil, an introduction to the *ladino* world, and the development of the conflict between the two. Along with the Chilean María Luisa Bombal and the Brazilian Clarice Lispector, she was a pioneer woman novelist in Latin America of the twentieth century.

Selected Work: Balún Canán (1957, *Nine Guardians: A Novel*, translation I. Nicholson, 1992); *Oficio de tinieblas* (1962, *The Book of Lamentations*, translation Esther Allen, 1998).

Castellanos Moya, Horacio [Biography] Novelist, short story writer, and journalist, he was born in Tegucigalpa, Honduras, in 1957, then living as a child in El Salvador, and is thus closely associated with both Central American nations. He was an outspoken critic of the ruling elites in El Salvador during the civil war from 1980 to 1992. In 1981 he went into political exile in Canada and then in Mexico, where he wrote on cultural and political topics for the newspaper *El Excelsior* and the magazine *Plural*. While in Mexico he also worked for several news agencies and as a foreign correspondent for the Brazilian journal *Cuadernos del Tercer Mundo*. In 2004 he sought political exile in Frankfurt, Germany.

Castellanos Moya began writing poetry and short fiction in the late 1970s and early 1980s and became one of Central America's more visible writers in the 1990s. In the early 1990s he wrote the volume of essays *Recuento de incertidumbre: cultura y transición en El Salvador* (1993, Review of uncertainty: culture and transition in El Salvador). His novel *La diáspora* (1988, The diaspora) deals with the diaspora of characters from El Salvador and the consequences of this movement. The protagonist takes exile in Mexico, where he can assess his experience in the armed conflict in El Salvador. Other characters also arrive in Mexico, and their discussions review their contradictory actions while still in El Salvador. The novel also introduces an opportunistic journalist and a failed revolutionary from El Salvador who ends up playing piano in bars as an alcoholic. Castellanos Mora's portrayal of the revolutionary cause in El Salvador is not flattering.

His recent novel *El arma en el hombre* (2001, The arm in the man) deals with some of the social problems Central American society faces after the civil wars: armed criminals, often working in gangs, who had been soldiers in the civil wars. The main character in this novel is Robocop, a former soldier whose only belongings after the war were weapons and whose only training in life has been to fight. He becomes a juvenile delinquent, and Castellanos Moya invites the reader to witness the broad range of problems that Central American governments and society face in the transition from civil strife to democracy.

Selected Work: La diáspora (1988); *Baile con serpientes* (1996); *El asco: Thomas Bernhart en El Salvador* (1997); *La diosa en el espejo* (1999); *El arma en el hombre* (2001); *Donde no andan ustedes* (2003).

Castillo, Ana [Biography] Novelist, short story writer, poet, translator, and editor, she is a leading novelist among Latina writers in the United States. She is known to be one of the prominent writers to bring a strong feminism into Latina writing and she is also known for her deft use of irony. She identifies her bold and assertive feminism as *Xicanisma*. She was born in Chicago in 1953 and as a youth read *As Tres*

Marias (*The Three Marias*) by the Portuguese writers Maria Isabel Barreno, Maria Teresa Horta, and Maria Velho da Costa; Castillo claims this book was an important beginning for her thinking as a Latina about issues such as patriarchy and incest. Her poetry and fiction began appearing in the 1980s. She received a BA from Northern Illinois University, majoring in art and secondary education, and she earned an MA in Latin American studies in 1979 from the University of Chicago. From 1989 to 1990 she was a dissertation fellow in the Chicano Studies Department at the University of California, Santa Barbara. She received a PhD in American studies from the University of Bremen, Germany, in 1991.

Castillo writes in English, but her debts to Latin American writing are obvious from her first novel, *The Mixquiahuala Letters* (1986), which is dedicated "in memory of the master of the game, Julio Cortázar" and was the recipient of the Before Columbus Foundation's American Book Award in 1987. Many critics consider *The Mixquiahuala Letters* to be her major novel; it is an epistolary work and fictional description of the relationship between the sexes that includes consideration of both Hispanic and Anglo forms of love and gender conflict.

Over the past decade she has been in consistent dialogue with Mexican writers such as Elena Poniatowska and she has made frequent visits as a guest lecturer at the National University in Mexico City (UNAM). In her book of critical essays, titled *Massacre of the Dreamers: Reflections on Mexican-Indian Women n the United States Five Hundred Years After the Conquest* (1992), she defines herself as a mestiza with a considerable portion of indigenous blood from a Mexican immigrant family that ended up in Chicago in the previous generation. She has dedicated a vast amount of time (over seven years) to researching family history, lamenting the general lack of information about the indigenous side of U.S. history as well as the history of Mexico or Central America. She considers both the racism and sexism of the ancient indigenous peoples as key issues for her understanding of her current situation as a female mestiza and as a writer. She also gives religiosity serious consideration, for she notes that a relatively high percentage of Mestiza and Latina women are Catholic.

Her fiction has been read in the context of gender, giving voice to the voiceless, and her work is also critical of male myths. Her work generally addresses the complexities of living on the boundaries of overlapping worlds. In her book of short stories *Loverboys* (1997) she challenges both the machismo of her male-dominated community and the ethnocentricity of some feminists. She writes linguistically nuanced fiction that includes many of the syntactical structures of the Spanish language affecting English syntax. Thus, when she moved to New Mexico late in her career, she began to make some modifications to her English, which in New Mexico is influenced by Spanish; in this sense her work is comparable to writers such as Frank Martinus Arion of Curaçao and Saúl Ibargoyen of Uruguay, whose writing in their respective languages is affected by other local languages. In both her poetry and her fiction she explores the meaning of random experience for life fulfillment.

Selected Work: The Mixquiahuala Letters (1986); *Sapogonia* (1990); *So Far from God* (1993).

Catania, Carlos [**Biography**] Argentine novelist, short story writer, essayist, and playwright, he was born in 1931. A relatively obscure novelist, he is known in Argentina as an experimental fiction writer. He lived in exile for twenty-three years, residing in Mexico, Guatemala, and Costa Rica. His creative writing began in his adolescence with the play *La nube en la alcantarilla* (The cloud in the sewer), which was not produced for another two decades. His first volume of short fiction, *La ciudad desaparece* (The city disappears), appeared in 1984. His first novel, *Las varonesas* (The baroness) appeared in 1977, followed by *El pintadedos* in 1981. He has written a critical essay on the fiction of Ernesto Sábato, *Entre la idea y la sangre* (1973, Between the idea and the blood). His work on film has appeared in Germany, and some of his plays have been translated into English.

Selected Work: Las varonesas (1977); *El Pintadedos* (1981).

Centauro no Jardim, O (1980, *The Centaur in the Garden*, Moaçir Scliar. Translation by Margaret A. Neves. New York: Available, 1984) [**Novel**] A prolific novelist who has written about a broad range of topics, Scliar approaches a theme in this novel that gets to the essence of his own identity: being Jewish in Brazil. The mythological Greek creature of the centaur appears in this book as a Jewish person living in Brazil, producing a humorous novel dealing not only with identity but also with sexual mores and life in general. In this case the centaur is named Guedali, a mestizo character with no fixed identity in either Greek mythology or Brazilian culture. Guedali's parents are Russian Jews, and their son is constantly perplexed about his own identity. Guedali finds solace in his attempts to see himself as a Brazilian man, a horse, a Jewish intellectual, and other potential beings that he imagines. For his parents, however, he is their Jewish son, so they follow the religious tradition of having him circumcised. As the son of educated parents who respect knowledge, Guedali follows their instructions to read, and he reads voraciously—from the Bible to Marx and Freud. Nevertheless, rational book knowledge does little to solve problems such as

his irrational desire to behave like a horse. He eventually marries a centauress, producing the expected conflicts and lessons involved in this relationship. After surgical operations, the pair live a "normal" life as human beings, but still miss the spontaneity that had characterized their lives as centaurs.

Cepeda Samudio, Alvaro [**Biography**] Colombian novelist and short story writer, he was a key player of Gabriel García Márquez's Barranquilla group—four intellectuals who met in the late 1940s and early 1950s in Barranquilla, Colombia. He was born in 1926 and died in 1972. As a part of the Barranquilla group, Cepeda Samudio, along with García Márquez, essayist Germán Vargas, and Felix Fuenmayor socialized in the late 1940s and early 1950s to share readings, discussions, and their early writing. They were particularly interested in work by William Faulkner, Jorge Luis Borges and Franz Kafka, all of whom offered new approaches to the predominant realist modes of Colombian fiction at the time. Cepeda Samudio was not highly productive; like Garcia Márquez during the same period, he experimented with Faulknerian modes of writing while simultaneously writing with an acute awareness of the social and political realities of uneven development in the Caribbean coastal region of Colombia. In 1954 he published a set of short stories under the title *Todos estábamos a la espera* (We were all waiting). His one novel, *La casa grande*, was a groundbreaking work in both political and aesthetic ways. In the political sphere it was the first novel to recover the forgotten history of the massacre of striking banana plantation workers by soldiers of the Colombian army in 1928. This national tragedy had been excluded from official histories of Colombia until the publication of this novel. The event was popularized beyond the borders of Colombia by Gabriel García Márquez in his novel *One Hundred Years of Solitude*. With respect to aesthetics, *La casa grande*, along with García Márquez's *La hojarasca* and Héctor Rojas Herazo's *Respirando el verano*, was a seminal work in the rise of modernist aesthetics in Colombia.

Selected Work: *La casa grande* (1962, translation Seymour Menton, 1991).

Céu Aberto, A (1996, To the open sky, by João Gilberto Noll. Written in Portuguese and untranslated. São Paulo: Companhia das Letras) [**Novel**] Noll writes in the postmodern mode, and the often shifting terrain and characters of fragile identity found in *A Céu Aberto* make this novel a unique experience. The unnamed protagonist begins the novel as an adolescent boy taking his sickly brother to a military encampment in hopes of finding their father, a misanthropic military officer. The protagonist is incorporated into the army as a sentinel, despite not knowing the enemy or why the war was begun, so he deserts his post. The protagonist reminisces about his time living with Arthur, a pederast pianist who cares for him. Neverthless, there is no chronological order of events. His brother, dressed as a bride, transforms into his wife and becomes impregnated during a ménage –à trois by either him or by Arthur's long-lost son, a Swedish writer. Unable to cope, he kills his wife and takes refuge on a ship. The captain forces him to be his sex slave until he escapes to a strange new land where he at last discovers his age to be approaching fifty and life still threatened by the dangers of the war. The gender-switching characters are unpredictable, and their homoerotic experiences are the only real interactions between them. The distinction between dreams and reality in this experimental novel of unfixed identities and locations is ambiguous. This Brazilian writes in the postmodern style of one of the early pi-oneers of fragile postmodern gender identity, the Cuban Severo Sarduy.

Chacón, Joaquín-Armando [**Biography**] Mexican novelist, playwright, short story writer, and essayist, he holds a well-earned reputation as one of the most talented novelists of his generation in Mexico. Born in Chihuaha in 1944, he studied theater at the undergraduate level in Mexico and has worked both as a teacher and journalist. He has also been quite involved in theater and film. He has published a volume of short stories under the title *Los extranjeros* (1983, The foreigners) and the plays *Dos meridianos a la misma hora* (1969) and *El hijo del hombre* (1983). His thematic interests and strategies for writing fiction are heterogeneous and have evolved over his writing career, making each of his novels distinctive. His subtle uses of self-conscious narrative technique relate his fiction to his compatriot Juan García Ponce and much postmodern fiction written in Latin America. His early fiction, including the novel *Los largos días* (1973, The long days), deals with unstable identity and emotional issues of adolescence. *Las amarras terrestres* (1982, Earthly ties) is different in tone and focuses on an entire town's dilemma in the context of dream and fantasy; some critics have compared this work to the magical realism of García Márquez. His ambitious and experimental novel *El recuento de los daños* (1987, The account of the damage) tells a vast array of stories constructed around the city of Cuernavaca. He has received several prizes in Mexico, including a national novel prize for *El recuento de los daños*.

Selected Work: *Los largos días* (1973); *Las amarras terrestres* (1982); *El recuento de los daños* (1987).

Chamoiseau, Patrick [**Biography**] Caribbean novelist and dramatist, he was born in Fort-de-France, Martinique, in 1953.

Along with Raphael Confiant and Jean Bernabé, he authored a manifesto in favor of creole language and culture, *Eloge de la créolité* (1989). He began writing theater in the 1970s. In his fiction he uses elements of French and the creole of the subculture of *djobeurs* (hustlers and handymen) in Fort-de-France. His first successful novel, *Chronique des sept misères* (1986, *Chronicle of the Seven Sorrows*) deals with the decline of Fort-de-France's vegetable market. He has also published *Solibo Magnifique* (1988, *Solibo the Magnificent*) and *Texaco* (1992).

Chamoiseau's fiction deals with the new urban landscape of the Caribbean. Many urban dwellers of Martinique had chosen self-marginalization as a response to the dominant system. In *Chronique des sept misères* Chamoiseau is the chronicler of the *djobeur* who is neither a full participant in the society of Martinique nor a totally marginalized or hopeless victim of the state. Rather, these writers live in a liminal state, improving an existence by their work with wheelbarrows. It is a fragile existence in which one character, unable to repair his broken wheelbarrow, ends up in an insane asylum and dies there.

In his more ambitious urban novel, *Texaco*, the main character is a female version of the *djobeur* from the previous novel. This woman's life story consists of multilayered texts, just as the edifice that she occupies—with a bar—is a multilayered building. The focus of *Texaco* is the founding and the historical development of the city. Thus the city is structured like a text and a language, making this novel a postmodern work par excellence. A novel rich in orality, it does not, nonetheless, privilege orality or writing, but maintains an unresolved tension between the two.

Chamoiseau is a serious and longtime reader of one of the most influential thinkers of the Caribbean, Eduoard Glissant.

Chamoiseau's novels are a fictionalization of Glissant's theory that liminality is a basic characteristic of the Caribbean.

Selected Work: Chronique des sept misères (1986, *Chronicle of the Seven Sorrows*, translation Linda Coverdale, 1999); *Solibo Magnifique* (1988, *Solibo the Magnificent*); *Texaco* (1992); *Bibliques des derniers gestes* (2002).

Changó, el gran putas (1993, Changó, the big SOB, by Manuel Zapata Olivella. Written in Spanish and untranslated. Bogotá: La Oveja Negra) [**Novel**] The major novel novel by this Colombian novelist, it offers a vast historic vision of the African diaspora to the Americas, both North and South. This is Zapata Olivella's culminating work, after a lifetime of research and writing about the African culture and history in Colombia and beyond, in this work the author incorporates cultural heroes such as Bentos Bioho, Francois Mackandal, and Nat Turner and ends with the death of Malcom X. Broad in scope, the novel spans three continents and six centuries of African and Afro-American history. It begins in Africa and then moves to Colombia and other regions of the Americas, ending in the United States. Zapata Olivella synthesizes multivocal oral cultures in this epic saga of a people's striving for liberation. As an Afro-Colombian writer, he writes in an Afro-Caribbean novelistic tradition of rewriting history that includes V. S. Reid and Maryse Condé.

Chávez Alfaro, Lizandro [**Biography**] Nicaraguan novelist, short story writer, and journalist, Chávez Alfaro was born in Bluefields, Nicaragua, in 1929. One of Nicaragua's major writers, his fiction tends to deal with historical events in Nicaragua, often returning to the Sandino war. While his readers learn of Nicaragua's history, he offers portraits of social life in this nation, with emphasis on the social injustice. He lived in Mexico from the 1940s to 1976, where he wrote fiction while working as a journalist, theater director, and radio announcer. Later he also served as director of an important publishing house in Central America, the Editorial Universitaria Centroamericana (EDUCA). After the triumph of the Sandinista Revolution he held positions in Nicaragua.

Chávez Alfaro's major work, *Trágame tierra* (1969, Swallow me earth), is a historical novel dealing with young men who, after suffering from corruption and social injustice, decide to become guerrilla fighters. The novel tells of two generations of a family's opposition to the dictatorship, and the dominance and terror of the dictatorship is portrayed throughout. In the novel's final pages the family desolately manages two funerals, for two sons are killed in the end.

Selected Work: *Trágame tierra* (1969).

Cheiro de Deus, O (2001, The scent of God, by Roberto Drummond. Written in Portuguese and untranslated. Rio de Janeiro: Objetiva) [**Novel**] The Drummond family from Belo Horizonte is the source of a tapestry of anecdotes and tall tales that constitute the plot for *O Cheiro de Deus*. Written in the tradition of magical realism, the story shares many qualities of Gabriel García Márquez's *Cien años de soledad*. Consequently, ghosts inhabit the city and a drunken werewolf terrifies the populace but is foretold to be the frog prince of Catula, the grandaughter of Vô Inacia who changes from being a cautious white girl to being a sensual black girl whenever the wind blows. The minority status of the hybrid Scottish Brazilian Drummond clan interacting with their inland Brazilian surroundings also makes this work comparable to other minority fictions currently being produced in Brazil, such as those by Milton Hatoum. Old Parr Drummond and Vô Inacia begin the tradition of naming their male offspring after bottles of Scotch—Johnnie Walker, Red Label, and the like. The family tree is a web of incest among nieces and uncles, aunts and nephews. Against the family is the indefatigable Coronel Bim Bim who rivals Vô Inacia for power over the region. Throughout the circular narrative Vô Inacia smells changes in the air, constantly hoping to smell God before she dies. The incredible and the mundane coexist in this recent example of magical realism as produced in Brazil.

Chicano novel [**Topic**] There is considerable debate about the use of any term applied to Hispanic writers in the United States of Mexican American origin, but many writers and scholars within this tradition refer to the novels produced by this group as the Chicano novel. The generally recognized founding fathers of the modern Chicano novel are Rudolfo Anaya, Miguel Méndez, Rolando Hinojosa-Smith, and Tomás Rivera, all of whom wrote major novels in the 1970s and were the first generation of Chicano novelists to be broadly recognized. Nevertheless, there were novelistic precedents to these important writers (such as Americo Paredes and John Rechy) as well as important novelists of the same period and later. Scholars of the Chicano novel point to origins in the Spanish colonial period in Mexico and the region of the southwestern United States with the writings of Spanish colonizers. In addition, recent research has identified important Hispanic texts of the nineteenth century that can be read as forerunners to modern Chicano literature. Widely recognized modern (now canonical) novels include Méndez's *Peregrinos de Aztlán*, Anaya's *Bless Me, Ultima*, and Tomás Rivera's *. . . y no se lo tragó la tierra*.

In the 1980s many of the most prominent writers have been women—Chicanas. They have questioned many of the totalizing projects and interests in national identity of the major male writers of the 1960s and 1970s, taking the lead from two of the most prominent Chicana intellectuals and writers of the 1980s, Gloria Andalzúa and Cherríe Moraga. Leading novelists of this period are Ana Castillo and Sandra Cisneros. Indeed, Cisneros's *House on Mango Street* and Castillo's *The Mixquiahuala Letters* have become modern classics among Chicano writers, read by a broad public beyond the limits of those specializing in Chicano literature. Castillo has been translated into Spanish and is read throughout the Americas, North and South. Other prominent Chicano novelists include Ron Arias, Oscar Zeta Acosta, Helena Maria Viramontes, and Denise Chavez.

Chile [Nation] The Chilean novel of the second half of the twentieth century inherited a strong literary tradition dating back to the nineteenth century. The tradition emphasized poetry, however, for the nation's young intellectuals could count two Nobel laureates among its poets (Gabriela Mistral and Pablo Neruda) and, until José Donoso, no internationally recognized novelists. Important forerunners of women's writing in Chile, in addition to Mistral, were the fiction writers Marta Brunet and María Luisa Bombal. Donoso gained international acclaim in the 1960s and 1970s as a participant in the 1960s Boom of the Latin American novel.

The overthrow of the democratically elected government of Salvador Allende in 1973, followed by the military dictatorship of Augusto Pinochet, produced both the novels of exile (of Antonio Skármeta, Ariel Dorfman, Poli Délano, and Isabel Allende) and a culture of resistance of writers who remained within (Diamela Eltit and Pedro Lemebel).

The major novelists of the post-1945 period have been José Donoso, Carlos Droguett, Jorge Edwards, Antonio Skármeta, and Diamela Eltit. New writers of the 1990s who have gained international recognition at a young age are Alberto Fuguet, Ramón Díaz Eterovic, Roberto Bolaño, Lina Meruane, Gonzalo Contreras, and Sergio Gómez.

Cidade de Deus (1997, City of God, by Paulo Lins. Written in Portuguese and untranslated. São Paulo: Companhia das Letras) **[Novel]** Lins captures a glimpse of the misery and violence of the notorious favela, Cidade de Deus, on the outskirts of Rio de Janeiro—from its construction in the 1960s to the drug turf wars of the 1970s. The novel is divided into three sections, each one following the life and death of a known criminal. One of the tougher of the three criminals robs and kills at will and is eventually gunned down by corrupt police armed with machine guns. In the second section the now more developed favela is taken over by the drug gang of Zé Miudo and Pardalhzinho, the latter of whom attempts to join the young kids of the beach scene who wear designer clothes and listen to rock and roll. In the third section Zé Miudo rules the city alone after Pardalzinho's death; his rape of a local girl sparks a gang war with Zé Bonito, a worker turned vigilante and drug lord. The increased violence and the youth of the combatants creates a media outcry that is met by a police crackdown—splintering the drug gang and eventually leading to Zé Miudo's betrayal and killing by some of his associates. The novel was adapted into a very successful film of the same title, directed by Fernando Meirelles in 2002.

Cidade Sitiada, A (1949, *Besieged City,* by Clarice Lispector. Translation by Giovanni Pontiero. London: Carcanet, 1999) [**Novel**] This work was an innovative and pioneering novel in Brazil when it appeared. In several ways it represented for the Brazilian novel what María Luisa Bombal's novels of the 1930s meant for Chile: both writers were pioneering feminist writers at a time when the novel was still a male preserve in Latin America. *A Cidade Sitiada* narrates an internal struggle of a woman attempting to adjust to her circumstances. She lives a precarious existence on the border between reality and her dreams. Lispector uses physical space to delineate between her two lives: in the small town of São Geraldo she is a young woman with ideals and hopes; in the large city she is the married woman and the materialist. In both spaces, however, she longs for another life, never satisfied with her immediate situation. Despite the ongoing suffering, this novel is an affirmation of a woman's ability to take control of her own life.

Cien años de soledad (1967, *One Hundred Years of Solitude,* by Gabriel García Márquez. Translation by Gregory Rabassa. New York: Random House, 1970) [**Novel**] One of the most widely read Latin American novels of the twentieth century, this is the Colombian writer's modern classic of magical realism. Easily accessible to a broad range of readers, this novel has been translated into over fifty languages, openly imitated throughout Latin America, and widely parodied. *Cien años de soledad* is the story of the Buendía family and the story of Macondo. An omniscient narrator tells the story of the family and the town from the foundation of Macondo in prehistoric times to the twentieth century. The novel's prodigious characters and events, told with the understatement and hyperbole that have become García Márquez's trademark, have made it one of Latin America's most entertaining and memorable novels. *Cien años de soledad* has been the object of multiple critical readings, having been interpreted as a historical, a political, and a mythic text and having been read as an exercise in the fantastic. Even though the roots of magical realism are to be found in Latin America in the 1920s and 1930s, it is often cited as the prototype of Latin American magical realism that has led to what some critics consider rewriting and others consider the imitation of writers such as Isabel Allende, Rosario Ferré, and Giaconda Belli. Other critics have noted the parodies of García Márquez in the 1970s novels of Colombian novelists Gustavo Alvarez Gardeazábal and Marco Tulio Aguilera Garramuño. Younger writers born in the 1960s, who began publishing in the 1990s, have almost uniformly rejected the writing of García Márquez, favoring urban settings and nonmagical realist approaches to storytelling (see generation of the 1990s).

Cisneros, Sandra [**Biography**] Novelist, short story writer, and poet, she is a leading Latina writer in the U.S. Her work is also well-known in Mexico and other nations of Latin America, where she is read in Spanish translation. She has spoken of her affinity with the work of Latin American novelists such as Juan Rulfo and Manuel Puig and considers herself a cartographer writing the stories that have not been written. Having published a relatively small amount of poetry and short fiction, she has, nevertheless, won numerous awards and been widely recognized as a major American writer. Born in Chicago in 1954 of a Mexican father and a Mexican American mother, she has drawn heavily on her childhood experiences of poverty and the specificity of her cultural heritage in her writing.

In fact, a turning point for her was at the Iowa Writer's Workshop in the late 1970s when, upon hearing a discussion of Bachelard and the poetics of space she decided to write of her own experience and space as a working-class Latina. As a child the family moved often between Chicago and Mexico, and important early readings for her were Virginia Lee Burton's *The Little House* and Lewis Carroll's *Alice's Adventures in Wonderland*. She began writing poetry while in high school and continued her creative process with experiments in fiction and poetry in the 1970s, exploring gender, poverty, self-identity, and cultural suppression. Among the numerous awards this author has received are fellowships from the National Endowment for the Arts and the MacArthur Foundation. She earned a BA in English from Loyola University in Chicago in 1976 and an MFA from the University of Iowa Writers' Workshop in 1978. She taught at the Latino Youth Alternative High School in Chicago from 1978 to 1980. She served as literature director at the Guadalupe Cultural Arts Center in San Antonio, Texas from 1984 to 1985, and has taught at California State University at Chico, the University of California, Berkeley, the University of California, Irvine, the University of Michigan, and the University of New Mexico. Her collections of poems include *Bad Boys* (1980), *My Wicked Ways* (1987), and *Loose Woman* (1994). Her poetry often alludes to her childhood roots in Chicago, including the sexual guilt associated with her rigid Catholic upbringing.

Cisneros has published three books of fiction, beginning with a volume of short stories titled *Woman Hollering Creek and Other Stories* (1991) and followed by the novels *The House on Mango Street* (1984) and *Caramelo* (2002). In this fiction she creates characters who are distinctively Latinos and Latinas and she uses language in ways that emphasize their isolation from mainstream American culture. Her fiction treats subjects such as the degradation associated with poverty and cultural conflict and, like many Latin American writers, she writes with an awareness of her need to address issues that are specifically Latina as well as more general, universal themes.

Her major novel, *The House on Mango Street*, is a volume of loosely structured vignettes that some readers prefer to consider as a set of stories. In this work an impoverished Latina, Esperanza, longs for a room of her own in a house of her dreams. Esperanza also questions the ambiguities and confusion of growing up Latina in the U.S., the possibilities of writing as an emotional defense, and whether to give marriage priority over her education. This novel has been a centerpiece for academic debates over mainstream literature versus multicultural literature in the high school and college classroom.

Like many Latin American writers of her generation writing in Spanish, she self-consciously attempts to avoid the stereotypes and clichés associated with magical realism. Like Ana Castillo, she also employs words and phrases in Spanish, where the cultural context obliges her to do so, as well as subtle shifts in rhythm, syntax, and vocabulary that reflect the nuances of Spanish speakers who are speaking or writing in English. One result of the cultural debates in U.S. academia that have often centered on the work of Cisneros has been her inclusion in the *Norton Anthology of American Literature*. Some critics have noted, however, that Cisneros's children's literature and writing dealing with adolescent themes have been more widely accepted in U.S. academia than her writing confronting cultural and ethnic issues in an adult context.

Selected Work: The House on Mango Street (1984); *Caramelo* (2002).

City of Night (1963, by John Rechy. Written in English. New York: Grove) [**Novel**] A pioneering gay Chicano novel, it was published by one of the most prolific Chicano novelists well before Chicano writers enjoyed the national and international visibility that characterized the 1970s and 1980s. *City of the Night* was Rechy's first novel, and it soon became intensely controversial. It deals with a young man from an abusive El Paso home who travels around the United States working as a gay prostitute. Chicano critics have tended to ignore Rechy, since many of the scenarios in his work are not specifically Hispanic and the culture of homosexuality was not a topic with which critics were as familiar in the early stages of Chicano literature as they are today. Nevertheless, some scholars have recovered this and other of Rechy's texts as foundational Chicano novels. The episodic structure of *City of the Night* has led many readers and critics to compare it with the picaresque. Some of these discussions about whether or not to define it as picaresque were used to reduce this novel to that category and, consequently, not really a novel. Other critics, however, have demonstrated that this work has as much structure and unity as any picaresque novel. The transgressive sexuality of *City of the Night* has also been understood in recent years as a way of being oppositional to mainstream American society.

Ciudad anterior, La (1991, The city before, by Gonzalo Contreras. Written in Spanish and untranslated. Buenos Aires: Planeta, 1993) [**Novel**] The first novel by one of Chile's more promising young writers, *La ciudad anterior* is as pessimistic as much Chilean fiction of the 1980s and 1990s, during and immediately following the military dictatorship: while the nation is undergoing an economic boom, the author keeps the reader in a melancholic city in the northern provinces of Chile. In this dull town the protagonist keeps busy playing electronic games and watching karate movies. He lives in a pension house with a family in which the father is physically handicapped and the son is a cretin. The protagonist has an affair with the father's wife; their first date is in a cemetery.

Ciudad y los perros, La (1963, *The Time of the Hero*, by Mario Vargas Llosa. Translation by Lysander Kemp. New York: Grove, 1966) [**Novel**] The earliest novel by this Peruvian writer, it is often cited as the first book of the 1960s Boom of Latin American fiction. Set in a military school in Lima, Peru, its main characters are adolescent cadets who represent a microcosm of Peruvian society. Faulkner was Vargas Llosa's idol, a fact that is evident in this neo-Faulknerian work with a fragmented structure and a variety of interior monologues. The plot involves a stolen exam and an eventual death among the cadets, the cause of which school officials cover up. The book's sex scenes and violence, as well as negative portrayal of military hierarchies, made it a scandalous book in Peru and an immediate best seller throughout Latin America. Vargas Llosa's debut showed him to be a master of portraying depravity, abuse, and the way that much human activity is merely the result of self-interest. He also develops in his mastery of the art of telling a story that is simultaneously complex, engaging, and accessible. In the early 1960s this was one of the first novels written by a Latin American writer to attain the status of best seller soon after its publication beyond the author's national borders. Read widely throughout Latin America in the early 1960s, it can indeed be seen as a beginning for what became known later as the 1960s Boom of Latin American fiction.

Cliff, Michelle [Biography] Caribbean novelist, poet, and essayist, she was born in Kingston, Jamaica, in 1946 and grew up in New York. She has experimented with several kinds of prose poetry in the collection *Claiming an Identity They Taught Me to Despise* (1980) and *Land of Look Behind* (1985). Her volume of short stories *Bodies of Water* (1990) interrogates issues of migration and fragile identity.

Cliff's fiction is directly autobiographical, often touching upon her identity as a light-skinned Afro-American. Her first two novels, *Abeng* (1984) and *No Telephone to Heaven* (1987), are fictionalizations of these issues of race and identity. Her later novel *Free Enterprise* (1993) focuses on slavery in the United States and includes historical characters.

Selected Work: Abeng (1984); *No Telephone to Heaven* (1987); *Free Enterprise* (1993).

Cobra (1972, *Cobra*, by Severo Sarduy. Translation by Suzanne Jill Levine. New York: Dutton, 1975) **[Novel]** A highly influential work for young Latin American writers interested in experimentation, *Cobra* is Sarduy's novelistic reflection on language and writing. The novel's title refers to a poem by Octavio Paz from *Conjunciones y disyunciones* that dramatizes the generation of language. The association of words in this poem creates more words, a process parallel to much of *Cobra*, which was one of the early Latin American texts to blur the line between fictional and theoretical discourse; this novel refers freely to the French theorists Derrida and Lacan, two theorists whom Sarduy parodies. The novel has a fragmented and digressive plot that takes the characters (who change in iden-

tity and gender as the novel develops) across several continents. More specifically, this novel consists of two interwoven narratives, the first of which, the Teatro Lírico de Muñecas (Lyrical Theater of Dolls), takes place in a burlesque house. The protagonist is Cobra, who is a transsexual star at the theater. Cobra and the owner of the theater, La Señora, are involved in a process to reduce the size of Cobra's feet, but the drug they take reduces the pair to dwarfs, now named Pup and La Señorita. Then Cobra goes to India in search of the proper oriental paints and colors for the theater. In the other narrative Cobra goes to Tangiers in search of a doctor famous for sex-change operations, Dr. Ktazob. In Tangiers some drug traffickers from Amsterdam direct Cobra to Dr. Ktazob. The novel concludes at the Chinese border of Tibet, where Cobra has gone with a group of motorcyclists. Both playful, enigmatic, and hermetic, *Cobra* was a unique and paradigm-shifting text to appear in Latin America in the early 1970s.

Cola de zorro (1970, Fox tail, by Fanny Buitrago. Written in Spanish and untranslated. Bogotá: Tercer Mundo) **[Novel]** The second novel by one of Colombia's most accomplished women writers, this one is also her most complex. More a novel of concept than of character or plot, *Cola de zorro* develops abstracts ideas about family tradition. This novel shares some of the generational attitudes found in her first novel: the characters lack clear direction and their existence tends to be boring. It deals with human relationships within the context of a large, extended family, telling the story of three generations.

Collyer, Jaime [Biography] Chilean novelist and short story writer, he is one of the leading writers of his generation in Chile, one that began writing during the dictatorship of Augusto Pinochet. Born in Santiago, Chile, in 1955, he studied psychology at the Universidad de Chile and then went to Spain in 1981 to study international relations and political science in Madrid. His generation was marked by a loss of innocence with the brutal regime of Pinochet, and Collyer's writing often takes place in an oppressive and asfixiating setting, an unnamed metropolis that is easily identifiable as the Santiago of the dictatorship.

Collyer's fiction is characterized by two opposing tendencies. On the one hand, he and some of his peers wrote a realist and conventional fiction that rejected the more technically audacious writing of the 1960s Boom, personified in Chile by the figure of José Donoso. He also rejected the hyperexperimention of postmodern writers such as Diamela Eltit. Thus Collyer, along with his contemporaries Gonzalo Contreras and Carlos Franz, writes linear stories with clearly identifiable plots. On the other hand, in contradistinction with his apparent conventionality, Collyer uses a parodic language that challenges established discourses. Even though Collyer sympathized with the political left during the dictatorship, his parodies included the leftist discourses of revolution and liberation.

In his novels Collyer writes of an anonymous city that is claustrophobic and oppressive. In his early novel *El infiltrado* (1989, The infiltrator) he offered a critique of much leftist political discourse in Chile, which he felt was incapable of taking Chile out of the dictatorship and moving forward. To the contrary, the dictatorship was eliminating all of Chile's young political idealists. In this work the protagonist is disenchanted with the left but his wife is a fervent militant. He believes that his love for her is the only thing of value in his life, even though he is in conflict with her throughout the novel. In the end, however, she is betrayed by her political cohorts, and

she reaches the same conclusion: her only tenable attachment is with her husband. In his novel *El habitante del cielo* (2002, The inhabitant of the sky) the protagonist György Nagy is a Hungarian obsessed with inventing airplanes in the nineteenth century. Given this inventor's creativity and vision, his project can be seen as a metaphor for writing.

Collyer's fiction promotes a respect for human beings as individuals independent of political persuasion. He believes in living beyond ideology, in a "supraideology" world. Collyer has won several literary prizes in Chile and Spain since the 1980s. His volume of short stories *Gente al acecho* (1992) appeared in English as *People on the Prowl* (1996).

Selected Work: Hacia el nuevo mundo (1985); *Los años perdidos* (1986); *El infiltrado* (1989); *Cien pájaros volando* (1996); *El habitante del cielo* (2002).

Como agua para chocolate (1989, *Like Water for Chocolate,* by Laura Esquivel. Translation by Margaret Sayers Peden. New York: Randon House, 1991) [**Novel**] One of the most widely read Latin American novels of the 1990s, *Como agua para chocolate* is the first novel by the enormously successful Esquivel. Along with Angeles Mastretta's *Arráncame la vida* (*Mexican Bolero*), this novel began a movement in Mexico that critics have called *literatura light*—easily accessible and entertaining works that are sold in an impressively high volume. Indeed, *Como agua para chocolate* has outsold the works not only of Esquivel's contemporaries in Mexico but also the novels of the 1960s Boom. This novel has been described as a fairy tale, a soap opera romance, a book of Mexican recipes, and a home remedies guide. Each of the novel's twelve chapters corresponds to a month of the year and begins with a recipe for a traditional Mexican dish. The recipe then moves into the narration of a love story. Like García Márquez and Rudolfo Anaya, Esquivel demonstrates the ability in *Como agua para chocolate* to create fictions that are accessible to her own cultural community as well as a broader literary establishment.

Company, Flavia [Biography] Argentine novelist, poet, and short story writer born in 1963, she has lived in Spain between Barcelona and Sant Carles de la Ràpita since 1973. She has published eight novels in addition to short stories, poems, and children's literature. She has written for the newspapers *ABC Cataluña* and *El Periódico de Cataluña*. Her fiction has been translated into French, Portuguese, Dutch, and Polish. Company writes fiction in which things are rarely what they appear to be on the surface and the laws of causality do not always work. In her volume of short stories *Género de punto* (2002) she writes nineteen short fictions about alcoholic mothers, unappreciative friends, disillusioned widows, lovers blinded by passion, and sincere imposters. Some of the characters implicated in evil deeds write letters to present their version of the facts, a strategy similar to those found in Company's novels.

Company calls her novel *Ni tú ni yo ni nadie* (2002) a "novel in three acts, three interviews and a monologue." In the preface the narrator claims that she will attempt to tell the story in a reliable way (*de manera fidedigna*). She then points out, however, that absolute veracity is impossible, for everything depends on one's point of view. All conclusions, she maintains, are provisional.

Selected Work: Querida Nélida (1988); *Fuga y contrapuntos* (1989); *Círculos en acíbar* (1992); *Saurios en el asfalto* (1997); *Luz de hielo* (1998); *Dame placer* (1999); *Melalcor* (2001); *Ni tú ni yo ni nadie* (2002).

Condé, Maryse [Biography] Caribbean novelist and essayist, she has become one of the major spokespersons for Francophone women writers. She writes of class, race, and the marginality of Caribbean women. As part of her Caribbean dialogue on identity, she has published an essay in favor of *créole*, *La civilisation du bossale* (1978). Born in Guadeloupe, she entered the literary scene of both the Caribbean and the broader francophone world in the 1970s. In 1976 she authored the first book-length project to convey the voices of francophone Caribbean women writers, *La parole des femmes: Essai sur les romancières des Antilles de langue française*; the women in this volume speak of issues such as politics, religion, education, and love. She published her first novel, *Segou*, in 1984. Her novel *Heremakhonon* (1976) is written in the confessional mode and tells the story of a woman in exile. She has also authored *Traversée de la Mangrove* (1984).

Condé is best known for her novel *Moi, Tituba, sorcière . . . noire de Salem* (1986, (*I, Tituba, Black Witch of Salem*, 1992). In this work Condé takes a historic character and writes a fictional biography.

Selected Work: Segou (1984); *Traversée de la Mangrove* (1984); *Moi, Tituba, sorcière. . . . noire de Salem* (1986, *I, Tituba, Black Witch of Salem*, translation Richard Philcox, 1992).

Conde, Rosina [Biography] Mexican novelist, short story writer, poet, playwright, and essayist, she is well known in Mexico, along with Federico Campbell and Luis Humberto Crosthwaite, as one of the prominent new border writers. Conde was born in Mexicali (state of Baja California) in 1954 and, after pursing a broad range of jobs and activities, studied Hispanic literature at the National University in Mexico City (UNAM). She is also known as a feminist writer concerned with the role of women in Mexico, particularly on the border. Several of her stories are critical of the foreign-owned cheap labor *maquiladora* industry along the border. She has taught creative writing in Baja California. Some of her works, such as *El agente secreto* (1990, The secret agent), can be read as a volume of short stories or as a novel; it consists of ten stories with thematic similarities. Similarly, *Volver* (1992, Returning) consists of four anecdotes that allow a reading of the text as a novel. Her novel *Arrieras somos* (1994) has been translated into English as *Women on the Road* and can also be read as a volume of short stories.

Selected Work: *El agente secreto* (1990); *Volver* (1992); *Arrieras somos* (1994, *Women on the Road*, translation Gustavo V. Segada and Patricia Irby, 1994); *La Genara* (1998).

Confiant, Raphael [Biography] Caribbean novelist and essayist, he was born in Fort-de-France, Martinique, in 1951. Known throughout the Caribbean and France as an activist in the *créolité* movement, he contributed to the manifesto *Eloge de la créolité* (1989) as one of three authors, along with Patrick Chamoiseau and Jean Bernabé. With roots in Martinique in the early twentieth century, the *créolité* movement was a reaction against the Europeanization of the Caribbean and also against the *negritude* movement. Confiant authored a provocative essay questioning the concepts of one of the father figures of modern thought in Martinique under the title *Aimé Césaire: une traversée paradoxale du siècle* (1993, Aimé Césaire: a paradoxical journey across the century).

Confiant's early novels were not written in French—the dominant literary language of Martinique—but in Creole. He gained international recognition with his parodic and postmodern work, written in both French and Creole. Titles include *Le Nègre e l'Amiral* (1988, The black guy and the admiral), *L'allée des soupirs* (1994, The walkaway of sighs), and *La vièrge du grand* (1996, The

virgin's great comeback). In *Le Nègre e l'Amiral* a variety of self-reflective texts tell the story of a writer, Amedée Mauville, who seems to practice a type of automatic writing along the lines of André Breton, but influenced by Aimé Césaire as well. The self-reflective quality of the text makes Confiant's writing comparable to postmodern Caribbean works such as those of the Cubans Guillermo Cabrera Infante and Severo Sarduy and the Haitian Dany Laferrière. In *L'allée des soupirs* a poet from Martinique and a white foreign critic engage in a lengthy debate over the most authentic possible form of literary expression. The foreigner defends the cause of *créolité*; the poet argues for French and pastoral poetry. In the end the debate is parodied by two champions of public defecation who perform their acts before a group of admiring spectators.

Confiant is a postmodern Caribbean writer who favors Creole language and culture and whose novels emphasize his interest in language, the obscene, and the scatological. He writes along the lines of Cuban's Cabrera Infante, Puerto Rico's Luis Rafael Sánchez, and Colombia's R. H. Moreno-Durán.

Selected Work: *Le Nègre e l'Amiral* (1988); *L'allée des soupirs* (1994); *La vièrge du grand* (1996).

Conteris, Hiber [Biography] Uruguayan novelist, playwright, and essayist, he has become internationally recognized in the 1990s. Born in 1933, he studied literature and theology in Montevideo, Buenos Aires, and Paris. His life and career have had two stages. In the first stage, from the early 1960s to the early 1970s, he wrote his early fiction. His first novel, *Cono Sur* (1963, The southern cone) received honorable mention in a novel contest sponsored by *Marcha* magazine in Montevideo. His other novels were *Virginia en flashback* (1966, Virginia in flashback) and *El nadador* (1968, The swimmer).

The second stage in Conteris's life and writing career was defined by the military dictatorship that took power in Uruguay in the early 1970s. During the military dictatorship Conteris was a political prisoner from 1976 to 1985, afterward publishing his most recognized novel, *El diez por ciento de la vida* (1985, *Ten Percent of Life*), which he wrote in prison. He also won the prestigious Letras de Oro prize for his volume of short stories *Información sobre la Ruta 1* (1987, Information on Route 1).

Selected Work: Cono Sur (1963); *Virginia en flashback* (1966); *El nadador* (1968); *El diez por ciento de la vida* (1985, *Ten Percent of Life*, translation Deborah Bergman, 1987); *La Diana en el crepúsculo* (1986); *El breve verano de Nefertiti* (1996); *Roundtrip* (1998).

Conti, Haroldo [Biography] Argentine novelist, short story writer, and playwright born in 1925, he began his literary career by winning a short story prize sponsored by *Life* magazine in 1960. A highly respected "writers' writer," as he began writing novels he had equally good fortune with prizes: the Argentine publishing firm Fabril Editora awarded him a national prize for his novel *Sudeste* (1962, Southeast); he received the Premio Municipal de Buenos Aires (a prize given by the city of Buenos Aires) in 1964 for his novel *Todos los veranos* (All the summers).

Conti portrayed alienated and marginalized individuals who lived isolated from society in a fashion similar to the characters of Juan Carlos Onetti. They tend to be outsiders and rebels. *Alrededor de la jaula* (1967, Around the cage) functions on the basis of allegory, fictionalizing a young boy who feels like a caged animal. The Universidad Veracruzana in Mexico gave him a prize for this novel in 1966. In *En vida* (1971, While alive) the alienated protagonist abandons his wife to live with a prostitute.

During the military dictatorship Conti was one of several prominent intellectuals who disappeared. He died in 1980.

Selected Work: Sudeste (1962); *Todos los veranos* (1964); *Alrededor de la jaula* (1967); *En vida* (1971).

Contreras, Gonzalo [Biography] Chilean novelist, journalist, magazine editor, and short story writer, he has been associated with the writers of the McOndo group. He can also be associated in a general sense with the generation of the 1990s in Latin America. He is a contemporary of the McOndo organizers Alberto Fuguet and Sergio Gómez as well as Arturo Fontaine Talavera, all of whom began writing in Chile under the dictatorship of Pinochet. His first book was a collection of short stories titled *La danza ejecutada* (1985).

Contreras writes fiction that can be read as a counterdiscourse to the positive economic discourse of the military regime and neoliberalism: this is a gloomy fictionalization of Chile. His first novel, *La ciudad anterior* (1991, The city before), is written along these pessimistic lines: while Chile is living its supposed economic boom, the author keeps the reader in a melancholic city in the northern provinces of Chile. In this dull town the protagonist keeps busy playing electronic games and watching karate movies. He lives in a pension house with a family in which the father is physically handicapped and the son is a cretin. The protagonist has an affair with the father's wife, and their first date is in a cementery. Contreras was awarded a national prize for this work.

Selected Work: La ciudad anterior (1991); *El nadador* (1995); *El gran mal* (1998); *La ley natural* (2004).

Conversación en La Catedral (1969, *Conversation in The Cathedral*, by Mario Vargas Llosa. Translation by Gregory Rabassa. New York: Harper and Row, 1975) [**Novel**] Vargas Llosa's third novel and a technical tour de force; it is his most complex work. The setting is 1950s Peru and the characters live under the dictatorship of Manuel Odría, who controlled Peru with an iron fist from 1948 to 1956, when Vargas Llosa was living there as a student. The point of departure is the following question, which is set forth on the novel's first page: exactly when did Peru "screw up?" Two characters meet in a bar in downtown Lima, La Catedral, and their dialogue is an attempt to reconstruct their lives in the context of national life under Odría. From this dialogue, however, Vargas Llosa takes the reader directly into numerous other overlapping dialogues, flashbacks, and interior monologues. The result is a complex mosaic that the reader can evaluate and judge in order to somehow respond to the questions of when and how Peru "screwed up." Once again, as in his previous novels, Vargas Llosa shows human depravity at its worst and individuals motived more by self-interest that any of their stated political, religious, or ethical objectives. This neo-Faulknerian work fully engages the reader in a complex web of plot development and relations between the characters.

Cony, Carlos Heitor [Biography] Brazilian novelist, essayist, and journalist born in 1926 in Rio de Janeiro, he is widely recognized in Brazil as one of the nation's most prolific and accomplished writers. He has published over thirty books of fiction as well as chronicles and journalism. He writes about human relations among middle-class Brazilians from Rio de Janeiro, with a focus on their inner lives. Portraying the privileged life of a small group of characters and the relations between them, he writes novels that are easily comparable to the small screen fiction of Sergio Galindo

in Mexico; in the case of Cony the focus is on relationships that lack substance, for his marriages lack love, and all human relationships lead inevitably to betrayal, violence, and death. His early fiction was exceptionally well-received in Brazil: his early novels *A Verdade de Cada Dia* (1957, The truth of every day) and *Tijolo de Seguranca* (1958, Security brick) received a prize for best novel, the Prêmio Manuel Antônio de Almeida. His novel *Matéria de Memória* (1962, Matter of memory) has been described by the renowned Brazilian novelist and essayist Antonio Callado as Cony's major work. It deals with the relationship of a married couple, with lengthy descriptions of a tense and occasionally torturous marriage, always burdened with unstable emotional connections. This novel's ending leaves the characters anguished and, in the end, on the verge of an outbreak or explosion of some sort.

In his youth he spent seven years in a seminary, emerging as a rebellious young man. He read the European classics with great enthusiasm, but considered the discovery of José Lins do Rêgo, the Brazilian writer of the 1930s and 1940s, a revelation. In the 1960s he was a journalist for the newspapers *Correio da Manhã* of Rio de Janeiro and *Folha de São Paulo* before being arrested for his political ideas by the military regime and being jailed for a few days. He has published three biographical essays: *Chaplin* (Chaplin), *Quem matou Vargas* (Who killed Vargas) and *JK: Memorial do Exílio* (JK: exile memorial). In 1993 he assumed a regular column in the *Fohla de São Paulo.*

With respect to his fiction, it tends to be critical of conventional values and pessimistic in tone to the point of cynicism; among his most cynical works is *Pilotos* (1973, Pilates), in which the protagonist is castrated and becomes totally skeptical about the possibilities of happiness. In 1995, after two decades without publishing fiction, he received the most prestigious literary award in Brazil, the Prêmio Jabuti, for *Quase Memória* (Nearly memory). Since his return to the novel in the mid-1990s, he has become quite active in fiction writing and since 2000 he has occupied the prestigious third seat in the Brazilian Academy of Letters. His recent *A Casa do Poeta Trágico* (1997) is the story of the relationship between a middle-aged man facing an intense midlife crisis and a young woman seeking advancement in the business world. Although the relationship seems to begin with passion, it ends after two decades in emptiness and divorce. In this work Cony uses a three-part structure to develop the story and employs the biblical allusions that appear throughout his work, inviting the reader to compare the characters to figures in the Bible. As for many writers of his generation in Latin America who emerged in the 1950s, Cony's writing is an ongoing search for the individual's significance in life within the context of pain, conflict, and crisis.

Selected Work: O Ventre (1957); *Tijolo de Seguranca* (1960); *Matéria de Memória* (1962); *Antes, o Verão* (1964); *Balé Branco* (1966); *Pessach: A Travessia* (1967); *Pilatos* (1973); *Quase Memória* (1993); *O Piano e a Orquestra* (1996); *A Casa do Poeta Trágico* (1997); *Romance Sem Palabras* (1999); *O Indigitado* (2001); *O Mistério das Aranãs Verdes* (2001); *A Tarde da Sua Ausência* (2003).

Coronel no tiene quién le escriba, El (1961, *No One Writes to the Colonel and Other Stories,* by Gabriel García Márquez. Translation by J. S. Bernstein. New York: Harper and Row, 1968) [**Novel**] An early masterpiece by the Nobel laureate most well known for *One Hundred Years of Solitude*, this is considered his best book by some Latin American writers. It belongs to the early group of fictions that García wrote in the 1950s set in the fictional town of Macondo and, consequently, often called his Macondo cycle. It is a short novel that tells the story of an aging colonel and life in Macondo in a simple, straightforward style. The colonel had been in Colombia's legendary War of a Thousand Days (1899–1902). The novel's "present" is the mid-1950s, a period of intense political violence in Colombia. Like the characters from García Márquez's novel *Leafstorm*, in the 1920s the colonel suffered from the decadence in the region that was associated with the arrival of the United Fruit Company. The novel covers a period of approximately three months and it presents the colonel's boredom and suffering. There is a political subtext that is to be found in the novel's silences—what is not stated. Despite the dismal situation of the colonel and the town, García Márquez offers notes of affirmation and optimism that are omnispresent in his fictions of Macondo.

Corpi, Lucha [Biography] Chicana novelist, poet, and essayist, she is one of the few U.S. Hispanic writers of detective novels or crime fiction. She was born in Jáltipan (state of Veracruz), Mexico, in 1945, and studied at the University of California, Berkeley, where she received her BA and MA in comparative literature. Her fast-moving plots are typical of the genre, but her detective figure, Gloria Damasco, broadens the classic representation of the Anglo-American detective. Her first novel, *Delia's Song* (1989), describes minority politics on the Berkeley campus. After that she turned to her highly successful detective fiction, creating Gloria Damasco in *Eulogy for a Brown Angel* (1992), a work some critics have identified as a feminist detective novel. Her detective seems to possess an understanding of reality that surpasses conventionally rational forms of logic.

Corpi continued her production of fast-paced crime fiction with *Cactus Blood* (1995), a novel set in the early 1970s in the context of the struggle of the United Farm Workers. She writes these novels in the English that she learned in the U.S. educational system; her most intimate poetry and short fiction are written in her native language of Spanish. She was awarded the PEN Oakland Josephine Miles Award and the Multicultural Publishers Exchange Best Book of Fiction Award for *Eulogy for a Brown Angel*.

Selected Work: *Delia's Song* (1989); *Eulogy for a Brown Angel* (1992); *Cactus Blood* (1995); *Black Widow's Wardrobe* (1999).

Cortázar, Julio [Biography] Argentine novelist, short story writer, essayist, and translator, he is one of the major intellectual figures of the century throughout Latin America. Along with Borges, he played a central role in promoting innovation and experimentation among several generations of Latin American writers in the second half of the twentieth century. For over three decades many of these Latin American writers have made reference to the singular importance of Cortázar for them, first as young readers, later as writers. Even many feminists, who might reject some of Cortázar's sexist language, refer to Cortázar's key role as a revolutionary writer. Many critics consider him at his best as a short story writer; some of his early stories of the 1950s are broadly considered modern classics. He was born of Argentine parents in Belgium in 1914 and, after spending his formative years in Argentina, moved to Paris permanently in 1951. The political atmosphere under Perón in the 1940s had become increasingly suffocating, and he began writing short stories during those difficult years. Cortázar published his early story "Casa tomada" in Borges's magazine *Los Anales de Buenos Aires*, and his first stories, written between 1937 and 1946, appeared in a volume titled *La otra orilla*. He wrote the novels *Divertimento* (Divertimento) and *El examen* (The exam) in 1949 and 1950, respectively, although he did not publish them during his lifetime. In the 1950s he published two volumes of short stories under the titles *Bestiario* (1951, *Bestiary*) and *Final del juego* (1956, *End of the Game and Other Stories*). These short fictions of the 1950s were pioneering works in the fantastic and other realms of the intangible and nonempirical world; many of them have been broadly read throughout Latin America by scholars and writers alike for decades. With this early writing Cortázar began a lifetime project of questioning Western rationality and subverting it. In the 1960s he continued publishing engaging and challenging volumes of short stories: *Historias de cronopios y de famas* (1962, *Cronopios and Famas*), *Las armas secretas* (1965, *The secret arms*), and *Todos los fuegos el fuego* (1966, *All Fires the Fire*). As his short fiction developed in the 1960s and 1970s, he found ways to incorporate subtle political themes into the stories. His commitment to social change and revolutionary politics was consistent from the early 1960s to his death; he fully supported Fidel Castro and the Sandinistas.

Cortázar wrote several novels, but his major work, according to most critics, consists of his short stories and his novel *Rayuela* (1963, *Hopscotch*). This experimental, ludic, and wide-ranging work offers the reader multiple possible alternative readings, questioning many of the conventions not only of traditional and modernist fiction but also of reading. In many ways, and for many reasons, *Hopscotch* has become a seminal work of the twentieth century in Latin America. Nevertheless, his novels *62: modelo para armar* (1968, *62: A Model Kit*) and *Libro de Manuel* (1972, *A Manual for*

Manuel) are novels that have been of interest to scholars of Latin American literature, writers, and a small sector of the general reading public. His novel *El examen*, written in the 1950s during the Perón regime in Argentina, was published posthumously in 1986. Another of his posthumous works was *Diary of Andrés Fava* (2005), a fragment from what had been *El examen*, consisting of the daily jottings of a marginal character in that novel. It was written in 1950 and is set in fog-bound Buenos Aires.

In the mid-1960s Cortázar declared his commitment to an increased political activism and a decreased literary experimentation. His writing and life of the 1970s and early 1980s (until his death in 1984) reflected the tensions of this dual commitment. At the beginning of the twenty-first century scholarly criticism and praise of his work from Latin American writers continue unabated.

Selected Work: Los premios (1960, *The Winners*, translation Elaine Kerrigan, 1965); *Rayuela* (1963, *Hopscotch*, translation Gregory Rabassa, 1966); *62: modelo para armar* (1968, *62: A Model Kit*, translation Gregory Rabassa, 1972); *Libro de Manuel* (1972, *A Manual for Manual*, translation Gregory Rabassa, 1978); *El examen* (1986); *Diary of Andrés Fava* (2005).

Costa Rica [Nation] Costa Rica gained its independence from Spain in the nineteenth century and has enjoyed more political and cultural autonomy than most of its neighboring nations in the region. It has also been free of the political strife and civil wars that have afflicted most Central American nations since 1945.

The major novelists of the post-1945 period have been Carmen Naranjo, Quince Duncan, Joaquín Gutiérrez, and Yoland Oreamuno. Oreamuno's *La ruta de su evasión* (1949, The route of her evasion) is a major modern novel, and Carmen Naranjo is the leading contemporary feminist writer in Costa Rica.

Costantini, Humberto [Biography] Argentine novelist and short story writer who was born in 1924 and died in 1987, he won the prestigious Casa de las Américas prize for his novel *De dioses, hombrecitos y policías* (1979, *The Gods, the Little Guys and the Police*). His writing of the 1970s and 1980s was an outgrowth of the military dictatorship in Argentina during this period. By using allegory in *De dioses, hombrecitos y policías*, he fictionalizes the multiple dangers of being an intellectual in a totalitarian society. The consequences of political repression are also developed in *La larga noche de Francisco Sanctis* (1984, *The Long Night of Francisco Sanctis*). Before the military dictatorship Costantini had published the more abstract and inventive volume of fiction that could be read as three tales or a novel, *Háblenme de Funes* (1970, Speak to me of Funes). Costantini invents a novelist-figure who, in turn, invents the main character, Corti, a pharmacist who inherits a card file of case histories from an acquaintance. Using information on these cards, Corti invents more characters, and the novel becomes increasingly complex. Corti eventually comes into conflict with his characters, and *Háblenme de Funes* develops other themes in its three parts, such as human relationships and the act of creation itself.

Selected Work: Háblenme de Funes (1970); *De dioses, hombrecitos y policías* (1979, *Of Gods, the Little Guys and the Police*, translation Tony Talbot, 1984); *La larga noche de Francisco Sanctis* (1984, *The Long Night of Francisco Sanctis*, translation Norman Thomas di Giovanni, 1985).

Coutinho, Sonia [Biography] Brazilian novelist, short story writer, translator, and essayist, she is known in Brazil as a spokesperson for women's rights. Born in Itabuna

(BA) in 1939, she was raised in a family of literati: her father was a poet. When she was a child her family moved to Salvador (Bahia), and she studied literature at the university in Bahia. She began writing journalism at the age of eighteen, and by the mid-1960s was working with a group of young writers on the magazine *Mapa*, an organ that questioned conventional literary norms. During this period she published her first short story in a literary supplement directed by the celebrity Brazilian film director Glauber Rocha. She traveled to Spain in 1964 to study film history and in 1966, back in Salvador, she published a small edition of her first volume of short stories, *Do Héroi Inútil* (1966, Of the useless hero). She moved to Rio de Janeiro in 1968 to practice journalism, and in 1983 she participated in the International Writers Program at the University of Iowa. Coutinho was awarded the Jabuti prize in 1978 for her volume of short stories *Os Venenos de Lucrecia* (1978, The poisons of Lucrecia). In much of her fiction she adopts feminist perspectives and portrays women characters in the process of transition. She is particularly well known for her novel *O Jogo de Ifá* (1980, The game of Ifa), which feminist critics have applauded as a successful rewriting of Brazilian history in the reconstruction of women's history. This novel and much of her other fiction is both historical and innovative in narrative technique. Her other books include the fiction collections *Atire em Sofia* (1989, Shoot in Sofia) and *O Ultimo Verão de Copacabana* (1985, The last summer of Copacabana) and a volume of essays, *Rainhas do Crime* (1994, Queens of crime).

Selected Work: *O Jogo de Ifá* (1980); *O Caso de Alice* (1990); *Os Seios de Pandora* (1992).

Crick Crack Monkey (1970, by Merle Hodge. Written in English. London: Heinemann, 1981) [**Novel**] One of the most accomplished Caribbean women writers presents two worlds: the creole world of the child growing up and the adult world that reflects upon the farmer. Ironic tension divides the perceptions of the child and the commentary of the adult. The protagonist suffers alienation in the face of her creole world being negated by a variety of factors: a colonial mentality and culture, a new American presence, and the like. She is also faced with negotiating the creole world she knows by experience with the outside world about which she learns in school. Her task is to reconcile multiple identities; despite these possibilities, she seems confused at the end. Thus the novel presents the possible negotiation between the colonial and the colonized as either positive syncretism or negative disorientation. Hodge offers a novel with complex and new understandings of race, class, and gender.

Cristóbal nonato (1987, *Christopher Unborn*, by Carlos Fuentes. Translation by Alfred MacAdam. New York: Farrar, Straus and Giroux, 1989) [**Novel**] This novel in itself is the twelfth cycle of Fuentes's fourteen-cycle lifelong writing project, which he calls *La Edad del Tiempo*, and is his novelistic approach to temporality. As in most of the other books in this cycle on time, Fuentes undermines any sense of linear time. A preeminent essayist in his own right, Fuentes often uses fiction to set forth ideas, and *Cristóbal nonato* is a wide-ranging comic tour de force replete with both stories and ideas. The point of departure for this novel is the announcement of a prize for the first child born on October 12, 1992, the five-hundredth anniversary of Columbus's arrival in the Americas. Fuentes's approach to time in this case is unique: the narrator turns out to be Christopher Columbus himself, whose conception and birth back the novel. Thus Columbus narrates a wild series of events from the tomb, including the transhistorical digressions and characters of multiple identity that have characterized several of Fuentes's more ambitious historical projects, such as *Terra Nostra* and *Change of Skin*. The grand finale of this work includes an apocalyptic vision of the destruction of a decadent and polluted Mexico City. The ecological disaster—with black acid rain falling on the corrupt and exhausted city—seems to reinforce Fuentes's dark vision for the future of his nation.

Crónica de una muerte anunciada (1981, *Chronicle of a Death Foretold,* by Gabriel García Márquez. Translation by Gregory Rabassa. London: Cape, 1982) [**Novel**] Published a year before his Nobel Prize in Literature, this work was this author's second novelistic tour de force. The first had been his 1975 novel *El otoño del patriarca* (1975, *The Autumn of the Patriarch*), where he demonstrated the ability to sustain the reader along seemingly endless sentences, culminating in a final chapter of one sentence of twenty-five to thirty pages, depending on which edition. In *Crónica de una muerte anunciada* the narrator announces the assassination of the protagonist in the first paragraph and then proceeds to hold the reader's attention until the novel's last page; thus the reader remains fully intrigued with the details of a plot set in the 1950s in small-town Colombia. This book can be read as a critique of the colonial legacy or the medieval codes of honor still intact in much of rural Latin America today.

Crosthwaite, Luis Humberto [**Biography**] Mexican novelist, short story writer, and essayist, he was born in Tijuana in 1962 and has lived there his entire life, defining himself as a border writer. He claims to have learned English by watching the *Flintstones*

on television. Along with Rosina Conde and Federico Campbell, he is one of Mexico's most prominent of the young new border writers. His stories *Instrucciones para cruzar la frontera* (2002, Instructions to cross the border) consist of eleven humorous anecdotes about border culture and society. His volume of stories *Estrella de la calle sexta* (1992, Star of sixth street) contains three fictions set in Tijuana. His novel *La luna siempre será un amor difícil* (1994) has been published in English translation as *The Moon Will Forever Be a Distant Love* (1997, translated by Debbie Nathan and Willivaldo Delgadillo). His novel *Idos de la mente* (2001, Mindless) is an homage to the popular music tradition in northern Mexico at the same time that it relates the adventures of two musicians. In this work he writes as a border novelist, freely incorporating words and phrases in English as well as moving smoothly across the cultural border of the United States (with references to the Beatles and Elvis Presley, among other pop culture icons) as do the Mexican workers in Tijuana who daily cross the border to work on the U.S. side. Crosthwaite is as comfortable and humorous parodying pop culture figures of the United States as he is ridiculing conventions of the traditional Catholic Church in Mexico.

Selected Work: La luna siempre será un amor difícil (1994, *The Moon Will Forever Be a Distant Love*, translation Debbie Nathan and Willivaldo Delgadillo, 1997); *Idos de la mente* (2001).

Cuarto mundo, El (1988, *The Fourth World,* by Diamela Eltit. Translation by Dick Gerdes. Lincoln: University of Nebraska Press, 1995) [**Novel**] One of the most intriguing and challenging novels by one of Latin America's most respected postmodern and feminist novelists, *El cuarto mundo* is Eltit's third work, having already published two radical novelistic experiments.

The novel is divided into two parts: the first, narrated by the male of a pair of fraternal twins, takes the reader from the womb through the teen years. It focuses on the mother's suffering and fear. The second part is narrated by the female twin counterpart and describes the impending birth of a deformed baby girl who has been conceived incestuously by the twins who, in turn, are eventually abandoned by their parents. This novel has been read as a metaphor for a variety of Latin American scenarios, particularly in the context of gender and violence. More specifically, some passages refer to a colonial power, which lead the reader to understand repression in a historic context, pointing to the original colonial empire of Spain. Eltit's sense of history, as in her previous novels, is deep but very abstract.

Cuba [Nation] The desire to be modern was evident in Cuba in the 1940s in the short fiction of the Cuban master of this genre, Lino Novás Calvo, and the content of the literary magazine *Orígenes* in the 1950s. The Cuban Revolution made Cuba a center for Latin American intellectuals, including its novelists, in the 1960s.

Major novelists of the post-1945 period have been Alejo Carpentier, José Lezama Lima, Guillermo Cabrera Infante, and Severo Sarduy. The most noteworthy innovators and experimentalists have been Cabrera Infante, Sarduy, and Reynaldo Arenas.

(Others noted: Eliseo Alberto, Miguel Barnet, Antonio Benítez Rojo, René Vásquez Díaz, Jesús Díaz, Norberto Fuentes, Senel Paz.)

Curaçao [Nation] A Dutch colony for several centuries, it still is not an independent Caribbean nation. Unlike Suriname, which gained independence from Holland, Curaçao still has a special relationship with the Dutch government, making it comparable to the situation of Puerto Rico—it is neither an independent nation nor a classic "colony." In the diverse cultural and linguistic environment of Curaçao—where Dutch and Papiamento are the major languages—Dutch is the most commonly used language for writing fiction and Papiamento is the language of poetry. One of the major novelists from Curçao during this period is Frank Martinus Arion.

Dadydeen, David [Biography] Caribbean novelist, poet, and essayist, he was born in Berbice, Guyana (formerly British Guyana), in 1945. He was reared as a child in rural Guyana, where the culture around him was still very much that of his family from India. He emigrated to Great Britain at the age of twelve and was eventually educated at Cambridge. He began writing poetry as an adolescent and began publishing poetry in the 1980s. A fellow of the Royal Society for the Arts, he won the Commonwealth Poetry Prize for his first collection of poems, *Slave Song* (1984), and was a finalist for the Geoffry Faber Memorial Prize for his second book of poetry, *Coolie Odyssey* (1988). He has taught at the University of Warwick in its Centre for Research in Asian Migration.

Daydydeen's first novel, *The Intended* (1991), was shortlisted for two prestigious prizes in Great Britain. In his second novel, *Disappearance* (1993), he expresses in a quiet way his outrage at having grown up in a colony. It is an allegorical tale with a subtle message, never being openly didactic. Dadydeen's fiction is informed by diverse cultural elements, including British literature (from Shakespeare to modern poetry), Caribbean writing, the culture of India as he experienced it in Guyana, and the English creole language of the Caribbean.

Selected Work: *The Intended* (1991); *Disappearance* (1993).

Danticat, Edwidge [Biography] Caribbean novelist and essayist from Haiti, she writes in English and is widely known throughout the United States and the Caribbean region. Her fiction is published in English, but her bicultural background and bilingual experience as a child in Haiti are an implicit presence in her fiction; Haitian Creole, for example, appears in her texts in occasional phrases.

Born in Haiti in 1969, she was raised by her aunt and, after moving to the United States, was reunited with her parents at the age of twelve. She began creative writing as an adolescent, and earned a BA in French from Barnard College, followed by an MFA from Brown University. She has published the short story collection *Krik? Krak!* (1995).

Danticat is best known for her novel *Breath, Eyes, Memory* (1994). In this work a young girl tells her own story of coming from a place (as she explains on the last page) where breath, eyes, and memory are one and the past is always alive in the present. She describes her childhood of economic poverty in Haiti, but is is a creole world rich in oral tradition and folklore. In addition to being an exceptional story of a rite of passage (as Caribbean immigrant stories have much potential to be), it eventually becomes a novel dealing with her mother's sexual abuse and gender issues in the United States. Read in the context of the Caribbean, this novel opens with a subtle linguistic layer of the Haitian creole language that affects interaction and the use of English. In this sense, this novel is comparable to Caribbean texts from Puerto Rico and Chicano texts from the United States.

Danticat's later fiction includes the novel *The Dew Breaker* (2004) and the children's fiction of the volume *Anacaona* (2005).

Selected Work: Breath, Eyes, Memory (1994); *The Dew Breaker* (2004).

Death of Artemio Cruz, The (See *Muerte de Artemio Cruz, La* by Carlos Fuentes) **[Novel]**

De perfil (1966, In profile, by José Agustín. Written in Spanish and untranslated. Mexico: Joaquín Mortiz) **[Novel]** The second novel by this Mexican novelist, it was a key text for the rise of postmodern fiction in Mexico in the 1960s, a movement called La Onda. This fragmented text consists of 8 unnumbered chapters and 122 segments. An unnamed first-person narrator is a young, upper-middle-class Mexican in Mexico City who lives comfortably with his parents and a younger brother. He openly relates intimate details of his thoughts, sexual fantasies, social activities, and attitudes toward society. He narrates in a continual present (in colloquial Spanish) and covers three days, affording him time to encounter rebellious friends and his first sexual partner, a female singer he meets at a party. In this text Agustín intercalates a variety of interruptions, such as phone calls and conversations. The colloquial language, humorous tone, and rebellious attitudes were all innovations for Mexican literature in the 1960s. This text and Gustavo Sainz's *Gazapo* were models for similar novels in homage to youth culture in the 1960s and 1970s. The Colombian Andrés Caicedo was one follower of this Mexican movement headed by Agustín and Sainz.

Dejemos hablar al viento (1979, *Let the Wind Speak*, by Juan Carlos Onetti. Translation by Helen R. Lane. London: Serpent's Tail, 1996) **[Novel]** Onetti portrays the life of Medina, who at different times plays the role of doctor, painter, and police chief, living across the river from Santa María (the fictional and mythical city of most of Onetti's fiction). At the beginning of the novel Medina lives in the house of an old friend, Frieda, and works as a night nurse until he loses his job. After this he engages in a series of ambiguous and tenuous relationships with relatives and friends from the present and the past. It is unclear, for example, if a character named Seone is his son or not. Medina is a skeptic who claims to put Catholics, Marxists, Freudians, and patriots "in the same bag." In the end Medina embodies the alienation, anguish, and doubts of many of Onetti's protagonists, providing what some critics have identified as the author's "thematic emptiness." Young writers throughout Latin America, writing in the 1990s, have considered Onetti's "emptiness" a model. The young Mexican David Toscana is one such writer of this generation.

Délano, Poli [Biography] Chilean novelist and short story writer, he was born in Madrid, Spain, in 1936, became a Chilean citizen, but then, after the Pinochet coup d'état, went into political exile in Mexico from 1974 to 1984. More of a traditional storyteller than an innovator, he has written accessible and entertaining books that treat the social and political circumstance in Chile. He was a professor of literature in Chile until 1973; in Mexico he taught creative writing workshops and wrote fiction. Délano has received national literature prizes in both Chile and Mexico. He has published twelve volumes of short stories and nearly an equal number of novels.

One of his major novels is *En este lugar sagrado* (1974, In this sacred place). The sacred place of the title refers to a restroom, for the protagonist finds himself locked in one at a movie theater while his entire country is in a crisis: the government of Salvador Allende's Unidad Popular is under attack.

Délano's light humor, often based on the use of colloquial, working-class language, as well as the absurdity of the basic situation, make *En este lugar sagrado* an entertaining novel, despite the seriousness of the topic. The humble protagonist, Gabriel Canales, struggles to find logic and order in an irrational and innocent world that, in the end, can only be understood as functioning under the rules of chance. Délano presents a critique of both the protagonist and the upper middle class to which he belongs. This novel has also been read as a metaphor for the political situation of Latin America in the 1970s, particularly that portion of Latin America suffering several brutal military dictatorships.

Selected Work: Cuadrilátero (1962); *Cero a la izquierda* (1966); *Cambalache* (1968); *El dedo en la llaga* (1974); *En este lugar sagrado* (1974); *En la misma esquina del mundo* (1981); *El hombre de la máscara de cuero* (1982); *El verano del murciélago* (1984); *Como si no muera nadie* (1988); *Como una terraza en la quebrada* (1988); *Casi los ingleses de América* (1990).

Denevi, Marco [Biography] Argentine novelist and short story writer, he is widely recognized as one of Latin America's pioneering writers of detective stories. Denevi claims to have learned the art of the detective story from the nineteenth-century writer Wilkie Collins. Born in the town of Saenz Peña in the province of Buenos Aires in 1920, he is best known for his detective novel *Rosaura a las diez*. He began writing in the early 1950s, and in 1960 was awarded a prestigious literary prize given by *Life en español* for the best short novel in Spanish America. The renowned judges for this prize, which was given to Denevi's *Ceremonia secreta* (1960, *Secret Ceremony*), included the Mexican writer Octavio Paz (later to win the Nobel prize) and the Uruguayan critic Emir Rodríguez Monegal (later to assume a professorship at Yale University and a leading promoter of the Boom). Considered by some to be an early magical realist, Denevi often describes objects that assume life and portrays characters who inexplicably go insane. Thus his fictions tend to offer not only the suspense of the crime thriller but the surprising transformations found in some magical realist texts.

Denevi's now classic crime novel, *Rosaura a las diez* (1955, *Rosa at 10 O'Clock*) has appeared in numerous national and international editions since its original publication. In this work Rosaura and four different characters provide five different accounts of the same event, including a letter written by Rosaura. The plot involves a homicide in a cheap hotel, and the resolution includes a novel within a novel. The novel has been questioned by some critics for its lack of social content: writers of the same generation, such as David Viñas, wrote on the basis of political experience and insisted on historical depth and political commitment. Nevertheless, *Rosaura a las diez* is a well-wrought story that has been widely read and appreciated throughout the Hispanic world; it has also been made into a film.

With the rise of the politically committed writer of the 1960s Boom, magical realism, and women's writing of the 1980s and 1990s, Denevi's work has been overshadowed. Nevertheless, his novel *Una familia argentina* (An Argentine family) came out in two editions (one in 1986 and another in 1998) and a collection of his short stories appeared in translation by Alberto Manguel in 1993 under the title *The Redemption of the Cannibal Woman and Other Stories*. He died in 1998.

Selected Work: Rosaura a las diez (1955, *Rosa at Ten O'Clock*, translation Donald A. Yates, 1964); *Ceremonias secretas* (1960, *Secret Ceremony*, translation Harriet de Onis, 1995); *Una familia argentina* (1986).

Denser, Márcia [Biography] Brazilian novelist, journalist, and short story writer, she has also been a promoter of women's writing in Brazil. She works in a neorealistic style that fictionalizes important moments of women's experience; she is widely recognized as one of Brazil's leading feminists. Born in 1949 in São Paulo, she studied communication at Mackenzie University in São Paulo. She began writing at an early age, publishing literary criticism and short fiction in her youth. She served as editor and writer for the magazine *Nova* from 1977 to 1979. In the 1990s she coordinated the literature and research section of the Centro Cultural São Paulo.

Denser published her first volume of short stories, *Tango Fantasma* (Tango ghost) in 1976. With respect to this first book, the author herself has spoken of her awareness of sexual liberation her exploration of women's space, and her confrontation with old demons. In her next book, *O Animal dos Motéis* (1981 The animal of the motels), her feminist search continues; it is an exploration of a woman's relationship to herself and others. This novel, as much of her fiction, is a postmodern feminist exercise in self-reflection and reflection on the genre of the novel in itself. Both books involve eroticism and a search for a language of the body. Some critics have also associated these two books with a "generation of the 1970s" with a connection to a counterculture and a satire of established societal norms. In her writing career in general she has been interested in exploring how female sexuality is linked to power, editing two volumes of erotic feminist short stories that explore this topic, *Muito Prazer* (1980, It's my pleasure) and *O Prazer é Todo Meu* (1984, The pleasure is mine). She has claimed that her writings are not exactly stories, but "fragments of reality." Her other fiction includes *Exercicios para o Pecado* (1984), *A Ponte das Estrelas* (1990), and *Toda Prosa* (2001).

Selected Work: *O Animal dos Motéis* (1981).

Depestre, René [Biography] Caribbean poet, novelist, and essayist, he was an intellectual leader in Haiti, the Caribbean, and Latin America for several decades. He lived most of his adult life in political exile from Haiti. Known as a political activist and enfant terrible at the age of twenty, he participated in protests leading to the downfall of the Elie Lescot regime of Haiti in 1945 and was in exile until 1958. When French surrealist André Breton arrived in Port-au-Prince in 1945, Depestre was collaborating with writer Jacques Stephen Alexis to publish the dissident literary and political paper *La Ruche*. They contributed to the overthrowing of the Lescot regime in the name of surrealism and Marxism. Depestre shared with many Caribbean writers of the time a great fear of isolation and parochialism, and thus wrote enthusiastically about not only the important presence of foreign cultures but also of the liberating contributions of writers.

Born in the small town of Jacmel in 1926, Depestre lost his father, who died when he was a child of ten, and was then reared by his grandmother. As an adolescent he moved to Port-au-Prince, where he lived with his mother and studied at the Lycée Pétion. After undergoing a mystical experience, he joined the Order of the Fathers of the Holy Spirit and remained with this group—which was critical of the government—from 1940 to 1943. During this period he read antiestablishment French rebels such as Baudelaire and Rimbaud. This was also the period in which Depestre discovered Marxism and surrealism, and the young mystic intellectual was transformed into an antibourgeous revolutionary intellectual. Depestre was also influenced by the Harlem Renaissance and the writings of Langston Hughes as well as other writers and artists from the United States.

Depestre's revolutionary fervor, political stances, and travels placed him in contact with Latin America and its intellectuals at large over the years. Cuban writer Alejo Carpentier spoke at the Paramont Theater in Port-au-Prince when Depestre was sixteen or seventeen. There Depestre heard Carpentier set forth for the first time his much-celebrated ideas about "marvelous realism." Later Depestre published essays on "marvelous realism" himself. In 1945 he met the writer Aimé Césaire of Martinique. While in political exile in Europe, Depestre was taken in by the Brazilian novelist Jorge Amado, who made Depestre his personal secretary. Depestre then spent three years living on Isla Negra off the coast of Chile as the guest of the Chilean poet Pablo Neruda. In 1959, with the triumph of the Cuban Revolution, Depestre moved to Cuba, although he became increasingly isolated there over the years.

With respect to his fiction, Depestre's novels *Hadriana dans tous mes rêves* (Hadriana in all my dreams) and *Le mât de Cocagne* (1979, *The Festival of the Greasy Pole*, 1990) have been widely recognized. The latter is a historical novel with ample references to the period of the Duvalier dictatorship and going back in history to the colonial periodo of French rule on the island. This novel includes anecdotes related to Haiti's independence movement in 1803 as well as the traumatic presence of U.S. marines in Haiti in 1915. The American occupation united the Haitians, creating a deep resentment that informs this novel and much of Depestre's writing throughout his lifetime. Like Gabriel García Márquez in Colombia, the experience of hearing of the American presence in their respective homelands—as a child—marked these writers for life as anti-American and pro-Cuban intellectuals.

Selected Work: Le mât de Cocagne (1979, The Festival of the Greasy Pole, translation Carrol F. Coates, 1990); Hadriana dans tous mes rêves (1988).

Desesperanza, La (1986, Curfew, by José Donoso. Translation by Alfred MacAdam. New York: Weidenfeld and Nicholson, 1988) [**Novel**] A later novel by Chile's major novelist of the post-WWII period, La desesperanza is Donoso's satire of political stereotypes, including the Chilean political left that survived the Pinochet dictatorship, mostly in exile. The central figure of this deconstruction is the renowned poet Pablo Neruda. The protagonist is a politically committed 1960s rock musician. After thirteen years in exile, he returns to a Chile that he barely recognizes. This return to Chile coincides with the death of Neruda's widow on January 5, 1985. With her death an era seems to have drawn to a close. An opportunist from the left attempts to use the funeral to revive his political party, but he looks as ridiculous as the protagonist does as the "guerrilla-singer" (1960s rock singer). At other moments in the novel the protagonist experiences rejection. This partially autobiographical novel communicates much of the author's sense of his homeland when he returned in the 1980s after over a decade in exile.

Después de las bombas (1979, After the Bombs, by Arturo Arias. Translation by Asa Zatz. Willimantic, CT: Curbstone, 1990) [**Novel**] A major novel from the Central American region, its author is Guatemalan novelist and critic Arturo Arias. The protagonist is a Guatemalan boy, Max, who suffers the 1954 bombing attack on the government of Jacobo Arbenz in Guatemala City. The opening is a powerful recreation of the attack itself, as experienced through Max's eyes and ears. In this highly effective first chapter, Arias uses a series of images and brief phrases rather than consistently full-length sentences to communicate the experience and effects of the bombing attack, turning the city into a living hell that seemingly shakes the whole world, at least from Max's perspective. Reminiscent of Asturias's use of language and style in El Señor Presidente, Arias uses oral effects and almost surreal imagery, such as the image of a set of false teeth rolling down a hill during the bombing. As the novel develops, Arias moves Max through various stages of life, from his exile from Guatemala to his search for identity and his father and, finally, his struggle to free his country. A novel typical of Latin America's post-Boom, Después de las bombas is written with a deep awareness of Guatemala's political, cultural, and literary history; this novel is a sophisticated coda to the classic El Señor Presidente by Arias's fellow Guatemalan Miguel Angel Asturias.

Detective novels/crime fiction [**Topic**] Latin American critics and writers associate detective fiction with the Anglo-American tradition. Nevertheless, since the 1940s pioneering essays and anthologies on detective fiction have been produced by such celebrity writers as the Argentines Jorge Luis Borges, Adolfo Bioy Casares, Marco Denevi, and, more recently, Ricardo Piglia. These Argentine writers have contributed enormously to legitimizing the hard-boiler as "literature." Denevi's Rosaura a las diez (1955, Rosa at 10 O'Clock) is a now classic detective novel, and the more recent Ricardo Piglia of Argentina and Paco Ignacio Taibo II of Mexico have popularized detective fiction in the region. There are over fifty novelists of the post-WWII period practicing in the genre, including such pioneers as Isaac Aisemberg (1918–1997), Enrique Anderson Imbert (1910–2000), Roberto Arlt (1900–1942), Velmiro Ayala Gauna (1905–1967), María Elvira Bermúdez (1916–1988), Rafael Bernal (1915–1972), Adolfo Bioy Casares (1914–1999), Jorge Luis Borges (1899–1986), María Angélica Bosco (b. 1917), Leonardo Bosco (b. 1917), Leonardo Castellini (1896–1980), Luiz Lopez Coelho (1911–1975), Marco Denevi (1920–1998), Alberto Edwards (1873–1932), Rubem Fonseca (b. 1925), Antonio Helú (1900–1972), José Martínez de la Vega (1908–1954), Manuel Peyrou (1902–1974), René Vergara (1921–1983), and Rodolfo Walsh (1927–1977).

Detective fiction written in Spanish and Portuguese is increasingly common; many major writers of both languages, in fact, have at least one detective novel in their repertoire. Argentina, Mexico, Brazil, Chile, and Cuba have active groups of writers currently producing detective fiction. Some writers, such as the Mexican Paco Ignacio Taibo II, dedicate themselves entirely to this genre. Taibo II has been highly prolific, publishing over twenty-five detective novels, including *Días de combate* (1976, Days of combat), *Cosa fácil* (1977, *An Easy Thing*, 1990), *No habrá final feliz* (1981, *No Happy Ending*, 1993), *Algunas nubes* (1985, *Some Clouds*, 1992), *Sombra de la sombra* (1986, *The Shadow of the Shadow*, 1991), *De paso* (1986, *Just Passing Through*, 2000), *68* (1991), and *Retornamos como sombras* (2001, *Returning as Shadows*, 2003).

The Uruguayan Hiber Conteris has published one of the more successful detective novels to appear in both English and Spanish, *El diez por ciento de la vida* (1985, *The Ten Percent of Life*). Conteris evokes classic detective novels with numerous tributes to Raymond Chandler and his Philip Marlowe. Far more than a detective novel, however, *El diez por ciento de la vida* is a political work written in the context of the 1970s military dictatorship of Uruguay.

Detective fiction in Brazil dates back to early in the twentieth century, but it was neither popular nor widely read until the 1960s and 1970s, with the appearance of writers such as Rubem Fonseca. His novel *Bufo & Spallanzani* is one of the most entertaining and successful of this genre in Brazil. The first detective novels to be published in Brazil appeared in newspapers as serials in the 1920s. In the 1930s the first Brazilian author to dedicate himself exclusively to detective fiction, Jerônimo Monteiro, began publishing novels. In the 1940s Luis Lopes Coelho and Anibal Costa also published detective novels. In addition to *Bufo & Spallanzani*, Fonseca is widely acclaimed for his novel *A Grande Arte* (1983, *High Art*, 1i86), which revolves around a series of murders in which the killer uses a knife to carve the letter "P" on the face of the prostitutes he slays. Fonseca's other detective novels include *O Caso Morel* (1973, The Morel case) and *O Buraco na Parede* (1995, The hole in the wall). Among recent Brazilian works in this genre, *Borges e os Orangotangos Eternos* (2000, *Borges and the Eternal Orangutans*, 2005), written by Luis Fernando Veríssimo is a parody of both Borges and the crime novel genre. Finally, Paulo Rangel has written a series of detective novels for young readers and adults. His novel *Assassinato na Floresta* (1991, Assassination in the jungle) is the third installment in the author's ongoing Ivo Cotoxó Adventure Collection, which he has constructed to vent Brazil's everyday problems within the framework of the juvenile detective novel. His other books in this series are *O Assassinato do Conto Policial* (1989, Assassination of the crime novel) and *Revisão Criminal: O Assasssinato* (1990,

Criminal Review: The Murder of Duclerc). His series of detective novels touch opon topics such as human rights violations and ecology.

In Chile an interesting case is the rise of Ramón Díaz Eterovic, whose main interest is detective fiction. His works include *La ciudad está triste* (1987, The sad city), *Solo en la oscuridad* (1992, Alone in the dark), *Nadie sabe más que los muertos* (1993, Nobody knows more than the dead), *Angeles y solitarios* (1995, Angels and solitaires), *Correr tras el viento* (1997, Chasing the wind), *Nunca enamores a un forastero* (1999, Don't fall in love with a stranger), *Los siete hijos de Simenon* (2000, The seven sons of Simenon), *El ojo del alma* (2001, The eye of the soul), and *El hombre que pregunta* (2002, The man who asks).

The U.S. Chicano novelist Rudolfo Anaya has written a series of detective novels including *Albuquerque* (1992), *Zia Summer* (1995), *Jalamanta* (1996), *Rio Grande Fall* (1996), and *Shaman Winter* (1999). Similarly, Chicana writer Lucha Corpi has written several detective novels, and, like those of Anaya, they are constructed with an awareness of local issues of Chicano culture in American society.

Many Latin American novelists not associated primarily with detective fiction, including such renowned figures as Carlos Fuentes, Mario Vargas Llosa, and Mempo Giardinelli, have at least one crime novel in their total work. Fuentes has published his tongue-in-cheek novel of this genre, *La cabeza de la hidra* (1978, *Hydra Head*) and Vargas Llosa has written *Quién mató a Palomino Molero?* (1986, *Who Killed Palomino Molero?*). Among the numerous other novelists from Mexico whose work includes at least one detective novel, the following authors and novels can be noted: Vicente Leñero, *Asesinato* (1985, Murder); Federico Campbell, *Máscara negra* (1995, Black

mask) and *Transpeninsular* (2000); Jorge Volpi, *Laz paz de los sepulcros* (1995, The peace of the tombs) and *En busca de Klingslor* (1999, *In Search of Klingsor*); Julieta Campos, *Muerte por agua* (1965, Death by water); David Martín del Campo, *El año del fuego* (1996, The year of fire). Among the numerous Argentines, Marco Denevi has published *Ceremonias secretas* (1960, Secret ceremonies) and Luisa Valenzuela has written *Novela negra con argentinos* (1990, Black novel with Argentines). In Colombia novelist and poet Darío Jaramillo Agudelo, author of several novels, has also published a crime thriller, *Memorias de un hombre feliz* (2000, Memories of a happy man). Alberto Duque López's one tribute to the crime novel is *Mi revolver es más largo que el tuyo* (1977, My revolver is bigger than yours). The young Colombian Hugo Chaparro Valderrama has written a parody of this genre, *El capítulo de Ferneli* (1992, The Ferneli chapter). Other contemporary Latin American writers with at least one detective novel incluye Martín Caparrós, José Pablo Feinman, Enrique Serna, Juan Martini, and Rafael Ramírez Ramírez.

Dézafi (1975, Challenge, by Frankétienne. Written in Haitian Creole and untranslated. Paris: Ventsd'ailleurs, 2002) [**Novel**] One of the most radical novelistic experiments to appear in the Caribbean region, this text is written in Haitian Creole, even though most Haitian writers have published in French. Originally published with a different orthography in 1975, this version reflects later standardization of written Haitian Creole. A text that can be read as a follow-up to Eduoard Glissant's theories and affirmations about *créolité* in the Caribbean region, this novel is as radically experimental as *Cobra* (1972) by the Cuban Severo Sarduy and comparable as a linguistic adventure to Martinus Arion's writings in Papiamento. In this work two nearby poor villages seem to be negatively affected by an outside agency. A voudou priest controls his daughter and mistress Sultrana, his henchman, and his zombie workers. He possesses these laborers after reanimating bodies he fetched from fresh graves. At the end, peasants and former zombies destroy the priest. This is an allegorical book of resistance about how human beings can lose their idols and even their will through starvation and fear. Written under the dictatorship of Duvalier in Haiti, it is comparable to some of the most grotesque allegories written under the dictatorships in Chile and Argentina as well as dictator novels such as García Márquez's *El otoño del patriarca*, which appeared the same year.

Di Benedetto, Antonio [Biography] Born in Mendoza, Argentina, in 1922, he has been an active presence on the Argentine cultural scene since the early 1950s as a journalist, writer, and screenwriter. In the 1950s he received a scholarship to study journalism in France, and he became a devotee of French avant-garde writer Alain Robbe-Grillet, a fact that explains Di Benedetto's simple and direct style, often described as "objective." His work that most closely approximates the "objective" style and immediate present of the French *nouveau roman* of Robbe-Grillet is *Declinación* (1958, Declination), a book that consists of a series of scenes with little plot. Di Benedetto's first volume of short fiction, *Mundo animal* (Animal world) appeared in 1953, and he has been writing fiction since that period. Interested in the absurd and the irrational, he is also known as a novelist with interests in history and capable of using strategies often associated with magic realism. His first novel, *El pentágano* (1955, The pentagon), is a set of stories that can be read as a novel,

with two love triangles and a lengthy interior monologue that unify the accounts.

His major work, *Zama* (1956) is a historical novel set in the eighteenth century in the Argentine province of Mendoza. Don Diego de Zama, the protagonist, is a twentieth-century antihero who suffers from existential anguish, who is living in the eighteenth century. Consequently, Di Benedetto makes the connection between the eighteenth century and the twentieth, and the author thus makes comments on life and society in both centuries. A magical realist early in his career, Di Benedetto uses unexplained phenomena to intensify the protagonist's varying moods. The magical events in *Zama* create a sense of being detached from time and place, an effect that relates to a sense of alienation found in some twentieth-century magical realist texts. His novel *Las suicidas* (1969) is an intimate study of emotional growth, written with the simplicity of style that some critics consider a sign of Di Benedetto's mastery. He received a national prize for his novel *El silenciero* (1964, The silencer), his critique of urban noise. Like many Latin American writers who gained prominence in the 1950s, he was overshadowed and often ignored with the rise of the 1960s Boom. Nevertheless, he died in 1986 as one of the most respected writers of his generation in Argentina.

Selected Work: *El pentágano* (1955); *Zama* (1956); *Declinación* (1958); *El silenciero* (1964); *Las suicidas* (1969).

Día en la vida, Un (1980, *A Day in the Life*, by Manlio Argueta. Translation by Bill Brow. New York: Random House, 1983) **[Novel]** One of the major texts to appear in El Salvador in recent years, it was widely read in several languages in the 1980s as an important Latin American *testimonio* concerning the political violence in Central

American nations. The text contains literally what the title suggests: an hour-by-hour account of one day in the life of peasant women in a rural village of El Salvador. The book opens with a section titled "5:30 am" and recounts in precise detail the rural environment, beginning with the presence of local birds called *clarineros* that fly over the peasants' hut. Other animals and objects are a vital part of this simple yet magical world. The second section, "5:45," begins with a similar detail from this rural world: "One day I was going to throw a stone at a frog." The narrator also observes the discovery of a new political voice, however, so not all the text consists of such basic observations. *Un día en la vida* contains a total of twenty-nine segments, each of which is an hour of the day and some of which are interior monologues by women in the town. The presence of an ominous Civil Guard threatens the minimal livelihoods and precarious lives of the peasants. Along with Nicaragua's Sergio Ramírez, Guatemala's Arturo Arias, and Honduras's Horacio Castellanos Mora, Manlio Argueta has been an influential political voice in Central America through his writing.

Día señalado, El (1964, The signaled day, by Manuel Mejía Vallejo. Written in Spanish and untranslated. Barcelona: Destino) [**Novel**] One of the classic novels of La Violencia in Colombia, this is also a major novel by one of Colombia's most respected modern novelists. The backdrop is the civil war of the 1940s and 1950s in Colombia that resulted in over three hundred thousand deaths and an ample literature about this traumatic period in the nation's history. Mejía Vallejo's portrayal of this conflict between Liberals and Conservatives is developed along two story lines. One story line is of a priest in a small town in rural Colombia; the other is told by a character who arrives in town to commit an act of revenge.

A six-page prologue tells the life story of a young man who sees the irrational political violence during the civil war.

Diaconú, Alina [**Biography**] Argentine novelist, short story writer, and journalist born in Romania in 1949, she moved to Buenos Aires in 1959 with her family and soon became an Argentine citizen. The author of eight novels, she writes as an act of resistance to authoritarianism and to recover the voices that have been silenced by the state. Her characters are often marginal to mainstream society. The child of an art critic and a native of Bucharest, Romania, she was reared in a lively intellectual environment: her early readings were in the French and Russian classics; later in Argentina she discovered Kafka, Joyce, Ionesco, Borges, and Cioran as her literary "parents." She also claims that movies, theater, and painting have been influential in her life. When she arrived from Europe at the age of ten, she wrote first in French, eventually starting to write in Spanish and publishing her first novel in 1975, *La señora* (1975, The lady), a novel that scandalized many middle-class readers in Argentina: a middle-age housewife rebels against several sexual mores and is eventually taken to an insane asylum.

In 1979 she received a national prize in Argentina for her novel *Buenas noches, profesor* (1979, Good evening, professor), a novel about an aging professor who falls in love with a student yet discovers at the end that his affair and his new life are all delusions. She claims that her life has been a product of politics, but that she attempts to write a literature that does not allude directly to politics, rather offering a broader vision and reflection on the human condition. Nevertheless, *Buenas noches, professor* was censored during the military dictatorship in Argentina (1976–1982). She has become increasingly autobiographical: in *El penúltimo viaje* (1989, The penultimate trip), the protagonist recalls a trip in Eastern Europe while traveling on a train in Argentina; *Los devorados* (1992, The devoured) offers a panoramic view of a desolate fictional city that could be partially Latin American, partially Eastern European. A growing volume of scholarly study has been produced on the creative work of Diaconú, including the book *Utopías, ojos azules y bocas suicidas. La narrativa de Alina Diaconú*, by coeditors Ester Gimbernat González and Cynthia Tompkins (1994). Diaconú has lived in Paris (1968–1970) and attended the University of Iowa's International Writing program (1985). She has received several acknowledgments for her journalism, including a Bronze Medal from the magazine *Cultura*; her cultural journalism appears throughout the Hispanic world.

    Selected Work: La señora (1975); *Buenas noches, profesor* (1979); *Enamorada del muro* (1981); *Cama de ángeles* (1983); *Los ojos azules* (1986); *El penúltimo viaje* (1989); *Los devorados* (1992); *Calidoscopio* (1998).

Días de combate (1976, Days of combat, by Paco Ignacio Taibo II. Written in Spanish and untranslated. Mexico: Grijalbo) [**Novel**] Mexico's most prolific writer of detective fiction, Taibo II began his lengthy hardboiled series with *Días de combate*. His detective figure is Héctor Belascoarán Shayne, the son of an Irish mother and Basque father who considers himself pure Mexican. The criminal whom Belascoarán pursues is not really an individual but institutions in Mexico: the police, the government, and the judicial system. Belascoarán does pursue an individual killer until he makes this realization. Meanwhile, the reader comes to appreciate the detective's intelligence and tenacity. This is the first of nine of Taibo's novels with Belascoarán as the detective. The crime and chaos of Mexico are not due to individuals, according to Taibo. Rather, they relate to larger and deeper problems that are systemic.

Díaz, Jesús (Jesus Díaz Rodríguez) [**Biography**] Cuban novelist, short story writer, and essayist born in 1941, he has been a professor of Marxism at the University of Havana in recent years. He writes social novels and historical critiques with the intention of defending the Cuban Revolution. He has been influenced by the historical and documentary trends of Cuban writers such as Alejo Carpentier and Miguel Barnet. Díaz has been a visible figure in Cuban fiction writing since 1966 when he was awarded the Casa de las Américas Prize in Cuba for his seminal volume of short fiction, *Los años duros* (1966). In this volume he portrays the abuse of revolutionaries by the police of the Cuban dictator Batista in the 1950s. The awarding of the Casa de las Américas Prize to Díaz was considered highly significant at the time in Cuba, for it indicated a relaxation of official restraints on Cuban writers, who were being increasingly censored by the government of Fidel Castro in the mid-1960s. The stories not only tell of the struggle against Batista but also of the cutting of sugarcane by volunteer workers and the fight against anti-Castro insurgents and the CIA. Some critics have suggested that Díaz's fiction in general has opened up new perspectives and possibilities for Cuban writers. Difficult to classify, he can be associated with both the modern and the postmodern, depending on which aspects of his work one chooses to emphasize. Like writers such as Gabriel García Márquez and Juan Rulfo, Díaz uses simple and straightforward language to portray basic human scenarios and the essence of human emotions. This Cuban author also uses individuals to present scenes with broader political and historical implications that may not be self-evident on first reading. His open-ended texts have invited some critics to associate him with the postmodern.

Díaz's first and major novel, *Las iniciales de la tierra* (1987, The initials of the land), is an implicit critique of the Cuban regime and modernist text with the multiple narrative strategies that characterize such fiction. The protagonist is an antihero figure who is caught up in the paradoxes of political systems in general as well as the contradictions of the Cuban regime in particular. Díaz shows how Cuba's history from 1959 to 1970 affects his present life. His memories include serving in the revolutionary militia, being trained in military school, and studying architecture. He also remembers having been a student activist. Throughout the novel he searches for ethical modes of conduct within the challenges he faces. One of his most difficult challenges is to overcome his own male attitudes (commonly associated with *machismo*) and accept that his wife should enjoy the same rights that he does. The Kafkaesque scenes, the masterful depiction of the sugarcane harvest, and the ability to tell a compelling story have made Díaz a novelist increasingly recognized beyond the borders of Cuba, with a growing number of readers throughout Latin America; *Las iniciales de la tierra* has been translated into German. Díaz has also written the novella *Gritar el amor* (1980, Scream love) and the screenplay for a video titled *Lejanía*, which is set in Cuba and portrays the awkward reunion between a Cuban son and his mother who left him when he was sixteen. His recent novel *Siberiana* (2000) is a love story.

Selected Work: *Las iniciales de la tierra* (1987); *Siberiana* (2000); *Las cuatro fugas de Manuel* (2002).

Díaz Eterovic, Ramón [Biography] With a growing reputation as one of Chile's most accomplished living writers of detective fiction, he began writing poetry in the early 1980s. Born in the Chilean city of Punto Arenas in 1956, he moved to Santiago to study at the University of Chile, where he received a degree in business administration. After writing two books of poetry, he published the volume of short stories *Atrás sin golpe* (1985, Backward without incident). He has edited an anthology of Chilean detective fiction under the title *Crímenes criollos: antología del cuento policial chileno* (1994, Creole crime: anthology of the Chilean crime story), with stories by Poli Délano, Alberto Edwards, and René Vergara.

Díaz Eterovic has created a central character, Heredia, for his hard-boilers. The private detective Heredia is a resident of Santiago who lives in an apartment in a bohemian neighborhood. His sidekick and confidant is a stray cat, Simenon. Heredia is an attractive character: he is reader of literature, an avid chronicler of the city of Santiago, and a sympathetic protector of his formerly homeless cat. Díaz Eterovic is a social critic who uses the crime novel to portray a corrupt society and social injustice. In this sense he follows the mode of Argentines Mempo Giardinelli and José Pablo Feinman and the Mexican Paco Ignacio Taibo II, all of whom use the crime novel for similar purposes.

Díaz Eterovic began his series with *La ciudad está triste* (1987, The sad city), a vivid portrayal of the destruction of Chilean society by the military government. Many of his cases relate to people who have disappeared under the dictatorship. The author continues his series with *Solo en la oscuridad* (1992, Alone in the dark), in which a flight attendant is murdered. The novels that follow become increasingly more engaged in political intrigues. His recent *El hombre que pregunta* (2002, The man who asks), however, departs from the rough world of urban Santiago to follow the death of a literary critic.

Selected Work: Pasajero de la ausencia (1982); *Atrás sin golpe* (1985); *La ciudad está triste* (1987); *Solo en la oscuridad* (1992); *Nadie sabe más que los muertos* (1993); *Angeles y solitarios* (1995); *Correr tras el viento* (1997); *Nunca enamores de un forastero* (1999); *Los siete hijos de Simenon* (2000); *El ojo del alma* (2001); *El hombre que pregunta* (2002).

Díaz Sánchez, Ramón [Biography] Venezuelan novelist, short story writer, journalist, literary critic, and politician born in 1903, he worked for a petroleum company in his youth, the background for his first novel, *Mene* (1936, Oil). With this novel Díaz Sánchez established his credentials as a classic Latin American protest novelist and social critic, taking to task not only the U.S. presence in Venezuela but also the generalized sexism and racism of Venezuelan society. In this first work the author employs basic dichotomies between good and evil, as was the common practice in social protest novels of the 1930s. After this relatively simplistic attempt at novel writing, Díaz Sánchez wrote two volumes of short stories in the 1940s and then produced his masterpiece, *Cumboto*. His other novels were *Casandra* (1958) and *Borburata* (1961). In *Casandra* Díaz Sánchez returned to his critique of foreign oil companies begun in *Mene* as well as a broader questioning of the modernization process in Venezuela.

Díaz Sánchez's most celebrated novel, *Cumboto*, like *Mene*, deals with social problems in the context of small-town Venezuela, but it is far more nuanced than *Mene* and the typical Latin American novel of social protest written in the 1930s and 1940s. The narrator is a black man who serves as mediator among forces creating cultural, economic, and class conflict. The four-part structure of *Cumboto* and its carefully controlled tone have engaged

readers for several generations. Díaz Sánchez died in 1968, recognized as one of Venezuela's major novelists of the century and one of Latin America's pioneering Afro–Latin American writers.

Selected Work: Mene (1936); *Cumboto* (1950, *Cumboto*, translation John Upton, 1969); *Casandra* (1958); *Borburata* (1961).

Dictator novels [Topic] One of the grimmest periods of twentieth-century Latin American literary history was popularized in fiction in the 1970s. These novels depicted numerous military dictatorial regimes in Latin America. The roots of the "novel of the dictator" are to be found in the Spanish writer Ramón del Valle-Inclán's *Tirano Banderas* and the Guatemalan Miguel Angel Asturias's *El Señor Presidente* (1946). In the 1970s the genre of the dictator novel was given prominence by the efforts of several celebrity novelists: García Márquez published *El otoño del patriarca* (1975, *The Autumn of the Patriarch*), Augusto Roa Bastos published *Yo, el supremo* (1977, *I the Supreme*), and Alejo Carpentier published *El recurso del método* (1974, *Reasons of State*). These three writers took very different approaches to the dictator novel. García Márquez drew from the historical record of some of Latin America's most infamous strongmen from the nineteenth and twentieth centuries, and his novel *El otoño del patriarca* is not located in any one identifiable nation. Carpentier's novel work's similarly (in search of the "universal" dictator figure), but Roa Bastos draws directly from the historical record of a particular strongman from Paraguay's past. Among the other authors of dictator novels, the Mexican René Avilés Fabila wrote *El gran solitario del palacio* (1971) and Peruvian Julio Ramón Ribeyro published *Cambio de guardia* (1976). More recently, Mario Vargas Llosa did extensive research on the political history of the Dominican Republic and published the dictator novel *La fiesta del Chivo* (2000, *The Feast of the Goat*).

Diez por ciento de la vida, El (1985, *Ten Percent of Life*, by Hiber Conteris. New York: Simon and Schuster, 1987) [**Novel**] On the surface this is a classic detective novel. Like much Latin American fiction of this genre, however, it both a detective novel and a self-reflective rewriting of this classic genre, thus inviting some critics to call it a postmodern detective fiction. As a detective novel, *Ten Percent of Life* is written as a tribute to Raymond Chandler; it even has Marlowe and other Chandler characters in it, including Chandler himself. The point of departure is the assassination of a literary agent, followed by the death of a reporter for the *Times*. The novel includes a discussion of detective novels and a questionnaire for the reader. This novel was written while Conteris was a political prisoner during the 1970s military dictatorship in Uruguay. Consequently, the novel needs to be read also with an awareness of the dominant discourse of the military government at the time it was written. The reader can find clues not only to the classic detective novel at hand but also to a political novel. In the end the reader never really knows what happens, yet another diversion from the classic mold. This is Conteris's best novel.

Diferentes razones tiene la muerte (1947, Death has various reasons, by María Elvira Bermúdez. Written in Spanish and untranslated. Mexico City: Plaza y Janés, 1987) [**Novel**] Bermúdez (1946–1988) was a pioneer of the detective novel in Mexico, and this was one of the most ambitious crime fictions to have ever appeared in Mexico when she published it in 1947. One of her consistent characters, Armando H. Zozoya, is the honest and logical journalist who is the protagonist of *Diferentes razones tiene la muerte*. He investigates two murders that have occurred at a gathering of friends. By studying fingerprints and other clues, Zozoya methodically and logically solves the crime. Another astute character is a woman named Georgina, one of several strong female characters in the fiction of Bermúdez.

Dois irmãos (2000, *The Brothers*, by Milton Hatoum. Translation by John Gledson. New York: Farrar, Straus and Giroux, 2002) [**Novel**] What might be called "minority" fiction traditionally has not occupied a significant cultural space in Brazil, but this and other works by Milton Hatoum are changing that situation, for through the 1990s he has been a successful writer. As a Lebanese Brazilian, he joins Jewish Brazilian writers as a minority writer of increasing visibility. Hatoum continues his family story with this second novel, which he had begun in *Relato de um certo oriente* (1989, *The Tree of Seventh Heaven*). *The Brothers* is a first-person narration in which one twin brother returns to Brazil from Lebanon after WWI. The narrator is the illegitimate son of one of the twins. It is the story of two generations of a Lebanese immigrant family, focusing on the twin brothers, Yaqub and Omar. The family is based in Manaus and São Paulo, and the book's twelve chapters describe the interactions between the family members. This is not a small screen novel, however, for it has a historical dimension, going back to the past as far as 1914. In an introductory section the mother Zana leaves Manaus, thus reliving her original departure from her home village in Lebanon. From the beginning it is evident that she is aware of tensions and conflicts between her two sons. In this work Hatoum explores topics such as the past as memory, ethnic identity, and aging. Among a growing number of minority writers publishing novels in Brazil, Hatoum is one of very few Lebanese Brazilian novelists.

Domecq, Brianda [Biography] Mexican novelist, short story writer, and essayist, she was born in New York in 1942, and her Mexican family lived in the northeast United States during her childhood. She has written of the cultural conflict and childhood crises associated with this binational background. She has been a permanent resident of Mexico since 1951. She studied literature as an undergraduate at the National University in Mexico City (UNAM) and then completed a doctorate at the Colegio de México in the capital. Her novelistic production has been relatively light, but she is highly regarded in Mexico as one of the more accomplished fiction writers of her generation. She has been associated with both Latin American *testimonio* and magical realism. In her first novel, *Once días . . . y algo más* (1979, *Eleven Days*) she fictionalizes her own kidnapping, which actually occurred in 1978, and the documentary qualities of the book relate it to *testimonio*. In this story a first-person narrator named Leo assumes the basic identity of Brianda Domecq, who was kidnapped for eleven days, and she tells the intimate story of not only the psychological stress and trauma of this event but also the positive relationship that developed with the kidnappers. It is a day-by-day account. This engaging text has some qualities of an autobiography in that she tells her life story, some of a novel in that it contains fiction, and some elements can be related to the documentary impulses of the Latin American *testimonio*. *La insólita historia de la Santa de Cabora* (1990, *The Astonishing Story of Saint Cabora*) is based on the life of the historic Teresa Urrea (the saint of Cobra, 1873–1906), an iconoclastic woman who attempted to overthrow the dictator-

ship of Porfirio Díaz and was sent into exile to the United States, where she died. Some of the more incredible events of this remarkable life have caused some critics to associate this novel with magical realism. Not a prolific writer, Domecq has the reputation in Mexico of producing a small number of high-quality stories.

Selected Work: Once días . . . y algo más (1979, *Eleven Days*, translation Kay S. García, 1995); *La insólita historia de la Santa de Cabora* (1990, *The Astonishing Story of Saint Cabora*, translation Kay S. García, 1998).

Dominican Republic [Nation] This Caribbean nation shares the island of Hispaniola with Haiti, with Spanish the national language since the arrival of the Spaniards in the sixteenth century. The Dominican Republic gained independence from Spain in the nineteenth century, and U.S. intervention in the nation in 1965 represented a turning point in this nation's politics for many of the writers and intellectuals in the 1960s. Writers such as Marcio Veloz Maggiolo and Efraín Castillo were profoundly affected by that entrance of U.S. marines in their homeland in the 1960s, and their writing shows evidence of this.

Major novelists have been Marcio Veloz Maggiolo, Aída Cartagena Portalín, Freddy Prestol Castillo, Pedro Mir, and Pedro Vergés. Younger writers include Andrés L. Mateo and Manuel García Cartagena.

Don Juan's Bar (See *Bar Don Juan* by Antonio Callado) **[Novel]**

Donoso, José [Biography] Chilean novelist, short story writer, and essayist, he was a major writer of the century, and closely associated with the 1960s Boom, which he wrote about in *Historia personal del Boom* (1972, *The Boom in Spanish American Literature: A Personal History*). In Chile he has been associated with the generation of 1950 that was interested in modernizing the national literary scene. His early works, *Coronación* (1957, *Coronation*) and *Este domingo* (1966, *This Sunday*) were his efforts in this direction. In these early novels he also portrayed characters representing the Chilean oligarchy in critical ways.

Donoso was born in Santiago in 1924 to a family of the professional middle class, with both grandfathers physicians. His father possessed strong literary and cultural interests. They sent their son to a prestigious private high school, the Grange School, where he began his adolescent incursions into fiction writing and met the Mexican writer Carlos Fuentes, who became a lifelong friend. Donoso was a failure in organized sports and other group activities, a fact that he attributes to his lifelong positioning as not only a writer but as a relatively isolated and marginalized intellectual who always considered himself to be an outsider. As a young adult, he traveled to Argentina, where he did manual labor, and later to the United States, where he studied at Princeton University and began writing in English. At Princeton he discovered literary critics such as R. P. Blackmur and Allen Tate. From his adolescence Donoso became an expert at feigning illnesses, which he used initially to be truant from school. Later real or imagined illness became intimately related with his creative process; many considered him a hypochrondriac. A long process of surgery became an important experience for the process of writing the novel *El obsceno pájaro de la noche* (1970, *The Obscene Bird of the Night*).

Not as much a celebrity figure in Latin America as his cohorts Carlos Fuentes, Gabriel García Márquez, and Mario Vargas Llosa of the 1960s Boom, Donoso was nevertheless a prominent Latin American novelist from the 1960s to the 1990s. His fiction tended to deal with psychological and emotional realities of characters, the surreal, the dreamworld of the characters, and subtle relations between individuals who were often either marginal to mainstream society or psychologically distant from their norms. Unlike his peers of the Boom, he was not interested in novelizing broad historical and cultural patterns of Latin America or even of Chile.

His major novel, and one of the major novels of the 1960s Boom, was *El obsceno pájaro de la noche* (1970, *The Obscene Bird of the Night*, 1973), a lengthy and highly fragmented worked that was written at a time when Donoso was suffering the effects of hallucinatory drugs ingested during surgery in a hospital in Fort Collins, Colorado. The major characters of this groundbreaking novel are an aristocratic couple, Jerónimo and Inés Azcoitía, with a deformed son whom they hide on their estate, La Rinconada. In addition to La Rinconada, the other main space for the novel's monstrous characters is a decadent convent. In the absence of any consistent narrator or consistent plot, many critics agree that in *The Obscene Bird of the Night* character, plot, and linear chronology are chaotic. Thematically the novel questions hierarchies of power as well as the basic tenets of the realist novel.

Donoso is also known for works such as *El jardin de al lado* (1981, *The Garden Next Door*), *Casa de campo* (1978, *A House in the Country*), and *La desesperanza* (1986, *Curfew*). In the last-mentioned work a "guerrilla-singer" (a 1960s rock singer) returns to Chile after a lengthy absence and finds his nation, now under a dictatorship, significantly transformed. He also finds few of his fellows citizens care about his plight as an aging leftist who has suffered in exile.

Near the end of his life Donoso wrote an autobiographical account of his life and interests, with focus on his family's past, under the title *Conjeturas sobre la memoria de mi tribu* (1996, Conjectures on the memory of my tribe). He died in Santiago in 1996.

Selected Work: Coronación (1957, *Coronation*, translation Jacosta Goodwin, 1965); *Este domingo* (1966, *This Sunday*, translation Lorraine O'Grady, 1967); *El lugar sin límites* (1966, *Hell Has No Limits*, translation Suzanne Jill Levine, 1972); *El obsceno pájaro de la noche* (1970, *The Obscene Bird of the Night*, 1973, translation Leonard Manes and Hardie St. Martin, 1973); *El jardín de al lado* (1981, *The Garden Next Door*, translation Hardie St. Martin and Leonard Manes, 1992); *Casa de campo* (1978, *A House in the Country*, translation David Pritchard with Suzanne Jill Levine, 1984); *La misteriosa desaparición de la marquesita de Loria* (1981); *La desesperanza* (1986, *Curfew: A Novel*, translation Alfred MacAdam, 1994); *Taratuta & Naturaleza muerta con cachimba* (1990, *Taratuta amp; Still Life with Pipe: Two Novellas*, translation Gregory Rabassa, 1993); *Donde van a morir los elefantes* (1995).

Dorfman, Ariel [Biography] Chilean novelist, playwright, short story writer, poet, and essayist, he became identified with Chilean writing in exile during the 1970s and 1980s. A supporter of Salvador Allende's Unidad Popular government in Chile in the early 1970s, he was forced into exile after the 1973 military coup. In recent years he has established an international reputation as a social critic, political activist, and essayist. Born in Argentina in 1942, he lived much of his early childhood in the United States and was later educated in his homeland of Chile, where he is a citizen. Early in his career Dorfman became known for the brilliant analysis of comic books and capitalism in his book *Para leer al Pato Donald* (1971, *How to Read Donald Duck: Imperialist Ideology in the Disney Comic*, 1975). This landmark book became a model for the study of ideology and popular culture in

Latin America and did much to popularize "dependency theory" in U.S. academia. In his cutting-edge analysis of kinship structures in Donald Duck, Dorfman demonstrates that there is no longer genealogy and kinships are thus unnatural. After going into exile he expanded his creative efforts beyond the essay to become a prolific writer of fiction, poetry, and plays, much of which has been translated into over twenty different languages. He has been on the faculty at Duke University since the 1980s.

His fiction is comparable in several ways to the novels of writers such as Carlos Fuentes: idea driven yet constantly on the border between empirical reality and some irrational or surreal sphere of time and/or space. His novel *La última canción de Manuel Sendero* (1983, *The Last Song of Manuel Sendero*, 1988) is comparable to Fuentes's *Christopher Unborn*, for both novels have a narrator who tells a story from the womb.

Selected Work: Moros en la costa (1973); *La última canción de Manuel Sendero* (1983, *The Last Song of Manuel Sendero*, translation G. R. Shivers, 1988); *Viudas* (1983, *Widows*, translation S. Kessler, 1989); *Máscaras* (1988, *Mascara*, translation by the author, 1988); *Terapia* (2001, *Blake's Therapy*, translation by the author, 2001).

Dos mujeres (1990, Two women, by Sara Levi Calderón. Written in Spanish and untranslated. Mexico: Diana) **[Novel]** Levi Calderón is a Mexican sociologist whose academic essays and fiction have been explorations of her cultural identity as a Mexican of Jewish heritage and her sexual identity as a lesbian in a male-dominated society. *Dos mujeres* is an autobiographical work dealing with lesbian women. The main story line recounts the experience of Valeria, a thirty-nine-year-old middle-class Mexican woman. She is of Jewish heritage and her mother, who is divorced, has a lesbian affair. This was a landmark novel in

Mexico for its overt treatment of lesbianism as well as its presentation of the suffering and marginalization experienced by lesbians in Mexico. Levi Calderón's pioneering texts are comparable to the work of Argentines Sylvia Molloy and Reina Roffé as well the Colombian Albalucía Angel and the Brazilian Márcia Denser.

Double Play (See *Dubbelspel* by Frank Martinus Arion) [**Novel**]

Dourado, Autran (Waldomiro Autran Dourado) [**Biography**] Brazilian novelist and short story writer, he is one of the major novelists of the post-1945 period in Brazil. He is a prolific novelist who wrote in the Faulknerian mode in the early stages of his career but developed a broad range of topics and strategies for writing from the 1940s to the 1990s. His fiction includes novels, novellas, and numerous volumes of short stories, and they deal primarily with the decadence of Minas Gerais. Dourado was born in Patos (state of Minas Gerais) in 1926 and spent his childhood in Santo de Minas before his family eventually went to Belo Horizonte, where he attended high school. When he was a young child his father was imprisoned for political reasons, an experience that left a lasting mark on Dourado. In 1945 he began working as a journalist at the same time that he pursued law studies in Minas Gerais. In the 1940s Dourado also began making his initial contacts on the literary and cultural scene of Minas Gerais; during this period he began writing his first stories. He served as press secretary for President Juscelino Kubitschek from 1956 to 1961. Among his essays his *Poética de Romance: Matéria de Carpintaria* (1976, The poetics of the novel: carpentry material) is his combination of a theory of the novel and explanation of some of his own texts. He argues in favor of the novelist's need to publish both literary criticism as well as creative work.

Dourado published his first novel, *Teia* (1947), at the age of seventeen, with his mother's financial support paying for the publication. It is the story of a young boy living "imprisoned" in a pension house with three women: an older woman who controls, the young woman who loves him, and the child with whom he empathizes. In this novel Dourado begins setting forth a common paradigm in his work: the playing out of interior labyrinths between characters who suffer from an inability to communicate and a generalized marginalization from both mainstream society and the people closest to them.

Dourado's most celebrated novels are *A Barca dos Homens* (1961, A ship of men), *Uma Vida em Segredo* (1964, *A Hidden Life*, 1969), *Opera dos Mortos* (1967, *The Voices of the Dead*, 1980), *O Risco do Bordado* (1973, *A Pattern for a Tapestry*, 1984), and *Os Sinos da Agonia* (1974, *The Bells of Agony*, 1988). *A Barca dos Homens* is a story of a symbolic voyage that is divided formally into two parts. The first part consists of eight fragments that tell of the preparations for the departure. The second part, "As Ondas em Mar Alto," deals with the end of the trip. *Uma Vida em Segredo* tells the story of a young country girl who is orphaned and adopted by relatives in the city; she suffers both cultural shock and marginalization from the family. *Os Sinos da Agonia* is one of Dourado's novels with the most overt political overtones; it is a love story set in the mining town of Minas Gerais in the eighteenth century. The context for this novel is a revolt of citizens of the region of Minas Gerais against the Portuguese colonial government. This revolt, the Inconfidência Mineira, was planned by a group of wealthy landowners, slave owners, and mine owners, and was a reaction against the taxes imposed by the Portuguese. Inspired by Enlightenment principles, the Inconfidência Mineira was fictionalized by Dourado so that his novel became an allegory of the political repression of the military dictatorship. Along with Guimarães Rosa and Clarice Lispector, Dourado is one of the major twentieth-century novelists of Brazil.

Selected Work: *Teia* (1947); *A Barca dos Homens* (1961); *Uma Vida em Segredo* (1964, *A Hidden Life*, translation Edgar H. Miller Jr., 1969); *Opera dos Mortos* (1967, *The Voices of the Dead*, translation John M. Parker, 1980); *O Risco do Bordado* (1973, *Pattern for a Tapestry*, translation John Parker, 1984); *Os Sinos da Agonia* (1974, *The Bells of Agony*, translation John Parker, 1988); *Novelário de Donga Novais* (1976); *Lucas Procopio* (1985); *Monte da Alegría* (1990); *Um Cavalheiro de Antigamente* (1992); *Confissões de Narciso* (1997); *Gaiola Aberta* (2000).

Droguett, Carlos [Biography] Chilean novelist of the generation of 1938 in Chile, he published a series of novels in the 1950s and 1960s written in the realist vein. He was not widely read outside of Chile, but commanded the respect of several generations of Chilean readers and intellectuals; he was awarded the Premio Nacional de Literatura de Chile (national literature prize) in 1970. Born in 1915, Droguett belonged to a generation of Chilean writers that shifted the focus of the novel from the country to the city and wrote in order to achieve social and political reform. His overall tone tends to be pessimistic, and his presentation of situations sensationalist. His characters tend to be marginal types. *Sesenta muertos en la escalera* (1953, Sixty dead on the staircase) portrays the massacre of students and the consequences for the survivors. Most critics consider his major novels to be *Eloy* (1960) and *Patas de perro* (1965, Dog's paw). The marginal character in *Eloy* is a criminal who lives his last hours before being fired upon by police; the main character in *Patas de perro* has dog's paws for feet. A definitive edition of his novel *Eloy* was published in Chile by Editorial Universitaria in 1994 and was also adapted for film and theater there. Droguett went into exile to Switzerland in 1975 after the military coup of Augusto Pinochet and never returned to his homeland, dying in 1997.

Selected Work: *Eloy* (1960); *Patas de perro* (1965); *El compadre* (1967); *El hombre que había olvidado* (1968).

Drummond, Roberto [Biography] Brazilian novelist and short story writer, he became an increasingly popular novelist in his homeland in the 1980s and 1990s, despite being an iconoclastic writer. He was born in Santana dos Ferros (state of Minas Gerais) in 1939 and died in 2002 after having published seven novels associated with international postmodern fiction. As an adolescent he began writing short stories and radio plays against his parents' advice. In the 1950s he worked as a journalist, writing critiques of the government in organs such as the *Folha de Minas,* in Minas Gerais, *Binômio,* and *Alterosa.* His political positions were fundamentally socialist; his life and career were seriously affected by the military dictatorship of 1964–1989. During much of this time, unable to write political journalism, he became a sports journalist as a way of making a living. Thus he is known in Brazil for his soccer column in the *Estado de Minas* newspaper. Humor and political satire are trademarks of his fiction; he wanted to create a "pop literature" that attempted to eliminate the intellectual pretensions found in much literature. In this sense he was interested in doing for literature what had been attempted by many writers during the 1920s with the playful avant-garde of the Semana de Arte Moderna. He also wanted to divorce literature from Brazil's deeply rooted regionalism—the much-celebrated *romance nordestino* (the traditional novel of the northeastern region).

Drummond's first literary achievement was winning a short story contest in the state of Paraná in 1971. His novels represent a specific project of rejecting traditional narrative paradigms and constructing a pop literature. Drummond collects and fictionalizes elements of pop culture such as advertising slogans, television and radio dialogues, and newspaper clippings. His first book of fiction was the volume of short stories *A Morte de D.J. em Paris* (The death of D.J. in Paris) published in 1975, and he was already including pop culture in his writing. His first novel appeared in 1978 under the title *O Dia em que Ernesto Hemingway Morreu Crucificado* (The day in which Ernest Hemingway died crucified). His two major novels are *Sangue de Coca-Cola* (1980, Blood of Coca-Cola) and *Hilda Furacão* (1991). In *Sangue de Coca-Cola* he appropriates the popular culture of the Carnival, carrying out a novelistic performance that can be described as a postmodern tour de force. Beneath the surface of popular music, however, is a rewriting of Brazilian history under the dictatorship. In this work Drummond has characters from old American movies, such as Tyrone Power, as well as the image of an upside-down Coca-Cola bottle printed on the page. Drummond's work contains many other images from pop culture, from Adidas shoes to Marilyn Monroe.

Hilda Furacão represents a change from his Coca-Cola cycle. It is a lightly humorous and nostalgic look at life in Brazil for the youth of his generation in the late 1950s and the early 1960s—the years leading up to the military coup of 1964. It tells the story of a generation's rite of passage not only in classic sexual terms but also with respect to politics. Thus it is the story of a generation that saw its political ideals vanish with the military coup.

Selected Work: O Dia em que Ernesto Hemingway Morreu Crucificado (1978); *Sangue de Coca-Cola* (1980); *Hitler Manda Lembranças* (1985); *Ontem à Noite era Sexta-Feira* (1988); *Hilda Furacão* (1991); *Inés é Morta* (1993); *O Cheiro de Deus* (2001); *Os Mortos não Dançam Valsa* (2002).

Duke, El (1974, *The Duke*, by Enrique Medina. Translation by David William Foster. London: Zed, 1985) [**Novel**] The third novel by one of Argentina's most prolific novelists, *El Duke* was written in the context of the brutal military regime in Argentina during the 1970s and 1980s. The protagonist, El Duke, is a small-time boxer who faces the degradation and dehumanization of the military regime. The novel consists of the predeath interior monologue of El Duke, thus allowing him to review the sordid details of his life as a hit man for the police. His interior monologue is interrupted by other voices that appear as fragments: postdeath interviews with the Duke by newspaper reporters, his miserable existence on the streets of Buenos Aires, the Duke's work with two others as a paid assassin for the government. Some readers find Medina's violent and sickly fictional world offensive. The author is committed, however, to criticizing this violence as well as the amoral nation and the victimization of humble individuals such as the protagonist. Medina's interest in depicting social reality in graphic terms also places him close to the writers of *testimonio*.

Duque López, Alberto [**Biography**] Colombian novelist, journalist, and film critic, he was a pioneer for experimental fiction in

Colombia with the publication of his first novel, *Mateo el flautista* (Mateo the flutist) in 1968. His later work is more accessible and has been written in the context of much international film and fiction from the United States and Europe. Duque López was born in Barranquilla, Colombia, in 1943 and was fascinated with going to the movies throughout his childhood, making film the central cultural reference in his writing. Early in his career he worked as a journalist with Colombian writer Alvaro Cepeda Samudio, who encouraged him to pursue his two passions: literature and film. Film has remained a passion and a means to make a living, for Duque López has divided his life between writing about film and writing fiction, publishing film reviews, feature stories, and reports on film festivals in newspapers and magazines. His novel *Mateo el flautista* was given a national literary prize, the Premio Esso, in 1968. Since then he has worked for a variety of venues to publish film reviews and criticism. He has also written several novels, including *Mi revolver es más largo que el tuyo* (1977, My revolver is longer than yours), his tribute to detective fiction. His novel *Alejandra* (1988,) can be read as a love story involving a love triangle or as a subtle novel of terror.

His most important novel is *Mateo el flautista*, his experimental fictional homage to Argentine writer Julio Cortázar. In this work the novel's two parts offer two different versions of the protagonist, Mateo, with no suggestion of resolution. One of the narrators, Ana Magdalena, formulates a concept of creation by juxtaposing words to create a new language, at one point suggesting the reader not believe some of the anecdotes. The concept of creation is the predominant theme in this wildly experimental and enigmatic work, a trailblazer for the postmodern novel in Colombia.

Selected Work: Mateo el flautista (1968); *Mi revolver es más largo que el tuyo* (1977); *El pez en el espejo* (1984); *Alejandra* (1988).

Dulce compañía (1995, *Angel of Galilea*, by Laura Restrepo, 1990). Translation by Dolores M. Koch. New York: Vintage, 1999) [**Novel**] A Colombian journalist who has become increasingly visible as a novelist since the early 1990s, Restrepo is a popular fiction writer that some critics have associated with the *literatura light* of Mexican writers such as Laura Esquivel and Angeles Mastretta. Her writing does play on the international interest in the exotic, fantasy, and related magical realist modes of fiction. In this novel Restrepo tells the story of la Mona, a reporter for the newspaper *Somos*. Among her trivial assignments as a reporter for this tabloid she is sent to an impoverished neighborhood in Bogotá called Galilea, where she is to cover the story of an angel sighting. Among the novel's other fantastic turns, la Mona marries the angel, and they have a spectacular wedding.

Duncan, Quince [**Biography**] Central American novelist and short story writer, he was born in San José, Costa Rica, in 1940. He is one of the major writers of African background in the Central American region. His grandparents immigrated to Costa Rica from Jamaica and Barbardos, and English was one of the family's languages. Duncan's work fits comfortably within the strong oral tradition of both Caribbean and Central American fiction. His first collection, *Una canción en la madrugada* (1970, *Dawn Song*), is comprised of stories that deal with migration to the Atlantic coast of Costa Rica and the oppression of minority immigrants. He followed with the stories collected in *La rebelión Pocomía* (1976, *The Pocomía Rebellion*), stories of women within the context of a rebellion in the early twentieth century that the oral tradition has preserved as part of Costa Rica's history. The conflicts centered on English-speaking Caribbean immigrants of black descent in Spanish-speaking Costa Rica.

His novel *Los cuatro espejos* (1973, The four mirrors), like Ralph Ellison's novel *The Invisible Man* (1954), deals with the position of the black man in a white world. His novel *La paz del pueblo* (1978, For the sake of peace) is a historical novel of five women, one of whom is raped and killed. The victim, who is the object of competition between two men, is cast into a river in Limón Province in Costa Rica. These personal conflicts take place in the context of labor strife during the depression era, although the narrated time in the novel goes back in history to the 1830s and Jamaican emigration to Costa Rica. Duncan's later novel *Final de la calle* (1981, Dead-end street) is an exploration of Costa Rica's history after a civil war in 1948. A watershed in Costa Rican history, this war marks the beginning of modern Costa Rica, when concepts of national identity and race were more firmly established. The main character of the novel questions his own participation in this civil war, thus questioning the modern state. The novel proposes a new understanding of Costa Rican identity, emphasizing the African element of that culture.

Selected Work: Los cuatro espejos (1973); *La paz del pueblo* (1978); *Final de la calle* (1981).

Duppelspel (1973, *Double Play*, by Frank Martinus Arion. Translation by Paul Vincent. London: Faber and Faber, 1998) [**Novel**] One of the most widely acclaimed Dutch-language novels of the Caribbean by one of the most prominent intellectuals of the nation of Curaçao, *Double Play* is the product of a writer who has dedicated a lifetime to studying and writing in Holland and its former colony, Curaçao. Martinus Arion is interested in the interactions among the numerous languages and cultures of the Caribbean; in Curaçao literary language is often affected by the Papiamento language, and this is the case in *Double Play*. In this sense the literary language of *Double Play* is comparable to the English used by Chicana author Ana Castillo when she writes in New Mexico and the syntax and vocabulary from Spanish affect her English in subtle ways. Like Castillo, the Argentine Julio Cortázar, and the Mexican Luis Arturo Ramos, Martinus Arion is also interested in the role of games and chance in human lives. In *Double Play* the central metaphor for life as a game is dominoes: the main characters play dominoes for a variety of reasons, including the exercise of male authority and power. The plot involves the relationship between a successful bailiff, Manchi Santiano, and his beautiful but adulteress wife as well as his relationship with others in the suburb of Wakota in Curaçao. Martinus Arion begins by citing a local term used by the people of Curaçao, *entre medio*, to describe the "in between" location of this town, explaining that the typical response from locals to the question "How are you?" would be *entre medio*. Political tensions of this (then) colonial state are in the background, and tensions related to sexuality and gender are explicit. The possible implications of the characters' playing dominoes are suggested in one of the novel's two epigraphs, the second being a quotation from the Antilles Broadcasting Service indicating that dominoes is a dangerous game: it was because of a domino tournament that the Dutch in 1625 were able to seize the fort of El Moro in Puerto Rico.

E

Edge of the Storm, The (See *Filo del agua, Al* by Agustín Yañez) [**Novel**]

Edgell, Zee [**Biography**] Novelist, essayist, and academic, she was born in Belize City, Belize in 1940, and has served as the director of the Women's Bureau in her homeland. She is the major novelist of this nascent country. Edgell writes in English, the language of slightly over half the population of Belize. Her first novel, *Beka Lamb* (1982), is an autobiographical account of a young girl of creole background. Her rite of passage is also a national coming-of-age—Belize's process of gaining its independence. *In Times Like These* (1991) is a continuation of her autobiographical fiction. Her more recent *The Festival of San Joaquin* (1997) is based on an historical event relating to the *mestizo* community in Belize and, more specfically, domestic abuse.

Selected Work: *Beka Lamb* (1982); *In Times Like These* (1991); *The Festival of San Joaquin* (1997).

Edwards, Jorge [**Biography**] Chilean writer and diplomat of the generation of 1950 in Chile, which included José Donoso and Enrique Lafourcade. His novels, essays, and memoirs have left Latin American readers with a virtual literary, cultural, and political history of Chile and Latin America in the 1950s, 1960s, and 1970s, a period in which Edwards was in personal contact with many of the leading intellectual and political figures—from Mario Vargas Llosa to Fidel Castro. Edwards's generation was interested in modernizing and internationalizing Chilean literature. Born in 1931, Edwards has served in the diplomatic corps

and had a distinguished career as a writer, beginning with his first novel, *El peso de la noche* (1964, The weight of the night). He began his writing career in the early 1950s with the publication of short stories and two decades later became widely known in the Hispanic world for his memoir about the Cuban period in his life, *Persona non grata* (1973); he broke with Castro while serving for four months as chargé d'affaires for the government of Salvador Allende. He writes of the period in the early 1970s when Castro's government was suffering an economic crisis as well as a crisis of legitimacy. During the first five years of the military dictatorship (1973–1978), Edwards went into political exile. He has also published a book of literary memoirs, *Adiós, poeta* (1990, Goodbye poet).

His two major novels are *El peso de la noche* (1965) and *Los convidados de piedra* (1978, The stone guests). In the former the two male protagonists alternate as the central focus, and each is a reflection of the family matriarch, a member of the Chilean oligarchy who is in the process of dying. The males are the matriarch's son and grandson, respectively, and they represent the potential continuation of two aspects of the traditions she embodies. Edwards moves deftly between narrators and varying dreamworlds of past and present. He became more politicized in his writings of the 1970s after the military coup overthrew President Salvador Allende and his Unidad Popular government in Chile. Consequently, his lengthy and historically ambitious novel, *Los convidados de la piedra*, comparable in its scope to works such as Vargas Llosa's *Conversación en La Catedral* and Fuentes's *Terra Nostra*, covers the entire history of twentieth-century Chile, with particular focus on the history of Allende's Unidad Popular party. Like the master texts by Vargas Llosa and Fuentes,

Los convidados de la piedra offers a fragmented structure and rapid shifts in narrative point of view.

Selected Work: El peso de la noche (1965); *Los convidados de piedra* (1978); *El museo de cera* (1981); *La mujer imaginaria* (1985); *El anfitrión* (1987); *El origen del mundo* (1996), *El sueño de la historia* (2000); *El inútil de la familia* (2004).

El Salvador [Nation] A history of civil strife and foreign intervention has been transcribed in a broad range of literary texts published in El Salvador. The colonial legacy of this small Central American nation (the smallest of mainland Latin America) is underscored by the fact that fourteen families have been the ruling class for the better part of the twentieth century. Among key events in the nation's twentieth-century political history are an armed insurrection in 1932 in which twenty thousand were killed by government soldiers and the civil war of the 1980s.

El Salvador's literary tradition includes the conventional short story writer Salarué, who portrayed peasant life in the 1930s, novelist Alvaro Menéndez Leal, and the poets Claudia Lars, Francisco Gavidia, and Roque Dalton. The latter is the most prominent modern poet as well as political activitist.

The major novelists in the latter half of the twentieth century have been Manlio Argueta, Hugo Lindo, and Claribel Alegría. Argueta is internationally recognized for his *testimonio* titled *Un día en la vida* (1980, *One Day in the Life*).

Elizondo, Salvador [Biography] Mexican novelist, short story writer, poet, playwright, and essayist, he was one of the most radical innovators of fiction in Mexico and Latin America in the 1960s. His early novels, *Farabeuf* (1965) and *El hipogeo secreto* (1968) were models for postmodern fiction in Mexico; they are celebrations of several of the concepts commonly associated with postmodern fiction such as unresolved contradiction and characters without fixed identity. Elizondo was born in Mexico City in 1932 and studied literature and film in several universities in Mexico and abroad. In the mid-1960s, when he was a student at the Centro Mexicano de Escritores, he worked on his most experimental fiction and was awarded an important national prize (Premio Xavier Villaurrutia) for *Farabeuf*. Elizondo has stated that all great literature is an attempt to confront death, and many of his texts do, indeed, have death at the forefront. This is evident in the context of a complex rewriting of literary and artistic theory in his novels.

Farabeuf is a paradoxical novel in many ways, narrating the same situations over and over. In this experimental work Elizondo discounts character and plot as significant elements and privileges language as a central element to fiction. *Farabeuf* is a recreation of both erotic scenarios and torture in different settings, all of which evoke Chinese historical rituals dating back at least a century. Elizondo places the reader before the novel's central image: a character sitting between mirrors looking at someone else. The repetitive acts of torture escape the world of the rational and moral judgment. *El hipogeo secreto* is a labyrinth of self-referential doubles that implicates the reader as an active agent. Elizondo has dedicated his entire writing career to experimentation and has theorized at length about the novel in books of essays such as *Cámera lúcida* (1983) and *Cuaderno de escritura* (1988). He also published a short book in 1988 that many critics considered a novel, *Elsinore*, with the subtitle of *cuaderno* (notebook); it can be considered either a self-conscious novel about writing a notebook or a fictionalized notebook about writing a novel.

Selected Work: Farabeuf o la crónica de un instante (1965, *Farabeuf*, translation

John Incledon, 1992); *El hipogeo secreto* (1968); *Elsinore* (1988).

Eltit, Diamela [Biography] Chilean novelist, short story writer, and essayist, she has become one of the most prominent women writers of her generation in Latin America. Born in Santiago, Chile, in 1949, she studied literature in Santiago during the 1970s under the dictatorship of Pinochet. Consequently, she belongs to a generation of writers who began writing in an "inner exile" situation within Chile. Along with Ricardo Piglia, she is one of the leading postmodern writers in Latin America, with both theoretically based and politically oriented interests in race, gender, and class. In the 1990s she became a prominent figure for many academic feminists in Europe, the United States, and Latin America and has lectured on numerous American campuses. During the 1980s Eltit collaborated with young writers and artists to create a cultural front of resistance to the military dictatorship. These writers and artists created innovative forms of popular theater, street "happenings," and visual arts that worked against the power structure of the regime in subtle ways. Eltit's fiction is often read as political allegory, and she has spoken of "scenes of power" as well as ideology in essays and interviews, making her work a lengthy reflection on theory, politics, and literature. In the 1990s she published *Vaca sagrada* (1991, *Sacred Cow*), *Los vigilantes* (1994, *Custody of the Eyes*), and *Los dictadores de la muerte* (1998, The dictators of death), political allegories that do not lend themselves easily to literal interpretation. Eltit's most experimental novel is *Lumpérica* (1981, *E. Iluminata*, 1991), a work with no linear plot or anything comparable to a sequence of actions that might be constructed as a plot. Rather, it consists of a series of fragments and situations located in a plaza near Santiago de Chile. The experimental uses of space and language suggest an analysis of the historical roots of the Spanish language as a language of repression. *El cuarto mundo* (1988, *The Fourth World*, 1995) is situated on the periphery of a periphery. This novel deals with family relations, but the ultimate implications of the work are not these interactions per se, but the politics of gender and class as well as the historical uses and abuses of power. Since the early 1990s, she has lived in Mexico City, Buenos Aires, and Santiago de Chile.

Selected Work: Lumpérica (1983, *E. Iluminata*, translation Ronald Christ, Gene Bell-Villada, Helen R. Lane, and Catalina Parra, 1997); *Por la patria* (1986); *El cuarto mundo* (1988, *The Fourth World*, translation Dick Gerdes, 1995); *Vaca sagrada* (1991, *Sacred Cow*, translation Amanda Hopkinson, 1995); *Los vigilantes* (1994, *Custody of the Eyes*, translation Helen R. Lane and Ronald Christ, 2005); *Los dictadores de la muerte* (1998); *Mano de obra* (2002).

En breve cárcel (1981, *Certificate of Absence*, by Sylvia Molloy. Translation by Daniel Balderston with the author. Austin: University of Texas Press, 1989) **[Novel]** One of the most influential feminist texts of the 1980s, *En breve cárcel* stood among several novels that marked a notably feminist direction for Latin American fiction. It is the story of an Argentine woman who returns to her former home in New England where she writes a memoir about an affair she had there with another woman. The narrator-protagonist is in an identity search at the same time that the text avoids fixed identities. The author avoids the use of the word *lesbian* in the text, thus undermining the possibility of any fixed identity. In the end the novel's process of coming into being is paralleled by the protagonist's coming into being. As these processes develop, the narrator-protagonist unravels a series of past relationships with her father, her mother, and her sisters that have affected her adult relationships, as she comes to understand them.

Escalante, Beatriz [Biography] Mexican novelist, short story writer, journalist, and essayist, she has become increasingly popular as a fiction writer in Mexico in the 1990s and the early twenty-first century. In Mexico she is associated with popular fiction written by women that some critics in Mexico have identified as *literatura light*. She was born in Mexico City in 1961, studied education as an undergraduate at the National University in Mexico City (UNAM), and completed a doctorate in education at the Universidad Complutense of Madrid. She has published journalistic pieces on literary and cultural topics in *Unosmásuno, Plural, Siempre!* and other newspapers and magazines in Mexico. She has compiled several anthologies of short stories. Her early publications in fiction were the volumes of short stories titled *Tiempo mágico* (1989, Magic time) and *El paraíso doméstico y otros cuentos* (1993, Domestic paradise and other stories). Her fiction is accessible to a broad readership in Mexico and abroad, with entertaining plots and the depiction of common people in their everyday lives as part of the working and middle class. Consequently, her fiction is easily comparable to the writings of Laura Esquivel and Angeles Mastretta. Her first novel, *La magia de la inmortalidad* (2001, The magic of immortality) is an imaginative work with a witch as the main character and an emphasis on fantasy. *Júrame que te casaste virgen* (1999, Swear to me that you were married virgin) begins with a postmodern variant on the classic ploy of the "found manuscript." In this case the author claims to have found a manuscript on a hard disk (and having edited it only slightly). A fictionalized author-figure, Diana Cóppola, provides commentary on the writing throughout this work, which offers a strong plot about a woman's failed sexual relationships. The humorous plot also involves intrigue with a group of criminals. *El marido perfecto* (2001, The perfect husband) consists of twenty anecdotes about Mexican women's strategies for the survival of their identities and their sexuality. *Como ser mujer y no vivir en el infierno* (2002, How to be a woman and not live in hell) includes fifty-two first-person accounts by a diverse group of Mexican women.

Selected Work: *Amor en aerosol* (1995); *La magia de la inmortalidad* (1996, *Magdalena: a fable of immortality*, translation Jay Miskowiec, 2002); *Júrame que te casaste virgen* (1999); *El marido perfecto* (2001); *Cómo ser mujer y no vivir en el infierno* (2002); *El paraíso secreto* (2003).

Espinosa, Germán [Biography] Colombian novelist, essayist, and poet, he was born in 1938. With keen interests in the historical novel, he generally does research in the colonial period and constructs novels around historic characters. His first work, *Los cortejos del diablo* (The devil's courtship), is of this type: it is set in Cartagena, Colombia, during the colonial period, when Cartagena was a major city of the Spanish colonial empire and center of the African slave trade. In this novel Espinosa fictionalizes the life of one of the major perpetrators of the Inquisition in Colombia. The work is a denunciation of both the inquisitor and the institution of the Inquisition. His later novel, *La tejadora de coronas* (1982, The weaver of crowns) also takes places during the Spanish colonial period. It consists of the life story as related by Genoveva Alcocer, a one-hundred-year-old woman accused of witchcraft, narrated in a lengthy interior monologue. He has also published *Sinfonía del nuevo mundo* (1990, Symphony of the new world), his most popular version of the history of the region. With emphasis on plot, relatively simplistic portrayal of characters, and short chapters of one to two pages in length, this fast-moving novel, set in the early nineteenth century, takes the reader from Paris to Jamaica, Haiti, and eventually to Venezuela and Colombia. It has a French hero who is imprisoned in Cartagena, only to be rescued by a French pirate disguised as a monk. The plot also includes a love story and action-packed conflict that reads more like the material of Hollywood movies than the historical work in the Caribbean region by writers such as George Lamming, Alejo Carpentier, or even Espinosa in his earlier fiction.

Selected Work: Los cortejos del diablo (1970); *El magnicidio* (1979); *La tejadora de coronas* (1982); *El signo del pez* (1987); *Sinfonía del nuevo mundo* (1990); *La tragedia de Beelinda Elsner* (1991); *Los ojos del basilisco* (1992); *La balada del pajarillo* (2000); *Rubén Darío y la sacerdotisa de Amón* (2003); *Cuando besan las sombras* (2004).

Esquivel, Laura [Biography] Mexican novelist and screenwriter, she became one of the most popular Latin American writers of the 1990s. Her first novel, *Como agua para chocolate* (1989, *Like Water for Chocolate*), immediately became a best seller in Mexico and the rest of Latin America (selling over three hundred thousand copies), and then Esquivel enjoyed overwhelming commercial success in the United States (over one million copies). Her later novels have garnered less critical and commercial success. Given the meteoric rise of women writers in Mexico during the 1990s, particularly in commercial venues, some critics in Mexico refer to the writing of Esquivel, Angeles Mastretta, and other commercially successful books as *literatura light* ("light literature").

Born in 1949, Esquivel worked in the medium of film before writing *Como agua*

para chocolate. Her script for a film titled *Guan, el Taco de Oro* (1985) was nominated for the most prestigious film prize in Mexico, the Ariel, but it was not until she wrote the screenplay version of *Como agua para chocolate*, directed by Alfonso Arau, that she won the coveted film prize. She has also written the books *La ley de amor* (1995, *The Law of Love*) and *Tan veloz como el deseo* (2001, *Swift as Dreams*), but none of her books has garnered either the critical acclaim or the huge sales of *Como agua para chocolate*. The characters of *La ley del amor* suffer psychological problems related to the acts they have committed in their previous lives. This multimedia text (which includes CDs) is set in Mexico City in the year 2200 and is a hybrid of science fiction and romance, Christianity and mysticism. The author describes the search for her protagonist's complementary soul mates across time and space. With respect to the CDs, they are to provide the reader with illustrations while the characters experience flashbacks into former lives. In the twenty-third century, Azucena is an astroanalyst in Mexico who joins her soul mate Rodrigo, whom she first met in 1521 during the sack of Tenochtitlan where he had been a conquistador and she a victim, only to have him disappear. In the intrigue that follows, planetary president "Mr. Bush" is assassinated, and Azucena must switch her soul out of her body in order to escape being murdered herself. Isabel is a cunning and Machiavellian politician who masterminds the operation to eliminate all who were or are witnesses to her various crimes. Azucena and her companions search the galaxy for Rodrigo, as the plot thickens.

The critique of her work as *literatura light* has been addressed by some feminist critics who connect *Como agua para chocolate* with the roots of nineteenth-century women's writing: the recipes that were published in women's magazines and the serial novels that grew directly out of these same magazines were the forerunners of Esquivel's novel; these texts were appearing in print in Latin America in the 1860s. The genre of the serial novel was, in effect, the first *literatura light*, for the literary establishment never considered it "literature." *Como agua para chocolate* can be read as a parody of these popular literary forms, for each chapter begins with a recipe and then moves to love stories set during the time of the narrator's great-aunt. Esquivel portrays a series of rural, middle-class women who must be strong and clever to survive. As such, this seemingly light series of recipes and love stories can be viewed as a woman's recuperation of artistic creativity as well as a celebration of this creativity.

Selected Work: Como agua para chocolate (1989, *Like Water for Chocolate*, translation C. Christensen and T. Christensen, 1992); *La ley del amor* (1995, *The Law of Love,* translation Margaret Sayers Peden, 1996); *Tan veloz como el deseo* (2001, *Swift as Desire*, translation Stephen H. Lytle, 2001).

Estación Tula (1995, *Tula Station*, by David Toscana. Translation by Patricia J. Duncan. New York: St. Martin's, 2000) [**Novel**] The first novel by this young Mexican writer to appear in English, it offers a complex web of characters, plot, and levels of time that recalls the early novels of Mario Vargas Llosa, such as *La ciudad y los perros* and *La casa verde*. A writer from the northern Mexican city of Monterrey, Toscana sets most of his fiction in this city or region. *Estación Tula* takes place in the rural town of Tula and is a multilayered exercise in the narration of human relations. With vague echoes of Cervantes, Fuentes, and García Márquez, it also interacts with film and television. Like many postmodern writers of the 1970s and 1980s in Latin America, Toscana creates situations in the text that

suggest that fiction not only affects empirical reality but seems to determine some aspects of everyday reality as well.

Estranha Nação de Rafael Mendes (1983, *The Strange Nation of Rafael Mendes,* by Moacir Scliar. Translation by Eloah F. Giacomelli. New York: Harmony, 1988) [**Novel**] One of Brazil's most prolific contemporary writers, Scliar often writes about his own Jewishness—Jewish history and what it means to be Jewish in Brazil. He considers Judaism itself to be dialectical, with the humanists, philosophers, and novelists in opposition to the more materialistically oriented. This is the vision presented in *A Estranha Nação de Rafael Mendes*, which recounts the history of a twentieth-century Brazilian Jew, Rafael Mendes, all the way back to the Old Testament. The novel begins in southern Brazil, Porto Alegre, in 1975, with its protagonist a partner in a corrupt investment firm, but more concerned about his rebellious daughter than his shaky financial status. The novel shifts to the past when a mysterious box arrives at his door, left by a genealogist who knew Mendes's father. The box contains a 1938 photo of Mendes as a baby with his parents, a notebook, and history books. The major part of the novel consists of anecdotes from the family past, which includes its presence in Spain under the Romans, its presence in Portugal during the Inquisition, and five centuries of experience in Brazil. The novel ends in the twentieth-century present of the beginning, with Mendes dramatically saving his daughter from marriage to one of his dishonest business partners. Some of the more incredible parts of this story, such as the Indian chief who speaks Hebrew, have been associated with magical realism.

Estrázulas, Enrique [**Biography**] Uruguayan novelist, short story writer, and poet, born in Montevideo in 1942, he began publishing literary criticism and journalism in his youth. In his fiction he is interested in experimentation and surprising the reader. In *Lucifer ha llorado* (1980, Lucifer has cried) he builds an intense and surprising relationship among three characters. *Tango para intelectuales* (1990, Tango for intellectuals) is a self-conscious metafiction in which the narrator is a writer.

Selected Work: *Pepe Corvina* (1974); *Lucifer ha llorado* (1980); *El ladrón de música* (1982); *El amante de paja* (1987); *Tango para intelectuales* (1990); *Los manuscritos del caimán* (2004).

Etienne, Franck (See Frankétienne) **[Biography]**

Eulogy for a Brown Angel (1992, by Lucha Corpi. Written in English. Houston: Arte Público) **[Novel]** A mystery novel by a Chicana writer who has dedicated most of her career to this genre, this book's protagonist, Gloria Damasco, is a Chicana feminist. The novel's intricate, fast-moving plot takes the reader across California—from the protests of the 1970s Chicano movement in Los Angeles to the late 1980s in Oakland. The novel begins with the brutal murder of a young Hispanic boy during the National Chicano Moratorium (of 1970) as well as the murder of an East Los Angeles gang member. Damasco's understanding of these two murders and related complications are mediated not only by her rational calculations but by her unexplicable perception of people and events. For example, when holding the newspaper clipping related to the first death, she sees visions that later prove useful in solving the mystery. Her solution leads her not only inside a Chicano family's personal and business relationships but also to international intrigue involving crime connections with a Brazilian brotherhood. Corpi's use of female detectives connects her to the detec-

tive novels of some U.S. Anglo writers; her special interest in unexplained visions associates her with the spiritually generated fictions of Rudolfo Anaya.

Eyherabide, Gley [Biography] Uruguayan novelist and short story writer, he was born in Melo (Uruguay) in 1934. His fiction is characterized by humor, satire, and use of the grotesque. He published his first volume of short stories, *Elotro equilibrista*, in 1967. His early novels were *En la avenida* (1970), *Gepeto y las palomas* (1972), and *Juego de pantallas* (finalist for the Seix Barral prize in 1973, published in 1987). This last is set in the early 1960s, when Latin American intellectuals were generally exuberant about the Cuban Revolution. He has also published the novel *En el zoo* (1988), a satirical account of the military dictatorship in the 1970s.

Selected Work: *En la avenida* (1970); *Gepeto y las palomas* (1972); *Juego de pantallas* (1987); *En el zoo* (1988).

Fallace, Tania Jamardo [Biography] Born in Porto Alegre, Brazil, in 1939, she began to publish well-received albeit conventional novels in the 1960s. Her first novel, *Fuga* (1964, Flight), deals with the monotonous and tedious daily life of an adolescent girl. It also relates some bitter experiences of her youth. She never reaches a full understanding of her predicament or what actions she might take to address it. Her second novel, *Adão e Eva* (1965, Adam and Eve) has a broader thematic focus, touching upon issues of free will, with mythical overtones to associated with the biblical story of Adam and Eve. *O 35 ano de Inês* (1974, The 35 years of Ines) also deals with themes such as liberty and dignity. This text contains three related narratives in which the characters search for an understanding of authenticity and the meaning of sacrifice.

Selected Work: *Fuga* (1964); *Adão e Eva* (1965); *O 35 Ano de Inês* (1974).

Farabeuf (1965, *Farabeuf*, by Salvador Elizondo. Translation by John Incledon. New York: Garland, 1992) [**Novel**] An early experiment in postmodern fiction in Latin America, *Farabeuf* is a paradoxical novel in which Elizondo narrates the same situations over and over. The author does not regard character and plot as significant elements, preferring to focus on language as the main interest. This novel is a recreation of both erotic scenarios and torture in different settings, all of which evoke historic Chinese rituals dating back at least a century. Elizondo places the reader before the novel's central image: a character sitting between mirrors looking at someone else. The repetitive acts of torture escape the world of the rational and moral judgment. One of the more complex novels to appear in Latin America during the 1960s, this pioneering work set the stage, along with José Emilio Pacheco's *Morirás lejos* (1968), for the publication of many experimental and postmodern fictions in Mexico during the 1970s, particularly during the early part of the decade.

Faria, Octavio de [**Biography**] Brazilian novelist and essayist, he was born in Rio de Janeiro in 1908 to a wealthy and conservative Catholic family and died in 1984. He wrote novels and essays to legitimate and defend these conservative values. In the 1930s he began publishing an ambitious cycle of novels under the general title Tragédia Burguesa, the first of which was *Mundos Mortos* (1937, Dead worlds). These novels relate to a broad range of personal, class, and societal conflicts of middle-class life in Rio de Janeiro in the 1930s, following several characters from adolescence to adulthood. In novels such as *Os Renegrados* (1947, The renegades), *Os Loucos* (1952, The insane), and *O Senhor do Mundo* (1957, The lord of the world) he depicts the world in Manichaean terms of good versus evil (with characters clearly representative of each side), emphasizing a reaffirmation of Christian values and the Brazilian Catholic Church as an institution. Writing in ways comparable to Lúcio Cardoso, he demonstrates the psychological consequences of his characters' actions. By 1976 he had published twelve of his planned fifteen volumes.

Selected Work: *Mundos Mortos* (1937); *Caminhos da Vida* (1939); *Os Renegrados* (1947); *Os Loucos* (1952); *O Señor do Mundo* (1957); *O Retrato da Morte* (1961); *Angela ou as Areias do Mundo* (1963); *A Sombra de Deus* (1966); *O Cavalero da Virgen* (1971); *O Indigno* (1976); *O Lodo das Ruas* (1976).

Feinman, José Pablo [**Biography**] Argentine novelist, essayist, and screenwriter, he was born in Buenos Aires in 1943. He studied philosophy and taught at the University of Buenos Aires in the early 1970s before the military dictatorship. In the 1970s he began publishing political essays and fiction; he has written several books in each genre. Several of his film scripts have been made into Argentine films. He published his first novel, *Ultimos días de la víctima* (The last days of the victim), in 1979.

Feinman's novel *Los crímenes de Van Gogh* (1994, The crimes of Van Gogh) is a parody of the crime thriller. The protagonist has two dismal jobs: assistant to a film producer and employee in a video club shop. His dream is to write the perfect film script, worth three million dollars to an international company for the best script based on a real event. In an attempt to escape from his tedious and mediocre life, he decides to commit a series of crimes and writes about them at the same time.

Feinman is a capable and sophisticated writer with a growing reputation in Argentina. Like his compatriots Borges and Piglia, he knows the detective genre well and is fully capable of making it into an entertaining game.

Selected Work: Ultimos días de la víctima (1979); *Ni tiro del final* (1982); *El ejército de la ceniza* (1986); *La astucia de la razón* (1990); *El cadaver imposible* (1992); *Los crímenes de Van Gogh* (1994).

Felinto, Marilene [Biography] Brazilian novelist, journalist, and translator, she was born in 1957 in Recife, and moved to São Paulo at the age of twelve, where she later studied literature. She has written journalism in the *Folha de São Paulo* since 1987 and has published a volume of her journalism under the title *Jornalisticamente Incorrecto* (2001, Journalistically incorrect). In 1982 she published her first novel, *As Mulheres de Tijucopapo* (1982, *Women of Tijucopapo*, 1994), which won a prestigious novel prize (Jabuti Prize) in Brazil and involves a series of returns that also constitute a search for origins on the part of the protagonist. This novel is written in a sharp, spirited, and discontinuous style that is well communicated in the English translation by Irene Matthews, published as *Women of Tijucopapo* (1994). In this novel the narrator, Risia, sustains a dialogue with herself and her memories. As Matthews explains in her afterword, the work can be read as a deviant version of strong memories and strong women. The question of optimistic or pessimistic attitudes, in the end, is ambiguous. She has also published a book-length study of the fiction of the Brazilian writer Graciliano Ramos, *Outros Heróis e Esse Graciliano* (1983).

Selected Work: As Mulheres de Tijucopapo (1982, *The Women of Tijucopapo,*

translation Irene Matthews, 1994); *O Lago Encantado de Grongonzo* (1987).

Fernández, Macedonio [Biography] Argentine novelist, short story writer, and poet, he was born in Buenos Aires in 1874; his impact in Argentina and throughout Latin America has been noteworthy since the 1960s. A humorist like Jorge Luis Borges, he has grown in stature with each passing decade since WWII, particularly among writers. With Borges he played a major role in the reaffirmation of the right of invention in Latin America. He wrote in opposition to the monumental figure of traditional and conservative literary values in Argentina, the early twentieth-century poet and essayist Leopolod Lugones. Consequently, the avant-garde *ultraísta* movement of the 1920s in Argentina adopted Fernández as their progenitor. He was also highly respected as a poet. His unconventional writings appeared in Spanish from the 1920s to the 1940s. Initially aligned with the Argentine avant-garde of the 1920s, Fernández published a fifty-page fictional text, *Papeles de recienvenido* (Papers of a recent arrival) in 1929. This unique text also shares qualities with the essay, albeit a rambling and chaotic one. The minimal story line involves a street accident soon after the *recienvenido* (newly arrived) reaches Buenos Aires. After this accident a first-person narrator leads the reader through a series of wild and humorous associations. Macedonio Fernández's typical procedure is to introduce the unexpected and to emphasize the irrational and the paradoxical. Not really a "novel" in any standard understanding of the term, *Papeles de recienvenido*, nevertheless, had an enormous impact on the development of the Latin American novel, particularly in the 1960s and 1970s, when Macedonio became fashionable among intellectuals. His later book, *Una novela que comienza* (1941, A novel that begins) is similar in style, but it reads at times like an essay about the process of writing, with occasional observations about women the narrator sees by chance. He needs to be in contact with one of them in order to complete his novel. Fernández died in 1952, well before becoming an icon of innovation among Latin American intellectuals.

Selected Work: *Papeles de recienvenido* (1929); *Una novela que comienza* (1941).

Fernández, Roberto [Biography] Cuban American novelist, short story writer, and essayist, he immigrated from Cuba with his family and the first wave of immigrants in 1962, at the age of fifteen. His writing covers a broad range of topics related to the immigration experience, from memories of the Cuba left behind to cultural tensions and conflicts. He does go beyond the usual topics of earlier exile writing—displacement and nostalgia. Fernández was born in Sagua la Grande, Cuba, in 1951, and after immigrating he received a BA and a PhD in linguistics in the United States. He began writing short fiction while in graduate school, and later published innovative novels consisting of multiple texts—monologues, dialogues, letters, and the like—in the fashion of writers such as Guillermo Cabrera Infante and Manuel Puig.

Fernández's fiction includes two volumes of short stories and three novels. His first novel, *La vida es un especial* (1982, Life is on special) is a satire of the materialism and commercialism of the Cuban community in Miami. His first novels written in English, *Raining Backwards* (1988) and *Holy Radishes!* (1995), are critical of the idealized past that many Cuban exiles hold of Cuba as well as of many aspects of their present life as Cuban Americans in the United States. *Raining Backwards* (1988) was well received by the critics and focuses on the generation of his parents and the tensions,

once in exile, between parents and children. In this work Fernández portrays the cultural malaise and failures of the Cuban community in the United States; its members are isolated individuals who destroy others and themselves. The novel contains some grotesque and sordid individual stories of corruption and failed relationships. In this novel and in *Holy Radishes!* Fernández uses linguistic and cultural referents (from Spanish) that make the experience of the novel different for bilingual readers. In this sense Fernández's interlingual work is comparable to some of the fiction of the Chicana Ana Castillo (who writes in English but uses referents from Spanish) and the Caribbean writer Frank Martinus Arion (of Curacão, who writes in Dutch with referents from a local creole called papiamento). *Holy Radishes!* has been read as a parody of García Márquez's *One Hundred Years of Solitude* and, more specifically, the Colombian's legendary village of Macondo, which becomes the idyllic Cuban village of Mondovi in Fernández's fiction. This novel follows the painful experience of a Cuban couple as they are forced to leave their home in Cuba. They are upper-class Cubans who suffer humiliation both in Cuba at the hands of revolutionaries and in the United States when they are eventually confronted by racist Americans who are hostile to Cuban immigrants. The novel's title comes from the fact that the formerly wealthy Cuban women work in a radish-packing house in Florida. One of the women dreams of an idealized past in a town she imagines as Mondavi in Cuba. Fernández leads the reader to an understanding, however, that dreams of a Cuban past, as well as the American Dream for the future, are nothing more than illusions for these Cuban exiles. Fernández's fiction presents the complexities of the Cuban exile circumstance with nuances not always seen in novels of exile. Despite his satire and critique, he leaves room for optimism: invention and imagination provide the characters with ways to survive. Some critics have also read Fernandez's fiction as a parody of Latin American magical realism in general. He has won several awards for his fiction and has taught linguistics at Florida State University.

Selected Work: La vida es un special (1981); *La montaña rusa* (1985); *Raining Backwards* (1988); *En la ocho y la doce* (1991); *Holy Radishes!* (1995).

Fernández, Sergio [Biography] Mexican novelist, short story writer, essayist, he was particularly recognized for his experimental fiction in the 1970s; he is more interested in intellectual experience than storytelling per se. His characters tend to be writers and intellectuals; his themes are the act of writing and the writer's identity. Fernández was born in Mexico City in 1926 and has dedicated a lifetime studying and teaching literature, with a graduate specialization in Spanish Golden Age literature and teaching experience in numerous Mexican and foreign universities. He has also published essays on art. His early fiction showed his interest in the French *nouveau roman. Los peces* (1968, The fish) is an exploration of the possibilities of the erotic. His most complex and successful novel, *Segundo sueño* (1976, Second dream), involves an elaborate plot constructed around the protagonist, a Mexican professor of art in Germany, and his numerous real and imaginary relationships with men and women. He is in Germany to teach do research on the painter Lucias Altner, on whom he is writing a biography. This novel is also a metafiction in which the narrator writes the biography and his own memoir as part of the novel, so the reader is privy to various versions of both. As the novel develops, the experience of the narrator himself and those of Altner tend to blur together. The novel also mixes the unlikely combination of critiques of certain nations (the United States, Germany, and Mexico) and dreams.

Selected Work: Los signos perdidos (1958); *En tela de juicio* (1964); *Los peces* (1968); *Segundo sueño* (1976).

Ferré, Rosario [Biography] Caribbean novelist, short story writer, poet, and essayist, she is one of the major contemporary women writers in Latin America. Like many Caribbean writers, she lives on a cultural and linguistic border between the United States and Latin America; in her case, she has written in both Spanish and English. She was born in Ponce, Puerto Rico, in 1942 to a prominent family in the region; her father had been governor of Puerto Rico. While studying at the University of Puerto Rico in the late 1960s, she became personally acquainted with the Peruvian writer Mario Vargas Llosa and the Uruguayan critic Angel Rama, both of whom served as mentors and role models for her literary career. The Argentine Julio Cortázar has also been a significant influence on her work. From 1971 to 1975 she directed a literary magazine, *Zona de carga y descarga*. She began publishing poems, essays, and short fiction in the 1970s. Associated with the post-Boom of the Spanish American novel of the 1980s, as well as the rise of women writers in the 1980s, she is also interested in politics and popular culture. She wrote *The House on the Lagoon* (1995) in English and subsequently published the work in Spanish as *La casa de la laguna* (1996). Most of her fiction involves family stories.

Ferré's novel *Maldito amor* (1986, *Sweet Diamond Dust*, 1988) is her major work and is based on a popular nineteenth-century love song. It consists of a short novel and three related stories; these are family stories concerning several generations of the De la Valle family. The main focus is on the women of the family—the loss of their sugarcane business destroys the family. Writing on the linguistic border, Ferré shares interests with writers such as the Chicana Ana Castillo and the Dutch Caribbean Frank Martinus Arion. *Maldito amor* also offers an obvious political reading, for the characters represent various positions with respect to the appropriate relationship with the United States. She continues telling family stories and setting forth Puerto Rico's social history in her more recent novel, *Vecindarios excéntricos* (1998, *Eccentric Neighborhoods*), a tale of two powerful families on the island.

Selected Work: La caja de cristal (1978, *The Glass* Box, translation by the author, 1986; *Maldito amor* (1986, *Sweet Diamond Dust*, translation by the author, 1988); *The House on the Lagoon* (1995, rewritten by the author in Spanish as *La casa de la laguna*, 1996); *Vuelo del cisne* (2002, *Flight of the Swan*, translated by the author, 2002).

Figueiredo, André de [Biography] Author of short stories and novels, this Brazilian writer was born in João Pessoa (state of Paraíba) in 1931. He began writing fiction in the early 1970s, publishing the volume of short stories *O Longo Aprendizado de Isaura* (The long learning of Isaura) in 1972. Several of these stories had earned local prizes before being collected in the volume. After publishing short stories, he was awarded a prestigious national prize (Walmap Prize) for his first novel, *Labirinto* (1971, Maze) in 1971, and it soon became a best seller. Considered by some critics the major Brazilian novel of the 1970s, it is a wide-ranging work that moves deftly between the realms of empirical reality and the fantastic. *Labirinto* has also been compared to Juan Rulfo's *Pedro Páramo* and Gabriel García Márquez's *Cien años de soledad*. Like these two Spanish American writers, Figueiredo uses the procedures of transcendent regionalism—using a real-world base to create mythic and universal experience. In his fictional world Figueredo goes back to his own youth, eventually evoking the fantastic to narrate the lives of his ancestors.

Selected Work: Labirinto (1971); *Alvorada* (1978).

Figueiredo, Rubens [Biography] Novelist and translator, he was born in Rio de Janeiro in 1956 and belongs to the generation of new Brazilian writers that Nelson de Oliveira and other critics have identified as the generation of the 1990s. He studied literature at the Universidade Federal do Rio de Janeiro. He has published short stories and novels. His novel *O Mistério da Samanbaia* (1986, The mystery of the samanbaia tree) uses the genre of detective fiction as its point of departure. *A Festa do Milenio* (1990, The party of the millennium) establishes surprising connections between the real and the symbolic, with characters such as an archpriest who is pursued by ghosts and a governor who loves parties, all of whom question established values.

Selected Work: O Mistério da Samanbaia (1986); *Essa Maldita Farinha* (1987); *A Festa do Milenio* (1990); *Barco a Seco* (2001).

Filho, Adonias (Adonias Filho Aguiar) **[Biography]** Brazilian novelist and essayist born in Itajuipe (state of Bahia) in 1915, he died in 1990 after a distinguished career in Brazil as an academic and creative writer. His books of essays include *Renascimento do Homen* (1937, Renaissance of man); *Modernos Ficcionistas Brasileiros I* (1958, Modern Brazilian fiction writers 1); *História da Bahia* (1963, History of Bahia); *Modernos Ficcionistas Brasileiros II* (1965, Modern Brazilian fiction writers 2); *O Romance Brasileiro de 30* (1973, The Brazilian novel of 1930).

Filho began writing fiction in the 1940s. Often compared to writers such as João Guimarães Rosa and William Faulkner, he uses settings in the interior of Brazil, in the southern part of the state of Bahia. His early novels, *Os Servos da Morte* (1946, The servants of death), *Memórias de Lázaro* (1952, Memories of Lazarus), and *Corpo Vivo* (1962, Live body), portray a nightmarish world of insanity and violence. A variety of narrators provide different perspectives on the uncivilized and brutal life of rural Bahia. Filho uses the *sertão* (the plains), that appears in much of Guimarães Rosa's work. Like Faulkner and Guimarães Rosa, he uses a clearly identifiable regional setting to attain a mythic understanding of the world.

Selected Work: Os Servos da Morte (1946), *Memórias de Lázaro* (1952, *Memories of Lazarus,* translation Fred P. Ellison, 1969), *Corpo Vivo* (1962); *O Forte* (1965); *As Velhas* (1975); *Noite sem Madrugada* (1983); *O Homen de Branco* (1987).

Filloy, Juan [Biography] Argentine novelist and essayist, he was a relatively unknown predecesor to Julio Cortázar and Guillermo Cabrera Infante with Joycean tendencies. Born in Argentina in 1894, he studied at the University of Córdoba in Argentina, then practicing law and serving as a judge. He was, nevertheless, active in Argentina's literary and cultural life in the 1930s and 1940s. He was a social critic from his earliest writings, beginning with *Periplo* (1931) and *Estafen* (1932). Compared to many other writers with similar novelistic production, he was not a widely known or popular novelist, but he enjoyed the dedicated following of a small group of intellectuals from the publication of his early novel *Op Oloop* (1934), an iconoclastic story of the disintegration of the protagonist over a period of twenty hours. In this novel Filloy gives the reader subtitles with the exact time, beginning at 10:00 am and ending at 5:59 am the next day. The protagonist is a resident in Buenos Aires from Finland who begins the novel with full confidence in the rationality of mankind and falls in love with a woman, later hosting a banquet for intellectuals. This soiree is full of artistic and philosophical allusions as well as humor with sexual overtones and Joycean wordplay. In the end the protagonist's apparently rational world falls apart, and he commits suicide. Filloy wrote this novel in Paris and published it with his own funds in Buenos Aires.

Many critics consider *Op Oloop* to be Filloy's major work, even though he published several other novel-like volumes that were heavily informed by his interest in poetry and surrealism. His gift for wordplay, his humor, and his publication of books that only vaguely related to the novel make him a predecessor to not only Cortázar and Cabrera Infante but also to writers such as the Argentine Leopoldo Marechal, the Mexican Carlos Fuentes, and the Brazilian João Guimarães Rosa.

Selected Work: Estafen (1932); *Op Oloop* (1934); *Caterva* (1937); *La purga* (1992).

Filo del agua, Al (1947, *The Edge of the Storm,* by Agustín Yáñez. Translation by Ethel Brinton. Austin: University of Texas Press, 1968) **[Novel]** A modern classic in Mexico, *Al filo del agua* takes place in a Mexican village during a period of a year and a half leading to the year 1910 and the outbreak of the Mexican Revolution (1910–1917). The novel begins with an "Acto Preparatorio," an introductory portrait of this somber and monotonous town. After the introduction the narrative moves rapidly from one character to another, juxtaposing personal desires with the opposing weight of traditions that stifle the realization of any hopes or desires. Several human dramas are developed during the course of this novel, including a priest who attempts to protect his followers from the influence of outsiders and modernity and a love triangle between a villager and an outsider. In this highly fragmented novel Yáñez uses interior monologues to capture the thoughts and feelings of the repressed characters, leaving the reader to decide what appears less attractive: a powerful and zealous religious institution or a chaotic revolution.

Fonseca, Rubem [Biography] Novelist and short story writer, he has been at the forefront of the Brazilian literary scene since the 1970s and read in Spanish and English translation throughout the Americas from the 1980s and through 1990s. He has done much to popularize detective fiction in Brazil. Born in Juiz de Fora (state of Minas Gerais) in 1925, Fonseca studied law in Brazil and later business administration in the United States. After becoming an executive in a private firm, he decided to dedicate himself to literature, gaining immediate recognition in Brazil for his short stories. His models have been such diverse figures as Alain Robbes-Grille and Jorge Luis Borges. In 1969 he won a national short story contest (II Concurso Nacional de Contos do Paraná). After his first novel, *O Caso Morel* (1973, The Morel case), he published a volume of fifteen satirical stories, *Feliz Ano Novo* (1975, Happy new year), which was censored by the government. His critique of technocracy and ecological destruction as well as his sardonic wit have made him one of Brazil's most admired and widely read novelists. He tends to use the detective novel as his model genre, but always with a parodic distance. *O Caso Morel* is a crime thriller dealing with a sexual relationship that might have led to a death. *A Grande Arte* (1983, *High Art*) is a crime novel in which the detective, Mandrake, not only searches for clues in

the rational fashion of the classic detective but also imagines situations—in good Borgesian fashion in which the act of imagination is central—that will lead him to solutions.

With *Bufo & Spallanzani* (1985), Fonseca entered into dialogue with international postmodern culture, constructing a parody of detective fiction, with a character who is a compulsive writer in the process of writing a book. Similarly, *Vastas Emoções e Pensamentos Imperfeitos* (1988, *The Lost Manuscript*) is a postmodern crime novel, with a Brazilian film director as the narrator-protagonist; he pays homage to the murder mystery, and Fonseca pays homage to American movies, film directors, and writers. When the protagonist is in Berlin, he is in the middle of cold war politics; when he is in Brazil he barely survives the labyrinth of crime and politics. Fonseca is satirical in tone and, as always, surprises the reader at the end. *Agosto* (1990, August) is another complex crime novel with satirical political implications. It deals with a series of real political events from 1954 that included the death of a businessman and the suicide of President Getúlio Vargas. The detective figure in this novel gets caught up in a complex web of criminal and political intrigue that eventually escapes rational explanation. Fonseca evokes the classic French writer Molière as the narrator-protagonist of his more recent novel *O Doente Molière* (2000, The sick Molière). In this work, which harks back to 1673 during the time of the court of Louis XIV, the French playwright Molière whispers, "I was poisoned" after a performance of his last play, *Le Malade imaginaire*, shortly before dying. In this historical detective fiction an anonymous marquise plays the sleuth in solving the mystery of who poisoned Molière. The narrative is filled with references to the theatrical giants of the period such as Racine and Corneille as well as Molière. Several chapters offer brief scenes from Molière's classics *Tartuffe* and *Don Juan ou le festin de pierre*. While investigating the crime, the narrator keeps his affair a secret. The narrator casts doubt, however, on the clergy and satirizes a broad range of social types.

Fonseca is widely known in Brazil beyond literary circles. His volume of short stories *Lúcia McCartney* (1969) has been adapted for Brazilian stage and television and has been reprinted in various editions.

Selected Work: O Caso Morel (1973); *A Grande Arte* (1983, *High Art*, translation Ellen Watson, 1986); *Bufo & Spallanzani* (1985, *Bufo & Spallanzini*, translation Clifford E. Landers, 1990); *Vastas Emocões e Pensamentos Imperfeitos* (1988, *The Lost Manuscript*, translation Clifford E. Landers, 1997); *Agosto* (1990); *O Doente Molière* (2000).

Forma de silencio, La (1987, The form of silence, by María Luisa Puga. Written in Spanish and untranslated. Mexico City: Grijalbo) [**Novel**] A book lacking a developed plot, *La forma del silencio* is a highly fragmented novel set in Mexico in the 1980s and intended to be a critique of Mexican politics and society in that period. The two main characters engage in a dialogue in an office building in Mexico City. In their conversation the female narrator seems to control what is said by her counterpart, Juan, suggesting that this conversation, like much else that transpires, is actually her imagination. Puga uses these characters to refere to different periods in Mexican history from the 1940s to the 1960s, with specific references to events and typical features of Mexican society in each period (i.e., the 1940s, the 1950s). She associates the 1980s with crises, and her critique points to the Americanization of Mexican society as well as it corruption and violence. *La forma de silencio* along with *Cuando el aire es azul*

(1990, When the air is blue) are two of the best novels by Puga, who is recognized as one of Mexico's most accomplished women writers.

França Junior, Oswaldo [Biography] Brazilian novelist, he was born in 1936 and died in an auto accident in June 1989. His professional career was clearly marked by the military dictatorship of the post-1964 period: with the military coup of 1964, the government revoked his pilot's license, ending his career as an airline pilot but opening the door to his future career as a writer. Once he turned to fiction writing, he came forth with *O Viúvo* (1965, Widower) and the highly successful novel *Jorge, um Brasileiro* in 1967, which was translated into English by Thomas Colchie as *The Long Haul* in 1980. His novels are characterized by strong plots and absurd, entertaining situations.

Selected Work: O Viúvo (1965); *Jorge, um Brasileiro* (1967, *The Long Haul*, translation Thomas Colchie, 1980); *Um Dia no Rio* (1969); *Um Homem de Macacão* (1969, *The Man in the Monkey Suit*, translation Gregory Rabassa, 1989); *A Volta para Marilda* (1974); *Dois Irmãos* (1976); *As Lembranças de Eliana* (1978); *O Passo-Bandeira* (1984); *No Fundo das Aguas* (1987, *Beneath the Waters*, translation Margaret A. Neves, 1990).

Franco, Jorge (Jorge Franco Ramos) [Biography] Colombian novelist and short story writer, he was born in Medellín in 1962. He belongs to the young generation of urban writers in Colombia that includes Santiago Gamboa and Mario Mendoza, similar in some ways to the young new urban writers in Brazil identified as the generation of the 1990s or the McOndo group organized by Fuguet and Gómez in Chile. He studied literature at the Universidad Javeriana in Bogotá and film in London. He also studied in a creative writing workshop directed by novelist Manuel Mejía Vallejo in Medellín. He received a series of literary prizes in Colombia and one in Spain for his writing, making him one of the most respected novelists of his generation in Colombia.

Franco is best known for his novel of disaffected youth in Medellín, *Rosario Tijeras* (1999), which has been successful throughout the Hispanic world and was made into a film in Colombia under the same title.

Selected Work: Maldito amor (1996); *Rosario Tijeras* (1999); *Paraíso Travel* (2001).

Franketienne [Biography] Caribbean novelist, poet, playwright, essayist, and painter from Haiti, he was the only major Haitian writer not to emigrate during the father-son Duvalier dictatorship from 1957 to 1986—and not to be imprisoned for his writing. He was refused a passport to leave Haiti. Born in 1936, he is known for being both a broad-ranging intellectual and the first writer to publish a novel in Haitian Creole in a nation where the standard had been to publish fiction in French. Etienne has promoted the idea of Spiralisme since the 1970s as a response to the dictatorship; this movement intends to offer the open-ended model of the spiral as opposed to the closed discourse of the dictatorship. Spiralisme was also intended to demystify the author, the text, and the very idea of authenticity.

Known also as Franketienne, he had already published a novel in French before coming forth with this linguistic and aesthetic experimentation Haitian Creole under the title *Dézafi* (1975, Challenge). His literary predecessors in Haitian Creole had published stories, fables, or poems. Etienne has enjoyed relative success with this novel, which is set during the Duvalier dictatorship and deals with the peasants in a small rural Haitian community. The impoverished and hopeless inhabitants of two villages suffer from hunger and fear. Etienne effectively uses a collective we as the narrative voice, and this we acts in opposition to a "they" who are the "enemies."

For writers of the Caribbean, as has been theorized by Edouard Glissant, language itself can be a political statement. For Franketienne, political resistance to the Duvalier regime has been writing *Dézafi* in Haitian Creole, followed by a novelistic experiment in the same language, which might be called a lyrical essay, *Ultravocal (Spiral)*. Its fragmented, visionary, and tormented style not only defies the genre of the novel but also seems to be an appropriate expression for the tortured existence of his island nation, which had been living under repressive dictatorial regimes for over two decades. His postmodern writing of resistance is comparable to the hermetic and tortured early novels of the Chilean Diamela Eltit, writing under the dictatorship of Pinochet in Chile. As an intellectual, Franketienne has also been compared to the major figures of the Caribbean—Aimé Césaire, Alejo Carpentier, and V. S. Naipul.

Selected Work: Ultravocal (1972, *Spiral*); *Dézafi* (1975, Challenge); *Les affres dún défi* (1979).

French Guyana (See Guadeloupe/Martinique/French Guyana) **[Nation]**

Fresán, Rodrigo [Biography] Argentine novelist and short story writer, he has been a practicing journalist since 1984, writing about such diverse topics as literature, film, gastronomy, and music. He belongs to the new generation of writers that the Chilean author Alberto Fuguet has labeled McOndo and that has been embraced in a variety of ways throughout Latin America. In the most general sense, he belongs to that young group of postmodern writers who began publishing in the 1990s that has also been referred to as the generation of the 1990s. Fresán was included in Fuguet's anthology *McOndo*.

Born in Buenos Aires in 1963, he has published several books of fiction, his first being a volume of short stories titled *Historia argentina* (1991, Argentine history), which received a prize in Argentina. He followed with the short fiction *Vidas de santos* (1993, Lives of saints) and *Trabajos manuales* (1994, Manual jobs). His first novel, *Esperanto* (1995), presents a protagonist, Federico, who is a musician living in constant crisis. The novel covers a week of time, but consists of numerous digressions to Federico's past; Federico attempts to order and make sense of his memories. Fresán intercalates fragments from different media to tell Federico's story, which involves an increasing awareness of aging and death. His second novel, the lengthy (539 pages) *Mantra* (2001), has received favorable critical readings and deals with the protagonist's relationship to media technology—television, radio, and film. This protagonist, Martín Mantra, lives in the world of the new media and, like characters of many novelists of the 1990s; he occupies an urban space. Mantra is saturated with a plethora of soap operas, movies, magazines, and photos. His dilemma, then, is the problem of his generation: what does one do with this excess and saturation of information? In addition to the key role of the media in *Mantra*, Fresán insists upon the impossibility of the totalizing projects that had been the objective of the writers of the 1960s Boom. Thus, although *Mantra* does have some of the encyclopedic impulses of the Boom novels, the numerous pieces of information found in this novel do not produce the totalizing, holistic vision of the modernist text explored by the masters of the Boom. Nevertheless, Fresán writes with an acute awareness of his predeces-

sors of the Boom. The use of a dead narrator in *Mantra* who watches television in hell evokes the Mexican classic novel *Pedro Páramo*.

The length of the novel, its fragmention, and its encyclopedic knowledge have lead some readers to compare *Mantra* to Cortázar's *Rayuela*. One important difference, though, lies in the function of information: in Cortázar the human mind is capable of processing all this information; in Fresán the mind cannot. If *Rayuela* is seen as the emblematic novel of the 1960s Boom, *Mantra* can be considered the novel par excellence of the generation of the 1990s. Fresán has received less critical attention than such high-visibility writers of his generation as Alberto Fuguet from Chile and Jorge Volpi from Mexico. Nevertheless, *Esperanto* and *Mantra* make Fresán a key figure of his generation in Latin America.

Selected Work: Esperanto (1995); *La velocidad de las cosas* (1998); *Mantra* (2001).

Fuentes, Carlos [Biography] One of the most prolific novelists of the generation of the 1960s Boom, Fuentes has published novels, short fiction, essays, and theater. His total writings have involved an ambitious rewriting of Latin American literature, history, and culture. Many critics considered Fuentes the most prominent political voice of the Boom, particularly in its early stages of alignment behind Fidel Castro and his Cuban Revolution. Born in Panama City in 1928, Fuentes is of Mexican nationality and the child of a diplomat who has lived in several nations of the Americas since his childhood, including Chile, Argentina, and the United States. In the 1930s he attended primary school in Washington, DC and has been fluent in English from an early age. He began writing as an adolescent in the 1940s, publishing his first stories in the early 1950s. Since the mid-1940s Fuentes's primary place of residence has been Mexico City, but he also lived several years in Paris in the late 1960s and 1970s, including a year as Mexico's ambassador to France. Since the early 1990s he has resided approximately half the year in Mexico City and the other half in London, with frequent public lectures in the United States. He is one of Latin America's most prominent public intellectuals.

Two of his most renowned novels are *La muerte de Artemio Cruz* (1962, *The Death of Artemio Cruz*, 1964) and *Terra Nostra* (1975, *Terra Nostra*, 1976). He considers his complete work, which consists of over twenty volumes of fiction, to be a corpus he identifies as "La Edad del Tiempo" (the epoch of time), which can be considered a lengthy fictionalized meditation on temporality. He divides this corpus into a set of fourteen cycles, which cover topics of cultural and political history from Roman times to the present, with particular focus on Latin American identity. His early novels *La región más transparente* (1958, *Where the Air Is Clear*, 1960) and *The Death of Artemio Cruz* concern Mexican history and identity; Fuentes has traced Mexican identity back to its pre-Columbian roots and offered severe critiques of the Mexican political establishment in power during the better part of the twentieth century. *Terra Nostra* is his most lengthy and complex novel to date and is his most daring statement about Latin American culture and identity and its historic roots with the Romans and in the Iberian peninsula. The primary setting for this work is the sixteenth-century Spain of Philip II.

Fuentes's writing has had enormous influence on the politics and writing of Latin America and the Caribbean; he shares the political and cultural interests of not only a vast range of Spanish American writers but also figures such as George Lamming and Daniel Maximim from the Caribbean and João Guimarães Rosa from Brazil.

Selected Work: La región más transparente (1958, *Where the Air Is Clear*, translation Sam Hileman, 1960); *Las buenas conciencias* (1959, *The Good Conscience*, translation Sam Hileman, 1961); *Aura*, (1962, *Aura*, translation Lysander Kemp, 1968); *La muerte de Artemio Cruz* (1962, *The Death of Artemio Cruz*, translation Ivan Obelensky, 1964); *Cambio de piel* (1967, *A Change of Skin*, translation Sam Hileman, 1968); *Zona sagrada* (1967, *Holy Cross*, translation Suzanne Jill Levine, in *Triple Cross*, 1972); *Cumpleaños* (1969); *Terra Nostra* (1975, *Terra Nostra*, translation Margaret Sayers Peden, 1976); *La cabeza de la hidra* (1978, *Hydra Head*, translation Margaret Sayers Peden, 1978); *Una familia lejana* (1980, *Distant Relations*, translation Margaret Sayers Peden, 1982); *Gringo viejo* (1985, *Old Gringo*, translation Margaret Sayers Peden and the author, 1985); *Cristóbal Nonato* (1987, *Christopher Unborn*, translaton Alfred MacAdam, 1989); *La campaña* (1990, *The Campaign*, translation Alfred MacAdam, 1991); *Diana cazadora* (1994, *Diana, the Goddess Who Hunts Alone*, translation Alfred MacAdam, 1995); *La frontera de cristal* (1995, *The Crystal Frontier*, translation Alfred MacAdam, 1997); *Los años con Laura Díaz* (1999, *The Years with Laura Díaz*, translation Alfred MacAdam, 2000); *Instinto de Inez* (2000, *Inez*, translation Margaret Sayers Peden, 2002); *La silla del águila* (2003).

Fuentes, Norberto [Biography] Cuban novelist, short story writer, and journalist, he was born in Havana in 1943 and has been amply recognized for his volumes of stories *Condenados de Condado* (1968, The condemned of Condado) and *Cazabandido* (1970, Bandido hunter). He was an intimate friend of Fidel Castro, working with him in close collaboration on the operations of the Cuban secret service during the 1980s. After many years of working with Castro for the Cuban Revolution, he attempted to escape Cuba and was arrested. With the support of Gabriel García Márquez and William Kennedy, he was freed from prison and currently lives in the United States. His fiction has received the praise of writers such as Italo Calvino, William Kennedy, Norman Mailer, and Gabriel García Márquez. His other books are *Dulces guerreros cubanos* (2000, Sweet Cuban fighters), *Posición uno* (Position number one), *Reencuentro con Hemingway* (Reencounter with Hemmingway), and *El último santuario* (The last sanctuary). In 2004 he published a voluminous (886-page) biography of Fidel Castro, *La autobiografía de Fidel Castro*.

Selected Work: *El último santuario, una novela de campaña* (1992).

Fuguet, Alberto [Biography] Chilean novelist, short story writer, playwright, film and music critic, and journalist, he has become a prominent spokesperson for the young generation of Latin American writers born since 1960, the generation of the 1990s. He has popularized the idea of a McOndo generation of write as an antidote to the more commercial and established modes of Latin American fiction, including magical realism. His writing represents an attempt to incorporate popular culture and downplay the central role of "literature" (as an elite writing culture).

Fuguet was born in Santiago, Chile, in 1964, but lived the first twelve years of his life in Los Angeles, California. After finishing his high school studies in Santiago, he completed a degree in journalism at the University of Chile and has been an active journalist much of his life. He studied creative writing under the mentorship of José Donoso. His volume of short stories *Sobredosis* (1990, Overdose) was proclaimed by many to herald a new type of fiction writing in Chile, as did his first novel, *Mala onda* (1991, *Bad Vibes*), both of which produced a sense of novelty, hip youth culture, and the new slang comparable to the phenomenon of the Onda in Mexico in the 1960s that some critics have associated with postmodern or a "post-postmodern" fiction in Latin America and critics in Brazil call the generation of the 1990s. He also gained considerable notoriety for a volume titled *Cuentos con walkman* (1993, Stories with walkman). His fiction has been read as chronicles of urban life in Santiago in the 1980s and 1990s. *Mala onda* is a novel of an adolescent protagonist's experiences in September 1980, beginning in Rio de Janeiro and continuing in Santiago, Chile. The date of this setting is in itself significant, for 1980 puts the protagonist at approximately the same age as the author in 1980 and September, of course, inevitably evokes the coup of September 11, 1973. It is noteworthy that the chapters are dated September 7, 8, 9, and 10, but then skip 11 to end on September 14. If *Bad Vibes* is the novel of the crisis of a future writer, his second novel, *Tinta roja* (1996, Red ink) is that of the adult writer in crisis, the fictional author of a work *Recursos humanos* who is described as having a modern voice of the capital. This urban chronicle contains some of the melodrama of Vargas Llosa's *Aunt Julia and the Scriptwriter* and some of the love-hate relationship toward the capital that Fuentes expresses in his first urban novel, *Where the Air Is Clear*. But the exact nature of this urban life and his particular use of colloquial language distances Fuguet from Vargas Llosa and Fuentes. His third novel, *Por favor, rebobinar* (1999, Please rewind), is the most complex of the three, consisting of a juxtaposition of multiple texts in eight sections or chapters that offer a diverse set of narrative voices, of urban inhabitants who, like many characters in Fuguet's fiction, are acutely aware of international postmodern culture and one of whom, Balthazar Daza (a name that resonates with the work of García Márquez), wants to write a family saga, but with a "virtual" magical realism, not one from García Márquez's Macondo or from Isabel Allende's *La casa de los espíritus.*

Among U.S. academics, Fuguet is best known for his already seminal anthology of short fiction, *McOndo* (1996), coedited with his compatriot Sergio Gómez, a novelist of the same generation. Offering the reader their selection of the new fiction by the youngest generation of writers in Latin America and Spain, their projection of the future of Hispanic letters includes several novelists that are now on the literary map with the publication of novels since the 1996 publication of *McOndo*: Rodrigo Fresán from Argentina, Edmundo Paz Soldán from Bolivia, Santiago Gamboa from Colombia, David Toscana from Mexico, and Jaime Bayly from Peru. Fuguet and Gómez offer a polemical "Presentación del País McOndo," as a preface to this anthology, rejecting all the modes of writing associated with the magical realism that U.S. publishers expect and demand of Latin American writers as well as the "the great theme of Latin American identity." They explain that the stories of this volume focus on private and individual realities. Referring to the lengthy discussions of Sartrean ilk about the writer's commitment to social and political change, they claim that the writer's task is no longer to decide between the pen or the rifle, but rather between Windows 95 or Macintosh.

Fuguet has recently published a 548-page volume of journalistic pieces that he titles *Primera parte* (2000, First part) with a noteworthy subtitle, *Crónicas, columnas y literatura instantánea* (Chronicles, columns, and instant literature, with the first three letters of *literatura* written and crossed out on the cover).

His recent *Las películas de mi vida* (2003, *The Movies of My Life*, 2003) is a sizable (385-page) work set in two worlds that Fuguet manages to construct as parallel in entertaining ways: the California of Richard Nixon and the Santiago of Augusto Pinochet. Thus this novel deals with two families, two languages, and two cultures.

Selected Work: Mala onda (1991, *Bad Vibes*, translation Kristina Cordero, 1997); *Tinta roja* (1996); *Por favor, rebobinar* (1999); *Las películas de mi vida* (2003, *The Movies of My Life*, translation Ezra F. Fitz, 2003).

Galeano, Eduardo (Eduardo Hughes Galeano) [Biography] Uruguayan novelist, historian, essayist, and journalist, he has been a major intellectual figure in Latin America and voice for progressive political causes since the 1970s. He was born in Montevideo in 1940 and was a political activist during his student days as well as an engaged and politically committed journalist and fiction writer in Montevideo during the 1960s and 1970s. He was in political exile from 1973 to 1985. He was the editor in chief for the cultural weekly *Marcha* in Montevideo and director of the newspaper *Epoca*. He first went into exile in Argentina in 1973, but soon had to find a haven in Spain, where he remained from 1977 to 1985. He is known as a master of the vignette; his ability to tell stories and describe situations in few words is unequaled in Latin America. The vignette is the main content in three of his books—*El libro de los abrazos* (1989, The book of embraces), *Las palabras andantes* (1993, Walking words), and *El futbol: a sol y sombra* (1995:

Soccer: in light and shade). By the time he wrote his second novel, *Dias y noches de amor y de guerra* (1978, *Days and Nights of Love and War*), his mastery of the vignette was well established.

He is best known for his historical essay *Las venas abiertas de América Latina* (1971, *Open Veins of Latin America*) and his award-winning novel *La canción de nosotros* (1975, Our song). Broad and sweeping in its historical scope, *Las venas abiertas de América Latina* is Galeano's view of the political, economic, social, and cultural history of Latin America. He calls it his history of plunder in Latin America, as well as a present-day account of the melodrama of dispossession. This book is also a history of the presence of foreign capitalists in Latin America and the collaborative rule of oligarchies in this region. Galeano continues his historical project in his novel *Dias y noches de amor y de guerra*, his testimony to the violence and repression so widespread in Latin America during the years he covers, from the 1950s to the 1970s. The 256 brief narratives in this novel include situations and characters from Latin American history, and Galeano emphasizes his documentary impulse by identifying himself within the text as Galeano. He has also published *Memoria del fuego*, a trilogy containing the books *Los nacimientos* (1982, The births), *Las caras y las mascaras* (1984, The faces and the masks), and *El siglo del viento* (1986, The century of wind).

Selected Work: Los días siguientes (1963); *La canción de nosotros* (1975); *Días y noches de amor y de guerra* (1978, *Days and Nights of Love and War*, translation Judith Brister, 1983).

Galindo, Sergio [Biography] Mexican novelist, short story writer, and novelist, he was one of Mexico's most accomplished modern writers in the second half of the twentieth century. He belongs to a generation of writers that identified themselves as the *Generación de Medio Siglo* (the mid-century generation) in Mexico; they were committed to modernizing Mexican culture and literature, which some writers of this group considered to be, in the 1950s, too nationalistic and even provincial. Born in Veracruz, Mexico, in 1926, he studied literature at the National University in Mexico City (UNAM) and in France; later he received a scholarship to study creative writing in the Centro Mexicano de Escritores (1955–56). He founded the university press (Editorial Veracruzana) at the University of Veracruz, which has had a prominent role in publishing new writing in Mexico and Latin America since the late 1950s. He also founded the prestigious literary journal *La Palabra y el Hombre*. Galindo served as director for both the press and the journal from 1957 to 1972. He published four volumes of short stories and nine novels, dying in 1993. He is known as a master of characterization and narrating human relations among an intimate, small group of characters (what some critics of Latin American literature have identified as the small screen novel).

His first novel, *Polvos de arroz* (1958, Dust of rice), portrays the tragic life of a solitary woman who hopes to find a relationship with a man with whom she corresponds by letters. This letter writing becomes an obsessive activity, and her opportunity to visit the city of the young man with whom she corresponds results in tragedy. His skill at depicting human relations is also evident in his second novel, *Justicia de enero* (1959, January justice), which is a cynical view of four immigration officers in pursuit an individual. The officers attempt to apprehend and deport this individual, and the novel shifts from one officer to another, focusing on their personal lives.

Galindo's major novels are *El bordo* (1960, *The Precipice*), *La comparsa* (1964, *Mexican Masquerade*), and *Otilia Rauda* (1986, *Otilia's Body*). *El bordo*, like *Polvos de arroz*, is a novel about a woman's self-realization, and informed scholars of Galindo's work consider it his most accomplished fictionalization of human relationships. *La comparsa* is a continuation of Galindo's saga of middle-class life in the state of Veracruz, but now the focus is a two-day period of carnival and the social scope is broader than in any of the previous novels. *Otilia Rauda* was widely read in Mexico and was the winner of a prestigious national prize in Mexico, the Premio Xavier Villarrutia, in 1986. Galindo now uses Mexican history to relate the story of an extraordinary woman and unforgettable passions. It appeared in English as *Otilia's Body* in 1994, and in this novel Galindo uses a backdrop of twentieth-century Mexican history and traditional narrative forms to tell the tale of an attractive and liberated woman, Otilia, and her lover. It is the most attractive story line constructed by Galindo in his career, leaving behind most of the strategies of the small screen fiction that had been his mainstay for most of his career.

Selected Work: Polvos de arroz (1958, *Rice Powder*, translation Bert Patrick and Lura Larsson Patrick, 1978); *Justicia de enero* (1959); *El bordo* (1960, *The Precipice*, translation John and Carolyn Brushwood, 1964); *La comparsa* (1964, *Mexican Masquerade*, translation Carolyn and John Brushwood, 1984); *Nudo* (1970); *El hombre de hongos* (1976); *Los dos ángeles* (1984); *Declive* (1985); *Otilia Rauda* (1985, *Otilia's Body*, translation Carolyn and John Brushwood, 1994); *Terciopelo violeta* (1985).

Gallardo, Sara [Biography] Argentine novelist, short story writer, and journalist born in Buenos Aires in 1934, she was a vis-ible and respected writer in Argentina in the 1960s and 1970s. During this period she traveled extensively throughout Europe, Latin America, and Asia, sending back articles on a variety of topics for publication in high-circulation magazines and newspapers. In 1978 she moved to Barcelona with her three children. In her fiction she writes about different forms of alienation and, more specifically, the difficulties of communication and the exploitation of the poor. She has also written some children's stories; some of this work pushes the limits of the fantastic and the magical.

Gallardo is best known for her first novel *Enero* (1958, January), an engaging and intimate story, set in rural Argentina, of a pregnant teenager. The novel shows her in a variety of settings as the pregnancy progresses, including confrontations with an abortionist and with her mother. Eventually, her godmother arranges a marriage with the biological father and not with the husband of the young girl's fantasies. The use of interior monologues and the development of her fantasies are factors that make *Enero* an attractive novel. It is also a story of the young girl's emotional growth, culminating in her acceptance of the fact that she was not seduced by a handsome ideal lover but by a very ordinary man.

Her next novels were *Pantalones azules* (1963, Blue pants) and *Los galgos, los galgos* (1968, The greyhounds). The latter is a first-person narrative that is more bold in narrative technique than her previous work. The greyhounds of the title represent specific people and the ruling class in Argentina. She also published the novels *Eisejuaz* (1971) and *La rosa en el viento* (1979). *El país del humo* (1977) is a volume consisting of a short novel and stories. She died in 1988.

Selected Work: Enero (1958); *Pantalones azules* (1963); *Los galgos, los galgos* (1968);

Eisejuaz (1971); *El país del humo* (1977); *La rosa en el viento* (1979).

Galmes, Héctor [Biography] Uruguayan novelist, essayist, and professor of literature, he was born in Montevideo in 1933, taught at both the high school and university levels, and died in Montevideo in 1986. He had a broad range of interests, serving on the editorial board for the local literary magazine *Maldoror*, writing essays on classical Greek and Latin literature, and publishing two books of essays on such topics. He is associated with a group of writers in Uruguay that published a significant body of fiction from 1970 to 1985, publishing a volume of short stories, *La noche del día menos pensado* (1981, The evening of the least expected day).

In his fiction he was more interested in the poetic effects of language and creating settings than strong plots, as is evident in his novels *Necrocosmos* (1971) and *Las calandrias griegas* (1977, Greek cramps). In the latter he creates scenes emphasizing certain colors. His later novel, *Final en borrador* (1985, Ending in rough draft) was influenced by the codes of film, particularly Hollywood westerns and spy thrillers.

His short fiction pushes the limits of the real and the fantastic further than his novels, and many critics in Uruguay considered him at his best in the genre of the short story.

Selected Work: Necrocosmos (1971); *Las calandrias griegas* (1977); *Final en borrador* (1985).

Gambaro, Griselda [Biography] Argentine playwright and novelist, she was born in Buenos Aires in 1928. After completing high school in 1943, she worked in the business office of a publishing company. Gambaro began writing at an early age and claims that she began writing as soon as she began reading. Nevertheless, her first publications came in the early 1960s when she published three novellas under the title *Madrigal en la ciudad* (1963, Madrigal in the city); she was awarded the prize of the Argentine Fondo Nacional de las Artes for this book. When Gambaro published the volume of fiction *El desatino* (1965, The blunder), she received another prestigious prize in Argentina, the Premio Emecé.

Gambaro published her first full-length novel, *Nada que ver con otra historia* (Nothing to do with another story) in 1972. Her novel *Ganarse la muerte* (1976, To earn death) was critical of the military regime in Argentina and much praised by critics in Spain. This novel also appeared in French translation. Gambaro's fiction generally presents matters that have been well developed in her theater as well: she has elaborated an aesthetics of violence and cruelty. By portraying this violence and cruelty, she intends to criticize the abuse of authority and the subsequent alienation of the individual.

Gambaro has been involved in theater since the early 1960s and is best known in Latin America as playwright. She has written over a dozen pieces of theater.

Selected Work: Nada que ver con otra historia (1972); *Ganarse la muerte* (1976).

Gamboa, Santiago [Biography] Colombian novelist, journalist, and short story writer, he belongs to the generation of the 1990s as one of the most prominent novelists in Colombia of this generation. He is interested in attempting to change the direction of national literature in a way that reflects the new urban life of drug trafficking and violence in recent decades; Jorge Franco and Mario Mendoza of the same generation in Colombia are involved with a similar aesthetic agenda. Like his compatriot Héctor Abad Faciolince, his fiction also exhibits the precariousness of urban life in Colombia.

Born in Bogotá in 1965, he studied literature in the Universidad Javeriana from 1982 to 1985 and did graduate studies in Hispanic literatures and philology at the Universidad Complutense in Madrid as well as in Paris. Certainly his novels *Páginas de vuelta* (1995, Pages written upon my return) and *Perder es cuestión de miedo* (1997, Losing is a question of fear) are remote from the modes of magical realism, for Gamboa's fiction is urban in setting and theme. *Páginas de vuelta* deals with the crisis of the youth of his generation, and *Perder es cuestión de miedo* focuses on the urban crime and violence of Bogotá. Gamboa's more recent *Los impostores* (2002, The impostors) is a wide-ranging work that demonstrates, once again, his playful interest in detective fiction. In 1990 he went to Paris and did a doctorate at the Sorbonne, specializing in Cuban literature. In his recent volume of short stories, *El cerco de Bogotá* (2003, The fence of Bogota), he constructs six accounts of journalists attempting to survive in a Bogotá under siege by armed guerrillas and drug traffickers.

Gamboa found a new setting for his most recent novel, *El síndrome de Ulises* (2005, Ulysses' syndrome), the precarious world of a young writer living in Paris with other immigrants.

Selected Work: Páginas de vuelta (1995); *Perder es cuestión de método* (1997); *Vida feliz de un joven llamado Esteban* (2000); *Los impostores* (2002); *El síndrome de Ulises* (2005).

Garcés, Gonzalo [Biography] Argentine novelist born in Buenos Aires in 1974, he has studied in Buenos Aires, the United States, and Germany. He writes cultural journalism for newspapers and magazines in Argentina and lives in Paris. Along with the Colombian Juan Gabriel Vásquez, he is among the youngest Latin American novelists to publish a noteworthy group of novels by the early part of the twenty-first century. He was awarded the prestigious Premio Biblioteca Breve in Spain for his second novel, *Los impacientes* (2000, The impatient ones). In this novel an enigmatic set of three young characters in Buenos Aires interact with one another. They have artistic and literary pretensions: one wants to be a writer, one wants to compose music, and the third has multiple desires but is also destructive. It is a story of vague relationships, desires, and affections among disaffected youth. His novel *El futuro* (2003, The future) is set in Paris during the 1995 workers' strike. The protagonist falls in love with his son's girlfriend in a provisional, unpredictable, and uncertain fictional world.

Selected Work: Diciembre (1997); *Los impacientes* (2000); *El futuro* (2003).

García, Cristina [Biography] Novelist, short story writer, and journalist, she has been the first Cuban American to attain mainstream success as a novelist. Her novel *Dreaming in Cuban* (1992) was a highly successful best seller in the 1990s, nominated for a National Book Award. She was born in Havana in 1958, immigrated to the U.S. with her parents, and was educated at Vassar College (BA in political science in 1979) and Johns Hopkins University (MA in Latin American studies 1981). After working at *Time* magazine as a journalist for nearly a decade, she took a leave of absence to write *Dreaming in Cuban* (1992), her chronicle of three generations of Cubans and her engaging comparison of the lives of those of the family in Cuba and those in the United States. It also communicates a sense of the fragmentation and crisis related to the difficult immigration experience from Cuba to the United States. Her second novel, *The Aguero Sisters* (1997) is a continuation of the family saga. With *Monkey Hunting* (2003) she tells an immigration and assimilation experience of much broader historical scope, following a family from China to Cuba to the U.S., beginning in 1857. She has been a recipient of a Guggenheim Fellowship and numerous writing prizes and has edited an anthology of Cuban writing, *Cubanísimo* (2002).

Selected Work: Dreaming in Cuban (1992, *Soñar en cubano,* translation Marisol Palés Castro, 1993); *The Aguero Sisters* (1997, *Las hermanas Aguero,* translation Alan West, 1997); *Monkey Hunting* (2003, *El cazador de monos,* translation María Eugenia Ciocchini, 2003).

García, Lionel [Biography] Chicano novelist and veterinarian, he was born in San Diego, Texas, in 1935 of a middle-class family that sent him to study at Texas A&M University, where he earned a BS in biology. He then received a degree in veterinary medicine from the same institution and has worked as both an assistant professor of anatomy and a veterinarian. His novel *Hardscrub* (1991) received the Best Novel Award from the Southwest Booksellers Association as well as the Jesse James Award for Fiction from the Texas Institute of Letters.

Selected Work: Leaving Home (1984); *A Shroud in the Family* (1987); *Hardscrub* (1990).

García Aguilar, Eduardo [Biography] Colombian novelist, short story writer, and journalist, he has lived abroad and written most of his fiction in Mexico and France. Born in Manizales, Colombia in 1953, he began writing poetry and short fiction in the early 1980s. He has dedicated a lifetime to writing against the conservative cultural traditions of his region, which during the first half of the twentieth century insisted upon constructing a literary tradition directly connected to Greek and Roman literature. Recognizing the absurdity of this anachronistic affiliation with the classics, García Aguilar followed the path of the modern Latin American writers whom he discovered in his adolescence: Miguel Angel Asturias, Ernesto Sábato, and the novelists of the 1960s Boom.

García Aguilar began writing prose in the late 1970s in Paris in a period when he was close to texts of the Boom that had been written in Paris—Vargas Llosa's *La ciudad y los perros* and Cortázar's *Rayuela*; García Aguilar has spoken of his admiration for these novels. He considers his first novel, *Tierra de leones* (1986, Land of lions), for example, to have been too much influenced by *La ciudad y los perros*. A writer's writer, he is interested in the exquisite production of turn-of-the-century *modernistas*. In actual practice, however, his work is distant from the *modernistas*: his urban novels involve an aesthetics of ugliness. In his later novel *El viaje triunfal* (1993, The triumphant trip) he returns to his interest in modernity, paying homage to the Latin American writers who desired to be modern in very different ways: the *modernistas* who sought transcendence through art and the *vanguardia* that equated European modernity with cosmopolitanism. The theme of modernity is developed in the characterization of a main character who is a hedonist Latin American poet living the life of a decadent an avant-garde writer.

His two major novels are *Tierra de leones* and *Bulevar de los héroes* (1987, Boulevard of the heroes). The first is his fictionalized autobiography of having grown up in Manizales and its cultural environment so strongly influenced by the Greco-Roman tradition. In it an employee suffers the illusion that he can transform his small town into a center of the arts. In *Bulevar de los héroes* a lawyer believes in another illusion: creating a world of happiness and justice. In these two novels and his other fiction García Aguilar seeks to demonstrate how post-Enlightenment belief in human reason is betrayed by the barbarity of modern society.

Selected Work: *Tierra de leones* (1986); *Bulevar de los héroes* (1987, *Boulevard of Heroes*, translation Jay Anthony Miskowiec, 1993); *El viaje triunfal* (1993); *Tequila coxis* (2003).

García Márquez, Gabriel [Biography] Colombian novelist, short story writer, essayist, and journalist, he has been a prominent figure in Latin America since publishing his landmark novel *Cien años de soledad* (*One Hundred Years of Solitude*) in the original Spanish in 1967 and being awarded the Nobel Prize in Literature in 1982. He was one of the leading members of the 1960s Boom of the Spanish American novel. Many biographies assert that he was born in 1928, which the author himself claimed for many years. Nevertheless, he was born in 1927 in Aracataca, Colombia; this birthplace became the mythical Macondo of his early fiction and the Caribbean coastal region is the backdrop for much of his writing. In his formative years he was an ardent reader of Faulkner, and he has claimed on more than one occasion that Faulkner and Borges gave him the key, at an early age, to becoming a fiction writer. He and his cohorts of the Barranquilla group, in fact, read Faulkner and other American and European modernists with great interest in the late 1940s and early 1950s, when García Márquez, Alvaro Cepeda Samudio, Germán Vargas, and Alfonso Fuenmayor met regularly to share their readings as they wrote their first texts themselves. Indeed, García Márquez's early fiction, such as *La hojarasca* (1955, *Leafstorm*) and *El coronel no tiene quién le escriba* (1961, *No One Writes to the Colonel*) was patently Faulknerian writing.

García Márquez's novelistic production can be divided into two periods. In the first period his Macondo cycle, he constructs his narrative around the fictionalized world of his hometown of Aracataca, which he calls Macondo. Making up this cycle are the novels *La hojarasca*, *El coronel no tiene quién le escriba* , and *La mala hora* (1962, *In Evil Hour*) as well as the short stories in *Los funerales de la mamá grande* (1962, *Big Mama's Funeral*) and the culminating novel *Cien años de soledad*. The books constitute both a family saga and a rewriting of Latin American history. They also question the power and authority of the traditional political elites of Colombia and Latin America. This is also the period in which García Márquez popularized the "magical realism" that many readers and critics consider the earmark of his writing.

After the Macondo cycle García Márquez explores a variety of new settings, themes, and modes of writing. He published a technical tour de force, *El otoño del patriarca* (1975, *The Autumn of the Patriarch*), a now classic portrayal of the archetypal dictator-figure in Latin America. It is a synthesis of several historical dictators and is located in an unnamed and imaginary Caribbean nation. His more recent novels, such as *Crónica de una muerte anunciada* (1981, *Chronicle of a Death Foretold*), *El amor en los tiempos del cólera* (1985, *Love in the Time of Cholera*), and *El general en su laberinto* (1989, *The General in His Labyrinth*) have been best-selling entertainments, with occasional touches of magical realism, Latin American history, and political critique. His more recent *Noticia de un secuestro* (1996, *News of a Kidnapping*) is a semidocumentary account of the real kidnapping of ten Colombian journalists by drug kingpin Pablo Escobar.

His major novel is *Cien años de soledad*, his family saga that has made him widely recognized as a master of magical realism. This novel can also be read as a history of Colombia and of Latin America. Despite its numerous fantasy elements, it also relates specific historical events, such as a massacre of striking banana plantation workers by government troops, an event that happened in Colombia in 1928. In this novel García Márquez draws upon oral tradition of the Caribbean region of Colombia. His recent book *Vivir para contarla* (2002) is his autobiography, replete with ample information about his lifetime literary interests and the readings that had the most impact on his later production.

Selected Work: La hojarasca (1955, *Leafstorm and Other Stories*, translation Gregory Rabassa, 1972); *El coronel no tiene quién le escriba* (1961, *No One Writes to the Colonel*, translation J. S. Bernstein, 1968); *La mala hora* (1962); *Cien años de soledad* (1967, *One Hundred Years of Solitude*, translation Gregory Rabassa, 1970); *El otoño del patriarca* (1975, *The Autumn of the Patriarch*, translation Gregory Rabassa, 1976); *Crónica de una muerte anunciada* (1981, *Chronicle of a Death Foretold*, translation Gregory Rabassa, 1983); *El general en su laberinto* (1989, *The General in His Labyrinth*, translation Edith Grossman, 1990); *Noticia de un secuestro* (1996, *News of a Kidnapping*, translation Edith Grossman, 1997); *Memoria de mis putas tristes* (2004, *Memories of My Melancholy Whores*, translation Edith Grossman, 2006).

García Ponce, Juan [Biography] Mexican novelist, short story writer, essayist, and art critic, with over forty books published he has been a major intellectual presence in Mexico. He also has the reputation as a "writers' writer" throughout Latin America, as one who has been uncompromising in his rejection of commercial literature. He is also known for his small screen fiction dealing with human relations, as opposed to the broad, panoramic historical novels published by many contemporary Latin American writers interested in rewriting national history. Born in Mérida, Mexico, in 1932, he devoted his entire life to reading and writing literature. His set of over thirteen abstract and often hermetic novels have had an enormous impact on the directions of the Mexican novel. His numerous essays and books on literature have focused on modern European writers such as Robert Musil, Pierre Klossowski, Thomas Mann, Rainier Maria Rilke, George Bataille, Marcel Proust, and Cesare Pavese, but for García Ponce, himself, Musil served as his most important model. His fiction tends to be a dialogue with writers such as these, as well as with the Argentine Jorge Luis Borges and the Mexican Sergio Pitol. A member of Mexico's *Generación de Medio Siglo* (the mid-century generation), García Ponce has been a central player in the modernization of Mexican literature since the 1950s.

Shortly before his death in 2003, he wrote that, given the reality of death, literature makes use of our brief lives to continue inventing stories, poems, novels, and essays. He began writing in the early 1960s, publishing *Figura de paja* in 1964. His fiction is an exploration of human relations, often posing the question of not only how intimate human relations operate but why they function the way they do. García Ponce's early novel *La invitación* (1972, The invitation) was his effort at novelizing abstract concepts rather than telling stories. It is an intellectual approach to a search for identity. In *Unión* (1974, Union) García Ponce clearly delineates the relationships in straightforward prose. Much of his fiction, such as *La cabaña* (1969, The Cabin), is more complex, particularly in the use of language. This work and *Unión* are among the best examples García Ponce's intricate and hermetic prose; His writing in the early 1970s can be seen as an exercise in fictionalizing uncertainty. His story is told through the voice of Elena, a young lawyer from Mexico City who visits an old friend, Marta, who lives in a beach house on the Yucatán peninsula with her husband Eduardo. Elena falls in love with her new surroundings and with Eduardo's best friend, a young doctor named Rafael. Gradually freeing herself from attachment to Mexico City (and her lover Pedro there), Elena enters the border space of the beach; halfway between the emptiness of the sea and the conventional social life of Merida. When Eduardo's elderly father dies, Elena becomes aware of her isolation in the world she has entered and plans her return to Mexico City. The vacation ends and Elena leaves the beach and her summer affair, facing the decision of whether he should follow her back to Mexico City or not. The focus of the novel is not so much on events as it is on human relations as well as subtle subjective and objective concepts of space.

Inmaculada, o los placeres de la inocencia (1989, Inmaculada or the pleasures of innocence) is an exploration of innocence within the context of the sexual in which the female character becomes involved in all types of sexual acts, searching for her true self by means of sexual apprenticeship. It is a linear work that follows the different stages of Inmaculada's sexual journey in chronological order. García Ponce's critics have viewed him as an elite, difficult, and detached writer; in addition, some critics have considered *Inmaculada, o los placeres de la inocencia* and some of his other works to be misogynist.

Selected Work: *Figura de paja* (1964); *La presencia lejana* (1965); *La casa en la playa* (1966); *La cabaña* (1969); *El libro* (1970); *El hombre olvidado* (1970); *La vida perdurable* (1970); *La invitación* (1972); *Unión* (1974); *El gato* (1974); *Crónica de la intervención* (1982, second part); *De anima* (1984); *Inmaculada, o los placeres de la inocencia* (1989); *Pasado presente* (1993).

García Saldaña, Parménides [Biography] Mexican novelist, short story writer, poet, journalist, and essayist, he was associated with the postmodern writing often identi-

fied in Mexico with the term *La Onda*. He was born in Orizaba (state of Veracruz) in 1944, studied literature in the National University in Mexico City (UNAM) and in the United States, at Louisiana State University in Baton Rouge, where he came into contact with Afro-American neighborhoods and was influenced by Afro-American culture. He died tragically at the age of thirty-eight in Mexico City (1982). He wrote in newspapers about pop culture and worked for many years as a disk jockey for a rock music radio station. He published his commentary on pop culture in magazines such as *Pop*, *Piedra Rodante*, and *Claudia*. His main contribution to Mexican literature was the writing of two books of fiction that were celebrations of 1960s youth culture, a volume of short stories titled *El rey criollo* (1970, The creole king), and his novel *Pasto verde* (1968, Green grass). Although his total novelistic production consisted of only one work, García Saldaña holds an important place in Mexican literary history because of his role with 1960s youth culture, the innovations of postmodern fiction, and his important position, along with José Agustín and Gustavo Sainz, in the group of writers in Mexico identified as La Onda. He wrote of this culture in his book-length essay *En la ruta de la Onda*. José Agustín has spoken and written of García Saldaña's contributions as an important writer who promoted verbal freedom and the ludic in literature.

Selected Work: *Pasto verde* (1968).

Gardea, Jesús [Biography] Mexican novelist, short story writer, and poet, he was the most visible as a novelist in the 1980s and early 1990s. He was born in Delicias (state of Chihuaha) in 1939, went to the University of Guadalajara to study dentistry, and lived in the border city of Juárez most of his adult life, where he practiced dentistry and taught at the University of Juárez. His identity as a writer in Mexico was regional: he was associated with his location in northern Mexico and on the border, as opposed to the center of Mexican literature, elite culture, and the cultural powers in Mexico City. His fiction tends to deal with everyday life in a small town in northern Mexico that is the setting for most of his novels.

Gardea did not write one novel that stands out as his most prominent work. His novel *El sol que estás mirando* (1981, The sun you are looking at) is typical of his fiction: it is set in northern Mexico and is the narration of a young boy who shares a series of reminiscences. There is no continuously developed plot in this work, although characters do reappear in the different anecdotes. In contrast to the bitter tone and cynical attitudes explored in much Mexican fiction published during this period, Gardea's nostalgic tone suggests transcendence by means of his own special type of *cariño*—a kind of love and cherishing of the people and the place. His total work is an expression of this attitude of respect for the people and the place in northern Mexico about which he wrote. He died in January 2000 in Mexico City.

Selected Work: El sol que estás mirando (1981); *La canción de las mulas muertas* (1981); *El tornavoz* (1983); *Soñar la guerra* (1984); *Los músicos y el fuego* (1985); *Sóbol* (1985); *El diablo en el ojo* (1989); *El agua de las esferas* (1992); *La ventana hundida* (1992); *Juegan los comensales* (1998); *El biombo y los frutos* (2001).

Garmendia, Salvador [Biography] Venezuelan novelist, short story writer, and scriptwriter, he was born in Barquisimento, Venezuela, in 1928, but then lived most of his adult life in Caracas. In the 1950s he was cofounder of the literary magazine called *Sardío* and the group of the same name; later he formed a splinter group called Te-

cho de la Ballena. He was a pioneer of the urban novel whose early novels of the late 1950s and early 1960s were extremely influential in setting a new and more modern direction for Venezuelan fiction. During this same period Garmendia and his cohorts of *Sardío* were commited to inserting Venezuelan culture and literature into the major directions of modern Western culture. Garmendia was considered a master of using details of the objective world that take on a special meaning. Rejecting the portrayal of epic heroes found in much previous Latin American writing, he attempted to characterize everyday people, as well as antiheroes, in an urban world from which they were alienated and in which they were often deemed failures.

In his first novel, *Los pequeños seres* (1959, The little beings), he tells the story of a working-class man, Mario Martín, who loses his job and becomes increasingly alienated. Martín suffers from identity problems that the reader can appreciate through interior monologues. In *Los pequeños seres* as well as *Los habitantes* (1961, The inhabitants) Garmendia experimented in both his urban settings and his new approaches to fiction writing. *Los pequeños seres* is a psychological presentation of Mateo Martin, who loses his boss and gradually his ability to deal with objective reality. Garmendia uses internal and external descriptions of the protagonist to underscore his sense of alienation.

Los habitantes deals with the frustrations and failures of a truck driver, Francisco, and his family. Francisco is unemployed, which is a crisis in itself, but the narrative also focuses on the different members of the family, and all this takes place in one day. Francisco's wife becomes a special character because of all of her efforts to save the situation, even though she fails. In this second novel the truck driver and his various family members are the

"little people," instead of the heroes of totalizing modern narratives.

Garmendia explored the uses of new
modernist narrative strategies to communicate urban experiences. In Garmendia's
later novels, *Los pies de barro* (1973, Feet of
mud) and *Memorias de Altagracia* (1974,
Memories of Altagracia), he moves from the
urban experience of the middle class and
working people to a fictional small town
with overtones of García Márquez's fictional Macondo. The author even mentions
García Márquez by name in *Los pies de
barro*, a novel in which the protagonist and
the town suffer from a growing sense of destruction. There are numerous fantastic
and prodigious memories in *Memorias de
Altagracia*, most of which take place in the
1930s and 1940s. The predominant attitude,
however, is of *asfixia*—a sensation of the
boredom that is pervasive in Garmendia's
fiction. The act of creation and humor seem
to be the only escapes from this dismal circumstance that Garmendia's characters
find.

He won the National Prize for Literature
in Venezuela in 1973 and wrote a highly
successful soap opera, *La hija de Juan Cre-
spo*. He died in May of 2001.

Selected Work: Los pequeños seres (1959);
Los habitantes (1961); *Días de ceniza* (1963);
La mala vida (1968); *Los pies de barro* (1973);
Memorias de Altagracia (1974, *Memories of
Altagracia*, translation Jeremy Munday,
1998); *El capitán Kid* (1989).

Garro, Elena [Biography] Mexican novelist, playwright, screenwriter, poet, and
short story writer, she has become increasingly recognized in recent years, particularly since her death in 1998. She was part
of what is called the *Generación de Medio
Siglo* (the mid-century generation) in Mexico, which promoted the modernizing of
Mexican culture and literature in the 1950s.
A marginalized and marginal figure in

Mexican literature in the 1970s and 1980s,
she has been reevaluated and reread in the
past decade as a major Mexican writer of
the second half of the twentieth century.

Garro was born in Puebla, Mexico, in
1920 and began studies in the humanities at
the National University in Mexico City
(UNAM) before pursuing further studies
of dance and theater. (Recent biographical
research in Mexico makes the case that
previous published studies are incorrect
and she was born, in reality, in 1916.) She
worked as an actress and choreographer for
the Teatro de la Universidad under the direction of Julio Bracho. She married the
Mexican poet Octavio Paz in 1937 after
working with Paz and the International
Brigades in the Spanish Civil War. Her
marriage with Paz was turbulent, and some
feminist scholars have argued recently that
Paz limited her creative activity from the
start of their marriage until their separation in the late 1950s. They lived together in
Paris and Switzerland from 1946 to 1952.
Shortly after her return to Mexico, in 1954,
she began working as journalist, writing
mostly on film and other cultural topics.
She became widely known in Mexico in
1957 when her one-act plays, *Un hogar sólido* (A solid home, published later in 1958)
were produced on the stage in Mexico City.
She later wrote the play *La señora en su balcón* (1963, The woman on her balcony). Her
first volume of short stories, *La semana de
colores* (1964, The week of colors) was an
early experiment in questioning the boundaries between the real and the fantastic.
Her short fiction has been amply antholo-
gized in Mexico, and some of it has been
translated into several other Western European languages.

Garro was a politically engaged intellectual in the 1950s and 1960s, and this involvement, as well as her poor relationship
with Octavio Paz, resulted in her going into
political exile twice in her career. In 1959

her support of antigovernment political activity resulted in her exile to Paris, where she stayed for several years, returning to Mexico in the mid-1960s. She went into exile to the United States and Europe again in 1972, not to return to Mexico until 1991, for an homage to her work, and then permanently in 1993. During this lengthy period of exile she lived in Madrid from 1974 to 1981 and then went to Paris. Since 1991 scholars in Mexico and beyond began a reevaluation of her work, and during the 1990s Garro published several volumes of fiction she had written in earlier stages of her life.

Garro's most important novel is her first one, *Los recuerdos del porvenir* (1963, *Recollections of Things to Come*). It is the story of the Mexican town of Ixtepec, and Garro employed an innovative method for telling the story: the collective voice of the town is the narrator. Garro's equally experimental use of time—bringing characters alive from the town's past—has led some critics to compare her work to the magical realism of some Latin American literature of the 1950s and 1960s. More important, in this novel she pioneered the concept of "inventing the past and remembering the future," an idea fully exploited by Carlos Fuentes and other Mexican intellectuals in the 1960s and 1970s.

After a hiatus of nearly two decades, Garro began publishing novels in the early 1980s and continued for more than another two decades. In this second stage of her work, much of her writing involved autobiographical reflections; the roots of her anguish and personal crises are the focus of several of these novels. Her novel *Y Matarazo no llamó* (1991) harks back to the late 1950s in the life of Garro and the conflicts in trade unions of that period.

Selected Work: Los recuerdos del porvenir (1963, *Recollections of Things to Come*, translation Ruth L. C. Simms, 1969); *Testi-monios sobre Mariana* (1981); *Reencuentro de personajes* (1982); *La casa junto al río* (1983); *Y Matarazo no llamó* (1991); *Inés* (1995); *Busca mi esquela y Primer amor* (1996; *First Love & Look for My Obituary*, translation David Unger, 1997); *Un traje rojo para un duelo* (1996); *Un corazón en un bote de basura* (1996); *Mi hermanita Magdalena* (1998).

Gay and lesbian Latin American novel [Topic] Argentine writer Manuel Puig was one of the writers most responsible for opening the Latin American novel to the possibilities of gay themes with his popular novel with a gay protagonist, *La traición de Rita Hayworth* (1968, *Betrayed by Rita Hayworth*). The history of fiction writing with gay themes begins well before, and an early example of pioneer novels was *Um Bom Crioulou* (1895, A good creole boy) by the Brazilian Adolfo Caminha.

The multiple discourses of gay and lesbian fiction became more common than ever in the 1980s and 1990s, although the Mexican José Caballos Maldonado had published *Después de todo* (After everything) in 1969 and the Chicano John Rechy had published *City of the Night* in 1963. *Después de todo* is a first-person account of the middle-age male protagonist's sexual encounters with teenage boys. With the writing of novelists such as Sylvia Molloy, Luis Zapata, and Fernando Vallejo, Latin American writers of the 1980s and 1990s are increasingly exploring the multiple discourses of gender and sexuality.

Noteworthy gay and lesbian novels of this period include Sylvia Molloy's *En breve cárcel* (1981, *Certificate of Absence*), Darcy Penteado's *Nivaldo e Jeronimo* (1981, Nivaldo and Jeronimo), José Rafael Calva's *Utopía gay* (1983, Gay utopia), Luis Zapata's *En jirones* (On tour), and Fernando Vallejo's *El fuego secreto* (1986, The secret fire). Among the Chicana and Chicano writers who produced gay and lesbian texts, Cherríe Moraga wrote the personal ethnic memoir *Loving in the War Years* (1983).

Luis Zapata and Fernando Vallejo played a major role in establishing a place for gay writing in Mexico and Colombia, and they are the most prominent gay writers in their respective homelands. Zapata's portrayal of gay characters questions the norms of the heterosexual order. His novel *En jirones* consists of a "notebook" that establishes relationships between gay love and writing. Fernando Vallejo's fiction represents an iconoclastic look at the sexual order in sectors of Colombian society that are supposedly conservative, traditional, and Catholic.

After Puig's implicit exploration of gay topics in *La traición de Rita Hayworth* and explicit treatment of the theme in *El beso de la mujer araña* (1976, *Kiss of the Spider Woman*), one of the most direct treatments of gay sex to appear in a novel was in the Brazilian *Risco de Vida* (1995, Risk of life) by Alberto Guzik. In this work a gay academic has an affair with a younger male in the setting of urban São Paulo, with emphasis on the cultural and intellectual scene in this city. *El beso de la mujer araña*, on the other hand, is exceptional in its demonstration of how sexual and political liberation must be viewed as integral parts of the same process. In this novel Puig explores the power of politics and gender and the relationship of the two. A well-distributed film has appeared under the same title, *Kiss of the Spider Woman*.

As a response to the colonial legacy, much writing identified as gay and lesbian literature of the 1980s and 1990s serves functions similar to that of many feminist and overtly political writers. Thus queer discourse has contributed as much to the questioning of the old patriarchal order of the colonial period as many texts of the feminist and postmodern writers have. The Mexican journal *Debate feminista* and the magazine *Fem* have promoted a new sexual politics in Mexico, and Nelly Richard's journal *Revista de crítica cultural* opened new space for heterogeneous writing in Chile. Autobiographical essays such as Jaime Manrique's *Eminent Maricones* (1993, Eminent gays) and Reynaldo Arenas's memoir *Antes que anochezca* (1992, Before night comes) present issues related to modern and postmodern writing as well as queer discourse in Latin America.

Gazapo (1965, *Gazapo,* by Gustavo Sainz. Translation by Hardie St. Martin. New York: Farrar, Straus and Giroux, 1968) [**Novel**] Along with the fiction of Mexican José Agustín, *Gazapo* was a key text in the 1960s Mexican postmodern and counterculture rebellion that some local critics called La Onda (or "new wave"). Some critics claim it was the first Mexican novel after Mariano Azuela's 1916 classic *Los de abajo* to be devoid of any mention of the Mexican Revolution. It was also one of the early works in Latin America to offer a set of voices and texts with no controlling narrator organizational entity of any sort, leaving the reader to arrange the various texts and anecdotes, including telephone conversations, tape recordings, diaries, dreams, and letters. The reader can place together a nonlinear plot in which an adolescent couple experiences the process of becoming adults. It is the story of an attempted seduction of an ingenuous girl by an inexperienced boy. The relationship is both humorous and tender. Sainz makes the two youths interesting enough to engage the reader with their rebellious attitudes toward society; his satire and humor make the process of constructing a novel well worth the task, even though there is never any resolution of the ill-defined plot.

General en su laberinto, El (1989, *The General in His Labyrinth,* by Gabriel García

Márquez. Translation by Edith Grossman, 1990) [**Novel**] One of the historical figures most widely discussed and written about is the liberator of several nations on the South American continent, Simón Bolívar. García Márquez selected this controversial leader of the Americas as the protagonist of a biographical novel written in the novelist's maturity, publishing it at the age of sixty-two as the second novel after his Nobel Prize in Literature in 1982. In this work García Márquez writes with absolute confidence and flair, evoking once again some of his magical realist repertoire in a world with prodigious rainfall, marvelous nature, and the like. All in all, however, this is more a novel of containment and limits than his exuberant and hyperbolic Macondo novels, and thus this novel harks back to the Colombian's earliest writings of the 1950s. This work focuses on the final months of Bolívar's life in the 1830s, as his deteriorating old body travels down the Magdalena River to his death. Occasional flashbacks round out the story of the general's life, which García Márquez presents as a tragic march toward nothingness.

Generation of the 1990s [Topic] Originally proclaimed in Brazil as the generation of writers born in the 1960s who began publishing in the 1990s, the term *generation of the 1990s* has also been used in Latin America in general to refer to this generation of writers. Several other local variants have arisen to refer to this generation, as well as the term *post-postmodern*. Author of two volumes on these young writers, the Brazilian fiction writer and critic Nelson de Oliveira (who belongs to this generation) has been the most responsible for promoting the generation of the 1990s in Latin America. In addition to his own fiction, he has published the anthologies *Geracão 90: Manuscritos de Computador* (2001, Generation of the Nineties: Computer manu-

scripts) and *Geração 90: Os Transgressores* (2001, Generation of the Nineties: The Transgressors). The writers in this volume include Marçal Aquino, Rubens Figueiredo, Cíntia Moscovich, and Mauro Pinheiro, among numerous others.

In Chile Alberto Fuguet and Sergio Gómez have published the volume *McOndo* as an anthology of writers from Latin America and Spain of this generation. Both the generation of the 1990s and the declarations in the anthology *McOndo* have underscored a critique of magical realism as a marketing strategy to sell Latin American literature to multinational publishing companies. These writers insist upon their commitment to nonmagical realist type stories, with emphasis on their urban life as part of the new global economy, as well as new forms of violence in the large cities that is part of their generation's life experience. Fuguet has enjoyed modest success in the international promotion of novels such as *Mala onda* (which appeared in English translation as *Bad Vibes*) and other works.

In Mexico Jorge Volpi, Ignacio Padilla, and a few others have called themselves the generation of the crack, referring to the *crack* in the sense of a radical change in direction. They claim to bring a new international cosmopolitism to Latin American literature and openly reject most of the writing of the 1960s Boom. Volpi has internationally promoted his most successful novel, the spy thriller *En busca de Klingsor*, which appeared in translation in several Western European languages, including an English version as *In Search of Klingsor*. Several talented Mexican writers of the same generation who have not enjoyed the international publicity of Fuguet in Chile or Volpi in Mexico, such as Cristina Rivera Garza and David Toscana, Mario Bellatín and Juan Villoro, have produced an impressive body of fiction. Rivera Garza's historical novel *Nadie me verá llorar* has appeared in English, under the title *No One Will See Me Cry*, and has also appeared in a Portuguese translation. Author of several books of fiction, Toscana has been highly successful with two novels in both Mexico and in the United States.

Several other writers of this generation have been productive in their young careers. In Colombia Santiago Gamboa has published a successful body of fiction, including the novel *Los impostores*, and his compatriots Mario Mendoza, Efraím Medina, Héctor Abad Faciolince, Jorge Franco Ramos, and Hugo Chaparro have each published more than one book of fiction as well. More recently, Ricardo Silva and Juan Gabriel Vásquez, both born in the 1970s, have already published noteworthy novels. Among Argentine writers of this generation, Rodrigo Fresán has been the most internationally visible and Flavia Company, living and writing in Spain, has published eight novels. Writing in his native Bolivia and in the United States, Edmundo Paz Soldán has had considerable impact as a novelist and essayist on this entire generation in Latin America. In Peru Jaime Bayly has produced a body of fiction that has made him the most visible fiction writer of this generation. In Uruguay Henry Trujillo has already published three novels, short fiction, and essays.

These writers have a common interest in the media and popular culture; two of the writers who have best articulated the role of the media and technology have been Rodrigo Fresán and Edmundo Paz Soldán. Paz Soldán's essays have established connections between writers such as the Argentine novelist Roberto Arlt (of the 1920s), the Argentine Adolfo Bioy Casares, and these new writers of the 1990s. In his novel *Mantra* Fresán presents the urban life of Mexico City as it is fully informed by the media and technology. Above all, the char-

acters in this novel seem to live more in the world of television than the empirical reality of Mexico City.

George Washington Gómez (1940, by Américo Paredes. Written in English. Houston: Arte Público) [**Novel**] Chicano writer Américo Paredes struggled through the Great Depression and the Second World War while working on this narrative about racism in the Rio Grande valley. The story contains a strong moral about the slim hope of peaceful diversity and the overpowering force of white racism against the Mexican population along the border. George Washington Gómez is raised by his mother Maria and his uncle Feliciano after Texas rangers assassinate his father. George is called Guálinto, as if it were an indigenous name, as he experiences discrimination at school. As a teen Guálinto overloads his studies with a miserable part-time job at a grocery store to save some money during the first year of the Great Depression. His girlfriend, the beautiful and wealthy Maria Elena, chooses a white identity and leaves him for an Anglo-American boy. Upon graduation from high school, the entire town rests its hopes on young Guálinto to go to college and return as a leader of the Mexican community. When he does return, however, it is in the capacity of a military agent to control the border. George's rejection of Mexico-Texan culture in favor of Anglo-America, in spite of the many reasons to be in opposition to the dominant Anglo culture, is the ultimate conclusion to this coming-of-age story.

Giardinelli, Mempo (Oscar Alfredo Giardinelli Alfaro) [**Biography**] Argentine novelist, short story writer, poet, and essayist, he is considered one of the major writers of the post-Boom of the Spanish American novel of the 1970s and 1980s. Giardinelli himself has written essays on his generation as the post-Boom generation. He is known as a writer of strong plots and fast-moving action and as an intellectual who believes in both the political role of the writer and the role of the writer in deciphering history. Born in Resistencia (province of Chaco) in 1946, he studied law in the National University of the Nordeste (in Corrientes, Argentina) and later, during the military dictatorship in Argentina, took political exile in Mexico from 1976 to 1984. Since the mid-1980s he has lived in Argentina, continuing to write novels, and was awarded the most prestigious novel prize in Spanish America (Premio Rómulo Gallegos) in 1993. He cofounded a literary magazine dedicated to the short story, *Puro Cuento*.

His major novels are *Luna caliente* (1983, *Sultry Moon*), which won the Premio Nacional de Novela (national novel prize) in Argentina, and *Santo Oficio de la memoria* (1991, Holy office of memory), a vast family saga covering several generations of Italians that immigrate to Argentina. This portrayal of adolescent sexuality in *Luna caliente* has made Giardinelli a controversial figure for some critics, particularly feminists, who have claimed that the author is misogynist. *Imposible equilibrio* (1995, Impossible balance) is an entertaining political satire that also develops his recent interest in ecological issues. His recent *Visitas después de hora* (2003, After-hour visits) is a gallery of women's voices that surface on the basis of a situation in which a man on his deathbed in Buenos Aires, in a coma, listens to his daughter tell her intimate stories of memories and feelings, becoming increasingly intimate as the novel develops.

Giardinelli lives in northern Argentina, where he writes and directs a center with a broad agenda—from promoting culture to protecting the environment.

Selected Work: Toño tuerto rey de ciegos (1976); *La revolución en bicicleta* (1980); *El cielo con las manos* (1982); *Luna caliente* (1983, *Sultry Moon*, translation Patricia J. Duncan, 1998); *¿Por qué prohibieron el circo?* (1983); *Qué solos se quedan los muertos* (1985); *Santo Oficio de la memoria* (1991); *Imposible equilibrio* (1995); *El décimo infierno* (1999, *The Tenth Circle*, translation Andrea G. Labinger, 2001).

Glantz, Margo [Biography] Mexican essayist, novelist, and academic, she was born in Mexico City in 1928. She is feminist who writes about the body and the text, among other topics. She completed undergraduate and graduate work at the National University in Mexico City (UNAM), later earning a doctorate at the University of Paris in 1958. She also studied related disciplines (art history, English, and Italian literatures) in Paris, London, and Perugia, Italy. She has held numerous faculty and administrative positions in universities and cultural institutions in Mexico as well as serving as the government's cultural attaché in London.

Glantz has been a key player in the cultural scene in Mexico since the 1960s, coordinating publications and literary events. She founded the magazine *Punto de Partida* (1966–1970) and, in the 1980s, directed the publication of several literary collections. Collaborating with Elena Poniatowska and Elena Urrutia, she organized the Fourth Interamerican Conference of Women Writers in 1981.

Best known for her essays, Glantz is the author of an influential book, *Onda y escritura en México* (Onda and writing in Mexico), her polemical anthology of the new writing of Mexico in the 1960s, with Gustavo Sainz and José Agustín at the forefront. In this work she proposed the term *onda* ("new wave") for the emerging young writers such as Sainz, Agustín, and García

Saldaña. This book contributed signficantly to the legitimacy of these counterculture, rebel writers. Throughout the latter half of the twentieth century, the term *Onda* has been institutionalized in Mexico. Glantz has also compiled a volume of biographical documents on the French adventurer Rousset-Boulbon, a count who attempted to conquer and colonize the Sonora region of Mexico in the nineteenth century in order to establish his own empire. This volume appeared under the title *Un folletín realizado: la aventura del conde Rousset-Boulbon.*

Glantz's creative writing includes a broad range of fictional texts, and she has received acknowledgment for this work in Mexico, including the prestigious national prize Premio Villaurrutia in 1984. Her novel *Las genealogías* (1981, The genealogies) is historical in vision, with a framework of international history covering the first half of the twentieth century. This novel has the format of a memoir: in the first half the female narrator asks her parents to answer questions about her life. Both the world history and the family story connect to Glantz's Jewish ancestry. Her interest in a woman's body and writing is evident in this novel and in her later *Síndrome de naufragios* (1984, Shipwreck syndrome). In the latter she leads the reader through a trip involving the readings and authors of her life. *De la amorosa inclinación a enrededarse en cabellos* (1984, On the loving inclination of getting tangled in hair) is a fictionalized erotic esssay on the topic of hair.

Glantz lives in Mexico City, where she is a retired academic who continues her scholarly activity and creative writing.

Selected Work: Las mil y un calorías, novela dietética (1978); *Doscientas ballenas azules* (1979); *Intervención y pretexto* (1980); *No pronunciarás* (1980); *Las genealogías* (1981, The Family Tree, translation Susan Bassnett, 1991); *Síndrome de naufragios* (1984); *De la amorosa inclinación a enrededarse en cabellos* (1984); *Zona de derrumbe* (2001); *El rastro* (2002).

Glissant, Edouard [Biography] Caribbean novelist, essayist, playwright, and poet, he is one of the most prominent theorists of Caribbean culture. Writing in dialogue with figures such as Aimé Césaire, Frantz Fanon, and Alejo Carpentier, his seminal essay on Caribbean culture, identity, and writing, *Le discourse antillais* (1981, *Caribbean Discourse*) was followed by *Poétique de la relation* (1990, Poetics of connectedness). In these two books he establishes a need for a cross-cultural poetics (or a "poetics of connectedness). In order to have a Caribbean poetics, Glissant underlines the need for unfettered literary expression, free from the poetics imposed by Europe. Glissant's theories of *créolité* differ significantly from the foundational thinkers on Caribbean identity—Césaire, Fanon, Carpentier.

Glissant was born in Sainte Marie, Martinique, in 1928 and, in addition to his essays, has published five novels and several volumes of poetry. He was a follower of Aimé Césaire and a contemporary of Frantz Fanon. He studied at the same Lycée Schoelcher as did Fanon and then went to Paris, where he remained for nineteen years. His first book of essays, *Soleil de la conscience* (1956, Sun of consciousness), underlined the diversity of the Caribbean region, and his interpretation of the region emphasized fluidity as opposed to the more fixed view of the dominant writers defending the positions of *négritude* and Marxist thinkers.

Glissant's early novels *La lézarde* (1958, The Ripening) and *Le quatrème siècle* (1964, The fourth century) brought him critical acclaim for their breaking of genre boundaries and unique treatment of the space and history of his native Martinique. His later novel *Malemort* (1975, Undead) presented a hopeless vision for the future of Martinique. He dedicated many years to anticolonial politics, opposing the modernization of Martinique along European models. To that end he worked with a political alliance called the Front Antillo-Guyanis and returned to Martinique in 1965 to found the Institut Martiniquais d'Etudes. In 1980 he went to Europe once again, now to assume a position as editor of UNESCO *Courier* in Paris.

Glissant's impact on contemporary Caribbean intellectuals and writers has been enormous. For example, the book *Eloge de la créolité*, which was written by three younger authors from the Caribbean, Rafael Confiant, Jean Bembé, and Patrick Chamoiseau, is an affirmation of many of Glissant's ideas. The radical writings of Frankétienne—which include books written in Haitain Creole—can be seen as a consequence of Glissant's theories. The Cuban essayist Antonio Benítez Rojo, who has developed a theory of Caribbean fluidity, can also be linked to the earlier theories of Glisssant. In recent years Glissant has become one of the Caribbean writers most widely read by academics in the Caribbean, the United States, and Europe.

Selected Work: La lézarde (1958, *The Ripening*, translation Michael Dash 1985, in Spanish *El lagarto*, translation M. Christine Chazell and Jaime Palacio, 2001); *Le quatrème siècle* (1965, *The Fourth Century*, translation Betsy Wing, 2001); *Malemort* (1975); *La case du commandeur* (1981); *Mahogony* (1987); *Tout monde* (1995); *Sartorius: Le roman des Batoutos* (1999); *Ormerod* (2003).

Goldemberg, Isaac [Biography] Peruvian novelist, poet, and academic born in 1945, he became widely known in Latin America

for his first novel, *La vida a plazos de don Jacobo Lerner* (1976, *The Fragmented Life of Don Jacobo Lerner*, 1979). Living in New York, Goldemberg had the English translation of his first novel published before the Spanish. It relates the experience of a Jewish immigrant to Peru and in a broader sense deals with the Jewish diaspora to Peru and the protagonist's disenfranchisement. This novel was a culturally pioneering work when it first appeared in Peru in the 1970s. In *Tiempo al tiempo* (1984, *Play by Play*) the protagonist is the son of a Russian Jewish father and a Peruvian Catholic mother. Goldemberg currently lives in New York, where he teaches and is widely recognized among Hispanic intellectuals, primarily as a poet.

Selected Work: La vida a plazos de don Jacobo Lerner (1976, *The Fragmented Life of Don Jacobo Lerner*, translation Robert S. Picciotto, 1979); *Tiempo al tiempo* (1984, *Play by Play*, translation Hardie St. Martin, 1985); *El nombre del padre* (2001).

Goloboff, Gerardo Mario [Biography] Argentine novelist born in 1939, he has authored several novels set in the provincial town of the pampas called Algarrobos. He began writing novels in the 1970s, and his first novel, *Caballos por el fondo de los ojos* (1976, Horses around the inside of eyes), is set in the town of Algarrobos. Goloboff uses this town to relate controversial elements of Argentine history, thus creating a social history that encompasses the conquest of the indigenous population, the foundation of the nation in the recent past, the impact of different immigrant populations (such as the Italian, Polish, and Jewish immigrants), and the violence and oppression inflicted by one group upon another.

Two of Goloboff's most noteworthy novels are *El soñador de Smith* (1990, The dreamer of Smith) and *Comuna verdad*

(1995, Common truth), both of which are set in Algarrobos. In *El soñador de Smith* an orphan continues learning the lessons he had begun learning in earlier works by Goloboff. This rite of passage harks back to the classic gaucho text of Argentina, *Don Segundo Sombra* (1926), as well as to other well-known texts of the gaucho tradition written by writers such as Hernández, Lugones, and Gerchunoff. The young boy becomes familiar with some of these traditions as well as his responsibility to become an adult in a nation with a history of wars. By learning his family's story, the boy learns some of the important elements of Argentine history. Among the immigrant stories included in this novel, the most prominent is the Jewish arrival in the pampas. In *Comuna verdad* Goloboff turns to a little-known chapter of Argentine history: the establishing of a utopian community in 1942 and its dissolution a year later. Goloboff uses multiple narrative voices to recreate and invent a mad vison of a town whose immigrants are Italians, Poles, and Jews who are idealist vegetarians, nudists, and students of Esperanto. Readers of this book as well as others by Goloboff can draw parallels with certain excesses to be found in modern Argentina, including the excesses of the dictatorship of the 1970s and early 1980s.

Selected Work: Caballos por los fondos de los ojos (1976); *Criador de palomas* (1984, The Algarrobos Quartet*, translation Stephen A. Sadow, 2002); *La luna que cae* (1989); *El soñador de Smith* (1990); *Comuna verdad* (1995).

Gómez, Sergio [Biography] Chilean novelist and short story writer, he has collaborated with Alberto Fuguet to promote a group of young Latin American writers they have labeled the McOndo generation in their co-authored anthology *McOndo*. They are writers who began to publish in

the 1990s that some critics have identified as the generation of the 1990s. Gómez and his collaborator Alberto Fuguet have been the most visible and successful of the groups across Latin American attempting to promote the generation of writers born in the late 1950s and 1960s. In their volume *McOndo* Gómez and Fuguet openly reject magical realism and related forms of literature they consider commercial writing for foreign consumption. The new writers whom they include in their volume are David Toscana from Mexico, Jaime Bayly from Perú, Edmundo Paz Soldán from Bolivia, and Rodrigo Fresán of Argentina, among others.

Born in 1964 in the town of Temuco in southern Chile, Gómez has been a literature teacher and has made scripts for television. He has been involved with the literary supplement for young readers of the newspaper *El Mercurio*, the major newspaper in Chile. He coedited a widely distributed and discussed volume of new fiction in Chile, *Cuentos con Walkman* (1993, Short stories with Walkman) with Alberto Fuguet. Gómez began publishing fiction in the early 1990s with the book of short stories *Adiós, Carlos Marx, nos vemos en el cielo* (1992, Good-bye, Karl Marx, we'll meet in heaven). He has also published the novel *Vidas ejemplares* (1994, Exemplary lives).

Selected Work: Vidas ejemplares (1994); *El labio inferior* (1998); *La mujer del policía* (2000); *La obra literaria de Mario Valdini* (2002).

González León, Adriano [Biography] Venezuelan novelist born in 1931, he is a major modern writer in Venezuela. He wrote one of the seminal novels in Venezuela in the 1960s, *País portátil* (1968, Portable nation), a work of Faulknerian structure as well as other overtones of the Mississippi novelist. It deals with urban revolutionaries in Caracas in the 1960s, but *País portátil* also expands to provide a larger sense of the city as well as the historical background to the protagonist's family, the Barazarte family. The basic present of the novel covers a span of a few hours, but the family story covers generations. Changes in time level and narrative voice make this a deeply intense story of family tradition, political commitment, and urban guerrilla activity. After this impressive novel, González León's novelistic career has been relatively insignificant.

Selected Work: *País portátil* (1968); *Linaje de árboles* (1988); *Viejo* (1995).

González Suárez, Mario [Biography] Mexican novelist, short story writer, and essayist, he is currently gaining a reputation as one of Latin America's most talented and accomplished younger writers. He was born in Mexico City in 1964 and has been working both as a university professor and giving writers' workshops in Mexico City. He has not been included in Jorge Volpi's group self-identified as the Generación del Crack, but can be associated with the group of Mexican writers born in the 1960s who began publishing fiction in the 1990s. His early books of fiction were *Nostalgia de la luz* (1996, Nostalgia for light) and the short stories *Materia del insomnio* (1997, Matter of insomnia). His novel *De la infancia* (1998) concerns a working-class adolescent's childhood growing up on the outskirts of Mexico City and begins with him and his siblings being abused by their sexist and violent father. The early parts of this work recount how his childhood dreams were shattered by his parents and how he experienced a series of events related to a rite of passage from childhood to adulthood. Much of the novel consists of his mental images of the world, which include both what he is experiencing and what he

is imagining. In this compelling and disturbing work, González Suárez begins to explore issues such as gender as social construct, domestic violence, authority, and institutionalized violence. The political subtext suggests that the traditional political parties and well-known ideologies of the twentieth-century do not offer solutions for the main characters (the abused boy or his abusive father). *El libro de las pasiones* (1999, The book of passions) consists of thirteen fictions that are only vaguely related, so this book can be considered a novel only with the broadest understanding of the genre. This volume of short fiction contributes to González Suárez's reputation. He was awarded a prestigious literary prize in Mexico, the Premio Gilberto Owen, in 1998.

Selected Work: *De la infancia* (1998); *El libro de las pasiones* (1999).

Gorodischer, Angélica [Biography] Argentine novelist and short story writer, she has received numerous recognitions for her work in her homeland as well as abroad, including translations into several languages. Much of her work is an exploration of the fantastic, and she holds the reputation of being one of the few science fiction writers in Latin America. She finds subtle ways of weaving gender issues into her stories of the fantastic and the world of science fiction. Among her numerous awards and prizes, she won the Sigriedo Radaelli Prize for the best short story of 1985. She claims that Argentine politics inevitably affect her work and that the stories in her book *Kalpa Imperial*, which were intended to be a dialogue with *A Thousand and One Nights*, became a dialogue with the political process of the military dictatorship. She currently lives in Rosario, Argentina.

Gorodischer was born in Buenos Aires in 1928 and studied liberal arts in Rosario, province of Santa Fe. Among the novelists she most admires are Aldous Huxley, Balzac, Borges, and Raymond Chandler. Her short fiction has received widespread critical acclaim in Argentina, particularly the volumes *Bajo las jubeas en flor* (1976, Under the jubeas in bloom) and *Casta luna electrónica* (1977, Chaste electronic moon). She has considerable experience abroad, having participated in the International Writing Program at the University of Iowa (1988) and having been a visiting lecturer at several venues in Europe and the United States. Her work spans the 1960s to the 1990s.

Selected Work: Opus dos (1967); *Floreros de Albastro, alfombras de Bokhara* (1985); *Jugo de mango* (1988); *Fábula de la virgen y el bombero* (1993); *La noche del inocente* (1996); *Doquier* (2002); *Tumba de Jaguares* (2005).

Grande Arte, A (1983, *High Art,* by Rubem Fonseca. Translation by Ellen Watson. New York: Harper and Row, 1986) [**Novel**] One of Fonseca's most widely read novels, this is a parody of detective fiction. Set in Rio de Janeiro, it follows the misadventures and sexual encounters of the male characters, with considerable satire and critique of the old aristocracy in Brazil. The novel consists of three parts and follows the path of Mandrake in his search for motives. Fonseca is a master of gaining the reader's attention from the outset, and in this novel he begins with an entertaining and humorous sex scene. The first-person narrator claims at the outset that he came to figure out the story through notebooks and stories from witnesses. He does admit to interpreting events and behaviors, thus undermining the fictional illusion of objectivity. He concludes the opening section of the novel by stating, "Am I not a lawyer professionally accustomed to the practice of hermeneutics?" He leads the reader through debauchery and mystery. This novel represents

Fonseca at his best and questions the very possibility of interpreting the events around him by means of human reason.

Grande Sertão: Veredas (1956, *The Devil to Pay in the Backlands,* by João Guimarães Rosa. Translation by James L. Taylor and Harriet de Onis. New York: Knopf, 1963) [**Novel**] Widely acclaimed as one of the major novels of the century in Brazil and Latin America, *The Devil to Pay in the Backlands* is a lengthy, complex and digressive monologue set in the backlands of northeastern Brazil called the *sertão*. Few Latin American novels have been the object of so many readings and studies in an attempt to clarify its plethora of ambiguities and themes. The narrator is an elderly *jagunço* (gunslinger or bandit) named Riobaldo. He relates anecdotes of his younger days, when he is befriended by his grandfather (eventually revealed to be his father), joins a band of *jagunços*, courts his future wife Otalícia, and eventually becomes a leader of the *jagunços*. Riobaldo's friend Diadorim kills their enemy Hermógenes, although Diadorim is also wounded and dies. Riobaldo discovers that Diadorim is actually a woman in disguise, Maria Diadorina. As this series of events unfold, Riobaldo struggles throughout the narrative to understand these happenings, the world around him, and himself. The reader shares in these struggles, in addition to numerous linguistic complexities, for Guimarães Rosa incorporates neologisms and words from several indigenous Brazilian languages. The novel has been read as an epic work and as a search for language. Along with *Paradiso* by Lezama Lima and *Terra Nostra* by Carlos Fuentes, this is a modern Latin American masterpiece of epic proportions.

Graviña, Alfredo Dante [**Biography**] Uruguayan novelist, poet, playwright, journalist, essayist, and short story writer, he was born in Tacuarembó, Uruguay, in 1913. He began writing short stories at an early age, publishing his first short fiction in the 1930s. He continued publishing short fiction throughout his career, and this work has been consistently high in quality.

Graviña began publishing novels in the 1940s, focusing on social and political critique in mostly rural settings, as was the case of his early novels *Historia de una historia* (1944, History of a story) and *Macadám* (1948). The latter is considered his best work. He depicts social injustice by creating clear divisions between the just and the unjust, the exploiter and the exploited. He was criticized for the simplicity of such schemes in his trilogy *Fronteras al viento* (1951, Borders to the wind), *El único camino* (1958, The only path), and *Del miedo al orgullo* (1959, From fear to pride). From 1976 to 1984 he wrote in political exile in Cuba, working for the Cuban cultural institution Casa de las Américas. While in Cuba he began writing poetry. He died in Montevideo in 1995.

Selected Work: Historia de una historia (1944); *Macadám* (1948); *Fronteras al viento* (1951); *El único camino* (1958); *Del miedo al orgullo* (1959); *Tiempo arriba* (1964); *Seis pares de zapatos* (1964); *Brindis por el húngaro* (1966); *La isla* (1970).

Green House, The (See *Casa verde, La,* by Mario Vargas Llosa) [**Novel**]

Gringo viejo (1985, *Old Gringo*, by Carlos Fuentes. Translation Margaret Sayers Peden. New York: Farrar, Straus and Giroux, 1985) [**Novel**] Published in different versions in Spanish and English, both the Spanish text titled *Gringo viejo* and the English text titled *Old Gringo* are border novels dealing with the life and death of Ambrose Bierce, a misanthropic American journalist and short story writer who ap-

parently crossed the border into Mexico during the Mexican Revolution in order to die. In a romanticized and mythic Mexico Bierce connects with the fictional character Harriet Winslow, becoming both a father figure and a lover. Bierce is the stereotypic American writer, Winslow the stereotypic American school teacher, and General Arroyo the stereotypic Mexican *caudillo*. The story is filtered through Winslow's memory. Bilingual readers of both texts, *The Old Gringo* and *Gringo Viejo*, can ascertain that there are important differences between the two: one has one less chapter, and Fuentes made other minor adjustments to the English translation. The historic setting is the early twentieth-century Mexican Revolution, but Fuentes once again attempts to create a timelessness beyond historic time, as he does in many of his novels. This novel is a small piece of Fuentes's dialogue between cultures.

Guadeloupe/Martinique/French Guyana [**Nation**] Technically not a nation, these three political entities are French overseas departments (DOM) of the Caribbean region. The French had been present in the Caribbean since 1635, coining the term *Latin America* in the nineteenth century to legitimate their own presence in the region. In the 1920s and 1930s Guadeloupe and Martinique established a strong tradition in poetry—promoting poetry of *négritude*—and relatively little novelistic production of any significance. The postwar generation, however, turned away from poetry toward the novel. Several of the writers of the region questioned the viability of speaking of a literary tradition; Aimé Césaire and Eduoard Glissant, for example, claimed that there were writers but no literary tradition. With neocolonial ties to France and little of their own literary tradition, this region differs considerably from much of Latin America, which traces a literary tradition back to the nineteenth century. Césaire never did favor the decolonization of this region—independence from France—but rather a transformation of French society into a socialist one of social and economic justice.

The major novelists from this region, in addition to Glissant, have been Maryse Condé, Raphael Confiant, Patrick Chamoiseau, Daniel Maximin, León Damas, Simone Schwarz-Bart, and Bertène Juminer.

Guardia, Gloria [Biography] Panamanian novelist and essayist, she was born in Panama City in 1940. She studied at Vassar College and Columbia University in the United States and the Universidad Complutense in Spain. A prolific writer, she has published thirteen books, some of which have been translated into Engish and Russian. Most of them are historical works that deal with political scenarios in Central America, and they are critical of both the United States and the local elites in Panama that collaborate with the United States.

One of her better-known novels, *El ultimo juego* (1997, The last game), is a critique of political corruption and Panama's dependency on the United States. An urban guerrilla commando kidnaps a group of politicians and multiple narrative voices communicate the sense of alienation of the characters in the new global economy of consumerism. In this novel the first person of the protagonist is the main voice, the revolutionary hero who maintains an imaginary dialogue with his lover. Revolutionary membership in the nation's old elite makes his political stance a rejection of patriarchal authority.

In *Libertad en llamas* (1999, Freedom in flames) the protagonist, Esmeralda Reyes-Manning, returns to her native Nicaragua to work under the command of the historic revolutionary figure César Augusto Sandino. Her job is to get information from elites in power and to establish links with other anti-U.S. nations. A novel about power and conflict, it contains documentary detail on the daily life and political history of Nicaragua in 1920s. Guardia's work in general questions patriarchal authority from a feminist perspective.

Selected Work: El ultimo juego (1997); *Libertad en llamas* (1999).

Guatemala [Nation] A strongly indigenous nation, Guatemala's recent history has been dominated by foreign intervention (the 1954 CIA attack on the government of Arbenz), civil strife, and the writing of Nobel laureate Miguel Angel Asturias. For the contemporary Guatemalan novel, all three elements are omnipresent. The classic *El Señor Presidente* (1945, *El Señor Presidente*) and the novels of Mario Monteforte Toledo were the key to the modernization of fiction in Guatemala.

The major novelists of Guatemala in the post-1945 period, in addition to Asturias and Monteforte Toledo, are Rodrigo Rey Rosa, Mario Roberto Morales, and Arturo Arias.

Guerra, Lucía [Biography] Chilean novelist, short story writer, essayist, and academic, she has been a practicing academic, as a scholar of Latin American literature, since the mid-1970s. She is currently a professor of Latin American literature at the University of California, Irvine, where she writes fiction and studies of nineteenth- and twentieth-century Latin American writers, particularly women writers and novelists from Chile. She researches and writes about issues of gender and urban spaces. Her book-length essay *La mujer fragmentada: historia de un signo* (1994) was awarded the prestigious Premio Extraordinario Casa de las Américas, in 1994 in Cuba. Her scholarly publications include over eighty articles and seven books. Invited to conferences and lectures in the 1980s and 1990s, she has become an influential voice for women writers both as a practitioner and a student of this writing, establishing herself as a leading theorist, along with scholars such as Jean Franco and Sara Castro-Klarén, of Latin American feminist thought. Her early work focused on a pioneer woman writer in Chile, María Luisa Bombal. Guerra also translated Bombal's fiction into English and was awarded a translation prize by Columbia University in 1979 for this work.

Guerra began a dual career as scholar and creative writer in the 1980s, publishing her first novel, *Más allá de las mascaras* (Beyond the masks) in 1984 as a part of her feminist project. This novel focuses on the biology of gender and is a reaffirmation of sexual identity. In general Guerra's work involves giving voice to women who have been historically silent. With the appearance of this work she became associated with the rise of feminist writing in the 1980s, a decade in which women's writing in general became more prominent than it had ever been in Latin America. She followed with the novel *Muñeca brava* (1993, Brave doll), using the figure of the female prostitute as a metaphor for resistance to the military dictatorship. She has also published two volumes of short stories, *Frutos extraños* (1991, Strange fruit) and *Los dominios ocultos* (1998, The hidden dominions), both of which question traditional masculine roles in society. *Frutos extraños* was awarded the Premio Letras de Oro given by the University of Miami and the Spanish government to a Hispanic writer in the United States.

Her most accomplished novel is the more recent *Las noches de Carmen Miranda* (2002, The nights of Carmen Miranda), her fictionalized story of the Brazilian actress of Hollywood fame in the 1940s and 1950s. In this account Guerra begins with Miranda's childhood, where she was born in 1909 in Portugal, and moves quickly to her family's emigration to Brazil. In Brazil the reader becomes privy to the future actress's abusive and violent father and the numerous difficulties of her childhood. At an early age she became fascinated with women's clothing and the different potential uses of the female body in a sexist society. The author digresses back to the historic past of the slave trade between Europe, Africa, and the Americas to provide background for the African influences in the music of Brazil (such as the samba) that Carmen Miranda eventually appropriated and popularized worldwide. This novel is a product of both historical research and creative writing. Some of her short fiction has been translated into English, German, and Italian. Guerra lives in Irvine, California, where she teaches and writes.

Selected Work: Más allá de las mascaras (1984); *Muñeca brava* (1993); *Las noches de Carmen Miranda* (2002).

Guido, Beatriz [Biography] Argentine novelist and short story writer born in Rosario in 1924, she studied literature at the University of Rome and philosophy in Paris. She is widely recognized in her homeland as a critic of the conventions of Argentine society who wrote in a more realist mode than most of her contemporaries. Her early novel, *La casa del angel* (1954, *House of the Angel*), is the characterization of a young women who suffers the sexual restrictions and repression of a conventional Catholic society. The first-person narrator, Ana, is a sixteen-year old who recreates the middle-class world of Buenos Aires in the 1920s, and La dueña is a young woman romantically committed to a friend of her father. The combination of psychological exploration and critique of middle-class conventions is essential to her work. She is more ambiguous in her treatment of the elite. In *La caída* (1956, The fall) a young university student from the provinces rents a room from a widow with four demonic children who, in turn, introduce her to their uncle. She resists the uncle's advances and leaves the home in order to write a novel.

She is best known for her novels *Fin de fiesta* (1958, End of the party) and *El incendio de las vísperas* (1964, End of the Day). The former deals with local patriarchs or *caudillismo*, telling the story of four cousins who grow up in the home of their grandfather, a classic *caudillo* figure. They develop from innocent adolescence to young adults with an increased political awareness. Alternating perspectives relate the aging and death of the *caudillo* and the rise of Perón in the 1940s as the new *caudillo*. Guido's novel suggests that the patriarchal authority implied in *caudillismo* remains strong as an institution in Latin America. This novel is also a portrayal of the Argentine oligarchy from 1930 to 1945. *El incendio de las vísperas* portays the decay of Argentine society under Perón. Guido fictionalizes Argentine history in 1952 and 1953, the fight against Peronism, violence instigated by the police, the burning of the Jockey Club on April 15, 1953, and the decadence of Argentina's middle class with the rise of Peronism. The artistic intellectual proves incapable of political confrontation; the young student defends his rights in the face of abuse.

Guido's husband, filmmaker Leopoldo Torre Nilsson, has made several of her novels into films, including *La casa del angel* and *La caída*. She has also published several volumes of fiction. She died in 1988.

Selected Work: La casa del ángel (1954, *The House of the Angel*, translation Joan Coyne MacLean, 1957); *La caída* (1956); *Fin de fiesta* (1958); *El incendio y las vísperas* (1964, *End of a Day*, translation A. D. Towers, 1966); *Escandalos y soledades* (1970); *Una madre* (1973); *La invitación* (1979); *Apasionadas* (1982).

Guimarães, Josué [Biography] Brazilian novelist, journalist, and short story writer, he was born in São Jeronimo (state of Rio Grande do Sul) in 1921, and surfaced on the Brazilian literary scene in 1969 when he won a national short story contest. He writes mostly conventional historical novels. The following year he published his first volume of stories, *Os Ladrões* (The thieves). During the government of João Goulart (1961–64) he served as director of the Agência Nacional de Noticias (National News Agency). He worked as a journalist for the newspapers *Zero Hora* in Porto Alegre and the *Folha de São Paulo*.

He has written a substantive corpus of historical fiction as well as some lighter and more humorous work. In the early 1970s he began a trilogy under the general title of *A Ferro e Fogo*, which begins with the colonization of Rio Grande do Sul in the nineteenth century. The first novel of the trilogy, *Tempo de solidão* (1972, Time of solitude) deals with marginalization and individual solitude and covers the historical period in Brazil of 1824 to 1835. The second historical novel of the trilogy, *Tempo de guerra* (1975, Time of war), covers from 1835 to 1845. These are written in the realist mode, and Guimarães has published other fiction independent of the trilogy. *E Tarde para Saber* (1977, It's late to know) is a love story between two adolescents and *Enquanto a Noite não Chega* (1978, As long as night doesn't arrive) is the story of a city that has been abandoned. *Dona Anja* (1978, Dona Anja) is a parody of the *folletín* (or serial novel) and of the venerable tradition of the

Spanish picaresque novel. He was awarded the Erico Verríssimo Prize in 1975 for his novel *Os Tambores Silenciosos* (The silent drums). Guimarães died in 1986.

Selected Work: Tempo de Solidão (1972); *Tempo de Guerra* (1975); *Os Tambores Silenciosos* (1975); *E Tarde para Saber* (1977); *Dona Anja* (1978); *Enquanto a Noite não Chega* (1978); *O Gato no Escuro* (1982).

Gusmán, Luis [Biography] Argentine novelist born in Buenos Aires in 1944, he is recognized and respected in Argentina as a writer not associated with the centers of cultural power in Buenos Aires. During the 1970s he was involved with a group of avant-garde artists in the journal *Litoral*. He gained national attention in Argentina for his short story "El frasquito" in 1973. He has published over ten books of fiction.

Gusmán wrote under the military dictatorship of the 1970s and 1980s in Argentina, and the result was sometimes similar to Piglia's response to repression and censorship. Gusmán's novel *En el corazón de junio* (1983, In the heart of June) is a highly fragmented work that is a series of enigmas. This novel, like Piglia's *Respiración oficial*, attempts to speak the unspeakable—writing under a dictatorship.

Selected Work: Brillos (1975); *Cuerpo velado* (1978); *En el corazón de junio* (1983); *La música de Frankie* (1993); *Villa* (1995); *Tennessee* (1997); *Hotel Edén* (1999); *Ni muerto has perdido tu nombre* (2002).

Gutiérrez, Joaquín [Biography] Costa Rican novelist and translator, he is the author of a canonical novel of Central America, *Puerto Limón* (1950, Port of Limón). The son of a plantation owner, he was born in 1918 in Costa Rica and studied economics in New York. Having lived for several years in Chile, he worked for the publishing houses Nascimiento and Chilena Quimantú. His creative activity includes translating both Shakespeare and Mao Tse-tung into Spanish. He received two national awards for his novel *Murámanos Federico* (1973, Let's die Federico).

Gutiérrez is best known for his novel of social protest *Puerto Limón*. In this work the protagonist is an eighteen year old, Silvano, who loses his parents and is forced to assist his uncle in managing the family banana plantation. When he arrives, however, the workers are on strike because of poor working conditions. In the process of learning about the life of workers and class difference, Silvano becomes increasingly aware of his own role as member of the land-owning elite and enters into a crisis. Nevethless, he does collaborate with the leadership of the United Fruit Company to strike a contractual agreement that both sides find acceptable.

Gutiérrez was more interested in a critique of local elites and foreign capitalists than the aesthetic agenda of modernism. Along with Miguel Angel Asturias, he is considered a major contributor to the legacy of social protest literature in the Central American region.

Selected Work: Manglar (1947); *Puerto Limón* (1950); *Murámanos Federico* (1973); *Te conozco mascarita* (1973); *Te acordás hermano* (1978); *Los azules días* (1999).

Guyana [Nation] Formerly known as the colony of British Guyana, this Caribbean nation received its independence in 1968. A triethnic culture with a signficant portion of its population of African origin, Guyana has also received an even larger population from India since the nineteenth century, and East Indians are currrently the ethnic majority. Commonly spoken languages in Guyana are English, English creole, and Spanish, and this nation enjoys a relatively high level of literacy.

Major novelists from Guyana are Jan Carew, Cyril Dadydeen, David Dadydeen, Fred D'Aguiar, Wilson Harris, Roy Heath, and Pauline Melville.

Guzik, Alfredo [Biography] Brazilian novelist, theater critic, playwright, theater director, and academic, he occupies a place in Brazilian society that defines him as a minority writer in several senses. First, he is one of the few writers in Brazil to deal explicitly with the issue of AIDS, the central topic of his one novel, *Risco de Vida* (1995, Life's risk). Second, he is one of the few Jewish novelists in Brazil, along with figures such as Moaçir Scliar. Third, he stands out as a cultural figure in Brazil who has had considerable impact on the literary scene with no prior credentials as a novelist per se.

Guzik was born in São Paulo in 1944 and has been active in the theater scene since his childhood participation in amateur productions. He entered the Escola de Arte Dramática (School of Drama) in São Paulo in 1964. He has taught theater at several institutions in Brazil, including the large and prestigious University of São Paulo (USPE). His additional work in theater has involved publishing theater criticism and reviews in the *Jornal da Tarde* since 1984.

His only novel, *Risco de Vida*, is a lengthy (492 pages), detailed, and lively chronicle of the cultural scene in São Paulo during the 1980s as well as one of the few extant narrative descriptions of gay life in the Brazilian capital. There are several erotic depictions of gay relationships in the novel, some with more detailed descriptions than is the case with earlier gay writers in Latin America, such as Manuel Puig, who tended to keep the precise details of gay sex more peripheral to the story. The plot in *Risco de Vida* involves a love affair between a young man named Cláudio who is twenty-six years old and a thirty-eight-year old Jewish Brazilian professor of theater and journalist named

Thomas Maicóvski, an alter ego of the author. The story includes an intimate and intense relationship between Thomas and Cláudio, which seems to function well until it is discovered that Cláudio has AIDS. In addition to the notoriety of the topic in Brazil, *Risco de Vida* can be read as a testimonial to the 1980s generation of artists and intellectuals in São Paulo.

Selected Work: Risco de Vida (1995).

Guzmán, Humberto [Biography] Mexican novelist, short story writer, and essayist, he was born in Mexico City in 1948 and studied economics at the college level before deciding to pursue literature. He has taught creative writing workshops and published essays in numerous Mexican literary and cultural journals. He began writing fiction in the mid-1960s and published volumes of short stories in 1967 and 1975.

Guzmán is a postmodern novelist who rewrites some of the most common topoi of Mexican literature. In his novel *Los buscadores de la dicha* (1990, The pleasure seekers) he uses a plot well known in Mexican literature: the man who is rejected by a woman. Guzman's postmodern reworking of this theme emphasizes the repetition and sameness of everything. The author sets this novel in Prague and uses foreign film as a framework.

Selected Work: El sótano blanco (1972); *Historia fingida* (1982); *Los buscadores de la dicha* (1990); *La caricia del mal* (1998); *Los extraños* (2001).

Háblenme de Funes (1970, Speak to me of Funes, by Humberto Costantini. Written in Spanish and untranslated. Buenos Aires: Sudamericana) **[Novel]** One of the more

experimental novels to appear in print in the 1970s, *Háblenme de Funes* is a three-part work that challenges the reader to find relationships among the parts. Associations among the parts create an implied, intuitive unity among apparently unconnected parts. The first part, and title story, "Háblenme de Funes," narrates the story of the life and death of the protagonist, a musician named Funes. Each musician who had worked with him tells some of his story, which includes a love affair with a woman. The second part, titled "Amarillo sol, Amarillo pétalo, Amarillo flamante, Amarillo poema" (Yellow sun, yellow petal, flaming yellow, yellow poem) captures a moment in the life of a neighborhood; it tells what each person is doing at exactly the same moment. Costantini's inventive and playful use of language in the second part is entertaining in itself. The third part, "Fichas" (Cards), is a metafiction about the creative process. Similar novelistic experiments had already appeared in Latin America, such as Manuel Puig's *La traición de Rita Hayworth* and José Agustín's *Inventando que sueño*, both of which appeared in 1968. Consequently, *Háblenme de Funes* was part of a then relatively new, postmodern direction of some Latin American fiction in the late 1960s and early 1970s.

Hadriana dans tous mes rêves (1988, Hadriana in all my dreams, by René Depestre. Written in French and untranslated. Paris: Gallimard, 1988) **[Novel]** Depestre is one of the leading intellectual figures of Haiti and the Caribbean region in the second half of the twentieth century. He sets this historical novel, which covers approximately three centuries of Haitian history, in the town of Jacmel. He tells the story of an idealized beautiful woman in a town that suffers decadence and decay after death. Before that, the town experiences political and economic viscissitudes, as well as a carnivalesque parade of historical figures from Haiti's past. Depestre portrays deep divisions in Haitian society along race and class lines, in addition to the contradictions of historical and political figures that have affected this nation's often unfortunate and sometimes bizarre history.

Haiti [Nation] The Haitian novel of the second half of the twentieth century inherited a literary tradition dating back to the nineteenth century and the first Haitian novel, *Stella* (1859), by Emérec Dergeaud. The imaginary construction of the Haitian nation in this new national literature (in this Francophone nation) was continued by turn-of-the-century realists Justin Lhérisson, Fernand Hibbert, Fréderic Marcelin, and Antoine Innocent. In the 1920s Jacques Rouman, Carl Brouard, Emile Roumer, and Phillippe-Thoby Marelin headed an antiestablishment movement to end Haiti's isolation by connecting Haitian culture to the Harlem Rennaissance, the remainder of the Caribbean, and Latin America. By the 1940s Haitian intellectuals were in dialogue with visitors to the island such as André Breton from France and Alejo Carpentier from Cuba.

The early classics of the post-1945 period were Rouman's peasant novel *Gouverneurs de la Rosée* (1945, *Masters of the Dew*, 1988) and Jacques-Stephan Alexis's *Les arbres musiciens* (1957, The tree musicians). Prominent novelists since the 1960s have been Frankétienne (also known as Frank Etienne), René Depestre, Anthony Phelps, Pièrre Clitandre, Marie Chauvet, Dany Laferrière, and Edwidge Danticat. The literary tradition of Haiti has been for the novel to be written in French, although by the 1970s French dominance was questioned by the production of fiction written in the lingua franca—Haitian Creole—by Frankétienne (who had also published amply in French) and Edwidge Danticat, who writes in English and publishes in the United States.

The international image and understanding of Haiti—the first African nation of the Americas—has been constructed less by Haitian writers than by foreign writers and journalists who have depicted and emphasized the nation's danger, irrationality, and African vodou religious practices. Danticat has provided, in effect, a counter-narrative in English for a wide readership in the United States, offering a human dimension to Haitian reality not clearly evident in the predominant imagery of voudou, the Duvalier dictatorship, and the like. The Duvalier dictatorship (1958–1971), on the other hand, resulted in numerous writers, such as Laferrière, taking political exile in Canada, Europe, and the United States. Unlike other regions of the Caribbean and Latin America, however, Haiti's exile writers did not produce a set of novels about the dictator figure.

Harp and Shadow, The (See *Arpa y la sombra*, El, by Alejo Carpentier) [**Novel**]

Harris, Claire [**Biography**] Caribbean novelist and poet from Trinidad, she was born Port of Spain in 1937. Harris is a postcolonial and innovative writer, comparable to Caribbean writers such as Frankétienne from Haiti and Astrid Roemer from Suriname. She studied at University College, Dublin, Ireland; the University of West Indies, Jamaica; and the University of Nigeria, Nsukka. Her poetry is experimental, and much of it is narrative in form, so that the description of her as "novelist and poet" is potentially misleading, for her writing is not easily associated with conventional forms of the novel or poetry. Many readers would consider Harris more a poet than a novelist. Her experimental writing often deals with topics such as racism, minority

rights, and expatriation. Author of several collections of this poetry, she won the Americas regional award of the Commonwealth Poetry Prize in 1985.

She is the author of *Drawing Down and Daughter* (1992), a "dream collage" that tells the story of her journey from Trinidad to Canada. It is a hybrid containing prose poetry, free verse, letters, short stories, journal writing, and autobiography. Much of the writing consists of elliptical configurations of images and metaphors that create a fragmented, dreamlike text with frequent use of stream of consciousness. She also recreates English as it was spoken in Trinidad during her childhood.

She emigrated to Calgary, Alberta in 1966 to teach, and since then has been active in the Canadian literary scene.

Selected Work: *Drawing Down and Daughter* (1992).

Harris, Wilson [**Biography**] Caribbean novelist and essayist, he was born in British Guyana (called Guyana today) in 1921. His first collection of essays, *Tradition, Writer and Society* (1967), was his opportunity to locate himself as a writer of the English language in the Caribbean region. In these essays he distinguishes between himself as an individual who writes and a writer belonging to a tradition. He wrote in favor of a radical politics; he was a postcolonial thinker deeply concerned with issues of race, class, and gender in the Caribbean. Nevertheless, he considered political radicalism merely a fashionable attitude unless it was accompanied by deep insights into the experimental nature of the arts and sciences.

Harris is best known for a trilogy of novels: *Carnival* (1983), *The Infinite Rehearsal* (1987), and *The Four Banks of the River Space* (1990). In these novels Harris plays with the identity of the author, using editor figures who supposedly find texts rather than writing them. The presence of multiple implied voices makes univocal and definitive interpretation a difficult proposition. *Carnival* consists of a series of conversations between two characters, which leads to a London flat and back in time, along a spiritual journey. The narrative constructed in the process of the conversation blurs reality and imagination as well as history and fiction. It is an allegorical evocation of a carnival, structured as a Dantean descent. In *Carnival* and in the rest of the trilogy, Harris's characters discuss race, class, and gender, but the author is less interested in social history and anthropology than in the authenticity of the individual as a moral being. Nevertheless, Harris's fiction does question traditional and fixed ideas about race and gender. It also reveals Harrris's faith in the possibility of reconciling opposites.

Selected Work: *Palace of the Peacock* (1960, *El palacio del pavorreal,* translation into Spanish Delia Mateovic, 2003; *Palacio do Pavâo,* translation into Portuguese Carlos Felipe Moisés, 1990); *The Far Journey of Oudin* (1961); *The Whole Armour* (1962); *The Secret Ladder* (1963); *Heartland* (1964); *The Eye of the Scarecrow* (1965); *The Waiting Room* (1967); *Tumatumari* (1968); *Ascent to Omai* (1970); *Black Marsden* (1972); *Companions of the Day and Night* (1975); *Da Silva da Silva's Cultivated Wilderness* (1977); *Genesis of the Clowns* (1977); *The Tree of the Sun* (1978); *The Angel at the Gate* (1982); *Carnival* (1983); *The Guyana Quartet* (1985); *The Infinite Rehearsal* (1987); *The Four Banks of the River Space* (1990); *Resurrection at Sorrow Hill* (1993); *Jonestown* (1996); *The Dark Jester* (2001); *The Mask of the Beggar* (2003).

Hatoum, Milton [Biography] Brazilian novelist, essayist, and translator, he has been an active presence on the Brazilian literary scene since the late 1980s. A child of early twentieth-century Lebanese immigrants, he has published three novels that deal with his ethnic background as a Lebanese-Brazilian writer. Born in the Amazon region in the city of Manaus in 1952, he began writing poetry and short fiction in the 1970s, going to France in 1980 to study Latin American literature in Paris (Sorbonne, Paris III) after studying architecture in São Paulo. In 1967 he left Manaus for Brasilia, and then spent the 1970s in São Paulo. His childhood experience in Manaus left a permanent mark, and he still refers to the importance of the oral tradition of the Amazonian region in his own understanding of the production of fiction. At the same time, he considers the fact that he left Manaus at the age of fifteen a decisive factor in his life experience as a writer. In France he became an informed reader of both Latin American and French literatures as well as a lifetime disciple of Flaubert. In 1984 he returned to Brazil from France and taught French literature at several universities. He currently lives in São Paulo, where he writes and occasionally gives public lectures.

Hatoum's first two novels, *Relato de um Certo Oriente* (1989, *The Tree of the Seventh Heaven*) and *Dois Irmãos* (2000, *The Brothers*), have won the most prestigious prize in Brazil, the Prêmio Jabuti. With his interests in human relationships, ethnic history, and the past, he uses a minimalist literary language reflective of his readings of writers such as Flaubert and the Brazilians Machado de Assis and Graciliano Ramos. He has also written essays on another major Brazilian writer who is significant for his own work: the canonical early twentieth-century writer Euclides da Cunha who lived in the Amazon region for a year and wrote about some of that experience. Both da Cunha and the Brazilian novelist Pedro Nava invoke memory to rewrite the past, a key element of Hatoum's fiction. Hatoum stands out as one of the most accomplished Brazilian novelists to appear on the scene in the latter part of the twentieth century and one of the most successful writers of his generation.

His novels evoke a specific past of Brazil, but the past has a special meaning for Hatoum: memory is the only challenge to the past, according to the author. He attempts to find this special meaning by means of an image, oral tradition, or literary tradition. In his first novel, *Relato de um Certo Oriente*, Hatoum begins his family saga with focus on a suffering mother; in this case, she endures the tragic loss of a son. He uses a first-person narrator whose story is continually affected by the direct and indirect presence of other voices. The novel is structured around the return of a son to his Lebanese family in the city of Manaus. Hatoum portrays an exotic and surprising fictional world that some readers might associate with the magical realism of the Spanish American novel. *Dois Irmãos* also uses a return as a central act in the fiction, but in this case it is the return of one of two twin brothers from Lebanon to Brazil after WWI. He also uses a first-person narrator in this work, but now the narrative voice itself remains more consistently and visibly in control of the story than in *Relato de um Certo Oriente*. *Dois Irmãos* tells the story of two generations of a Lebanese immigrant family, focusing on a pair of twin brothers, Yaqub and Omar. The twelve-chapter book deals with the interactions of the family whose members live in Manaus (the main setting) and São Paulo. As in *Relato de um Certo Oriente*, the mother is also an important figure: in a two-page introductory section, the mother Zana leaves Manaus and in the process relives her original departure from her village in Lebanon. She awaits the return of her son Omar, but at the end of this introductory section she is nearing her death. She also wonders if her two sons have made peace with one another, an early indicator of an intense conflict and central tension of the novel. The novel goes back in time as far as 1914, when the early members of the family opened their first restaurant in Manaus. In both novels the first-person narrator is an entity slightly outside the inner circle of the families involved. In addition to exploring family relationships and the past as memory, Hatoum is interested in subjects such as identity, origins, and aging. He currently lives in São Paulo, Brasil, where he writes and occasionally lectures on literary topics.

Selected Work: *Relato de um Certo Oriente* (1989, *The Tree of the Seventh Heaven*, translation Ellen Watson, 1994); *Dois Irmãos* (2000, *The Brothers*, translation John Gledson, 2002); *Cinzas do Norte* (2005).

Heart of Aztlán (1976, by Rudolfo Anaya. Written in English. Berkeley: Justa) [**Novel**] The second novel in Anaya's widely read New Mexican trilogy, *Heart of Aztlán* followed *Bless Me, Ultima*, the story of an indigenous folk healer's attempts to cure the psychological wounds of the protagonist. In *Heart of Aztlán* Anaya follows the travels of the protagonist, a journey that can be considered a mythic quest. This character's search for self-identity is part of a larger search for integration in his community. Anaya's context, however, is also social and political, as he suggests in his dedication: "This book is dedicated to the good people of Barlas . . . and to people everywhere who have struggled for freedom, dignity, and the right of self-determination." The protagonist climbs a mountain in search of the essence of Aztlán and then sets forth to liberate his people. The novel continues to recount his adolescent maturing process.

More than in his first novel, in *Heart of Azt-lán* Anaya attempts to balance spiritual needs with social circumstance. He ends it on an affirmative note, with the people marching as a voice is heard saying *adelante* ("forward"). Anaya's storytelling strategies and affirmations link him directly to the master for many Chicano writers, the Colombian Gabriel García Márquez.

Heath, Roy [Biography] Caribbean novelist, short story writer and essayist, he is a major writer from the only Anglophone nation of the South American continent, Guyana (formerly British Guiana). He grew up in Guyana as a child and emigrated to Great Britain in his early twenties. Health writes of both the colonial and the postcolonial experience in Guyana, which gained independence from Great Britain in 1968. He writes of the forlornness individuals feel in the context of social malaise.

In his novels, *From the Heat of the Day* (1979) and *Shadows Round the Moon* (1990), this individual and collective malaise is evident. The characters in *From the Heat of the Day* suffer from a social and political fate from which there is no escape. It is the story of a young postal worker of working-class and humble origins who marries a more sophisticated middle-class woman from the major city, Georgetown. Eventually, alienation and family conflict become a problem for the couple, and the marriage becomes akin to death. The young man seeks escape from the marriage with prostitutes and an affair with the maid, eventually growing so alienated that he loses his job. In the end the characters have few redeeming qualities. In his memoir-novel *Shadows Round the Moon* Heath offers reminiscences of colonial life and Caribbean culture. His reproductions of Guayanese dialect, as well as his descriptions of the Creole (black), Hindu, and Muslim communities are noteworthy.

Selected Work: *A Man Come Home* (1974); *The Murderer* (1978); *From the Heat of the Day* (1979); *Genetha* (1981); *One Generation* (1981); *Kwaku or the Man Who Could Not Keep His Mouth Shut* (1982); *Orealla* (1984); *Shadows Round the Moon* (1990); *The Shadow Bride* (1991); *The Ministry of Hope* (1997).

Heker, Liliana [Biography] Argentine novelist, short story writer, and essayist born in 1943, she began writing in the 1960s. She has edited two literary magazines, *El Escarabajo de Oro* and *El Ornitorrinco*. She began publishing short fiction in the 1960s and published her first volume of stories, *Los que vieron la zarza*, in 1966. In addition to the collections of stories *Acuario* (1972), *Un resplandor que se apagó en el mundo* (1977), and *Las peras del mal* (1982), she has collected her complete stories in the volume *Los hordes del real* (1991).

Her first novel, *Zona de clivaje* (1986, Zone of cleavage), deals with the complex relationship between a young student and a well-known and narcissistic intellectual. Heker explores the depths of human emotions in the context of human relationships.

Selected Work: *Zona de clivaje* (1986); *El fin de la historia* (1996); *La crueldad de la vida* (2001).

Hernández, Felisberto [Biography] Uruguayan short story writer and novelist, he was born in Montevideo in 1902 and earned a reputation as a short story writer who cultivates his own very special version of the fantastic. Before becoming a writer, he was a concert pianist in the 1920s and 1930s and performed in various cities of Uruguay and in Buenos Aires. His knowledge of avant-garde music is one source for his writing. Between 1925 and 1931 he published four short and modest books without book jackets; the author maintained that his books were presented without covers because they were open and free. In 1929 he published a book with a title reflecting this interest: *Libro sin tapas* (Book without covers).

Hernández was best known for his inventive and fantastic short stories, which, along with Jorge Luis Borges's *Ficciones*, represented a paradigm shift for Latin American fiction of the 1940s and 1950s. In 1942 Hernández gained recognition in Latin America for his volume *Por los tiempos de Clemente Colling* (The times of Clemente Colling) a memoir-novel. He followed with the collection *Nadie encendía las lámparas* (1947, No one lit the lights). His novel, *Tierras de la memoria* (Lands of memory), published posthumously in 1965, is a humorous series of sketches that have invited critics to compare him to the Mexican writer José Arreola. More of a classic oral storyteller than a traditional novelist, he relates his stories in the first person in *Tierras de la memoria*, telling episodes from his childhood and adolescence. His use of point of view is often playful; at one point he refers to his own body in the third person, and his fingers refuse to follow his orders when he plays the piano.

Throughout his career Hernández placed together disparate and fragmented pieces of fiction from sources he claimed not to know; freed from the restrictions of the known genres of history and the novel, he pursued self-exploration and liberation. These strategies made him a master of metafiction, of a poetics of the unknown.

His iconoclastic and humorous short stories appeared in a series of volumes from the 1920s to the 1950s. His fantastic stories of the 1940s played a significant role in the reaffirmation of the right of invention for the Latin American writer in general. Along with Borges, he was a pioneer innovator. His stories appeared in English translation as *Piano Stories* (1993, translation Luis Harss, from the original Spanish *Nadie encendía las lámparas*, 1947). Like Borges, he never published a novel, but his impact on the Latin American novel was comparable to that of Borges. Hernández died in 1963, and his legacy has grown over the years, with editions of his work appearing in several languages in addition to English. A volume of selected short fiction appeared in Spanish in 1990 under the title *Narraciones incompletes*. This volume offers a sampler of Hernández from every stage of his career.

Selected Work: *Libro sin tapas* (1929); *Por los tiempos de Clemente Colling* (1942); *Tierras de la memoria* (1965); *Narraciones incompletas* (1990); *Nadie encendía las lámparas* (1947, *Piano Stories*, translation Luis Harss, 1993).

Hernández, Luisa Josefina [Biography]
Mexican novelist, short story writer, playwright, and translator, she has been central to the Mexican cultural scene since the 1960s. Born in Mexico City in 1928, she studied theater at the National University in Mexico City (UNAM), was awarded a Rockefeller Fellowship to study theater at Columbia University, has taught theater at the university level, and in 1991 was the first woman to be awarded the title *Profesora Emérita* at the UNAM. In addition to her distinguished career as an academic, an essayist, and a playwright, she has published a substantial body of fiction. Her life's work includes over forty plays and sixteen novels.

Her first novel, *El lugar donde crece la hierba* (1959, The place where the grass grows) emphasized the creation of atmosphere and relations among the characters. *Los palacios desiertos* (1963, The deserted palaces) deals with the relationship between two characters who are ill-adjusted to life. *Nostalgia de Troya* (1970, Nostalgia of Troy) is another of her intimate portrayals of relationships. Her fiction tends to portray a small number of characters dealing with issues of authenticity and personal identity. She was awarded a prestigious national literary prize (Premio Xavier Villarrutia) for her novel *Apocalipsis cum figuris* (1982, Apocalypse cum figuris).

Selected Work: *El lugar donde crece la hierba* (1959); *La plaza Santo* (1962); *Los palacios desiertos* (1963); *La primera batalla* (1963); *La cólera secreta* (1964); *La noche exquisita* (1965); *El valle que elegimos* (1965); *La memoria de Amadís* (1967); *Nostalgia de Troya* (1970); *Los trovadores* (1973); *Apostasía* (1978); *Las fuentes ocultas* (1979); *Apocalipsis cum figuris* (1982); *La cabalgata* (1988); *Almeida danzón* (1989); *En una noche como ésta* (1994).

Hijuelos, Oscar [Biography] Caribbean/Latino/American novelist and short story writer, he was born in New York City in 1951 of Cuban parents and studied at the City College of City University of New York, where he received a BA and an MA in English. He studied under the tutelage of American writer Donald Barthelme and later participated in the prestigious Breadloaf Writers Conference. His awards include the American Academy in Rome Fellowship, the National Endowment for the Arts Fellowship (1985), and the Guggenheim Fellowship (1990).

Hijuelos became a noteworthy presence in the North American literary scene with his fictionalization of Cuban American culture and music with his novel *The Mambo King Plays Songs of Love* (1989). He has published five novels. As a Caribbean/Latino novelist writing in the English language in the United States, he shares linguistic and cultural issues with writers such as Ana Castillo in the United States, Rosario Ferré in Puerto Rico (writing in both English and Spanish), and Frank Martinus Arion in Curaçao (writing fiction in Dutch and poetry in Papimentu). Along with these writers, Hijuelos writes in the dominant language (in this case, English), but is occasionally affected by other languages and cultures, in this case by the Spanish spoken by the Caribbean population in the northeastern United States.

Selected Work: *The Mambo King Plays Songs of Love* (1989, *Los reyes del mambo tocan canciones de amor*, Spanish translation Alejandra García Reyes, 1996); *The Fourteen Sisters of Emilio Montez O'Brien* (1993, *Las catorce hermanas de Emilo Montez O'Brien*, 1994, Spanish translation Maribel de Juan); *Our House in the Last World* (1991, *Nuestra casa del fin del mundo*, Spanish translation Jordi Mustieles, 1991); *Mr. Ives' Christmas* (1996); *Empress of the Splendid Season* (2000, *La emperatriz de mis sueños*, Spanish translation Jaime Zulaika, 2001); *A Simple Habana Melody* (2003, *Una sencilla melodía habanera*, Spanish translation José Lucas Badue, 2003).

Hilda Furacão (1991, by Roberto Drummond. Written in Portuguese and untranslated. São Paulo: Siciliano) [**Novel**] Drummond blurs the boundaries between fiction and autobiography in this postmodern, playful, and nostalgic memoire of life in Brazil in the late 1950s and early 1960s. The narrator (an author figure named Roberto Drummond in the text) satirizes the political and religious establishment of the period, narrating from a "present" at the end of the twentieth century and often utilizing a lightly humorous critique of the pro-Cuban, pro–Che Guevara leftist movement in which he participated. The setting is the city of Belo Horizonte where the narrator-protagonist was a student who idolized politically "committed" writers, such as Jorge Amado and Graciliano Ramos, and belonged to the Young Communist Party. He becomes a militant student leader and reporter for a local newspaper. Belo Horizonte is also the setting for a former prostitute of the time, Hilda Furacão, who is demonized by middle-class women and the

Catholic Church. For the young men of Belo Horizonte, however, she is a legendary figure, even something of a myth. This playfully self-reflective text is considered to be more of a *brinquedo lúdico* (ludic game) than a novel by the narrator, who offers frequent digressions about literature, politics, and himself. At one point he even leaves most of the page blank for the reader's notes. A playful look at a period that represented an end to a traditional way of life for much of Brazil's middle class, this novel's satirical tone is as much a mockery of youthful militancy as it is of traditional and proper social mores in Brazil in the 1950s.

Hilst, Hilda [Biography] Brazilian novelist, poet, and playwright, she is one of the most innovative and challenging contemporary writers in Brazil. She has blurred genre boundaries with prose poetry writings that some critics associate with the postmodern. Hilst was an iconoclastic intellectual figure who assumed various roles in the different stages of her career. Early in her career, in the 1950s, she was known as a poet. In the 1960s she continued with her poetry but also became involved with the theater scene in São Paulo. In the 1970s and 1980s she continued writing poetry and plays but also began experimenting with short fiction written in a poetic mode. In her later years her erotically charged writing was considered pornographic by some traditional critics. In addition to her numerous books of poetry and theater, she published thirteen books of fiction.

Born in Jaú, São Paulo, in 1930, she studied law in São Paulo but soon thereafter committed herself to literature. She traveled to Europe and the United States in the 1950s and 1960s. Her early writings were in poetry, publishing the *Presaggio* (Foreshadower) in 1950 and winning prizes for her poems in the 1960s. In 1982 she was artist in residence at the Universidade Estadual de Campinas. Some critics have described this early writing as a mystical exercise or spiritual search.

Hilst began writing experimental fiction in the 1970s. Her book *Fluxo Floema* (1970) is an abstract and hermetic experiment with her own special prose poetry; she followed with another experimental book of fiction, *Qadós*, in 1973. Her novel *Cartas de um Sedutor* (1991, Letter from a seductor) is a more standard narrative; it is a first-person account of a male protagonist's love life. In the 1980s and 1990s she continued writing poetry and experimental fiction, publishing one of her fictional experiments under the title *Rutilo Nada* (Nothing Rutilo) in 1993. Several scholars have pointed to theosophical and surrealist elements in her fiction. In her later years she claimed to communicate with the dead and to have contact with extraterrestrial beings. She also received awards and recognition for her career, and translations of her work appeared in German and French. In 2000 an exposition of her work was organized in São Paulo by the architect Gisela Magalhães. Hilst is one of Brazil's major innovators of the post-WWII period, along with innovators such as Osman Lins, Clarice Lispector, and João Guimarães Rosa. She died in 2004.

Narrative: *O Vergudo* (1969); *Fluxo Floema* (1970); *Qadós* (1973, also appears under title *Kadosh*); *Júbilo Memória da Paixão* (1974); *Ficções* (1977); *Tu Não te Moves de Ti* (1980); *A Obscena Senhora D* (1982); *Com Meus Olhos de Cão e Outras Novelas* (1986); *O Caderno Rosa de Lori Lamby* (1990); *Contos D'escárnio/Textos Grotescos* (1990); *Cartas de um Sedutor* (1991); *Rutilo Nada* (1993); *Estar Sendo/Ter Sido* (1997); *Cascos e Carícias: Crônicas Reunidas* (2000); *Do Desejo* (1992); *Do Amor* (1999).

Hinojosa, Rolando [Biography] Chicano novelist, short story writer, and essayist, he is widely considered one of the foundational figures of the modern Chicano novel. Along with Miguel Mendes, Rudolfo Anaya, and Tomás Rivera, Hinojosa became visible through his early fiction in the 1970s. He gained international acclaim when he received the Casa de las Américas Prize. He writes of the common people of the south Texas border region where he grew up—the valley along the Rio Grande.

Born in Mercedes, Texas, in 1929, he is the son of a Mexican American father and an Anglo-American mother. On the Mexican side of the family, he belongs to a clan that arrived at the banks of the Rio Grande River from Santander, Spain, in the eighteenth century. He was interested in creative writing at an early age and won a writing contest in high school. Hinojosa completed his undergraduate studies at the University of Texas at Austin, although these studies were interrupted twice for military service, including a stint in Korea he later fictionalized. After completing his BS in Spanish literature in 1954, he taught for two years in high school in Brownsville; he began his creative writing at that time, after which he received an MA in Spanish at New Mexico Highlands University and a PhD in Spanish at the University of Illinois. After serving as professor and chair at Texas A and M University, he joined the faculty at the University of Texas at Austin, where he currently holds a named chair.

His lifelong project has been the rewriting of the history of the valley of the Rio Grande River, a project that has been identified as his Klail City cycle. Writing in the Faulknerian mode, Hinojosa has created a fictional Belken County and developed a series of multilayered historical novels rich in the region's history, culture, language, and oral tradition. Not a realist, he uses a modernist's eye for irony and humor that gives his writing his special mark. The novels in this Klail City cycle are *Estampas del Valle y otras obras* (1973, *Sketches of the Valley and Other Works,* 1977), *Klail City y sus alrededores* (1976), *Generaciones y semblanzas* (1977), *Korean Love Songs* (1978), *Mi querido Rafa* (1981, Dear Rafa), *Rites and Witnesses* (1982), *The Valley* (1983), and *Partners in Crime: A Rafe Buenrostro Mystery* (1985). With this cycle Hinojosa exhibits a desire for the "total" novel that characterized much of the writing the 1960s Boom writers in Latin America that he admires—García Márquez, Fuentes, Vargas Llosa, and Cortázar. In the 1970s and 1980s Hinojosa read and interacted with these writers, whom he met in a variety of settings in the United States, Cuba, and Mexico.

In *Klail City y sus alrededores* (Klail City Death Trip), Hinojosa affirms the human spirit and struggle of the Mexican Americans in Texas through the use of language and humor, often recalling similar affirmations in the early writing of García Márquez dealing with the common folk. Once again, workers and their families suffer, but they survive. This is the work most independent of Hinojosa's Klail City cycle and also the most innovative: it is an anthology of postmodern motifs, as told by four generations of storytellers. By receiving the prestigious Casa de las Américas Prize in Cuba for this work, Hinojosa expanded the borders of Chicano literature, which received little recognition in the United States and Latin America before the 1970s.

A hardcore modernist along the lines of William Faulkner and Carlos Fuentes, Hinojosa is well aware of more postmodern writing and, like Fuentes, occasionally engages playfully in the motifs and strategies of postmodern fiction. He currently lives in Austin, Texas, where he teaches and writes.

Selected Work: *Estampas del Valle y otras obras* (1973, *Sketches of the Valley and Other Works,* translation Gustavo Valadéz and

José Reyna, 1977); *Klail City y sus alrede-dores* (1976, Klail City Death Trip); *Genera-ciones y semblanzas* (1977); *Korean Love Songs* (1978); *Mi querido Rafa* (1981, *Dear Rafa/Mi querido Rafa*, bilingual edition, 2005); *Rites and Witnesses* (1982); *The Valley* (1983); *Partners in Crime: A Rafe Buen-rostro Mystery* (1985); *Claros varones de Belken* (1986; *Fair Gentlemen of Belken County,* translation Julia Cruz, 1986); *Friends of Becky* (1989, *Amigos de Becky,* 1991); *The Useless Servants* (1993); *Ask a Policeman* (1998).

Hiriart, Hugo [Biography] Mexican novel-ist, short story writer, playwright, essayist, and screenwriter, he has been active in the Mexican cultural scene since the early 1980s. His fiction is marked by humor based on hyperbole and is often of a satirical tone. He was born in Mexico City in 1942, stud-ied philosophy at the National University in Mexico City (UNAM), and was awarded a Guggenheim Fellowship in 1983. Early in his career, in the 1970s, he dedicated his ef-forts mostly to theater, although some of his iconoclastic fiction began to appear in the 1970s as well. His particular brand of inven-tive and postmodern fiction is not easily comparable to the main currents of writing in Mexico and Latin America. His work is more erudite and historical than the writ-ings of the Onda in Mexico. Writing against the grain, his first novel, *Galaor* (1972), is a historical piece that evokes both classical writing and the tradition of the medieval novel of chivalry.

Hiriart has published two books of fic-tion that can be called highly inventive narratives or experimental novels. The first, *Disertación sobre las telarañas* (1980, Dis-sertation on the spider web), is a discontin-uous series of short fictions and essays, and the second, *Cuadernos de Gofa* (1981, Gofa's notebooks), is a wildly inventive, entertain-ing, and discontinuous set of notebooks written by an erudite fictional professor with encyclopedic impulses. His volume ti-tled *Discutibles fantasmas* (2001, Debatable ghosts) is a humorous set of reflections on a wide gamut of unrelated subjects, from the aesthetics of poetry to the flight of flies and the perfect goal in a soccer match. His novel *La destrucción de todas las cosas* (1992, The destruction of everything) pres-ents an apocalyptic vision of the conquest of Mexico by a foreign power. It is a cruel, violent, and entertaining satire of the PRI regime in its final years of power in Mexico. His recent *El actor se prepara* (2004, The actor prepares) is a seven-part novel—a de-tective fiction and a treatment of the theme of religion. The mixture of the spy thriller and theological meditation make it an ex-ceptional example of the hybrid. The main character contemplates the possibility of a life of isolation at the same time that he participates in life.

Selected Work: *Galaor* (1972); *Disert-ación sobre las telarañas* (1980); *Cuadernos de Gofa* (1981); *La destrucción de todas las cosas* (1992); *El actor se prepara* (2004).

Hodge, Merle [Biography] Caribbean nov-elist and essayist, she was born in Trinidad in 1944. In the 1940s she grew up in a soci-ety with three clear class divisions: a very small white elite, a small mulatto middle class, and a large African underclass of the underprivileged and the impoverished. In her major novel, *Crick Crack Monkey* (1970), Hodge describes what it is like growing up in this colonial Trinidadian society as a member of the small and privileged middle class. The author has explained that when she wrote this work she did not yet know the word *feminism* and was only vaguely aware of the women's movement. She was aware of strong women figures, however, and these were the individuals whom she most admired. Since her childhood she was impressed with women who did not accept their place in Caribbean society, refusing to pattern their lives after the rules set down by Trinidadian society. As an adult and as a writer, Hodge believes in the power of the written word to transform the world.

Hodge began writing for the same fundamental reason that the Peruvian Mario Vargas Llosa did: as a protest against society. *Crick Crack Monkey* is a picaresque-type work in which the protagonist tells her story while describing all three classes of Trinidadian society. This character strives to move from her indigenous Afro-Trinidadian culture to the middle class—where she suffers alienation. It is a story of psychological disintegration. Writing on topics that make her comparable to Caribbean writers Edwidge Danticat and Jamaica Kincaid, Hodge creates with a Caribbean consciousness of her positioning as an African and as a woman.

Selected Work: *Crick Crack Monkey* (1970); *The Life of Laetitia* (1993).

Honduras [Nation] This Central American nation lived the twentieth century at the mercy of foreign banana companies at the same time that well over half the population is one of the most impoverished in Latin America and the Caribbean. U.S. troops used Honduras as a base for the Contra war against the Sandinistas in Nicaragua; since then Honduras has suffered the destruction of agricultural land as well as an increase in drug trafficking, gang warfare, and prostitution.

Honduras has a more noteworthy tradition in short fiction than in the novel per se. The major short story writer of the 1940s and 1950s was Víctor Cáceres Lara (born 1915). The most visible contemporary novelists have been Horacio Castellenos Mora, Ramán Amaya Amador, Julio Escoto, and Roberto Quesada. The work of Castellanos Mora has circulated through-out Latin America in Spanish and Quesada has appeared in English translation.

Hopscotch (See *Rayuela* by Julio Cortázar) **[Novel]**

Hora da Estrela, A (1977, *The Hour of the Star,* by Clarice Lispector. Translation by Giovanni Pontiero. Manchester: Carcanet, 1986) **[Novel]** Written in the last stage of Lispector's career, this novel offers a synthesis of much of her thought and writing as it points toward her death. A male narrator tells of eight other characters, including the protagonist, Macabéia, an orphan from the northeastern state of Algaoas who attempts to escape her humdrum existence with a love affair and fantasies of imitating the life of celebrities like Greta Garbo and Marilyn Monroe. Thus, the "star" in the title refers to the movie stars that are Macabéia's idols. Her banal life is matched by the narrator's focus on everyday objects and a straightforward style using short sentences. The urban setting is Rio de Janeiro; the city seems to work in opposition to Macabéia's life and desires. When she vomits blood, it seems to evoke the red lips of Marilyn Monroe and serve as a central metaphor of the book's movement toward the protagonist's death. The protagonist's agony in living parallels the agony of the act of writing in *A Hora da Estrela*. This novel is also a dialogue with a wide range of texts, from the Brazilian classic *Os Sertões* and Lispector's own *Agua Viva* to numerous texts of international postmodern fiction.

Hora dos ruminantes, A (1966, *The Three Trials of Manirema,* by José J. Veiga. Translation by Pamela G. Bird. New York: Knopf, 1970) **[Novel]** The most renowned novel of a highly productive Brazilian novelist, this work has overtones of Faulkner and García Márquez and his magical world of Macondo. Written in a terse, simple style, it consists of three parts: "The Arrival," "The Time of the Dogs," and "The Time of the Oxen." Each of the three describes a borderline and absurd situation: in the first the arrival of some "strangers" to a small town, in the second the presence of dogs, and in the third the invasion of oxen. Inexplicably, these threatening outsiders depart in a manner that is as mysterious as their arrival. A Kafkaesque quality of the fictional world makes it both as attractive and as dangerous as the pistol that one character inexplicably holds under his shirt. Like the Mexican Juan Rulfo and the García Márquez of his early fiction, Veiga is a minimalist whose language suggests a mythic or allegorical reading of the text.

Hour of the Star, The (See *Hora da Estrela, A,* by Clarice Lispector) [**Novel**]

Ibañez, Jaime [**Biography**] Colombian novelist, he is associated with psychological fiction published in Colombia in the 1940s and 1950s. His novel *Cada voz lleva su angustia* (1944, Every voice has its anguish), however, deals with an external and not a strictly psychological matter: the erosion of land and the effects this problem has on the workers of the land. When Ibáñez began writing fiction in the 1940s, Colombian literature was one of the most tradition-bound in Latin America, and the dominant mode of writing was realist and folkloric, with an emphasis on regional values. Modernist aesthetics from the United States and Europe had exercised little impact on Colombian literature, which was still imitative of the canonic *La vorágine* (1924, *The Vortex*) by José Eustacio Rivera

or the urban social protest work that was being published by José Antonio Osorio Lizarazo. Thus Ibáñez's interest in urban and psychological fiction—with its focus on the middle class—was something of a novelty in Colombia in the early 1940s. *Cada voz lleva su angustia* was an effort to break with the predominant modes.

Selected Work: Cada voz lleva su angustia (1944); *Donde moran los sueños* (1947); *No volverá la aurora* (1948); *Un hueco en el aire* (1968).

Ibargoyen, Saúl [**Biography**] Uruguayan novelist, short story writer, journalist, translator, and poet, he is well known in both Uruguay and Mexico, since he wrote in political exile in Mexico from 1976 to 1984, and has been prolific—publishing over thirty books. He writes on a broad range of topics, from the standards of social injustice and violence to his concern over the loss of diversity caused by globalization. He is known for exploring linguistic boundaries between Spanish and Portuguese. In his recent book of poetry, *Grito de perro*, he questions processes of globalization and suggests the breakdown of classic divisions between species. He believes that identification with animal species (such as dogs) places us in a better position to resist globalization.

Ibargoyen was born in Montevideo in 1930 and began writing poetry in his youth, publishing his first volumes of poetry in the 1950s. In Montevideo he directed the poetry magazine *Aquí poesía* as part of the *Generación de Crisis* (generation of crisis) in Uruguay. He has published a complete collection of his short stories, *Cuento a cuento* (2001). *Toda la tierra* (2002, All the land) is his fourth novel, and it continues his border saga of Uruguay/Brazil, which he had begun with *La sangre interminable* (1982, The endless blood) and continued with *Noche de espaldas* (1987, Night of spears) and *Soñar la muerte* (1993, Dream death).

In his best-known novel, *La sangre interminable*, he experiments with several aspects of the novel, with a minimal description of the characters and a scanty plot. The narrator and the characters make vague references to the assassination of four characters who seem to be ordinary people resisting the order of the elite. This nonlinear text moves from one narrative voice to another. One of the most noteworthy aspects of this text is the use of a "border" Spanish that shows the influence of Portuguese. Uruguayans who live along the border with Brazil speak a *portuñol* that is sometimes reflected in this text.

Selected Work: La sangre interminable (1982); *Noche de espaldas* (1987); *Soñar la muerte* (1993); *Toda la tierra* (2002).

Ibarguengoitia, Jorge [Biography] Mexican novelist, playwright, short story writer, essayist, and journalist, he was a major intellectual in Mexico in the second half of the twentieth century, and his fiction is read throughout the Hispanic world. Much of his fiction is closely related to Latin American *testimonio*, crime fiction, or both. He was born in Guanajuato in 1928, studied engineering and literature at the National University in Mexico City (UNAM), and died in an airplane accident in Madrid in 1983. In his distinguished career he was awarded numerous literary prizes and recognitions in Mexico; two of his international recognitions were the Guggenheim Fellowship and Cuba's prestigious Casa de las Américas Prize (1963). In the 1950s and early 1960s he was active both in theater and teaching at several universities, and in his total career he wrote thirteen plays. He was interested in detective fiction, and several of his novels are closely related to this genre. His novel *Dos crímenes* (1979,

Two crimes) fits squarely in this tradition and is divided into two parts. The first is narrated by Marcos González, who escapes the police and takes refuge in the home of his uncle, where the inhabitants' reactions lead him to the crime. The second follows the British model of the classic crime novel: the courteous detective attempts to discover the author of the crime, using logic.

Of his six novels, the most recognized were *Los relámpagos de agosto* (1964, The August lightning), *Estas ruinas que ves* (1975, These ruins that you see), and *Las muertas* (1977, The dead women). In *Estas ruinas que ves* the ruins of the title are those of a decadent small town. The novel consists of chapters that can stand as independent short stories about the town, vignettes that can be read as a light parody of nineteenth-century *costumbrismo*. The main characters are the rural people of this village, who leave for the capital never to return, as well as a young intellectual who comes back to the town after having been educated in Mexico City. In addition to the parody of literary precedents, Ibarguengoitia is critical of social injustice.

Selected Work: Los relámpagos de agosto (1964); *Maten al león* (1969); *Estas ruinas que ves* (1975); *Las muertas* (1977); *Dos crímenes* (1979); *Los pasos de López* (1982).

Icaza, Jorge [Biography] Ecuadorian novelist, he was considered a leading writer of the Latin American *indigenista* movement. He was born in 1906 and died in 1978. His novel *Huasipungo* (1934) has become a classic work of Spanish American *indigenismo*, which intended to portray the indigenous groups in a manner that would be realistic in sociological and anthropological terms, as opposed to the romanticized portrayals of Native Americans by previous generations. Indeed, Icaza did studies in sociology and anthropology.

A social protest novel, *Huasipungo* deals with the brutal exploitation of the indigenous population by the dominant white elite of Ecuador. The writer sets forth the classic triangle of exploitation in Latin America, with the collaboration of the government, the landowners, and the leaders of the Catholic Church. Icaza shocks readers into reacting against those who exploit other human beings. The author successfully humanizes his characters more than is often the case of typical novels of social protest; he is a master of irony, describing a *patrón*, Don Alfonso, who sends his Indians workers to labor in the swamps even though he openly admits that some of them will die. He portrays the protagonist, Andrés, with fuller human dimensions. Using interior and exterior presentation of the characters and their conflicts, Icaza successfully compels the reader to be indignant over their situation.

Selected Work: Huasipungo (1934, *Huasipungo,* translation Mervyn Savill, 1962); *Huairapamushcas* (1948).

In the Castle of My Skin (1953, by George Lamming. Written in English. New York: McGraw Hill, 1954) **[Novel]** One of the classic modern novels of the English-speaking Caribbean, it has been read widely across the cultural borders of the region. Lamming was reared in a village in Barbados, and he lived in Barbados from his birth in 1927 to 1950, at which point he emigrated to England; much of the experience related in the novel is autobiographical: the coming of age of a young boy and of an island society. This was a formative period for Barbados, as the traditional rural society was being modernized. The novel begins with the protagonist's seventh birthday, and the voice of the island is filtered through the figures of Ma and Pa, who articulate broader historical concerns going beyond the immediate world of the boy.

The novel also begins, then, with a critique of British colonialism as represented in an educational system that taught only British history and in which the schoolmaster is dismissed for sexual misconduct. Lamming then proceeds to show how the British arranged land sales to deprive the original inhabitants of their traditional rights. The totality of these events leads to the political riots of the 1940s in Barbados and points to the eventual independence of Barbados from Great Britain. The synthesis of personal experience, national history, and political critique make *In the Castle of My Skin* comparable to novels such as Fuentes's *La muerte de Artemio Cruz* and several of García Márquez's early novels.

Indigénisme (Caribbean) [Topic] The *indigénisme* of the French Caribbean differs considerably from Spanish American *indigenismo* and Brazilian *indigenismo*. *Indigénisme* was a cultural and political movement of the French Caribbean; it developed in Haiti as a response to the U.S. marine occupation in 1915. Writers such as Jean Price-Mars argued for the ideological base of *indigénisme*, but most scholars considered it more a poetic vision than a doctrine based on history or politics. Those who argued in favor of the poetic vision felt that the poets would be the keepers of knowledge. *Indigénisme* offered a critique of the decadent values of the West and was a celebration of Caribbean folk culture. An anti-American and anti-Enlightenment movement, *indigénisme* is unique in being based on nativist thought originating entirely in the Caribbean. Like Spanish American *indigenismo*, it was at its apogee in the 1930s.

Indigenismo (Spanish American) [Topic] Spanish American *indigenismo* differs considerably from the *indigénisme* of the

French Caribbean and Brazilian *indigenismo*. Mexican writers Mauricio Magdaleno and Rosario Castellanos, the Peruvian writers José María Arguedas and Ciro Alegría, as well as the Ecuadorian Jorge Icaza are generally recognized as the modern masters of *indigenista* fiction, but this writing dates back to the 1930s. In the 1930s and 1940s the Spanish American *indigenista* movement in the novel was spearheaded by Jorge Icaza and Ciro Alegría. Unlike nineteenth-century *indianismo* (which offered a romantic and idealized portrayal of the Indians), Spanish American *indigenismo* underscored an anthropologically sound and socially just representation of the indigenous population. These were novels of social protest, written in a realist mode that often denounced the classic triangle of power used to exploit the impoverished indigenous groups: the Catholic Church, the government, and the white elite who were the landowners.

Two of the more successful novelists of the *indigenista* tradition were Rosario Castellanos of Mexico and José María Arguedas of Peru, both of whom lived inside and outside of the Native American cultures about which they wrote. They have also written novels that avoid many of the clichés of more classic *indigenista* fictions. Castellanos lived her childhood and some of her adult life in Chiapas, Mexico, where she was in close proximity to the Chamula Indians of that region. Thus, even though she wrote as an outsider, she was relatively well informed. Arguedas actually grew up bilingual (Spanish and Quechua) in an Indian village, leaving it in his adolescence to fully join the white and *mestizo* society of Lima. In *Los ríos profundos* he communicates an indigenous vision of language, culture, and society in the Spanish language, based on his childhood experience. All in all, Castellanos's *Oficio de tinieblas* and Arguedas's *Los ríos profundos* are widely considered two of the most accomplished texts for the modern reader of the *indigenista* vein.

Other major works of the *indigenista* movement in Spanish America were Mauricio Magdaleno's *El resplandor* (1937, Sunburst, 1944), Gregorio López y Fuentes's *El indio* (1935, *El Indio/The Indian*, 1937), Ciro Alegría's *La serpiente de oro* (1935, *The Golden Serpent*, 1963), and José María Arguedas's *Yawar fiesta* (1940, *Yawar fiesta*, 1985). Other less prominent contributors to *indigenismo* include the Colombian César Uribe Piedrahita, author of the novel *Toá* (1934).

Inventando que sueño (1968, Inventing that I dream, by José Agustín. Written in Spanish and untranslated. Mexico: Joaquín Mortiz) [**Novel**] Along with Manuel Puig's *La traición de Rita Hayworth* (1968) and Humberto Costantini's *Háblenme de Funes* (1970), this was one of the most experimental novels to appear in Latin America in the late 1960s. As was the strategy of Puig and Costantini, Agustín leaves the reader with the task of organizing and associating a set of apparently disparate narratives. *Inventando que sueño* (Inventing that I dream) consists of four narratives (which the author calls "a drama in four acts"), some of which have appeared in anthologies of short stories. The work's unity is not to be found in its plot or themes, but in a comic tone that assures the reader that an absurd world is at least consistently entertaining. Among the entertainments in this book, the story "Cuál es la Onda" is one of the best examples: a young couple spends the evening wandering from one hotel to another in Mexico City, entertaining themselves and the reader with their indifference to almost everything and their satire of established norms. They are 1960s counterculture adolescents, and their spoken Spanish is replete with the colloquialisms of their generation and the U.S. English language of drugs and rock-and-roll.

Isla de Cundeamor (2000, *Island of Cundeamor,* by René Vásquez Díaz. Translated by David E. Davis. Pittsburgh: Latin American Literary Review Press, 2000) [**Novel**] A Cuban exile living in Sweden in recent years, Vásquez Díaz develops the exile theme in a novel with a fast-moving plot. Two story lines tell the experiences of Cuban exiles in Miami. In one the wife of a demented immigrant has an affair with the owner of a Cuban restaurant where she works as a waitress. After that job and the affair end, she befriends a homeless black woman who is eventually killed. Thus the protagonist ends up working with a street-wise pawnbroker and junk-store owner, a man she hopes to commit to a permanent relationship, but fails. The second story line relates the intrigues of a private investigation firm that also deals in Cuban contraband. This story line also develops some romantic liaisons, and eventually this story line connects with the other. One character contemplates writing a novel about all this, with the thought that it will be an "untruthful" and "chaotic" book. The Island of Cundeamor serves as a metaphor for another Cuba, a false one.

Ivo, Lêdo [**Biography**] Brazilian novelist, poet, short story writer, and essayist, he was born in Maceió, the setting for most of his fiction, in 1924. After receiving his early education in Recife, he moved to Rio de Janeiro in 1943, where he worked as a journalist and received a law degree in 1949. He gained national attention in Brazil in 1944 with his first book of poems, *As Imaginacões* (Imaginations), and soon became a prominent member of a group of poets identified as the generation of 1945. It was a group interested in breaking most of the established norms for 1940s Brazilian po-

etry. Since then, he has been prolific as a poet and as a translator of fiction.

Lêdo's novel *As Alianças* (1947, The alliances), a conventional yet psychologically probing work, was awarded the Prêmio Graça Aranha by the Brazilian Academy of Letters. His novel *Ninho de Cobras* (1973, *Snake's Nest*) won a national prize (Prêmio Nacional Walmap); in this novel an unreliable narrator tells a mystery story. The author has explained that under a dictatorship all narrators are unreliable, making this novel implicitly much more political than would be the case had it been written elsewhere. The author has also called this work a "transgressional" text that he considers more of a "hybrid" genre than a novel. It is set in the early 1940s during the Novo Estado ("new state") of Brazil (the semifascist government of Getúlio Vargas, 1930–1945). In the novel, life in the city of Maceió is basically a representation of conditions under the government of Vargas. Since the novel was published under a later dictatorship, readers have found parallels between the two. Maceió is a town of violence and corruption, and at the end the unreliable narrator leaves the reader unsure if the final actions lead to a murder.

Selected Work: As Alianças (1947); *Ninho de Cobras* (1973, *Snake's Nest*, translation Jon M. Tolman).

Jacobs, Bárbara [**Biography**] Mexican novelist, short story writer, and translator, she has been an active fiction writer since the early 1980s. She was born in 1947 in Mexico City, completed high school in Canada, and earned a degree in psychology at the National University in Mexico City (UNAM). She has participated in government-sponsored writing workshops (Centro de Escritores Mexicanos) and has taught both English and French at universities in Mexico City. Her first volumes of short fiction were *Un justo acuerdo* (1979, A just agreement) and *Doce cuentos en contra* (1982, Twelve oppositional stories).

Jacobs's first novel, *Las hojas muertas* (1987, The dead leaves), partially autobiographical, is the story of her father's experience of immigration to Mexico from Spain, rearing a family, dealing with Fascism in Spain, and confronting old age. This first novel received a prestigious national literary prize in Mexico, the Premio Xavier Villaurrutia. The fictions of *Escrito en el tiempo* (1985, Written in time) are in the form of letters written to *Time* magazine but never sent; these narratives have been read as a novel. *Vida con mi amigo* (1994, Life with my friend) is a novel of mostly dialogue concerning a couple's relationship with literature and each other. *Adiós humanidad* (1999, Good-bye humanity), Jacobs's most experimental text, consists of the narrative fragments of several characters and has numerous metafictional qualities.

Selected Work: Las hojas muertas (1987); *Las siete fugas de Saab, alias el Rizos* (1992); *Vida con mi amigo* (1994); *Adiós, humanidad* (1999).

Jamaica [Nation] Jamaica's rich intellectual tradition includes political activitists and writers within the British Commonwealth who preceded the island's independence in 1962. Thus political activists such as Marcus Garvey of the 1920s and novelists such as V. S. Reid were important contributors to a black nationalist awareness in Jamaica. Reid's novels offer a historically based critique of the colonial legacy of slavery. An early case of a Caribbean (or West Indian) perspective on race appeared in his novel *New Day* (1949), in which he makes the claim for a role for a former slave in the new society. In the 1960s poetry, narrative with popular speech, and music flourished in Jamaica as part of this construction of a new nation. The BBC radio program *Caribbean Voices* offered an important platform for writers.

In addition to Reid, major novelists from Jamaica in the post-1945 period have been Erna Brodber, Michelle Cliff, Roger Mais, and Andrew Salkey. Salkey was born in Panama City but lived in Jamaica and wrote about the island.

Jandra, Leonardo Da (Leonardo Breogán Cohen) [Biography] Mexican novelist and essayist, he is an anomaly in the Mexican literary scene, operating at the margins of the literary and academic world. He was born in Pichucalco (state of Chiapas) in 1951 and was educated abroad, going to Spain at the age of fifteen and doing his undergraduate studies at the University of Santiago de Compostela in Galicia and in Madrid. He received his doctorate in philosophy at the University of Santiago de Compostela, after which he returned to Mexico to complete a doctorate in the philosophy of mathematics at the National University in Mexico City (UNAM). After establishing contact with writers such as Gustavo Sainz and José Agustín, he left Mexico City for the village of Huatulco (state of Oaxaca) and was cofounder of the Calmecac Chinanteco, a research center dedicated to the recovery of pre-Hispanic culture in Mexico and its application to contemporary life. His writing is experimental, conceptual, and, like that of Mexican novelist Hugo Hiriart, enough of an anomaly to make it difficult to place within the main currents of Mexican fiction of recent decades.

Da Jandra's first three novels consist of a trilogy (titled *Entrecruzamientos*) all dealing with the same basic situation, with two characters in the tropics, the one an elderly

Spaniard and the other a young Mexican student who has just completed his studies in philosophy. They discuss the concept of *mexicanidad* in a broad historical context of Western culture, with particular focus on this idea within the cultural traditions of Spain and Mexico. The individual volumes of the trilogy appeared in 1986, 1988, and 1990. Da Jandra continues to explore the origins of Mexican culture and its relationship with Spain in his later fiction. Along with the Mexican Homero Aridjis and the Argentine Mempo Giardinelli, Da Jandra is one of the few writers in Latin America who expresses his ecological interests in fiction.

Selected Work: *Entrecuzamientos I* (1986); *Entrecruzamientos II* (1988); *Entrecruzamientos III* (1990); *Samahua* (1997); *En el corazón de un sol herido* (2000).

Joana and Louisa Will Come Home (1980, by Erna Brodber. Written in English. London: Villier, 1980) **[Novel]** Brodber has written essays and fiction about race and class issues for Africans in Jamaica. The protagonist of this novel, Nellie Richmond, grows up in an idyllic world; she feels safe within fertile nature and a protective family. As she reaches adolescence, however, her world begins to fall apart because of her race and class, and soon her existence is under attack. Nellie loses her psychic balance and becomes sickly, and is often described as "cold" or "frozen." She begins her journey to recovery when she connects to Baba, a Rastafarian who is a positive, calming presence and even a Christ-like figure. Nellie slowly recovers her health and is returned to health or transformed from a symbolic death to life. This complex novel, with ongoing flashbacks, develops from fragmentation to wholeness.

Jaramillo Agudelo, Darío [Biography] Colombian novelist, poet, and essayist, he is among the leading writers of his generation in his homeland. Known primarily as one of Colombia's most talented poets in the early stages of his writing career in the 1970s, he has become increasingly known throughout the Hispanic world for his postmodern fiction as well as an active presence in several spheres of intellectual life in Colombia. Born in Santa Rosa de Osos (department of Antioquia) in 1947, he studied social sciences and law at the Universidad Javeriana in Bogotá. He began publishing poetry at an early age, his first poems appearing in print in the late 1960s and early 1970s. His generation of poets was identified as both the "disenchanted generation" by some critics and as the generation of the literary magazine *Golpe de Dados* by others. His poetry, which has received several prizes in Colombia, is often ironic, playful, and irreverent, although he is more of a traditionalist in his love poetry. He participated in the International Writing Program at the University of Iowa, and this experience was important for the writing of his first novel, *La muerte de Alec* (1983, The death of Alec), an epistolary work about a young man's experience in the United States, an experience involving a spiritual search. His major novel, *Cartas cruzadas* (1995, Crossed letters), is a substantive contribution to an understanding of urban life in Colombia in the 1970s and 1980s as well as an ambitious fictionalization of an individual's search for meaning in life. His two lighter and more entertaining fictions are the novel *Novela con fantasma* (1996, Novel with a ghost) and *Guía para viajeros* (1991, Guide for travelers). He lives in Bogotá, where he plays a central role as a cultural administrator for the Banco de la República in Colombia and editor of its cultural journal.

Selected Work: *La muerte de Alec* (1983); *Cartas cruzadas* (1995); *Novela con fan-*

tasma (1996); *Memorias de un hombre feliz* (1999); *El juego del alfiler* (2002).

Jardín de al lado, El (1981, *The Garden Next Door,* by José Donoso. Translation by Hardie St. Martín and Leonard Mares. New York: Grove, 1992) [**Novel**] A novel about a failed Latin American novelist of the 1960s Boom in political exile, this work has obvious autobiographical qualities. The protagonist is living in a community with other Latin American writers in Spain while his mother is dying in Chile (Donoso's mother died in Chile in 1975). The novelist who is the main character, however, is not the narrator, for at the end it is revealed that the assumed narrator's wife tells the story. This is a dark and bitter approach to Chile's somber dictatorship (1975–1989), as well as Donoso's attempt to exorcise himself of his own personal demons. Donoso falls into the nostalgic tone of much exile fiction only briefly (when speaking of his mother in Chile); the remainder of the novel relates defeats and failure. Like Fuentes, Donoso is a deeply committed modernist; his writing career harks back to the classic Anglo-American modernists who know all the motifs, strategies, and games of the postmodern—several of which he displays proudly in this novel.

Johns, Per [**Biography**] Brazilian novelist, short story writer, translator, and essayist, he was born in Rio de Janeiro 1933 of Danish parents who immigrated to Brazil in 1922. Johns is a versatile intellectual who was trained in law but never practiced the profession. He has been involved most of this life in business and diplomacy as well as a broad range of cultural activities. He has published five novels in Portuguese and several literary essays in Danish, including a study in Danish published on modern Brazilian literature in 1985. He has also translated several of his own novels from

Portuguese into Danish, as well as several major foreign writers, such as Isak Dinesen, from Danish into Portuguese. His fiction explores fragile terrain and ambiguous spaces and identities, with resonances of Joyce, Guimarães Rosa, and the international postmodern. Three of his novels constitute a trilogy. *Cemitérios Marinhos as Veces São Festivos* (1990, Navy cemeteries are sometimes festive) is a self-conscious metafiction with two main characters who are doppelgangers. He was awarded a prestigious national prize, the Prêmio Jabuti, in 1991, for his novel *As Aves de Cassandra* (1995, The birds of Cassandra), an autobiographical fiction about a young man's coming-of-age living between two cultures, one Danish, the other Brazilian. In *O Navegante de Opereta* (1998, The opera's navigator), he continues the trilogy with his ongoing questioning of identity.

Selected Work: A Revolução de Deus (1977); *Morte na Rodovia Galileo Galilei* (1978); *As Aves de Cassandra* (1990); *Cemitérios Marinhos às Vezes São Festivos* (1995); *Navegante de Opereta* (1998).

Jurado, Alicia [**Biography**] Argentine essayist, scholar, and novelist, she has been a major presence in Argentine intellectual life since the 1960s. She was born in Buenos Aires in 1922 and first studied the natural sciences at the University of Buenos Aires before turning to her lifetime passion of literature. She took courses in literature at the University of London in 1961. In 1971 she published a biography of W. H. Hudson, which she had begun under the auspices of a Guggenheim Fellowship. Her essays have appeared in such prominent venues as the cultural journal *Sur* as well as in the newspapers *La Nación* and *La Prensa.* Her stellar scholarly and literary career have given her a prominent institutional role in Argentine cultural life as a member of the Argentine Academy of Letters and of the board of directors of the Argentine National Arts Fund. In 1986 she delivered the invitational Jorge Luis Borges Lecture to the Anglo-Argentine Society. Her fiction tends to deal with the literati and her settings involve arts and letters. For example, her novel *Los hechiceros de la tribu* (1980, The sorcerers of the tribe) is a representation of Argentine cultural life as seen by its writers; the main character is an author.

Selected Work: Los hechiceros de la tribu (1980).

K

Kincaid, Jamaica [Biography] Caribbean novelist, short story writer and essayist, she was born in St. John's, Antigua in 1949. Her father, from Antigua and her mother, of half-Carib descent from Dominica, had named her Elaine Potter Richardson, but she moved to New York in 1966 and adopted her writing name in 1973. She became a staff writer for the *New Yorker* in 1976. With her first volume of stories, *At the Bottom of the River* (1983), and the polemical essay *A Small Place* (1988), she established a reputation as an important new Caribbean voice. As such, she is one of the many Caribbean writers who left their respective homes at a young age to become important writers abroad.

She received critical acclaim for her first novel, *Annie John* (1985), which deals with female autonomy. In this work a seventeen-year-old girl leaves her idyllic life in Antigua to migrate to London. Facing this important change in her life, the young protagonist finds strength in the adult women around her and in the traditions of oral storytelling. Kincaid tells her own life story as a woman in Dominica in *The Autobiography of My Mother* (1996). In her writ-

ing she positions herself as a writer from Antigua who celebrates the fact that she is black and a woman.

Selected Work: Annie John (1985); *Lucy* (1991); *The Autobiography of My Mother* (1996).

Kohan, Martín [Biography] Argentine novelist, short story writer, and essayist, he teaches literary theory at the University of Buenos Aires. Born in Buenos Aires in 1967, he began publishing fiction in the 1990s and belongs to the generation of the 1990s, or the McOndo generation, that has been identified with several names throughout Latin America. He has not been active in the international promotion of his fiction, however, unlike several other writers of this generation. He has published the volumes of short stories *Muero contento* (1994, I die content) and *Una pena extraordinaria* (1998, An extraordinary pain). His novels are *La pérdida de Laura* (1993, The loss of Laura); *El informe* (1997, The report); *Los cautivos* (2000, The captives), and *Dos veces junio* (2002, June twice). In his latest work, *Dos veces junio*, he goes back to June of 1978 and the early stages of the military dictatorship in Argentina and experiments with new approaches to communicating the experience of the oppression and horror of those years in his homeland.

Selected Work: La pérdida de Laura (1993); *El informe* (1997); *Los cautivos* (2000); *Dos veces junio* (2002).

Krauze, Ethel [Biography] Mexican novelist, short story writer, essayist, and poet, she has been publishing novels since the mid-1980s. Born in Mexico City in 1954, she studied literature at the National University in Mexico City (UNAM), has taught in a variety of settings, and has written on literary and cultural topics in magazines such as *Proceso*, *Plural*, and other venues. Her volumes of short stories include *Inter-*

medio para mujeres (1982, Intermediary for women), *Niñas* (1982, Girls), *Nana María* (1987, Nana Maria), and *El lunes te amaré* (1987, On Monday I will love you). She has published several books of poetry as well as a book introducing readers to the study of poetry, *Cómo acercarse a la poesía* (1992, How to approach poetry). Her novels include *Donde las cosas vuelan* (1985, Where things fly); *Infinita* (1992, Infinite); *Mujeres en Nueva York* (1995, Women in New York).

Selected Work: *Donde las cosas vuelan* (1985); *Infinita* (1992); *Mujeres en Nueva York* (1995).

L

Labrador Ruiz, Enrique [Biography] Cuban novelist, poet, essayist, short story writer, and journalist, he was a boldly experimental writer of the Latin American avant-garde of the 1920s and 1930s. Labrador was well known in Cuba as a short story writer, and many Cuban readers considered his volumes of short stories *Trailer de sueños* (1949, Dream trailer) and *El gallo en el espejo* (1953, The rooster in the mirror) to be classics of Cuban literature. As a novelist he is best-known for his wildly experimental novel *El laberinto de sí mismo* (1933, The labyrinth of he himself). His entire writing career was an assault on conventional, traditional, and realist modes of literature, which had been predominant in Cuba until the 1930s.

Born in 1902, he wrote an autobiographical trilogy of novels that consists of *El laberinto de sí mismo, Cresival* (1936), and *Anteo* (1940, The olden days), which he called *novelas gaseiformes* ("gaseous" novels). Labrador Ruiz claimed that his fragmented and nonlinear narratives were his attempts to guide his characters so that they might follow their own will. *El laberinto de sí mismo* is an introspective and playful work in which the author invites the reader to observe the process of creation and enjoy (with the hypercreative author) language for the sake of language and creation for the sake of creation. He adopted a more serious tone in his later novel, *La sangre hambrienta* (1951, The hungry blood), a portrayal of desperate and disillusioned characters in a boardinghouse along the lines of the writing at the same time of Uruguayan Juan Carlos Onetti. His iconoclastic methods were matched by his irreverent treatment of matters such as politics and sex. He also wrote short fiction in a similar vein, calling them "cloudy little novels."

Labrador Ruiz died in the United States in 1991. Before moving to Miami in 1979, he had left Cuba for Spain in 1976, where he continued writing and interacting with Latin American intellectuals until the late 1970s.

Selected Work: *El laberinto de sí mismo* (1933); *Cresival* (1936); *Anteo* (1940); *La sangre hambrienta* (1951); *El pan de los muertos* (1958).

Laferrière, Dany [Biography] Caribbean novelist and journalist, he was born in Port au Prince, Haiti, in 1953. A practicing journalist under the dictatorship of Duvalier, he was working at this profession at a time when journalists were being assassinated by the government, so Laferrière went into political exile in Montreal, Canada, in 1978. After taking a job in Canada as a laborer, he began writing his first novel, *Comment Faire l'amour avec un Nègre* (1985, How to Make Love to a Negro), the story of an immigrant. This erotico-satiric novel plays with many of the racial and sexual stereotypes of African Americans. When Laferrière describes himself and his friends, he uses the word *nègre* ("Negro" and even "nigger") rather than the more politically and socially correct *noire*. A wild and irreverent metafiction with many digressions, it does, nevertheless, deal constantly with issues of race, class, and gender. Self-referential and postmodern, this novel is a parody of numerous Caribbean literary and cultural topics and movements. As in much postmodern fiction, the written word takes priority over empirical reality and, in this provocative novel, the textual is also sexual. Comparable to writers such as Charles Bukowski in the United States and R. H. Moreno-Durán in Colombia with respect to his explicit and playful attitude toward sexuality and textuality, his specifically Caribbean postmodern turn also recalls writers such as Maryse Condé and Marie Chauvet. He dedicates his novel *Eroshima* (1987) to Rita Hayworth, the actress the author claims introduced him to sexual desire. After living in Montreal, he moved to Miami, Florida, and wrote *L'Odeur de Café* (1991, *An Aroma of Coffee*).

An iconoclast who readers of English will associate with Henry Miller and Jack Kerouac, he also links himself directly with the Latin American innovators Borges, Cortázar, and Fuentes and the Caribbean writer Alejo Carpentier.

Selected Work: Comment Faire l'amour avec un Nègre sans se Fatiguer (1985, *How to Make Love to a Negro*, translation David Homel, 1987); *Eroshima* (1987, *Eroshima*, translation David Homel, 1991); *Pays sans Chapeau* (1996); *La Chair du Maitre* (1997); *Le Charme des après Midi sans Fin* (1997); *Cette Grenade dans la Main du Jeune Nègre est-elle une Arme ou un Fruit?* (1993, *Why Must a Black Writer Write About Sex?* translated by David Homel, 1994).

Lafourcade, Enrique [Biography] Chilean novelist, essayist, he belongs to the generation of 1950 in Chile that includes José Donoso and Jorge Edwards. In their writing this group was less committed to social and political change than their predecessors of the 1930s and 1940s; rather, their literary models were the European and North Americanist modernists such as Joyce, Woolf, and Faulkner. Lafourcade was born in 1927 and began publishing novels in the early 1950s. This generation also read the French writers Sartre and Camus with great interest.

His first novel, *Pena de muerte* (1952, *Death penalty*), was exceptional for its time, for it portrayed the tragic life of a gay protagonist. *Para subir al cielo* (1954, To go up to the sky) is a love story of existential anguish with overtones of these two French writers. His novel *La fiesta del Rey Acab* (1959, The fiesta of King Acab) is a forerunner of the 1970s "novels of dictators" written by authors such as García Márquez and Carpentier. He becomes interested in experimentation in the two novels *Invención a dos voces* (1963, Invention for two voices) and *Frecuencia modulada* (1968, Modulated frequency). His most widely read works are *Palomita blanca* (1971, Little white dove) and *Adiós al Fuehrer* (1982, Good-bye to the Fuhrer). *Palomita blanca* is a love story set during the election campaign for Salvador Allende in the late 1960s; *Adiós al Fuehrer* is a grotesque novel about the authoritarian and repressive politics of the time in Chile.

Selected Work: Para subir al cielo (1954); *La fiesta del Rey Acab* (1959); *Invención a dos voces* (1963); *Frecuencia modulada* (1968); *Palomita blanca* (1971); *Adiós al Fuehrer* (1982).

Lago, Sylvia [Biography] Uruguayan novelist, short story writer, essayist, and academic, she was born in Montevideo in 1932. She won a local literary prize with her first novel, *Trajano*, in 1956, which is a family story focusing on a child and his dog. Lago began writing fiction as a conventional realist, and this first novel was a typical critique of middle-class values in Uruguay in the 1950s. Lago remained a conventionalist in her second novel, *Tan solos en el balneario* (1962, All alone in the pool). In her short fiction that followed in the mid-1960s, she was a pioneer with the use of colloquial and vulgar language. In her later novels, *La última razón* (1968, The last reason) and *Saltos mortales* (2001, Mortal jumps), she uses a more bitter tone to satirize intellectuals.

In addition to her eight books of fiction, Lago has been an active academic, publishing scholarly studies and anthologies of Latin American literature, with particular focus on the literatures of Uruguay and Argentina. She currently lives in Montevideo, where she is the director of the Department of Uruguayan and Argentine Literature at the University of the Republic.

Selected Work: Trajano (1956); *Tan solos en el balneario* (1962); *La última razón* (1968); *Saltos mortales* (2001).

Lamming, George [Biography] Caribbean novelist and essayist, he is one of the leading intellectual figures of the region, which, along with Alejo Carpentier (writing in Spanish), Aimé Césaire and Eduoard Glissant (writing in French), and Frank Martinus Arion (writing in Dutch), has set the direction for modern fiction and Caribbean postcolonial discourse. He has contributed considerably to an understanding of the colonial experience and the postcolonial circumstance. Born in Carrington, Barbados, in 1927, he grew up in Trinidad and taught there until emigrating in 1950 to England, where he became a prominent figure of the London West Indian literary movement through the 1950s.

He has attracted a wide readership in the Caribbean and beyond with his seven novels and his seminal essay *The Pleasures of Exile* (1992). His novels address the condition of the colonial subject from a variety of perspectives—the experience of colonial education, the experience of exile, the experience of racism, and the like. After his semiautobiographical first novel, *In The Castle of My Skin* (1953), he followed with *The Emigrants* (1954), narrating the destinies of West Indians in London who seek a fulfillment in Britain they were unable to attain back in their colonial homeland. In the end their lives are confused and chaotic in London. His next two novels, *Of Age and Innocence* (1958) and *Season of Adventure* (1960) are explicitly political works, the former portraying a fictional Caribbean island's political processes before independence and the latter treating the situation after independence. In both novels the promoters of political independence and progress face obstacles and setbacks, but Lamming also offers a final vision that could be interpreted as hopeful.

Many critics consider *Natives of My Person* to be Lamming's finest novel. Set in the sixteenth century, this complex and highly poetic work follows a slave ship without slaves but with utopian dreams as it crosses the Atlantic. The poor moral decisions of the captain and the crew, however, lead to the experiment's failure. Lamming offers a ray of hope: the women on the ship are sent ahead and seem capable of creating a better society.

Creating complex works that avoid many of the stereotypes of Caribbean culture as well as the clichés of postcolonial discourse, Lamming is considered a major literary and cultural voice in the Caribbean.

Selected Work: In the Castle of My Skin (1953); *The Emigrants* (1954); *Of Age and Innocence* (1958); *Season of Adventure* (1960); *Water with Berries* (1972); *Natives of My Person* (1972).

Lange, Norah [Biography] Argentine novelist born in 1906, she wrote a set of novels that passed by with relatively little recognition during her lifetime. She died in 1972, having published the novels *Voz de vida* (1927, Voice of life), *45 días y 30 marineros* (1933, 45 days and 30 sailors), and *Antes que mueran* (1944, Before they die), *Personas en la sala* (1950, People in the room), and *Los dos retratos* (1956, The two portraits). She participated in the most sophisticated of literary circles in Buenos Aires. Many scholars and critics consider her an early feminist, and several critics have pointed to the high quality of novels such as *45 días y 30 marineros*. In this work a young girl is aboard a ship with a group of men traveling to Norway on a freighter. Feminist in perspective, it portrays the young girl's autonomy and sophistication. Her early *Voz de vida* is an epistolary novel that relates a love affair between two married individuals and represents an iconoclastic call for sexual freedom. Along with María Luisa Bombal and Marta Brunet, Lange was a pioneer woman novelist in Latin America.

Selected Work: Voz de vida (1927), *45 días y 30 marineros* (1933), and *Antes que mueran* (1944), *Personas en la sala* (1950); *Los dos retratos* (1956).

Lara Zavala, Hernán [Biography] Mexican novelist, essayist, and short story writer, he has both produced and promoted experimental fiction in Mexico and Latin America. He was born in Mexico City in 1946 and studied literature at the National University in Mexico City (UNAM), followed by graduate work at both the UNAM and in East Anglia, Great Britain. In 1987 he participated in the International Writing Program at the University of Iowa. In the 1990s he was editor of a series (Serie Rayuela) at the press of the UNAM that published innovative and experimental fiction. His first novel, *Charras* (1990), is a reconstruction of a variety of voices and texts to relate the story of a student leader assassinated in Yucatán in 1974.

He lives in Mexico City, where he holds faculty and administrative posts at the UNAM.

Selected Work: El mismo cielo (1987); *El hombre equivocado* (1988); *Charras* (1990).

Leñero, Vicente [Biography] Mexican novelist, journalist, playwright, and screenwriter, he has been a major intellectual presence in Mexico in the second half of the century. He was born in Guadalajara, Mexico, in 1933, studied engineering at the National University in Mexico City (UNAM), and later journalism at the Escuela Carlos Septién García. His fiction tends to blur traditional genre boundaries, particularly the line between fiction and *testimonio* or documentary writing. His writing tends to escape easy description or classification, for it is at the same time superficially quite traditional yet, in reality, quite innovative. His most widely read book, *Los albañiles* (1964, The bricklayers), pushes the limits of the genres of the testimonial novel; on the surface it appears similar to a detective novel (posing the question of who committed a murder), but it is really a novel about justice. His first novel, *La voz adolorida* (1961, The pained voice), is narrated by a supposedly insane person, but the work questions the very categories of sanity and insanity. *El garabato* (1967, The scribbling) is a self-conscious metafiction comparable to the early postmodern fiction of the period of José Emilio Pacheco, Salvador Elizondo, and Carlos Fuentes. *A fuerza de palabras* (1976, The force of words) and *El evangelio según Lucas Gavilán* (1979, The evangelicals according to Luke Gavilán) are rewriting of other texts, the former of his own first novel *La voz adolorida*, the latter of a narrative from the Bible. One of his more ambitious and lengthy works (329 pages), his recent *La* *vida que se va* (1999, The life that goes away), is an elderly woman's memoir of real and an imagined past lives.

Selected Work: La voz adolorida (1961); *Los albañiles* (1964); *Estudio Q* (1965); *A fuerza de palabras* (1967); *El garabato* (1967); *Redil de ovejas* (1973); *Los periodistas* (1978); *El evangelio según Lucas Gavilán* (1979); *La gota de agua* (1983); *La vida que se va* (1999).

Levinson, Luisa Mercedes [Biography] Argentine novelist, short story writer, playwright, and journalist born in 1909, she is known for her collaborations with Jorge Luis Borges, having coauthored the volume of fiction *La hermana de Eloísa* (1955) with him. She has written numerous journalistic pieces on cultural topics and travel chronicles for the newspaper *La Nación*. She has published the volumes of short stories *La pálida Rosa de Soho* (1959) and *Las tejadoras sin hombres* (1967) as well as several theater pieces.

Levinson is best known for her novel *La casa de los Felipes* (1951, The house of the Felipes). In this novel, which has been associated with the tradition of the gothic novel, a townhouse is torn down and the reader is privy to the mad life of an eccentric family. It includes ghosts, incest, a mistress, and an alcoholic. Levinson has the ability to develop and deepen mystery, and this capacity is fully on display in this novel, as is her ability to shift smoothly and effectively from one narrative point of view to another. She also portrays a decadent aristocracy, offering a class critique that appears in several of her novels. She died in 1988.

Selected Work: La casa de los Felipes (1951); *Concierto en mí* (1956); *La isla de los organilleros* (1964).

Leyva, Daniel [Biography] Mexican novelist and poet, he is known among well-informed Mexican writers and intellectuals as an experimental novelist. He was born in Mexico City in 1949, studied linguistics and literature at the University of Paris VIII, and has been awarded prestigious literary prizes in Mexico (Premio Xavier Villarrutia, 1976) as well as receiving a Guggenheim Fellowship (1982). His most radical narrative experiment is *Una piñata llena de memorias* (1984, A piñata full of memories). In his recent *El cementerio de los placeres* (2000, The cementery of pleasures), he places into doubt the ontological status of his characters as people and as characters. Although he is relatively uknown outside Mexico, all of his writing can be associated with the trends of international postmodern fiction.

Selected Work: ¿ABCDerio o ABeCeDamo? (1980); *Una piñata llena de memoria* (1984); *El cementerio de los placeres* (2000).

Lezama Lima, José [Biography] Cuban poety, essayist, and novelist, he was known most of his life as one of Cuba's premier poets but was later recognized as the author of the celebrated novel *Paradiso* (1966, *Paradise*). His much admired poetry is considered hermetic and baroque, offering multiple allegorical readings. Born in 1912, in the military camp Columbia near Havana, he read Spanish classics as a child and was writing poetry as an adolescent. By the time he entered the University of Havana, he was seriously committed to poetry. When the university went on a four-year strike, he dedicated himself to reading the Western classics in Spanish, French, Italian, and German.

Lezama Lima was the founder of the influential literary magazine *Orígenes*, which was in circulation from 1944 to 1957 and was the centerpiece for an entire generation of Latin American writers both inside and outside of Cuba. The writers of the 1960s Boom, for example, have spoken of how important *Orígenes* had been in their readings as young intellectuals.

Many critics consider his novel *Paradiso* the most important Cuban novel of Lezama Lima's generation and of the period. This lengthy and complex novel is as hermetic and baroque as the author's poetry and has been read as an intellectual history of homosexuality from San Agustín to Nietzsche. On a more literal level, it is the semiautobiographical account of an adolescent's experience of entering the world of sexuality and creative work. The novel includes numerous digressions, including lengthy discussions on the meaning of life and the nature of the universe. Upon appearing in print, *Paradiso* was immediately acclaimed by Julio Cortázar and the other writers of the Boom. The protagonist's spiritual guide, Oppiano Licario, becomes the title of his posthumous novel, *Oppiano Licario* (1977, Oppiano Licario), in which Lezama Lima continues developing some of the topics he had set forth in his fiction, poetry, and essays. The protagonist moves forward in his poetic apprenticeship and finds some unity in the fragments of his life and work.

Despite the hermetic qualities of his poetry and his fiction, Lezama Lima was one of the most heralded and influential writers of Cuba in the twentieth century. Since his death in 1976, his stature as one of the giants of Latin American and Caribbean literature has grown.

Selected Work: Paradiso (1966, *Paradise*, translation Gregory Rabassa, 1974); *Oppiano Licario* (1977).

Libertella, Héctor [Biography] Argentine novelist, short story writer, editor, and essayist, born in Bahia Blanca (Argentina) in 1945, he has been a leading innovator of Argentine and Latin American fiction since the late 1960s. Along with the Mexican Salvador Elizondo and the Cuban Severo Sarduy, he is one of the model postmodernists among Latin American writers. He has taught literary theory at the University of Buenos Aires, New York University, and the National University in Mexico City (UNAM). His fiction has received numerous international recognitions, including prestigious prizes in Buenos Aires (Premio Paidós, 1968), in Venezuela (Premio Internacional Monte Avila, 1971), and in Paris (Premio Juan Rulfo de Cuento, 1986).

His hermetic and innovative short fiction includes volumes such as *Cavernícolas!* (1985, Caverniculas!), and his essays (some of which read like experimental fiction) include *Nueva escritura en Latinoamérica* (1977, New writing in Latin America), *Ensayos o pruebas sobre una red hermética* (1990, Essays and tests on an hermetic network), *Los juegos desviados de la literatura* (1991, The digressive games of literature), and *Las sagradas escrituras* (1993, The sacred writings). The books include an implicit theory of literature that he elaborates more fully in his fiction. His early novels, *El camino de los hiperbóreos* (1968, The road of the arctics) and *Personas en pose de combate* (1975, People in combat pose), were already literary experiments that challenged the active postmodern reader to join with the characters in a search for meaning. His later fiction, such as *El paseo internacional del perverso* (1990, The international walk of the perverse), is less experimental.

His recent *Memorias de un semidiós* (1998, Memoires a demigod) is one of his most conventional works, with a protagonist and plot line that involves intrigue from Buenos Aires to New York; it is Libertella's closest approximation of detective fiction. He lives in Buenos Aires, where he does editorial work, teaches, and writes.

Selected Work: El camino de los hiper-bóreos (1968); *Personas en pose de combate* (1975); *El paseo internacional del perverso* (1990); *Memorias de un semidiós* (1998).

Lihn, Enrique [Biography] Chilean poet, essayist, playwright and novelist, he is widely considered a major Latin American poet and one of Chile's major poets of the century. Best known for his antipoetry, he is associated with the Chilean antipoet Nicanor Parra. Born in Santiago in 1929, he spent most of his life writing a skeptical poetry that parodied not only traditional forms of poetry but even poetry manifestos and the very concept of poet as hero. He remained in Chile during the dictatorship, writing subtle satires of all forms of authority. Much of his writing was experimental and he was often involved in poetry performances. In his later years, before his untimely death in 1988, he was a professor and researcher in the Department of Humanistic Studies at the University of Chile. He was not well-known outside of Chile as a novelist; nevertheless, he did publish innovative and experimental postmodern fiction. His novel *El arte de la palabra* (1980, The art of the word) involves discussions among writers and intellectuals about the work of such individuals. He also published the experimental novel *La orquesta de cristal* (1976, The crystal orchestra), which contains obscure and hermetic footnotes that critique authoritarian governments.

Selected Work: Batman en Chile (1971); *La orquesta de cristal* (1976); *El arte de la palabra* (1980).

Lindo, Hugo [Biography] Novelist, journalist, diplomat and poet from El Salvador, he was born in 1917 and studied law in El Salvador and in Chile. He directed the newspaper *La Tribuna* in El Salvador and wrote essays from several literary journals, including *Ars* and *Guión literario*. He served as El Salvador's ambassador to Chile, Colombia, and Spain, and was also director of the Academy of the Language of El Salvador.

Selected Work: El anzuelo de dios (1956); *Cada día tiene su afán* (1965); *Justicia señor gobernador* (1966); *Yo soy la memoria* (1983).

Lins, Osman [Biography] Novelist, short story writer, essayist, and playwright, Lins is recognized as one of Brazil's most erudite and experimental writers and has been compared to Joyce because of similar interests in exploring the possibilities of language. His work is also easily comparable to international postmodern fiction and to Spanish American writers such as the Cuban Severo Sarduy, the Argentines Héctor Libertella and Julio Cortázar, and the Mexicans Salvador Elizondo and José Emilio Pacheco. He was also a writer committed to social change who wrote of his admiration for writers who were known as social critics, such as the Brazilians Lima Barreto and Graciliano Ramos. Lins has written some of his fiction as a protest against poverty in Brazil. (He deals with this and other related areas in his volume of essays *Guerra sem testamunha*.) He was born in 1924 in Vitória de Santo Antão (state of Pernambuco), and lost his mother in his infancy, a tragedy that marked him for life; he grew up as an orphan. He did his university studies in economics and theater in Recife, completing a degree in finance in 1964 after a degree in theater in 1960. He earned a doctorate in literature in 1973, with a dissertation on the topic of the writing of Lima Barreto and novelistic space. He later published this study as a book as well as other book-length essays on literary and cultural topics.

While pursuing his university studies in literature and theater, Lins was writing his first stories and publishing them in newspapers under the titles *O Visitante* (1955, The visitor, his first novel), *O Fiel e a Pedra* (1961, The faithful and the stone, a novel), and *Os Gestos* (1957, The gestures, short stories). His interest in intellectual themes and language per se was evident in his first intensely interior novel, *O Visitante*, divided into three notebooks. He also questions traditional codes and conventions of society in the stories of *Os Gestos* and in *O Fiel e a Pedra*. In 1961 he won a contest sponsored by the French government for a trip to France, during which he wrote what he called a "false diary" published later under the title *Marinheiro de Primeira Viagem* (1962, Sailor on a first trip). A fragmented work, it is considered a predecessor to his later fiction *Nove, novena* (1966, *Nove novena*) and *Avalovara* (1975). With this trip to France and the writing of his travel journal, Lins reached an inner equilibrium that allowed him to consolidate his career. Lins began thinking and writing about the relationship between writing and the plastic arts, a relationship that remained important in all is writing. In 1962 he settled in São Paulo and he then began moving toward more abstract treatments of character and themes in the stories *Nove, novena*. His masterpiece and most renowned work is *Avalovara*, is one of the most experimental novels to be published in Brazil in the century. The options and challenges for the reader of *Avalovara* are similar to those in Cortázar's *Rayuela*. In it the narrator-protagonist, Abel, has three women who are both real and abstractions, located in three different geographical locations: one in Europe, one in São Paulo, and one in Pernambuco. The first two women are identified by name; the third is identified with a graphic symbol rather than a name and represents an idealized synthesis of all three. As in Cortázar's *Rayuela*, the reader is invited to join the protagonist in constructing a path toward the absolute and an abstract paradise. Readings of this novel also invite the reader to search for resources in the plastic arts, architecture, music, and astrology. Lins continues in the experimental line in *A Rainha dos Cárceres da Grécia* (1976, The queen of the jails in Greece), his sixth and final book of fiction, published posthumously. Translated into English as *The Queen of the Prisoners of Greece* (translation Adria Frizzi, 1995), this postmodern text is an anonymous high school teacher's journal about an unpublished novel written by his deceased lover, a young woman named Julia Marguerim Enone. The journal is the teacher's attempt to understand Julia, her novel, and their relationship.

Along with Lispector, Hilst, and Guimarães Rosa, Lins is one of the major innovators of the second half of the twentieth-century in Brazil. Numerous article-length studies and some books have been written about his fiction. He died in 1978, leaving his fifth novel, *A Cabeça Levada em Triumfo* (The head lifted in triumph) unfinished. In honor of the eightieth anniversary of his birth, a group of Brazilian scholars published a volume of critical essays, *O Soprona Argila* (2004), offering nineteen illuminating essays on Lins's complete work.

Selected Work: O Visitante (1955); *O Fiel e a Pedra* (1961); *Avalovara* (1973, *Avalovara*, translation Gregory Rabassa, 1979); *A rainha dos cárceres da Grécia* (1976, *The Queen of the Prisoners of Greece*, translation Adria Frizzi, 1995).

Lispector, Clarice [Biography] Novelist, essayist, and short story writer, she was a major innovator in Brazil and one of Latin America's leading women writers. Unconventional uses of language and other subversive strategies have marked her work.

Many scholars consider her first novels a watershed for the Brazilian novel. Born in the Ukraine in 1924, she immigrated to Brazil as an infant, living in the northeastern region until she was twelve years old and then moving to Rio de Janeiro with her family. After studying law and practicing journalism in the 1940s, she lived abroad and established a career inside and outside of Brazil as one of the nation's leading novelists before dying in 1977.

Lispector's writing career developed along three stages. Her early work, which was nonlinear from the beginning, included *Perto do Coração Selvagem* (1944, *Near to the Wild Heart,* 1990), *O Lustre* (1946, The luster), *A Cidade Sitiada* (1949, *The Besieged City,* 1997), and *A Maçã no Escuro* (1961, *The Apple in the Dark,* 1967). These early writings were influenced by Sartre, Camus, and other figures of existentialism; many of her characters were engaged in a search for the meaning of life and also suffered from existential anguish. This was also Lispector's most explicitly feminist work, one in which some female characters were seen in creative activities related to literature or painting. In her next period, with the publication of *A Paixão Segundo G. H.* (1964, *The Passion According to G. H.*) and *Uma Aprendizagem ou o Livro dos Prazeres* (1969, *An Apprenticeship, or the Book of Delights,* 1986), Lispector became radically experimental in her style. In the former the protagonist eats a cockroach as a symbolic and quasi-spiritual act, part of his effort to free herself from society's conventions. This is her Brazilian rewriting of Kafka's *The Metamorphosis.* The stories in *Laços de Família* (1960, *Family Ties,* 1972), which some have read as a novel, portray women who suffer from the meaningless in their lives and their unwillingness to accept the conventions of everyday middle-class life. Her third and last stage consisted of the novels *Agua Viva* (1973,

White water), *A Hora da Estrela* (1977, *The Hour of the Star*), and the posthumously published *Um Sopro na Vida* (1978, A breath of life) They are the works of what Lispector herself called her "trash" period, i.e., a last stage that related to a final exhaustion pointing to her death. It was also a period in which she became even more radical in her writing, using extreme fragmentation; these texts were collages with minimal unity. In *Agua viva* a female painter-narrator directs the narrative to a male reader, writing in a subjective and constant present. Lispector's last novel, *A Hora da Estrela*, written in the spirit of Julio Cortázar, offers the reader the choice of thirteen possible titles and is a synthesis of much of her thought and writing as well as a daring revision of ideas predominant among intellectuals about Brazil's national identity. In this work the main character, Macabéia, an orphan who eventually works as a typist, has a love affair, loses her boyfriend (the narrator), and at the end of the novel is run over by a car and killed. There is a considerable amount of the narrator's self-reflection concerning his relationsip with Macabéia. This narrator is a sadomasochistic transvestite who claims he writes because there is nothing left to do in the world. By the end of her career, Lispector wrote in a dialogue with international postmodern culture. She is one of the major Brazilian writers of the second half of the century, along with João Guimarães Rosa, Autran Dourado, Jorge Amado, Rubem Fonseca, and Antonio Callado.

Selected Work: Perto do Coração Selvagem (1944, *Near to the Wild Heart,* translation Giovanni Pontiero, 1990); *O Lustre* (1946); *A Cidade Sitiada* (1949, *The Besieged City,* translation Giovanni Pontiero, 1997); *A Maçã no Escuro* (1961, *The Apple in the Dark,* translation Gregory Rabassa, 1967); *A Paixão Segundo G. H.* (1964, *The Passion According to G. H.,* translation Ronald W.

Sousa, 1988); *Uma Aprendizagem ou o Livro dos Prazeres* (1969, *An Apprenticeship, or the Book of Delights*, 1986); *Agua Viva* (1973, *White Water*, translation Elizabeth Lowe and Earl Fitz, 1975); *A Hora da Estrela* (1977, *The Hour of the Star*, translation Giovanni Pontiero, 1986); *Um Sopro de Vida: Pulsações* (1978).

Lo anterior (2004, What was before, by Cristina Rivera Garza. Written in Spanish and untranslated. Barcelona: Tusquets) [**Novel**] Young Mexican writer Cristina Rivera Garza is the author of several engaging and abstract books of fiction, and most of them deal with not only gender, but the relationships between gender and language. In this short novel, Rivera Garza approaches love in relationship to language. The plot focuses on various beings of ambiguous gender, creating permeable boundaries between the various men and women. The novel begins in the desert, where a female photographer encounters a comatose man with a note in his hand: "Love always occurs afterwards, in retrospect." The photographer rescues the man and cares for him in her home during his mute convalescence. In the second part the chapters alternate fonts and between numbers and the four suits of cards. Now a man is in love with a woman he suspects is from outerspace; another man in a restaurant captivates a woman who acts as a listener and as a writer. The final fusion of characters in their desire for love and through the medium of writing makes this poetic novel seem experimental. Rivera Garza's mastery in creating fragile gender boundaries and questioning their relationship with writing makes her comparable to such postmodernists as the Cuban Severo Sarduy and the Brazilian Ignacio Loyola Brandão.

Lobato, Manoel [**Biography**] Brazilian novelist and short story writer, he pub-

lished conventional fiction in the 1960s and 1970s. He was born in Açaraí (state of Minas Gerais) in 1925 and studied both pharmacy and law. He portrays characters with moral dilemmas that put them in conflict with society. His novel *Mentira dos Limpos* (1967, The lie of the clean) depicts a protagonist with Christian ethics in conflict with social norms. In addition to several volumes of short stories, he wrote a later novel, *A Verdaderia Vida do Irmão Leovelfildo* (1976, The true life of brother Leovelfildo), in which he continues his questioning of the ability of the ethical individual to survive in a society in continual degeneration.

Selected Work: Mentira dos Limpos (1967); *A Verdadeira Vida do Irmão Leovelfildo* (1976).

Lonely Londoners (1956, by Samuel Selvon. Written in English. London: Wingate, 1956) [**Novel**] The third novel by one of the pioneer Caribbean novelist of the English language, this is the story of a West Indian family that immigrates to London. Selvon, George Lamming, and other writers in exile had already begun publishing a series of novels on the immigrant experience in London. Selvon adds a political touch to a collection of sketches on the frivolous aspects of life in London. Underlying their seemingly pleasant life are concerns over exile and cultural rootlessness. The common thread to these sketches is Moses Aloetta, who finds solace in humor. Selvon is from Trinidad, but the characters that populate this fiction come from a broad range of Caribbean nations, underlining the potential cultural unity of the region.

Lopes, Moacir Costa [**Biography**] Brazilian author of novels, novellas, short stories, essays, and children's literature, he was born in Quizadá (state of Ceará) in 1927. He is well known in Brazil as a storyteller and commercial writer. He garnered considerable attention with the publication of his first novel *Maria de Cada Porto* (1959, Maria of every port), which became an immediate best seller; it is about the Brazilian marines in WWII, written by an ex-combatant with little formal training in literature. After that, Lopes continued writing full time, and his major novel is *A Ostra e o Vento* (1964, The oyster and the wind), a work about violence.

Selected Work: Maria de Cada Porto (1959); *A Ostra e o Vento* (1964).

Loubet, Jorgelina [Biography] Argentine novelist, short story writer, playwright, and essayist, she has been prominent in the Argentine cultural scene since the early 1960s. She was born in Buenos Aires in 1918 and studied mathematics in both Bahia Blanca and Buenos Aires. She taught at the University of Buenos Aires but decided to take an early retirement in order to dedicate herself to her writing. From an early age she was interested in French existentialism and the writing of Virginia Woolf. She was the founder of the Argentine chapter of International PEN. She won the Plaza y Janés Prize for Argentine novel for her work *El biombo* (1963, The screen), which she later rewrote as a play that was produced in Brazil.

More recently, she has served as the secretary general of the Argentine Academy of Letters.

Selected Work: El biombo (1963).

Louzada Filho, Oswald Corrêa [Biography] Brazilian novelist and journalist, he became associated with the procedures of the French *nouveau roman*, as evidenced in the novels he published in the 1960s and 1970s. He was born in São Paulo in 1943 and studied both electrical and civil engineering. His novels *Dardará* (1965) and *Diario de Bordo* (1975, Diary on board) are abstract and complex works that are exercises in using the objective camera-eye point of view of the world as pioneered in the French *nouveau roman*. His later novel *A Luz do Dia* (1977, The light of day) connects more directly with the empirical reality of Brazil, examining the relationship between intellectuals and the armed forces.

Selected Work: Dardará (1965); *Diario de Bordo* (1975); *ALluz do Dia* (1977).

Love in the Time of Cholera (See Amor en los tiempos del cólera, El, by Gabriel García Márquez) **[Novel]**

Luces artificiales (2002, Artificial lights, by Daniel Sada. Written in Spanish and untranslated. Mexico City: Alfaguara) **[Novel]** Set in Mexico City, this novel depicts an artificial society in the context of an adventure story. Using language that alternates between the erudite and the commonest of street slang, this young Mexican author plays with his narrative voice, frequently focusing on flights of fancy about trivial details to suggest the neurotic nature of his characters. Ramiro Cinco is a failure at the age of thirty six: upon his father's death, he inherits most of the family fortune under the stipulation that he undergo plastic surgery to correct his facial ugliness. In Mexico City he surreptitiously hears of a plot to rob a bank once a mysterious man named Liborio returns from abroad. In the meantime he uses his new face to interest a waitress and proves his love by writing her a check for a million pesos. Unfortunately, the plastic surgeon gave him the face of a wanted criminal, the bank robber Liborio Cantu. Fleeing from possible incarceration, Rodrigo returns to his town and must deal with his family and the remains of his inheritance. Sada is a master of language and of the bizarre, two elements that keep the reader engaged in descriptions of much of the worst of urban life as it can be lived and imagined in Latin America.

Luft, Lya [Biography] Brazilian novelist, poet, essayist, and translator, she has been publishing fiction since the 1980s. She writes small screen fiction in which she portrays the minute details of family relations. She has spent a lifetime attracted to what she calls the "dangerous shadows" of emotional and psychological states in the everyday lives of her middle-class characters, whose relationships are often torturous, rather than focusing strictly on social reality. Born in Santa Cruz (state of Rio Grande do Sul) in 1938, she studied Anglo-American and Germanic letters and made a first career translating foreign fiction into Portuguese, translating authors such as Virginia Woolf, Doris Lessing, Gunter Grass, and Thomas Mann. She began publishing poetry while teaching linguistics and translating.

Luft was forty years old when she wrote her first novel, *As Parceiras* (1980). She has called her novel *O Quarto Fechado* (1984, *The Island of the Dead*) one of her studies of "closed family relationships"; the action takes place during a wake and consists of the thoughts of the family members, with no omniscient narrator. *Exílio* (1988, *The Red House*) is a first-person account of a woman's experience with an alcoholic mother, an unfeeling husband, and loss of her only child. She is sent to reside with misfits in a space called the Red House. As in her previous work, Luft sets forth problems of existence for characters who are haunted by morbid realities of the past, at best, and traumas, at worst. As dark as Luft's fictional world may be, she considers herself an optimisit who observes, contemplates, and invents the world.

Luft also writes short fiction and poetry, and some of her writing escapes genres; her volume of prose titled *O Rio do Meio* (1982,

The river in the middle) is similar to literary essay and memoir; she has explained that much of her fiction is about women because she has spent a lifetime observing the hopes and aspirations of everyday women vanish as marriages do not foster the realization of their dreams. Luft also observes that men, too, are often trapped in unsatisfactory relationships and lives. Her collection of essays is titled *Matéria do cotidiano* (1978).

She currently contributes editorials in the weekly news magazine *Veja* and writes fiction.

Selected Work: As Parceiras (1980); *A Asa Esquerda do Anjo* (1981); *Reunião de Família* (1982); *O Quarto Fechado* (1984, *The Island of the Dead*, translation Carmen Chaves McClendon and Betty Jean Craige, 1986); *Exílio* (1988, *The Red House*, translation Giavanni Pontiero, 1994).

Lynch, Marta [Biography] Argentine novelist born in 1929, she was a major presence on the national novel scene from the early 1960s until her death in 1985. By the 1970s her work was also widely recognized in Latin America. Like many writers of her generation, she wrote critically of the experience of living in Argentina during the 1940s and 1950s under the Perón regime, but her main interest was less politics and society than communicating the intimate lives of her characters. Her stories *Cuentos tristes* (1967, Sad stories) relate the painful experience of growing up. Her three novels with more political themes were *La alfombra roja* (1962, The red carpet), *Al vencedor* (1965, The winning), and *La senora Ordóñez* (1968, Mrs. Ordóñez).

Lynch's most recognized work, *La alfombra roja*, is a psychological study of what happens to a group of people during an election campaign. It is a first-person account of the protagonist's use of people and their response to him, and in some chapters the narrative point of view changes. At the end the focus is on election day and the transformation of the candidate into a powermonger. Some critics have compared this novel to such political classics as Asturias's *El Señor Presidente* and Martín Luis Guzman's *La sombra del caudillo*. Her later novels show the ill effects of a corrupt society on the individual. The stories in her later *No te duermas, no me dejes* (1985, Don't sleep, don't leave me) can be read as a novel of intimate personal relationships in the context of frequently extreme situations and abstract conflicts.

Selected Work: *La alfombra roja* (1962); *Al vencedor* (1965); *La señora Ordóñez* (1968); *No te duermas, no me dejes* (1985).

Magical Realism [Topic] Most associated with the fiction of Gabriel García Márquez and Isabel Allende, the concept of magical realism began to circulate in Latin America in the 1940s and 1950s. The most classic magical realist texts from Latin America are Gabriel García Márquez's *Cien años de soledad* (1967, *One Hundred Years of Solitude*) and Isabel Allende's *La casa de los espíritus* (1984, *The House of the Spirits*). Scholars have pointed to the early uses of the term in connection with the painting of Franz Roh in Switzerland in the 1920s. The term has been discussed among scholars of Latin American literature since the 1950s. It is generally applied to a wide variety of texts that employ a base of concrete reality in conjunction with fantastic events or elements. Some scholars have made distinctions between the fantastic and magical realism. Others have pointed to the fact that much of what is called magical realism

is actually close to oral tradition. Recent generations of Latin American writers have either parodied or rejected magic realism, although the commercial success of Mexican Laura Esquivel points to its ongoing viability. Parodies of the style include works by the Cuban-American Roberto Fernández, the Colombian Marco Tulio Aguilera Garramuño, and the Colombian Gustavo Alvarez Gardeazábal. The generation of the 1990s in Brazil and the generation of crack in Mexico, as well as the international group McOndo (headed by the Chileans Alberto Fuguet and Sergio Gómez) have openly rejected magic realism.

Mainardi, Diogo [Biography] Brazilian novelist and journalist, he has become one of the more productive and noteworthy among the latest generation of Latin American novelists born since 1955. Born in São Paulo in 1962, he has studied economics and worked as a journalist and scriptwriter, living much of the time in Italy since the 1990s. He is widely known in Brazil as a regular columnist in the weekly news magazine *Veja*, where his irreverent and iconoclastic writings have gained him both celebrity and infamy among Brazil's middle-class readers and intellectuals. Identified by some critics as a postmodern novelist, he is an avid reader of Raymond Roussel, Donald Barthelme, Flann O'Brien, Italo Calvino, and Robert Coover. A satirical tone and parodic mode have marked his fiction since his first novel, *Malthus* (1989), titled after the British economist Thomas Robert Malthus (1766–1834). His second novel, *Arquipélago* (1992, Archipelago), uses as its point of departure the inundation of the city of Pedranópolis, where the narrator is located at the top of a church.

Two of Mainardi's most accomplished recent works are *Polígano das Secas* (1995, Poligano of the dry plains) and *Contra o Brasil* (1998, Against Brazil). The fragmented and multitextured *Polígano das Secas* is a parody of the Brazilian regionalist novel of the northeast. In this work Mainardi carries out a dialogue with writers such as Jorge Amado, José Lins de Rêgo, Rachel de Queiroz, Graciliano Ramos, and João Guimarães Rosa and sets forth a severe critique of the novel of the Brazilian northeastern region known as *sertão*. Given the canonical position of these works, *Polígano das Secas* is a polemical work that questions the essential and broadly cherished values of Brazilian literary tradition and national culture. This innovative, provocative, and humorous novel has been amply discussed among critics and could well be his major work to date. In *Contra o Brasil* the protagonist travels throughout Brazil following the footsteps of Claude Lévi-Strauss. This polemical satire begins with Pimenta Bueno, a self-titled ethnologist who probes the infamy of Brazilian culture while naked on his sofa humming an antinationalistic song. Bueno recites from memory anecdotes and quotes from famous scientists and travelers such as Lévi-Strauss as well as Theodore Roosevelt, who visited Brazil from Europe and the United States and found fault with Brazil. After burning down an old movie theater owned by his family and inhabited by a colony of beggars, Bueno travels to the jungles of Mato Grosso hoping to find the Nambiquara people, a tribe described by Lévi-Strauss as being Stone Age savages. Bueno thinks nothing of exploiting and abusing those whom he encounters. The experiment in going native fails, and Bueno flees to Europe where he continues to embody the infamy that he vehemently denounces in Brazil while searching in vain for Claude.

Arquipélago is an allegorical satire of the authoritarian uses of power based on an absurd situation: a group of Brazilians are shipwrecked on an island. Initially, they are stranded on the top of a church, surrounded by water. One by one, the members of the group attempt to abandon the island and die. The narrator-protagonist becomes the authoritarian leader of the group and soon begins to abuse his power. Eventually, his followers consider him a god. The novel contains tour stories taken from the history of different attempts at establishing quasi-utopias on islands, relating humorous versions of failed attempts by Rousseau, St. John, Plato, and a Frenchman named Nicolan Durant de Villegagnon, who spent four years (1555–1559) attempting to rule an island off the coast of Brazil to establish religious freedom for French religious exiles. Mainardi makes it clear that he is skeptical of all religious belief systems.

Selected Work: *Malthus* (1989); *Arquipélago* (1992); *Polígano das Secas* (1995); *Contra o Brasil* (1998).

Mallea, Eduardo [Biography] Argentine novelist and essayist who was born in 1903 and died in 1979, he was a major intellectual figure in Latin America at midcentury. He published the seminal essay *Historia de una pasión argentina* in 1937. In his fiction he was a pioneer of his time in that he moved the focus from a broad panoramic vision to the details of his characters' interior lives. During the 1940s and 1950s he was considered a major novelist in Argentina and throughout Latin America. In his most renowned novel, *Todo verdor perecerá* (1941, *All the Green Shall Perish*), Mallea portrays the relationship between a married couple, with the main focus on the woman, Agata Cruz. Mallea communictes a sense of a sterile long-term relationship, and, at the novel's end, Agata is alone, frustrated, and disoriented. Since the rise of the 1960s Boom of the Latin American novel, Mallea's work has been increasingly ignored for both aesthetic and political reasons.

Selected Work: La ciudad junto al río inmóvil (1936); *Fiesta en noviembre* (1938, *Fiesta in November*, translation Alis de Sola, 1966); *La bahía de silencio* (1940, *The Bay of Silence*, translation Stuart Edgar Grummon, 1944); *Todo verdor perecerá* (1941, *All Green Shall Perish*, translation John B. Hughes, 1967); *Las aguilas* (1943); *Los enemigos del alma* (1950); *La torre* (1951); *Chaves* (1953, *Chaves*, translation María Mercedes Aspiazu, 1966); *La sala de espera* (1953); *Simbad* (1957); *El resentimiento* (1966); *La penúltima puerta* (1969); *Gabriel Andaral* (1961), *Triste piel del universo* (1971).

Manjarréz, Héctor [Biography] Mexican novelist, short story writer, poet, essayist, and playwright, he was associated with the rebellious new writers of the 1960s Onda in Mexico. He was born in Mexico City in 1945. He has taught, edited, and worked for the media in the arts. He has translated a broad range of writers, from Artaud to Tristan Tzara, and has also written a book of essays on writers such as Malcolm Lowry, Juan Rulfo, and Julio Cortázar. His writings are generally irreverent in tone and connected to the counterculture of his generation—a group born in the 1940s who surfaced in the Mexican literary scene in the 1960s. He is broadly recognized in Mexico for his humor and colloquial language. After Gustavo Sainz and José Agustín, Manjarrez has been one of the most productive members of the Onda group. He was awarded a prestigious national literary prize, the Premio Xavier Villarrutia, in 1983 for his volume of short fiction *No todos los hombres son románticos* (1983, Not all men are romantic), a book that fictionalizes many of the political positions, cultural preferences, and sexual mores of his generation. He also published another volume of short fictions of a personal tone, *Ya casi no tengo rostro* (1996, I almost don't have a face anymore). His book *Acto propiciatorio* (1970, Propitiatory act) has been read both as a set of short stories and as a novel. In his self-conscious and playful *Lapsus* (1971), the narrator invites the reader to invent a chapter. Manjarrez is a noteworthy contributor to postmodern fiction in Mexico and Latin America.

Selected Work: Acto propiciatorio (1970); *Lapsus* (1971); *Pasaban en silencio nuestros días* (1987); *El otro amor de su vida* (1999); *Rainey, el asesino* (2002); *La maldita pintura* (2004).

Mansilla, Margarita [Biography] Mexican essayist, poet, translator, and novelist, she has published one patently experimental novel, *Karenina express* (1995), which was awarded a national prize, the Premio de Narrativa Colima. She was born in Mexico City in 1953 and studied English at the National University in Mexico City (UNAM), then continuing graduate study at El Colegio de México in Hispanic Linguistics. She has also done graduate work in London and at Brywn Mawr College in the United States. The protagonist in *Karenina express* is an unemployed woman who proposes to write a novel with a love story, but then works on various alternative directions for the novel. It includes a multiplicity of voices and discourses such as diaries, aphorisms, and poems.

Novel: Karenina express (1995).

Mar de lentejas, El (1985, *Sea of Lentils*, by Antonio Benitez-Rojo. Translation by James Maraniss. Amherst: University of Massachusetts Press, 1985) **[Novel]** Benítez-Rojo was a major intellectual presence in Cuba before taking exile in the United States, and, until his death in late 2004, he continued writing hybrid texts (essays and novels). This work consists of stories of conquest and conflict. Benítez-Rojo draws upon the oral storytelling tradition, but also employs the discourses of autobiography, economics, and history to construct a pastiche of Caribbean history from approximately the conquest up until the death of King Phillip II of Spain. The plot involves King Phillip II's final thoughts about the New World, memories of the failed Armada against England, and the spread of the Reformation in Europe before illness claims him. There are also anecdotes of the brutality of the conquistadors in Florida who massacre French Huguenot colonists, Anton Babtista following Colombus's second exploration and setting himself up as a feudal lord of a clan of Indians on Haiti, and English piracy. Throughout the various narrative lines, the Caribbean is portrayed as a sea of material goods, for which one geographer labeled it the Sea of Lentils.

Marechal, Leopoldo [Biography] Argentine novelist who was born in 1900 and died in 1970, he is the author of one of the major novels of the century in Latin America, *Adán Buenosayres* (1948). He played a major role in the reaffirmation of the right of invention in the 1940s in Latin America. In the 1920s he was involved with the avant-garde literary magazine *Martín Fierro*. He also made two trips to Europe, where he was in contact with avant-garde writers in Spain and France. In 1931 he began writing *Adán Buenosayres* during a spiritual crisis. This lengthy, complex, and Joycean work centers on the character Adán Buenosayres and his cohorts. They travel to obscure places and discuss literary topics. In addition to being a satire of literary life in Buenos Aires in the 1920s, the novel delves deeply into the protagonist's psyche and insanity.

Marechal's use of literary language was special for the 1940s, for it involved a humorous juxtaposition of the pretentious and the vulgar. The vulgar language emphasizes the anal, creating a humorous deflation of the pretentious. Along with Miguel Angel Asturias, Clarice Lispector, and Alejo Carpentier, Marechal was a pioneer modern writer of the 1940s.

Selected Work: Adán Buenosayres (1948); *El banquete de Severo Arcángelo* (1965); *Megafón o la Guerra* (1970).

Martín del Campo, David [Biography] Mexican novelist, short story writer, and screenwriter, he has been active in the Mexican literary scene in the 1980s and 1990s. Born in Mexico City in 1952, his fiction reflects the generalized skepticism and disenchantment of his generation with the political establishment in Mexico and status quo. He has two prestigious novel prizes in Mexico (Premio Internacional de Novela Diana-Novedades, Premio José Rubén Romero). His novel *Las rojas son las carreteras* (1976, The red ones are highways) portrays Mexico's youth confronting the pain and injustice of the tragic events of the conflict in October 1968 in Mexico City. *Isla de lobos* (1987, Island of wolves) deals with issues of cultural conflict between the country and the city. *Alas de angel* (1990, Angel wings) is a historic work, looking back at the Mexico of the 1940s.

Selected Work: Las rojas son las carreteras (1976); *Esta tierra del amor* (1982); *Isla de lobos* (1987); *Todos los árboles* (1987); *El hombre equivocado* (1988); *Alas de ángel* (1990); *Dama de noche* (1990); *Quemar los pozos* (1990); *Las viudas de blanco* (1993); *El año de fuego* (1996).

Martínez, Tomás Eloy [Biography] Argentine novelist and essayist born in 1934, he went into political exile when in 1974 a bomb destroyed the building where he was working as a journalist. He became widely known in Latin America and beyond with the publication of his novel *Santa Evita* (1995), which appeared in English under the title *Evita* in 1996 and was followed by the release of a film of the same title starring the media celebrity Madonna. This novel popularized the historic character Evita Peron in the international scene as much as had been the case in Argentina: as a sexual persona as well as a political figure. *Santa Evita* connects directly in historic context and themes with his earlier *La novela de Perón* (1985, The Peron novel). Both novels are postmodern fictions in the sense that they are self-reflexive and historically based. Martínez claims that he writes "intimate history," for he uses real historical figures to explore the personal fantasies that individuals can have of political figures. Since the mid-1980s he has worked as an academic in the United States.

Selected Work: *Sagrado* (1969); *La novela de Perón* (1985, *The Peron Novel*, translation Asa Zatz, 1988); *La mano del amo* (1991); *Evita* (1995, *Evita*, translation Helen R. Lane, 1996); *Las memorias del General* (1996); *El vuelo de la reina* (2002); *El cantor del tango* (2004).

Martínez Moreno, Carlos [Biography] Uruguayan novelist, journalist, theater critic, and literary critic, he is one of the major fiction writers in Uruguay of the second half of the century. He was born in Colonia, Uruguay, in 1917, practiced law, and in the mid-1970s went into exile in Mexico, where he died in 1986. He is recognized in his fiction as an innovator who played a major role in the modernization of the Uruguayan novel. He began writing in the 1950s, and won his first literary prize from the magazine *Número* in 1956 for his novella *Cordelia* (1961). He published his first full-length novel, *El paredón* (The wall) in 1963. His questioning of reality itself is carried out in his novels *Con las primeras luces* (1966, With the first lights), *Coca* (1970, Coca), and *Tierra en la boca* (1974, Dirt in the mouth). He has also published several books of short fiction and book-length lit-

erary essays. His major novels are *Con las primeras luces* and *Tierra en la boca*.

Selected Work: *Cordelia* (1961); *El paredón* (1963); *Con las primeras luces* (1966); *Las cuatro* (1967, collection of short novels including *Cordelia*); *Coca* (1970); *Tierra en la boca* (1974); *El color que el infierno me escondiera* (1981, *El Infierno*, translation Ann Wright, 1988).

Mastretta, Angeles [Biography] Mexican novelist, poet, journalist, translator, and essayist, she is one of the most broadly read women writers in Latin America today. She gained instant fame in Mexico for her novel *Arráncame la vida* (1988), which appeared in English as *Mexican Bolero*. Born in Puebla in 1949, she studied communication at the National University in Mexico City (UNAM). She received the prestigious Rómulo Gallegos Novel Prize, given in Caracas in recognition of a major writer in Latin America.

Her more recent *El cielo de los leones* (2003, Sky of lions) is a semiautobiographical survey of the dreams and desires that she finds in everyday life. The work is made up of thirty-eight small essays, poems in prose, and reflections about the various people and passions of her life. In a semichronological manner, the first pieces deal with Mastretta's memories of her grandfather, who embraced the changing times and technology of the twentieth century. A dynamic great aunt is described as a role model and poet Jaimes Sabines is given a eulogy in one chapter entitled "Si sobrevives, canta." Mastretta's children are described as miracles in her life in several later chapters. The eponymous "El cielo de los leones" is a reflection on seduction toward all of the miracles in life and its catalyst—the craziness of some very private dreams.

Selected Work: *Arráncame la vida* (1988, *Mexican Bolero*, translation Ann Wright, 1989); *Mal de amores* (1996, *Lovesick*, translation Margaret Sayers Peden, 1997); *Ninguna eternidad como la mía* (1999); *El cielo de los leones* (2003).

Medina, Enrique [Biography] Argentine novelist born in 1937, he has been one of the most prolific writers in Argentina during the post-WWII period. He writes fiction that tests the limits of censorship and middle-class moral codes. His major novel is *El Duke* (1976, *The Duke: Memories and Anti-Memories of a Participant in the Repression*, 1985), a fictionalization of the life of a boxer famous in Argentina. In this novel and others, he explores the underworld of sex, violence, and crime. Some readers consider his work borderline pornography; Medina and some scholars consider his fictions an exploration of a world where neither morality nor immorality are legitimate concepts.

Selected Work: *Transparente* (1974); *El Duke* (1976, *The Duke: Memories and Anti-Memories of a Participant in the Repression*, translation David William Foster, 1985); *Perros de la noche* (1978); *Las muecas del miedo* (1981); *Con el trapo en la boca* (1983); *Los asesinos* (1984); *Colisiones* (1984); *Año nuevo en Nueva York* (1986); *Las hienas* (1986); *Buscando a Madonna* (1987); *La espera infinita* (2000).

Mejía Vallejo, Manuel [Biography] Colombian novelist, short story writer, poet, and essayist, he was born in 1923 in the department of Antioquia in the small town of Jericó. Reared in a rural setting, he lived on a farm near the town of Jardín, which is still isolated from mainstream urban society in Colombia. His parents sent him to Medellín for high school, and he has written that his literary vocation arose during those years. In the 1940s he studied at the Universidad Bolivariana in Medellín. While doing his college-level studies, he began to write for a local newspaper and composed much of his first novel, *La tierra éramos nosotros* (1945, We were the land). This early experiment in fiction writing was an account of his youth in rural Antioquia. In his youth he experienced La Violencia. In addition to that first novel, he published short fiction beginning in the late 1940s, but is best known for his novel on the period of La Violencia, *El día señalado* (1963, The signaled day). A synthesis of various elements from his previous fiction, *El día señalado* is set in a mythical invented town and develops along two narrative lines, one, written in the third person, deals with the small town, and the other tells a story of personal revenge. The basic context is La Violencia, yet this is Mejía Vallejo's most internationally recognized work.

He was also widely recognized in Colombia for his novel, *Aire de tango* (1975, Tango air), written in homage to the legendary Argentine singer Carlos Gardel.

Selected Work: *La tierra éramos nosotros* (1945); *Al pie de la ciudad* (1958); *El día señalado* (1963, The signaled day); *Aire de tango* (1975); *Tarde de verano* (1980); *La casa de dos palmas* (1988).

Melo, Patrícia [Biography] Brazilian novelist, playwright, and screenwriter, she has become an accomplished writer of criminal suspense novels closely allied to the genre of detective fiction. She was born in 1962 and lives in São Paulo. In 1999 *Time* magazine included her among fifty Latin American leaders for the new millennium. Her novels are typically fast-paced, action intense, and brazen in both language and content, offending conventional sensibilities. *Acqua Toffana* (1994) provides powerful insight into the mindset of a violent criminal who kills women. The first half of the novel is narrated by the women with whom the protagonist lives and the second half by the protagonist himself. This is the first of several works by Melo in which socially deviant characters have normalized violent crime as common, everyday activities.

Selected Work: *Acqua Tiffana* (1994); *O Matador* (1995, *The Killer*, translation Clifford E. Landers, 1997); *Elogio da Mentira* (1998, *In Praise of Lies*, translation Clifford E. Landers); *Inferno* (2000, *Inferno*, translation Clifford E. Landers, 2002); *Valsa Negra* (2003, *Black Waltz*, translation Clifford E. Landers, 2004).

Memory Fever (1993, by Ray Gonzalez. Written in English) [**Novel**] The border between Mexico and the United States serves as the setting for many Chicano novels, and one of the pioneers of the Chicano novel, Rolando Hinojosa, has used the valley of the Rio Grande in Texas for his entire set of fictions. The same politically charged Rio Grande, in this case near El Paso, is the setting for this book by Chicano author and poet Ray Gonzalez. A collection of short memoirs about the author's youth along the banks of the Rio Grande, it is laden with metaphorical language. The vignettes range from prose poems about items such as an encounter with a rattlesnake and the memory of an elderly grandmother making tamales to short essays about writing poetry and the racism of the dominant Anglo-American culture of the region. In its totality the author's past covers early youth—being a boy playing along the river—to involvement in high school football and the racism found in those arenas, to being a young poet at the University of Texas at El Paso. At the end the author describes his return to the area years later—now as an established poet and editor—encountering his past in a series of objects that a part of his memory.

Menchú, Rigoberta [**Biography**] Guatemalan writer and activist, she won the Nobel Peace Prize in 1992. She is known throughout the world for her now classic coauthored testimonial work, *Me llamo Rigoberta Menchú y así me nació la conciencia* (1984, *I Rigoberta Menchú*), which was transcribed by anthropologist Elizabeth Burgos-Debray. In this work she tells her story—as an indigenous woman—of surviving the abuses of the military regime that injured and murdered the indigenous population.

Selected Work: *Me llamo Rigoberta Menchú y así me nació la conciencia* (1984, *I, Rigoberto Menchú: An Indian Woman in Guatemala*, translation Ann Wright, 1984).

Méndez, Ariel [**Biography**] Uruguayan novelist, short story writer, and journalist, he has written amply about the effects of human relations and urban life on the individual. He was born in Castillos, Uruguay, in 1919 and moved to Montevideo when he was eighteen years old. His major novels are *La encrucijada* (1949, *The crossroad*), *La ciudad contra los muros* (1961, *The city against the walls*), *La otra aventura* (1962, *The other adventure*), and *Los escándalos* (1970, *The scandals*). Later in his career he wrote some short fiction of a light and humorous tone: *Chocolate con sardines* (1982) and *Ayer comí con los Borgia* (1986).

Selected Work: *La encrucijada* (1949); *La ciudad contra los muros* (1961); *La otra aventura* (1962); *Los escándalos* (1970).

Mendoza, Mario [**Biography**] Colombian novelist and short story writer, he was born in 1964 and belongs to the generation of the 1990s in Latin America that began publishing fiction in the 1990s. His short fiction has won several awards in Colombia, and much of his writing represents an effort to offer a new vision of urban reality in Latin America. Author of several novels, his recent novel *Satanás* (2002, Satan) was the 2002 winner of a very prestigious international prize in Spanish, the Seix

Barral Premio Biblioteca Breve, offered by the Spain-based publishing house. *Satanás* is a horror-inspiring historic fiction set in contemporary Bogotá. The pervasive vision of evil triumphing over good throughout Colombian society reveals a deep malaise in the country. Maria is a young woman caught up with a band of thieves who drug and then rob wealthy executives. Andrés is an artist who paints portraits complete with the hidden interior horrors of the models exposed. Padre Ernesto is the doubting priest who means well but is incapable of saving any of his parishioners who lust, host demons, or murder their family. As the nexus to these other interwoven stories, Campo Elias is an English teacher in Bogotá who served with the U.S. army in Vietnam. Inspired by the duality of humanity found in books such as *Dr Jekyll and Mr. Hyde* by Robert Louis Stevenson, Elias eventually snaps and converts himself into an exterminating angel on the streets of Bogotá, claiming over twenty lives. Mendoza's deep pessimism leaves many victims, and most are also also executioners.

Selected Work: *La ciudad de los umbrales* (1992); *Scorpio City* (1998); *Relato de un asesino* (2001); *Satanás* (2002).

Mexican Bolero (See *Arráncame la vida* by Angeles Mastretta) [**Novel**]

Miranda, Ana [**Biography**] Brazilian novelist, poet, and short story writer, she was born in Fortaleza (state of Ceará) in 1951. She moved to Rio de Janeiro in 1969, where she lived until 1999, when she moved to São Paulo. Much of her work recreates Brazilian historical moments or the lives of writers. She writes novels with strong plots and elaborate historical content; *Boca do Inferno* (1989) and *O Retrato do Rei* (1991, The portrait of the king) are historical works. Her first novel, *Boca do Inferno* (1989), appeared in English as *Boy of All Saints and Every Conceivable Sin*, translated by Giovanni Pontiero, is an intriguing story of murder and revenge set in the Bahia of the seventeenth century, when it was a major city of the Portuguese Empire. In this novel she includes historical figures as characters. *Sem Pecado* (1993, Without sin) is not a historical work: the protagonist is a contemporary adolescent girl who emigrates from the provinces to the city to pursue a career in theater. Miranda fictionalizes the life of writer Augusto dos Anjos (1884–1914) in *A última Quimera* (1995, The last sin) and creates a fictional Clarice Lispector as a character in her novel *Clarice* (1999). Her work has been translated into several languages, and she received the prestigious BrazilianPrêmio Jabuti in 1990. Her recent *Dias y Dias* (2002, Days and days) relates a love story as it unfolds between three characters.

Selected Work: *Boca do inferno* (1989, *Boy of All Saints and Every Conceivable Sin*, translation Giovanni Pontiero, 1991); *O Retrato do Rei* (1991); *Sem Pecado* (1993); *A última Quimera* (1995); *Desmundo* (1996); *Amtrik* (1997); *Clarice* (1999); *Noturnos* (1999); *Dias y Dias* (2002).

Modernismo (Brazil) [**Topic**] A literary movement specific to Brazil and different from both Spanish-American *modernismo* and Anglo-American modernism, Brazilian *modernismo* is best associated with the broad literary and cultural desire to be modern of the 1920s, 1930s, and 1940s. A much-celebrated Semana de Arte Moderna (week of modern art) in 1922 came about with the growing awareness of European futurism as well as other European art movements. In Brazil (as opposed to the rest of Latin America), *modernismo* was the dominant cultural trend from the 1920s to the 1940s. Held in São Paulo's Municipal

Theater, the Semana de Arte Moderna was a platform for many young writers, artists, and musicians. Most critics think of the period from 1922 to 1945 as that of Brazilian *modernismo* at its height. During the middle years of this period, the regionalist novel was important, followed by more psychological novels in the later years.

Iconoclastic and irreverent fiction writers of this period were Oswald de Andrade, Mário de Andrade, and Antônio de Alcântara Machado.

Molloy, Sylvia [Biography] Argentine novelist, essayist, and academic, she is a leading novelist and theorist of feminism in Latin America. Born in Buenos Aires in 1938, she has been a practicing academic in the United States for over three decades. She is widely known for her novel *En breve cárcel* (1981, *Certificate of Absence*), which deals with the construction of a woman's identity and of a text. It is the story of an Argentine woman who returns to an apartment in New England where she once had an affair with another woman and where she writes a memoir about that experience. The narrator-protagonist struggles with both expressing herself in this memoir and with her own identity. Like much postmodern and recent feminist fiction written in Latin America, this novel destabilizes any notion of fixed identity.

Selected Work: *En breve cárcel* (1981, *Certificate of Absence*, translation Daniel Balderston, 1989); *El común olvido* (2002).

Monteforte Toledo, Mario [Biography] Guatemalan novelist, poet, translator, and essayist, he was born in 1911 and later studied law in Costa Rica and sociology at the Sorbonne in Paris, receiving a degree in 1946. He was expelled from the University of San Carlos because of his opposition to President Ubico of Guatemala and studied in Paris in the 1930s. He has carried out much of his professional career as a writer, academic, and politician in exile in Mexico, holding positions as both a professor and a researcher at the National University in Mexico City (UNAM) and as president of the Association of Academics at that same institution in 1974–75. He was the representative of socialist president Jacobo Arbenz to the United Nations, a post he received in 1951. He has also served as editor of the Mexican cultural organ *Siempre*.

He began writing in the 1930s and claims to have completed his first novel in Haiti in 1938, even though he did not publish it until much later. His novels are partially the product of his experience living in the countryside with indigenous groups upon his return from Paris. They are social realist presentations of native American peoples that reflect many of the methods and motifs of *indigenismo*. His major novels, *Anaité* (1948) and *Entre la piedra y la cruz* (1948, Between the rock and the cross), hark back to the Latin American novel of the 1920s, although the latter represents an effort to develop the characters in psychological depth. In *Anaité* the protagonist goes to the most remote and exotic region of Guatemala to find his fortune and plays out a classic *civilización* versus *barbarie* scenario. Monteforte Toledo's most widely read novel was *Donde acaban los caminos* (1952, Where the roads end).

After living in exile for thirty-five years, he returned to Guatemala in 1986, receiving a prestigious national literary prize there, the Miguel Angel Asturias prize, in 1992. He was working on a screenplay version of his novel *Donde acaban los caminos* when he died in 2003.

Selected Work: *Anaité* (1946); *Entre la piedra y la cruz* (1948); *Donde acaban los caminos* (1953); *Una manera de morir* (1957); *Llegaron del mar* (1966); *Los desencontrados*

(1976); *Unas vísperas muy largas* (1989); *Los adoradores de la muerte* (2001).

Montello, Josué [Biography] Brazilian author of novels, short stories, theater, poetry, literary criticism, and journalism, he used fiction to portray his home state of Maranhão. He was born in São Luís in 1917 and has served as director of the National Library, the National Museum of History, and the National Theater. He is known for the psychological development of characters in his novels. His novel *Cais da Sagração* (1971, *Coronation Quay*), which critics consider his major work, tells the story of an individual's attempts at maintaining a family's maritime customs and traditions. He also published a saga of an Afro-Brazilian family, *Os Tambosres de São Luís* (1975, The drums of San Luis). He has published seven novels and numerous volumes of short stories.

Selected Work: *Janelas Fechadas* (1941); *A Luz de Estrela Morta* (1948); *Labirinto de Espelhos* (1952); *Os Degraus do Paraíso* (1965); *Cais da Sagração* (1971, *Coronation Quay*, translation Myriam Hendersen, 1975); *Os Tambores de São Luís* (1975); *Noite sobre Alcantara* (1978); *A Coroa de Arcia* (1979); *O Silêncio da Confissão* (1980); *Largo do Desterro* (1981); *Aleluia para os Bentevis* (1989); *A Ultima Convidada* (1989); *O Camarote Vazio* (1990); *O Baile da Despedida* (1992); *A Viagem sem Regresso* (1993); *Uma Sombra na Parede* (1995); *A Mulher Proibida* (1996); *Enquanto o Tempo não Passa* (1996); *Sempre Serás Lembrada* (2000); *A Mais Bela Noiva de Vila Rica* (2001).

Morales, Mario Roberto [Biography] Guatemalan novelist, poet, essayist, and journalist, he is one of Central America's most prominent young writers. Born in 1947, he has studied both the social sciences and literature at the undergraduate and graduate levels in Costa Rica and in the United States. To date, his most renowned novel is *El esplendor de la pirámide* (1986, The splendor of the pyramid). After completing a PhD in literature at the University of Pittsburgh, he returned to Guatemala, where he is a journalist and writes fiction.

Selected Work: *Los demonios salvajes* (1978); *El esplendor de la pirámide* (1986); *Señor bajo los árboles* (1994, *Face of the Earth, Heart of the Sky*, translation Edward Waters Hood, 2000); *El ángel de la retaguardia* (1996).

Moreno Durán, R. H. (Rafael Humberto Moreno Durán) [Biography] Colombian novelist, short story writer, and essayist, he is one of the country's foremost postmodern writers. After spending several years in Spain writing and working as an editor, he returned to Colombia in 1987 to become a major presence as a novelist, essayist, and public intellectual. He has published several books of essays on elegant literary topics, most of which focus on the writers of the 1960s Boom and the masters of Anglo-American modernism. His recent book of essays, *Mujeres de Babel* (2004), for example, is a discussion of verbal excess in Joyce.

Born in Tunja (department of Cundinamarca) in 1946, he studied law in the National University in Bogotá and then went to Spain in the early 1970s. Writing in Spain, he surfaced on the literary scene in Colombia with the novel *Juego de damas* (1977, Lady's game) and essay *De la imaginación a la barbarie* (1976, From imagination to barbarism). His first fiction was an impressive trilogy that he called Femina Suite, and included the titles *Juego de damas*, *Toque de Diana* (1981, Diane's touch), *Finale capriccioso con Madonna* (1983, Capricious end with Madonna). He has also enjoyed considerable success with his novel *El caballero de la invicta* (1987,

The gentleman of the undefeated). He is interested in topics such as the relationship between language and sexuality. His novels are playful and entertaining; nevertheless, his dense and complex fiction is too hermetic to have gained a large reading audience in Latin America, but Moreno-Durán is widely admired in Colombia and well respected among Latin America's most elite and urbane intellectuals. Among his other writings, he published the volume of short stories *Cartas en el asunto* (1995, Letters on the subject) and four other books of short stories as well as a play, *Cuestión de hábitos* (2004, A question of habits).

Selected Work: *Juego de damas* (1977); *Toque de Diana* (1981); *Finale capriccioso con Madonna* (1983); *Los felinos del Canciller* (1987); *El caballero de la invicta* (1993); *Mambrú* (1996); *La conexión africana* (2003).

Moscovich, Cíntia [Biography] Brazilian novelist and short story writer, she was born in Porto Alegre (state of Rio Grande do Sul) in 1958. She has taught and worked as a journalist in addition to working as a translator. Moscovich won a prestigious prize (Concurso de Contos Guimarães Rosa) for her short stories. She published her first novel, *Duas Iguais: Manual de Amor e Equívocos Assemelhados* (Two of the same: manual of love and assimilated errors) in 1998; she claims in the preface that her only intention with this book is to tell a love story, although she also points to the fragmented nature of the facts and "suspicioius" coherence and logic. It is a first-person account. Some critics have associated her with the new generation of writers born since 1955 who have published their first work in the 1990s, known as the generation of the 1990s. Her recent book of fiction is the volume of stories *Anotacões durante o Incendio* (2000).

Selected Work: *Duas Iguais: Manual de Amor e Equívocos Assemelhados* (1998).

Mujica Lainez, Manuel [Biography] Argentine novelist and short story writer who was born in 1910 and died in 1984, he was a prolific author of works that tended to portray a fantasy world in the context of Argentina's decadent society. Mujica Lainez was interested in exploring a variety of utopias (often in the arts and in a distant historic past) as an antidote to mortality. He is best known for his novel *Bomarzo* (1962), which appeared in English translation under the same title.

He began writing fiction in the late 1930s, publishing his first relatively unknown novel, *Don Galaz de Buenos Aires* (Don Galaz of Buenos Aires) in 1938. In this work a seventeenth-century page dreams of El Dorado, but finds death. His volumes of short fiction, written in the 1940s and 1950s, include *Aquí vivieron*, *Misteriosa Buenos Aires*, and *Crónicas reales*. His early novel *La casa* (1954, The house) treats the house itself as the central character. The novel covers seven decades of this house's life on the elegant Calle Florida in the center of Buenos Aires. (In the early 1950s future Nobel laureate Gabriel García Márquez and his friend Alvaro Cepeda Zamudio were also writing novels with the tentative title of "la casa"; Garcá Márquez eventually changed the title of his first novel to *La hojarasca* and Cepeda Zamudio eventually published his only novel under the title *La casa grande*.)

Mujica Lainez's major novel *Bomarzo* is a detailed account of cultural life in Italy during the sixteenth-century Renaissance, with references to the intellectual and artistic setting. It is a first-person account of the Duke of Bomarzo's search for immortality, with ample development of his family history and fantasy life. In the end the duke drinks of the poison that substitutes for a magic elixir of immortality. With its well-developed plot, minute descriptions of cultural artifacts, and utopian search for immortality, this novel represents Mujica Lainez at his best.

Selected Work: *Don Galaz de Buenos Aires* (1938); *Idolos* (1953); *La casa* (1954); *Los viajeros* (1955); *Invitados en el Paraíso* (1957); *Bomarzo* (1962); *El unicornio* (1965, *The Wandering Unicorn*, translation Mary Fitton, 1983).

Muñiz-Huberman, Angelina [Biography] Mexican novelist, short story writer, translator, and essayist, she has become a major representative of Jewish-Mexican fiction writing. She was born in France in 1936 and became a nationalized Mexican citizen in 1942. She studied literature at the National University in Mexico City (UNAM), where she received an MA, and later completed her PhD at the University of Pennsylvania and CUNY. She has published several volumes of short stories as well as the novels *Morada interior* (1972, Inner dwelling), *Tierra adentro* (1977, Inland), *La guerra del unicornio* (1983, The war of the unicorn), *Hacia Malinalco* (1986, Toward Malinalco). Her fiction addresses issues of ethnicity, gender, and identity.

Selected Work: *Morada interior* (1972), *Tierra adentro* (1977), *La guerra del unicornio* (1983), *Hacia Malinalco* (1986); *Dulcinea encantada* (1992); *Castillos en la tierra* (1995); *El mercader de Tudela* (1998); *Molinos sin viento* (2001); *Areúsa en los conciertos* (2002).

Murena, Héctor A. [Biography] Argentine novelist, short story writer, and essayist who was born in 1923 and died in 1975, he is a well-known satirist of the nation's institutions. He portrays the absurd and nightmarish aspects of life in the 1940s and 1950s under the Perón regime in his trilogy, which consists of *La fatalidad de los cuerpos* (1955, The fatality of bodies), *Las leyes de la noche* (1958, The laws of the night), and *Los herederos de la promesa* (1965, The laws of the night). The raucous and satirical *Epitalámica* (1969, Epithalamic) is his most entertaining and acerbic critique of Argentine society.

Selected Work: *La fatalidad de los cuerpos* (1955); *Las leyes de la noche* (1958); *Los herederos de la promesa* (1965); *Epitalámica* (1969).

Mutis, Alvaro [Biography] Colombian novelist and poet who has become internationally recognized since the 1980s. Born in Bogotá in 1923, he lived in Belgium for much of his childhood but often returned to Colombia with his parents, who owned an hacienda there. He belonged to what has been called the *Generación de Mito* (the generation centered around the 1950s magazine *Mito*, 1955–1962). He was first known in Colombia as a poet, publishing in that genre from the 1950s to the 1970s. He wrote little fiction during this period and published his first short story in 1948. In the 1970s he began publishing a series of highly successful novels, all of which focused on the mythical character Maqroll. Among Mutis's better-known novels is *Un bel morir* (1989, A better death) and *Maqroll el gaviero* (1973, Maqroll the Topman).

A predecessor to his fiction was his *testimonio* to his experience in prison in Mexico, *Diario de Lecumberri* (1956, Diary of Lecumberri). His first novel, *La mansión de Aracaíma* (1973, The mansion of Aracaíma), contains many elements of the classic Gothic novel. It is a nostalgic look at an idyllic place like the region of his childhood experience. In his novels Mutis constructed a protagonist, Maqroll, who travels around the world; Mutis has dedicated a lifetime to relating the life experience, spiritual search, and adventures of this character of both his poetry and fiction. He has enjoyed considerable success in English translation and has been awarded several important international prizes in the Hispanic world as well as the Neustadt Prize in 2002.

Selected Work: *La mansion de Aracaíma* (1973); *La nieve del almirante* (1973); *Maqroll el gaviero* (1973, *The Adventures of Maqroll: Four Novellas*, translation Edith Grossman, 1995); *Ilona llega con la lluvia* (1988); *La última escala del Tramp Steamer* (1989); *Un bel morir* (1989); *Amirbar* (1990); *Abdul Bashur soñador de navíos* (1991); *Tríptico de mar y tierra* (1993).

Naranjo, Carmen [Biography] Costa Rican novelist and poet, she is one of the major woman writers of the Central American region. Born in 1928, she studied literature at the National University in Mexico City (UNAM), later living in both the United States and Venezuela. She has held several government positions, serving as Costa Rica's ambassador to Israel, director of the National Museum, and director of the major publishing house in the Central American region (EDUCA). She is also a member of the Academy of Language in Costa Rica. She began writing fiction in the 1960s, and her novels deal with issues of personal identity and gender. Since the late 1980s, she has been a leader in the women's rights movement in Costa Rica.

Her major novel, *Diario de una multitud* (1974, Diary of a multitude), was awarded a prize by the Superior Council of Central American Universities.

Selected Work: *Los perros no ladraron* (1966); *Camino al mediodía* (1968); *Memorias de un hombre palabra* (1968); *Responso por el niño Juan Manuel* (1971); *Diario de una multitud* (1974); *Sobrepunto* (1985); *Más allá del Parismina* (2004).

Nascimento, Esdras do [Biography] Brazilian novelist, translator, journalist, and academic, he was born in Teresina, Brazil in 1934, and completed his high school studies in the city of Fortaleza, later moving to Rio de Janeiro, Porto Alegre, and eventually Brasília. He studied philosophy as an undergraduate and literature at the graduate level in Brazil. In 1977 he was a pioneer in Brazil by having a creative work—the novel *Variante Gotemburgo* (Gotemburgo variant)—accepted as his doctoral dissertation. He lived abroad for ten years in Amsterdam, London, and New York. His conventional and linear novels set forth critique of Brazil's classist society and social norms, particularly the institution of marriage. He is known as an urban writer interested in developing the psychological states of characters who suffer from alienation and existential anguish. His novels include *Solidão em Família* (1963, Solidarity in the family), *Tiro na emória* (1965, Memory shot), and *Paixão bem Temperada* (1970, Temperate passion), and he has published several volumes of short fiction and essays.

Selected Work: *Solidão em Família* (1963); *Convite ao Desespero* (1964); *Tiro na Memória* (1965); *Engenharia do Casamento* (1968); *Paixão bem Temperada* (1970); *O Ventre da Baleia* (1980); *Jogos da Madrugada* (1983); *Lição da Noite* (1998).

Nassar, Raduan [Biography] Novelist and journalist, he is known for his unique novel—a major work of the 1970s—*Lavoura Arcaica* (1975, Old fashioned farming). Born in Pindorama, São Paulo in 1935, he studied philosophy and law in São Paulo, also studying classical literature, but he did not receive a degree in any of these fields. Lacking the desire to practice law, he became a rancher and began working as a journalist, writing pieces on political and cultural topics. His fiction writing is patently lyrical and allegorical. He began taking notes for his novel *Lavoura Arcaica* in 1968, developing the work in the years that followed. A modern rewriting of stories from the Bible and *The Thousand and One Nights*, it resulted in several prizes and recognition for Nassar in Brazil. Translated into Spanish in 1982 and also produced as a successful film, it has resonances with the story of the prodigal son. *Um Copo de Cólera* (1978, A cup of anger) narrates a few days in the life of a married couple and fictionalizes marital tensions. It was also made into a film. Nassar has not gained notoriety outside of Brazil, but his writing of the 1970s is widely respected in his homeland. In 1997 he published a collection of previously published short stories under the title *Menina a Caminho* (1997). In recent years he has returned to the passion of his youth—ranching.

Selected Work: *Lavoura Arcaica* (1975); *Um Copo de Cólera* (1978).

Niet Wat Pijn Diet (1985, Nothing that causes pain, by Astrid H. Roemer. Written in Dutch and untranslated. Amsterdam: In de Knipscheer, 1993) [**Novel**] Roemer is a major writer of the Dutch-speaking Caribbean. The protagonist of this novel is an adult woman who writes of her childhood experience and young adulthood. She emigrates from Suriname to Holland as a child. At the beginning of the novel, she describes minute physical details of her mother's body as well as the social world around her: the cultural conflict of an immigrant of African descent in Holland and the racial tensions involved. In the present the adult woman still dreams of an idealized mother's body and an idealized relationship with her, as opposed to the conflicts and fears remembered from that period of her life. She recalls her ninth birthday, when she

and her mother built a kite and flew it. She remembers this day fondly as the most important one in her life—the day she learned to construct a kite. This was also the day she and her mother moved from congested low-income housing to a house with fresh paint and warm concrete. The narrator-protagonist also learned an important lesson from her mother that day, when she lost her kite in the wind: freedom and possession can cause pain, so one must learn to cope with freedom, possession, and pain. The novel contains many more key anecdotes of her rite of passage and later life, but the main themes that surfaced early reappear later. Roemer's story as a Caribbean immigrant and a woman addressing gender issues makes her work comparable to the writing of the Argentine Sylvia Molloy and the Haitian Edwidge Danticat.

Nocturno de Chile (2000, *By Night in Chile,* by Roberto Bolaño. Translation by Chris Andrews. London: Harvill, 2003) [**Novel**] Written by one of Chile's most accomplished young novelists, this story weaves between the real world of post-Allende Chile and the surreal world of the protagonist's inner reverie. An aging writer, priest, and teacher, Sebastián Urrutia Lacroix travels from Chile to Europe and back while contemplating nature, urban society, and the culture of contemporary Chile. The work is a sophisticated "writer's novel," in dialogue with Chile's most venerable literary figures, from nineteenth-century novelist Alberto Blest Gana to twentieth-century figures such as Manuel Rojas, Pablo Neruda, and José Donoso. His ironical detachment from Chilean society produces humorous and often cynical social commentary as he reads Greek texts and observes social unrest. As he travels, reads, teaches, and contemplates, the protagonist assesses the ebb and flow of his own existence as well as that of persons surrounding him, searching for a meaningful answer in literature, the arts, national culture, and some kind of "final truth." Bolaños is also interested in memory, and the seemingly endless paradoxes involved in life and death, and is more concerned with communicating these themes to the reader than with technical experimentation. Along with the recent fiction of Mexicans Cristina Rivera Garza and David Toscana, as well as the Brazilians Bernardo Carvahlo and Diogo Mainardi, this novel is among the most attractive and evocative to have been published by this generation.

Noll, João Gilberto [Biography] Novelist and short story writer, he is widely considered one of the leading exponents of postmodern fiction in Brazil. He was born in Porto Alegre in 1946 and studied literature at the university level. He entered the literary scene in Brazil in 1980 with the publication of a volume of short stories, *O Cego e a Dançarina*, and then spent the 1982–83 academic year at the International Writing Program at the University of Iowa. Later he taught at the University of California, Berkeley. He was trained as a Marxist, but his characters suffer from a lack of belief in systems, and they tend to be failures in society with questionable individual identities. The author claims to write because of an "organic" need to do so.

Noll's substantive set of novels vary in style, from the baroque and dense style of his early writing to the minimalist approaches found in *Bandoleiros* (1985, Bandoleros), *Rastros do verão* (1986, Traces of the summer), and *Hôtel Atlântico* (1989, *Hotel Atlantico*, 1997). Populated with the alienated, the uprooted, and the marginalized, from prostitutes to street people, his fiction tends to depict a fragile, unstable, and disintegrating world. In many ways, both in form and content, he writes a literature of exhaustion. In his first novel, the baroque *A Fúria do Corpo* (1981, The fury of the body), his main characters are trapped in a petty everyday world, imprisoned by language and mass culture. *Bandoleiros* (1985) is written in a minimalist style and portrays violence. *Rastros do Verão* (1986) is set in Porto Alegre, but Noll creates ambiguity between the real space of this city and the time and space of the fiction. The main character in *Hôtel Atlântico* is a washed-up opera star facing a world of disintegration. Characters with no fixed identity inhabit *O Quieto Animal da Esquina* (1991, The still animal on the corner), a short novel of fragile time and space. An ex-lawyer in *Harmada* (1993) lives isolated in a home for street people, unable to understand himself or those around him. *A Céu Aberto* (1996, The open sky) has a first-person narrator whose identity is indefinite and androgynous. *Canoas e Marolas* (1999, Canoes and ocean waves) depicts a world of prejudice. In *Berkeley em Bellagio* (2002, Berkeley in Belagio) the narrator is a digressive, narcissistic, and gay writer-figure whose own story is the story of writing a novel titled *Berkeley em Bellagio*. His recent book *Mínimos, Múltiplos, Comuns* (2003) is a lengthy volume of very short narratives.

Selected Work: *A Fúria do Corpo* (1981); *Bandoleiros* (1985); *Rastros do Verão* (1986); *Hôtel Atlântico* (1989, *Hotel Atlantico*, translation David Treece, 1997); *O Quieto Animal da Esquina* (1991); *Harmada* (1993); *A Céu Aberto* (1996); *Canoas e Marolas* (1999); *Berkeley em Bellagio* (2002).

Obligado, Clara [Biography] Argentine novelist, short story writer, and essayist, she is one of Argentina's leading women writers in the generation born since WWII. Persecuted by the military dictatorship in Argentina in the 1970s, she took political exile in Spain, where she has been living since 1976. She was born in Buenos Aires in 1950 into a conservative family with strong literary and academic backgrounds. She has spent a lifetime working and writing against that conservative tradition; her relatives were mostly poets on the political right; in contrast, she has written narrative and positioned herself on the political left. She has spoken of being a "mestizo" writer in the sense that she employs double linguistic registers (those of Spain and Argentina); she considers writing for a readership in both her nations (Spain and Argentina) one of her important challenges. She began creative writing in Spain, but did not publish her first fiction until her volume of short stories *Una mujer en la cama y otros cuentos* (A woman in bed and other stories) appeared in Spain in 1990. She has written essays on feminist topics and is currently completing a book of biographies on distinguished women. She was awarded a prestigious award for women writers, the Premio Femenino Lumen, for her novel *La hija de Marx* (The daughter of Marx) in 1996. Obligado wrote a book about food and literature, *Manjares económicos* (1996, Economical caramels). Her more recent novels are *Si un hombre vivo te hace llorar* (1998, If a clever man makes you cry), *Qué me pongo* (2000, What do I put on), *Salsa* (2002), and *No le digas que lo quieres* (2002, Don't tell him what you want). She has used her exile experience in Spain as a point of departure in fictionalizing topics such as immigration and globalization. She has stated that she now considers herself a foreigner in both Spain and Argentina.

Selected Work: *La hija de Marx* (1996); *Si un hombre vivo te hace llorar* (1998); *Qué*

me pongo (2000); *No le digas que lo quieres* (2002); *Salsa* (2002).

Oliveira, Nelson de [Biography] Brazilian novelist, short story writer, essayist, and critic, he has been the central figure in promoting the idea of a generation of the 1990s in Brazil. Born in 1966, he himself belongs to the group of writers he is promoting. He studied literature at the University of São Paulo (USP). He has published two anthologies of his generation's work: *Geração 90: Manuscritos de Computador* (2001) and *Geração 90: Os Transgressores* (2003), seminal books for readers of contemporary fiction in the Portuguese language. His volumes of short stories include *Fábulas* (1995, Fables); *Os Saltitantes Seres da Lua* (1997, The hopping beings of the moon); *Fátima Fez os Pés para Mostrar na Choperia* (1998, Fátima did her feet to show in the bar); *Naquela Época Tínhamos um Gato* (1998, At that time we had a cat); *Treze* (1999, Thirteen); *As Moscas, Armas!* (2000, The flies, weapons!); *O Filho do Crucificado* (2001, The son of the crucified). Oliveira uses direct, sexually explicit, and often vulgar language. Critics have compared his writing with that of the French fiction writer Céline and of Henry Miller. He has published the novel *O Azul do Filho Morto* (2002, The dead child's blue).

He is currently doing graduate work in the literature of Portugal at the University of São Paulo.

Selected Work: *Subsolo Infinito* (2000); *O Azul do Filho Morto* (2002).

Onetti, Juan Carlos [Biography] Novelist and short story writer, he is the major Uruguayan novelist of the twentieth century and one of the major writers in Latin America of the generation preceding the 1960s Boom writers. He wrote fiction of existential anguish, alienation, and skepticism. Born in Montevideo in 1909, he did not finish high school because of his parents' constant moves from place to place. He was an avid reader of literature from an early age and an admirer of the fiction of the Scandanavian writer Knut Hamsun. He married and moved to Buenos Aires to work in private business in 1930; the remainder of his life he would marry and move several more times. Political unrest in Argentina resulted in his return to Montevideo in 1939, where he began writing for the new weekly magazine *Marcha*, to which he contributed pieces on cultural topics. That same year he published his first novel, *El pozo* (*The Pit and Tonight*). In 1941 he published a longer novel, *Tierra de nadie* (*No Man's Land*), introducing his character Larsen and the mythical city of Santa María of much of his later fiction. In this novel an entire generation of intellectuals suffers aimless lives and a hopeless future. Onetti assumed several different positions in the editorial and public sphere, all related to culture, as his life became increasingly more that of a full-time professional writer. In 1974 he went into political exile in Spain, where he remained and where he began to receive the international acclaim he deserved.

Onetti published one of his major novels, *La vida breve* (*A Brief Life*) in 1950, set in the fictional and mythical city of Santa María, the setting for a number of his fictions. Employing many of the technical strategies of European and North American modernist fiction, he became a major force in the rise of the new novel in Latin America in the 1940s and 1950s. The protagonist of this novel suffers the existential crisis in the mediocre world of most of the major characters in Onetti's universe. The author characterizes dopppelgangers, or doubles, and masterfully questions the limits of everyday reality.

Onetti's major works are *La vida breve*, *Los adioses* (1951, *Goodbyes and Other Sto-*

ries), and *El astillero* (1961, *The Shipyard*). *Los adioses* expresses many of the same individual crises seen in *La vida breve*, but the plot involves an impossible love story; the narrator's multiple versions of the protagonist's life leave the text inevitably ambiguous. *El astillero* continues Onetti's saga of anguish in Santa María and was awarded a certificate of merit by the Faulkner Foundation in 1963.

The international recognition of Onetti's work came relatively late. His reputation in the Hispanic world grew throughout the 1960s and 1970s, well after he had published much of his major fiction. In the 1980s and 1990s, however, the critical assessment of his writing, the symposia in his honor, the translations into English and several other languages, and the literary prizes have done justice to Onetti's stellar career as one of the major Latin American novelists of the century. In 1980 he was awarded the most prestigious literary prize given in Spain (Premio Cervantes), a fitting honor to a remarkable career. His novel *Dejemos hablar al viento* (1979, *Let the Wind Speak*) can also be read as his culminating work, portraying a character with the "thematic emptiness" that all of Onetti's protagaonists suffer. This character also believes that Catholics, Freudians, Marxists, and patriots can all be considered the same. In summary, Onetti's characters are sometimes nihilists and often skeptics at best.

Selected Work: *El pozo* (1930, published in English with another short novel under the title *The Pit and Tonight*, translation Peter Bush, 1991); *Tierra de nadie* (1941, *No Man's Land*, translation Peter Bush, 1994); *Para esta noche* (1943, published in English with another short novel under the title *The Pit and Tonight*, translation Peter Bush, 1991); *La vida breve* (1950, *A Brief Life*, translation Hortense Carpenter, 1976); *Los adioses* (1954, published in English with other fiction under the title *Farewells and a Grave with No Name*, translation Peter Bush, 1992); *Una tumba sin nombre* (1959, published in English with other fiction under the title *Farewells and a Grave with No Name*, translation Peter Bush, 1992); *El astillero* (1961, *The Shipyard*, translation Rachel Caffyn, 1968); *Juntacadáveres* (1964, *Junta, the Body Snatcher*, translation Suzanne Jill Levine, 1976); *Obras completas*, edited by Emir Rodríguez Monegal (1970); *Dejemos hablar al viento* (1979, *Let the Wind Speak*, 1996).

Opio en las nubes (1998, Opium in the clouds, by Rafael Chaparro Madiedo. Written in Spanish and unstranslated. Bogotá: Proyecto) [**Novel**] One of the several new urban novels to appear in Colombia that have been referred to as acid novels, this work deals with drugs, alcohol, and violence in Bogotá. A paradoxical combination of intensity and emptiness, along with the horror of urban life in Colombia in the 1990s, this work became one of the most widely read novels in that nation in the latter part of the century. Some critics have claimed that this novel defined a generation in Colombia that was as dedicated to Donna Sommer and American rock music as it was to heroin and Colombian *aguardiente* drinks. This is a fragmented text that is narrated in the continuing present of the frenetic action. Full of the colloquial language of Bogotá's youth, this novel creates more sensory perceptions than plot, with violence and aggression taking priority over any other aspect of human life.

Oreamuno, Yolanda [**Biography**] Costa Rican novelist and journalist, she was born in 1916, studied in Costa Rica, and lived in Guatemala, Chile, and Mexico while developing her writing career. Before dying in 1956, she had become a major woman writer in the Central American region. Her major work, *La ruta de su evasión* (1949, The route of her evasion), received a major novel prize in Guatemala in 1948, the Premio Centroamericano 15 de Septiembre. In it she explores a women's psychological and emotional states, making her a pioneer of her time.

Selected Work: *Por tierra firme* (1946); *La ruta de su evasion* (1949).

Ortiz, Adalberto [**Biography**] Ecuadorian novelist born in 1914, he has been a major exponent of Afro-Ecuadorian literature. He also belongs to that nation's generation of 1930, which intended to reform social and political injustice. He is most widely recognized for his novel *Juyungo* (1942, *Juyungo: A Classic Afro-Hispanic Novel*, 1982), which portrays the black protagonist's search for identity. Ortiz's language and narrative technique make him a forerunner to the new novel of the 1940s and 1950s. He also published *El espejo y la ventana* (1967, The mirror and the window), a historical novel placed in the Ecuador of the 1920s and 1930s.

Selected Work: *Yuyungo* (1942, *Juyungo: A Classic Afro-Hispanic Novel*, translation Susan F. Hill and Jonathan Tittler, 1982); *El espejo y la ventana* (1967).

Otero Silva, Miguel [**Biography**] Venezuelan novelist and essayist born in 1905, he established a record as one of the major modern novelists in Venezuela and Latin America by the time he died in 1985. His impressive career extended from the 1930s to the 1970s. His early fiction followed the conventions of social realism. His novel *Casas muertas* (1955, Dead houses) is a Faulknerian work set in a dying town that is ignored by the central authorities and almost a ghost town. Eventually, the reader makes connections between the condition of the town and the condition of the nation. His equally engaging *Cuando quiero llorar no lloro* (1970, When I want to cry I don't cry) tells the story of three youths who eventually die simultaneously. They are all victims of the established order, even though each comes from a different social class. These two novels are among the finer modernist fictions produced in Venezuela in the twentieth century along with Adriano González León's *País portátil*.

Selected Work: *Casas muertas* (1955); *Cuando quiero llorar no lloro* (1970).

Pacheco, José Emilio [Biography] Mexican novelist, poet, short story writer, and essayist, he is one of the leading writers of his generation in Latin America. Born in 1939, he began publishing poetry, short fiction, and essays in Mexico in the 1960s. Primarily known in Mexico as one of the nation's major poets, he has, nevertheless, penned high quality and innovative postmodern fiction. His short fiction includes the volumes *El principio de placer* (1972, The principle of pleasure) and *La sangre de Medusa* (1990, Medusa's blood). His one novel, *Morirás lejos* (1967, *You Will Die in a Distant Land*), was a watershed book for postmodern fiction in Mexico and Latin America. This Borgesian postmodern experiment is set in two entirely different venues: WWII Germany and ancient Roman times in the region of present-day Israel, inviting the active postmodern reader to find parallels in the acts of repression and oppression exercised by the Nazis and the Romans. Following the lead of Cortázar's similar invitation in *Hopscotch*, Pacheco offers the reader the opportunity to choose between alternate story lines.

Morirás lejos was one of the early successes in carrying out the postmodern kind of fiction implicitly proposed by Borges and Cortázar.

Novel: *Morirás lejos* (1967, *You Will Die in a Distant Land*, translation Elizabeth Umlas, 1991).

Padilla, Ignacio [Biography] Mexican writer of the self-described generation of the crack, he was born in 1968 in Mexico City. Along with Jorge Volpi, Pedro Angel Palou, and a few other Mexican writers born in the 1960s, he has proposed to place a "crack" in the hegemony of Mexican letters held by the major figures of novel such as Carlos Fuentes and Elena Poniatowska. In many ways his literary interests and fiction are comparable to that of the same generation in Brazil, the generation of the 1990s. He studied literature and communication at the undergraduate level in Mexico, later doing graduate work in Spanish literature in Spain, completing a doctorate at the University of Salamanca on Cervantes. His irreverent and surprising fiction has been compared to Gothic writing as well as to Borges and tends to operate in the intangible spaces of the fantastic and dream.

He has published the volumes of short fiction *Subterráneos* (1990) and *Ultimos trenes* (1996). Of his four novels, the most celebrated has been the recent *Amphitryon* (2000), a suspense thriller set in the 1916 of WWI, the 1943 of WWII, and the 1960 of a Nazi refugee in Buenos Aires. A novel of intrigue and dubious identities, it was awarded a prestigious prize in Spain for a first novel (Premio Primavera de Novela) in 2000. He has been awarded several literary prizes in Mexico and presently teaches literature at the University of the Americas in Puebla, Mexico.

Selected Work: *Imposibilidad de los cuervos* (1994); *La catedral de los abogados*

(1995); *Si volviesen Sus Majestades* (1996); *Amphitryon* (2000).

Paiva, Marcelo Rubens [Biography] Brazilian novelist, he has been writing innovative fiction since the early 1980s. His work includes the widely read *Feliz Ano Velho* (Happy old year) which he claims to have written in 1981–82 while listening to the music of Bill Evans, The Clash, and Steve Wonder. Along the same lines, he claims to have written *Blecaute* (1986) in 1985–86 while listening to Tom Waits, King Crimson, and Duke Ellington. In the case of both novels the writer has referred to his love for adolescence and hatred of truth as the background and context of the writing. More recently, he has published *Não es tu, Brasil* (1996, It's not you, Brazil).

Selected Work: *Feliz Ano Velho* (1982); *Blecaute* (1986); *Não es tu, Brasil* (1996).

Pallotini, Renata [Biography] Brazilian novelist, poet, playwright, translator, and essayist, she was born in São Paulo in 1931 and studied law in São Paulo at the state university and then philosophy at the private Pontifícia Universidade Católica. She also studied theater at the Escola de Arte Dramática of São Paulo. She holds a professorship in the school of communications and arts in the Universidade de São Paulo. She began writing poetry and theater in the 1950s, although her major publications appeared in the 1980s and 1990s. She has published several volumes of poetry and fiction.

Selected Work: *Nosotros* (1989); *Ofícios e Amargura* (1998).

Palmério, Mário [Biography] Active in literature, politics, and education throughout his life, he has served in the Brazilian congress and the diplomatic core while writing novels. Born in Monte Carlos (state of Minas Gerais) in 1916, he has used the set-ting of his native region of Minas Gerais for his fiction. His first and most widely read novel, *Vila dos Confines* (1956, House of limits), portrays two political parties vying against each other during the elections in rural Minas Gerais. Palmério describes all-too-typical scenarios of greed, corruption, and deception among traditional politicians. *Chapado do Bugre* (1965) also describes typical characters and life in the *sertão*.

Selected Work: *Vila dos Confines* (1956); *Chapado do Bugre* (1965).

Palou, Pedro Angel [Biography] Mexican writer of the self-described generation of the crack, he was born in Puebla, Mexico, in 1966. In many ways his group of writers in Mexico, which includes Jorge Volpi and Ignacio Padilla, is comparable to the generation of the 1990s in Brazil and the McOndo group organized out of Chile: they are the newest generation of young writers born in the 1960s who began publishing in the 1990s. They are particularly interested in breaking away from any of the restrictions placed on Mexican writing by the cultural nationalists; their writing is invariably international in setting and tone. In Palou's case, he regularly explores a variety of realms of the fantastic. Palou began publishing short fiction and novels in the early 1990s, including the volume of short stories *Amores enormes* (1991, Enormous loves), which won a fiction prize in Mexico (Premio Jorge Ibarguengoitia). He has published several novels; *Memorias de los días* (1995, Memories of the days) is work that tells an elaborate fantastic tale of a 1999 end-of-the-century apocalypse. In *Bolero* (1998) the protagonist is a man in his fifties who returns to his hometown of Puebla after an absence of over two years; the work is structured around a series of songs popular in Mexico. Of all Palou's fiction, this one has the least international tone, although it can be read throughout the Hispanic world, where the music of the *bolero* transcends national borders. The protagonist in *Demasiadas vidas* (2001, Too many lives) is involved with a search, the settings more fantastic than real.

In *Con la muerte en los puños* (2003, With death in the fists) Palou tells a rise-and-fall story from the memory of a battered old boxer. Consisting of fifteen chapters or *raunds* to match the format of a boxing match, the work introduces "Baby" Cifuentes, who, while shining shoes in Mexico City in 1965, befriends Juan Gavito, an intellectual who provides him with a notebook to record his memories. Within those pages Baby writes about his painful childhood. He recounts how he was abused in the military by corrupt superiors. After leaving the military, Baby trains with irascible old Don Lupe and eventually becomes the welterweight champion of the world, boxing in the United States, Europe, and Asia. His success brings only troubles as he divorces his wife, in the process losing his children and half his fortune. He falls for Marisol, a beautiful cabaret singer who lives with the dangerous drug dealer Tomás Chavez, who later frames him for her murder. After coming back from physical and emotional trauma, Baby is blamed for the death of a woman in a car accident that leaves him a cripple and ends his boxing days. Working as a bartender in New York, he finally receives his chance to return to Mexico for revenge upon Tomás Chavez; all of which is contained within the notebook he gives back to Juan Gavito.

Selected Work: *Como quien desangra* (1991); *Memoria de los días* (1995); *Bolero* (1998); *Demasiadas vidas* (2001); *Con la muerte en los puños* (2003); *Malheridos* (2003).

Parra Sandoval, Rodrigo [Biography] Colombian novelist and essayist, he has been an innovator since the publication of his first novel, *El album secreto del Sagrado Corazón* (1978, The secret album of the Sacred Heart). He was born in Colombia in 1937 and did graduate study in sociology at the University of Wisconsin, Madison. Since then, he has lived in Colombia and worked as a practicing sociologist his entire professional career. *El album secreto del Sagrado Corazón* was one of the most experimental novels to appear in Colombia in the 1970s. It is a collage of a variety of texts—letters, newspaper articles, and the like—that creates an ambiguous understanding of the main character. Parra Sandoval questions traditional institutions of Colombia at the same time that he questions the potential of the novel as a genre.

Among his more recent works, his novel *Tarzán y el filósofo desnudo* (1996, Tarzan and the nude philosopher) is a satire of academic life and *El don de Juan* (2002, The don of Juan) is inspired thematically by the Don Juan literature of the Hispanic tradition and stylistically by Paul Auster.

Selected Work: *El album secreto del Sagrado Corazón* (1978); *Un pasado para Micaela* (1988); *La amante de Shakespeare* (1989); *Tarzán y el filósofo desnudo* (1996).

Paso, Fernando del [Biography] Mexican novelist and essayist, he was born in 1935 and has been a major literary presence in Mexico since the 1960s. His work has also been amply recognized throughout the Hispanic world, culminating in his receiving one of the most prestigious novel prizes in all of Latin America, the Rómulo Gallegos novel prize in 1975. He is known as a novelist with encyclopedic interests who writes lengthy works of vast historic proportions. Several of his most informed critics have referred to the "totalizing" effects of his ambitious novels. His first three novels, *José Trigo* (1966), *Palinuro en México* (1975, Palinuro in Mexico), and *Noticias del*

Imperio (1987, News from the empire) lived up to these grand dimensions. They are also his major novels. Del Paso has also written several works along a lighter vein, including some detective fiction.

Selected Work: *José Trigo* (1966); *Palinuro de México* (1975); *Noticias del Imperio* (1987); *Linda 67: Historia de un crimen* (1995).

Patán, Federico [Biography] Mexican novelist, poet, translator, essayist, he is one of Mexico's most gifted writers and informed literary critics. Born in Spain in 1937, he was trained in comparative literature at the National University in Mexico City (UNAM). He emigrated with his family from Spain in 1939 after his father was on the losing side in the Spanish Civil War. This exile left a permanent mark on Patán's life and work; his first novel, *Ultimo exilio* (1986, Last exile) deals with internal and external exile. After living in the provinces of both northern and eastern Mexico, his family moved to Mexico City in 1945, where he has lived since. He began writing poetry in the 1960s, establishing his first literary identity in Mexico as one of the premier poets of his generation. After writing his early poetry, he began publishing short stories. His short fiction is hermetic, with abstract and subtle allusions to his literary idols of British and American literature. His poetry, short fiction, and translations have secured his reputation as a writer's writer in Mexico. His early work with the novel began in the late 1960s; he wrote the drafts for three novels between 1967 and 1982 without publishing any of them during this period. A highly productive essayist and book reviewer, he provided readers and scholars of Mexican fiction ongoing weekly book reviews, most of which appeared in the literary supplement *Sábado* of the newspaper *Uno Más Uno*.

Patán's major novels are *Ultimo exilio* and *Angela, o las arquitecturas abandonadas* (2001, Angela, or the abandoned architectures). Both books are complex and labyrinthine works directed to the sophisticated reader well versed in the Western literary tradition.

Selected Work: *Ultimo exilio* (1986); *Puertas antiguas* (1989); *La ceremonia perfecta* (1994); *Mujeres ante el espejo* (1996); *Angela, o las arquitecturas abandonadas* (2001); *Esperanza* (2001).

Peri Rossi, Cristina [Biography] Uruguayan novelist, short story writer, journalist, and poet, she was born in Montevideo in 1941 and brought up in the midst of an impressive library collection owned by an uncle. She studied at the University of Montevideo and wrote journalism and taught in order to make a living. She has been publishing creative work since the 1960s and went into exile to Spain in 1972. Her narrative and poetry speak against numerous forms of oppression and some of her writing is a celebration of homosexuality. She writes with an explicit understanding of social and political tensions and often satirizes traditional family structures. She published her first volume of short stories, *Viviendo* (Living) in 1963.

Peri Rossi's first novel, *El libro de mis primos* (1969, The book of my cousins) has a child as a first-person narrator in order to satirize the conventions of a patriarchal society. Nevertheless, it contains numerous perspectives, as do most of her novels. Her narrative text *Indicios pánicos* (1970, Signs of panic) consists of a series of brief fragments and is only vaguely related to the genre of the novel. *El museo de los esfuerzos inútiles* (1983, The museum of useless efforts) is an even more radical collections of texts. Many critics consider *La nave de los locos* (1984, Ship of fools), which underlines the injustice of modern capitalist society, her most important novel. It also celebrates homoerotic relations. In 1992 she published *La última noche de Dostoievsky* (1994, *Dostoevsky's Last Night*), a novel about chance in which the main character is a gambler.

Selected Work: *El libro de mis primos* (1968); *Indicios pánicos* (1970); *El museo de los esfuerzos inútiles* (1983); *La nave de los locos* (1984); *La última noche de Dostoievky* (1992, *Dostoevsky's Last Night*, translation Laura C. Dail, 1994).

Piglia, Ricardo [Biography] Argentine novelist, short story writer, and essayist, since the 1980s he has become one of the most prominent novelists in Latin America. Born in 1942, he belongs to the generation of Argentine intellectuals whose lives and careers were seriously marked by the military dictatorship of the 1970s and 1980s. He began writing fiction in the late 1960s, publishing his first volume of short fiction, *La invasion* (The invasion), in 1967. His volume of short fiction *Nombre falso* (1975, False name) later appeared in a revised and expanded version under the title *Prisión perpetua* (1988, Perpetual prison); some critics have considered this book a novel.

Piglia studied history at the Universidad de la Plata and later served as director of the collection of detective novels—well distributed throughout Latin America—that included Spanish translations of writers such as Hammett, Chandler, Goodis, and McCoy. Between 1986 and 1990 he taught at Princeton and Harvard Universities. His work in film includes the screenplay for the film *Foolish Heart*, which was directed by Héctor Babenco, as well as the screenplay for the film *La sonámbula*, directed by Fernando Spiner.

Piglia's fiction is an ongoing dialogue with the Argentine literary tradition, particularly with master innovators Jorge Luis Borges, Roberto Arlt, and Macedonio Fernández. At different periods in Argen-

tine history these three writers were marginalized and criticized by a cultural elite in Argentina that favored traditionalists that supported the official nationalist state culture. In his fiction, which in many ways reads like essays on culture, Piglia analyzes the key roles of Borges, Arlt, and Fernández in Argentine society while simultaneously questioning the viability of more conservative writers.

Piglia's major novel is *Respiración artificial* (1979, *Artificial Respiration*), a seminal novel that was widely read in the 1980 and 1990s throughout Latin America and positioned Piglia among the most respected novelists publishing in Latin America during this period. Piglia explores the relationship between literature and history in this two-hundred-page meditation on Argentine cultural and political history. A pastiche of the philosophical style explored by Borges and others, it delves into questions related to the construction of national histories.

More recently, Piglia has published *Plata quemada* (1997, *Money to Burn*), a novel taken straight from the pages of a newspaper, based on a bank robbery and related events that took place in Buenos Aires and Montevideo in 1965. It deals with a complex political scandal—a series of betrayals and deceptions—from real history. This novel, which received the prestigious (and controversial) Planeta Novel Prize in Argentina, has kept Piglia at the forefront of Argentine letters. Many writers and critics consider him one of the major writers of his generation throughout Latin America.

Selected Work: *Respiración artificial* (1979, *Artificial Respiration*, translation Daniel Balderston 1993); *Prisión perpetua* (1988); *Plata quemada* (1997, *Money to Burn*, translation Amanda Hopkinson, 2003).

Piñón, Nélida [Biography] Brazilian novelist and short story writer, she has dedicated a lifetime to the production of fiction. She began publishing in the 1960s and has become one of Brazil's major novelists of the century, with translations of her work widely available in translation. Along with figures such as Jorge Amado and Rubem Fonseca, she has been translated amply into Spanish and is one of the few contemporary Brazilian novelists read throughout Latin America. Born in Rio de Janeiro in 1937, she was reared in an upper-middle-class family with roots in Galicia, Spain. After studying in a private German high school, she studied journalism in the Pontifícia Universidade Católica in Rio de Janeiro. She published her first novel, *Guia Mapa de Gabriel Arcanjo* (Guide map of Gabriel Arcanjo) in 1961 and has published over eight novels since this first work appeared. In 1989 she was elected to the Brazilian Academy of Letters. She was the Brazilian correspondent for the Latin American magazine *Mundo Nuevo* and is an assistant editor of *Cadernos Brasileiros*.

Piñón is recognized as a writer dedicated to describing the customs of the small city, thus making her comparable to writers such as the Brazilians Luiz Vilela and Josué Guimarães. She portrays the absurdity of everyday social life in an urban setting, portraying the internal psychology of her characters and their difficulty in making the small changes that are metaphors for more comprehensive social change. In the small-city setting Piñón depicts resistance to globalization, mass media, and numerous other signs of postmodern culture. Thus her writing describes a sector of Brazilian upper-middle-class urban society that is deeply conservative.

Her longest and most recognized novel, *A Doce Canção de Caetana* (1987, *Caetana's Sweet Song*), concerns an actress who returns to her provincial town of Trinidade after a twenty-year absence. She intends to become the lead in a local production of *La Traviata*, although this plan is a failure.

Her return to the town is ostensibly to reconnect with her lover of twenty years before. She represents a variety of characters, from the volatile Maria Callas to the leaders of Brazil in the early 1970s and the presidency of Medici during the military dictatorship.

Piñón's other novels include *Fundador* (1969, Founder) and *Tebas do Meu Coração* (1974, Tebas of my heart). *Fundador* was one of the early books that brought recognition to Piñón. Replete with magical elements, *Fundador* offers a reinterpretation of the conquest of the Americas by the Europeans. *Tebas do Meu Coração* is a broad Faulknerian story with numerous characters who appear and disappear from the scene. She is also broadly recognized for her historical novel *A Republica dos Sonhos* (1984, The republic of dreams).

Selected Work: *Guia Mapa de Gabriel Arcanjo* (1961); *Madeira Feita Cruz* (1963); *Fundador* (1969); *A Casa da Paixão* (1972); *Tebas do Meu Coração* (1974); *A Força do Destino* (1977); *A Republica dos Sonhos* (1984, *The Republic of Dreams*, translation Helen R. Lane, 1989); *A Doce Canção de Caetana* (1987, *Cateana's Sweet Song*, translation Helen R. Lane, 1992).

Pitol, Sergio [Biography] Mexican novelist, short story writer, and essayist, he is one of the most respected contemporary novelists in Mexico among writers and intellectuals. Born in Veracruz in 1933, he belongs to Mexico's *Generación de Medio Siglo*, the generation of Carlos Fuentes, which wanted to modernize and universalize Mexican literature during the 1950s, when he began publishing his first short stories. He is widely recognized in Mexico as one of the nation's most sophisticated and "literary" writers, and his writing is well-known throughout Latin America. Pitol spent several years living in Eastern Europe, and much of his fiction bears the traces of European literature and culture in general.

Selected Work: El tañido de una flauta (1972); *Juegos florales* (1982); *El desfile del amor* (1984); *Domar a la divina garza* (1988); *Vals de Mefisto* (1989); *La vida conyugal* (1991); *El viaje* (2000).

Poniatowska, Elena [Biography] Mexican novelist, short story writer, essayist, and journalist, she is a prominent public intellectual in Latin America and considered by many to be the major female writer of the Spanish language. Born in Paris in 1933, she arrived in Mexico as a young child with French as her first language. She studied in a private British school in Mexico City and then spent two years in a private Catholic school in Philadelphia. She learned Spanish by speaking with the domestic workers in her home. In the early stages of her career, in the 1950s and 1960s, her principal identity was that of a journalist who wrote on both cultural and political issues. She began her journalistic career writing for *El Excelsior* in Mexico City in 1954, the same year she published the volume of short stories *Lilus Kikus*. She is best known for her book *Hasta no verte Jesús mío* (1968, *Here's to You, Jesusa*), which marked the beginning of a literary career that has included a series of narratives published well into the twenty-first century.

Selected Work: Hasta no verte Jesús mío (1968, *Here's to You, Jesusa,* translation Deanna Heikkinen, 2001); *La noche de Tlatelolco* (1971, *Massacre in Mexico,* translation Helen R. Lane, 1975); *Querido Diego, te abraza Quiela* (1976, *Dear Diego,* translation Katherine Silver 1986); *De noche vienes* (1979); *Fuerte es el silencio* (1980); *La "Flor de Lis"* (1988); *Nada, nadie* (1988, *Nothing, Nobody: The Voices of the Mexico City Earthquake,* translation Aurora Camacho de Schmidt and Arthur Schmidt, 1995); *Tinísima* (1991, *Tinisima,* translation Kath-

erine Silver, 2006); *Paseo de la Reforma* (1997); *La piel del cielo* (2001); *El tren pasa primero* (2005).

Porzecanski, Teresa [Biography] Uruguayan novelist and anthropologist, she was born in 1945. In addition to several books and numerous articles in the field of anthropology, since the late 1960s she has published a great many works of fiction. She has been awarded local prizes in Uruguay and a Guggenheim Fellowship in 1992, and distinguished scholars such as Angel Rama have praised her work. Her early novel *Una novela erótica* (1986, An erotic novel) garnered her critical acclaim in Uruguay. Her fiction also includes the novels *Intacto el corazón* (1976, The heart intact) and *Perfumes de Cartago* (1994, Perfumes of Carthage). She is one of the more experimental and postmodern writers in Uruguay.

Selected Work: Intacto el corazón (1976); *Una novela erotica* (1986); *Perfumes de Cartago* (1994).

Post-Boom novel [Topic] A term frequently used to describe certain fiction published after the 1960s Boom in Spanish America. The writers most frequently associated with the post-Boom who have discussed it in essays and interviews are the Argentine Mempo Giardinelli and the Chilean Antonio Skármeta. Other writers commonly associated with the post-Boom are Isabel Allende and Luisa Valenzuela.

The novels of the post-Boom represent a continuation of the modernist project initiated in Latin America in the 1940s and continued masterfully by novelists such as García Márquez and Vargas Llosa. Writers such as Skármeta and Giardinelli share generational attitudes that separate them from the novelists of the Boom. Nevertheless, the fiction of Skármeta and Giardinelli is fundamentally a continuation of modernist aesthetics. These writers are by no means traditionalists; indeed, they employ narrative strategies explored and refined by modernist writers since the 1940s. As such, Skármeta, Giardinelli, Allende, and a host of other Latin American storytellers belong to the tradition of the modernist novel. The post-Boom represents a return to accessibility, more realism, and pop elements that reflect greater cultural autonomy and the revival of democracy in parts of the continent during the late 1980s and early 1990s. Several writers and critics associated with the post-Boom have spoken of the pessimism of this generation.

Several of the writers associated with the post-Boom are politically committed storytellers whose writing can be seen as a post-Macondo phenomenon: they write either with or against the storytelling vitality and magical realist approaches of García Márquez. Writers such as Isabel Allende and Luis Sepúlveda produced fiction with many of the overtones and stylistic characteristics of García Márquez's magical fictional worlds. On ther other hand, writers such as the Colombian Gustavo Alvarez Gardeazábal and Marco Tulio Aguilera Garramuño have written parodies of such fiction. Other writers that can be associated with the post-Boom are Elena Poniatowska, Sergio Galindo, Arturo Azuela, and Rosario Ferré.

Postmodern novel [Topic] Latin American fiction of the 1970s and 1980s that shares many qualities of international postmodern fiction. Leading exponents of postmodern fiction in Latin America are the Argentine Ricardo Piglia, the Chilean Diamela Eltit, the Mexican José Emilio Pacheco, the Cuban Severo Sarduy, the Colombian R. H. Moreno-Durán, and the Brazilians Osman Lins, João Gilberto Noll, and Rubem Fonseca.

The historical roots of postmodern fiction in Latin America are to be found in the volume titled *Ficciones* (1944) of Jorge Luis Borges and the novel *Rayuela* (1963) by Julio Cortázar. Early postmodern novels began appearing in Latin America in the 1960s with such titles as *Tres Tristes Tigres* (1967) by Guillermo Cabrera Infante and *Cobra* (1972) by Severo Sarduy.

Prado, Adélia (Adélia Luiza Prado de Freitas) [Biography] Poet, short story writer, and novelist, she was born in Divinópolis (state of Minas Gerais), Brazil, in 1935 and has remained living there. She studied philosophy and has dedicated much of her life to the teaching of philosophy and the writing of poetry. She has recently published anthologies of her prose (*Prosa Reunida*, 1999) and poetry (*Poesia Reunida*, 10th edition, 2001). Her novels include *Os Componentes da Banda* (1992, The components of the band) and *O Homen da Mão Seca* (1994, The man of the dry hand). Both are first-person narratives that involve a philosophical and spiritual search. She is a defender of traditional values and has recently headed public campaigns against corruption in Brazil.

Selected Work: *Os Componentes da Banda* (1992); *O Homen da mão seca* (1994).

Prata, Mario [Biography] Brazilian novelist, author of the experimental novel *Buscando o Seu Mindinho* (2002, Searching for Mr. Pinky), he was born in Uberaba (state of Minas Gerais) in 1946. He lives in São Paulo, where he has worked as a journalist, screenwriter, and playwright. In 1998 he published an innovative autobiographical text, *Minhas Mulheres e Meus Homens* (My women and my men), with brief sketches of well over one hundred friends and acquaintances that have been important in different stages of his life. His novel *Minhas Vidas Passadas (a limpo)* (1998, My previous lives [cleaned]) consists of a six-part story that tells the six past lives of the protagonist, Leonardo Ramos. He calls his wildly inventive novel *Os Anjos do Badaró* (2000, The angels of Badaró) a "police comedy."

Selected Work: *Minhas Vidas Passadas (a limpo)* (1998); *Os Anjos do Badaró* (2000); *Buscando o Seu Mindinho* (2002).

Puig, Manuel [Biography] Argentine novelist and playwright, he was one of the major contemporary novelists in Latin America. He was born in 1932 in provincial Argentina, and much of his early fiction uses as its main referent the stifling atmosphere of conventional, middle-class life there. His escape from this atmosphere as a child was Hollywood movies. He spent a lifetime fascinated with the classical Hollywood and European film of the 1930s and 1940s, and this passion has been evident in all his fiction. His first novel, *La traición de Rita Hayworth* (1968, *Betrayed by Rita Hayworth*) was a literary bombshell throughout the Hispanic world: his depiction of the popular culture of Hollywood film and homosexual experience had rarely been so openly explored in a Latin American novel. It is the story of a young boy growing up in provincial Argentina; it is also a semiautobiographical account of Puig growing up as a gay youth in a conservative and traditional town, finding refuge in the fantasy world of the movies. In a subtle narrative move Puig put the story together as a gallery of independent voices, with no controlling narrator or voice.

Puig is also broadly recognized for his novel *El beso de la mujer araña* (1977, *Kiss of the Spider Woman*), his novel about two prisoners sharing a cell, one of whom is a leftist activist and the other a homosexual.

In this work Puig explores the politics of sexuality and the sexuality of politics. He died in Mexico City in 1990.

Selected Work: *La traición de Rita Hayworth* (1968, *Betrayed by Rita Hayworth*, translation Suzanne Jill Levine, 1971); *Boquitas pintadas* (1969, *Heartbreak Tango*, translation Suzanne Jill Levine, 1973); *The Buenos Aires Affair* (1973, *The Buenos Aires Affair*, translation Suzanne Jill Levine, 1976); *El beso de la mujer araña* (1977, *Kiss of the Spider Woman*, translation Thomas Colchie, 1979); *Eternal Curse to the Reader of These Pages* (1980, *Maldición eternal a quien lea estas páginas*, written in English, Spanish translation by the author, 1982).

Queiroz, Rachel de [Biography] Novelist, short story writer, and playwright, she was one of the major Brazilian novelists of the 1930s and 1940s, but of only marginal importance in the post-WWII period. She was born in Fortaleza, Brazil, in 1910, but her early life on the *sertão* (backlands) provided valuable life experience for her later regionalist fiction. Her first novel, *O Quinze* (1930, The fifteen) depicted life on the *sertão* of the northeastern region of Brazil. Most of her fiction was published before 1945. She published five books of fiction, including *As Tres Marias* (The three Marias) in 1939 and *O Galo de Ouro* (The gold rooster) in 1950.

Selected Work: *O Quinze* (1930); *As Tres Marias* (1939); *O Galo de Ouro* (1950).

Quesada, Roberto [Biography] Honduran novelist, he is one of the few writers of his nation who has been able to successfully continue writing despite the lack of opportunity and space for writers of that nation. Born in 1962, this young writer has written a corpus of imaginative and lively fictions, much of which has found its way into English translation. In *Los barcos* (1988, *The Ships*) Quesada describes the occasional triumphs of daily life, usually in the form of silent laughter, in a world of poverty. In this novel a young writer comes to the Honduran coastal town of La Ceiba to work at a pineapple plantation. His days are governed by hard work in the shadow of military exercises conducted by U.S. naval and air forces. As the story develops, the characters hear of a revolution in nearby Nicaragua. In the end Quesada defends human values over the forces of the military and big business in the region.

Selected Work: *Los barcos* (1988, *The Ships*, translation Hardie St. Martin, 1992); *El lector que de repente quedó ciego* (1994); *El humano y la diosa* (1996, *The Human and the Goddess*, 2002); *Big Banana* (1999, *The Big Banana*, translation Walter Krochmal, 1999); *Nunca entres por Miami* (2002, *Never Through Miami*, translation Patricia Duncan, 2002).

R

Ramírez, Sergio [Biography] Nicaraguan novelist, short story writer, and essayist, he was a leader of the Sandinista Revolution in the late 1970s, serving as vice president of Nicaragua in 1985 with the Sandinista government. He writes about the politics, culture, and history of Nicaragua. Born in Masatepe, Nicaragua, in 1942, he received a law degree from the National University of Nicaragua in 1964 and began writing fiction in the 1960s. He went to Costa Rica in 1964 and then into political exile to Germany during the Somoza dictatorship in Nicaragua. In 1975 he joined Sandinista forces to overthrow Somoza. After the subsequent downfall of the Sandinista regime in 1990, he was elected the representative of the minority Sandinista Party in the parliament, a position he held until 1994. His numerous essays include the volume of political writings titled *Confesión de amor* (1991, Confession of love). A highly respected short story writer from an early age, his volumes of short fiction include *Clave de sol* (1992, Key of the sun). In 1998 he was awarded one of the most prestigious prizes of the Spanish-speaking world, the Premio Internacional Alfaguara de Novela.

His major novels are *¿Tio dio miedo la sangre?* (1977, *To Bury Our Fathers*) and *Margarita, está linda la mar* (1998, Margarita, the sea is beautiful). In his recent *Mil y una muertes* (2004, A thousand and one deaths) he evokes the historical and literary past of Nicaragua and of his own readings.

Selected Work: *Tiempo en fulgor* (1970); *¿Te dio miedo la sangre?* (1977, *To Bury Our Fathers*, translation Nick Caistor, 1984); *Castigo divino* (1988); *Baile de máscaras* (1994); *Margarita, está linda la mar* (1998); *Sombras nada más* (2002).

Ramos, Graciliano [Biography] Novelist, journalist, and short story writer, he is one of the major twentieth-century fiction writers in Brazil. Five of his six books of fiction, however, appeared before 1945, although *Insônia* (1945, Insomnia) is a noteworthy book of the post-WWII period. He was born in Quebrangúlo (state of Alagoas) in 1892, dedicated a career to teaching and writing, and died in 1953. In 1936 he was imprisoned for his critical writings and socialist views; he was released in 1937. He is best known for his classic novel *Vidas Secas* (1938, *Barren Lives*).

Selected fiction: Vidas Secas (1938, *Barren Lives*, translation Ralph Edward Dimmick, 1971); *Insônia* (1945); *Caetés* (1947).

Ramos, Luis Arturo [Biography] Mexican novelist and short story writer, he belongs to the generation of Mexican intellectuals who were marked by the events of October 1968 in Mexico City and has often discussed the meaning of that political watershed in his life and writing. He was born in Minatitlán (state of Veracruz) in 1947 and has spoken of the seminal importance of this region in his writing: the setting was stimulating in every sense, not just because of the semitropical environment but also because of the way it influenced his multifaceted personality. At the age of thirteen he moved to the port city of Veracruz, and Ramos believes this change to a more Caribbean setting left a permanent mark on him and his work, much of which has the Caribbean in the background as some type of referent. One of his early stories, for example, deals with Columbus's arrival at the Caribbean, and the sea is a constant presence. In Ramos, however, this is not the sea of empirical reality but the Caribbean rewritten within the context of fantastic literature. He studied literature at the University of Veracruz and creative writing at the Centro Mexicano de Escritores (1972–73). His first writing project, which grew out of his experience at the Centro Mexicano de Escritores, was the volume of short fiction *Junto al paisaje* (1985, Together with the countryside, published much later in revised form). He has assumed a variety of roles at the University of Veracruz, including director of publications, and he currently divides his time between this university and the University of Texas–El Paso, where he teaches creative writing in Spanish. He began publishing short fiction in the 1970s and has become one of the most accomplished writers of his genera-

tion in both Mexico and the Hispanic world. His early volumes of short fiction, *Del tiempo y otros lugares* (1979, Of time and other places) and *Los viejos asesinos* (1981, The old murderers) were his initial explorations into the potentially ambiguous spaces that traditionally divide one space from another, such as windows, stairs, and the like. A disciple of Julio Cortázar's early stories, Ramos is more interested in raising questions about the nature of reality than affirming social or political values. His postmodern fiction places an emphasis on intriguing plots, ambiguous spaces, and characters of fragile psychic states that have difficulty understanding the world they inhabit in rational terms.

Ramos's work can be divided into three periods. In the first he established his identity as a writer of the fantastic with the publication of the short fiction *Del tiempo y otros lugares* (1979), the novel *Violeta-Perú* (1979, Violet-Peru), and the short stories *Los viejos asesinos* (1981). His first experiment with novelistic form appeared in the form of a short novel about an individual's experience in an urban setting, *Violeta-Perú*, in 1979. This urban setting is only a backdrop for a story that increasingly blurs the fragile line between empirical reality and fantasy, and this is the model for much of Ramos's fiction. His second period, which consists of the novel *Intramuros* (1983, Inside the walls) and the novella *Junto al paisaje* (1985), is a return to a more conventional and realist style. The third period consists of Ramos's most accomplished and mature writing and includes the novels *Este era un gato* (1987, This was a cat), *La casa del ahorcado* (1993, The house of the hanged one), and *La mujer que quiso ser Dios* (2000, The woman that wanted to be God), as well as the short fiction in the volume *Señora de la Fuente y otras parábolas de fin de siglo* (1996, Señora de la Fuente and other end-of-century parables).

Many critics consider his most accomplished novel to be *Este era un gato*, a novel set in Veracruz from 1914 to 1974. The point of departure is 1914, the year the U.S. marines invaded the port of Veracruz and took over the city, inflicting numerous deaths in the process. This novel tells the story of Roger Copeland, an American from Oklahoma who participates in the 1914 invasion and returns six decades later to Mexico to die. During his second trip to Mexico he mysteriously abandons his Caribbean cruise ship and isolates himself in Veracruz. Along with this story, a first-person narrator tells the story of a small group of Mexicans, including one who dies in 1914 in the Veracruz invasion, as well as the story of Copeland's relationship with a Mexican woman. As in much of Ramos's fiction, there is a fine line between the imagined and the real, and the play between the two in encounters between the characters creates much of the novel's intrigue. Like Cortázar, Ramos has a unique ability to undermine any fixed and stable understanding of empirical reality, and invites the reader to consider ways in which these fixed understandings are nothing more than mental constructs. He has well-established credentials as one of Mexico's most accomplished postmodern writers after the generation of the Boom.

Selected Work: *Violeta-Perú* (1979); *Intramuros* (1983); *Este era un gato* (1987); *La casa del ahorcado* (1993); *Señora de la Fuente y otras parábolas de fin de siglo* (1996); *La mujer que quiso ser Dios* (2000).

Recurso del método, El (1973, *Reasons of State*, by Alejo Carpentier. Translation by Francis Partridge. London: Writers and Readers, 1977) [**Novel**] One of Carpentier's relatively late novels, *Reasons of State* is known as one of the major works in the genre of dictatorship novels. The writing is comparable to much postmodern, experimental writing of 1970s, with the Cuban author's trademark baroque style. He places the work in an unspecified but vaguely Caribbean nation and continues some of the classic dichotomies of Latin American literature (i.e., *civilización* versus *barbarie*) as well as other clichés of Caribbean society—economic dependence on single-crop agriculture, authoritarian government, rampant corruption, and the like. Over all rules the unnamed prime minister modeled after Cuban dictator Gerardo Machado. Between persecuting mutinous officers such as his friend Colonel Walter Hoffmann, crushing opposition leaders such as the socialist leader The Student, and attempts at modernizing the country with a new capital building and an opera house, he spends long periods in Paris where he feels among his equals. After an economic crash following the end of WWI, dissenters finally achieve an ouster of the prime minister, exiling him to Paris with the complicity of the United States. The rise-and-fall story of the prime minister draws together the methods of many Latin American dictators and systematizes them within the arrogant and ruthless ruler who is the main character. This novel has been compared with two others of this type in the 1970s, Gabriel García Márquez's *El otoño del patriarca* and Augusto Roa Bastos's *Yo, el supremo*.

Rêgo, José Lins de [**Biography**] Brazilian novelist who was born in the state of Paraíba in 1901 and died in Rio de Janeiro in 1957, he was a major regional writer. Most of Rêgo's important fiction appeared in the 1930s and 1940s and much of it corresponds to the dictatorship of Vargas. He was from a family of landowners with deep roots in the land. From his early years as a writer, he associated with the regionalist movement founded in 1926 in Recife under the leadership of Gilberto Freyre. He published important regionalist novels before

1945, with a total of twelve novels in his career. In the latter part of this career he published a "sugarcane cycle" of novels that included *Cangaçeiros* (1953, Bandits), his last novel. In 1956 he published his memoirs under the title *Meus Verdes Anos* (My green years). Other than *Cangaçeiros*, his post-WWII fiction consisted of *Eurídice*.

Selected Work (after 1945): *Eurídice* (1947); *Cangaçeiros* (1953).

Respiración artificial (1979, *Artificial Respiration,* by Ricardo Piglia. Translation by Daniel Balderston. Durham: Duke University Press, 1993) [**Novel**] A key novel that was widely read in the 1980s and 1990s throughout Latin America, it placed Piglia among the most respected novelists in Latin America during this period. It opens with the question "Is there a story?" and then keeps the reader intrigued until the end, although the action is minimal. Piglia explores the relationship between literature and history in this two-hundred-page meditation on Argentine cultural and political history. The novel consists of two parts, the first of which is narrated primarily by an aspiring writer named Emilio Renzi and concerns Enrique Osorio, a private secretary of the nineteenth-century dictator Juan Manuel Rosas. The second part is narrated by a Pole named Vladimir Tardewski living in Argentina and recreates a lengthy conversation about Argentine political and cultural history. This pastiche of the philosophical style explored by Borges, Cortázar, and Macedonio Fernandez delves into the question of how national histories are constructed and institutionalized. Piglia returns to the roots of Argentine nationhood in the nineteenth century, as national history and family history are fused in this novel. On another level of reading, *Respiración artificial* evokes the question of "how to speak the unspeakable," thus referring to issues related to the censorship of the military dictatorship in Argentina under which this novel was written.

Restrepo, Laura [Biography] Colombian novelist, essayist, and journalist, she has taught literature at the National University in Bogotá, Colombia, and has been the director of the important news weekly *Semana*. She has lived in Colombia, Spain, and Mexico. Since the 1990s she has been one of Colombia's most widely read and commercially successful women writers and increasingly recognized beyond the borders of her homeland. She is a storyteller best associated with commercial fiction and the post-Boom.

In her novel *Dulce compañía* (1995, *Angel of Galilea*) Restrepo tells the story of la Mona, a reporter for the newspaper *Somos*. Among her assignments as a reporter for this tabloid, she is sent to an impoverished sector in Bogotá called Galilea to cover the story of an angel sighting. Restrepo does not challenge the reader with her writing style or any other aspect of this novel, justifying those who categorize this type of fiction as *literatura light*.

Selected Work: *Leopardo al sol* (1993, *Leopard in the Sun*, translation Steven A. Lytle, 1999); *Dulce compañía* (1995, *The Angel of Galilea*, translation Dolores M. Koch, 1995); *La novia oscura* (1999).

Revueltas, José [Biography] Mexican novelist, short story writer, essayist, playwright, and scriptwriter, he was born in Mexico City in 1944. He is widely known in Mexico as a left-wing public intellectual self-educated by reading books in the public library. He became a political activist at a young age; in 1929 he was arrested for his political activity and jailed for six months. He was active in the Communist Party, which was banned in Mexico between 1929 and 1934. In 1943 he was expelled from the

Communist Party and readmitted in 1995, only to be ejected again in 1960. He participated in the 1968 protests at Tlatelolco and was jailed from 1968 to 1971. Between 1944 and 1975 he wrote twenty-six film scripts; these films included an adaptation of the novel *El apando* (1969, The punishment cell).

Revueltas wrote three volumes of short stories and several novels. His political agenda is evident throughout his fiction, with reference to ideas originating in Christian principles, existentialist thought, and socialist humanism. He died in 1976.

Selected Work: *Los días terrenales* (1949); *En algún valle de lágrimas* (1956); *Los motivos de Caín* (1957); *Los errores* (1964); *El apando* (1969).

Rey Rosa, Rodrigo [Biography] Guatemalan novelist and short story writer, he has emerged in the 1990s as one of the leading young writers of the Central American region. Born in Guatemala City in 1958, he completed his studies there and in recent years has lived in Tangier, Morocco, New York, and Guatemala's remote Petén region. In 1995 he directed the film *The Proof* and scripted one of the stories in this production for Laurie Parker in Los Angeles, California. Rey Rosa's fiction has been translated into English, French, German, Dutch, and Japanese. He is the author of *The Path Doubles Back* (1982), *El cuchillo del mendigo* (1986, The Beggar's Knife), *Dust on Her Tongue* (1989), *El agua quieta*, (1989, The quiet water) and *Ningún lugar sagrado* (1998, No sacred place). He wrote the text accompanying Miguel Barceló's *Toros*, published by Galerie Bruno Bischofberger (Zurich, 1991).

Selected Work: *El Salvador de buques* (1990); *Cárcel de árboles* (1991, The Peleari Project*, translation Paul Bowles, 1997); *Lo que soñó Sebastián* (1994); *El cojo bueno* (1996); *Que me maten si* (1997); *La orilla africana* (1999); *El tren a Travancore* (2001); *Piedras encantadas* (2001).

Ribeiro, Carlos [Biography] Born in Salvador, Bahia, in 1958, he has been identified by critics in Brazil as one of the promising new writers of the generation of the 1990s in Brazil. He has written one novel, short stories, and essays and has worked as a journalist and professor at the UFB. In his novel *O Chamado da Noite* (1997, The call of the night), he explores the terrain of dreams, memory, and fantasy. In this five-part novel he is interested in everyday situations and common people—this is not the fiction of heroes of the grand narrative. The author along with his characters live in a world of new technology and the popular postmodern culture of globalization, from computers to Romy Schneider, Monica Vitti, and Blauber Rocha.

Novel: *Abismo* (1994); *O Chamado da Noite* (1997).

Ribeiro, Darcy [Biography] Known in Brazil primarily as an anthropologist and an academic, he has also had a career as a politician and a novelist. Born in 1922, he has long been engaged in research on folklore, ethnology, and popular culture in Brazil. In the early 1960s he held several high-level government posts, but his career in public service was interrupted by the military dictatorship in 1964. He entered the public sphere later, in the 1980s. He is widely recognized for his penetrating analysis of Brazilian culture and society, which he has set forth in books such as *O Processo Civilizatório* (1968, The Civilization Process) and *O Povo Brasileiro* (1995, The Brazilian people). After establishing his credentials in the social sciences, Ribeiro turned to the novel. Since then he has published the trilogy *O Mulo* (1981, The mule), *Utopía Selvagem* (1982, Wild utopia); and *Maíra* (1983, *Maíra*). One prominent critic in Brazil has compared the breadth of *O Mulo* to Guimarães Rosa's *Grande Sertão: Veredas*; other readers have remarked that *O Mulo* is a mirror of the distorted image of Brazil created by official institutions. Considered by some critics a benchmark of Brazilian fiction, *Maíra* is a work of social protest set in the Amazon, and Ribeiro's anthropological research is exhibited in the book. His more recent *Migo* (1988) is an experiment that recalls Julio Cortázar's *Hopscotch*; like the Argentine's paradigm-shifting text, *Migo* is structured in such a way that the author offers the reader numerous possible methods of reading from the outset.

Selected Work: *O Mulo* (1981); *Maíra* (1983, *Maíra*, translation E. H. Goodland and Thomas Colchie, 1984); *Utopía Selvagem* (1982); *Migo* (1988).

Ribeyro, Julio Ramón [Biography] Peruvian novelist and short story writer, he was born in 1929 and died in 1996 shortly after being internationally recognized with a prestigious literary prize (Premio Juan Rulfo). He was considered one of Latin America's most accomplished short story writers. His first novel, *Crónica de San Gabriel* (1960, Chronicle of Saint Gabriel), is a critique of the decadent elite among large landowners in Peru. His later novel *Cambio de guardia* (1976, Change of guard) deals with the same period of dictatorship in Peru as Mario Vargas Llosa's *Conversación en La Catedral*: the 1950s dictatorship of Odría in Peru.

Selected Work: *Crónica de San Gabriel* (1960); *Los geniecillos dominicales* (1965); *Cambio de guardia* (1976).

Rivera Garza, Cristina [Biography] Mexican novelist, short story writer, poet, historian, and essayist, she is currently gaining the reputation as one of Latin America's most accomplished young writers. She belongs to the generation referred to as the generation of the crack in Mexico, but has not associated with the central figures of that group, such as Jorge Volpi and Pedro Angel Palou. In general she has demonstrated less interest in the machinations of the world literary market than many of the writers of this group or the generation of the 1990s in Brazil. Her challenging novels, interest in gender issues, and low-profile approach to writing places her closer to certain writers of the previous generation, such as Diamela Eltit and Sylvia Molloy. She was born in Matamoros, Mexico, in 1964, and has lived in several cities in northern and central Mexico since her childhood. The daughter of a Mexican scientist, she studied sociology at the National University in Mexico City (UNAM) and completed her PhD in history at the University of Houston. Since then she has assumed several positions in U.S. academia and is currently is on the faculty in the Department of History at San Diego State University in California. During her tenure at San Diego State she has offered creative writing workshops in nearby Tijuana and worked closely with emerging writers and artists in the border region.

Rivera Garza's transgeneric, transnational, and interdisciplinary writing puts into question conventional understandings of gender, genre, and human relations. She began publishing poetry and fiction in the early 1980s, the story "Parto del Horizonte" appearing in an anthology in Mexico City in 1982. In 1984 she received a poetry prize organized by the literary magazine *Punto de Partida* in Mexico. In 1985 she was awarded another prize (the Salvador Novo scholarship) by the Centro Mexicano de Escritores. Her first volume of fiction was a collection of seven short stories titled *La guerra no importa* (1991, War does not matter) that was awarded a national short story prize in Mexico (Premio de Cuento San Luís Potosí). In 1997 she received a prestigious national prize (Premio Nacional de Novela José Rubén Romero) for her novel *Nadie me verá llorar* (1999, *No One Will See Me Cry*). Her most recent fiction is the novel *La cresta de Ilión* (2002, Ilion's hip bone) and the volume of short stories *Ningún reloj cuenta esto* (2002, No clock counts this). The novel is a subtle and engaging exploration of gender, and *Ningún reloj cuenta esto* is a set of eight fictions that portray fragile individual identities, ambiguous human relationships, and characters who consistently face the possibility of absolutely no transcendence or meaningful significance in life.

Selected Work: Nadie me verá llorar (1999, *No One Will See Me Cry*, translation Andrew Hurley, 2003); *La cresta de Ilión* (2002); *Lo anterior* (2004).

Roa Bastos, Augusto [Biography] Paraguay's major twentieth-century novelist, he was born in 1917 and has been an active presence in Latin America since the 1960s. His international renown, however, became widespread in the 1970s when he published his masterpiece, *Yo, el supremo* (1974, *I, the Supreme*), an ambitious "total" novel comparable in many ways to the massive projects of the 1960s Boom. In both the Spanish and English editions, there is a lengthy glossary of the terms used in the text in the Guaraní indigenous language.

Selected Work: Hijo de hombre (1960, *Son of Man*, translation Rachel Caffyn, 1965); *Yo, el supremo* (1974, *I the Supreme*, translation Helen R. Lane, 1986).

Rodríguez Juliá, Edgardo [Biography] Puerto Rican novelist, short story writer, and essayist, he was born in Rio Piedras, Puerto Rico, in 1946. An innovator, he writes postmodern texts that challenge conventional boundary definitions. He combines photography and narrative in his book *Puertorriqueños: Album de la sagrada*

familia puertorriqueña (1990, Puerto Ricans: Album of the Puerto Rican Holy Family). His book *Cámara secreta* (1994, Secret camera) has been described as an "erotico-pornographic visual essay." On the other hand, *Sol de medianoche* (1995, Midnight sun) is a detective novel.

Rodriguez Juliá's major novels are *La renuncia del héroe Baltasar* (1974, Resignation of the hero Baltasar) and *Las tribulaciones de Jonás* (1981, Jonah's tribulations). The novels are part of the author's broader interest in rewriting the history of Puerto Rico—with emphasis on the lives of working people—to provide a counterdiscourse to official and institutionalized histories that have legitimized the rule of the elite. His best-selling work is his short novel *El entierro de Cortijo* (1993, *Cortijo's Wake*), his chronicle of the funeral of a popular working-class musician in Puerto Rico.

Selected Work: La renuncia del héroe Baltasar (1974); *Las tribulaciones de Jonás* (1981); *El entierro de Cortijo* (1993, *Cortijo's Wake*, translation Juan Flores, 2004); *Cámara secreta* (1994); *Sol de medianoche* (1995).

Roemer, Astrid H. [Biography] Caribbean novelist, playwright, poet, and short story writer, she was born in Paramaribo, Suriname, in 1947. She writes in Dutch, the language of most prose and fiction in Suriname as well as the oficial language of education in that multilingual nation. She writes about issues of gender, race, and class from the perspective of a woman of African descent growing up in Suriname (where the majority of the population is of African descent) and in Holland (where Afro-Caribbeans are a minority). In one of her major novels, *Niets Wat Pijn Doet* (1985, Nothing that causes pain), the protagonist is an adult woman who writes of her childhood experience as an immigrant from Suriname to Holland. At the beginning of the novel she describes the cultural conflict of an immigrant of African descent. She learns important lessons about how to cope with freedom, possession, and pain. The novel contains many more key anecdotes of her rite of passage and later life, but the main themes that surfaced early on reappear later. Although Roemer writes in Dutch, her work is comparable to that of the Cuban Zoé Valdés, who immigrated to Paris. As a Caribbean woman of African descent who is interested in issues of gender and class, Roemer's work can be linked in different ways to that of the Puerto Rican Rosario Ferré, the Argentine Sylvia Molloy, and the Haitian Edwidge Danticat.

Fiction: *Neem mij terug Suriname* (1974); *De wereld heeft gezicht verloren* (1975); *Over de gekte van een vrouw* (1982); *Nergens Ergens* (1983); *Niets Wat Pijn Doet* (1985); *Levdenslang gedicht* (1987); *Het spoor van de jakhals* (1988); *De achtentwingigste dag* (1988); *De orde van de dag* (1998); *Alles wat gelukkig maakt* (1989); *O Post west Holland best* (1989).

Rojas Herazo, Héctor [Biography] Colombian novelist, poet, and painter born in 1922, he is one of Colombia's foremost neo-Faulknerian writers. From the same Caribbean coastal region of Gabriel García Márquez and of the same generation, he grew up idolizing writers such as Faulkner. His novel *Respirando el verano* (1962, Breathing the summer) was one of three landmark neo-Faulknerian novels that modernized fiction in Colombia in the 1950s and 1960s, along with Gabriel García Márquez's *Leafstorm* (1955) and Alvaro Cepeda Samudio's *La casa grande* (1962). He followed the same family story in his next novels, *En noviembre no llega el arzobispo* (1967, In November the archbishop does not arrive) and *Celia se pudre* (1986, Celia rots). These novels evoke the pre-

modern world of Celia, the central character of these three novels, and her family. *Respirando el verano* focuses on the aging matriarch and her grandson Anselmo. Celia is a minor character in *En noviembre no llega el arzobispo*, a denunciation of the local oligarchy's absolute domination of all sectors of society in the town of Cedrón. It carries with it, in addition, a consistent subtext of terror and violence. *En noviembre no llega el arzobispo* characterizes a broader spectrum of society than did the first novel, its social critique being more strident than that of *Repirando el verano*. Just as García Márquez's *Cien años de soledad* (1967) was a synthesis of his world of Macondo, the massive (811-page) *Celia se pudre* is the summa of the world of Cedrón. Although this hermetic work has multiple narrative voices, the decadence of Cedrón is primarily filtered through Celia's memory. As in *Respirando el verano*, the central image of *Celia se pudre* is the home—*la casa*—and the predominant tone accentuates the hatred that permeates Cedrón as well as Celia's life.

In addition to his novels, Rojas Herazo produced a significant body of poetry and painting, devoting much of his later life to painting. He died in 2002.

Selected Work: *Respirando el verano* (1962); *En noviembre no llega el arzobispo* (1967); *Celia se pudre* (1986).

Rosa, João Guimarães [Biography] Novelist, short story writer, and essayist, he is one of the major figures of the twentieth-century Brazilian novel and, with the Argentine Julio Cortázar, one of the seminal innovators of the century in Latin America. He was born in Cordisburgo (state of Minas Gerais) in 1908 and, after spending a lifetime writing stories about his native northeastern region of the *sertão*, died in 1967. After a rural childhood on a cattle ranch, he was trained in medicine and spent much of his life in the diplomatic corps. His encyclopedic knowledge of cultures, languages, religions, and science, the study of which are often described as his "hobbies," appear in his fiction, which is as complex, multilayered, and hermetic as his vast knowledge. His esoteric fiction consists of writings in a variety of lengths and linguistic registers. Consequently, these writings often escape easy genre classification. For the sake of introductory description, it can be stated that he published one lengthy novel and six volumes of shorter fiction.

Guimarães Rosa's major work is the novel *Grande Sertão: Veredas* (1956, *The Devil to Pay in the Backlands*), one of the groundbreaking works for the novel in Brazil and Latin America. In it a variety of narrators tell a multiplicity of stories, many of which digress considerably from the main story line.

Selected Work: *Sagarana* (1946); *Grande Sertão: Veredas* (1956, *The Devil to Pay in the Backlands*, translation James L. Taylor and Harriet de Onis, 1963); *Corpo de Baile* (1956); *Primeiras Estórias* (1962); *Tutaméia* (1967); *Estas Estórias* (1969); *Ave, Palabra* (1970).

Rubião, Murilo [Biography] Brazilian short story writer, journalist, and novelist, he was born in Silvestre Ferraz (state of Minas Gerais) in 1916. He studied law in Belo Horizonte, receiving his degree in 1942. He has served in several major capacities to promote Brazilian writing and culture, such as president of the Association of Journalists in Minas Gerais and director of a seminal and often-remembered conference of Brazilian writers, the I Congresso Brasileiro de Escritores. Critics in Brazil consider him one of the nation's primary exponents of surrealism. He began publishing short fiction in the 1940s, with his first volume, *O Ex-mágico*, appearing in 1947. Later he published the stories *Os Dragões e*

Outros Contos (1965) and *O Convidado* (1974) as well as the novel *O Pirotécnico Zacarías* (1974, Zacarías the pyrotechnic). His total production of fiction and essays consists of six books.

Selected Work: *O Pirotécnico Zacarías* (1974).

Rulfo, Juan [Biography] Mexican novelist and short story writer, he wrote one of the masterpieces of the century, *Pedro Páramo* (1955, *Pedro Páramo*) and intrigued many of his readers and critics by never publishing another novel before his death in 1986; his family has published posthumous fragments of his other writings. He was born in 1918, in the rural area of the state of Jalisco in the small town of Apulco. Soon after his birth his family moved to a town called San Gabriel, a location that he later fictionalized. After the death of his parents when he was ten years old, he and his two brothers were sent to an orphanage in Guadalajara, where he remained until the age of fourteen. He eventually began studies of law at the National University in Mexico City (UNAM), but a lack of financial support forced him to withdraw and take a job as an immigration officer in the Department of the Interior, where he worked from 1935 to 1945. He began writing fiction in the late 1930s and early 1940s, although the writings from that period were published only as fragments many years later. It appears that he was working on a novel in the early 1940s, although it was never published. Rulfo published his first story, "La vida no es muy seria en sus cosas," ("Life is not very serious in its things") in the literary magazine *America* in 1945. Later that year he published two better-known stories, "Macario" and "Nos han dado la tierra" ("They have given us the land"), which later appeared in the volume *El llano en llamas* (1954, *The Burning Plain*). He received a fellowship from the Centro de Escritores Mexicanos, where he wrote some portions of *Pedro Páramo*. He died in 1986.

Rulfo was a Faulknerian-type writer who used his native region of rural Jalisco as the setting for both *Pedro Páramo* and his one volume of short stories, *El llano en llamas*. *Pedro Páramo* is a relatively short novel, but its complex imagery, multiple points of view, and always shifting space and time have intrigued, challenged, and perplexed readers since its publication. The novel begins in a realist mode, with the arrival of a character named Juan Preciado in Comala, but as the situation unfolds it becomes evident that the scenario is far from real, for all of the characters, in fact, are dead. With ample overtones of a wide variety of Western myths, *Pedro Páramo* is also a novel about lost love and the abuse of power by a local political boss, a classic Latin American *caudillo*. Early reviews and commentary in Mexico were mostly negative, but by the 1960s it became increasingly evident that Rulfo had written a major work that was, in many ways, ahead of its time in Latin America. Writers of the Boom and post-Boom in Latin America have made frequent reference to this novel as a masterpiece of narrative that has served both as model and inspiration.

Selected Work: *Pedro Páramo* (1955, *Pedro Páramo*, translation Lysander Kemp, 1959).

Ruy Sánchez, Alberto [Biography] Mexican novelist, short story writer, poet, translator, and essayist, he was born in Mexico City in 1951. He has a reputation for writing erotic books, but he describes them as "sensual" rather than erotic. He considers it necessary to write fiction to communicate what is not possible to express in the genre of the essay or scholarly study. He studied both communications and creative writing in Mexico City as well as both communications and literature at the University of Paris. He has written essays about film and translated essays on film from the French. During his eight-year stay in France, he visited Morocco for three months, which was a defining experience for his later writing, for it was in this African nation that Ruy Sánchez came to appreciate the nonrational, nonscientific, and magical aspects of reality. His novels can be divided into two general categories—those of the universe of guilt and those in which desire is played out without concern over guilt. Within the universe of guilt is his historical novel *Los demonios de la lengua* (1987, Devil of the tongue), which deals with the excesses of the Spanish Inquisition. His novels of desire are *Los nombres del aire* (1987, The names of the air), *Los labios del agua* (1996, Lips of water), and *Los jardines secretos* (2001, The secret gardens). *Los labios del agua* deals with masculine desire, and *Los jardines secretos* is the story of a pregnant woman. His fiction is characterized by fast-moving plots and an interest in the Anglo-American tradition of the detective novel. His first novel, *Los nombres del aire*, won a prestigious novel prize in Mexico (Premio Villarrutia, 1987). He has published numerous essays on literary topics, including a book-length study on the writing of Octavio Paz. Among his numerous recognitions, he has been awarded a Guggenheim Fellowship.

Selected Work: *Los demonios de la lengua* (1987); *Los nombres del aire* (1987); *En los labios del agua* (1996); *Los jardines secretos* (2001).

Sábato, Ernesto [Biography] Argentine novelist and essayist, he is a major intellectual figure of the post-WWII period in

Latin America. He was born in Rojas (province of Buenos Aires) in 1911 and went to the city of La Plata in southern Argentina in 1924 for his high school studies; he remained in La Plata for his undergraduate education in physics and mathematics. With the military coup in Argentina in 1930, Sábato became increasingly politicized and joined the Communist Party, although he later became skeptical of most mainline ideologies and political parties and left the Communist Party. In 1934 he attended an anti-Fascist conference in Brussels and visited Paris from there. He returned to Buenos Aires in 1936, marrying the woman who would remain his wife for the rest of his life, and began graduate studies in physics, completing his doctorate in 1937. With a scholarship for postdoctoral study in Paris in 1938, he met French surrealist André Breton and other European writers of the avant-garde. After studies at MIT in the United States, he returned to Buenos Aires in 1940 and became involved in the literary world of Adolfo Bioy Casares and Victoria Ocampo, publishing essays in the prestigious magazine *Sur* and the cultural supplement of the newspaper *La Nación*. In 1943, suffering from an existential crisis, he left the discipline of science and began writing the literary-philosophical essay *Uno y el universo* (One and the universe), which he published in 1945. In 1948 he published his first novel, *El túnel*, which appeared in English in 1950 as *The Outsider* with a French version the following year. It is a novel of love, jealousy, and murder, but the thematic focus is the protagonist's alienation. He published a book of essays, *Heterodoxia*, in 1953. After holding several government positions in the cultural sphere, he wrote his major novel, *Sobre heroes y tumbas* (1961, *On Heroes and Tombs*). For the early part of the novel, it is the story of two characters, then focusing on a third character, Fernando Vidal, whom many

readers consider the protagonist. It is a lengthy and complex work that is best understood as an examination of values and an effort to reconsider human beings as individuals in contemporary society. The first volume of his *Obras completas* (Complete works) appeared in 1966, and the second volume in 1970. He received several prizes in Argentina, among them the Gran Premio de Honor de la Sociedad Argentina, for his novel *Abaddón, el exterminador* (1974, *The Angel of Darkness*), his most enigmatic and provocative work. In 1981 Seix Barral, in Spain, published his *Narrativa completa* (Complete narrative). He was active in the political process in Argentina after the military dictatorship in the 1980s and was involved with the evaluation of the military legacy.

Selected Work: El túnel (1948, *The Outsider*, translation Harriet de Onís, 1950); *Sobre heroes y tumbas* (1961, *On Heroes and Tombs*, translation Helen R. Lane, 1981); *Abaddón, el exterminador* (1974, *The Angel of Darkness*, translation Andrew Hurley, 1991).

Sabino, Fernando Tavares [Biography] Brazilian novelist and journalist, he was born in Belo Horizonte (state of Minas Gerais) in 1923. He was a voratious reader of literature as a child, a period when he read everything from Portuguese classics to detective novels. He was also a competitive swimmer. After holding several government positions, he began publishing journalism in the 1940s. He began publishing fiction in the 1950s.

He has published over forty books of fiction, *crônicas*, travel books, and children's literature, and his work has been included in an anthology of the nation's one hundred best short stories. He has also worked as a journalist in several important venues in Brazil, including the *Fohla de São Paulo*. Serving in the diplomatic corps in New

York and London in the 1950s and 1960s, he became well-known among Brazilian readers as the author of *crônicas*—short and light vignettes of urban life. His novel *O Encontro Marcado* (1956, The appointment) harks back to the Vargas dictatorship of the 1930s and 1940s, and tells the story of an alienated boy's spiritual search for meaning in life.

Selected Work: *A Cidade Vazia* (1950); *O Encontro Marcado* (1956); *O Homen Nu* (1960); *A Mulher do Vizinho* (1962); *A Companheira de Viagem* (1965); *A Inglesa Deslumbrada* (1967); *O Menino Espelho* (1982); *Zelia, uma Paixão* (1991); *Os Movimentos Simulados* (2004).

Sada, Daniel [Biography] Mexican novelist, short story writer, and poet, he was born in Mexicali (state of Baja California del Norte) in 1953. After beginning his writing career as a poet, and short story writer, he has become one of the most prominent novelists of his generation with stories of minimal survival in Mexico, conflict, and black humor. His novel *Porque parece mentira la verdad nunca se sabe* (1996, Because it seems like a lie the truth is never known) is a political intrigue dealing with the potential for truth in Mexican politics. Fraudulent elections and a protest against them are the basis of this novel's plot, which is not centered on one protagonist but on a group of characters all somehow related to each other by blood, political affiliation, or the workplace. Most of them have suffered a death or disappearance of someone close to them. The reader places together the events and relationships as they appear in a series of fragments, often written in a telegraphic style and not lacking in humor. At the end the characters abandon the town of Remadrín, and all that remains are rumors. His recent *Luces artificiales* (2002, Artificial lights) is an urban chronicle survival with Sada's trademark black humor.

Selected Work: *Lampa vida* (1980); *Albredrío* (1989); *Una de dos* (1994); *Porque parece mentira la verdad nunca se sabe* (1996); *Luces artificiales* (2002).

Saer, Juan José [Biography] Argentina novelist, short story writer, and essayist born in Serodino (province of Santa Fe) in 1937, he has become one of the most productive and widely read novelists of his generation in his homeland and increasingly known throughout Latin America. He was a professor at the Universidad Nacional del Litoral, where he taught film and film criticism. His literary essays include the books *El río sin orillas* (1991, River without banks), an antiliterary polemic, and later came forth with *El concepto de ficción* (1997, The concept of fiction) and *La narración-objeto* (1999, Narrative-object), the latter a group of essays on writers such as Cervantes, Faulkner, and Borges. He began publishing fiction in the early 1960s with the volume of short stories *En la zona* (1960, In the zone); his total fiction includes four volumes of short stories and eleven novels. In 1986 he received the Nadal Prize in Spain for his novel *La ocasión* (1986, The Event). His one book of poetry is titled, paradoxically, *El arte de narrar* (1977, The art of narrating).

Selected Work: *Responso* (1964); *La vuelta completa* (1966); *Cicatrices* (1969); *Nadie, nada, nunca* (1980); *El entenado* (1983); *Glosa* (1985); *La ocasión* (1986, The Event, translation Helen R. Lane, 1988); *Lo imborrable* (1992); *La pesquisa* (1994); *Las nubes* (1997); *La mayor* (1998).

Sainz, Gustavo [Biography] Mexican novelist, screenwriter, short story writer, and essayist, he was born in Mexico City in 1940. He studied law and then literature at the National University in Mexico City (UNAM). Sainz and José Agustín are best known in Mexico and Latin America as the central figures of the Onda, a countercultural rebellion against the established norms of both the traditional and modern cultures of Mexico. Inspired by the work of J. D. Salinger, the American Beats, and rock music, they produced a fiction in tune with youth culture and the colloquial language of 1960s Mexico. In many ways this fiction was in dialogue with international postmodern fiction. Sainz's first novel, *Gazapo* (1965), was the first work of the Onda and has remained the signature novel of this movement. His second novel of this type was *Obsesivos días circulares* (1969, Obsessive circular days). Sainz began writing against the Onda with *Compadre lobo* (1977, Friend wolf), *Ojalá te mueras y otras novelas clandestinas mexicanas* (1982, I hope you die and other clandestine Mexican novels), and *Fantasmas aztecas* (1982, Aztec phantoms).

Sainz has received numerous prizes and recognitions, including a Guggenheim Fellowship and thePremio Xavier Villarrutia in Mexico.

Selected Work: *Gazapo* (1965); *Obsesivos días circulares* (1969); *La princesa del Palacio de Hierro* (1974); *Compadre lobo* (1977); *Fantasmas aztecas* (1982); *Ojalá te mueras y otras novelas clandestinas mexicanas* (1982); *Muchachos en llamas* (1987).

Salazar Bondy, Sebastián [Biography]
Peruvian novelist and short story writer, he was born in 1924 and died in 1965. His publications in fiction were sparse, but he commanded the respect of his readership in Peru, including such prominent novelists as Mario Vargas Llosa. He published the volume of short stories *Náufragos y sobrevivientes* (1954, Shipwrecks and survivors). His posthumous novel *Alférez Arce, Teniente Arce, Capitán Arce* (1969, Ensign Arce, Lieutenant Arce, Captain Arce) describes the inner life of a political prisoner.

Selected Work: *Alférez Arce, Teniente Arce, Capitán Arce* (1969).

Sales, Herberto [Biography] Born in Andaraí (state of Bahia) in 1917 in Brazil, he has written detailed fictionalized descriptions of his native region, which is well-known for its diamond panners as well as the violence associated with such activities. He is a conventional realist and social critic who constructs linear plots and well-rounded characters. His first novel, *Cascalho* (1944), deals with the criminal activity and everyday life among the diamond hunters, and this novel gained Sales considerable notoriety in Brazil. His second novel, *Além dos Marimbas* (1961, Beyond the marimbas), is a travel narrative that offers the reader extravagant descriptions of the flora and fauna of the region of Matas de Andaraí in Brazil. In the process he tells the story of a man involved in the lumber industry. His work *Einstein, o Minigênio* (1983, Einstein the minigenius) is his satire of certain aspects of modernization, such as education in the computer age.

Sales's typical work includes *Os Pareceres do Tempo* (1984, The appearances of time), a lengthy (454-page) historical novel set in eighteenth-century Brazil. In this work Sales describes the colonizing process in which Portugal destroyed the people and nature of Brazil. He also relates a love story through a portrait of the process of "Christianizing" the Native American population.

In 1986 he wrote a work of science fiction, *A Porta de Chifre* (Door of Cypress). Set in Amazonia in the year 2352, in this ecological tragedy there is no more petroleum on earth: the people live off the mud they dig out of the ground. His more recent *Rebanho de Odio* (1995, Herd of hate) is a lengthy (502-page) intergenerational saga dealing with the loves and conflicts of a traditional family in a small town near Rio de Janeiro.

Selected Work: *Cascalho* (1944); *Além dos Marimbas* (1961); *Dados Biográficos do Finado Marcelino* (1965); *Einstein, o Minigenio* (1983); *Os Pareceres do Tempo* (1984); *A Porta de Chifre* (1986); *Na Selva da tua Lembrança* (1988); *Rio dos Morcegos* (1993); *Rebanho do Odio* (1995); *A Prostituta* (1996).

Salvador, Humberto [Biography] Ecuadorian novelist born in 1909, he was associated with that nation's generation of 1930, a group committed to social and political reform. He was as committed to these ideals as his contemporaries, but more interested in portraying the psychological depth of his characters and the human relationships among them in such novels as *La fuente clara* (1946, The clear fountain), *Silueta de una dama* (1964, Silhouette of a lady), and *Viaje a lo desconocido* (1967, Voyage into the unknown).

Selected Work: *La fuente clara* (1946); *Silueta de una dama* (1964); *Viaje a lo desconocido* (1967).

Sánchez, Héctor [Biography] Colombian novelist, essayist, and short story writer, he became prominent in the late 1960s and 1970s as part of the generation that had a double task in Colombia; dealing with how to fictionalize the experience of the 1950s civil war called La Violencia and dealing with the shadow of celebrity writer Gabriel García Márquez. He was born in Guamo (department of Tolima), Colombia, in 1940. He began writing in the late 1960s and published his first volume of short stories, *Cada viga en su ojo* (Each branch in his eye) in 1967; he has published two other volumes of short fiction as well as a collection of essays and short fiction, *Literatura y chantaje* (1973). Sánchez and others who began writing in the late 1960s and early 1970s also became known in Colombia as the "Generation of the Blockade and the State of Siege" because of the blockade against

Cuba and the numerous governmental crises in Colombia that caused the central government to regularly declare a state of siege, suspending many normal democratic processes and human rights protections. Sánchez earned a reputation with the publication of his prize-winning first novel, *Las causas supremas* (1969, The supreme causes), followed by *Las maniobras* (1969, The schemes), but then went to Barcelona for the better part of the 1970s and 1980s to write and pursue his literary career. In these two early novels, Sánchez presents characters who are frustrated in any attempt to participate in society and improve their lot. While in Barcelona Sánchez wrote *Los desheredados* (1974, The disinherited), *Sin nada entre las manos* (1976, Nothing in the hands), and *El tejemaneje* (1979, The operator).

Selected Work: *Las causas supremas* (1969); *Las maniobras* (1969); *Los desheredados* (1974); *Sin nada entre las manos* (1976); *El tejemaneje* (1979).

Sánchez, Luis Rafael [Biography] Puerto Rican novelist, essayist, and playwright born in Humaco, Puerto Rico in 1936, he is the major contemporary novelist of that island. He began writing plays in the late 1950s and enjoyed his first major success in 1968 with his play *La pasión según Antígona Pérez* (The passion according to Antigone Perez). His early plays were existentialist in theme, and his later ones were lighter in tone, celebrating the entertainment value of language in itself. Sánchez has also published essays throughout his career, including *La guagua aérea* (1994, The aerial bus). He began publishing fiction in the late 1960s.

He is best-known for his novel *La guaracha del Macho Camacho* (1977, *Macho Camacho's Beat*), an important incursion into the postmodern and popular culture in Puerto Rico. This novel is a playful and humorous fictionalization of a pop culture figure, as is his later novel *La importancia de llamarse Daniel Santos* (1988, The importance of calling oneself Daniel Santos).

Selected Work: *La guaracha del Macho Camacho* (1977, *Macho Camacho's Beat*, translation Gregory Rabassa, 1980); *La importancia de llamarse Daniel Santos* (1988).

Sánchez, Néstor [Biography] Argentine novelist born in 1934, he became known as one of Argentina's most radically experimental novelists in the late 1960s. He was much acclaimed for his early novel *Siberia Blues* (1968), one of the most audaciously experimental books to be published in Latin America.

Selected Work: *Siberia Blues* (1967); *Cómico de la lengua* (1973); *La condición efímera* (1988).

Sánchez (Yoss), José Miguel [Biography] Caribbean novelist and short story writer, he was born in Havana, Cuba, in 1969. He is one of the few Latin American writers writing in Spanish, along with the Argentine Angélica Gorodischer, who is interested in science fiction. He studied biology and has received prizes in Cuba for both his short stories and novels, including a local prize for science fiction (David de Ciencia-Ficción) at the age of nineteen. His 1994 novel *Jugando a rumiarse el tiempo* (Playing at contemplating time) was a finalist for the Casa de las Américas Prize. He has published two volumes of science fiction short stories, *Timshel* (1990) and *W* (1997), as well as the novel *Los pecios y los náufragos* (2000, The fish and the shipwrecks).

Selected Work: *Jugando a rumiarse el tiempo* (1994); *Los pecios y los náufragos* (2000).

Sant'Anna, Sérgio [Biography] Novelist, poet, and short story writer, he is known in Brazil as a satirist and experimentalist. He combines humor with critique and successfully juxtaposes formal language with the colloquial. Born in Rio de Janeiro, Brazil, in 1941, he studied law before embarking on a career as a writer and becoming involved with *Estórias*, a magazine of experimental fiction (later closed down by the military regime in the 1960s). He was also associated with the literary supplement of a newspaper in Minas Gerais. His writing arose as part of the expression of a generation influenced by the Beat generation and 1960s counterculture in the United States, constantly challenging limits and conventions, and is easily associated with international postmodern fiction. After publishing his first volume of short stories, *O sobrevivente* (1969, The survivor), he participated in the International Writing Program at the University of Iowa. His first novel, the parodic *Confissões de Ralfo (uma autobiografía imaginária)* (1975, Ralfo's confessions), was remarkably successful in Brazil. Its wild adventures and experimental style hark back to inventive fictions as far ranging as *Don Quijote* to a Brazilian classic of the 1920s, *Macunaíma*; in fact, the book has been called an "anti-*Don Quijote*." It is inspired as much by Jack Kerouac as by Cervantes, however, and the author explains in the prologue that the book treats the "real life of an imaginary man or the imaginary life of a real man." A first-person account divided into nine books of thoughts and fantasies, this novel is only vaguely related to the genre of the novel. The antihero Ralfo undertakes a psychological voyage that is highly imaginative. On another level of reading, it is a subtle and subversive political work, with one section dealing with torture: the author uses humor to present violence. His novel *Simulacros* (1977, Simulacra) is a self-conscious metafiction that exhibits the crisis of the novelistic form as well as the crisis of middle-class values. *Um*

Romance de Geração (1980, Generational novel), which the author calls a "dramatic comedy in one act," is about a frustrated, alcoholic writer. Sant'Anna received a prestigious Brazilian literary prize (Prêmio Jabuti) for two of his texts, *O Concerto de João Gilberto no Rio de Janeiro* (1982, João Gilberto's concert in Rio de Janeiro) and *Amazônia* (1986, Amazon), the latter a soap opera parody of the political establishment. His volume *A Senhorita Simpson* (1989, Ms. Simpson) can be read as a two-part novel or seven stories. The second part of the book consists of a novella titled "A senhorita Simpson (uma novela)," and tells the story of cultural and personal encounters between students of English in Copacabana. His recent short novel *Um Crime Delicado* (1997, A delicate crime) is a postmodern text with vague links to the spy thriller as well as to criticism and memoir. In 1997 he published a volume of his collected short stories and novellas, *Contos e Novelas Reunidos* (Stories and novels) with texts originally published from 1969 to 1990.

Selected Work: *Confessões de Ralfo (una autiobiografia imaginária)* (1975); *Simulacros* (1977); *Um Romance de Geração* (1980); *Amazônia* (1986); *A Senhorita Simpson* (1989); *Um Crime Delicado* (1997).

Santiago, Silviano [Biography] Brazilian novelist, poet, short story writer, and scholar, he holds a doctorate in French literature from the Sorbonne and is a leading exponent of postmodern fiction in Brazil as well as an outspoken critic of the military regime (1964–1989). He is also considered an authority in French literature. Born in Formiga (state of Minas Gerais) in 1936, he has taught in the United States, Canada, and Europe. His essays have appeared in volumes titled *Uma literatura nos trópicos* (1971, A literature in the tropics) and *Vale quanto pesa* (1982, You get what you pay for). He has established a well-earned repu-

tation as an experimentalist both in fiction and his poetry. In 1970 he published a book of poems titled *Salto* (Jump). His novel *O Olhar* (1974, The look) deals with a mother-father-child triangle and is written in the mode of the French *nouveau roman*. He was awarded the prestigious Prêmio Jabuti in 1982 for his novel *Em Liberdade: Uma Ficcão de Silviano Santiago* (1981, At liberty: a fiction by Silviano Santiago). Narrated through the eyes of a fictionalized version of the Brazilian novelist Graciliano Ramos, this novel questions the nature of personal liberty. *Stella Manhattan* (1985) is set in New York during the years of the military dictatorship in Brazil and deals with subjects such as exile, leftist guerrillas, and gender. His later novel *Uma História de Família* (1992, A family story) is an atypical family story, for it is a disturbing account of human relations: it consists of a series of ramblings by an unnamed narrator-character who makes frequent references to a silent interlocutor, Uncle Mário, who is the personification of misfortune. His antisocial, obsessive, and at times sadomasochistic behavior presents a fearful vision of domestic life.

Selected Work: *O Olhar* (1974); *Em Liberdade* (1982); *Stella Manhattan* (1985, *Stella Manhattan,* translation George Yudice, 1994); *Uma História de Família* (1992); *Viagem ao México* (1995); *De Cócoras* (1999).

Santos-Febres, Mayra [Biography] Puerto Rican novelist, short story writer poet, essayist, and academic, she was born in 1966. The child of teachers who grew up with asthma, she lived in a world of books from an early age and was writing as a child. In high school a mentor taught her several of the disciplines that support a writing career. She holds a PhD in literature from Cornell University. Santos-Febres writes about the experience of urban life in the Caribbean, and she is particularly interested in exploring ways to reproduce the subtle tones and rhythm of Caribbean popular language as it is used in music. She writes as a marginalized black woman, but does not consider marginality a fixed category: in some spheres of her life (for reasons associated with class and education) she considers herself more in the center than in the margins. She has also been involved with television, appearing as a poet in the show *Grado Zero*.

Santos-Febres has published several volumes of short fiction and novels. Her first novel, *Sirena Selena vestida de pena* (2000, Selena Siren dressed in sorrow), was the product of her experience working as a volunteer in an organization assisting AIDS victims. On the basis of people she met doing this volunteer work, she wrote this highly successful novel—the story of a gay male adolescent who works in the streets as a performer and singer. She has already received several prizes and international recognition for her work, which has much in common with Caribbean women writers such as Edwidge Danticat and Paule Marshall.

Selected Work: *Sirena Silena vestida de pena* (2000); *Cualquier miércoles soy tuya* (2002).

Sarduy, Severo [Biography] Cuban novelist , essayist, and poet, he was a leading innovator of his generation in Latin America and one of the most complex and hermetic writers of the Caribbean region. Influenced by French structuralism and poststructuralism, he is known as a theoretical, postmodern novelist and essayist who challenged many of the traditional and even modern tenets of Latin American culture and thought. He wrote at length about the "empty center," and many critics considered his novels a parody of poststructuralist thought in general and deconstructionist theory in particular.

Sarduy was born in Camaguey, Cuba, in 1937, of a working-class family, and he graduated from high school there in 1955. He began writing poetry in the 1950s, publishing in local newspapers, and in 1958 he published a poem in an important literary magazine in Havana, *Ciclón*. In his literary career he published six books of poetry, as well as several books of essays. He moved to Havana in 1956 to study medicine, but was soon involved in Havana's literary world, writing literary criticism for both *Ciclón* and another prestigious journal, *Orígenes*.

Sarduy was strongly committed to the revolution promoted by the government of Fidel Castro and began writing literary and political essays for a variety of new cultural organs in the early 1960s. He received a fellowship to study art criticism at the Ecole du Louvre in Paris in 1959, and in 1961 he decided to stay in Paris rather than return to Cuba. He continued studying art, wrote his first novel, *Gestos* (1963, Gestures), and eventually studied with French theorist Roland Barthes, bringing Sarduy into the group involved with the publication of the renowned French journal of literature and theory, *Tel Quel*. He worked closely with Barthes and renowned structuralist philosopher François Wahl. Under the influence of French structuralism, Sarduy reread a large number of Cuban literary texts. In addition to *Gestos*, he published a total of seven novels before his death in 1994. In his later *Maitreya* (1978), another bizarre plot leads the reader to understand that Sarduy's real concern is how Western culture is destroying Eastern religions. In his last novel, *Pájaros de la playa* (1993, Beach birds), an island is populated by the aged and infirm, with multiple allusions to Latin American writing from the early twentieth century. The plot involves a conflict between competing healers, or *curanderos*, for the sick. Following the postmodern strategies of his earlier writing, Sarduy engages in an overt rewriting of the Latin American tradition. His essays made Sarduy a leading cultural critic of the 1970s and 1980s, and one of his most representative essays is available in English under the title *Written on a Body* (1989).

Sarduy's major novels are *Gestos* (1963, Gestures), *De donde son los cantantes* (1967, Where the birds sing), and *Cobra* (1972). Sarduy is not transparent about his interests in history, but all three are historical works in the most abstract sense. *Gestos* was the author's attempt to grasp "Cubanness," to satirize the 1950s dictatorship of Batista in Cuba, and to relate the history of Cuba. A technically sophisticated work for its time, it was an experiment in using multiple voices. *De donde son los cantantes* contains three overlapping plots involving the Chinese, African, and white segments of the Cuban people. In the first plot a transvestite entertainer named Lotus Flower is pursued and murdered by a Spanish general; in the second an Afro-Cuban woman from a rural area marries a politician in Batista's congress; the third reviews Cuban history, culminating in the trek of two white transvestites who carry a statue of Christ symbolic of Castro from Santiago to Havana. In *Cobra* a white transvestite who has undergone a sex-change operation becomes the star of a plush theater-brothel, an exceptional place that includes characters such as La Cadillac, Cobra's double who has also undergone a sex-change operation. In accordance with the historic interests Sarduy shows in the first two novels, the third part of *Cobra* is a quote from Columbus's diary, his voyage being seen as the first example of the Latin American (and perhaps Western) search for the mythic, utopian East as a resolution to the violent contradictions of Western civilization.

Sarduy died in Paris in 1993, succumbing to complications of AIDS at the age of fifty-five. A posthumous volume of poems and short prose pieces appeared in 1994 under the title *Epitafios. Imitación. Aforismos* (Epitaphs, imitations, aphorisms). Anticipating those who might write epitaphs after his own death, in this volume he wrote a jocular epitaph that reflected his playful view of life. He also evokes the religious tradition of Spain's Golden Age, writing an imitation of the spiritual poetry of San Juan de la Cruz. In this and several other pieces in the collection, Sarduy wrote about the enigmas related to the presence or absence of God.

Selected Work: *Gestos* (1963); *De donde son los cantantes* (1967); *Cobra* (1972, *Cobra*, translation Suzanne Jill Levine); *Maitreya* (1978, *Matreya*, translation Suzanne Jill Levine, 1987); *Colibrí* (1982); *Cocuyo* (1990); *Pájaros de la playa* (1993).

Schwarz-Bart, Simone [Biography] A leading writer of the French Caribbean, she was born in 1938 in France but grew up in Guadeloupe from age three. She has dedicated most of her writing to fiction and theater and authored the play *Ton beau capitane* (1987). With her novel *Pluie et vent sur Telumée Miracle* (1972, Between two worlds) she was soon recognized as one of the major women's voices in the Caribbean. She writes in French, but her literary language reflects a sense of the French creole spoken in Guadeloupe. Her fiction deals with the colonial legacy in the Caribbean—slavery, the uneven distribution of wealth, and the breakdown of traditional family relationships. Her second novel, *Ti-Jean L'horizon* (1979, Your handsome captain), deals with similar issues in a more explicitly political manner.

Selected Work: *Pluie et vent sur Telumée Miracle* (1972); *Ti-Jean L'horizon* (1979).

Scliar, Moacyr [Biography] Brazilian novelist and short story writer, he has cultivated a set of fantastic fictions that have invited many readers and critics to compare him to the Argentine master Jorge Luis Borges as well as the exponents of magical realism in Spanish America. A prolific writer, Scliar has published over thirty books of fiction. Born in Porto Alegre in 1937 of a Jewish Brazilian family, he is a descendent of a Russian Jewish family that came to Brazil in the early twentieth century; he has also been compared to international Jewish writers, primarily because of the particular type of humor apparent in much of his work and the fact that his writing fictionalizes the Jewish cultural legacy in Brazil. He received a medical degree in 1962 and since then has been a practicing doctor as well as writer. During the 1970s and the 1990s he published a journalistic column regularly in the newspaper *Folha de São Paulo*.

Scliar entered the Brazilian literary scene with a volume of short stories, *O Carnival dos Animais* (1968, Carnival of the animals), and then began a long and distinguished career as a novelist with *A Guerra do Bom Fim* (1972, The war with a good ending), the story of a boy growing up in the Jewish sector of Porto Alegre. Most of his fiction since has underscored Jewish difference. His next novel, *O Exército de Um Homen Só* (1973, *The One-Man Army*) is the story of a Jewish real-estate agent in Porto Alegre who seems to be struck by madness and attempts to form a utopian society. The protagonist in *Deuses de Raquel* (1975, *The Gods of Raquel*) is a Jewish woman who immigrates to Porto Alegre. *O Ciclo das Aguas* (1976, The cycle of waters) deals with a Jewish street prostitute in Porto Alegre. *O Centauro no Jardim* (1980, *The Centaur in the Garden*) is the story of a Jewish centaur, and depicts Brazilian reality by means of myth and allegory. *A Majestade do Xingu* (1997, Xingu's majesty) focuses on a Russian Jewish immigrant, a doctor who dedicates himself to working with indigenous groups; the novel

reflects a broad range of race and class. Scliar's deft handling of allegory and history are apparent in his later novel, *Cenas da Vida Minúscula* (1991, Scenes of minuscule life), which spans the biblical creation and King Solomon to the European Renaissance and a modern "1984" Brazil in which the protagonist, who is married and has several children, carries on secret affairs with a woman ten centimeters tall. In this novel the author satirizes Brazilian ideals of being "big" and "bigger" and draws upon the teachings of the Bible and the Kabbalah to emphasize, as the narrator-protagonist states, "small is beautiful." This novel, like several of Scliar's fictions, offers not only a critique of traditional machismo and authoritarianism but also a playful approach to feminism and different forms of consumerism.

A volume of his short stories appeared in English in 1999, *The Collected Stories of Moacyr Scliar*, translated by Eloah F. Giamelli, and with an introduction by Ilan Stavans (University of New Mexico Press).

Selected Work: *O exército de um Homen Só* (1973, *The One-Man Army*, 1986); *Os deuses de Raquel* (1975, *The Gods of Raquel*, translation Eloah F. Giamelli, 1986); *O centauro no jardim* (1980, *The Centaur in the Garden*, translation Margaret A. Neves, 1985); *Max e Os felinos* (1981, *Max and the Cats*, translation Eloah F. Giamelli, 1990); *A Estranha Nacão de Rafael Mendes* (1983, *The Strange Nation of Rafael Mendes*, translation Eloah F. Giacomelli, 1988); *Cenas da Vida Minúscula* (1991); *A Colina dos Suspiros* (1999); *Os Leopardos de Kafka* (2000); *Cenas Médicas* (2002); *Edén-Brasil* (2002).

Sea of Lentils by Antonio Benitez-Rojo (See *Mar de lentejas*) [**Novel**]

Selvon, Samuel [**Biography**] Caribbean novelist, short story writer, poet, journalist, and screenwriter, he was born on the island of Trinidad, then a British colony, in 1923. Selvon grew up on the island's second-largest city, San Fernando, as part of its middle class: his father was a dry goods merchant who had immigrated from India and his mother was half Scottish and half Amerindian. Selvon claims to have grown up completely Westernized, even though many Indians choose to live in Trinidad practicing the customs and religions of India. He served in the British navy during WWII and worked as a journalist for the *Trinidad Guardian*. As a youthful journalist, he also began writing short stories and poems. His early work was heard throughout the British Empire on a *Caribbean Voices* program of the BBC in the 1950s. Selvon immigrated to Great Britain in 1950 and published his first novel, *A Brighter Sun*, in 1952.

Author of ten novels and two volumes of short stories, Selvon is recognized as a pioneer, along with V. S. Reid, in incorporating Caribbean creole language in the novel. Related to his attention to Trinidadian English is Selvon's deft use of the strong oral tradition of the islands in his fiction. Having grown up in a hybrid milieu with inhabitants originally from Africa, India, Europe, and the Americas, Selvon was interested in writing about the creolization of his homeland. His other main themes are the identity of Trinidadians and self awareness.

Like many other writers of his generation throughout Latin America, such as the Mexican Carlos Fuentes, Selvon was interested from his youth in placing the literature of his homeland on the international literary map. Indeed, Selvon belongs to the generation that is associated with the emergence of Caribbean literature, or a West Indian literature (as Caribbean literature is often termed in the Anglo-American context), written in English.

Selvon is best known for his early novels *A Brighter Sun* (1952), and its sequel, *Turn Again Tiger* (1958), as well as his London trilogy *The Lonely Londoners* (1958), *Moses Ascending* (1975), and *Moses Migrating* (1983). *A Brighter Sun* is the novel of a quest: the protagonist, Tiger, is an Indian youngster who searches for identity in colonial society, supporting a wife as a newlywed. His search leads him to an increasingly macabre understanding of his role, even to a special kind of wisdom gained through experience, as well as a new social and political awareness. Tiger's need to better understand himself and the social world continues in *Turn Again Tiger*. In *The Lonely Londoners* Selvon uses a Caribbean creole as the narrative voice, and the strategies of oral storytelling are central to the novel's construction; several critics have associated its episodic structure to both the carnival and to calypso music. This novel and the later *Moses Ascending* are chronicles of the immigrant experience of Trinidadians in London. The main theme of the three novels set in London is cultural assimilation. Selvon adopts a satiric attitude toward narratives that celebrate the symbiotic relationship between Caribbean (West Indian) culture and European (British) culture. This satire implies a critique of many basic assumptions about the relationship between developing and developed nations.

Selvon left Great Britain for Canada in 1978 and has since lived in Calgary, where he continues writing.

Selected Work: A Brighter Sun (1952); *The Lonely Londoners* (1958); *Turn Again Tiger* (1958); *Moses Ascending* (1975); *Moses Migrating* (1983).

Señor Presidente, El (1946, *The President,* by Miguel Angel Asturias. Translation by Francis Partridge, 1978) [**Novel**] A classic dictator novel by the Nobel laureate of

Guatemala, it is based on the dictatorship of Manuel Estrada Cabrera from 1898 to 1920. Asturias began a short story, "Los mendigos" (The beggars), in Guatemala in 1922 and continued its development as a novel in Paris in the 1930s. A pioneer novel at the time, it is an anthology of modernist narrative techniques, with fragmention, interior monologue, neologisms, and the like. Many readers have pointed out an anomaly: the dictator is omnipresent yet does not actually appear as a character. This physical invisibility is typical of many Latin American dictators (and dictator novels). The novel's opening scene is on a street populated with beggars and Pelele, an idiot, who kills Colonel Parrales Sonriente, a key officer for the dictator. The dictator uses this death as an excuse to assassinate General Eusebio Canales and the lawyer Miguel de Carvajal. The central character is Cara de Angel, an encarnation of evil. Asturias uses other characters to represent the forces of good and evil and incorporates numerous elements of Mayan mythology into the work. He presents ongoing scenarios that underscore human depravity. In the end, however, he also offers hope in the characters of the young Miguel as well as other affirmations of human values.

Sepúlveda, Luis [Biography] Chilean novelist, he has gained a broad international readership in the Hispanic world with best sellers such as *Un viejo que leía novelas de amor* (1992, An old man who read love stories), which was translated into fourteen languages. His novel *Hot Line* (2002) is a detective story. In a prologue to this work, the author claims that, on a trip to the Aysén fjord in Patagonia, a Mapuche Indian told him the story which he originally published in the style of nineteenth-century journalism called

the *folletín*. Most scholars and critics in Latin America consider him a commercial writer.

Selected Work: *Un viejo que leía novelas de amor* (1992); *Hot Line* (2002).

Serna, Enrique [Biography] Mexican novelist, essayist, and short story writer, he has become increasingly visible on the Mexican literary scene since the late 1990s. His novel *El seductor de la patria* (1999, Seductor of the fatherland) was highly circulated and commented upon in Mexico. It is a historical novel that tells the story of a controversial nineteenth-century figure, Santa Anna (Antonio López de Santa Anna, commonly known as "Santa Anna," 1794–1986), from his youth in Xalapa to his death in Mexico City. A novel of historical research, it is written using the epistolary tradition in fiction, with letters from a series of historical figures and versions of events and motives that contradict each other. In this fictionalized biography, his son of eighty years of age uses memory and a series of letters to relate his father's fictitious life. Born into a conservative Catholic family in Mexico, Santa Anna joined the army at the age of sixteen and worked his way up the military hierarchy. Always motivated by the desire to control and exercise power, in this novel Santa Anna eventually becomes a pathetic figure. Serna shows him as a person willing to sell his family's properties and lose the confidence of the townspeople to promote his career. Serna weaves a complex and engaging plot through a series of characters, ranging from military figures to relatives to the women in his life. In the end Santa Anna is an embittered and destroyed figure. In the process of reconstructing Santa Anna's story, Serna questions the motives of more traditional historic writing, suggesting new and modern methods might be more appropriate.

Selected Work: *Amores a segunda mano* (1991); *Jorge el bueno, la vida de Jorge Negrete* (1993); *Las caricaturas me hacen llorar* (1996); *La caverna encantada* (1997); *El seductor de la patria* (1999); *Uno soñaba que era rey* (2000); *El orgasmografo* (2002); *El miedo a los animales* (2003).

Serrano, Marcela [Biography] Chilean novelist, she studied art before beginning to write fiction in the 1990s. She has published four novels that have been highly successful best sellers in Chile. Comparable in many ways to writers such as Isabel Allende, Laura Esquivel, and Luis Sepúlveda, Serrano is widely known as a commercial writer.

Selected Work: *Nosotras que nos queremos tanto* (1991); *Para que no me olvides* (1993); *Antigua vida mía* (1995); *El albuerque de las mujeres tristes* (1997).

Shaman Winter (1999, by Rudolfo Anaya. Written in English. New York: Warner) **[Novel]** Author of classic Chicano fictions of the 1970s and 1980s, Anaya published a series of mystery novels in the 1990s and early in the twenty-first century. In *Shaman Winter* the author weaves a tale of abduction, murder, nuclear threat, cultural history, and Native American religion. The protagonist, a private investigator named Sonny Baca, is wheelchair bound, facing his own physical and spiritual recovery as well as discovery. He is called upon to help find young women who are being abducted in a pattern that parallels his dreams, where he encounters his ancestors and historic figures from New Mexico's beginnings in 1598. Anaya displays his craftsmanship by weaving a postmodern mystery with cultural contexts alluding to traditional New Mexico and its people. The reader moves between multiple times and spaces, with dialogues strongly influenced by the Spanish of the region and cultural allusions relating to the Native American as well as Hispanic traditions.

Shipyard, The (See *Astillero, El* by Juan Carlos Onetti) **[Novel]**

Shua, Ana María [Biography] Argentine novelist, short story writer, journalist, playwright, screenwriter, and poet, she born in Buenos Aires in 1951. She studied literature at the University of Buenos Aires, where she received an MA in literature and has made a living in journalism and screenwriting. She began publishing poetry in the 1960s and saw her first volume of poems, *El sol y yo* (The sun and I), published at the age of sixteen. During the military dictatorship she took refuge in Paris, where she worked as a journalist for the Spanish press. Her novel *Soy paciente* (1980, *Patient*) received the prestigious Premio Losada in Argentina. She has published two novels that were made into films: *Soy paciente* (*Patient*) and *Los amores de Laurita* (Little Laura's loves). In 1993 she received a Guggenheim Fellowship to complete her novel *El libro de los recuerdos*, which appeared later in translation under the title *The Book of Memories* in 1999. Her recent novel *La muerte como efecto secundario* (1997, Death as a secondary effect) presents an invented future for a nation in political and economic crisis. Much of her work consists of volumes of short fiction that escape easy genre definition. Her 1984 volume *La soñera* (The dreamer) is of this type, consisting of *historias brevísimas* ("very short stories"), and her volumes *Viajando se conoce gente* (1988, Traveling one meets people) and *Casa de Geishas* (1992, Geisha house) are also short fictions.

In *El libro de los recuerdos* Shua offers a fictionalized account of her family's life in Buenos Aires, drawing on the collected memory of several of the family's members. Utilizing a Yiddish convention of relating a story on the basis of two men talking, she tells a multiplicity of entertaining albeit contradictory stories. Criticized for trying too hard to explain these contradictions, Shua sometimes loses the storytelling potential of her anecdotes. She has also published children's fiction. Shua lives in Buenos Aires with her husband and three children, where she writes.

Selected Work: *Soy paciente* (1980, *Patient*, translation David William Foster, 1977); *Los amores de Laurita* (1981); *El libro de los recuerdos* (1994, *The Book of Memories*, translation Dick Gerdes, 1999); *La muerte como efecto secundario* (1997).

Silva, Abel [Biography] Brazilian novelist, short story writer, and journalist, he has held academic positions and has served as editor for newspapers. Born in Cabo Frio (Rio de Janeiro) in 1943, he studied literature at the Universidade Federal de Rio de Janeiro. His novel *O Afogado* (1971, The drowned man) deals with a man who is metaphorically "drowned" in the sense that he suffers the paralysis and atrophy of the mediocre atmosphere he inhabits. Most of the first-person narrative is a lengthy flashback. His second book, *Açogue das Almas* (1973) is a group of short stories dealing with solitary and marginalized individuals.

Selected Work: *O Afogado* (1971); *Açogue das Almas* (1973).

Silva, Ricardo [Biography] Colombian novelist, short story writer, poet, and film critic, he was born in Bogotá in 1975. He completed his undergraduate studies in literature at the Universidad Javeriana in Bogotá, followed by graduate work in film and television in Barcelona. His first novels were *Relato de Navidad en la Gran Vía* (2001, Christmas tale on the grand avenue)

and *Tic* (2003). Silva has received a number of literary prizes in Spain and Colombia, and several critics consider him the most prominent new novelist in Colombia to be born in the 1970s.

Selected Work: *Relato de Navidad en la Gran Vía* (2001); *Tic* (2003).

Skármeta, Antonio [Biography] Chilean novelist, short story writer, and screenwriter, he is widely considered a leading writer of the post-Boom of the Spanish American novel. Born in 1940, he began publishing highly successful short fiction in the late 1960s. He writes stories about working people and common folk, often using colloquial, everyday language. A supporter of leftist president Salvador Allende, Skármeta went into political exile to West Germany during the military dictatorship, holding a faculty position in the Academy of Cinema in Berlin. He is widely known as one of the major writers of the exile experience among those southern cone writers who went into political exile in the 1970s. His first novel, *Soñé que la nieve ardía* (1975, *I Dreamt the Snow Was Burning*), recounts a series of events leading up to the military coup and immediately following it.

In his recent *La boda del poeta* (1999, The poet's wedding) Skármeta begins with a prologue in which he establishes a personal link between himself and Esteban Coppeta, one of the novel's main characters. Using childhood memories from his youth in Antofagasta, Chile, as a point of departure, Skármeta relates a sad story from the island of Gema, located in the Adriatic Sea, during a period covering much of the second half of the twentieth century.

Selected Work: *Soñé que la nieve ardía* (1975, *I Dreamt the Snow Was Burning*, translation Malcolm Coad, 1985); *No pasó nada* (1980, Nothing happened); *La insurrección* (1982, *The Insurrection*, translation

Paula Sharp, 1983); *Ardiente paciencia* (1985, *Burning Patience*, translation Katherine Silver, 1987); *La boda del poeta* (1999); *La chica del trombón* (2001); *El baile de la Victoria* (2004).

So Far from God (1993, by Ana Castillo. Written in English. New York: Norton) **[Novel]** This is a story about the unique circumstance of strong women in Chicana society, written by one of the leading contemporary Chicana novelists. Castillo tells of the New Mexican desert town of Tomé and its incredible happenings. She writes in imitation of oral tradition; the narrator uses the same tone as the bilingual female characters. The plot centers on Sofi and the lives and deaths of her four daughters. The hard-working Sofi struggles to rear her girls and eventually manages to appoint herself mayor of Tomé in order to ease some of the poverty in her town. Esperanza, her oldest daughter, is an ambitious girl and social activist who pursues her career as a reporter to Saudi Arabia where she is kidnapped and killed. The physically attractive Caridad plays the role of bar girl, then becomes a *curandera* (healer), and finally follows the woman she loves into death. Fe is a serious girl who dies from the poisons in the factory where she works. La Loca is the youngest daughter and, after dying at the age of three and then being resurrected, lives as a recluse until she succumbs to AIDS. Sofi, bereft of her girls, founds M.O.M.A.S., the Mothers of Martyrs and Saints Society.

Solares, Ignacio [Biography] Mexican novelist, short story writer, playwright, and essayist, he is one of the leading writers of his generation. Born in 1945 in Chihuahua, he is known as a novelist who writes on the tenuous border between fantastic and empirical reality and has explored the historic reality of Mexico at the same time that much of his fiction puts into question the very nature of empirical reality. He tells stories of urban life in one of the largest cities in the world, Mexico City, with emphasis on human relationships and frequent excursions into the realm of the fantastic or supernatural. Most of his novels can be read as metaphors for urban life in postmodern Mexico, although he sometimes looks back nostalgically at Mexico City of the period from the 1940s to the 1960s. Although his work is postmodern in a general sense, he is an accessible writer with a relatively large readership in Mexico.

His novel *Anónimo* (1980, Anonymous) is among his more fantastic works. He began writing in the 1970s, publishing his first novel under the title *Puertas al cielo* (Doors to the sky) in 1976, the story of a boy of modest background who works as a bellboy, but the novel soon moves into the realm of the supernatural, as the boy receives visits from angels. *Casas de encantamiento* (1987, Houses of enchantment) focuses on 1940s Mexico City, but Solares blends together three different time periods. His first historical novel, *Madero, el otro* (1989, *Madero's Judgement*), also deals with the supernatural, for it not only relates the history of the period of President Madero but also tells of the ex-president's supernatural conversations with his deceased brother. Solares continued in a political vein with *El gran elector* (1991, *The Great Mexican Electoral Game*), his satire of the political process in Mexico, in which the main character is a synthesis of several historic presidents of Mexico. *Columbus* (1996) deals with the invasion of the United States by Pancho Villa. Solares was awarded the prestigious Premio Villarrutia in 1998 for his novel *El sitio* (1998, The place), a novel that begins in the realm of urban reality in Mexico City (an apartment building), but then moves toward a horrific world of the fantastic in which the inhabitants of the twenty apartments are shut off from all contact with the outside world and seem to be under siege. His recent novel *El espía del aire* (2001, The spy in the air) begins as a nostalgic look at the 1960s in Mexico City, then goes back to the 1940s and 1950s. This brief, self-reflexive work can also be read as an autobiography of a writer and of the generation in Mexico that was educated in the 1960s and began writing in the 1970s. Two of his novellas have appeared in English translation under the title *Lost in the City: Tree of Desire and Serafin* (1998, translation by Carolyn and John Brushwood) and demonstrate his unusual adeptness in portraying the complexities of the lives of young people in Mexico.

Solares has served in numerous roles in the cultural and academic spheres in Mexico, including editor of the weekly magazine *Siempre*, director of the Department of Literature at the National University in Mexico City, the UNAM, and director of cultural diffusion at the UNAM. He writes essays on literary and political topics and has written a documentary-type work on alcoholism titled *Delerium Tremens* (1979) as well as a recent book on the Argentine writer Julio Cortázar, a literary father figure to whom Solares owes many debts. In addition to the Villarrutia prize, Solares has been recognized with several other prizes and honors, including a Guggenheim Fellowship in 1996. He currently lives in Mexico City and holds an administrative position in the cultural sphere at the UNAM.

Selected Work: *Puertas al cielo* (1976); *Anónimo* (1980); *Madero, el otro* (1989, *Madero's Judgment,* translation Alfonso González and J. Wong, 1999); *El gran elector* (1993, *The Great Mexican Electoral Game,* translation Alfonso González, 1999); *Nen, la inútil* (1996); *Columbus* (1997); *El sitio* (1998); *El espía del aire* (2001).

Sombras nada más (2002, No more than shadows, by Sergio Ramírez. Written in Spanish and untranslated. Mexico: Alfaguara) **[Novel]** Ramírez is known as a former Sandinista leader in Nicaragua as well as one of the major contemporary novelists of the Central American region. *Sombras nada más* tells the story of the capture of Alirio Martinico in the days leading up to the fall of the Somoza regime in Nicaragua. Somoza's former private secretary is accused of illicit acts and is taken to a popular court. The reader is introduced to the social and economic conditions in Nicaragua, including repression, poverty, and imprisonment. The reader also has access to several documents—texts that, in the mode of Jorge Luis Borges, are in fact false documents and, in reality, just more fiction. Ramírez leads the reader to speculate on the nature of historical truth in politically intense environments, and with this work contributes to his rewriting of the history of Nicaragua. He portrays a contradictory and bleak environment.

Sommers, Armonía (Armonía Etchepare de Henestrosa) [Biography] Uruguayan novelist, short story writer, and essayist, she is one of the major contemporary women writers in Latin America. There is no common agreement about her exact birth date; she was born approximately in 1920. She has dedicated much of her life to education, but since the early 1970s has concentrated primarily on her writing. Her fiction tends to emphasize sexuality, the fantastic, and the exceptional; the world she fictionalizes is senseless and cruel, with characters who suffer from solitude and anguish. Since publishing her first novel, *La mujer desnuda* (The nude woman) in 1950, she has written novels and short fiction from the 1950s to the 1990s. In *La mujer desnuda* she relates an allegorical story of a young woman's rebellion against the norms of conventional society, and this novel was considered scandalous in

Uruguay. Her second novel, *De miedo en miedo* (1965, From fear to fear), consists of a monologue by a nameless man and the adulterous relationship he has with a woman. In the end he suffers anguish and confronts nothingness. Her third novel, *Un retrato para Dickens* (1969, A portrait for Dickens), is the story of an orphaned girl, but the complex narrative lines and multiple narrators make it one of her most challenging novels. Her later *Sólo los elefantes encuentran mandrágora* (1986, Only elephants find mandrake roots), however, is her most lengthy and complex novel to date, telling the story of a woman's searching for self-realization and meaning, but this is only the central story to a multilayered narration. *Viaje al corazón del día* (1986, Voyage to the heart of the day) tells both a family story and a story within a story.

Selected Work: *La mujer desnuda* (1950); *De miedo en miedo* (1965); *Un retrato para Dickens* (1967); *Sólo los elefantes encuentran mandrágora* (1986); *Viaje al corazón del día* (1986).

Soriano, Osvaldo [Biography] Argentine novelist born in 1943, he became an important figure as a writer in exile during the military dictatorship of the 1970s and 1980s. After the dictatorship he returned to Argentina and published a set of essays titled *Artistas, locos y criminales* (1983, Artists, lunatics and criminals).

Selected Work: *No habrá más penas ni olvido* (1980, A Funny Dirty Little War, translation Nick Caistor, 1986); *Cuarteles de invierno* (1982); *Triste, solitario y final* (1983); *A sus plantas rendido un león* (1986).

Sorrentino, Fernando [Biography] Argentine novelist born in 1942, he belongs to a venerable tradition of writers in his nation who, in the face of humiliating social circumstances and codes, have opted for black humor as a response. He has published an entire corpus of grotesque fictions replete with dark irony and allegory, much of which alludes to Argentine history.

One of his more typical texts, *El rigor de las desdichas* (1994, The rigors of calamities), consists of three narratives, two of which are historical chronicles and one of which is a fantastic allegory. The first of the chronicles, a narrative titled "Carta a Graciela Conforte de Sicardi" is about a failed dramatist, told in a setting of class and social conflict. It also involves self-humiliation, as does "Historia de don José Montilla," the story of a haberdasher's suicide. In the allegorical "Cuaderno del ingeniero Sismondi," Sorrentino invents a República Autónoma that is even more capable of producing injustice than is Argentina itself.

Selected Work: *El rigor de las desdichas* (1994).

Soto, Pedro Juan [Biography] Puerto Rican novelist who belongs to that nation's generation of 1940, he was born in Castaño, Puerto Rico, in 1929 and died in Puerto Rico on November 6, 2002. When in the maturity of his academic career, he was devastated by the assassination of his son by the Puerto Rican police because the youth worked in favor of Puerto Rican independence. He is well-known for his volume of short stories, *Spiks* (1957, Spics). He was one of the first modern Puerto Rican novelists to gain an international reputation, although critics and scholars were slow to recognize his presence and enormous impact in Caribbean letters. He is best known for his novel *Usmail* (1959, U.S. mail).

Selected Work: *Usmail* (1959); *El francotirador* (1969).

Souza, Márcio [Biography] Novelist, playwright, and filmmaker, he has gained a considerable literary reputation in Brazil and beyond since the publication of his first novel in 1976, *Galvez, Imperador do Acre* (*The Emperor of the Amazon*). He is known as one of Brazil's masters of parody and satire who frequently employs pastiche and carnivalization. Souza was born in Manaus in the Amazon region in 1946, has been writing fiction and theater since the 1960s, and has established a publishing company as well as headed the National Book Department of the National Library in the early 1990s. His fiction is highly accessible, widely read, and entertaining. A writer who also has significant themes to develop, his work is comparable to the writings of the Nobel laureate of Colombia, Gabriel García Márquez.

Souza is best known as the political satirist who penned the works *Galvez, Imperador do Acre* and *Mad María* (1980, *Mad Maria*). *Galvez, Imperador do Acre* is a parody of the Spanish picaresque novel set in the nineteenth century. In it he tells the wild adventures of a nineteenth-century entrepreneur in the Amazon whose amorous conquests put him by chance into the political arena. This first novel is critical of local institutions in the Amazon. He continues his political satire in *Mad María* and later works. *O Brasileiro Voador* (1986, The flying Brazilian) is a fictionalized biography of Alberto Santos Dumont, a national hero whom the Brazilians consider the first man to have flown an airplane. Souza calls his text *A Resistível Ascensão do Boto Tucaxi* (1982, The resistable ascention of Boto Tucaxi) a *folhetim*, and it is a parodic satire of a Brazilian political figure.

His later novel *O Fim do Terceiro Mundo* (1990, The end of the third world) is another exercise in satire, pastiche, and carnivalization. The targets of his parody are the Anglo-American detective novel, Brazilian regionalism, and the Spanish picaresque, among other genres. In this metafiction Souza names writers who are his friends as well as figures from Brazilian novels and real political life.

Selected Work: *Galvez, Imperador do Acre* (1976, *The Emperor of the Amazon*, translation Thomas Colchie, 1980); *Mad María* (1980); *Operação Silêncio* (1980); *A Resistível Ascensão do Boto Tucaxi* (1982); *A Ordem do Día* (1983); *A Condolência* (1984, *Death Squeeze*, translation Ellen Watson, 1992); *O Brasileiro Voador* (1986); *O Fim do Terceiro Mundo* (1990); *Lealdade* (1997).

Spota, Luis [Biography] Mexican novelist, short story writer, and playwright, he was widely read in Mexico during the 1950s and 1960s as a critic of Mexican society and its political structure. He wrote for the masses in Mexico, and his novels reflect many of the aberrations and scandalous aspects of Mexican society. He published his first volume of short stories, *De la noche al día* (From night to day) in 1944 and also published two book-length biographies and two plays in the 1940s. As a novelist he was a conventional social critic. He published novels from the late 1940s until his death in 1985 and is known for his best-selling *Casi el paraíso* (1956, *Almost Paradise*). He was born in Mexico City in 1925 and was self-educated. He worked as a journalist for several newspapers in Mexico City and was director of *Novedades* and *El Heraldo Cultural*. He was president of the Mexican Boxing Association from 1958 to 1984. Between the 1940s and the 1980s he received several literary prizes, including the Premio Mazatlán de Literatura in 1984 for his novel *Paraíso 25* (1983, Paradise 25). In the 1950s and 1960s he was one of the few Mexican novelists who could make a living writing novels.

Spota published twenty-five novels, and his most noteworthy work, *Casi el paraíso*, is his critique of café society. Spota has been taken to task by critics for expressing himself so strongly that sometimes he can appear to be silly. The novel is a journalistic exposé, denouncing the corruption of power in Mexico City, including both Mexican and foreign powermongers. In this work Spota does not attempt to probe the deeper realities of the Modernists such as his contemporaries Agustín Yáñez or Juan Rulfo; his main contribution is his cosmopolitanism and his concern for the disenfranchised in Mexico. It is also an important contribution to the novel of social protest: he criticizes Mexico's elite not only for their excessive interest in wealth but also for their lack of interest in the common good and the common people.

Selected Work: *Murieron a mitad del río* (1948); *La estrella vacía* (1950); *Más cornadas da el hambre* (1950); *Vagabunda* (1950); *Las grandes aguas* (1954); *Casi el paraíso* (1956, *Almost Paradise*, 1965); *Las horas violentas* (1958); *La sangre enemiga* (1959); *El tiempo de la ira* (1960); *La carcajada del gato* (1964); *Los sueños del insomnio* (1964); *La pequeña edad* (1965); *La plaza* (1971); *El viaje* (1973); *Palabras mayores* (1975); *Retrato hablado* (1975); *Sobre la marcha* (1976); *El primer dia* (1977); *El rostro del sueño* (1979); *Las vísperas del trueno* (1980): *Mitad oscura* (1982); *Paraíso 25* (1983); *Los días contados* (1984); *Días de poder* (1985); *De cuerpo presente y otros textos* (1991).

Steen, Edna Van [Biography] Brazilian short story writer, screenwriter, and playwright, she has had a multifaceted career in Brazil, including film and acting. She was born in the state of Santa Catarina in 1936 of parents from Germany and Belgium. At an early age she was involved with the media—radio, broadcasting, film, and journalism—and began writing short stories in the late 1950s. Her fiction has received praise from critics in Brazil and has been widely read. Much of her writing involves women's lives that have been a failure. Her first novel, *Memórias do Medo*

(1974, Memories of fear), is a subtle critique of the military dictatorship under which it was written. Her second novel, *Corações Mordidos* (1983, *Village of the Ghost Bells*), begins with an epigraph from Pirandello and is her first piece of postmodern metafiction, questioning the ability of a novel to represent reality. The portrayal of a woman protagonist without a fixed identity also associates the novel with postmodern and feminist theory. Men are vague and tenuous images, and the dead rise from their graves. Her novel *Madrugada* (1992, *Early Morning*) received two prizes in Brazil. Covering a single night, this third novel portrays an eerie urban landscape of São Paulo, with characters from all sectors of Brazilian society. Her terse, virtually minimalist style seems to correspond to the minimalist lives of the city's inhabitants, and the novel ends with multiple images of death. Her volume *Cheiro do amor* (1996, *Scent of Love*) consists of two lengthy stories. Recently she has been involved in writing plays and promoting women writers, in addition to other feminist activism.

Selected Work: *Memórias do Medo* (1974); *Corações Mordidos* (1983, *Village of the Ghost Bells*, translation David S. George, 1991); *Madrugada* (1992, *Early Morning*, translation David S. George, 1997); *Cheiro do amor* (1996, *Scent of Love*, translation Edna Van Steen, 2001).

Steimberg, Alicia [Biography] Argentine novelist, short story writer, and essayist, she was born in Buenos Aires in 1933. She was the child of immigrants from Romania and Russia who were among the early Jewish immigrants to Buenos Aires. A common theme of her fiction is economic and psychological instability, with which her childhood was marked: her father died when she was eight years old and her mother lost her position as a dentist because she refused to sign a loyalty oath to Perón. She studied English at the Instituto de Lenguas Vivas and was engaged in creative writing from her youth but did not begin publishing until relatively late in her life. She published her first novel, *Músicos y relojeros* (*Musicians and Watchmakers*) in 1971.

Steimberg's novel *La loca 101* (1973, Crazy 101) deals with the political tensions of the 1970s in Argentina as well as the violence that has become a central part of life in that nation. She touches upon more social and psychological matters in her next novel, *Cuando digo Magdalena* (1992, *Call Me Magdalena*, 2001); it deals with a visit to an estate of the old aristocracy where a homocide occurrs. Steimberg is a master of the fictionalization of human relations, producing work comparable in many ways to Clarice Lispector in Brazil and Sergio Galindo in Mexico.

Selected Work: *Músicos y relojeros* (1971, *Musicians and Watchmakers*, translation Andrea G. Labinger, 1998); *La loca 101* (1973); *Cuando digo Magdalena* (1992, *Call Me Magdalena*, translation Andrea G. Labinger, 2001).

Taibo II, Paco Ignacio [Biography] Mexican novelist, short story writer, historian, translator, journalist, and essayist, he is widely recognized in Mexico as one of the nation's leading writers of detective fiction. Born in Gijón, Spain, in 1949, he is a naturalized Mexican citizen. He has been a professor and researcher at the National University in Mexico City (UNAM) and editor of the Spanish book series called Etiqueta Negra. He has held a variety of positions in the sphere of journalism, including director of the magazine *Bronca*, codirec-

tor of *La Semana*, and head of information at *Fin de Siglo*. He began writing detective fiction in the 1970s, publishing his first detective novel, *Días de combate* (Combat days) in 1976; it has received national and international prizes and has been translated into several languages, including English, French, German, and Italian. He has published over ten books of essays on topics relating to labor history and class conflict, most of which focuses on Mexican and Cuban politics.

Taibo II has published over twenty-five novels; he often writes more than one book a year. One of his more substantial and noteworthy works, *La bicicleta de Leonardo* (1993, Leonardo's bicycle), is an exercise in excess and is more voluminous than most of his fictions. An elaborate metafiction, this novel deals with the effects of popular culture on individual characters along the border and in the capital. More specifically, it tells the store of how a Mexican detective fiction writer falls in love with an adolescent basketball player. The novel, however, takes the reader into a series of digressions beyond this basic plot, including Leonardo Da Vinci's invention of the bicycle, a worker's strike in Barcelona in 1921, and the American invasion of Saigon in the 1960s.

Selected Work: *Días de combate* (1976); *Cosa fácil* (1977); *No habrá final feliz* (1981); *Héroes convocados: Manuel para la toma del poder* (1982); *De paso* (1986); *Sombra en la sombra* (1986); *La vida misma* (1987); *La bicicleta de Leonardo* (1993).

Tavares, Zulmira Ribeiro [Biography] Tavares writes stories of families she envisions as microcosms of Brazilian society. She began her career as a satirist of the Brazilian family with her first novel, *O Nome do Bispo* (1985, The bishop's name).

In *Jóias de Família* (1990, Family jewels) Tavares continues her family satire, constructing another intimate family story as opposed to the broad, panoramic works that many Latin American writers use to portray society. An elderly and dignified widow, Maria Bráulia Munhoz, is the protagonist; her affluent days are over, but she follows the daily rituals that have characterized her entire life with her faithful black maid, Maria Preta. As suggested by the title, family jewels are also central to this narrative: an omniscient narrator establishes the connection between these objects and empty family values. Maria Preta is also equated to one of these antiquated, expensive objects. This maid's grandniece, however, rejects the values, behaviors, and expectations of the maid, choosing a more modern set of values and independent life. Despite all these negatives with respect to Maria Bráulia, the narrator creates empathy for the protagonist.

Selected Work: *O Nome do Bispo* (1985); *Jóias de Família* (1990).

Telles, Lygia Fagundes [Biography] Novelist and short story writer, she is a popular fiction writer in Brazil. Born in São Paulo in 1924, she has been active in the Brazilian literary scene since the 1940s and began publishing short stories when she was young, gaining a reputation over the years as skilled master of the craft of fiction. Her first volume of stories, *Porão e Sobrado* (1938, Basement and Two-Story House), appeared in 1938. She was reared in several rural towns in the interior of the state of São Paulo, as her family moved often; her father was a chief of police and criminal prosecutor. Telles studied law in São Paulo at a time when Brazilian society was rigidly conventional with respect to women. Consequently, her early professional career and her early writing represented a rejection of many of the norms of Brazilian society in the 1940s and 1950s. As her career developed, so did Brazilian society's acceptance of professional women who were writers and intellectuals. She was associated with a group of writers identified as the generation of 1945 who reacted against the avant-garde and the experimental excesses of some Brazilian writing of the 1920s and 1930s. Thus Telles and the generation of 1945 were conventionalists who returned to some of the traditional literary forms. She has been involved in journalism since the 1940s, writing regular pieces for the *Folha de São Paulo*. She became a member of the Academia Brasileira de Letras in 1982 and died in 2003.

In Brazil Telles is widely recognized for her novels *Cirandra de Pedra* (1954, *The Marble Dance*) and *As Meninas* (1973, The girls). The former is a psychological novel that was widely read in Brazil and later serialized on television. It tells the story of a young girl whose parents divorce, after which the girl finds no solace in either home. *As Meninas* is an ambitious open novel dealing with three progressive young girls involved in sex, drugs, and politics. The multiple first-person and multigenerational story make this an engaging work.

Selected Work: *Cirandra de Pedra* (1954, *The Marble Dance*, translation Margaret A. Neves, 1986); *As Meninas* (1973).

Testimonio [Topic] A type of fiction that was popularized in the 1980s and 1990s in Latin America, it is based on reality as testimonial or documentary writing. Rigoberta Menchú, Elizabeth Burgos, Eduardo Galeano, Miguel Barnet, Elena Poniatowska, and Rodolfo Walsh and others have popularized the genre since the late 1960s. *Testimonio* has no exact equivalent in the English language or the Anglo-American literary tradition, but it is closely allied to genres such as American New Journalism and the documentary novel.

In the *testimonio* there is often an interaction between an interviewer and a witness, a special relationship between the editor and the interlocutor, and intellectual commitment and solidarity with the causes of the marginalized and their need to have a voice. In *Biografía de un cimarrón* (1966, *Autobiography of a Runaway Slave*) Miguel Barnet engages in ethnographic research to tell the story of Afro-Cubans who have been marginalized. *Me llamo Rigoberta Menchú y así me nació la conciencia* (1983, *I Rigoberta Menchú*), on the other hand, is the result of Elizabeth Burgos Debray's interviewing the Guatemalan Rigoberta Menchú and then editing the volume. In contrast, in Rodolfo Walsh's *Operación massacre* (1965, Operation massacre) and Elena Poniatowska's *La noche de Tlatelolco* (1970, *Massacre in Mexico*) historical events are covered in a fashion comparable to New Journalism.

As opposed to much of the postmodern fiction being published at the same time these *testimonios* were written, the *testimonio* genre is less formally innovative and more committed to the idea of truth than is experimental postmodern fiction in general. Rather than novels, *testimonios* are closely aligned to postmodern ethnography.

Tezza, Cristovão [Biography] Brazilian novelist, poet, actor, and teacher, he was born in Lages (state of Santa Catarina) in 1952. He is known as an irreverent and innovative writer in Brazil. At the age of ten he moved with his family to the city of Curitiba. He became active in theater in the 1960s and involved with the Pocket Theater group in 1968, writing scripts. Shortly thereafter he also became involved in writing for film with Ari Para-Raio and Oraci Gemba. In 1970 he completed his studies at the State College of Paraná. In the following years he wrote for various theater groups and also participated as an actor. He went to Portugal to study, but the University of Coimbra was closed by the dicta-

tor Salazar. While traveling through Europe after the closure of the university, he began his prolific output of short stories. In Frankfurt, Germany, he worked illegally as a house cleaner. In 1977 he married and moved to Rio Branco in Brazil, where he wrote his novel *Gran Circo das Américas* (Great circus of the Americas). At the University of Florianopolis, Santa Catarina, he worked as an instructor of Portuguese and published *Trapo* (1982, Rag) and *Aventuras Provisórias* (1984, Provisional adventures). In 1986 he returned to Curitiba to be a professor of Portuguese. He defended his dissertation for a master's degree in Portuguese in 1987.

With funding from the Bolsa Vitea of Literature, Tezza wrote a hybrid playful text, *A Suavidade do Vento* (1991, The softness of the wind) that contains elements commonly associated with prose fiction as well as theater. The first-person narrator is a grammar teacher with an extravagant personality: he is as obsessed with tobacco and alcohol as he is with writing and with women. His wanderings only briefly allude to a military dictatorship in the background, for his more immediate concerns are matters such as finishing his first novel and escapes into Paraguayan casinos.

In 1994, together with writers from Germany, Slovakia, and the United States, Tezza worked in an isolated cabin in upstate New York, funded by the Art-Omi Foundation and Ledig House, where he completed *Uma Noite em Curitiba* (A night in Curitiba). In 1998 he was a nominee for the Machado de Assis Prize from the National Library for his novel *Breve Espaço entre Cor e Sombra* (Brief space between the heart and the shadow).

Selected Work: Gran circo das Américas (1979); *O Terrorista Lírico* (1981); *Ensaio da Paixão* (1986); *Trapo* (1988); *Aventuras provisórias* (1989); *Juliano Pavollini* (1989); *A Suavidade do Vento* (1991); *O Fantasma da*

Infancia (1994); *Uma Noite em Curitiba* (1995); *Breve Espaço entre Cor e Sombra* (1998); *O Fotografo* (2004).

Tierra de nadie (1941, *No Man's Land,* by Juan Carlos Onetti. Translated by Peter Bush. London: Quartet, 1994) [**Novel**] A key novel in Onetti's cycle of works, the author introduces the character Larsen-the-corpse-gatherer and begins to create the Uruguayan master's imaginary town of Santa María. He also depicts a generation of frustrated and alienated intellectuals and political activists. The basic plot involves a group of characters, the central one of which is Aránzuru, a lawyer who has relationships with two women, Nené and Nora. His friend is Num. Aránzuru has relationships with several other women, including a prostitute with whom he lives for a while. Other members of the group include artists and intellectuals. Larsen seems to belong to the world of crime, but the exact nature of his shady activities is ambiguous. Two characters live closer to the world of politics and a "revolutionary" cause, but the ethics of their work is questionable. The book's sixty-one brief chapters are written in a cinematic style, and the novel is fragmented. The fact that many chapters seem unconnected is one of the novel's salient features. Related to this fragmented structure is the creation of fragmented characters who are in a constant process of change. The protagonist's quest is a confrontation of an alienated self in an urban environment.

Tizón, Héctor [**Biography**] Argentine novelist born in 1929, he writes of the region in and around Salta. He began publishing fiction in the early 1960s, issuing his first volume of short stories, *A un costado de los rieles* (At a side of the rails). He is a modernist who writes fragmented fiction, often in a biblical and mythical tone that represents a search for the authentic values of Argentina. He relies heavily on the oral tradition of the region, evoking popular songs and legends; these traditional motifs of gaucho literature in Argentina are counterbalanced by modernist strategies, including the use of interior monologues. He is widely recognized in Argentina as one of the nation's most accomplished contemporary short story writers, and he published an anthology of his personal favorites among his short stories under the title *Recuento* in 1984. He is also becoming increasingly recognized as a novelist.

Tizón's novel *Fuego en Casabindo* (1967, Fire in Casabindo) is a questioning and critique of rural life in Argentina. The main character, Carmen Real, analyzes three basic problems of this life: the search for identity in a rural setting, the ownership of the land, and oral tradition as the vehicle for constructing the historical and social identity of a people. The basic conflict deals with the humble peasants who demand that the government return their land. The novel can be read as an allegory of the power of the central government versus the powerlessness of the rural people.

Selected Work: *Fuego en Casabindo* (1967); *El hombre que llegó a un pueblo* (1988).

Todas las sangres (1964, All bloods, by José María Arguedas. Buenos Aires: Losada) [**Novel**] A Peruvian novel that focuses on the power struggles between the modernizing forces of Peru's entrepreneurs and multinational mining corporations and the feudal lords who hold the local Incan population as serfs on their ancient haciendas, this is one of Arguedas's best-known works. Using dialogue in Quechua as well as songs, Arguedas evokes the eternal Incan presence of the high Andes as well as the Castillian world of government and power. The cruel don Bruno aids his ambitious brother Fermin in creating a mine by providing the unremunerated labor of his Indians. Rendon Wilkes becomes the leader of the indigenous workers and befriends Bruno. Through Rendon's influence, the indigenous people throughout the district restore Incan social structures to avert famine and consolidate their ability to earn a wage for their labor. The possibility of silver discoveries in the town of San Pedro attracts the Wisther Bozart mining conglomerate, which brutalizes the community, shooting into an angry crowd and burning down the local church. Any reproaches against the company are met with the accusation of communist sympathies and immediate incarceration or execution. Bruno's fanatical religious traditionalism leads him to attack the feudal injustice he inherited. The company's exploitation and continuation of the colonial legacy is met by stoic indigenous resistance.

Torres, Antônio [Biography] Born in Junco in the state of Bahia, Brazil, in 1940, he is a novelist who has worked professionally in journalism and advertising. He has written for newspapers in São Paulo and Rio de Janeiro. Being from the northeastern region of Brazil, however, his novels are populated with characters suffering the difficulties of the harsh life in that region, where attempts at agrarian reform have been resisted by large landowners. Torres has the reputation for being a political writer: he is viewed as a spokesman for the poor migrants from the northeastern region; he has inherited this position from generation of socially conscious writers that include Jorge Amado, Graciliano Ramos, and Rachel de Queiroz. Many novelists writing under the military dictatorship of the 1960s and 1970s have been seen as fundamentally apolitical; Torres rejected this position by returning to the ethical positions of his forerunners from the northeastern region. In his later and more recent fiction he has been less overtly political. He focuses on the disinherited in his first novel, *Um Cão Uivando para a Lua* (1972, A dog howlng at the moon), a work that deals with radically different perceptions of Brazilian society as seen through two characters, one more conventional, one less so. Set in an insane asylum, this novel has been read as a metaphor for Brazilian society of the 1970s. His second novel, *Os Homens dos Pés Redondos* (1973, The men with round feet), is set in Portugal and deals with the effects of political oppression on the individual; this novel directly refers to the dictatorship of Antônio de Oliveira Salazar in Portugal and indirectly to the military dictatorship in Brazil. In *Essa Terra* (1976, That land) he tells the story of a family's exodus from their traditional home in Bahia to São Paulo and the attendant economic and social crises that follow. In his *Balada da Infância Perdida* (1986, *Blues for a Lost Childhood*) Torres continues with the story of the protagonist from the previous work, who recalls his childhood of poverty and exploitation. It covers a period of thirty years, and we see his engagement in politics as a worker. The narrative fragments also contain nightmares influenced by alcohol and multiple conversations and thought processes, many of which involve his fear of losing his job. In *O Chorro e o Lobo* (1997, The pup and the wolf) he has his main character return to his home in the northeast of Brazil after a lengthy absence and reconsiders this character's relationship with the land and the region. In his more recent work Torres has changed focus; *Um Taxi para Viena d'Austria* (1991, A taxi for Vienna of Austria) is a parodic and satirical detective novel. His fiction has been translated into several languages.

Selected Work: Um Cão Uivando para a Lua (1973); *Essa terra* (1976, *The Land*, translation Margaret A. Neves, 1987); *Carta ao Bispo* (1979); *Adéus, Velho* (1981, Goodbye, old man); *Balada da Infância Perdida* (1986, *Blues for a Lost Childhood*, translation John A. Parker, 1989); *Um Taxi para Viena d'Austria* (1991); *O Cachorro e o Lobo* (1997); *Meu Querido Canibal* (2000).

Toscana, David [Biography] Mexican novelist, short story writer, translator, and essayist, he is a leading writer of his generation who has quickly gained recognition in Spain and the U.S. He belongs to the generation of writers born in Mexico in the 1960s who began publishing in the 1990s and has been associated with the McOndo group of Chilean writers Alberto Fuguet and Sergio Gómez. This group openly defies the methods of magical realism and tends to prefer a fiction with more urban or interior spaces or both. Toscana's work is characterized by strong plots, memorable characters, and a complex interweaving of subplots and different levels of time. Toscana is a follower of the Peruvian master Mario Vargas Llosa precisely because of Vargas Llosa's commitment to engaging the reader with strong, complex plots and enigmatic characters. Toscana is also an avid reader of the fiction of Uruguayan Juan Carlos Onetti, admiring the Uruguayan writer's skepticism and tendencies toward nihilism, two attitudes that pervade Toscana's writing.

Toscana was born in Monterrey, Mexico, in 1961, studied industrial engineering in the Instituto Tecnológico de Monterrey, and worked as an engineer in Monterrey for several years before deciding to dedicate himself to writing as a full-time profession. He spent a year in 1990–1991 in the Centro de Escritores of the state of Nuevo León and soon thereafter published his first novel, *La bicicleta* (1992, The bicycle). In his recent *Duelo por Miguel Pruneda* (2002, Mourning for Miguel Pruneda) he recounts the macabre story of the assassination of a

foreigner and the finding of both a cadaver and the bones of a woman.

His two major novels, *Estación Tula* (1995, *Tula Station*) and *Santa Maria del Circo* (1998, *Our Lady of the Circus*) were reviewed well in both the Mexican and U.S. press. In *Estación Tula* the intricate plot operates on several levels of the past and present of a small town in northern Mexico. *Santa Maria del Circo* is a novel about how a ghost town in the desert of northern Mexico is transformed into the living community of Santa Maria del Circo when a troupe of performers abandon their circus in order to settle down. Interwoven into the complicated plot are the strange life stories of the nine new residents. They include a midget, a bearded lady, an overweight strongman, a contortionist, a human cannonball, a magician, a female trapeze artist, and an elderly ringmaster. After an elaborate series of events, the midget and the strongman lock themselves in the abandoned church, leaving little hope beyond a darkly ironic sense of humor regarding the indefatigable march of humanity along an empty path.

Constructing a career in defiance of the cultural powers of Mexico located in Mexico City, Toscana lives and writes in Monterrey, Mexico.

· *Selected Work*: *La bicicleta* (1992); *Estación Tula* (1995, *Tula Station*, translation Patricia J. Duncan, 1999); *Santa María del Circo* (1998, *Our Lady of the Circus*, translation Patricia J. Duncan, 2001); *Duelo por Miguel Pruneda* (2002).

Tovar, Juan [Biography] Mexican novelist, playwright, screenwriter, and short story writer, he was born in Puebla (state of Puebla), Mexico, in 1941. He began studies in engineering and then abandoned this field in order to pursue studies on the theory and practice of theater with Luisa Josefina Hernández. In the late 1960s and early 1970s Tovar taught theater himself in several institutions in Mexico City. He has also taught screenwriting. He has published essays in numerous Mexican literary magazines as well as the prestigious Cuban *Casa de las Américas*. His early fiction was associated with the rebellious counterculture group of the Onda in 1960s Mexico. His first short fiction appeared in the mid-1960s, and his first novel, *El mar bajo la tierra* (1967, The sea below the earth), deals with growing up and generational differences in the context of the 1960s counterculture.

Selected Work: *El mar bajo la tierra* (1967); *La muchacha en el balcón o la presencia del coronel retirado* (1970); *Criatura de un día* (1984).

Traición de Rita Hayworth, La (1968, *Betrayed by Rita Hayworth,* by Manuel Puig. Translation Suzanne Jill Levine. New York: Dutton, 1971) **[Novel]** The town of Coronel Villegas is the setting for this novel of a middle-class family in the 1930s and 1940s. The main characters are the parents, Berto and Mita, and their son Toto. The dull and monotonous life of this town has one saving grace: a movie house where Toto can escape into the glamorous world of the Hollywood movies of Vivien Leigh, Clark Gable, Rita Hayworth, and the like. The book's sixteen chapters consist of sixteen monologues and dialogues, with no controlling third-person voice. Thus the active postmodern reader must make corrections among the characters, situations, and chapters. The protagonist, Toto, is the speaker of the monologues of chapters 3 and 5, and the writer of chapter 13. He is also the character most discussed. Underneath the apparently banal anecdotes, a complex series of power relations unfold, and the reader becomes aware that Toto's story is that of a gay boy in the process of becoming an artist.

Treinta años (1999, *Leaving Tabasco,* by Carmen Boullosa. Translation by Geoff Hargreaves. New York: Grove, 2001) **[Novel]** With elements of the classic bildungsroman and the Spanish picaresque, this novel relates the story of a young Mexican girl growing up and discovering her sexuality. She comes of age in rural Mexico, then going into exile in Germany, where she lives for thirty years. With some allusions to Latin American magical realism, Boullosa evokes García Márquez in her use of a small town as a microcosm of Latin American society suffering numerous social problems and injustices. These allusions make the novel more a parody than a reproduction of the Colombian master's work. The protagonist struggles to recover her memory in the face of modernization and globalization, and the importance of memory as part of identity is underlined. A satire of numerous professions, this novel is also a parody of several novelistic traditions beyond the bildungsroman and the picaresque. Easily accessible, *Treinta años* is one of the works that has made Boullosa one of Mexico's most widely read novelists. This novel belongs in a venerable tradition of Latin American novels that challenge conventional ideas about the value of Western progress and modernization.

Trevisan, Dalton Jérson [Biography] Brazilian short story writer and novelist, he was born in Curitiba in 1925. His first stories were published as imitations of the traditional *Literatura de cordel* of the northeastern region of Brazil. Trevisan has disavowed authorship of his first works of short stories, *Sonata ao Luar* (1945, Sing to the night) and *Sete Anos de Pastor* (1946, Seven years as pastor), both created in this style. From 1946 until 1948 he edited a literary magazine, *Joaquim*, which he designed to be the voice of his generation, that included such prominent names in Brazil as Antônio Candido, Mario de Andrade, Otto Maria Carpeaux, and Carlos Drummond de Andrade. During this time Trevisan began avoiding publicity—refusing to have his picture taken or give interviews. He worked as a journalist—often covering crime stories—and married in 1953.

Trevisan became widely recognized as a fiction writer in Brazil in the late 1950s with his *Novelas nada Exemplares* (1959, Not exemplary novels), which won the prestigiousPrêmio Jabuti in 1959. By 1970 his works were being translated for an international market that was attracted to his often critical and pessimistic portrayal of urban life in Brazil. His works have been translated into English, Spanish, German, Italian, Polish, and Swedish. His dark humor depicts frustrated souls with serious character defects and moral contradictions. Some of his characters simply have difficulties in dealing with everyday life. Trevisan has won numerous awards for other books of short stories including *Cemiterio de Elefantes* (1964, Elephant cemetery), also a Jabuti prizewinner and the winner of another national literary prize. His *Morte na Praça* (1964, Death in the plaza) received the Premio Luis Claudio de Sousa of the Brazilian PEN Club. His book *Guerra Conjugal* (1969, Conjugal war) was made into a film by Joaquim Pedro de Andrade in 1975. In 1996 he received the Premio Ministerio da Cultura de Literatura for lifetime achievement in literature. In 2003 he won another important literary prize in Brazil jointly with Bernardo Carvalho.

Selected Work: *Novelas nada exemplares* (1959); *Morte na Praça* (1964); *Guerra conjugal* (1969).

Trevisan, João Silverio [Biography] Brazilian novelist, screenwriter, film director, translator, essayist, and short story writer, he was born in 1944. He has published a book-length essay, *Devassos no Paraíso* (1985, Missteps in paradise), on gay life and

culture in Brazil. He began publishing short fiction in the 1970s, and since the early 1980s has been publishing complex novels in dialogue with international postmodern fiction. He is the author of the volume of short stories *Troços e Destroços* (Bits and destructions).

His first novel, *En Nome do Desejo* (1983, In the name of desire) is a complex, tenpart experimental novel. *O Libro do Avesso* (1992) is a novel on the life of a young man who discovers he is a poet. This book is basically a parody of the Argentine master Jorge Luis Borges and literary theory. In this work Borges and other writers convene to call the author a plagiarist.

Ana em Venezia (1994, Ana in Venice) is a vast (649-page) novel set in the late nineteenth century, from 1858 to 1891, and dealing with the roots of Germanic culture in Brazil. It contains encyclopedic quantities of history and philosophy, making Trevisan comparable to writers such as Thomas Pynchon, Carlos Fuentes, Fernando del Paso, and Jorge Volpi.

Selected Work: *Em Nome do Desejo* (1983); *Vagas Notícias de Melinha Marchiotti* (1984); *O Libro do Avesso* (1992); *Ana em Veneza* (1994).

Ubidia, Abdón [Biography] Ecuadorian novelist, essayist, and journalist, he has been associated with several cultural and political movements in Ecuador. In the 1960s he was involved with the progressive Tzántzico movment. He collaborated with the magazine *La Bufanda del Sol* and later founded the magazine *Palabra Suelta*.

With respect to his fiction writing, Ubidia has been committed to taking fiction of this region from its traditional location in the jungle and rural areas to the city. He was also interested in experimenting with the technical innovations associated with high modernism. Ubidia is a leading Ecuadorian urban writer who often writes about the *hampa*—the marginalized—in these urban spaces. Much of his novel *Sueño de lobos* (1986, *Wolves' Dream*) concerns the daily lives and everyday anecdotes in an underworld of crime, drugs, pool halls, street vendors, and the like. The action, which leads to a bank robbery, takes place over a period of several months in 1980. The innovative structure consists of a rotating focus on the approximately half-dozen main characters. Ubidia does not construct fast-moving plots, but he does create memorable characters. He has received several literary prizes in Ecuador, including a national prize for *Sueño de lobos*.

Selected Work: *Ciudad de invierno* (1984); *Sueño de lobos* (1986, *Wolves' Dream*, translation Mary Ellen Fieweger, 1996).

Urrea, Luis Alberto [Biography] Chicano author who has spent a lifetime on or near the U.S./Mexican border of Tijuana, he has written several books of fiction and nonfiction describing the experience of border life. Born in Tijuana in 1955, his focus is on the marginalized: he travels back and forth between Tijuana and the United States, and on the Mexican side he moves amidst garbage dumps, cardboard houses, impoverished communities on hillsides dominated by roving gangs. In his book *Across the Wire, Life and Hard Times on the Mexican Border* (1993) he describes the random violence of these gangs, as well as the environmental violence of whole neighborhoods appearing and disappearing seemingly overnight, constructed on garbage dumps oozing toxic fumes. The Tijuana that Urrea describes is beyond the control of the Mexican police, who are portrayed as totally corrupt.

Selected Work: Across the Wire, Life and Hard Times on the Mexican Border (1993).

Uslar Pietri, Arturo [Biography] Venezuelan novelist born in Caracas in 1906, he is best known for his novel *Las lanzas coloradas* (1933, *The Red Lances*). As a young child, his family moved to Cagua, a small town near Caracas, where he became familiar with the land and nature in general that would appear regularly in the fiction he later wrote. In Cagua and later in Maracay he also became aware of the folklore and oral tradition that grew to be essential to his writing. This physical setting and the characters who peopled his fiction were often part of this rural experience. He read avidly in his youth and began publishing essays, short fiction, and poetry at an early age—he published his first article (at the age of fourteen) on bananas in a local newspaper. He studied law at the Universidad Central de Caracas during the 1920s, a period when he was actively involved with the intellectual life and literary world of young intellectuals. With his cohorts he not only read the major exponents of Spanish American *modernismo* but also such writers as Oscar Wilde, Leo Tolstoy, Gabriel Miró, Azorín, and other European writers. Uslar Pietri and other upstarts, inspired by the new writing of the European avant-garde, founded the magazine *Válvula* in 1928, in which they attacked the "rancid" tradition of Venezuelan letters. That same year Uslar Pietri published his first volume of short fiction, *Barrabás y otros relatos* (1920, Barrabás and other stories). In addition to publishing over forty books of fiction, essays, and theater, Uslar Pietri has dedicated a lifetime to diplomacy, editing, public service, and teaching.

Uslar Pietri's major novels are *Las lanzas coloradas* (1931, *The Red Lances*, 1963) and *Oficio de difuntos* (1976, Funeral mass).

The latter is a story about a dictator with similarities to thehistoric Venezuelan figure Juan Vicente Gómez of the 1950s. It is a novel about power and the lengthy process of obtaining absolute political power in a nation such as Venezuela.

Selected Work: *Las lanzas coloradas* (1931, *The Red Lances*, 1963); *Oficio de difuntos* (1976).

Valdés, Zoé [Biography] Cuban novelist, poet, short story writer, and screenwriter, she has been working in exile in Paris since 1995 and enjoying remarkable international success. She writes of the experience of being a woman, of being a foreigner in exile in Europe, and of her own tenuous cultural identity as a Cuban exile. Born in Havana in 1959, she studied philology at the University of Havana. She worked in the Cuban delegation before the UNESCO in Paris from 1983 to 1987 and returned to Cuba to work in a variety of capacities, among them subdirector of the *Revista de Cine Cubano* until late 1994.

Valdés has refreshingly new ideas about exile and the literature of exile. Writing after the onslaught of novels written in the 1980s by Latin American political exiles (mostly from Chile, Argentina, and Cuba), she has rejected many of the clichés about living and writing in exile. Most important, she rejects and mocks the nostalgia that pervades much of this fiction. She has enjoyed considerable success in Latin America and Europe with her novel *Café nostalgia* (1997, Nostalgia café), one of the works in which nostalgia is the object of satire rather than the traditional emotion of attachment to the past—a type of postmodern nostalgia.

Selected Work: *Sangre azul* (1993); *La hija del embajador* (1995); *Le néant quotidien* (1995, translated into Spanish by the author as *La nada cotidiana* in 1995 and into English as *Yocandra in the Paradise of Nada*, translation Sabina Cienfuegos, 1997); *Te di la vida entera* (1996); *Cólera de angeles* (1996); *Café nostalgia* (1997); *Traficantes de belleza* (1998); *Querido primer novio* (2002, *Dear First Love*, translation Andrew Hurley, 2002).

Valenzuela, Luisa [Biography] Argentine novelist, short story writer, and essayist, she is a major contemporary woman writer in Latin America, an urban writer with interests in politics and feminism. Valenzuela was born Buenos Aires in 1938 and reared in a family of intellectuals: her mother is the writer Luisa Mercedes Levinson. As a child, Valenzuela had ample access to a vast array of books, and as a young woman she read modern masters such as William Faulkner, Graham Greene, and Somerset Maugham. Jorge Luis Borges and Cortázar, whom she knew personally, were also important to her literary formation. She left Argentina for France at age twenty, after marrying a French sailor, and her experience in Paris led her to the writing of her first novel, *Hay que sonreír* (1966, *Clara*). Over the years she has been engaged in wide-ranging studies and activities, from the "pataphysics" of the French writer Alfred Jarry to the study of the Mapuche Indians in Chile and shamans in Mexico.

Valenzuela's major novels are *Cambio de armas* (1982, *Other Weapons*), *Cola de lagartija* (1983, *Lizards Tale*), and *Novela negra con argentinos* (1990, *Black Novel*). The last is only a detective novel on the surface, for it operates on many levels and, like many detective novels written in Latin America, is more a reflection on the genre than a true participant in it. There is a murder to be solved, although the victim and the motive become increasingly vague as the novel progresses. The protagonist takes literature too seriously, making him a murderer, and literature makes another character lose track of reality. Many of the chararacters in this postmodern text fluctuate in their sexual orientation, from bisexual to homosexual and heterosexual relationships. Their names also change in this novel of constant flux. With numerous allusions to other Argentine writers, this is a novel of seemingly infinite levels of self-reflection as well as reflection upon the sometimes nightmarish social and political reality of Latin America.

Selected Work: *Hay que sonreír* (1966, *Clara*, translation Hortense Capentier and J. Jorge Castello, 1976); *Los heréticos* (1967); *El gato eficaz* (1972); *Aquí pasan cosas raras* (1975, *Strange Things Happen Here*, translation Helen R. Lane, 1979); *Como en la guerra* (1977, *He Who Searches*, translation Helen R. Lane, 1987); *Libro que no muerde* (1980); *Cambio de armas* (1982, *Other Weapons*, translation Deborah Bonner, 1985); *Donde viven las águilas* (1983, *Up Among the Eagles*, 1988); *Cola de lagartija* (1983, *Lizards Tale*, translation Gregory Rabassa, 1983), and *Novela negra con argentinos* (1990, *Black Novel*, translation Tony Talbot, 1992).

Vallejo, Fernando [Biography] Colombian novelist, biologist, and screenwriter, he was awarded one of most the prestigious literary prizes in Latin America (Premio Rómulo Gallegos) in 2003. He began writing scandalous satires of Colombia's upper crust and their mores in the 1980s, bring out a trilogy of novels he has titled *El río del tiempo* ("The river of time"). He is also the most recognized writer of gay themes in Colombia. Born in Colombia, he has lived the major portion of his adult life in Mexico. He has published two books of nonfiction: a biography of an early-century Colombian poet and a study of literary

language, *Logoi: una gramática del lenguaje literario* (1997, Logoi: a grammar of literary language).

He gained widespread recognition throughout Latin America with his novel *La virgen de los sicarios* (1994, The virgin of the assassins), which deals with a young gay boy who returns to his home in Medellín, Colombia, from abroad and finds himself in immediate conflict with his parents and relatives because of their traditional, conservative, Catholic values. In this, as most of his writing, Vallejo satirizes the values of Colombia's traditional institutions.

Selected Work: *El fuego secreto* (1986); *Los caminos a Roma* (1988); *Años de indulgencia* (1989); *El mensajero* (1991); *La virgen de los sicarios* (1994); *Chapolas negras* (1995); *El desbarrancadero* (2001).

Vargas Llosa, Mario [Biography] Peruvian novelist, short story writer, playwright, and essayist, he is associated with the 1960s Boom and widely recognized as one of the leading writers of the twentieth century in Latin America. He was been actively involved in Latin American culture and politics since the 1960s, establishing a reputation as one of the leading novelists writing in the Spanish language. He was born in Arequipa, Peru, in 1936, and became a world-class writer of Peruvian nationality before eventually assuming Spanish nationality, too, making him a writer of dual citizenship since the early 1990s. In Latin America he was widely recognized for his first novel, *La ciudad y los perros* (1962, *The Time of the Hero*), his critique of corruption in a military school and the beginning of a life-long career denouncing Peruvian institutions. The complex juxtaposition of different narrative planes, with multiple narrative voices, is reminiscent of Faulkner, who was Vargas Llosa's idol when he became interested in fiction writing. In fact, on several occasions Vargas Llosa has described how, as a student beginning to write, he read Faulkner "with my pen in hand." Vargas Llosa has also written less Faulknerian, light, and humorous works, such as *La tía Julia y el escribidor* (1977, *Aunt Julia and the Script Writer*).

The overall quality of Vargas Llosa's fiction is impressively consistent. Nevertheless, most critics agree that his major novels are *La casa verde* (1966, *The Green House*), *Conversación en La Catedral* (1969, *Conversation in The Catedral*), *La guerra del fin del mundo* (1981, *The War of the End of the World*), and *La fiesta del Chivo* (2000, *Feast of the Goat*). These are four lengthy, complex, and dense works with ample historical breadth and rich mythical overtones. In *La casa verde* and *Conversación en La Catedral* he continues his Faulknerian project, and with increased technical complexity. *La casa verde* is set in the jungles of Peru (upper Amazon area) and the city of Piura (northern desert of Peru) and consists of four apparently disconnected narrative lines that eventually intersect to tell the story of a small group of characters whose lives cross paths in the jungle, in Piura, or both. Vargas Llosa uses a variety of styles and voices (exterior and interior to the action) in this critique of the practices of the state, the church, and the military. *La casa verde* represents a more ambitious approach to fiction writing than anything Vargas Llosa had written to date, and his next novel, *Conversación en La Catedral* is an even more complex work of epic proportions. In it Vargas Llosa explores the military dictatorship in Peru in the 1950s, a repressive period for both the nation and the generation of young intellectuals to which the author belongs. He was a student and a journalist during the 1950s. In *La guerra del fin del mundo* the technical complexity is less evident; nevertheless, it is another epic approach to a historic period, in this case an exceptionally violent civil war in Brazil in the early twentieth century. In this novel Vargas Llosa sets forth another of his lifelong concerns and literary themes: his critique of political fanaticism, which, in turn, is a questioning of all types of fanaticism. His more recent *La fiesta del Chivo* is a rewriting of the history of a dictatorship in the Dominican Republic, and it is another multilayered and multivoiced political novel that presents much of the most horrific side of the abuse of political power. Along with Gabriel García Márquez, Clarice Lispector, Carlos Fuentes, João Guimarães Rosa, and Julio Cortázar, Vargas Llosa is one of the major Latin American novelists of the twentieth century.

Selected Work: La ciudad y los perros (1962, *The Time of the Hero*, translation Lysander Kemp, 1966); *La casa verde* (1966, *The Green House*, translation Gregory Rabassa, 1973); *Conversación en La Catedral* (1969, *Conversation in The Catedral*, translation Gregory Rabassa, 1975); *Pantaleón y las visitadoras* (1974, *Captain Pantoja and the Special Service*, translation Ronald Christ and Gregory Kolovakos, 1978); *La tía Julia y el escribidor* (1977, *Aunt Julia and the Script Writer*, translation Helen R. Lane, 1983); *La guerra del fin del mundo* (1981, *The War of the End of the World*, translation Helen R. Lane, 1984); *Historia de Mayta* (1984, *The Real Life of Alejandro Mayta*, translation Alfred MacAdam, 1986); *Quién mató a Palomino Molero?* (1986, *Who Killed Palomino Molero?* translation Alfred MacAdam, 1987); *El hablador* (1987, *The Storyteller*, translation Helen R. Lane, 1989); *Elogio de la madrasta* (1988, *In Praise of the Stepmother*, translation Helen R. Lane, 1990); *Lituma en los Andes* (1993); *Los cuadernos de don Rigoberto* (1997); *La fiesta del Chivo* (2000, *Feast of the Goat*, translation Edith Grossman, 2001); *El paraíso en la otra esquina* (2003).

Vasquez, Juan Gabriel [Biography] Colombian novelist, short story writer, essayist, and journalist, he was born in Bogotá in 1973. He is one of the most noteworthy novelists in Colombia to be born in the 1970s.

Selected Work: *Persona* (1997); *Alina suplicante* (1999); *Los informantes* (2004).

Vasquez Díaz, René [Biography] Cuban novelist, journalist, and translator, he went into exile in 1975 and has been writing in Sweden ever since. He writes of social injustice, political exile, and the consequences of these two. In his fiction he engages in some of the self-referential play commonly associated with postmodernism.

His novel *Querido traidor* (1993, Beloved traitor) refers to an unnamed Latin American country in the River Plate region during the period of the military dictatorships of the 1970s and 1980s and the *desaparecidos* ("missing") in Argentina and Chile. It begins as a classic novel of social protest of the 1930s and 1940s in Latin America, but as the work progresses it becomes evident that it has more affinity to the large number of Latin American novels of political exile. The "beloved traitor" of the title is a profesor who is politically disengaged until he is recruited by his activist daughter to participate in a leftist movement, resulting in his imprisonment and torture. After feigning a heart attack, he goes into political exile in Sweden. His daughter marries and rears a child in Finland, and she is the narrator of this novel. In a postmodern turn at the novel's end, the narrator suggests that the entire story might just be an act of her imagination, based on reading her father's papers. The novel also becomes overtly political in its focus, for the professor is tormented by the fact that he broke under the pressure of torture, leading to the torture of others. In the end this book is critical of both the left and the right, thus questioning the recent political align-

ments in Latin America, but particularly the acute politization of the extreme left and the extreme right in Cuba.

Selected Work: *Querido traidor* (1993); *Isla de Cundeamor* (2000, Island of Cundeamor, 2000).

Veiga, José J. [Biography] Short story writer, novelist, and journalist, he is known in Brazil as an allegorical writer who offers statements about the human condition. Born in Corumbá (state of Goiás) in 1915, he studied law before embarking on a career in radio and literature. His fiction often portrays bored characters who suffer attempting to tolerate the mediocrity of everyday existence. In his novel *A Hora dos Ruminantes* (1966, *The Three Trials of Manirema*), a foreign group takes control of a town through intimidation and fear. His volume of short stories *A Máquina Extraviada* (1968, *The Misplaced Machine and Other Stories*) appeared in English translation.

Of his more recent fictions, *O Risonho Cavalo do Príncipe* (1992, The prince's smiling horse) is a short (124-page) work directed as much to young readers as adults, and his more recent *Relógio Belisario* (1995, Belisario's watch) is a thirteen-part short novel of 147 pages. In it a magical old clock tells metaphorical stories.

Selected Work: *A Hora dos Ruminantes* (1966); *Sombras dos Reis Barbudos* (1972); *Aquele Mundo de Vasabarros* (1982); *Torrelinho Dia e Noite* (1985); *O Almanaque de Piunhy* (1988); *A Casca da Serpente* (1989); *O Risonho Cavalo do Príncipe* (1992); *O Relógio Belisario* (1995).

Verbitsky, Bernardo [Biography] Argentine novelist who was born in 1907 and died in 1979, he is known as one of Argentina's most accomplished social realists. In many of his novels, he fictionalizes the experience of the working class in Buenos Aires during the 1930s and 1940s. His novel *Un noviazgo* (1956, An engagement) describes the decline of the working class under the 1930s military dictatorship in Argentina. In *Villa miseria también es América* (1957, Shanty town also is America) he portrays the South American continent suffering a spiritual crisis.

Selected Work: *Un noviazgo* (1956); *Villa miseria también es América* (1957).

Veríssimo, Erico [Biography] Author of over thirty books, he was best known in Brazil as a regionalist novelist who situated himself as a witness for political rights and freedom of expression. He was born in Cruz Alta, Brazil, in 1905 and died in 1975, leaving behind a legacy as one of Brazil's major novelists of the century. He also began writing journalism in the 1930s and continued actively in journalism throughout much of his life. After publishing the regionalist novel *Clarissa* (Clarissa) in 1933, he used urban settings in the novels *Caminhos Cruzados* (1935, Crossed paths) and *Olhai os Lirios do Campo* (1938, Look at the flowers in the field); in the last two works he began exploring the use of techniques associated with the Anglo-American and European modernist novel. He published a trilogy of novels over a three-year period under the title *O Tempo e o Vento* (The time and the wind, appearing in 1949, 1951, and 1952), broadly conceived historical novels that tell a family saga over several centuries, set in the region of Rio Grande do Sul from 1745 to 1945. In the 1960s he changed his geographical and thematic focus entirely, moving his fiction to Washington, DC in *O Senhor Embaixador* (1965, Mr. Ambassador) and Vietnam in *O Prisionero* (1967, The prisoner). Veríssimo used humor and satire in his return to a Brazilian setting with *Incidente em Antares* (1971, The incident in the Antares).

Selected Work: *O Tempo e o Vento* (1949, 1951, 1952); *O Señor Embaixador* (1965); *O Prisionero* (1967).

Veríssimo, Luis Fernando [Biography] Brazilian novelist, short fiction writer, playwright, and journalist, he has made a career as a journalist and television scriptwriter. Born in 1936 in Brazil, he is known in that country as a journalist with a regular column in several major newspapers and a humorous chronicler of urban life. He is also an amateur saxophonist. In recent years he has become increasingly noteworthy as a novelist. *O Clube dos Anjos* (1998, *The Club of Angels*) is a crime novel about ten men who suffer from gluttony, although the novel can be read as a text on gastronomy as cultural pleasure. *Borges e os Orangotangos Eternos* (2000, *Borges and the Eternal Orangutans*) is both a detective story and a parody of the genre of the detective story; in it the narrator-protagonist (self-declared unreliable narrator) tells of his role in a crime in Buenos Aires, where he attends a conference with the Argentine master Jorge Luis Borges.

Selected Work: *O Clube de Anjos* (1998, *The Club of Angels*, translation Margaret Jull Costa, 2001); *Borges e os orangotangos eternos* (2000, *Borges and the Eternal Orangutans*, translation Margaret Jull Costa, 2004).

Vilela, Luiz [Biography] Brazilian short story writer, journalist, and novelist, he has published several volumes of widely recognized experimental short fiction in Brazil. He is also considered a master of the dialogue and portraying problems of communication. Born in Ituiutaba (state of Minas Gerais) in 1942, he went to Minas Gerais at the age of fifteen. He studied philosophy before becoming involved with the avant-garde short story magazine *Estória* in 1963 as well as working with the journal *Texto*; both organs promoted experimental fiction. He has worked as an editor and reporter for the newspaper *Jornal da Tarde*. Vilela began writing in his adolescence and moved to São Paulo in 1968, traveling to Europe in 1969. He has also lived in the United States, receiving a fellowship to participate in the International Writing Program at the University of Iowa. In 1973 the founded the small press Editora Libertade. He gained recognition in Brazil for his first volume of short stories, *Tremor de Terra* (Earthquake), which was awarded a prestigious literary prize, the Prêmio Nacional de Ficção, in 1956. Among his other volumes of short stories are the titles *No Bar* (1968, In the bar), *Tarde da Noite* (1970, Late at night), *O Fim de Tudo* (1973, The end of everything), *Contos Escolhidos* (1978, Selected stories), *Lindas Pernas* (1979, Beautiful legs), *Uma Seleção de Contos* (1986, A selection of stories), *Os Melhores Contos de Luiz Vilela* (1988, The best stories by Luis Vilela).

His novel *Os Novos* (1971, The new ones) reveals his background in philosophy and his ability creating dialogue; it is also a borderline subversive work when read in the context of the military dictatorship under which it was written and published. Vilela has published two short novellas: *O Choro no Tavesseiro* (1979) is an exercise in nostalgia; *Te Amo Sobre Todas as Coisas* (1994, I love you above all things) includes the title novella and nine other previously published stories.

Selected Work: *Os Novos* (1971); *O Choro no Tavesseiro* (1979); *O Inferno é Aqui Mesmo* (1979); *Entre Amigos* (1983); *Graça* (1989); *Te Amo Sobre Todas as Coisas* (1994).

Villoro, Juan [Biography] Mexican novelist, journalist, and short story writer. Born in Mexico City in 1956, he has not been as-

sociated with the group in Mexico identified as the *Generación del Crack*, but he is, nevertheless, one of the most accomplished writers of his generation. He has been a visiting professor at Yale University and a cultural journalist in Mexico City. He became known first in Mexico as a short story writer and has also written a volume of chronicles, *Palmeras de la brisa rápida* (1989, Palms of fast breeze).

His first novel, *El disparo de Aragón* (1991, The shot of Aragon), is easy to associate with the American spy thriller, although Villoro's success in using this genre has been questioned in Mexico. A first-person narrator tells a love story about Mónica, although it never becomes clear exactly what degree of interest Mónica might have in the protagonist. The narrator, Fernando Balmes, is a bumbling thirty-six-year-old retina surgeon who grew up in the San Lorenzo neighborhood of Mexico City and has difficulty organizing his life. The plot is intriguing: Antonio Suarez is mysteriously missing and the ambitious doctor Iniestra is secretly involved in black-market organ trade. The light tone is one of the novel's numerous successes, as are the descriptions of the urban spaces of Mexico City. Near the end it becomes evident that Villoro has interests that go beyond simply constructing a good plot for a spy thriller, for he sets forth a point of view that underlines the fragile, shifting, and postmodern quality of contemporary life in a Mexico City where all its inhabitants are living, in effect, under siege.

Selected Work: *El disparo de Aragón* (1991); *Materia dispuesta* (1997); *La casa pierde* (1998).

Viñas, David [Biography] Argentine novelist, poet, short story writer, literary critic, and essayist, he is a major intellectual figure in Latin America in this century. Born in

1929, he belongs to a generation of Argentine writers who have been critical of the Perón dictatorship, the Argentine oligarchy, and most of the nation's institutions. They were called the generation of the parricides and their work began appearing in the 1950s; their revisionist attitudes distinguished them from their contemporaries. In Viñas's work commonly used concepts of Argentine history are questioned, and his critique includes many aspects of Argentine life that conventional citizens consider the essence of what it means to be Argentine.

The fiction of Viñas and his generation tended to be neorealistic, revealing an interest in attempting to portray the nation "as it really was." He has been a prolific writer; his early work *Los años despiadados* (1956, The pitiless years) is the story of a young boy who feels imprisoned by the restrictions of his conventional, middle-class family. His best friend, an immigrant, on the other hand, seems freer to act as a proletarian *peronista*. The author makes his point by comparing the two characters, and he uses a similar method in *Los dueños de la tierra* (1959, The lords of the earth), which begins with a lengthy historical overview of those who own land in Argentina and tells the story of the frontier movement of conquering and settling the land in the Patagonia region. Near the end of the novel Viñas introduces a schoolteacher with progressive ideas as a counterbalance to the exploiters and the traditionalists.

His most accomplished novels, according to most critics, are *Cayó sobre su rostro* (1955, He fell on his face) and *Los hombres de a caballo* (1967, The men on horseback). One of Viñas's several targets of questioning in *Cayó sobre su rostro* is General (later President) Julio A. Roca, the "Conquerer of the Desert." He is a legendary figure in Argentina because of his campaign against the Indians of Patagonia in 1879. He is linked to the violence and dishonesty associated with the campaign. The novel is an example of Viñas's militant debunking, and he uses of multiple points of view to enhance the story and give it a human dimension within the larger historical context. His later work, *Los hombres de a caballo*, contains both regionalist and cosmopolitan features and represents a continuation of the author's skeptical attitudes toward Argentine history.

Selected Work: *Cayó sobre su rostro* (1955); *Los años despiadados* (1956); *Los dueños de la tierra* (1958); *Los hombres de a caballo* (1967).

Virgen de los sicarios, La (1994, The virgin of the hit men, by Fernando Vallejo. Written in Spanish and untranslated. Bogotá: Alfaguara, 1994) [**Novel**] The most widely read and acclaimed novel by one of Colombia's most accomplished writers after Gabriel García Márquez, this work is set in Medellín, Colombia, the center of drug trafficking and related violence in the 1980s and 1990s. The narrator-protagonist, Fernando, is a Colombian of one of the city's respected upper-middle-class families who returns to Medellín after an extended stay abroad. Given his status as a gay intellectual, Fernando finds himself in conflict with his family, which espouses traditional conservative values. The family lives a social life centered on the Catholic Church; Fernando lives in the community of gays and *sicarios* (lower-class paid gunslingers). The novel relates Fernando's memory of the stable and secure world of his grandparents, which contrasts with the decentered and violent world in which he lives with the young gays and *sicarios,* or hit men, of Medellín. Fernando also suffers conflicts related to love and violence. Vallejo parodies many of the well-known official discourses of the government and the Catholic Church as part of his biting satire of the Colombian establishment in Medellín and the region of Antioquia, one of the most deeply entrenched in centuries-long tradition and conservative values.

Volpi, Jorge [**Biography**] Mexican novelist and essayist, he is widely recognized in Mexico as a leader of the self-described generation of the crack that was popularized in Spain and Mexico in 1996 and 1997. Born in Mexico City in 1968, he belongs to the generation of writers that became visible in the 1990s and have attempted to "crack" open the sacred cows of Mexican literature, thus creating new possibilities for fiction in Mexico and Latin America. As such, he is one of the leading figures of the generation of the 1990s in Latin American in general. He has made numerous public statements about the state of modern and postmodern international culture and literature and is often cited in the international press in Mexico and Spain. He has claimed, for example, that the genre of the novel is not in danger of disappearing, but of becoming banal. Rejecting the trend toward "light" and commercial literature that was prominent in Mexico in the 1990s, he has argued that novels should be searches for knowledge. Indeed, his fiction tends to be encyclopedic pieces full of diverse ranges of knowledge, including Western European history and esoteric science; they are the products of research. He writes complex novels that are highly respected among writers and intellectuals in Mexico.

Volpi studied law and literature at the National University in Mexico City (UNAM), and he completed a doctorate in Hispanic philology at the University of Salamanca in Spain. He writes regularly in the cultural organs *Letras libres*, *Viceversa*, and *Letra Internacional*. He has published a lengthy essay that constitutes an intellectual history of 1968 in Mexico, *La imaginación y el poder* (1998, Imagination and power). He began publishing novels in the early 1990s with *A pesar del oscuro silencio* (1992, In spite of the dark silence), which was based on research in literary criticism, and has continued publishing fiction since then. In this novel a first-person narrator named Jorge researches the life of Jorge Cuesta, a poet and essayist of the 1920s avant-garde in Mexico. An enigmatic figure, he collaborated with the literary group that published the magazine *Contemporáneos* in Mexico, suffered numerous professional and personal crises, and eventually died in a psychiatric hospital in 1942, perhaps as a suicide. Volpi operates on a fine line between biography and fiction. Eventually, the narrator realizes that his life is following patterns similar to those of the insane poet he is researching and writing about. Volpi's most ambitious novel of the 1990s was *El temperamento melancólico* (1996, The melancholy temperament), a psychological analysis in which the author constructs several levels of plot overlap involving a film, a painting, and the novel. His novel *Sanar tu piel amarga* (1997, Heal your skin) portrays couples involved in love triangles, with computers part of the scheme for matching couples.

Volpi is best known for his internationally acclaimed and prize-winning novel *En busca de Klingsor* (1999), a spy novel and intellectual game set toward the end of WWII Germany that appeared in English under the title *In Search of Klingsor*. Based on research in quantum mechanics and game theory, it was awarded the prestigious Biblioteca Breve Prize in 1999. In this work Volpi recounts the story of a military intelligence operation. The young protagonist loses his position as a physicist at Princeton University over a love affair, so his mentor, who is German, recommends him for a mission in Germany during WWII: he is assigned to discover the identity of Hitler's main scientific consultant—the man behind everything from the Nazi biological experimentation to the research for the atomic bomb. Thus, the progatonist, whose name is actually Francis Bacon, gains a connection to a German mathematician named Links and immediately falls in love with a German woman, Irene, his assistant in this special research project. The plot becomes complex as Irene turns out to be an operative for Russian intelligence, and the Russians suspect that Links is Klingsor. These events take place right after WWII, beginning in 1946, but Links is the novels's narrator in 1989, the week the Berlin Wall falls.

Volpi's more recent *El fin de la locura* (2003, The end of insanity) deals with the end of revolutionary utopias. Volpi consistently interrogates the possibility of knowledge, for he sees novels as a vehicle for exploring these possibilities as well as a number of questions related to human society, such as ethical behavior and its related enigmas and paradoxes.

Selected Work: *A pesar del oscuro silencio* (1992); *Días de ira* (1994); *La paz de los sepulcros* (1995); *El temperamento melancólico* (1996); *Sanar tu piel amarga* (1997); *En busca de Klingsor* (1999); *El juego del apocalipsis* (2001); *El fin de la locura* (2003).

Wacquez, Mauricio [Biography] Chilean novelist, short story writer, essayist, and academic, he dedicated a lifetime to innovation and experimentation with fiction. Born in 1939, he taught philosophy at the Universidad de Chile, the Universidad de Habana, and La Sorbonne. He settled permanently in Calaceite, Spain, in 1972, and lived the remainder of his life in Spain, where he worked in publishing houses and did translations from the French. In the 1980s he published essays in newspapers and magazines in Spain such as *La Vanguardia* defending humanistic values of tolerance and writing against hardline politics of either the left or the right. He died in Spain in 2000.

Wacquez began publishing fiction in the early 1960s with the volume of short stories *Cinco y una ficciones* (1963, Five and one fictions) and later published short fiction under the title *Excesos* (1971, Excesses). He was among the avant-garde of experimental novelists in Chile when he published his novels *Toda la luz del mediodía* (1965, All the midday light) and *Paréntesis* (1975, Parenthesis). His other novels included *Frente a un hombre armado* (1981, In front of an armed man) and *Ella o el sueño de nadie* (1983, She or the dream of no one). His last novel to appear was *Epifanía de una sombra* (2001, Epiphany for a shadow), the first volume of an unfinished trilogy titled *Trilogía de la oscuridad* (Trilogy of darkness). It is an autobiographical novel about the author's adolescence in Santiago—recreating the experience of growing up on a vineyard among the nation's elite.

Selected Work: *Toda la luz del mediodía* (1965); *Paréntesis* (1975); *Frente a un hombre armado* (1981); *Ella o el sueño de nadie* (1983); *Epifanía de una sombra* (2001).

Walcott, Derek [Biography] Caribbean poet, novelist, essayist,and short story writer, Walcott was born in 1930 in Castries, St. Lucia. A Nobel laureate, he is best known as a playwright and poet. He has been working in theater since the 1950s and has been publishing poetry since the 1960s.

His experimental work *Omeros* (1990) can be read as a book-length poem or as an innovative novel. In this work Walcott assumes four fictious identities as novelist, autobiographer, playwright, and poet.

Omeros is an adaption of the Greek for Homer; this protagonist appears as a St. Lucian fisherman and an East Asian shaman as well as a variety of other characters who might drift through the Caribbean from all continents. In this ambitious and wide-ranging work Walcott covers topics such as spiritual alientation, exile, racism, and class conflict. He sees all these matters as they relate to the centuries-old colonial heritage of the Caribbean region.

Selected Work: *Omeros* (1990).

Walsh, Rodolfo [Biography] Argentine novelist who was born in 1927 in the province of Río Negro and died in 1977, he was a prolific writer. His work as a fiction writer, journalist, and playwright has been increasingly recognized since his disappearance on March 24, 1977, during the military dictatorship. In the 1940s he worked as a copy editor and translator of detective fiction in Buenos Aires. He began writing fiction in the early 1950s, and in 1953 he published a pioneering anthology of detective fiction as well as the volume of short stories *Variaciones en rojo* (Variations in red). His interest in detective fiction and some of the stylistic nuances of his fiction link him to Jorge Luis Borges. He has also worked in theater and published the plays *La Granada* (1965, The grenade) and *La batalla* (1965, The battle). His books of fiction and *testimonio* include, in addition to *Variaciones en rojo*, the volumes of short stories *Los oficios terrestres* (1965, Earthly professions), *Un kilo de oro* (1967, A kilo of gold), *¿Quién mató a Rosendo?* (1969, Who killed Rosendo?); *Un oscuro día de justicia* (1973); and *El caso Satanowsky* (1973).

Walsh is best known for his book *Operación massacre* (1957, Operation massacre), a work of investigative journalism first published in 1957 and then expanded by him into increasingly refined forms in later editions.

Selected Work: *Operación massacre* (1957).

Wide Sargasso Sea (1966, by Jean Rhys. Written in English. New York: Norton, 1982) **[Novel]** One of the major novels of Caribbean women's writing, it deals with women who are victims of the colonial legacy. Rhys reinvents the past of a character considered insane, but the author explores the way in which the colonial environment is significant to the protagonist Antoinette's psychological state, as is her mother's indifference to her. The destructive relationship between mother and daughter is the basis for the plot. After Antoinette marries, she is rejected by her husband because of her race. Part Spanish and part French, she is less desired because of her mulatto status. In the last part of the novel she searches for and establishes a connection with her mother that had always been lacking. Antoinette also finds a way to accept herself as the racial being that she is. Rhys's novel is an in-depth exploration of race and gender in the Caribbean.

Women novelists [Topic] Women's writing in Latin America has been prominent since the early 1980s, but women have had a literary presence in the region throughout the twentieth century. Women have consistently addressed issues directly related to the colonial legacy in Latin America: racism as rooted in the European attitudes toward indigenous groups in the Americas upon their arrival, racism that began with the African slave trade, gender issues that were inherited from the patriarchal society established by the colonizers from Spain, Portugal, France, Great Britain, and Holland.

Pioneering women novelists of the first half of the century were the Chileans María Luisa Bombal and Marta Brunet as well as the Venezuelan Teresa de la Parra. The last published one of the major novels of the 1920s, *Las memorias de la Mamá Blanca* (1929, Memoirs of Mama Blanca).

Laura Esquivel, Isabel Allende, Angeles Mastretta, Marcela Serrano, and Laura Restrepo have been highly visible commercial women writers, popular in Europe, the United States, and Latin America in recent years. Indeed, Esquivel's *Como agua para chocolate* (*Like Water for Chocolate*) .and Allende's *La casa de los espíritus* (*The House of the Spirits*) were among the most widely read novels of the century in Latin America. Among many scholars and critics of women writers in the post-WWII period, however, more substantive novels have been written by novelists such as the Brazilian Clarice Lispector and the Mexicans Rosario Castellanos, Elena Poniatowska, and Elena Garro. Garro's novel *Los recuerdos del porvenir* (1963, Memories of the future) has been described as one of the early texts of magical realism and shares several characteristics of the novels of the 1960s Boom, which did not include any women writers. In recent years Garro has been increasingly recognized in Mexico as a major writer who had been ignored for most of her writing career.

With the rise of modernist fiction throughout Latin America in the 1940s, the female counterparts to this transformation of literary production were the Brazilian Clarice Lispector, the Colombian Elissa Mújica, the Mexicans Rosario Castellanos, Elena Garro, Josefina Vicens, and Elena Poniatowska, and the Argentines Beatriz Guido, Luisa Mercedes Levinson, Sara Gallardo, and Marta Lynch.

Brazil and the Caribbean region both have a strong tradition of women writing. Brazil is the nation with the strongest tradition in Latin America of women novelists, from Clarice Lispector to Nélida Piñón, including such practitioners as Lygia Fagundes Telles, Alice Barroso, Patrícia

Bins, and Márcia Denser. Lispector wrote from the 1940s to the 1970s, and her work has been amply translated into English and other languages. Caribbean women writers often address the fragmentation that results from their relationship to African and European cultures, and novelists who write in English and articulate these concerns are Zee Edgell (Belize), Merle Hodge (Trinidad), Jamaica Kincaid (Antigua), Paule Marshall (Barbardos), Jean Rhys (Dominica), and Sylvia Wynter (Jamaica). Haiti's Edwidge Danticat also writes in English, and the major women novelists of the French Caribbean are Maryse Condé, Maurice Chauvet, Simone Scharz-Bart, Myriam Vieyra, Michèle Lacrosil, and Myotte Capecia. Suriname's Astrid Roemer writes in Dutch of her experience as a Caribbean woman of African descent and now lives in the Netherlands.

With respect to recent women writers who are neither highly commerical nor already recognized as masters of the modern novel, the generation of postmodern writers in Latin America—often experimental and feminist—includes the Chileans Diamela Eltit and Lucía Guerra Cunningham, the Argentines Sylvia Molloy and Alicia Borinsky, the Mexicans Carmen Boullosa and Brianda Domecq, and the Colombian Albalucía Angel. They are increasingly read and recognized among academic specialists in the United States as well among intellectuals in Latin America.

Storytellers that are often feminists yet less interested in technical experimentation and questioning the borders of the genre of the novel include the Puerto Rican Rosario Ferré, the Argentine Luisa Valenzuela, the Brazilians Lygia Fagundes Telles and Nélida Piñón, the Colombian Fanny Buitrago, the Costa Rican Carmen Naranjo, and the Ecuadorian Alicia Yáñez-Cossío.

The youngest women writers, of the generation of the 1990s, includes the Mexican

Cristina Rivera Garza, the Argentine Clara Obligado, and the Brazilians Cíntia Moscovich and Patrícia Melo. Rivera Garza has published poetry, short fiction, and several novels that question conventional understandings of gender, and she has had the novel *Nadie me verá llorar* (2003) published in English translation under the title *No One Will See Me Cry*. Melo has published novels in Brazil that push the limits that many Brazilian readers are willing to tolerate with respect to explicit violence and sex.

Wynter, Sylvia [Biography] Jamaican novelist, playwright, and essayist, she was born in Holguín, Cuba, in 1928 of Jamaican parents. She was educated in London, where she studied Spanish and promoted indigenous West Indian drama. Her play *Under the Sun* (1962) was developed into the novel *Hills of Hebron* (1962). She has written essays in favor of a Caribbean African-based culture.

Selected Work: *Hills of Hebron* (1962).

Yáñez, Agustín [Biography] Mexican novelist and essayist, he was born in Guadalajara in 1904. He studied law in Guadalajara, receiving his degree in 1929. He was involved with Mexico's innovative avant-garde literary movements and editor of the important literary magazine *Bandera de Américas*, whose mission was to recognize and promote the modern, the cosmopolitan, and the universal of Mexican letters. Yáñez eventually moved to Mexico City, where he taught literature and aesthetics at the National University (UNAM). He is known as the author of one of the modern classics of the Mexican novel, *Al filo del agua* (1947, *The Edge of the Storm*), publishing six novels in the course of his writing career as well as some autobiographical pieces. His historical research resulted in the publication of studies on Mexican historical figures such as Fray Bartolomé de las Casas, Justo Sierra, and José Joaquín Fernández de Lizardi. He spent much of his life involved in public service, serving as governor to his native state of Jalisco from 1953 to 1959 and later as secretary of education in the cabinet of President Gustavo Díaz Ordaz. He died in 1980.

Selected Work: *Al filo del agua* (1947, *The Edge of the Storm*, translation Ethel Brinton, 1963); *La creación* (1959); *Las tierras flacas* (1962, *The Lean Lands*, translation Ethel Brinton, 1969).

Yañez Cossio, Alicia [Biography] Ecuadorian novelist, poet, short story writer, and professor of literature, she is the leading contemporary woman writer from this nation. Born in 1929 in Quito, she was educated at the Sacred Hearts Catholic School. She received a scholarship to study journalism in Madrid. Her early writing consisted of poetry, her first collection of poems entitled *Luciolas* (1949).

Yáñez Cossío appeared as a novelist on the literary scene in the early 1970s, winning a national literary prize for her first novel *Bruna, soroche y los tíos* (1971, *Bruna and Her Sisters in the Sleeping City*). In this novel Bruna is a young girl raised by uncles in a highland area where the soroche, a type of altitude sickness unique to the Andes, kills off the older generation. The novel refers to several classic motifs of magical realism. In *La casa del sano placer* (1989, *The house of healthy pleasure*) she uses a bordello as the focus of her critique of government and religious institutions; she also contemplates ways in which to collaborate. The grand dame who operates the bordello soon has it competing with the town's other institutions. By questioning the conventional norms of Ecuador, Yañez Cossío subverts some of the nation's most venerable institutions. An indicator of her importance in Ecuador is the fact that the province of Pichincha holds a yearly literary prize for women authors named for her. In 1997 she won the prestigious Premio Sor Juana Inés de la Cruz for her novel *El cristo feo* (1996, The ugly Christ). She is a member of the National Academy of the Language in Ecuador.

Selected Work: *Bruna, soroche y los tíos* (1971, *Bruna and Her Sisters in the Sleeping City*, translation Kenneth J. A.Wishnia, 1999); *La casa del sano placer* (1989).

Z

Zapata, Luis [Biography] Mexican novelist and screenwriter, he is widely recognized as one of the foremost exponents of gay themes in the Mexican novel. Zapata was born in 1951 in Chilpancingo, Guerrero. His youth was marked by cinema and his early writing was fiction and screenplays. He studied French language at the National University in Mexico City (UNAM). Zapata is known as a polemic author who crosses many social boundaries in his writing. He has offended many conventional Mexican readers with his intimate descriptions of gay sex and his use of gay language. Zapata uses a mixture of writing styles in order to present a variety of Mexican homosexual personalities and situations.

His best-known novel, *El vampiro de la colonia Roma* (1979, *Adonis García*), won a national prize in Mexico, the Premio Grijalbo, and was later translated into English. His third novel, *De pétalos perennes* (1981, Perenniel petals), was adapted to film by the film director Jaime Humberto Hermosillo. In this three-part novel, *La más fuerte pasión* (1995, The strongest passion), Zapata constructs a fiction around two male characters, the entire novel consisting of a dialogue between the two. The pair spends a few months in Houston, then Mexico City, and the third part transpires upon their return to Houston. They resolve differences and interests and eventually decide to remain together. In *Siete noches junto al mar* (1999, Seven nights by the sea) Zapata again exercises his abilities at forming a novel out of dialogue. The four protagonists, Ivan, Fernando, Lucia, and Nidia, portray Mexican society in a manner that highlights both its grotesque and intimately quotidian aspects. The protagonists endure seven nights without television, where they entertain themselves by telling stories.

Selected Work: *Hasta en las mejores familias* (1976); *El vampiro de la colonia Roma* (1979, *Adonis García*, translation Gaysunshine Press, 1981); *De pétalos perennes* (1981); *Melodrama* (1983); *La más fuerte pasión* (1995).

Zapata Olivella, Manuel [Biography] Colombian novelist, short story writer, playwright, and essayist, he has been a major exponent of Afro-Colombian culture; in the latter half of his career he gained international recognition for his work. He was active on the Colombian intellectual scene from the late 1940s to the 1990s, and he is known as a social critic. He was born in Lorica, a small town on the Caribbean coast of Colombia (department of Córdoba) in 1920 and grew up in this town on the Sinú River, an area historically populated by Arawak-Carib Indians and later by African slaves brought by the Spaniards to work in the agricultural and mining industries. From his childhood Zapata Olivella heard the myths and tales of oral tradition, as passed down through indigenous and

African traditions. When he was seven years old his family moved to the city of Cartagena, and he was educated in Cartagena and later in Bogotá, where he completed studies in medicine.

Zapata Olivella began writing and traveling in the 1940s and published his first novel, *Tierra mojada* (1947, Wet land) as a work of social protest. The novels that followed, *He visto la noche* (1953, I have seen the night) and *La calle 10* (1960, 10th street), were also works of social protest that defended the poor and the exploited. More specifically, *La calle 10* deals with the period of La Violencia—the civil war of the 1950s in Colombia.

Zapata Olivella's major works are *En Chimá nace un santo* (1964, A Saint Is Born in Chimá) and *Changó, el gran putas* (1983, Chango, the big SOB), two very different kinds of novels. The latter is his panoramic historical overview of the African diaspora in the Americas.

Selected Work: *Tierra mojada* (1947); *He visto la noche* (1953); *La calle 10* (1960); *Detrás del rostro* (1963); *Chambacú, corral de negros* (1963); *En Chimá nace un santo* (1964, *A Saint is Born in Chimá*); *Changó, el gran putas* (1983).

Zeta Acosta, Oscar [Biography] Novelist and short story writer, he was a pioneer in developing a Chicano novelistic aesthetic in the early 1970s. He was born in El Paso, Texas, in 1935 and studied law in California in the mid-1960s. During a trip in northern Mexico in 1974 he disappeared. His writings promoted ethnic identity, rejected the established order, and identified with the working class, all of which later became commonplace in U.S. Hispanic literature of the 1980s and 1990s. His representation of the U.S. he experienced as well as his critique of it were marked by humor. His two novels are fictionalized, "false" autobiographies.

Selected Work: *The Autobiography of a Brown Buffalo* (1972); *The Revolt of the Cockroach People* (1973).

Zink, Rui [Biography] Brazilian novelist, Zink is known as a writer who has reacted against much of the experimental and postmodern fiction of Brazil, writing that he considers an importation from Europe, particularly from France. He, on the other hand, has written a series of works with the strong plots and accessibility of popular American fiction. He also likes to associate himself with such writers as Swift and Montesquieu. In addition to his allusions to American fiction, he writes with full awareness of popular film in the United States. His novel *Apocalipse Nau* (1996) mimics the title of Francis Ford Coppola's film *Apocalypse Now*.

His is novel *Hotel Lusitano* (Hotel Lusitano) originally published in 1987, has two young American men as the main characters, an aspiring novelist who serves as narrator and a novice painter who is his roommate. The narrator recounts their trip to Europe, which eventually leads them to an extended stay in Portugal. They stay in Lisbon, where they meet an artist and his girlfriend. The four develop strong personal bonds (including sexual relationships) and spend a considerable portion of the novel drinking, consuming drugs, and talking about Portugal. Their lengthy analysis of the country leads them to the conclusion that it is a soft-core nation. Later, the narrator is arrested upon entering the U.S. for the possession of drugs and sent to prison, where he contemplates writing a novel with similar plot and characters, only set in Rio de Janeiro. He also imagines the possibility of it becoming a popular movie.

Selected Work: *Hotel Lusitano* (1987); *Apocalipse Nau* (1990).

Zurita, Raúl [Biography] Chilean poet and novelist born in Santiago in 1950, he was associated with Chile's underground writing of resistence in the 1980s during the military dictatorship. Known most widely as an irreverent poet, he has also published fiction. In the late 1960s and early 1970s he studied civil engineering in Valparaíso. In the 1970s he began publishing poetry and has published five books. He is known in Chile and Latin America for his public performances; in 1982 he wrote a poem in the sky in New York. He was the cultural attaché of Chile in Italy from 1990 to 1994. His first novel was *El día más blanco* (1999, The whitest day).

Selected Work: *El día más blanco* (1999).

Annotated Bibliography

General Introductions to the Latin American and Caribbean Novel

Alegría, Fernando. *Nueva historia de la novela hispanoamericana*. Hanover, NH: Ediciones del Norte, 1986.

Chronological discussion of the major movements in Latin American literature during the nineteenth and twentieth centuries. Includes analysis of the emergence of the new novel in the 1950s.

Amorós, Andrés. *Introducción a la novela hispanoamericana actual*. Salamanca: Anaya, 1973.

A study of the contemporary novel in Latin America with some discussion of antecedents of the new novel. Analysis of works by Ernesto Sábato, Julio Cortázar, Juan Rulfo, Carlos Fuentes, Alejo Carpentier, José Lezama Lima, Juan Carlos Onetti, Mario Vargas Llosa, Gabriel García Márquez.

Arnold, James, ed. *A History of Literature in the Caribbean*. 3 vols. Amsterdam and Philadelphia: Benjamins, 1994.

The most complete overview of Caribbean literature written in Spanish, French, English, Dutch, and creole languages of the region.

Arrom, José Juan. *Esquema generacional de las letras hispanoamericanas: Ensayo de un método*. Bogotá: Instituto Caro y Cuervo, 1963.

A pioneering study of Latin American literature using a generational approach, including discussion of many major writers.

Avelar, Idelbar. *The Untimely Present: Postdictatorial Latin American Fiction and the Task of Mourning*. Durham: Duke University Press, 1999.

In-depth readings of novels published in the southern cone region after the dictatorships there in the 1970s and 1980s.

Bellini, Giuseppe. *Historia de la literatura hispanoamericana*. Madrid: Castalia, 1985.

A well-informed chronological overview of the development of the Spanish American literature from the pre-Columbian period to the twentieth century, with the emphasis on writers and the movements. Introduces both major and minor writers.

Brotherston, Gordon. *The Emergence of the Latin American Novel*. Cambridge: Cambridge University Press, 1977.

A well-informed introduction to the Latin American novel, with the emphasis on the development of the modern novel and on the writers who contributed to the rise of the new novel: Asturias, Carpentier, Onetti, Rulfo, Cortázar, Arguedas, Vargas Llosa, and García Márquez. Lengthy discussion of major works.

Brushwood, John S. *The Spanish American Novel: A Twentieth-Century Survey*. Austin: University of Texas Press, 1975.

A well-informed and analytical introduction to the Spanish American novel from 1900 to 1970. Clear and precise style avoids jargon and makes this book accessible to the nonspecialist.

Cudjoe, Selwyn, ed. *Caribbean Women Writers*. Wellesley: Calaloux, 1990.

Informed and useful essays on women writers from the Caribbean region.

Dash, Michale J. *The Other America: Caribbean Literature in a New World Context*. Charlottesville: University of Virginia Press, 1998.

Insightful analysis and discussion of Caribbean writers who write in English, French, and Spanish.

Foster, David W. *Gay and Lesbian Themes in Latin American Writing*. Austin: University of Texas Press, 1991.

Informed and pioneering study on gay fiction in Latin America.

Franco, Jean. *Spanish-American Literature*. Oxford: Oxford University Press, 1969.

Deals with much literature published before 1945, but there are chapters that treat regionalism, realism, and the Indianist novel. Closes with a glimpse of the Boom.

Gallagher, D. P. *Modern Latin American Literature*. Oxford: Oxford University Press, 1973.

An introduction Latin American literature, it includes chapters on poetry and novel. Focus on major writers, including Borges, Vargas Llosa, García Márquez, and Cabrera Infante.

Glissant, Eduoard. *Caribbean Discourse: Selected Essays*. Trans. Michael Dash. Charlottesville: University Press of Virginia, 1989.

Translation from the French of a seminal essay on Caribbean culture.

Goiá, Cedomil. *Historia de la novela hispanoamericana*. Valparaíso: Universitaria, 1972.

A classic history of Latin American novel, it offers incisive readings of individual texts, including some thirty novelists from Fernández de Lizardi to Mario Vargas Llosa.

González Echevarría, Roberto. *Myth and Archive: A Theory of Latin American Literature*. Durham: Duke University Press, 1990.

One of the most influential theories about Latin American literature, based on vast readings of Latin American culture, literature and theory.

—— *Voice of the Masters: Writing and Authority in Latin American Literature*. Austin: University of Texas Press, 1985.

Influential and seminal readings of modern Latin American writers.

Lindstrom, Naomi. *The Social Conscience of Latin American Writing*. Austin: University of Texas Press, 1998.

Discussion and analysis of major directions of modern Latin American writing with emphasis on the social.

Lorenz, Günter W. *Diálogo con Latinoamérica*. Valparaíso: Universidad Católica de Valparaíso, 1972.

A collection of conversations with Latin American writers such as Ernesto Sábato, Ricardo E. Molinari, Antonio Di Benedetto, Mario Vargas Llosa, Rosario Castellanos, and João Guimarães Rosa. Each chapter also includes biography of the writer and the bibliographical reference of his/her works.

Ludmer, Josefina. *El cuerpo del delito: un manual*. Buenos Aires: Perfil, 1999.

A lengthy (508-page), informed and insightful study of various literary topics related to gender issues and transgression.

Shaw, Donald. *Antonio Skármeta and the Post Boom*. Hanover, NH: Edicíones del Norte, 1994.

Shaw emphasizes that the "extreme pessimism" characteristic of the Boom shifted to a new optimism in the Post-Boom.

Sommer, Doris. *Foundational Fictions: The National Romances of Latin America*. Berkeley: University of California Press, 1991.

Insightful and influential essays on the novels that preceded the post-WWII novel.

Williams, Raymond L. *The Twentieth-Century Spanish American Novel*. Austin: University of Texas Press, 2003.

General introduction to the twentieth-century Spanish American novel.

Studies on the National Novel

Argueta, Mario. *Diccionario de escritores hondureños*. Tegucigalpa: Letras Hondureñas No. 61, 1993.

Contains very brief entries on major and minor writers from Honduras.

Brushwood, John S. *Mexico in Its Novel*. Austin: University of Texas Press, 1966.

A well-informed and thorough introduction to the Mexican novel, with literary contexts and critical reading of the nineteenth and twentieth century Mexican novels.

Castillo, Debra. *Easy Women: Sex and Gender in Modern Mexican Fiction*. Minneapolis: University of Minnesota Press, 1998.

Feminist readings of modern Mexican novels from the early twentieth century to the present.

Curcio Altamar, Antonio. *Evolución de la novela en Colombia*. Bogotá: Instituto Colombiano de Cultura, 1975.

A classic study of the Colombian novel orginally published in 1952, it provides an introduction to the Colombian novel from the colonial period to the 1940s. A traditional literary historian of his time, Curcio Altamar demonstrates a thorough knowledge of the Colombian novel.

DiAntonio, Robert F. *Brazilian Fiction: Aspects of Evolution in Contemporary Narrative*. Fayeteville: University of Arkansas Press, 1989.

Discussion of a broad range of topics and many modern Brazilian novels. Very useful for its breadth.

Forero Villegas, Yolanda. Un eslabón perdido: la novela de los años cuarenta (1941–1949), primer proyecto moderno en Colombia. Bogotá: Kelly, 1994.

Pioneer work into an unknown area of Colombian literary history: the early modern novel of the 1940s, including relatively unknown novelists, such as Jaime Ardila Casamitjana.

García Corales, Guillermo. *Relaciones de poder y carnalización en la novela chilena contemporánea*. Santiago: Asterión, 1995.

Insightful and informed analysis of major contemporary novelists of Chile.

López Tamés, Román. *La narrativa actual de Colombia y su contexto social*. Valladolid: Universidad de Vallodolid, 1975.

A reading of the modern Colombian novel with emphasis on the sociopolitical context as well as the topics of solitude and the civil war of La Violencia. Major writers include Gabriel García Márquez and Manuel Mejía Vallejo.

Masiello, Francine. *Between Civilization and Barbarism: Women, Nation, and Literary Culture in Argentina*. Lincoln: University of Nebraska Press, 1992.

Pioneering research on the predecessors to the WWII novel in Argentina.

Menton, Seymour. *Historia crítica de la novela guatemalteca*. Guatemala: Universitaria, 1960.

A history of the Guatemalan novel. Dividing thirty-six novelists into eight generations, he includes works published up until 1958.

——— La novela colombiana: planetas y satélites. Bogotá: Plaza y Janés, 1978.

In-depth analysis of major novels ("planets") and minor novels ("satellites") from Colombia, including classic novels published before 1945 as well as modern authors, such as Gabriel García Márquez and Héctor Rojas Herazo.

Schwarz, Roberto. *O pai de família e outros estudos.* Rio de Janeiro: Paz e Terra, 1978.

Fifteen informed and illuminating essays on literary and cultural topics related to modern Brazil.

Silverman, Malcom. *Protesto e o novo romance brasileiro.* Rio de Janeiro: Civilizacão Brasileira, 2000.

A lengthy and in-depth study of social themes in a broad range of Brazilian novels.

Steele, Cynthia. *Politics and Gender in the Mexican Novel, 1968–1988.* Austin: University of Texas Press, 1992.

Well-informed feminist and political analysis of two decades of Mexican fiction.

Süssekind, Flora. *Cinematograph of Words: Literature, Technique and Modernization in Brazil.* Trans. Paul Henriques Britto. Stanford: Stanford University Press, 1997.

A refined study of early twentieth-century Brazilian literature.

Stegagno Picchio, Luciana. *História da literatura brasileira.* Rio de Janeiro: Nova, 1997.

A well-informed and encyclopedic introduction to Brazilian literature in all genres from the colonial period to 1996. Useful and accurate information on recent fiction of the 1980s and 1990s.

—— *La letteratura brasiliana.* Milan: Sansoni-Accademia, 1972.

An informed and encyclopedic introduction to Brasilian literature of all genres until 1971.

Studies on Specific Topics of Latin American and Caribbean Fiction

Adams, M. Ian. *Three Authors of Alienation: Bombal, Onetti, Carpentier.* Austin: University of Texas Press, 1975.

Perceptive analysis of alienation in the selected works of María Luisa Bombal, Juan Carlos Onetti, and Alejo Carpentier. Begins with the brief theoretical discussion and continues with analytical reading.

Alonso, Carlos. *The Burden of Modernity: The Rhetoric of Cultural Discourse in Spanish America.* Oxford: Oxford University Press, 1998.

An informed and theoretical discussion of rhetoric, cultural discourse, modernity, and related subjects in a selection of major Latin American texts.

Ainsa, Fernando. *Identidad cultural de iberoamérica en su narrativa.* Madrid: Gredos, 1986.

A study of Latin American identity as it appears in fiction in each region, the author argues that Latin America's diverse nations share a common culture.

Aldama, Frederick Luis. *Postethnic Narrative Criticism: Magicorealism in Oscar "Zeta" Acosta, Ana Castillo, Julie Dash, Hanif Kureishi, and Salman Rushdie.* Austin: University of Texas Press, 2003.

A bold approach to magical realism in U.S. Latino and British postcolonial novel and film. Offers both theoretical breadth and depth of reading individual texts by the authors in the title.

Arias, Arturo. *Gestos ceremoniales: narrativa centroamericana 1960–1990.* Guatemala: Artemis-Edinter, 1998.

A well-informed study of nine representative authors of the period from 1960 to 1980, with emphasis on the sociohistorical context.

—— *La identidad de la palabra: narrativa guatemalteca a la luz del Siglo Veinte.* Guatemala: Artemis-Edinter, 1998.

A well-informed critical anlaysis of the twentieth-century Guatemalan novel, taking into account recent theory and self-searching on the part of the critic as writer.

Balderston, Daniel, ed. *The Historical Novel in Latin America: A Symposium*. Gaithersburg, MD: Hispamérica, 1986.

A volume of articles written in English and Spanish originally presented at a 1985 symposium of the historical novel. Studies of topics, authors, and novels.

Benedetti, Mario. *El recurso del supremo patriarca*. México: Nueva Imagen, 1979.

Critical essays on Carpentier, Roa Bastos, García Márquez, original approach to the works of these writers. Benedetti writes as an intellectual and fiction writer, rather than strictly a scholar.

Beverley, John and Marc Zimmerman. *Literature and Politics in the Central American Revolutions*. Austin: University of Texas Press, 1990

A discussion of Central American literature as a struggle for national liberation.

Biron, Rebecca E. *Murder and Masculinity: Violent Fictions of Twentieth-Century Latin America*. Nashville: Vanderbilt University Press: 2000.

An exploration of masculinity in *A maçã no escuro* (Lispector), *The Buenos Aires Affair* (Puig), and *El asalto* (Arenas), in addition to some short fiction.

Blanco Aguinaga, Carlos. *De mitólogos y novelistas*. Madrid: Turner, 1975.

Five essays written between 1968 and 1977 concerning the relationship between literature and history in new novel in Latin America, including books by Octavio Paz, García Márquez, Alejo Carpentier, and Carlos Fuentes.

Borinsky, Alicia. *Theoretical Fables: The Pedagogical Dream in Contemporary Latin American Literature*. Philadelphia: University of Pennsylvania Press, 1993.

Informed and insightful discussions of major writers of Spanish America, including Borges, Cortázar, García Márquez.

Bruce-Novoa, Juan. *Retrospace: Collected Essays on Chicano Literature*. Houston: Arte Público, 1990.

A set of fourteen informed and insightful essays on Chicano literature, including comparisons with Mexican literature. Bruce-Novoa enters into several polemical terrains with respect to literary criticism and, specifically, the critique of Chicano literature.

Camayd-Freixas, Erik, and José Eduardo González, eds. *Primitivism and Identity in Latin America: Essays on Art, Literature, and Culture*. Tucson: University of Arizona Press, 2000.

Essays on the notion of primitivism and its implications in contemporary Latin American society, art, and literature. Includes writers such as Julio Cortázar and Rómulo Gallegos.

Chamberlain, Bobby J., ed. *The City in the Latin American Novel*. Michigan State University, 1980.

A volume of articles presented in at the 1979 annual meeting of the MALAS, held at Michigan State University in 1979. Papers are divided into categories that deal with Buenos Aires, Lima, and Brazilian cities and include studies of the theme of the city in works by Mario Vargas Llosa, Graciliano Ramos, Jorge Amado, and others.

Conte, Rafael. *Lenguaje y violencia*. Madrid: AL-Borak, 1972.

An exploration of the phenomenon of the new novel in Latin America, including its origins and influences, context and precursors, general tendencies. The focus on the works by specific writers, such as Miguel Ángel Asturias, Alejo Carpentier, Juan Rulfo, and Juan Carlos Onetti, with analysis of language and violence.

Craft, Linda J. *Novels of Testimony and Resistance from Central America*. Gainesville: University Press of Florida, 1997.

Includes chapters on novels by Arturo Arias of Guatemala, Claribel Alegría and Manlio Argueta of El Salvador, and Giaconda Belli of Nicaragua. While formulating a theory of the Central American testimonial novel, Craft argues that the main function of such novels is to provide a voice for the underrepresented.

Dorfman, Ariel. *Imaginación y violencia en América*. Santiago de Chile: Universitaria, 1970.

A classic and thought-provoking look at violence and its role in Latin American literature.

——— *Some Write to the Future: Essays on Contemporary Latin American Fiction*. Trans. George Shivers and Ariel Dorfman. Durham, NC: Duke University Press, 1991.

A collection of essays dealing with genres, specific works, or authors. The main focus is reader participation in contemporary Latin American fiction.

Eltit, Diamela. *Emergencias: escritos sobre literatura, arte y política*. Edited and with a prologue by Leonidas Morales T. Santiago: Planeta/Ariel, 2000.

Well-argued and carefully construed essays on topics such as gender, power, feminism, visual arts, and democracy in Latin America.

Favre, Isabelle. *La Différrance Francophone*. New Orleans: Presses Universitaires du Nouveau Monde, 2001.

Well-informed analysis of several French Caribbean writers in the larger context of Francophone writing.

Fernández Retamar, Alberto. *Ensayo de otro mundo*. Santiago: Universitaria, 1969.

An examination of the concept of development as well as the struggle to forge a national identity.

García Márquez, Gabriel, and Mario Vargas Llosa. *Diálogo sobre la novela Latinoamericana*. Lima: Perú-Andino, 1988.

A transcript of a conversation between the two authors in 1967, including a speech by García Márquez entitled "La Soledad de América Latina." The issues explored include the purpose of literature, the characteristics of a good literary work, the definition of a novelist, as well as personal influences.

González, Aníbel. *Killer Books: Writing, Violence, and Ethics in Modern Spanish American Narrative*. Austin: University of Texas Press, 2001.

An informed and insightful discussion of the persistence of graphophobia, or the fear of writing, in Latin American fiction. The author also analyzes the ethical difficulties and the love-hate relationship between writers and writing, emphasizing the exposition of many forms of abuse in the contemporary narrative. Valuable readings of Cortázar, Borges, Carpentier, as well as discussion of important writers of the pre-1945 period.

González, Eduardo. *The Monstered Self: Narratives of Death and Performance in Latin American Fiction*. Durham: Duke University Press, 1992.

An analysis the importance of death in Latin American fiction, addressing both the short story and the novel. González emphasizes the equal importance of life and death in fiction and considers the performance aspect of the latter. The writers analyzed include Borges and Vargas Llosa.

Guibert, Rita. *Seven Voices*. New York: Knopf, 1972.

This useful book consists of conversations with seven Latin American writers: Pablo Neruda, Jorge Luis Borges, Miguel Ángel Asturias, Octavio Paz, Julio Cortázar, Gabriel García Márquez, and Guillermo Cabrera Infante.

Harss, Luis, and Barbara Dahmann. *Into the Mainstream: Conversations with Latin American Writers.* New York: Harper, 1966.

This is a very useful book that examines prominent authors and how their life experiences affect their works. Authors include Miguel Angel Asturias and his concern for the disenfranchised, Julio Cortázar's confrontation with the realities of modernity, and Carlos Fuentes's concern for the power struggles within postrevolutionary Mexico.

Herrera-Sobek, María, ed. *Reconstructing a Chicano/a Literary Heritage.* Tucson: University of Arizona Press, 1993.

Essays on early colonial Hispanic literature in the southwestern region of the United States by major scholars of Chicano literature, including Herrera-Sobek, Juan Bruce-Novoa, Tino Villanueva, Ramón Gutiérrez, Francisco Lomelí, and Luis Leal.

Hoeg, Jerry. *Science, Technology, and Latin American Narrative in the Twentieth Century and Beyond.* Bethlehem, PA: Lehigh University Press, 2000.

This book explains the importance of science and technology in Latin American literature. Works include *One Hundred Years of Solitude, The House of the Spirits, Gabriela, Clove and Cinnamon, Like Water for Chocolate,* and *Única mirando al mar.*

Juan-Navarro, Santiago. *Archival Reflections: Postmodern Fiction of the Americas (Self-Reflexivity, Historical Revisionism, Utopia).* Lewisburg, PA: Bucknell University Press, 2000.

A thought-provoking discussion of the postmodern aspects of historical fiction of the United States and Latin America written in the 1970s. Authors include Carlos Fuentes, Ishmael Reed, Julio Cortázar, and E. L. Doctorow.

Kadir, Djelal. *Questing Fictions: Latin America's Family Romance.* Minneapolis: University of Minnesota Press, 1986.

A study of pertinent texts and, specifically, how they are direct responses to the historical, social, and cultural conditions and bias under which they are produced. Most of the discussions are based on readings in theory and philosophy.

Kulin, Katalin. *Modern Latin American Fiction: A Return to Didacticism.* Budapest: Akadémiai Kiadó, 1988.

This book belongs to a series entitled Studies in Modern Philology and explores the works of Rulfo, Onetti, García Márquez, Vargas Llosa, and Cortázar, analyzing each author's image of the world. The author discusses how Latin America's unique social and political history has prevented what was believed to be the inevitable death of the novel. Specifically discussed are myth, narratology, setting, nature, chronology.

Libertella, Héctor. *Nueva escritura en Latinoamérica.* Caracas: Monte Ávila, 1977.

An analysis of the phenomenon of the new literature in Latin America. The writer examines factors, such as tradition, language, and particularities of the continent and its history, that influence the literature. The last chapter is dedicated to analysis of novels by writers such as Osvaldo Lamborghini, Salvador Elizondo, Severo Sarduy, and Manuel Puig.

MacAdam, Alfred J. *Modern Latin American Narratives.* Chicago: University of Chicago Press, 1977.

An examination of a number of modern Latin American narratives, including novels by Julio Cortázar, João Guimarães Rosa, Gabriel García Márquez, and Juan Rulfo.

McCracken, Ellen. *The Feminine Space of New Latina Narrative.* Tempe: University of Arizona Press, 1999.

Well-informed readings of recent Latina narrative, with emphasis on subjects such as postmodern ethnicity, collective narration of history, and transgressive narrative tactics.

Menton, Seymour. *Latin America's New Historical Novel*. Austin: University of Texas Press, 1993.

A study of Latin American historic novels published between 1979 and 1992. Menton's basis of analysis is that of periodization rather than motifs, country, or theory. He seeks to distinguish the presentation of the themes (such as war, power, imperialism, subversion, exile, and religion) and techniques of these novels from previous historical novels.

Miller, Yvette E., and Charles M. Tatum, eds. *Latin American Women Writers: Yesterday and Today*. Pittsburgh: Latin American Literary Review Press, 1977.

A collection of criticism on literature from Latin America (poetry, narrative), originally presented at a conference on women writers. Most of the essays are detailed exploration of the works of women writers such as Ronni Gordon Stillman, Elena Poniatowska, María Angélica Bosco, Beatriz Guido, Silvina Bullrich, and others. A pioneering volume in the area of women's writing in Latin America.

Minc, Rose S., ed. *Literature and Popular Culture in the Hispanic World: A Symposium*. Gaithersburg, MD: Hispamérica, 1981.

This volume combines the critical works on Latin American literature that were presented in a conference at Montclair State College in 1981. Includes essays on Puig, Arlt, and Luis Rafael Sánchez.

Nagel, Susan. *The Influence of the Novels of Jean Giraudoux on the Hispanic Vanguard Novels of the 1920s–1930s*. Lewisburg, PA: Bucknell University Press, 1991.

An examination of the influence of Jean Giraudoux on the Latin American vanguardist novel of the 1920s and 1930s. Nagel cites many of his innovations, such as reader participation, the importance of the creative process, metalepsis, ellipsis, decharacterization, pneumatic metaphor, metafiction, all of which have been employed by vanguardist novelists in Spanish America. The often-ignored Latin American works examined include *Víspera del gozo* by Pedro Salinas, *Cuentos para una iglesia desesperada* by Eduardo Mallea, and *Novela como nube* by Gilberto Owen.

Patai, Daphne. *Myth and Ideology in Contemporary Brazilian Fiction*. London: Associated University Presses, 1983.

Analytical essays on major Brazilian writers, including Mary Alice Barroso, Clarice Lispector, Jorge Amado, Carlos Heitor Cony, Adonias Filho and Autran Dourado.

Peavler, Terry J., and Peter Standish, eds. *Structures of Power: Essays of Twentieth-Century Spanish-American Fiction*. Albany: State University of New York Press, 1996.

A collection of essays that address issues of hegemony and power with regard to politics, social issues, religion, economics, gender, and sexual orientation in Latin American fiction. Authors studied include José Donoso, Mario Vargas Llosa, Gabriel García Márquez, Julio Cortázar, Macedonio Fernández, Augusto Roa Bastos, Juan Rulfo, Guillermo Cabrera Infante, Alejandra Pizarnik, and Luisa Valenzuela.

Rama, Angel. *La riesgosa navegación del escritor exiliado*. Montevideo: Arca, 1993.

A compilation of essays about various novels and novelists, including *La hojarasca* by Gabriel García Márquez, Puig, Fuentes, Donoso, Cortázar, Carpentier, and *La guerra del fin del mundo* by Mario Vargas Llosa. He also discusses the vanguardist movement in Latin America in general, the Mexican narrative, modernity as expressed in literature, exile, as well as censorship and its effect on self-expression.

Randall, Margaret. *Risking a Somersault in the Air: Conversations with Nicaraguan Writers*. San Francisco: Solidarity, 1984.

Interviews with fourteen Nicaraguan writers, including Sergio Ramírez and Giaconda Belli. Includes poets and novelists.

Rodríguez, Ileana. *Women, Guerrillas, and Love: Understanding War in Central America*. Minneapolis: University of Minnesota Press, 1996.

Offers a reading of politically committed texts by such authors as Sergio Ramírez and Arturo Arias. Within a political context it explores topics of gender, sexuality, and feminism.

Rodríguez-Alcalá, Hugo. *Narrativa Hispanoamericana*. Madrid: Gredos, 1973.

Nine critical essays on the Latin American narrative. Seven of the essays are dedicated to the short narrative and discuss stories by Carpentier, Roa Bastos, and Rulfo. The last essay investigates seventy years of the Paraguayan narrative, with emphasis on the work of Roa Bastos.

Rodríguez Monegal, Emir. *El arte de narrar—Diálogos*. Caracas: Monte Avila, 1968.

The author narrates interviews he has conducted with celebrated authors and other artists, such as Cabrera Infante, Fuentes, Sarduy, Sáinz, Beatriz Guido, and Juan Goytisolo. Cabrera Infante discusses how orality converts the horizontal language of the mundane into the vertical language of literature without losing its validity. Fuentes, however, seems more concerned with the explosive power of language as well as the cannibalism of Mexican cultural life.

—— *El Boom de la novela latinoamericana*. Caracas, Venezuela: Tiempo Nuevo, 1972.

A study of the phenomenon of the Boom in Latin American literature, which includes discussion of origins, development, and national and international interests.

Saldívar, José David. *Border Matters: Remapping American Cultural Studies*. Berkeley: University of California Press, 1997.

Well-informed and theoretically sophisticated reconsideration of Chicano culture, including literature.

—— *The Dialectics of Our America: Genealogy, Cultural Critique, and Literary History*. Durham: Duke University Press, 1991.

A comparative analysis of writing on both sides of the border, including a proposal for a "pan-American" literary tradition.

Saldívar, Ramón. *Chicano Narrative: The Dialectics of Difference*. Madison: University of Wisconsin Press, 1990.

An incisive analysis of Chicano narrative, with a strong historical introduction and deft use of theory.

Schwartz, Marcy E. *Writing Paris: Urban Topographies of Desire in Contemporary Latin American Fiction*. Albany: State University of New York Press, 1999.

An examination of the role of Paris as a setting for many contemporary Latin American novels. Focus on *Rayuela* by Julio Cortázar (among his other novels), *La danza inmóvil* by Manuel Scorza, and *La vida exagerada de Martín Romaña* and *El hombre que hablaba de Octavia de Cádiz*, both by Alfredo Bryce Echenique.

Schwartz, Ronald. *Nomads, Exiles, and Emigres: The Rebirth of the Latin American Narrative, 1960–80*. Metuchen, N.J.: Scarecrow, 1980.

An examination of ten major contemporary authors whose novels have been translated into English. Among the writers presented are Carpentier, Cortázar, Lezama Lima, García Márquez, and Vargas Llosa.

Simpson, Amelia S. *Detective Fiction from Latin America*. Rutherford, NJ: Fairleigh Dickinson University Press, 1990.

A study of the development of detective fiction in Latin America, a genre often ignored. Simpson begins with an outline of the emergence of the detective novel in the nineteenth century and follows with an analysis of the phenomenon in the region, focusing specifically on the River Plate, Brazil, Mexico, and Cuba, the principal settings of such works. Simpson additionally conducts a comparison between Latin American detective novels and those of the United States, much more popular in Spanish America than those produced in the region. She notes that the Latin American works address moral, social, and political issues, while North American detective novels tend to be more superficial, devoid of ideological or societal implications.

Souza, Raymond D. *La historia en la novela hispanoamericana moderna*. Bogotá: Tercer Mundo, 1988.

In this book Souza emphasizes that the theme of the past and the desire to understand and/or explain it is rampant in the Latin American novel, a phenomenon that started in the first novels of the region, shortly after the conquest. The search for the past in literature represents, according to Souza, a search for national and personal identity. He specifically focuses on historical novels written between 1961 and 1984, emphasizing the works of Alejo Carpentier, José Lezama Lima, Mario Vargas Llosa, Ernesto Sábato, Mariano Azuela, Carlos Fuentes, and Gustavo Alvarez Gardeazábal.

Tittler, Jonathan. *Violencia y literatura en Colombia*. Madrid: Orígenes, 1989.

Selected essays from an international conference on violence and literature in Colombia, these pieces, written by specialists on Colombian literature, offer solid insights into the topic at hand.

Vidal, Hernán. *Literatura Hispano-Americana e ideología liberal: Surgimiento y crisis (Una problemática sobre la dependencia en torno a la narrativa del Boom)*. Buenos Aires: Hispamérica, 1976.

A study of Latin American literature as a manifestation of Latin American economic dependence and the sociopolitical praxis of certain classes and groups within this framework. The author focuses especially on the possible definitions of literary discourse as liberal ideology.

Volek, Emil. *Cuatro claves para la modernidad: Análisis semiótico de textos hispánicos*. Madrid: Gredos, 1984.

The author analyzes literary texts as representations of the phenomenon of modernity. The discussion includes works by Borges, Carpentier, and Cabrera Infante.

Williams, Raymond L. *The Postmodern Novel in Latin America*. New York: St. Martin's, 1995.

Analysis of postmodern fictions of the 1970s and 1980s.

Studies on Individual Authors of Latin America and the Caribbean

Jorge Amado

Chamberlain, Bobby. *Jorge Amado*. Boston: Twayne, 1984.

General introduction to Amado's fiction, with brief biography.

Miguel Ángel Asturias

Bellini, Giuseppe. *La narrativa de Miguel Ángel Asturias*. Buenos Aires: Losada, 1969.

A critical discussion of the fiction of Asturias, with chapters on dictatorship, myth, and reality, banana plantation settings, and social protest.

Callan, Richard. *Miguel Ángel Asturias*. New York: Twayne, 1970.

A clear and informed introductory study to the life and works of Miguel Ángel Asturias, including chapters on his major novels and other works.

Couffon, Claude. *Miguel Ángel Asturias*. Paris: Seghers, 1970.

> A critical study of Miguel Ángel Asturias, written in French, with biography. Includes a selection of translated poems and a chronology of Asturias's life and works.

Prieto, René. *Miguel Ángel Asturias's Archaeology of Return*. Cambridge: Cambridge University Press, 1993.

> Emphasizes the originality and aesthetic value of *Leyendas de Guatemala, Hombres de maíz,* and *Mulata de tal*. Argues against Asturias's assertion that the sole function of a Latin American novelist is to portray political and social realities.

Sáenz, Jimena. *Genio y figura de Miguel Ángel Asturias*. Buenos Aires: Universitaria, 1974.

> Biography and criticism. Ten chapters. Includes bibliography of Asturias's first editions, translations done by him, and limited critical bibliography.

Chico Buarque

Zappa, Regina. *Chico Buarque*. Rio de Janeiro: Relume Dumará, 1999

> Informed and useful introduction to the life and work of this multitalented Brazilian musician and writer.

Guillermo Cabrera Infante

Souza, Raymond D. *Guillermo Cabrera Infante: Two Islands, Many Worlds*. Austin: University of Texas Press, 1996.

> Well-informed biographical introduction and analysis of fiction.

Antônio Callado

Moraes, Ligia Chiappini. *Quando a patria viaja: uma leitura dos romances de Antônio Callado*. Havana: Casa de las Américas, 1983.

> Informed and insightful essays on the complete fiction of Callado published up to the early 1980s. This book was awarded the prestigious Casa de las Americas prize for essay.

Alejo Carpentier

González Echevarría, Roberto. *Alejo Carpentier: The Pilgrim at Home*. Ithaca: Cornell University Press, 1977.

> A seminal study for an understanding of Carpentier and modern Latin American literature.

Rosario Castellanos

O'Connell, Joanna. *Prospero's Daughter: The Prose of Rosario Castellanos*. Austin: University of Texas Press, 1995.

> Reading and analysis of the complete work of Castellanos.

Julio Cortázar

Boldy, Stephen. *The Novels of Julio Cortázar*. Cambridge: Cambridge University Press, 1980.

> An introduction to the novels of Cortázar.

Carlos Fuentes

Van Deldon, Maarten. *Carlos Fuentes, Mexico and Modernity*. Nasheville: Vanderbilt University Press, 1998.

> Well-argued study of modernity in the fiction of Fuentes.

Williams, Raymond L. *The Writings of Carlos Fuentes*. Austin: University of Texas Press, 1996.

   Analysis of the writings of Fuentes, preceded by a biographical introduction.

Gabriel García Márquez

Minta, Stephen. *Gabriel García Márquez*. New York: Harper and Row, 1987.

   Introduction to the writer and his context.

Ortega, Julio, Editor. *Gabriel García Márquez and the Powers of Fiction*. Austin: University of Texas Press, 1988.

   Insightful essays on the Colombian writer.

Williams, Raymond L. *Gabriel García Márquez*. Boston: Twayne, 1984.

   Introduction to the Colombian writer's work.

Elena Garro

Stoll, Anita K. *Studies on the Work of Elena Garro*. Lewisburg: Bucknell University Press, 1990.

   A compilation of fourteen valuable essays on the work of Mexican writer Elena Garro. Authors include Catharine Larson, Vicky Unruh, and Beth Miller. Analysis of marginality and alienation in the complete work of this Mexican writer.

Rolando Hinojosa

Saldívar, José David, Editor *The Rolando Hinojosa Reader: Essays Historical and Critical*. Houston: Arte Público, 1985.

   Essays by established scholars on a variety of topics in the writings of Rolando Hinojosa.

Clarice Lispector

Alonso, Cláudia Pazos, and Claire Williams, Editors. *Closer to the Wild Heart: Essays on Clarice Lispector*. Oxford: European Humanities Research Centre, 2002.

   A volume of twelve informed and well-conceived essays on the individual works of Clarice Lispector as well as topics relating to several works. Topics include gender, class, race, nation, and autobiography.

Rigoberta Menchú

Arias, Arturo, ed. *The Rigoberta Menchú Controversy*. Minneapolis: University of Minnesota Press, 2001.

   A set of polemical essays on the Guatemalan writer and activitist.

Miguel Méndez

Keller, Gary D., Editor. *Miguel Méndez in Aztlán*. Tempe: Bilingual, 1995.

   Useful companion to the reading of Miguel Méndez, this volume contains biographical overviews, critical readings, and bibliography. Contributors include David W. Foster, Luis Leal, Francisco Lomelí, Charles Tatum, and Miguel Méndez himself.

Manuel Puig

Kerr, Lucille. *Suspended Fictions: Reading the Novels of Manuel Puig*. Urbana: University of Illinois Press, 1987.

   Insightful and lucid readings of Puig.

Levine, Suzanne Jill. *Manuel Puig and the Spider Woman: His Life and Fictions*. New York: Farrar, Straus, and Giroux, 2000.

> A comprehensive and thorough biography of the Argentine writer.

Joâo Guimarâes Rosa

Vincent, Jon. *Joâo Guimarâes Rosa*. Boston: Twayne, 1978.

> Introductory readings to the Brazilian master's fiction.

Juan Rulfo

Leal, Luis. *Juan Rulfo*. Boston: Twayne, 1983.

> A complete study of Juan Rulfo's life and work.

Mario Vargas Llosa

Kristal, Efraín. *Temptation of the Word: The Novels of Mario Vargas Llosa*. Nasheville: Vanderbilt University Press, 1998.

> Informed and lucid readings of Vargas Llosa.

Oviedo, José Miguel. *Mario Vargas Llosa: la invención de una realidad*. Barcelona: Seix Barral, 1972.

> Key readings by an insider of Vargas Llosa's life and writing.

Williams, Raymond L. *Mario Vargas Llosa*. New York: Ungar, 1972.

> Introductory analysis on the novels of Vargas Llosa.

Index

Abad Faciolince, Héctor, Columbian writer, 77

Abbadón, el exterminador (Sábato), 78, 310

Abeng (Cliff), 78, 162

Aberracão (Carvalho), 148

Abreu, Caio Fernando, Brazilian writer, 78

Açogue das Almas (Silva, A.), 322

Acosta, Oscar "Zeta," Chicano writer, 79

Acqua Toffana (Melo, P.), 278–79

Across the Wire, Life and Hard Times on the Mexican Border (Urrea, L.), 336

Acto propiciatoria (Manjarréz), 275

El actor se prepara (Hiriart), 250

Adán Buenosayres (Marechal), 15–16, 56, 79, 276

Adán, Martín, Peruvian writer, 52

Adão e Eva (Fallace), 200

Adiós al Fuhrer (Lafourcade), 262

Adiós humanidad (Jacobs), 257

Los adioses (Onetti), 80, 289

Adoum, Jorge Enrique, Ecuadorian writer, 80

O Afogado (Silva, A.), 322

African diaspora, 133

Afro-Antillean poetry, 35

Afro-brasileiro, 81

Afro-Latin American novel, 80–81, 84

Age of Innocence (Lamming), 263

El agente secreto (Condé), 165

Agosto (Fonseca), 81, 208

Agua quemada (Fuentes, C.), 81–82

Agua viva (Lispector), 19, 269

Agudelo, Darió Jaramillo, Columbian writer, 51

The Aguero Sisters (García, C.), 218–19

Aguilar Camín, Héctor, Mexican writer, 82

Aguilar, Rosario, Nicaraguan writer, 82

Aguilera Garramuño, Marco Tulio, Columbian writer, 83

Aguilera Malta, Demetrio, Ecuadorian writer, 83, 140

Aguinis, Marcos, Argentinian writer, 84

Aguirre, Eugenio, Mexican writer, 85

Agustín, José, 27, 32; Mexican writer, 86, 174, 255–56

Aimé Césaire: une traversée paradoxale du siècle (Confiant), 165

Aire de tango (Mejía Vallejo), 278

Airó, Clemente, Columbian writer, 87–88

Al filo del agua (Yáñez), 15–16, 24–25, 92, 207–8

Alas de angel (Martín del Campo), 276

Alatriste, Sealtiel, Mexican writer, 88

Los albañiles (Leñero), 27, 264

Alberto, Eliseo, Cuban writer, 42, 88

El album secreto del Sagrado Corazón (Parra Sandoval), 52, 293

Albuquerque (Anaya), 99

Alegría, Ciro, Peruvian writer, 46, 89

Alegría, Claribel, El Salvadorian writer, 90

Alegría, Fernando, Chilean writer, 56, 90–91

Alejandra (Duque López), 193

Além dos Marimbas (Sales), 312

Alexis, Jacques Stephan, 91

Alférez Arce, Teniente Arce, Capitán Arce (Salazar Bondy), 312

La alfombra rojo (Lynch), 272–73

Allende, Isabel: Latin American writer, 12, 18, 20, 22, 42, 92–93; post-Boom writer, 62

Alrededor de la jaula (Conti), 166

Alvarez Gardeazábal, Gustavo, Columbian writer, 6, 20, 53, 83, 94–95, 116–17

Alvarez, Julia, Dominican Republic writer, 45, 93

Amado, Jorge, Brazilian writer, 17–19, 72, 95–96

Amasijo (Brunet), 133

Amaya Amador, Ramón, Honduran
writer, 96–97
Ambert, Alba, 97
American Connection (Brodber), 133
La amigdalitis de Tarzán (Bryce
Echenique), 134–35
Las ammaras terrestres (Chacón), 155
O Amor é uma Dor Feliz (Bonasi), 126
Amor en los tiempos del cólera, El (García
Marquez), 97–98, 220
El amor y la muerte (Aguilera
Garramuño), 83
Los amores de Afrodita (Buitrago), 13,
53–54
Los amores de Laurita (Shua), 321
Amores enormes (Palou), 292
Amphitryon (Padilla), 98, 291
Ana em Venezia (Trevisan, J.), 335
Anaité (Monteforte Toledo), 281
Anaya, Rudolfo: Chicano writer, 9, 19, 39,
98–99, 180, 244–45, 321; post-Boom
writer, 42–43
Las andariegas (Angel), 100
Andean region: Boom in, 49–50;
Faulknerian influence in, 47–48; novels
of, 46, 54–55; post-Boom writing in,
53–54; postmodern writing in, 50–51
Andrade, Mário de, 66
Andrés, Jorge, 45
Angel, Albalucía, Columbian writer,
12–13, 99–100
Angela, o las arquitecturas abandonadas
(Patán), 294
Angêlo, Ivan, Brazilian writer, 100–101
Angosta (Abad Faciolince), 77
O Animal dos Motéis (Denser), 176
Os Anjos do Badaró (Prata), 299
Annie John (Kincaid), 260
Anónimo (Solares), 323
Anônimo Célebre, O (Brandão), 67, 101
Los años con Laura Díaz (Fuentes, C.), 31,
101
Los años despiadados (Viñas), 343
Los años duros (Díaz, J.), 183
Anotacões durante o Incendio (Moscovich),
283
Antes (Boullosa), 102, 130
Antes, o verão (Cony), 18, 101
Antõnio, João, 102

El apando (Revueltas), 304
Apocalipsis cum figuris (Hernández, L.),
247
*Uma Apprendizagem ou o Livro dos
Prazeres* (Lispector), 19
Aqua (Arguedas), 46
Aquí, también, Domitila (Barrios), 14
Arana, Federico, 102–3
Les arbres musicians (Alexis), 91
Arcadia todas las noches (Cabrera Infante),
142
Ardiles Gray, Julio, Argentinian writer,
103
Arenas, Reynaldo, Cuban writer, 4, 9,
103–4
Argentina: detective novels in, 202–3, 266,
295, 337, 346; government of, 10–11,
145, 192, 239, 343; novels about, 4, 11,
104–5, 303; postmodern fiction in,
58–59; women writers of, 105, 137–38,
145, 197–98, 245, 263–64, 281, 287–88.
See also Perón, Juan Domingo
Arguedas, José María: *indigenista* tradition
and, 255; Peruvian writer, 46, 105–7
Argueta, Manlio, El Salvadorian writer,
32, 34, 106, 181–82
Arias, Abelardo, Argentinian writer, 106–7
Arias, Arturo, Guatemalan writer, 5,
32–33, 107
Aridjis, Homero, Mexican writer, 107–8
El arma en el hombre (Castellanos), 152
El arpa y la sombra (Carpentier), 108, 148
Arquipélago (Mainardi), 273–74
Arráncame la vida (Mastretta), 30, 108,
277
Arreola, Juan José, Mexican writer, 108
Arrieras somos (Condé), 165
El arte de la palabra (Lihn), 267
El Arte de vivir sin soñar (Caballero
Calderón), 140
As Alianças (Ivo), 256
As Aves de Cassandra (Johns), 259
As Iniciais (Carvalho), 148–49
As Meninas (Telles), 329
As Mulheres de Tijucopapo (Felinto), 203
As Parceiras (Luft), 272
As Tres Marias (Queiroz), 299
El asalto (Arenas), 104
El asedio (Valcárel), 38

Así en la paz como en la guerra (Cabrera Infante), 141–42

Assassinato dos Pombos (Bins), 121

Assassinato na Floresta (Rangel), 179

Assunciāo de Salviano (Callado), 143

El astillero (Onetti), 109, 289

Asturias, Miguel Angel, Guatemalan writer, 5, 7–8, 32–33, 109–10, 319–20

Asuntos de un hidalgo disoluto (Abad Faciolince), 77

At the Bottom of the River (Kincaid), 260

Atrás sin golpe (Díaz Eterovic), 184

Aura (Fuentes, C.), 110

The Autobiography of a Brown Buffalo (Acosta), 79

The Autobiography of My Mother (Kincaid), 260

El autor de mis días (Burel), 138

Avilés Fabila, René, Mexican writer, 110–11

Avolovara (Lins), 19, 21, 66, 110, 268

Azuela, Arturo, Mexican writer, 20, 30, 111–12

Azuela, Mariano, Mexican Revolution novel by, 4, 24, 112

O Azul do Filho Morto (Oliveira), 288

A Bag of Stories (Van Steen), 112

Bahia Sonora (Buitrago), 137

Bahr, Eduardo, Guatemalan writer, 34

Bajo las jubeas en flor (Gorodischer), 234

Balada da Infância Perdida (Torres), 332

Balza, José, Venezuelan writer, 52, 113

Bandoleiros (Noll), 287

Bar Don Juan (Callado), 113–14, 143

Barbados, 114

A Barca dos Homens (Dourado), 18, 64, 190

Los barcos (Quesada), 300

Barletta, Leónidas, Argentinian writer, 114

Barnet, Miguel, Cuban writer, 39, 114–15

Barrabás y otros relatos (Uslar Pietri), 336

Barranquilla group, 154

Barreto, Benito, Brazilian writer, 115

Barrios, Domitila, 14

Barroso, Maria Alice, Brazilian writer, 64–65, 116

Basura (Abad Faciolince), 77

Bayly, Jaime, Peruvian writer, 228

El bazar de los idiotas (Alvarez Gardeazábal), 20, 53, 94–95, 116–17

Os Bêbedos e os Sonâmbulos (Carvalho), 148

Bebel que a Cidade Comeu (Brandāo), 131

Beira Rio, Beira Vida (Brasil), 131

Beka Lamb (Edgell), 195

Un bel morir (Mutis), 284

Beleño, Joaquín, Panamanian writer, 117

Beliz, 117, 195

Bellatín, Mario, Mexican writer, 117–18

Belli, Giaconda, Nicaraguan writer, 32, 118

Benedetti, Mario, Uruguayan writer, 57, 91, 118–19

Benítaz Rojo, Antonio, Cuban writer, 4, 42, 119–20

Benjamin (Buarque), 69, 120, 135–36

Berkeley em Bellagio (Noll), 120

Berlinalexanderplatz (Doblin), 17, 27

Bermúdez, María Elvira, 186

Bernabé, Jean, 156

El beso de la mujer araña (Puig), 120, 136, 226, 299

Bestiario (Cortázar), 169

La bicicleta (Toscana), 333

La bicicleta de Leonardo (Taibo II), 328

Bins, Patrícia, Brazilian writer, 70, 121

Biografía de un cimarrón (Barnet), 39, 115, 121–22, 330

El biombo (Loubet), 271

Bioy Casares, Adolfo, Argentinian writer, 122–23

Blecaute (Paiva), 292

Bless me, Ultima (Anaya), 19, 43, 98–99, 123

Boca do Inferno (Miranda), 280

La boda del poeta (Skármeta), 123, 322

Bodas de cristal (Bullrich), 137

Bodies of Water (Cliff), 162

Boedo group, 114

Boguitas pintadas (Puig), 127–28

Bolaño, Roberto, Chilean writer, 124–25, 286–87

Bolero (Palou), 292–93

Bolívar, Simón, 4

Bolivia, 125; postmodern fiction in, 53

Um Bom Criolou (Caminha), 225

Bomarzo (Mujica Lainez), 283–84

Bombal, María Luisa, Chilean writer, 12, 125–26

Bonasi, Fernando, Brazilian writer, 71, 126
Boom: in Andean region, 49–50; fiction of, 7, 15, 17–20, 30, 33, 42, 50, 187–88; major novels of, 22, 126–27, 161–62. *See also* Post-Boom novel
El bordo (Galindo), 26, 128, 216
Borges e os Orangotangos Eternos (Vérissimo, L.), 129, 179, 341
Borges, Jorge Luis: Argentinian writer, 11, 15, 128–29; politics of, 73; postmodern fiction and, 21–22, 50, 59, 98, 122
Borinsky, Alicia, Argentinian writer, 129–31
La borra del café (Benedetti), 119
Boullosa, Carmen, Mexican writer, 22–23, 28, 30, 32, 102, 130–31, 334
Brandão, Ignácio de Loyola, Brazilian writer, 67, 101, 131
Braschi, Giannina, 45
Brasil, Assis, Brazilian writer, 65, 131–32
O Brasileiro Voador (Souza), 326
Brazil, 132; colonial legacy of, 3; detective novels in, 179–80, 206, 208–9, 278–79; experimental fiction in, 66, 110, 126, 148–49, 267–68, 314–15; generation of 1965 in, 64–65; government in, 9, 63, 70, 81, 113–14, 132, 135, 302, 332; major novelists of, 72, 143, 167, 190–91; *modernismo* of, 280–81; modernist novel in, 63–64, 96; novels of, 21, 96, 112, 131; politics in, 5, 7; post-Boom writing in, 70–72; postmodern fiction in, 66–68, 70, 155, 315; *saudade of*, 113; *vazio cultural* of, 66
Breath, Eyes, Memory (Danticat), 174
Breve Espaço entre Cor e Sombra (Tezza), 330
Breve historia de la novela hispanoamericana (Alegría, F.), 91
Breve historia de todas las cosas (Garramuno), 20
A Brighter Sun (Selvon), 319
Brinquedo lúdico, 248
Brodber, Erna, Caribbean writer, 3, 132, 258
Bruna, soroche y los tíos (Yañez Cossio), 348
Brunet, Marta, Chilean writer, 12, 133–34
Bryce Echenique, Alfredo, Peruvian writer, 54, 134–35

Buarque, Chico, 69, 120, 135–36
Budapeste (Buarque), 136
El buen salvaje (Caballero Calderón), 140–41
Buenas noches, professor (Diaconú), 182
The Buenos Aires Affair (Puig), 136
Bufo & Spallanzani (Fonseca), 136, 179, 208
Buitrago, Fanny, 13, 53, 136–37, 162
Bulevar de los héroes (García Aguilar), 219–20
Bullrich, Silvina, Argentinian writer, 137–38
Burel, Hugo, Uruguayan writer, 138
Burgos Cantor, Roberto, Columbian writer, 138–39
Burgos, Elizabeth, 14, 138
Los burgueses (Bullrich), 138
Los buscadores de la dicha (Guzmán, H.), 240
Buscando o Seu Mindinho (Prata), 139, 298
Butazzoni, Fernando, Uruguayan writer, 139–40

Caballero Calderón, Eduardo, Columbian writer, 140–41
El caballero de la invicta (Moreno Durán), 283
Los caballeros del sol (Aguilera Malta), 140
Caballos por el fondo de los ojos (Goloboff), 231
La cabaña (García Ponce), 221
La cabeza de la hidra (Fuentes, C.), 141
Cabrera, Estrada, 7–8
Cabrera Infante, Guillermo, Cuban writer, 4, 17, 21, 39, 141–42
Caçada de Memórias (Bins), 121
Cactus Blood (Corpi), 169
Cada voz lleva su angustia (Ibañez), 252
Cadáver exquisito (Aguirre), 86
Café nostalgia (Valdés), 45, 337
Caicedo, Andrés, Columbian writer, 51–52, 142–43
La caída (Guido), 238
Cais da Sagração (Montello), 282
Las calandrias griegas (Galmes), 217
Callado, Antonio, Brazilian writer, 9, 64–65, 70, 72, 143
La Calle 10 (Zapata Olivella), 46, 350

Cámara secreta (Rodríguez Juliá), 306

Cambio de guardia (Ribeyro), 305

Cambio de piel (Fuentes, C.), 27, 143–44, 186

Caminha, Adolfo, Brazilian writer, 225

El camino de los hiperbóreos (Libertella), 266

Caminos subterráneos (Caballero Calderón), 140

Campbell, Federico, Mexican writer, 144–45

Campos, Julieta, 145

La canción de nosotros (Galeano), 215

Una canción en la madrugada (Duncan), 193

Cangaçeiros (Rêgo), 303

Canoas e Marolas (Noll), 287

Canto castrato (César), 87

Canto, Estela, Argentinian writer, 145–46

Um Cão Uivando para a Lua (Torres), 332

Caparrós, Martín, Argentinian writer, 146

Caperucita en la zona roja (Argueta), 106

Caracol Beach (Alberto), 42, 89

Caramelo (Cisneros), 146, 160

Carballo, Emmanuel, 16

Cárdenas, Lázaro, 24

Cardoso, Lúcio, Brazilian writer, 146–47

Caribbean: colonial legacy of, 3, 36, 78, 263; Cuban revolution and, 36; diaspora novels, 44–45; modernist novels in, 37; postmodern novels of, 39–41, 165, 262; writing about, 33–36, 119

Carnival (Harris, W.), 147, 242, 243

O Carnival dos Animais (Scliar), 318

Carpentier, Alejo: Cuban writer, 5, 7, 16, 35–37, 39, 147–48, 177; dictator novel by, 185; post-Boom writer, 42

Cartagena, Manuel García, Dominican Republican writer, 44

Cartas cruzadas (Jaramillo Agudelo), 258

Cartas de um Sedutor (Hilst), 248

Cartas en el asunto (Moreno Durán), 283

Carvalho, Bernardo, Brazilian writer, 22, 71, 148–49

Carvalho-Neto, Paulo de, 149

La casa (Mujica Lainez), 283

Casa de encantamiento (Solares), 323

La casa de la laguna (Ferré), 205

La casa de los espíritus (Allende), 12, 62, 92–93, 149–50

La casa de los Felipes (Levinson), 265

A Casa de Vidro (Angêlo), 100

La casa del angel (Guido), 57, 237–38

La casa del sano placer (Yañez Cossio), 348–49

A Casa do Poeta Trágico (Cony), 150, 168

La casa grande (Cepeda Samudio), 150, 154

La casa verde (Vargas Llosa), 49, 65, 150–51, 339

Casaccia, Gabriel, Paraguayan writer, 151

Casas muertas (Otero Silva), 48, 290–91

Cascalho (Sales), 312

Casi el paraíso (Spota), 26, 326–27

Casta luna electrónica (Gorodischer), 234

Castellanos Moya, Horacio, 152

Castellanos, Rosario: *indigenista* tradition and, 255; Mexican writer, 12, 17, 25–26, 151–52

Castillo, Ana, 13–14, 39, 152–53

Castillo, Efraím, 41

Castro, Fidel, 36, 183, 195, 212–13

Catania, Carlo, Argentinian writer, 153–54

Caudillismo, 238

Las causas supremas (Sánchez, H.), 313

Cavernícolas! (Libertella), 266

Cayó sobre su rostro (Viñas), 17, 57, 343

Cazabandido (Fuentes, N.), 212

O Cego e a Dançarina (Noll), 287

Celestino antes del alba (Arenas), 103–4

Celia se pudre (Rojas Herazo), 307

El cementerio de los placeres (Levya), 265

Cemirérios Marinhos as Veces São Festivos (Johns), 259

Cenas da Vida Minúscula (Scliar), 318

O Centauro no Jardim (Scliar), 154, 318

Cepeda Samudio, Alvaro, Columbian writer, 154

Ceremonia secreta (Denevi), 175

El cero de Bogotá (Gamboa), 218

Césaire, Aimé, Caribbean writer, 16, 36, 73

César, Aira, Argentinian writer, 87

Céspedes, Augusto, Bolivian writer, 125

A Céu Alberto (Noll), 155, 287

O Céu e o Fundo do Mar (Bonasi), 126

Chacón, Joaquín-Armando, Mexican writer, 155

O Chamado da Noite (Ribeiro, C.), 304

Changó, el gran putas (Zapata Olivella), 81, 156, 350

Chapado do Burge (Palmério), 292

Charmoiseau, Patrick, Caribbean writer, 155–56

Charras (Lara Zavala), 264

Chávez Alfaro, Lizandro, Nicaraguan writer, 156–57

O Cheiro de Deus (Drummond), 157

Cheiro do amor (Steen), 327

Cheísmo, novels of, 4

Chicano novels, 157–58; detective, 180, 201; gay, 161

Chile: colonial legacy of, 3; detective novels in, 180, 184, 320; government in, 10, 60–61, 91, 124–25, 158, 163 178, 189, 196, 259, 262; novels of, 158, 163; postmodern fiction in, 59–60, 124

Chin-Chin el Teporocho (Ramírez, A.), 20

O Chorro e o Lobo (Torres), 332

Chronique des sept miséres (Charmoiseau), 156

Chungara, Domitila Barrios de, Bolivian writer, 47

O Ciclo das Aguas (Scliar), 318

Ciclo do Terror (Brasil), 131

Cidade de Deus (Lins), 158

A Cidade Sitiada (Lispector), 159, 269

El cielo de los leones (Mastretta), 277

Cien años de soledad (García Márquez), 17, 50, 65, 159, 220–21; parodies of, 20, 95, 116–17, 204

Cifuentes, Edwin, Guatemalan writer, 34

Cinco y una ficciones (Wacquez), 345

Cine continuado (Borinsky), 129

Cirandra de Pedra (Telles), 329

Cisneros, Sandra, 3, 14, 22, 35, 159–60; post-Boom writer, 42–44

City of Night (Rechy), 161

La ciudad anterior (Contreras), 161, 166

La ciudad ausente (Piglia), 59

La ciudad está triste (Díaz Eterovic), 184

Ciudad real (Castellanos), 151

La ciudad y los perros (Vargas Llosa), 17, 49, 161, 338

La civilisation du bossale (Condé), 164

Clarissa (Veríssimo), 341

Clave de sol (Ramírez, S.), 300

La clave morse (Campbell), 144

Cliff, Michelle, Caribbean writer, 78, 162

O Clube de Anjos (Veríssimo, L.), 341

Cobra (Sarduy), 39–41, 162, 180, 317

Cola de lagartija (Valenzuela), 13, 62, 337

Cola de zorro (Buitrago), 13, 53, 137, 162

Colibrí (Sarduy), 40

Collyer, Jaime, Chilean writer, 162–63

Colombia: detective novels in, 193, 218; massacre in, 154–55; modern writing in, 150; politics in, 6–7, 94; postmodern writing in, 51, 193; writings of, 54, 140

Colombus (Solares), 323

Colonial legacy, 3, 14

Colosanti, Marina, Brazilian writer, 13

Comment Faire l'amour avec un Nègre (Laferriére), 261–62

Cómo acercarse a la poesía (Krauze), 261

Como agua para chocolate (Esquivel), 22, 30 163–64

Como ser mujer y no vivir en infierno (Escalante), 198

Company, Flavia, Argentinian writer, 164

La comparsa (Galindo), 216

Os Componentes da Banda (Prado), 298

Comuna verdad (Goloboff), 231–32

Con la misma herradura (Amaya Amador), 97

Con la muerte en los puños (Palou), 293

Con las primeras luces (Martínez Moreno), 277

Condé, Maryse, Caribbean writer, 3, 12, 35, 39, 42, 164

Conde, Rosina, Mexican writer, 164–65

Condenados de Condado (Fuentes, N.), 212

La condesa sangrienta (Pizarnik), 11

Cóndores no entierran todos los días (Gardeazábal), 6, 53, 94

Confabulario (Arreola), 108

Confesión de amor (Ramírez, S.), 300

Confiant, Raphael, Caribbean writer, 156, 165

Confissões de Ralfo (uma autobiografia imaginária) (Sant'Anna), 68, 314

Cono Sur (Conteris), 165

Conteris, Híber, Uruguayan writer, 60, 165–66, 179, 186

Conti, Haroldo, Argentinian writer, 166

Contra o Brasil (Mainardi), 273–74

Contreras, Gonzalo, Chilean writer, 161, 166

Conversación én La Catedral (Vargas Llosa), 6, 8, 49, 166–67, 339

Los convidados de piedra (Edwards), 195–96

Cony, Carlos Heitor, Brazilian, 17, 64–65, 70, 101, 167–68

Um Copo de Cólera (Nassar), 286

Corações Mordidos (Steen), 327

Cordelia (Martínez Moreno), 277

Coronacíon (Donoso), 57, 188

El coronel no tiene quién le escriba (García Márquez), 168, 220

Corpi, Lucha, Chicana writer, 44, 168–69, 180

Cortázar, Julio, Argentinian writer, 7, 11, 14, 16–17, 21–22, 29, 39, 50, 58, 119, 127, 169–70, 211

Los cortejos del diablo (Espinosa), 53, 198

Costa, Moreira da, 67

Costa Rica, 170; government in, 32; novels of, 194

Costantini, Humberto, Argentinian writer, 58–59, 170, 240–41

Cota-Cárdenas, Margarita, 13–14

Countess Báthory, 11

Coutinho, Sonia, Brazilian writer, 170–71

Creolité, 80, 165, 180, 230

La cresta de Ilión (Rivera Garza), 31, 306

Crick Crack Monkey (Hodge), 171, 250–51

Um Crime Delicado (Sant'Anna), 315

Los crímenes de Van Gogh (Feinman), 202–3

El cristo de espaldas (Caballero Calderón), 140

El cristo feo (Yañez Cossio), 349

Cristóbal nonato (Fuentes, C.), 171–72

Critical generation. *See* Uruguay

Crônica da Casa Assasinada (Cardoso), 147

Crónica de San Gabriel (Ribeyro), 305

Crónica de una muerte anunciado (García Márquez), 172, 220

Crónica del gato que haye (Burel), 138

Crônicas, 310–11

Crosthwaite, Luis Humberto, Mexican writer, 31, 172

La cruz invertida (Aguinis), 85

Cuadernos de Gofa (Hiriart), 250

Cuando digo Magdalena (Steimberg), 328

Cuando quirero llorar no lloro (Otero Silva), 291

El cuarto mundo (Eltit), 60, 172–73, 197

Cuba, 173; novels about, 103–4, 204, 316; revolution in, 3–4, 36–37, 45, 103, 114–15, 119, 126, 141, 177, 183–84, 212. *See also* Castro, Fidel

Cuento a cuento (Ibargoyen), 252

Cuentos con walkman (Fuguet and Gómez), 213

Cuentos tristes (Lynch), 272

La cuidad y el viento (Airó), 88

Cumboto (Díaz Sánchez), 185

Cumpleaños (Fuentes, C.), 27–28

El cumpleaños de Juan Angel (Benedetti), 118

Cunha, Helena Parente, Brazilian writer, 13, 68

Curação, 173

D (Balza), 52

Da Silva, Francisco Maldonado, 85

Dabeibia (Alvarez Gardeazábal), 94

Dadydeen, David, Caribbean writer, 173–74

Danticat, Edwidge, Caribbean writer, 22, 42, 174, 347

La danza ejecutada (Contreras), 166

Dardará (Louzada Filho), 271

Los de abajo (Azuela, M.), 4, 24, 112

De amor y de sombra (Allende), 20, 92–93

De dioses, hombrecitos y policías (Costantini), 170

De donde son los cantantes (Sarduy), 317

De gozos y desvelos (Burgos Cantor), 139

De la amorosa inclinacíon a enrededarse en cabellos (Glantz), 230

De la imaginación a la barbarie (Moreno Durán), 282

De la infancia (González Suárez), 233

De la noche al día (Spota), 326

De miedo en miedo (Sommers), 325

De noche vienes (Poniatowska), 13

De perfil (Agustín), 27, 86, 174

De pétalos perennes (Zapata, L.), 349

De un salto descabalga la reina (Boullosa), 130

Death of Somoza (Alegría, Claribel, and Flakoll), 90

Declinación (De Benedetto), 181

Défazi (Frankétienne), 210

Dejamos hablar al viento (Onetti), 174–75, 289

Del tiempo y otros lugares (Ramos, L.), 301

Délano, Poli, Chilean writer, 175

Delia's Song (Corpi), 168

Demasiadas vidas (Palou), 293

Los demonios de la lengua (Ruy Sánchez), 309

Denevi, Marco, Argentinian writer, 175–76

Denser, Márcia, Brazilian writer, 176–77

Depestre, René, Caribbean writer, 177, 241

Dergeaud, Emérec, Haitian writer, 241

Derrida, Jacques, 40

El desatino (Gambardo), 217

Descanso de caminantes (Bioy Casares), 122

La desesperanza (Donoso), 178, 188

Los desheredados (Sánchez, H.), 313

Después de las bombas (Arias), 5, 32, 34, 107, 178

Después de todo (Maldonado), 225

Desterrados al fuego (Huidobro), 43

La destucción de todas las cosas (Hiriart), 250

Detective novels: Argentinian, 202–3, 266, 295, 337, 346; Brazilian, 179–80, 206, 208–9, 278–79; Chicano, 180, 201; Chilean, 180, 184, 320; Colombian, 193, 218; Latin American, 175–76, 178–79; Latino-written, 44; Mexican, 180, 183, 186, 250, 264, 294, 309, 328; Paraguayan, 306; parody of, 234, 326, 332, 341; as post-Boom, 44; postmodern, 186; Uruguayan, 186; women writer and, 201, 278–79

Los detectives salvajes (Bolaño), 124

Deuses de Raquel (Scliar), 318

Los devorados (Diaconú), 183

Dézafi (Frankétienne), 11, 180

Di Benedetto, Antonio, Argentinian writer, 181

O Dia em que Ernesto Hemingway Morreu Crucificado (Drummond), 192

Un día en la vida (Argueta), 32, 106, 181–82

El día más blanco (Zurita), 351

El día señalado (Mejía Vallejo), 6, 18, 48, 182, 278

Diaconú, Alina, Argentinian writer, 182–83

Diario de bordo (Louzada Filho), 271

Diario de Lecumberri (Mutis), 284

Diario de una multitud (Naranjo), 34, 285

Los días contados (Alegría, F.), 56, 91

Días de combate (Taibo II), 183, 328

Los días enmascarados (Fuentes, C.), 16

Dias y Dias (Miranda), 280

Dias y noches de amor y de guerra (Galeano), 215

Diaspora: African, 133; Caribbean, 44–45; Jewish, in Peru, 54. *See also* Exile, novel of

La diáspora (Castellanos Moya), 152

Díaz Eterovic, Ramón, Chilean writer, 180, 184–85

Díaz, Jesús, Cuban writer, 4, 43, 183–84

Díaz, Porfirio, Mexican regime of, 4, 16, 24–25

Díaz Sánchez, Ramón, Venezuelan writer, 185

Dicen que de noche tú no duermes (Valcárel), 38

Dictator novel, 19, 185–86

El diez por ciento de la vida (Conteris), 60, 166, 179, 186

Diferentes razones tiene la muerte (Bermúdez), 186

Disappearance (Dadydeen), 173

Discutibles fantasmas (Hiriart), 250

Disertación sobre las telarañas (Hiriart), 250

El disparo de Aragón (Villoro), 342

Divertimento (Cortázar), 169

A Doce Canção de Caetana (Piñón), 296

O Doent Moliére (Fonseca), 208

Dois Irmãos (Hatoum), 186, 243–44

DOM. *See* French overseas departments

Domar a la divina garza (Pitol), 29

Domecq, Brianda, Mexican writer, 29, 187

Dominican Republic, 187; government in, 8, 94

Los dominios ocultos (Guerra), 237

El don de la palabra (Azuela, A.), 111–12

Don Galaz de Buenos Aires (Mujica Lainez), 283

Don Goyo (Aguiler Malta), 84

Don Segundo Sombra (Güiraldes), 5

Dona Anja (Guimarães), 238–39

Doña Bárbara (Gallegos), 5

Dona Flor e seus dois maridos (Amado), 18, 65, 95–96

Donde acaban los caminos (Monteforte Toledo), 33, 281

Donoso, José, Chilean writer, 17–18, 40, 57, 59, 178, 187–89, 259

Dorfman, Ariel, Chilean writer, 189

Dos crímenes (Ibarguengoitia), 253

Dos mujeres (Levi Calderón), 189–90

Dos Passos, John, 16

Dos veces junio (Kohan), 260

Dourado, Autran, Brazilian writer, 18–19, 21, 63–64, 190–91

Os Dragões não Conhecem (Abreu), 78

Drawing Down and Daughter (Harris, C.), 242

Dreaming in Cuban (García, C.), 218

Droguett, Carlos, Chilean writer, 56, 191

Drummond, Roberto, Brazilian writer, 67, 191–92

Duas Iguais: Manual de Amor e Equívocos Assemelhados (Moscovich), 283

Duelo por Miguel Pruneda (Toscana), 333

Los dueños de la tierra (Viñas), 343

Duerme (Boullosa), 130

El Duke (Medina), 192, 278

Dulce compañía (Restrepo), 47, 193, 303

Dulcinea encantada (Muñiz-Huberman), 30

Duncan, Quince, Central American writer, 193–94

Duppelspel (Martinus Arion), 35, 194

Duque López, Alberto, Columbian writer, 50, 192–93

Duvalier, François "Papa Doc," 10–11

Duvalier, Jean-Claude, 10–11

Ecuador, 52, 83–84

La edad del Tiempo (Fuentes, C.), 171, 212

Edgell, Zee, Caribbean writer, 195

Edwards, Jorge, Chilean writer, 195–96

Eguez, Iván, Ecuadorian writer, 52

Einstein, o Minigênio (Sales), 312

El Salvador, 152, 196

Elizondo, Salvador, Mexican writer, 27–28, 196–97, 202

Eloge de la créolité (Chamoiseau, Confiant and Bernabé), 156, 165

Eloy (Droguett), 191

Elsinore (Elizondo), 196

Eltit, Diamela: Chilean writer, 3, 10–13, 21–23, 172–73, 197; postmodern writing of, 60, 74

Em Liberdade: Uma Ficção de Silviano Santiago (Santiago), 315

The Emigrants (Lamming), 263

En breve cárcel (Molloy), 11, 59, 197–98, 281

En busca de Klingsor (Volpi), 31, 344–45

En el corazón de junio (Gusmán), 11, 239

En este lugar sagrado (Délano), 175

En jirones (Zapata, L.), 226

En la zona (Saer), 311

En Nome do Desejo (Trevisan, J.), 335

En una ciudad llamada San Juan (Marqués), 38

En vida (Conti), 166

O Encontro Marcado (Sabino), 311

La encrucijada (Méndez, A.), 279

Enero (Gallardo), 216

Engagé writer, Sartre theory of, 16

Enlightenment, 4

El entierro de cortijo (Rodríguez Juliá), 40–41

Entre la idea y la sangre (Catania), 154

Entre la piedra y la cruz (Monteforte Toledo), 32–33, 281

Entre Marx y una mujer desnuda (Adoum), 80

Entre medio, 194

Entrecruzamientos (Jandra), 257–58

Epifanía de una sombre (Wacquez), 345

Epitalámica (Murena), 284

Ergens Nergens (Roemer), 80

Escalante, Beatriz, Mexican writer, 198

Escoto, Julio, Honduran writer, 33–34

Escrito en el tiempo (Jacobs), 257

El espejo y la ventana (Ortiz), 290

Esperanto (Fresán), 211

El espía del aire (Solares), 324

Espinosa, Germán, Colombian writer, 53, 198–99

El esplendor de la pirámide (Morales), 282

Esquivel, Laura, Mexican writer, 22, 32, 42, 164–65, 199–200

Essa Terra (Torres), 332

Estación Tula (Toscana), 23, 200, 333

Estado Novo, 5

Estampas del Valle y otras obras
(Hinojosa), 249

Estas ruinas que ves (Ibarguengoitia), 253

Este era un gato (Ramos, L.), 29, 302

"Este mar narrativo" (Balza), 52

Estorvo (Buarque), 135

A Estranha Nação de Rafael Mendes
(Scliar), 200

Estrázulas, Enrique, Uruguayan writer,
200–201

Estrella de la calle sexta (Crosthwaite), 172

Estrella distante (Bolaño), 124

La eternidad por fin comienza un lunes
(Alberto), 89

Etienne, Franck. *See* Frankétienne

Eulogy for a Brown Angel (Corpi), 168–69,
201

Eurídice (Rêgo), 16, 64, 303

Eva Luna (Allende), 92–93

El examen (Cortázar), 170

O Exército de Um Homen Só (Scliar), 318

Exile, novel of, 4, 8–9, 44

Los exiliados (Casaccia), 151

Exílio (Luft), 272

Existentialist fiction, 88

O Ex-mágico (Rubião), 308

Eyherabide, Gley, Uruguayan writer, 201

La fabula de José (Alberto), 42, 89

Fallace, Tania Jamardo, Brazilian writer,
201–2

Una familia argentina (Denevi), 176

Una familia lejana (Fuentes, C.), 28

Family Album (Alegría, Claribel), 90

Farabeuf (Elizondo), 27, 196, 202

Faria, Octavio de, Brazilian writer, 202

Faria, Octávio de, 63

Faulkner: Barranquilla group and, 154;
influence of, 15–17, 19, 27, 47, 50, 150,
161, 167, 338–39

Fazendo modelo: novela pecuária
(Buarque), 135

Feinman, José Pablo, Argentinian writer,
202

Los felinos del canciller (Moreno-Durán), 51

Felinto, Marilene, Brazilian writer, 203

Feliz Ano Novo (Fonseca), 208

Feliz Ano Velho (Paiva), 292

Femina Suite (Moreno Durán), 50, 282

La feria (Arreola), 108–9

Fernández, Macedonio, Argentinian,
203–4

Fernández, Pablo Armando, Cuban writer,
38

Fernández, Roberto, Cuban American
writer, 9, 204–5

Fernández, Sergio, Mexican writer, 205

Ferré, Rosario: Caribbean writer, 12–14,
18, 22, 42, 205–6; post-Boom writer,
42–43

A Ferro e Fogo (Guimarães), 238

A Festa (Angêlo), 100–101

A Festa do Milenio (Figueiredo, R.), 206

Ficciones (Borges), 15, 21, 50, 128, 298

Fictions of resistance. *See* Resistance

O Fiel e a Pedra (Lins), 268

La fiesta del chivo (Vargas Llosa), 7–8,
185–86, 339

La fiesta del Rey Acab (Lafourcade), 262

Figueiredo, André de, Brazilian writer, 206

Figueiredo, Rubens, Brazilian writer, 206

Figura de paja (García Ponce), 221

Filho, Adonias, Brazilian writer, 206–7

Filloy, Juan, Argentinian writer, 207

O Fim do Terceiro (Souza), 326

Fin de fiesta (Guido), 238

El fin de la locura (Volpi), 345

Final de la calle (Duncan), 194

Final del juego (Cortázar), 169

Final en borador (Galmes), 217

Finale capriccioso con Madonna (Moreno-
Durán), 51

First Congress of Black Writers and
Artists, 92

Flakoll, Darwin, 90

La "flor de Lis" (Poniatowska), 13, 30

Fluxo Floema (Hilst), 248

Fonseca, Rubem, Brazilian writer, 68, 179,
208–9

La forma de silencio (Puga), 29, 209

45 días y 30 marineros (Lange), 264

The Four Banks of the River Space (Harris,
W.), 242

França Junior, Oswaldo, Brazilian writer,
209

France, 3

Franco, Jorge, Columbian writer, 55, 209–10

Frankétienne, Haitian writer, 10–12, 35, 39, 41, 180–81, 210

Free Enterprise (Cliff), 162

French Guyana, 235–36

French overseas departments (DOM), 235–36

Frente a un hombre armado (Wacquez), 345

Fresán, Rodrigo, Argentinian writer, 210

From the Heat of the Day (Heath), 245

Frutos extraños (Guerra), 237

Fuego en Casabindo (Tizón), 331

Fuentes, Carlos, 211–12; Boom writing of, 18, 22, 27, 127; detective novels by, 141; on Mexican Miracle, 7, 24–26; Mexican writer, 3, 11, 16–18, 30–31, 36, 101, 235; politics of, 73; post-Boom writer, 42; postmodern writing by, 28, 32, 143–44

Fuentes, Norberto, Cuban writer, 212–13

Fuga (Fallace), 200

Fuguet, Alberto, Chilean writer, 54, 62–63, 213–14

Fundador (Piñón), 296

A Fúria do Corpo (Noll), 287

El futuro (Garcés), 218

Gabriela, Cravo e Canela (Amado), 95

Galaor (Hiriart), 250

Galeano, Eduardo, Uruguayan writer, 214–15

Los galgos, los galgos (Gallardo), 216

Galindo, Sergio, Mexican writer, 20, 26, 30, 128–29, 215

Gallardo, Sara, Argentinian writer, 216–17

Gallegos, Rómulo, Venezuelan writer, 5

Galmes, Héctor, Uruguayan writer, 217

O Galo de Ouro (Queiroz), 299

Galvez, Imperador do Acre (Souza), 326

Gambardo, Griselda, Argentinian writer, 217

Gamboa, Santiago, Columbian writer, 54–55, 217–18

Ganarsa la muerte (Gambardo), 217

El garabato (Leñero), 264

Garcés, Gonzalo, Argentinian writer, 218

García Aguilar, Eduardo, Columbian writer, 219–20

García, Cristina, Cuban American writer, 218–19

García, Lionel, Chicano writer, 219

García Márquez, Gabriel, 220–21; Barranquilla group of, 154; Boom and, 42, 127; Columbian writer, 4, 6, 16–17, 20, 47, 65, 97, 172, 226–27; dictator novel by, 185; Faulknerian influence on, 47–48; Macondo cycle of, 48, 168, 220; parody of, 77, 83; politics of, 73

García Ponce, Juan, Mexican writer, 221

García Saldaña, Parménides, Mexican writer, 222

Gardea, Jesús, Mexican writer, 222–23

Garmendia, Salvador, Venezuelan writer, 17–18, 223–24

Garramuno, Mario Tulio Aguilera, 20

Garro, Elena, Mexican writer, 12, 18, 26, 30, 224–25

El gato eficaz (Valenzuela), 62

Gay and lesbian Latin American novel, 161, 225–26, 349

Gazapo (Sainz), 27–28, 226, 312

Las genealogías (Glantz), 230

Generacíon de Medio Siglo (Galindo), 215, 221, 224

Generacíon de Mito, 284

Generacíon del Crack, 23, 31, 98, 291–92, 305, 344–45

Generaciones y semblanzas (Hinojosa), 249

El general en su laberinto (García Márquez), 4, 140, 226–27

Generatión de Medio Siglo, 16, 296–97

Generation of 1938, 90–91

Generation of 1956, 64

Generation of forty-five. *See* Uruguay

Generation of the 1990s, 148, 206, 227–28; women writers of, 347–48. *See also* Post-postmodern writers

Generation of the Blockade and the State of Siege, 313

Generation of the crack. *See Generacíon del Crack*

Generation of the parricides, 343

Género de punto (Company), 164

Los geniecillos dominicales (Ribeyro), 49

Gente al acecho (Collyer), 163

George Washington Gómez (Paredes), 228

Geração 90: Manuscritos de Computador (Oliveira), 71, 102, 227, 288

Geração 90: Os Transgressores (Oliveira), 227, 288

La german de Eloísa (Borges and Levinson), 265

La gesta del marrano (Aguinis), 85

O Gestos (Lins), 268

Gestos (Sarduy), 316–17

Giardinelli, Mempo, Argentinian writer, 8–9, 19–20, 22, 62, 228–29

Giraldo, Octavio Escobar, 54

Glantz, Margo, Mexican writer, 229–30

Glissant, Edouard, Caribbean writer, 230

O Globo da Morte (Barroso), 116

Goldemberg, Isaac, Peruvian writer, 53–54, 231

Goloboff, Gerardo Maro, Argentinian writer, 231

Gómez, Sergio, Chilean writer, 232

González, José Luis, 38–39

González León, Adriano, Venezuelan writer, 10, 12, 232–34

Gonzalez, Ray, Chicano writer, 279

González Suárez, Mario, Mexican writer, 233

Gonzalo Guerrero (Aguirre), 85

Gorodischer, Angélica, Argentinian writer, 233–34

Gouverneurs de la rosée (Roumain), 36

Gran Circo das Américas (Tezza), 330

El gran elector (Solares), 25, 30, 323

El gran solitario del palacio (Avilés Fabila), 111, 186

Gran teatro del fin del mundo (Aridjis), 107

A Grande Arte (Fonseca), 179, 208, 234

Grande Sertão: Veredas (Guimarães Rosa), 17, 21, 64, 234, 308

Graviña, Alfredo Dante, Uruguayan writer, 234–35

Great Britain, 3

Gringo viejo (Fuentes), 235

Grito de perro (Ibargoyen), 252

Grupo de los Cien, 107

Guadeloupe, 235–36

Guan, el Taco de Oro (Esquivel), 199

La guaracha del Macho Camacho (Sánchez, L.), 40–41, 67, 313–14

Guardia, Gloria, Panamanian writer, 236–37

Guatemala, 236; Mayan presence in, 32; politics in, 5, 7–8, 14, 32, 34, 97

Guerra conjugal (Trevisan, D.), 335

La guerra del fin del mundo (Vargas Llosa), 8, 339

A Guerra do Bom Fim (Scliar), 318

Guerra, Lucía, Chilean writer, 10, 236–37

La guerra no importa (Rivera Garza), 305

El guerrillero (Aguilar), 82

Guevara, Che, 4

Guia mapa de Gabriel Arcanjo (Piñón), 296

Guía para viajeros (Jaramillo Agudelo), 258

Guido, Beatriz, Argentinian writer, 12, 57, 237–38

Guimarães, Josué, Brazilian writer, 238–39

Guimarães Rosa, João, Brazilian writer, 7, 17, 21, 64, 66, 70, 72, 307–8

Güiraldes, Ricardo, Argentine, 5

Gusmán, Luis, Argentinian writer, 11, 239

Gutiérrez, Joaquín, Costa Rican writer, 33, 239

Guyana, 239–40

Guzik, Alberto, Brazilian writer, 72, 226, 240

Guzmán, Humberto, Mexican writer, 240

Guzmán, Jorge, Chilean writer, 59

Guzmán, Nicomedes, Chilean writer, 56

El habitante del cielo (Collyer), 163

Los habitantes (Garmendia), 18, 223–24

Háblenme de Funes (Costantini), 59, 170, 240–41

Hadriana dans tous mes rêves (Depestre), 177, 241

Haiti, 241–42; government of, 9–11, 92, 177–78, 242; *indigénisme* movement of, 36, 91; post-*indigeniste* writing in, 92; postmodern fiction of, 41

Hardscrub (García, L.), 219

Harmada (Noll), 287

Harris, Claire, Caribbean writer, 242

Harris, Wilson, 147

Hasta no verte Jesús mío (Poniatowska), 13, 297

Hatoum, Milton, Brazilian writer, 70–72, 186–87, 243–44

Hay que sonreír (Valenzuela), 337
Heart of Aztlán (Anaya), 99, 244–45
Heath, Roy, Caribbean writer, 245
Los hechiceros de la tribu (Jurado), 260
Heker, Liliana, Argentinian writer, 245
Herazo, Rojas, 48
Heremakhonon (Condé), 164
Hernández, Felisberto, Uruguayan writer, 245–46
Hernández, Luisa Josefina, Mexican writer, 246–47
Heterodoxia (Sábato), 310
La hija de Marx (Obligado), 288
Hijo de hombre (Roa Bastos), 57
Hijuelos, Oscar, 44, 247
Hilda Furacão (Drummond), 192, 247–48
Hills of Hebron (Wynter), 348
Hilst, Hilda, Brazilian writer, 248
Hinojosa, Rolando, Chicano writer, 19, 39, 248–50
El hipogeo secreto (Elizondo), 28, 196
Hiriart, Hugo, Mexican writer, 250
La historia (Caparrós), 146
Historia argentina (Fresán), 211
Uma História de Família (Santiago), 315
História de un Casamento (Barroso), 116
Historia de una historia (Graviña), 235
Historia de una pasión argentina (Mallea), 274
Historia personal del Boom (Donoso), 187
Historias brevísimas, 321
Hodge, Merle, Caribbean writer, 171, 250–51
Un hogar sólido (Garro), 224
La hojarasca (Márquez), 16–17, 47–48, 220
Los hojas muertas (Jacobs), 257
Holland, 3
Holy Radishes (Fernández, R.), 204
El hombre de paja (Buitrago), 137
El hombre del crepúsculo (Canto), 145
El Hombre que pregunta (Díaz Eterovic), 184
Los Hombres de a caballo (Viñas), 343
Hombres de maíz (Asturias), 33, 109
O Homen da Mão (Prado), 298
Os Homens dos Pés Redondos (Torres), 332
Honduras, 97, 251
A Hora da Estrela (Lispector), 19, 251, 269
Hora dos Ruminantes (Veiga), 251–52, 340

El Hostigante verano de los dioses (Buitrago), 137
Hot Line (Sepúlveda), 320
Hôtel Atlântico (Noll), 287
Hotel Lusitano (Zink), 350
The House on Mango Street (Cisneros), 14, 38, 43, 160
The House on the Lagoon (Ferré), 43
How the García Girls Lost Their Accents (Alvarez), 45, 94
Huasipungo (Icaza), 46, 253–54
Huerto cerrado (Bryce Echenique), 134
Hughes, Langston, 36
Huidobro, Montes, 43
Humo hacia el sur (Brunet), 133

Ibañez, Jaime, Columbian writer, 252
Ibargoyen, Saúl, Uruguayan writer, 252
Ibarguengoitia, Jorge, Mexican writer, 253
Iberia, 3
Icaza, Jorge, Ecuadorian writer, 46, 253–54
Idos de la mente (Crosthwaite), 172
La Ilaga (Casaccai), 151
Imaginacões (Ivo), 256
Immaculada, o los placeres de la inocencia (García Ponce), 222
Los Impacientes (Garcés), 218
La importancia de llamarse Daniel Santos (Sánchez, L.), 40, 314
Imposible equilibrio (Giardinelli), 229
Los impostores (Gamboa), 218
In the Castle of My Skin (Lamming), 254, 263
In the Time of the Butterflies (Alvarez), 94
El incendio y las vísperas (Guido), 238
Incidente em Antares (Vérissimo, E.), 341
Independence, novels about, 3–4
Indianismo, 255
Indicios pánicos (Peri Rossi), 294
Indigénisme movement: Caribbean, 36, 254; Haitian, 36, 91
Indigenismo, Spanish American, 254–55; Aguerdas and, 255; Castellanos and, 255
Indigenismo writing, 46, 89, 105–6, 151, 253, 281
Indigenista fiction, 46, 253, 255
Indo-Afro-Ibero America, 3
El infiltrado (Collyer), 163

The Infinite Rehearsals (Harris, W.), 242

Las iniciales de la tierra (Díez), 4, 184

El inocente (Ardiles Gray), 103

La insólita historia de la Santa de Cabora (Domecq), 187

Insônia (Ramos, G.), 15–16, 64

Instrucciones para cruzar la frontera (Crosthwaite), 172

La insurrección (Skármeta), 20

Intacto el corazón (Porzecanski), 297

Intramuros (Ramos, L.), 301

La invasión (Piglia), 295

La invención de Morel (Bioy Casares), 122

La invención del poder (Campbell), 144

Inventando que sueño (Agustín), 28, 38, 86, 255–56

La invitación (García Ponce), 221–22

Isabel entre las plantas (Canto), 145

Isla de Cundeamor (Vásquez Díaz), 256

Isla de lobos (Martín del Campo), 276

Islas, Arturo, 41

Ivo, Lêdo, Brazilian writer, 9, 256

Jacobs, Bárbara, Mexican writer, 256–57

Jamaica, 3, 257

Jandra, Leonardo Da, Mexican writer, 257–58

Jane and Louisa Will Soon Come Home (Brodber), 133, 258

Jaramillo Agudelo, Darío, Columbian writer, 258–59

El jardín de al lado (Donoso), 259

Los jardines secretos (Ruy Sánchez), 309

Las jiras (Arana), 103

Job-Boj (Guzmán, J.), 59

O Jogo de Ifá (Coutinho), 171

Johns, Per, Brazilian writer, 69, 259

Jóias de Família (Tavares), 328–29

Jorge, um Brasileiro (França), 209

José Reigo (Paso), 293–94

Joyce, James, influence of, 21–22, 39, 122

Juego de damas (Moreno Durán), 50–51, 282

Juego de pantallas (Eyherabide), 201

Juego florales (Pitol), 29

Los juegos (Avilés Fabila), 111

Los juegos verdaderos (Ríos), 4

Jugando a rumiarse el tiempo (Sánchez, J.), 314

Junto al paisaje (Ramos, L.), 301

Jurado, Alicia, Argentinian writer, 259–60

Júrame que te casaste virgen (Escalante), 198

Justicia de enero (Galindo), 215

Juyango (Ortiz), 290

Kalpa Imperial (Gorodischer), 234

Karenina express (Mansilla), 275

Kincaid, Jamaica, Caribbean writer, 260

Klail City y sus alrededores (Hinojosa), 19, 249

Kohan, Martin, Argentinian writer, 260

Korean Love Songs (Hinojosa), 249

Krauze, Ethel, Mexican writer, 260–61

Krik? Krak! (Danticat), 174

La Violencia, Columbia's, 6, 18, 48, 94, 100, 150, 182, 313, 350

El laberinto de sí mismo (Labrador Ruiz), 261

Los labios del agua (Ruy Sánchez), 309

Labirinto (Figueiredo, A.), 206

Labrador Ruiz, Enrique, Caribbean writer, 261

Laços de Familia (Lispector), 269

Os Ladrões (Guimarães), 238

Laferriére, Dany, Caribbean writer, 261–62

Lafourcade, Enrique, Chilean writer, 262

Lago, Sylvia, Uruguayan writer, 262–63

Lainez, Manuel Mujica, 57

L'allée des soupirs (Confiant), 165

Lamming, George, Caribbean writer, 8–9, 35, 37, 263

Lange, Norah, Argentinian writer, 263–64

Language: Caribbean fiction and, 35; Spanish speakers and, 160

Las lanzas coloradas (Uslar Pietri), 336

Lapsus (Manjarréz), 275

Lara Zavala, Hernán, Mexican writer, 264

Latin America: avant-garde of, 261; censorship in, 63, 65; colonial legacy of, 3, 73; cultural heritage of, 3; detective novels in, 175–76, 178–79; modernist aesthetics in, 7; novel of exile in, 8; politics and writing in, 4, 7, 65, 73, 101, 175; younger writers in, 67, 74

Lavoura Arcaica (Nassar), 285–86

The Law of love (Esquivel), 30, 199
Le discourse antillais (Glantz), 230
Lemebel, Pedro, 10
Leñero, Vicente, Mexican writer, 27, 264
León, Luis de, Guatemalan writer, 34
Levi Calderón, Sara, Mexican writer,
    189–90
Levinson, Luisa Mercedes, Argentinian
    writer, 265
Levya, Daniel, Mexican writer, 29–30, 265
La ley del amor (Esquivel), 199
La leyenda de los soles (Aridjis), 107
Leyendas de Guatemala (Asturias), 109
Lezama Lima, José, Cuban writer, 37–39,
    103, 265–66
Liano, Dante, Guatemalan writer, 34
Libertad en llamas (Guardia), 236
Libertella, Héctor, Aregentinian writer, 21,
    58–59, 266–67
El libro de las pasiones (González Suárez),
    233
El libro de los recuerdos (Shua), 321–22
El libro de mis primos (Peri Rossi), 294
O Libro do Avesso (Trevisan, J.), 335
Libro sin tapas (Hernández, F.), 246
La liebre (Aira), 87
Lihn, Enrique, Chilean writer, 59–60, 267
Limité Branco (Abreu), 78
Lindo, Hugo, El Salvadorian writer, 267
Lins, Osman, Brazilian writer, 19, 66,
    267–68
Lispector, Clarice, Brazilian writer, 5,
    12–13, 17–19, 66–67, 251, 268–70
Literatura de cordel, 334
Literatura light, 163, 193, 198–99, 303
La literatura nazi en América (Bolaño),
    124
Literatura testimonial. See Testimonios
Llamadas telefónicas (Bolaño), 124
Lo amodor (Burgos Cantor), 139
Lo anterior (Rivera Garza), 270
Loayza, Luis, Peruvian writer, 48–49
Lobato, Manoel, Brazilian writer, 270
La Loca 101 (Steimberg), 328
The Lonely Londoners (Selvon), 270, 319
O Longo Aprendizado (Figuiredo, A.), 206
Lopes, Moacir Costa, Brazilian writer, 66,
    270–71
Loubet, Jorgelina, Argentinian writer, 271

Louisa in Realityland (Alegría, Claribel),
    90
Louzada Filho, Oswaldo Carrêa, 65, 271
Loverboys (Castillo), 153
Loyola Brandão, Ignácio de, 22
Luces artificiales (Sada), 271–72, 311
Lucifer ha Ilorado (Estrázulas), 201
Luft, Lya, Brazilian writer, 272
El lugar donde crece la hierba (Hernández,
    L.), 246
Lumpérica (Eltit), 10, 60, 197
Luna caliente (Giardinelli), 229
Luna verde (Beleño), 117
La luz argentina (Aira), 87
A Luz do Dia (Louzada Filho), 271
Lynch, Marta, Argentinian writer, 272–73

Machismo: Mexican, 83, 86, 108; role of,
    100
Macunaíma (de Andrade), 66
Mad María (Souza), 326
Madero, el otro (Solares), 323
Madiedo, Rafael Chapparo, Columbian
    writer, 290
Madrigal en la ciudad (Gambardo), 217
Madrugada (Steen), 327
Maggiolo, Veloz, 41
La magica de la inmortalidad (Escalante),
    198
Magical realism, 273; novels of, 15–17, 20,
    50–51, 149–50, 187
Mainardi, Diogo, Brazilian writer, 71,
    273–74
Maíra (Ribeiro, D.), 304–5
Maitreya (Sarduy), 40, 316
A Majestade do Xingu (Scliar), 318
Mal de amores (Mastretta), 30, 277
La mala hora ((García Márquez)), 6, 220
Mala onda (Fuguet), 213
Maldito amor (Ferré), 205–6
Maldonado, José Caballos, Mexican writer,
    225
Maleita (Cardoso), 147
Malemort (Glantz), 231
Mallea, Eduardo, Argentinian writer, 57,
    274–75
Malthus (Mainardi), 273
The Mambo King Plays Songs of Love
    (Hijuelos), 247

Una manera de morir (Monteforte Toledo), 33

Manhattan Transfer (Dos Passos), 17

Manifestación de silencios (Azuela, A.), 20, 111

Las maniobras (Sánchez, H.), 313

Manjarréz, Héctor, Mexican writer, 275

Mansilla, Margarita, Mexican writer, 275

La mansión de Aracaíma (Mutis), 284

Mantra (Fresán), 211, 228

Maqroll el gaviero (Mutis), 284

A Máquina Extraviada (Veiga), 340

El mar bajo la tierra (Toscana), 334

El mar de las lentejas (Benítez Rojo), 43, 119, 275–76

Marechal, Leopoldo, Argentinian writer, 15, 56, 276

Margarita, está linda la mar (Ramírez, S.), 300

Maria de Cada Pôrto (Lopes), 271

María Luisa (Azuela, M.), 112

Mariátegui, José Carlos, neo-Marxist critic, 73

El marido perfecto (Escalante), 198

Marinheiro de Primeira Viagem (Lins), 268

Martín del Campo, David, Mexican writer, 276

Martínez Moreno, Carlos, Uruguayan writer, 277

Martínez, Tomás Eloy, Argentinian writer, 6, 276–77

Martinique, 235–36

Martinus Arion, Frank, Caribbean writer, 35, 194

Marzo anterior (Balza), 113

Más allá de las mascaras (Guerra), 237

La más fuerte pasión (Zapata, L.), 349

Massacre of the Dreamers: Reflections on Mexican-Indian Women in the United States Five Hundred Years After the Conquest (Castillo), 153

Massiani, Francisco, 52

Mastretta, Angeles, Mexican writer, 30, 32, 277–78

Le mât de Cocagne (Depestre), 177

El matemático (Azuela, A.), 112

Mateo el flautista (Duque López), 50, 52, 193

Matéria de Memória (Cony), 167

Matéria do cotidiano (Luft), 272

Matías no baja (Burel), 138

McOndo (Soldán and Fuguet), 23, 62, 117, 211, 214, 227, 232

McOndo group, 54, 124, 166, 210, 292, 333

Me llamo Rigoberta Menchú y así me nació la conciencia (Burgos and Menchú), 14, 114, 279; as *testimonios*, 330

Medina, Enrique, Argentinian writer, 129, 192, 278

Medo de Sade (Carvalho), 149

Medoza, Mario, Columbian writer, 54–55

Mejía Vallejo, Manuel, Columbian writer, 6, 17–18, 48, 182, 278

Mejor desaparece (Boullosa), 130

Melo, Batista, 72

Melo, Patrícia, Brazilian writer, 278–79

Memoria del fuego (Galeano), 215

Memorias de Altagracia (Gardea), 224

Memorias de los días (Palou), 292

Memorias de un semidiós (Libertella), 266

Memorias del nuevo mundo (Aridjis), 107

Memórias do Medo (Steen), 327

Memory Fever (Gonzalez), 279

Menchú, Rigoberta, Guatemalan writer, 14, 32, 34, 279

Méndez, Ariel, Uruguayan writer, 279

Méndez, Miguel, Chicano writer, 19

Mendoza, Mario, Columbian writer, 279–80

Mene (Díaz Sánchez), 185

Menina a Caminho (Nassar), 286

Mentira dos Limpos (Lobato), 270

Mercado, Tununa, Argentinian writer, 9

Mestizo writer, 288

Metatrón (Giraldo), 54

Mexican Miracle, 6–7, 24–26

Mexican Revolution, novels about, 3–4, 24–26, 112, 207–8

Mexicanidad, 258

Mexico: colonial legacy of, 3; detective novels of, 180, 183, 186, 250, 264, 294, 309, 328; *Generación del Crack in*, 98; *machismo* of, 83, 86, 108; *modernismo* of, 336; novel of social protest in, 327; politics in, 6, 12, 15, 24–26, 30, 144; postmodern writing in, 51, 200, 240, 265, 291. *See also* La Onda; Tlatelolco massacre

Mi querido Rafa (Hinojosa), 249

Mi revolver es más largo que el tuyo (Duque López), 193

El miedo de perder a Eurídice (Campos), 145

Mientros ca la noche (Prada Oropeza), 53

Migo (Ribeiro, D.), 305

Migrant Souls (Islas), 41

Mil y una muertes (Ramírez, S.), 300

La milagrosa (Boullosa), 30, 130

Minhas Mulheres e Meus Homens (Prata), 298–99

Minhas Vidas Passadas (Prata), 298–99

Mir, Pedro, 42

Miranda, Ana, Brazilian writer, 280

Mirisolo, Marcelo, 72

Misiá señora (Angel), 100

O Mistério da Samanbaia (Figueiredo, R.), 206

The Mixquihuala Letters (Castillo), 14, 153

Modernismo: Brazilian, 280–81; Mexican, 336

Modernist writing, 15–22, 26–27, 32–33, 41–44, 46; Andean region, 47; Caribbean, 37; Puerto Rican, 38–39; in southern cone region, 56

Modernistas, 219

Moi, Tituba, sorciére . . . noire de Salem (Condé), 164

Molloy, Sylvia, Argentinian feminist writer, 11, 13, 197–98, 281

Mongólia (Carvalho), 149

Monkey Hunting (García, C.), 219

Monteforte Toledo, Mario, Guatemalan writer, 32, 281–82

Montello, Josué, Brazilian writer, 282

Montero, Marya, Puerto Rican writer, 42–43

Montés, José W., 53

Morales, Mario Robert, Guatemalan writer, 34, 282

Moreno Durán, R. H., Columbian writer, 50, 282–83

Morirás lejos (Pacheco), 27, 291

A Morte de D.J. em Paris (Drummond), 192

Morte na Praça (Trevisan, D.), 335

Moscovich, Cíntia, Brazilian writer, 283

Moses Ascending (Selvon), 319

Moses Migrating (Selvon), 319

MRTA. *See* Peruvian Tupac Amaru Revolutionary Movement

Las muertas (Ibarguengoitia), 253

La muerte de Alec (Agudelo), Columbian writer, 51, 258

La muerte de Artemio Cruz (Fuentes, C.), 4, 17, 24–25, 27, 101, 212

Muito Prazer (Denser), 176

La mujer desnuda (Sommers), 324

Una mujer en la cama y otros cuentos (Obligado), 288

La mujer fragmentada: historia de un signo (Guerra), 236

La mujer habitada (Belli), 32, 118

Las mujeres de Adriano (Aguilar Camín), 83

Mujeres de Babel (Moreno Durán), 282

Mujica Lainez, Manuel, Argentinian writer, 283–84

Mulher no Espelho (Parente Cunha), 68

O Mulo (Ribeiro, D.), 304–5

El mundo alucinante (Arenas), 104

El mundo es ancho y ajeno (Alegría, Ciro), 46, 89–90

Mundo Neuvo, 127

Un mundo para Julius (Bryce Echenique), 53, 134

Mundos Mortos (Faria), 202

Muñeca brava (Guerra), 237

Muñiz-Huberman, Angelina, Mexican writer, 28–30, 284

Murámanos Federico (Gutiérrez), 239

Murena, Héctor A., Argentinian writer, 284

El muro de mármol (Canto), 145

El museo de los esfuerzos inútiles (Peri Rossi), 294

Músicos y relojeros (Steimberg), 328

Mutis, Alvaro, Columbian writer, 16, 284–85

My Invented Country (Allende), 93

Myal (Brodber), 133

Nada, nadie (Poniatowska), 30

Nadie encendía las lámparas (Hernández, F.), 246

Nadie me verá llorar (Rivera Garza), 23, 31, 306

Não verás país nenhúm (Loyola Brandão), 22, 67, 131

Naranjo, Carmen, Costa Rican writer, 34, 285

Nascimento, Esdras do, 64; Brazilian writer, 285

Nassar, Raduan, 285–86

Natives of My Person (Lamming), 263

La nave de los locos (Peri Rossi), 294–95

O Navegante de Opereta (Johns), 259

Le nègre e l'Amiral (Confiant), 165

Négritude movement, 5, 35, 165, 235

Ni tú ni yo ni nadie (Company), 164

Nicaragua, 90, 300

Niets Wat Pijn Doet (Roemer), 286, 306

Niggli, Josephina, 45

Ningún reloj cuenta esto (Rivera Garza), 306

Ninho de cobras (Ivo), 9, 256

Los niños se despiden (Fernández, P.), 38

No te duermas, no me dejes (Lynch), 273

No telephone to Heaven (Cliff), 162

No todos los hombres son románticos (Manjarréz), 275

La noche abierta (Buttazoni), 139

Una noche con Iris Chacón (Rodríguez Juliá), 41

La noche de Tlatelolco (Poniatowska), 13, 26

La noche del día menos pensado (Galmes), 217

La noche oscura del Niño (Rodríguez Juliá), 41

Las noches de Carmen Miranda (Guerra), 10, 237

Nocturno de Chile (Bolaño), 124–25, 286–87

Uma Noite em Curitiba (Tezza), 330

Noll, João Gilberto, 68, 120, 155, 287

Nolla, Olga, Puerto Rican writer, 42–43

Los nombres del aire (Ruy Sánchez), 309

O Nome do Bispo (Tavares), 328

Um Nome para Matar (Barroso), 116

Nostalgia de Troya (Hernández, L.), 246

Noticia de un secuestro (García Márquez), 220

Noticias del Imperio (Paso), 293–94

Nouveau roman, 271

Nove Noites (Carvalho), 23, 149

Nove, novena (Lins), 268

Novela con fantasma (Jaramillo Agudelo), 258

Novela de espectáculo, 129

La novela de Perón (Martínez), 6

Una novela erótica (Porzecanski), 297

Novela negra con argentinos (Valenzuela), 337–38

Una novela que comienza (Fernández, M.), 203–4

Novelas gaseiformes, 261

Novelas nada Exemplares (Trevisan, D.), 335

Una novelita lumpen (Bolaño), 125

Un noviazgo (Verbitsky), 56, 341

El noviembre no llega el arzobispo (Rojas Herazo), 307

Os Novos (Vilela), 342

Nueva Generación, 141

Obligado, Clara, Argentinian writer, 287–88

El obsceno párajo de la noche (Donoso), 18, 59, 188

Obsesivos días circulares (Sainz), 312

La ocasión (Saer), 311

L'Odeur de Café (Laferriére), 262

Oficio de difuntos (Uslar Pietri), 336–37

Oficio de tinieblas (Castellano), 18, 25, 151–52, 255

O Olhar (Santiago), 315

Oliveira, Nelson de, Brazilian writer, 71, 227, 288

Omeros (Walcott), 345–46

Once días . . . y algo más (Domecq), 187

La Onda, 20, 51, 67, 86, 102–3, 142, 174, 222, 226, 229–30, 275, 312, 334

Onda y escritura en México (Glantz), 229

Onde Andará Dulce Veiga (Abreu), 79

Onetti, Juan Carlos, Uruguayan writer, 16–17, 56, 109, 288–90

Onze (Carvalho), 148

Op Oloop (Filloy), 207

Operación massacre (Walsh), 330, 346

Opio en las nubes (Madiedo), 290

Oppiano Licario (Lezama Lima), 266

Oreamuno, Yoland, Costa Rican writer, 170, 290

La orquesta de cristal (Lihn), 267

Ortiz, Adalberto, Ecuadorian writer, 290

Ostornol, Antonio, Chilean writer, 62

A Ostra e o Vento (Lopes), 271

Otero, Lisandro, Cuban writer, 36–38, 42

Otero Silva, Miguel, Venezuelan writer, 6, 16, 48, 290–91

Otilia Rauda (Galindo), 20, 216

El otoño del patriarca (García Márquez), 6–7, 172, 185, 220

La otra gente (Buitrago), 137

La otra orilla (Cortázar), 169

Otra vez al mar (Arenas), 104

Pacheco, José Emilio, Mexican writer, 27, 32, 98, 291

Padilla, Ignacio, Mexican writer, 98, 291–92

Páginas de vuelta (Gamboa), 218

O País do Carnival (Amado), 95

País portátil (González León), 12, 232–33

Paiva, Marcelo Rubens, 70, 292

Paixão bem Temperada (Nascimento), 285

A Paixão Segundo G.H. (Lispector), 18

Pájaros de la playa (Sarduy), 316

El palacio de las blanquísimas mofetas (Arenas), 104

Los palacios desiertos (Hernández, L.), 246

Palinuro en México (Paso), 293

Pallotini, Renata, Brazilian writer, 292

Palmério, Mário, Brazilian writer, 292

Palomita blanca (Lafourcade), 262

Palou, Pedro Angel, Mexican writer, 292–93

Panama, 236

Los pañamanes (Buitrago), 13, 53

Pánico o peligro (Puga), 29

Pantaleón y las visitadoras (Vargas Llosa), 8

Pantalones azules (Gallardo), 216

Papeles de recienvenido (Fernández, M.), 203

Para leer al Pato Donald (Dorfman), 189

Para subir al cielo (Lafourcade), 262

Os Paraceres do Tempo (Sales), 312

Paradiso (Lezama Lima), 37, 265–66

Paraguay, 8, 151, 306

Paraíso 25 (Spota), 326

Paredes, Américo, Chicano writer, 228

El paredón (Martínez Moreno), 277

Parétesis (Wacquez), 345

La parole des femmes: Essai sur les romanciéres des Antilles de langue française (Condé), 164

Parra Sandoval, Rodrigo, Columbian writer, 52, 293

Partido Revolucionario Institucional (PRI), Mexican, 12, 24–26

Partners in Crime: A Rafe Buenrostro Mystery (Hinojosa), 249

Paso, Fernando del, Mexican writer, 293–94

Los pasos perdidos (Carpentier), 16

Pasto verde (García Saldaña), 222

Patán, Frederico, Mexican writer, 9, 29–30, 32, 294

Patas de perro (Droguett), 191

Paula (Allende), 93

La paz del pueblo (Duncan), 194

Paz, Senel, 43

Los peces (Fernández, S.), 205

Los pecios y los náufragos (Sánchez, J.), 314

Pedro Páramo (Rulfo), 16, 26–27, 308–9

Las peliculas de mi vida (Fuguet), 214

Pena de muerte (Lafourcade), 262

El penúltimo (Diaconú), 182–83

Los pequeños seres (Garmendia), 18, 223

Percusión (Balza), 113

Perder es cuestión de miedo (Gamboa), 218

Peregrinos de Aztlán (Méndez, M.), 19

Perfumes de Cartago (Porzecanski), 297

Peri Rossi, Cristina, Uruguayan writer, 61, 294–95

Permiso para vivir: antimemorias (Bryce Echenique), 134

Perón, Juan Domingo, 6, 55–56, 105, 238, 284

Perros heroes (Bellatín), 117

Persona non grata (Edwards), 195

Personas en pose de combate (Libertella), 266

Perto do Coração Selvagem (Lispector), 15, 64, 269

Peru: Jewish diaspora in, 54; leadership of, 6, 49–50, 167; novels about, 17, 105–6; postmodern writing in, 52–53

Peruvian Tupac Amaru Revolutionary Movement (MRTA), 90

A pesar del oscuro silencio (Volpi), 344

El peso de la noche (Edwards), 195
La piel del cielo (Poniatowska), 30–31
Los pies de barro (Gardea), 224
Piglia, Ricardo, Argentinian writer, 4,
    10–12, 21–22, 74, 295, 303
Pilotos (Cony), 167
Una piñata Ilena de memoria (Levya), 30
Pinheiro, Mauro, 71
Piñón, Nélida, Brazilian writer, 18, 295–96
Pitol, Sergio, Mexican writer, 28–29, 296
Pizarnik, Alejandro, 11
El plan infinito (Allende), 93
Plata quemada (Piglia), 295
Plataforma Vazia (Barreto), 115–16
The Pleasures of Exile (Lamming), 263
Pluie et vent sur Telumeé Miracle
    (Schwarz-Bart), 317
Pocho (Villarreal), 17, 46
Poética de Romance: Matéria de
    Carpintaria (Dourado), 190
Poétique de la relation (Glantz), 230
Polígano das Secas (Mainardi), 273–74
Polvos de arroz (Galindo), 215
Ponce de León, Baccino, 61
Ponce, May Helen, 41
Poniatowska, Elena, Mexican writer,
    12–13, 17, 30, 32, 297
Por favor, rebobinar (Fuguet), 213–14
Por la patria (Eltit), 10–11
Por los tiemps de Clemente Colling
    (Hernández, F.), 246
Porão e Sobrado (Telles), 329
Porfiriato, 24–25
Porque hay silencio (Ambert), 97
Porque parece metira la verdad nunca se
    sabe (Sada), 311
Portugal, 3
El porvenir de un pasado (Benedetti), 119
Porzecanski, Teresa, Uruguayan writer,
    297
Os Posseiros (Barroso), 116
Post-abertura. See Post-Boom novel
Post-Boom novel, 18–21, 30–34, 66, 69,
    127, 134, 228–29, 322; in Andean
    region, 53–54; in Brazil, 70–72;
    definition of, 297–98; detective novel as,
    44; exile, 12, 61–62; in Southern cone
    region, 61; women writers of, 12–13,
    42–44; writers of, 42, 50, 61–62, 187

Postmodern novel: Andean region, 50–51;
    Argentinian, 21–22, 50, 58–59, 98, 122,
    266; Brazilian, 66–68, 70, 101, 131, 155,
    315, 325–26; Caribbean, 39–41, 165,
    262; Central American, 33; Chilean, 60,
    74; Columbian, 51, 193; Cuban, 37;
    definition of, 298; detective, 186; Haitian,
    41; Mexican, 27–32, 51, 143–44, 200,
    240, 265, 291; Peruvian, 52–53; Puerto
    Rican, 40; of resistance, 210; southern
    cone region, 58, 61; Uruguayan, 60–61,
    186; Venezuelan, 52, 112
Post-postmodern writers, 54, 213, 227
Praça Mauá (Carvalho-Neto), 149
Prada Oropeza, Renato, Bolivian writer, 53
Prado, Adélia, Brazilian writer, 298
Prata, Mario, Brazilian writer, 139, 298–99
O Prazer é Todo Meu (Denser), 176
Los premios (Cortázar), 17
Pretexta (Campbell), 144
PRI. *See* Partido Revolucionario
    Institucional
Price-Mars, Jean, *indigénisme* movement
    leader, 36
Prieto, José Manuel, 44
Primera parte (Fuguet), 214
La princesa del Palacio de Hierro (Sainz),
    20
Prisión perpetua (Piglia), 295
Prova Contrária (Bonasi), 126
Puerrtorriqueños: Album de la sagrada
    familia puertorriqueña (Rodríguez
    Juliá), 306
Puertas al cielo (Solares), 323
Puerto Limón (Gutiérrez), 33, 239
Puerto Rico: colonial legacy of, 3;
    immigrants from, 38; modernist fiction
    in, 38; postmodern fiction of, 40
Puga, María Luisa, 29
Puig, Manuel: Argentinian writer, 17, 21,
    120–21, 127–28, 136, 225–26, 299;
    postmodern writing of, 59
Puppet (Cota-Cárdenas), 14

Qadós (Hilst), 248
O Quarto Fechado (Luft), 272
Quarup (Callado), 143
Quase Memória (Cony), 168
Os Que Bebem Como as Cães (Brasil), 65

¡Qué viva la música! (Caicedo), 51–52, 142
Queiroz, Rachel de, Brazilian writer, 299
Querido Diego, te abraza Quiela
    (Poniatowska), 13
Querido traidor (Vásquez Díaz), 340
Quesada, Roberto, Honduran writer,
    299–300
Quién de nosotros? (Benedetti), 118
O Quieto Animal da Esquina (Noll), 287
O Quinze (Queiroz), 299

Rain of Gold (Villaseñor), 41–42
A Rainha dos Cárceres da Grécia (Lins), 268
Raining Backwards (Fernández, R.), 204
Ramírez, Armando, 20
Ramírez, Sergio, Nicaraguan writer,
    32–33, 300, 324–25
Ramos, Franco, 55
Ramos, Graciliano, Brazilian writer, 15,
    300–301
Ramos, Luis Arturo, 28–30, 32, 301
Rangel, Paulo, 179
Rastro do Verão (Noll), 287
Rayuela (Cortázar), 14, 21, 30, 51, 53, 58,
    66, 169, 211, 268, 298
Realist writing, 63–65, 112, 116
Rebanho de Odio (Sales), 312
La rebelión Pocomia (Duncan), 193–94
Recabarren (Alegría, F.), 91
Rechy, John, 161
Recuento de incertidumbre: cultura y
    transición en El Salvador (Castellanos
    Moya), 152
El recuento de los daños (Chacón), 155
Los recuerdos del porvenir (Garro), 18, 26,
    225
El recurso del Método (Carpentier), 7, 42,
    302
Reflexos de Baile (Callado), 143
La región más transparente (Fuentes, C.), 7,
    16, 26–27, 212
Rêgo, José Lins de, Brazilian writer, 15,
    63–64, 302–3
El reino de este mundo (Carpentier), 15–16,
    37, 148
Los relámpagos de agosto (Ibarguengoitia),
    253
Relato de Navidad en la Gran Vía (Silva),
    322

Relato de um certo oriente (Hatoum), 186,
    243–44
Relógio Belisario (Veiga), 340
La renuncia de héroe Baltasar (Rodríguez
    Juliá), 41, 306
A Republica dos Sonhos (Piñón), 296
Requiem por un suicida (Avilés Fabila), 111
Resistance: language and, 11; novels of,
    10–12, 30, 61, 337; postmodern writing
    of, 210
A Resistível Ascensão do Boto Tucaxi
    (Souza), 326
Respiración artificial (Piglia), 4–11, 59, 295,
    303
Respirando el verano (Rojas Herazo), 307
El resplandor de la madera (Aguilar
    Camín), 83
Restrepo, Laura, Columbian writer, 47,
    193, 303
Un retrato para Dickens (Sommers), 325
The Revolt of the Cockroach People
    (Acosta), 79
Revueltas, José, Mexican writer, 303–4
El rey criollo (García Saldaña), 222
Rey del albor, Madrugada (Escoto), 33
Rey Rosa, Rodrigo, Guatemalan writer,
    304
Reynoso, Oswaldo, Peruvian writer,
    48–49
Rhys, Jean, Caribbean writer, 346
Ribeiro, Carlos, Brazilian writer, 304
Ribeiro, Darcy, Brazilian writer, 304–5
Ribeiro, João Ubaldo, 70, 96
Ribeyro, Julio Ramón, Peruvian writer,
    48–49, 305
The Rigoberto Menchú Controversy (Arias),
    107
El rigor de las desdichas (Sorrentino), 325
El río del tiempo (Vallejo), 338
O Rio do Meio (Luft), 272
Ríos, Edmundo de los, Peruvian writer, 4
Los Ríos profundos (Arguedas), 105, 255
Risco de Vida (Guzik), 226
O Risonho Cavalo do Príncipe (Veiga), 340
Rites and Witnesses (Hinojosa), 249
Rivera Garza, Cristina, Mexican writer,
    22–23, 31, 270, 305–6
Rivera, Tomás: Chicano writer, 19, 39;
    post-Boom writer, 42

Roa Bastos, Augusto, Paraguayan writer, 8, 57, 306

Rodríguez Juliá, Edgardo, Puerto Rican writer, 40–41, 306

Roemer, Astrid, Caribbean writer, 3, 42, 286, 306–7

Rojas Herazo, Héctor, Columbian writer, 307

Las rojas son las carreteras (Martín del Campo), 276

Rojos, Manuel, 57

Um Romance de Geração (Sant'Anna), 314–15

Romance nordestino, 192

Rosario Tijeras (Franco), 55, 210

Rosaura a las diez (Denevi), 175–76

Rossi, Alejandro, 52

Roumain, Jacques, 36

Royal Circo (Barletta), 114

Rubião, Murilo, Brazilian writer, 308

Rulfo, Juan, Mexican writer, 5, 16, 308–9

La ruta de su evasión (Oreamuno), 170

Rutilo Nada (Hilst), 248

Ruy Sánchez, Alberto, Mexican writer, 309

Sábato, Ernesto, Argentinian writer, 78, 88, 309–10

Sabino, Fernando Tavares, Brazilian writer, 310–11

Sada, Daniel, Mexican writer, 271–72, 311

Saer, Juan José, Argentinian writer, 311

Sainz, Gustavo, 20, 27–28, 32, 311–12

Salazar Bondy, Sebastían, Peruvian writer, 312

Sales, Herberto, Brazilian writer, 312

Salinger, J. D., 86

Salón de belleza (Bellatín), 117

O Salto do Cavalo Cobridor (Brasil), 131

Salvador, Humberto, Ecuadorian writer, 313

Samudio, Alvaro Cepeda, Colombian writer, 150

Sanar tu piel amarga (Volpi), 344

Sánchez (Yoss), José Miguel, Caribbean writer, 314

Sánchez, Héctor, Columbian writer, 313

Sánchez, Luis Rafael, Puerto Rican writer, 22, 39–40, 313–14

Sánchez, Néstor, Caribbean writer, 21, 314

La sangre hambrienta (Labrador Ruiz), 261

La sangre interminable (Ibargoyen), 252–53

Sangue de Coca-Cola (Drummond), 192

Santa Anna, 320

Santa Evita (Martínez), 276–77

Santa Maria del Circo (Toscana), 333

Sant'Anna, Sérgio, Brazilian writer, 67–68, 314–15

Santiago, Silviano, Brazilian writer, 9, 315

Santo oficio de la memoria (Giardinelli), 229

Santos-Febres, Mayra, Puerto Rican writer, 315–16

Sarah e os Anjos (Bins), 121

Sarduy, Severo, Cuban writer, 21, 39, 162, 316–17

Sartre, Jean Paul, 16, 73

Satanás (Mendoza), 279–80

Schwarz-Bart, Simone, Caribbean writer, 317

Scliar, Moacir, Brazilian writer, 70, 72, 132, 154, 200, 317–18

Season of Adventure (Lamming), 263

El Seductor de la patria (Serna), 320

Segundo sueño (Fernández, S.), 205

Selvon, Samuel, Caribbean writer, 270, 318–19

Sem Pecado (Miranda), 280

La semana de colores (Garro), 224

Sempreviva (Callado), 143

O Senhor Embaixador (Vérissimo, E.), 341

A Senhorita Simpson (Sant'Anna), 315

El Señor Presidente (Asturias), 7–8, 15, 26, 33, 109–10, 185, 319–20

La señora (Diaconú), 182

La señora de la Fuente y otras parábolas de fin de siglo (Ramos, L.), 29

La señora en su balcón (Garro), 224

Señora Honeycomb (Buitrago), 137

Sepúlveda, Luis, Chilean writer, 20, 320

Serialized novel, 127

Serna, Enrique, Mexican writer, 320–21

La serpiente de oro (Alegría, Ciro), 89–90

Serrano, Marcela, Chilean writer, 321

Os Servos da Morte (Filho), 207

Sesenta muertos en la escalera (Droguett), 191

Sete Anos de Pastor (Trevisan, D.), 334

Shadows Round the Moon (Heath), 245

Shaman Winter (Anaya), 321

Shaw, Donald, 19–20

Shua, Ana María, Argentinian writer, 321–22

"*Si me permiten hablar . . .* " (Barrios), 14

Siberia Blues (Sánchez, N.), 21, 314

Siete lunas, siete serpientes (Aguilera Malta), 84

Siete noches (Zapata, L.), 349

El siglo de las luces (Carpentier), 81, 148

El silenciero (Di Benedetto), 181

El sillón del águila (Fuentes, C.), 141

Silva, Abel, Brazilian writer, 322

Silva, Ricardo, Columbian writer, 322

Silviano, Santiago, Brazilan writer, 68

Simulacros (Sant'Anna), 314

Sin nada entre las manos (Sánchez, H.), 313

Síndrome de naufragios (Glantz), 230

Sinfonía del nuevo mundo (Espinosa), 198–99

Os Sinos da Agonia (Dourado), 190

Sirena Selena vestida de pena (Santos-Febres), 316

El sitio (Solares), 323–24

La situación (Otero), 36–38

Skármeta, Antonio, Chilean writer, 19, 22, 61–62, 123–24, 135, 322–23

Slave Song (Dadydeen), 173

A Small Place (Kincaid), 260

So Far from God (Castillo), 323

Sobre heroes y tumbas (Sábato), 310

Sobredosis (Fuguet), 213

Sobrepunto (Naranjo), 34

Sobrevivo (Alegría, Claribel), 90

Sodoma está Velha (Brasil), 131

O Sofoco, 65

Sol de medianoche (Rodríguez Juliá), 306

El sol que estás mirando (Gardea), 223

Solares, Ignacio, Mexican writer, 10, 12, 25, 28–30, 32, 323–24

Soldán, Edmundo Paz, 54–55, 125

Soleil de la conscience (Glantz), 230

Solidão em Família (Nascimento), 285

Solo en la obscuridad (Díaz Eterovic), 184

Sólo los elefantes encuentran mandrágora (Sommers), 325

Sombras nada más (Ramírez, S.), 324

Something to Declare (Alvarez), 93

Sommers, Armonía, Uruguayan writer, 61, 324–25

Son vacas, somos puercos (Boullosa), 130

El soñador de Smith (Goloboff), 231–32

Sonata ao Luar (Trevisan, D.), 334

Soñé que la nieve ardía (Skármeta), 322

Soriano, Osvaldo, Argentinian writer, 325

Sorrentino, Fernando, Argentinian writer, 325

Soto, Pedro Juan, Puerto Rican writer, 37–38, 325

Southern cone region: modernist fiction in, 56; politics in, 55–56; post-Boom writers in, 61; postmodern fiction in, 58, 61

Souza, Márcio, Brazilian writer, 68, 325–26

Soy paciente (Shua), 321

Spain, 3

Spiks (Soto), 38, 325

Spiralisme, 210

Spota, Luis, Mexican writer, 26, 326–27

Steen, Edna Va, Brazilian writer, 327

Steimberg, Alicia, Argentinian writer, 327–28

Stella (Dergeaud), 241

Stella Manhattan (Santiago), 9, 68, 315

A Suavidade do Vento (Tezza), 330

Subterráneos (Padilla), 291

Sudeste (Conti), 166

La sueñera (Shua), 321

Sueño de lobos (Ubidia), 336

Sueños del seductor abandonado (Borinsky), 129–30

Las suicidas (Di Benedetto), 181

Suriname, 3

El Sustituto (Mazzanti), 57

Taibo II, Paco Ignacio, Mexican writer, 183, 328

Un tal José Salomé (Azuela, A.), 20, 111

El tamaño del infierno (Azuela, A.), 20, 111

Os Tambores Silenciosos (Guimarães), 239

Os Tambosres de São Luís (Montello), 282

Tango Fantasma (Denser), 176

Tango para intelectuales (Estrázulas), 201

Tarzán y el filóso desnudo (Parra Sandoval), 293

Tavares, Zulmira Ribeiro, Brazilian writer, 328

Um Taxi para Viena d'Austria (Torres), 332

Tebas do Meu Coração (Piñón), 296

Teia (Dourado), 190

La tejadora de coronas (Espinosa), 198

Teléfono ocupado (Bullrich), 137–38

Telles, Lygia Fagundes, Brazilian writer, 66, 329

El temperamento melancólico (Volpi), 344

O Tempo e o Vento (Vérissimo, E.), 341

Terciopelo violeta (Galindo), 20

Tereza Batista cansada de guerra (Amado), 19

Terra Nostra (Fuentes, C.), 27–29, 144, 212

Testimonios, 329–30; Argentinian, 346; Caribbean, 39; Colombian, 284; Cuban, 114–15, 121, 330; El Salvadoran, 106, 181–82; Honduran, 97; women writers and, 13–14, 187, 225

Texaco (Charmoiseau), 156

Tezza, Cristovão, Brazilian writer, 330–31

Theoretical Fables (Borinsky), 129

O 35 Ano de Inês (Fallace), 201–2

La tía Julia y el escribidor (Vargas Llosa), 339

Tiempo al tiempo (Goldemberg), 231

Tierra de la memoria (Hernández, F.), 246

Tierra de leones (García Aguilar), 219

Tierra de nadie (Onetti), 289, 331

Tierra en la boca (Martínez Moreno), 277

La tierra éramos nosotros (Mejía Vallejo), 278

Tierra mojado (Zapata Olivella), 350

Ti-Jean L'horizon (Schwarz-Bart), 317

Tijolo de Seguranca (Cony), 167

Tijuanenses (Campbell), 144

Tinísima (Poniatowska), 30

Tinta roja (Fuguet), 213

¿Tio dio miedo la sangre? (Ramírez, S.), 300

Tipocoque: estampas de provincia (Caballero Calderón), 140

Tiro na emória (Nascimento), 285

El titiritero (Alvarez Gardeazábal), 95

Tizón, Héctor, Argentinian writer, 331

Tlatelolco massacre, 24–25, 28–29

Toda la luz del mediodía (Wacquez), 345

Toda la tierra (Ibargoyen), 252

Todas las sangres (Arguedas), 105, 331–32

Todo lo de las focas (Campbell), 144

Todo verdor perecerá (Mallea), 274

Todos estábamos a la espera (Cepeda Samudio), 154

Tonito de Bryce, 134

Toque de Diana (Moreno-Durán), 51

Torres, Antônio, Brazilian writer, 332–33

Tortuga (Anaya), 99

Toscana, David, Mexican writer, 22–23, 31, 200, 227–28, 333

Tovar, Juan, Mexican writer, 333–34

Tradition, Writer and Society (Harris, W.), 242

Trágame tierra (Chávez Alfaro), 157

La traición de Rita Hayworth (Puig), 21, 59, 128, 225, 299, 334

Trajano (Lago), 262–63

La tregua (Benedetti), 118–19

Treinta años (Boullosa), 334

Trejo, Oswaldo, Venezuelan writer, 52

Tremor de Terra (Vilela), 342

Tres ejercicios narrativos (Balza), 113

Tres tristes tigres (Cabrera Infante), 4, 21, 36, 39, 142

Trevisan, Dalton Jérson, Brazilian writer, 334–35

Trevisan, João Silverio, Brazilian writer, 335

Triángulos das Aguas (Abreu), 79

Las tribulaciones de Jonás (Rodríguez Juliá), 40, 306

Trinidad, 250, 319

Trujillo, Henry, Uruguayan writer, 228

El túnel (Sábato), 310

Turn Again Tiger (Selvon), 319

Ubico, Jorge, 5, 8

Ubidia, Abdón, Ecuadorian writer, 52, 335–36

La última niebla (Bombal), 125–26

La última noche de Dostoievky (Peri Rossi), 295

A última Quimera (Miranda), 280

Ultimo exilio (Patán), 29–30, 294

El ultimo juego (Guardia), 236

Ultimos días de la victimia (Feinman), 202

Ultimos trenes (Padilla), 291

Ultraísta (Fernández, M.), 203

Ultraísta movement, 203

Ultravocal (Frankétienne), 11, 210

A un costado de los rieles (Tizón), 331

Unión (García Ponce), 221

United Fruit Company, 5, 7, 32

Urrea, Luis Alberto, Chicano writer, 336

Urrea, Teresa, 187

Uruguay: detective novels of, 186; generation of forty-five in, 118; novels of, 109, 139, 166; postmodern writers of, 60–61, 186

Uslar Pietri, Arturo, Venezuelan writer, 336–37

Usmaíl (Soto), 38, 325

Valcárel, Emilio Díaz, 37–38

Valdés, Zoé, Cuban writer, 4, 9, 35, 44–45, 337

Valenzuela, Luisa, Argentinian writer, 12–13, 62, 337

Vallejo, Fernando, Columbian writer, 47, 226, 338, 343

The Valley (Hinijosa), 249

Valverde, Umberto, 52

El vampiro de la colonia Roma (Zapata, L.), 349

Van Steen, Edna, 112–13

Vanguardia, 128

Vargas, Getúlio, 5

Vargas Llosa, Mario: dictator novel by, 185–86; Peruvian writer, 5–8, 16–17, 22, 49, 150–51, 161, 166–67, 338–39; politics of, 73; postmodern works by, 53

Variaciones en rojo (Walsh), 346

Variante Gotemburgo (Nascimento), 285

Vásquez Díaz, René, Cuban writer, 45, 256, 340

Vasquez, Juan Gabriel, Columbian writer, 339–40

Vásquez, Miguel Angel, Guatemalan writer, 34

Vastos Emocões e Pensamentos Imperfeitos (Fonseca), 208

Veiga, José J., Brazilian writer, 240, 251–52

Las venas abiertas de América Latina (Galeano), 215

Venezuela: politics in, 6–7, 12, 185, 337; postmodern fiction in, 52, 112

Verbitsky, Bernardo, Argentinian writer, 56, 340–41

A Verdade de Cada Dia (Cony), 167

A Verdadeira Vida do Irmão Leovelfildo (Lobato), 270

Verges, Pedro, 42

Veríssimo, Erico, Brazilian writer, 341

Vérissimo, Luis Fernando, 179

Viaje al corazón del día (Sommers), 325

El viaje triunfal (García Aguilar), 219

La vida a plazos de don Jacobo Lerner (Goldemberg), 54, 231

Um Vida am Segredo (Dourado), 190

La vida breve (Onetti), 16–17, 56, 289

Vida con mi amigo (Jacobs), 257

La vida es un especial (Fernández, R.), 204

La vida que se va (Leñero), 264–65

Vidas ejemplares (Gómez), 232

Vidas Secas (Ramos, G.), 301

Un viejo que leía novelas de amor (Sepúlveda), 320

Los viejos aesinos (Ramos, L.), 301

Vila dos Confines (Palmério), 292

Vilela, Luiz, Brazilian writer, 341–42

Villa, Francisco "Pancho," 24

Villa miseria también es América (Verbitsky), 341

Villarreal, José Antonio, 17, 39, 45

Villaseñor, Victor, 41–42

Villoro, Juan, Mexican writer, 342

Viñas, David, Argentinian writer, 16–17, 56, 342–43

Violeta-Peru (Ramos, L.), 301

La virgen de los sicarios (Vallejo), 338, 343

O Visitante (Lins), 268

Visitas después de hora (Giardinelli), 229

La víspera del hombre (Marqués), 38

Viviendo (Peri Rossi), 294

Vivir para contarla (García Márquez), 221

Volpi, Jorge, Mexican writer, 22–23, 31, 98, 344–45

Volver (Condé), 165

La vorágine (Rivera) *The Vortex*, 5

Voyeurs (Andrés), 45

La voz adolorida (Leñero), 264

Voz de vida (Lange), 264

Wacquez, Mauricio, Chilean writer, 60, 345
Walcott, Derek, Caribbean writer, 345–46
Walsh, Rodolfo, 330, 346
War of the Saints (Amado), 95
The Wedding (Ponce), 42
Wide Sargasso Sea (Rhys), 346
Women Hollering Creek and Other Stories (Cisneros), 160
Women writers, 125–26, 130, 153; Andean region, 47; Argentinian, 105, 137–38, 145, 197–98, 245, 263–64, 281, 287–88; Brazilian, 69, 159, 171, 176, 268–69; Caribbean, 171, 242, 250, 346; Central American, 82, 236–37; Chicano, 146; Chilean, 172–73; Columbian, 99–100, 136–37; Costa Rican, 285, 290; detective novels by, 201, 278–79; Ecuadorian, 348–49; Francophone, 164; generation of the 1990s, 347–48; Latina, 42, 45, 152, 160; Mexican, 18, 26, 151, 199–200, 229–30, 297; post-Boom, 12–13, 42–44; *testimonios* by, 13–14, 187, 225. *See also Literatura light*
World War II, 5
Wynter, Sylvia, Caribbean writer, 348

Xicanisma (Castillo), 152

Y Matarazo no llamó (Garro), 225
Y no se lo tragó la tierra (Rivera), 19
Ya casi no tengo rostro (Manjarréz), 275
Yáñez, Agustín, Mexican writer, 5, 24–26, 92, 348
Yañez Cossio, Alicia, Ecuadorian writer, 348–49
Yawar fiesta (Arguedas), 105
Yo, el Supremo (Roa Bastos), 8, 185, 306
Yo me llamo Rigoberta Menchú y asi me nació la conciencia (Menchú), 34
Yo-yo boing! (Braschi), 45
Yugo de niebla (Airó), 88

Zama (Di Benedetto), 181
Zapata, Emiliano, 24
Zapata, Luis, Mexican writer, 226, 349
Zapata Olivella, Manuel, Columbian writer, 46, 81, 156, 349–50
Zero (Brandão), 22, 131
Zeta Acosta, Oscar, Chicano writer, 350
Zink, Rui, Brazilian writer, 350
Zona de clivaje (Heker), 245
Zona sagrada (Fuentes, C.), 27
El zorro de arriba y el zorro de abajo (Arguedas), 106
Zurita, Raúl, Chilean writer, 351